Health and Human Behavior

Health and Human Behavior

Robert M. Kaplan
Department of Family and Preventive Medicine
University of California, San Diego

James F. Sallis, Jr.
Department of Psychology
San Diego State University

Thomas L. Patterson
Department of Psychiatry
University of California, San Diego

McGraw-Hill, Inc.
New York / St. Louis / San Francisco / Auckland
Bogotá / Caracas / Lisbon / London / Madrid
Mexico / Milan / Montreal / New Delhi / Paris
San Juan / Singapore / Sydney / Tokyo
Toronto

Health and Human Behavior

Copyright © 1993 by McGraw-Hill, Inc. All rights reserved. Printed in the United States of America. Except as permitted under the United States Copyright Act of 1976, no part of this publication may be reproduced or distributed in any form or by any means, or stored in a data base or retrieval system, without the prior written permission of the publisher.

2 3 4 5 6 7 8 9 0   AGM   AGM   9 0 9 8 7 6 5 4 3

ISBN 0-07-033566-4

This book was set in Palatino by Better Graphics, Inc.
The editors were Christopher Rogers and Eleanor Castellano;
the production supervisor was Kathryn Porzio.
The cover was designed by Rafael Hernandez.
Arcata Graphics/Martinsburg was printer and binder.

Cover photograph: Goffrey Gove

Library of Congress Cataloging-in-Publication Data

Kaplan, Robert M.
    Health and human behavior / Robert M. Kaplan, James F. Sallis,
Jr., Thomas L. Patterson.
        p.   cm.
    Includes bibliographical references and index.
    ISBN 0-07-033566-4
    1. Clinical health psychology.   I. Sallis, James F.
II. Patterson, Thomas L.   III. Title.
R726.7.K33   1993
616' .0019—dc20   92-44553

Robert M. Kaplan is professor and chief of health care sciences in the department of family and preventive medicine at the University of California, San Diego. His research has focused on health outcome measurement and on behavioral interventions in chronic illnesses, including diabetes mellitus, chronic obstructive pulmonary disease, and arthritis. Over the years, his research has been supported by a variety of agencies including the National Institute of Health, the National Science Foundation, NATO, the National Center for Health Services Research, the American Diabetes Association, and the Arthritis Foundation. He serves on many NIH, WHO, and other agency committees, including study sections for both the Agency for Health Care Policy and Research (AHCPR) and the Veterans Administration. Having spent most of his career in San Diego, Dr. Kaplan has been active in the development of many new training programs. He helped found a new graduate school of public health at San Diego State, and he was active in the development of a new Ph.D. program that combined the resources of an academic psychology department and a school of medicine. In addition, he helped develop a general preventive medicine residency. Dr. Kaplan is the former recipient of an NIH Research Career Development Award and the Award for Outstanding Scientific Contribution to Health Psychology from the American Psychological Association. He is currently an associate editor for *The Annals of Behavioral Medicine,* and he serves on several other editorial boards. In 1988–1989 he served as the program chair for the Society of Behavioral Medicine, and he has held elected offices in several organizations including the Society of Behavioral Medicine, the American Association for the Advancement of Science, and the American Psychological Association. In 1992–1993 he was president of the division of health psychology of the American Psychological Association. Dr. Kaplan is the author or editor of 13 books and over 200 publications. He enjoys outdoor sports such as surfing, running, and tennis.

James F. Sallis, Jr., received his doctorate in clinical psychology in 1981 from Memphis State University, with an internship at Brown University. He was a postdoctoral Fellow in cardiovascular disease prevention and epidemiology at the Stanford Center for Research in Disease Prevention. He is currently professor of psychology at San Diego State University and assistant adjunct professor of pediatrics at the University of California, San Diego. Dr. Sallis is the author of over 100 scientific publications. He is on the editorial boards of *Health Psychology* and *Medicine, Exercise, Nutrition, and Health,* and has consulted with numerous government agencies, corporations, and research projects concerning health promotion. His research explores methods of keeping people healthy through regular physical activity, prudent dietary habits, and abstention from tobacco. Dr. Sallis has studied varied populations, such as adults, children, adolescents, families, and Latinos. He has conducted research in schools, work sites, churches, clinics, and homes. Dr. Sallis teaches undergraduate health psychology as well as the behavioral medicine seminar for the SDSU-UCSD Joint Doctoral Program in Clinical Psychology. To improve his own quality of life, he jogs and plays drums in a rock-and-roll band.

Thomas L. Patterson received his master's degree from the University of Georgia and his Ph.D. from the University of California, Riverside. He is currently associate professor in the department of psychiatry at the University of California, San Diego. His broad field of interest lies in behavioral medicine and the biological basis of behavior. He has authored numerous papers investigating stressful life events, coping, and social support and their relationship to physical and psychological health. He has also published a number of papers investigating aggregation of various health habits. His current studies include how the stress of caring for Alzheimer's patients impacts the caregiver's health. Other work focuses on how stress, coping, and social support may impact HIV disease progression. Dr. Patterson serves as reviewer for a number of journals and granting agencies, and is a member of various community boards including the Board of Directors of the San Diego Alzheimer's Association. However, he feels most at home on the beach, where he is a competitive body surfer. He placed fifth in his age class in last year's world championships.

For health in three generations, to Cameron and Seth for adult questions only a child could raise, to Cathie for love and support, and to Oscar and Rose for believing this line of work is respectable.

RMK

To Asante sana Shemi Amarsi-Sallis and my parents, for nourishing me body and soul. To new and old friends and collaborators from many places and walks of life, who make it enjoyable. To those who conducted and participated in the research on which we rely so heavily.

JFS

I am grateful for the patience and support of my family, Suzi, Carly, Jessie, and Leroy, who have reduced my stress level while I increased theirs. Many thanks to all the friends and colleagues who have provided ideas, critiques, and laughs.

TLP

CONTENTS

ix

SECTION 2

Life Stress

SECTION 3

Chronic Illnesses

SECTION 5

Summary

The first wealth is health.
   Ralph Waldo Emerson, *The Conduct of Life*, 1860.

Health is important. That is why we direct our lives toward achieving it. Wellness enables the pursuit of life's accomplishments and its pleasures. The days that marked the completion of this book were not unlike many others in which health items dominated the national news. Two of the most popular athletes in professional sports ended their careers because of health problems. Magic Johnson, a long-standing basketball star with the Los Angeles Lakers, announced that he had developed AIDS after an unprotected sexual encounter. In early 1992, Bo Jackson, perhaps the most gifted athlete in professional sports, announced that a damaged hip would forever limit his athletic performance. Jackson retired and sought surgery for an artificial hip.

Health and human behavior are inseparably intertwined. This book reviews numerous studies demonstrating that human behaviors are related to health status. Health and illness can be influenced by diet, exercise, stress, social relationships, and coping behaviors. A healthful lifestyle promotes health. Magic Johnson's health problems may have resulted from a lifestyle that included multiple sexual partners. Most of the major chronic illnesses have been connected, at least to some extent, with lifestyle. The most common cause of lung cancer, for example, is smoking behavior. Much of our message in this book is that we can, at least partially, control our health by controlling our behavior.

In addition to behavior affecting health, health can affect behavior. For Bo Jackson, a health condition dramatically affected behavior. Behavioral science, in its quest to identify the causes of behavior, often neglects one of the most important influences. Health status may determine whether you will play tennis, stay in bed, perform up to your potential on the midterm exam, or choose a particular vacation destination. Illness disrupts daily life. When illness strikes, the desire to get better is usually accompanied by motivation to get back to regular activities.

This book is about health and about behavior. More specifically, it is about the science that connects behavior to health and health to behavior.

WHY WE WROTE THIS BOOK

There are other excellent books about health psychology. However, they are different. Most of them place the greatest emphasis on psychological processes, such as coping with stress, and upon personality factors, such as the Type A personality. These are important topics. However, the study of health and behavior has become even broader and extends far beyond the individual. Sometimes several different perspectives are needed in order to understand complicated problems. For example, heart disease might be preventable through changes in diet and exercise behaviors. In order to accomplish this, we can work with individuals by providing in-depth counseling and behavior modification. Another approach is to work with small groups of individuals, while a third approach is to use the mass media in an attempt to affect entire communities. The media approach may have only a small effect upon any one individual, but collectively a community may lower its risk. This latter approach reflects the public health perspective. We attempt to cover the field of health and human behavior broadly by including a wide variety of topics and perspectives.

Although the study of health and human behavior has interested scholars for centuries, it has only recently become legitimized. The Institute of Medicine of the National Academy of Sciences is probably the most prestigious collection of recognized biomedical scholars in the world. In 1982 it released a report suggesting that individual behaviors—such as cigarette smoking, diet, and exercise—may be associated with at least 50 percent of all chronic illness (Hamberg, Elliott, & Parron, 1982). Within a decade similar reports were offered by other distinguished organizations, including the World Health Organization and the National Institutes of Health. These reports and related developments stimulated a whole new scientific field. It is this new and exciting young discipline that we attempt to summarize in this book. Throughout the book, we make reference to an important document known as *Healthy People 2000*. This book, released in 1991 by the U.S. Department of Health and Human Services, lays out the objectives for improving the health of the U.S. population by the year 2000. Most of the objectives emphasize changing human behavior.

WHY THE THREE OF US?

None of us remembers exactly how this project got started. However, we agree that each of us thought it was a good idea and that each author needed the other two. San Diego is a good place for professors interested in health and human behavior. The three of us have been friends and colleagues for years (for one pair the friendship goes back to junior high school). In some ways we are an unlikely threesome— by avocation two surfers and a rock-and-roll drummer. Yet we have similar academic interests, and we represent complementary per-

spectives. At times we have worked collaboratively on research projects, and at other times we have criticized each other's work. For many years we have run together, partied together, and worked together in the supervision of students. Our personal work has become focused in slightly different areas, which represent the diversity of topics in this book. Jointly our expertise is in chronic illness, stress and coping, and health promotion/disease prevention. We work in different settings—a medical school department focusing on public health, a psychology department with a strong emphasis on applied and clinical issues, and a university psychiatry department based in a hospital. This diversity has helped us identify what we know, and what we collectively need to learn.

WHAT DOES THE BOOK COVER?

This book presents 20 chapters divided into four general categories. The first section of the book reviews methods and issues. Within this section we will review behavioral epidemiology. *Epidemiology* is the study of the distribution and determinants of disease. Behavioral factors are important in the establishment of risk factors for various illnesses. The chapter considers not only the behavioral risk factors but also the methods that are used in establishing which behaviors are associated with risk. Next, Chapter 3 reviews models of health behavior. The chapter focuses on the principles of learning and on other social influences that may affect health behavior. Chapter 4 is an overview of the health care system; it discusses many contemporary issues relevant to today's "health care crisis." Chapter 5 also reviews interactions with the health care system and problems in compliance with medical recommendations.

The second section of the book reviews stress and coping. Chapter 6 provides an overview of stress, the relationship between stress and immunity, and techniques that are used to manage stress. Chapter 7 goes into more depth on social support; it considers social support as a risk factor for illness and reviews evidence for and against the assumption that social relationships can influence health outcomes.

The third section of the book focuses on chronic illnesses. Chapter 8 reviews chronic pain and arthritis. Chapter 9 goes into more detail on diabetes; it considers various types of diabetes and relates each to behavioral determinants and behavioral interventions. Chapter 10 focuses on cardiovascular disease, Chapter 11 reviews cancer, while Chapter 12 goes into detail about one of our major current public health threats, AIDS. Chapter 13 discusses injury, violence, and alcohol, three major threats to public health.

The final section of the book is devoted to health behavior and health promotion. Chapter 14 reviews diet, Chapter 15 considers physical activity, and Chapter 16 focuses on smoking. Each of these chapters reviews current epidemiology and describes interventions. Chapter 17 reviews the relationship between obesity and disease, Chapter 18 considers the relationship between personality and disease, while Chapter 19 evaluates community interventions. The final chapter will be used to provide information for those students who want to continue their study of health and human behavior. The chapter summarizes organizations devoted to the field as well as training opportunities. Finally, the book has several special features, including special boxes that focus on areas such as ethnic diversity and women's issues. Most of the chapters are framed in relation to the U.S. health objectives for the year 2000.

WHO DO WE OWE?

We are pleased to take credit for completing this book, but must admit that many others helped us get this far. The following reviewers provided many important insights: Glen Albright, Baruch College; Robert Croyle, University of Utah–Salt Lake City; Charles Kaiser, College of Charleston; Edward Krupat, Massachusetts College of Pharmacy and Allied Health Sciences; Connie Schick, Bloomsburg University; and Mervyn K. Wagner, University of South Carolina. Graduate students Liz Eakin and several members of our first-year Ph.D. class read various parts of the manuscript and provided important critical appraisal. The manuscript was read by 45 undergraduate students enrolled in health psychology at San Diego State University in the Fall of 1991, and we are indebted to those who identified countless problems. We take responsibility for any that remain. Of course, the book contains some opinions and personal interpretations. We hope the reader will enjoy agreeing or disagreeing with these comments.

We are especially appreciative to Robin Nordmeyer for taking the role of oversight mother hen, and to Rachel Ingram and Bev Jones for helping put the manuscript together. Computer wizardry and sharp eyes were provided by Kecia Carrasco throughout the manuscript preparation phase. Finally, to our three editors at McGraw Hill—Jim Anker, Jane Vaicunas, and Chris Rogers—and the editorial staff Eleanor Castellano and Kathy Porzio for sticking with us through the process, we offer our most sincere appreciation. To all who have helped us by either encouraging or criticizing the manuscript, we express our sincere appreciation.

Robert M. Kaplan
James F. Sallis, Jr.
Thomas L. Patterson

Methods and Issues

CHAPTER 1

Introduction

For Susan, life changed suddenly. At age 54, life had gone well. Susan had a good job, a faithful husband, and two loving children. It happened on a Saturday morning after a long workweek. Susan was warming up to play tennis with Tom, her 18-year-old son who was home from college for the first time. At first she felt sick to her stomach. Then she felt a sharp pain in her left shoulder. Could the pain be a pulled muscle from throwing the tennis ball? It certainly did not feel like anything Susan had experienced before. This pain was deeper and more intense, and it moved all the way down her left arm. Seconds later, Susan was lying on the tennis court. She tried to reassure Tom that she was OK, but both mother and son recognized that it was not true. However, Susan convinced Tom that she must be getting the flu. Tom helped her to the car, and they went home. Two hours later, the situation had become much worse. Susan was vomiting, and pains in her shoulder and chest had become unbearable. When Susan's husband returned home from a golf game, he was certain something was seriously wrong. He called the family doctor, who, upon hearing the story, insisted that the family call 911. Seven minutes later the paramedics arrived.

Susan had a heart attack. Heart attacks vary in severity, and unfortunately, this was a bad one. The situation was made worse because there was a delay of several hours between the time Susan had her first symptoms and the time her husband called 911. Heart attaks result from clots in the major arteries that feed blood to the heart. New medications, if administered promptly, can disolve the clots. If there is a delay, as in Susan's case, permanent damage to the heart muscle often results.

At the hospital, Susan's condition was critical for several days. She was hooked to monitors, fed by tubes, and her life was completely placed in the hands of other people. However, it was on the fourth day of her hospitalization that Susan got a report from her doctor that stung like a gunshot. She learned that she would be permanently disabled. The damage to her heart muscle was so severe that resumption of her normal activities would be unlikely. Furthermore, the doctor felt that narrowing of her arteries placed her at risk for another heart attack. So she recommended a complicated surgery that would take veins from Susan's legs and use them to bypass the narrowed arteries that fed blood to Susan's heart. The doctor believed that the operation would help Susan, but was unwilling to give her any guarantees. Furthermore, she said that there would be risks. About 2 percent of those who undergo the operation die on the operating table. The doctor refused to make the decision, but Susan decided to go ahead.

Recovery from the surgery seemed like it took forever. Even after 6 months, Susan still felt pain in her leg and chest. Her recovery from the heart attack was only partial. She would never play tennis again, and she was short of breath after only brief walks. Although Susan returned to work, she did so only on a limited and part-time basis. Because of this, the family financial picture changed. Tom left the private college he was attending and returned home to attend a state university. The relationships between Susan and her family also changed. They worried about her and often treated her like a fragile piece of china. Susan hated this. On the other hand, she was dependent, and she needed help doing most things she formerly did for herself. Over the course of a year, Susan became depressed and at times just wanted to die.

The interactions with the health care system were also a new experience for Susan. The only time she had previously been in a hospital was to have her babies. Now she needed to visit doctors regularly and take a whole series of different medications. All of this was time-consuming and, at times, demeaning. Susan felt that she was a mature adult, but the health care system often treated her like a helpless child. That hurt! To make the matter worse, all of this health care was very expensive. When Susan became unemployed after the heart attack, she lost her health insurance. Her husband did not have insurance because he was self-employed. When the family applied for insurance, they were turned down because of Susan's health condition. Health insurance, it seemed, was only for those who did not need it. As the bills came in, the family holdings declined.

Susan's life took an important turn for the better when she enrolled in a cardiac rehabilitation program. The program helped her to increase her level of activity, to resume some everyday life, and to stay on the right medications. As a result, she became less dependent on the health care system and she regained much of her self-worth. Although Susan was still disabled, she overcame her depression and eventually was able to return to work. Most important for Susan, she came to be satisfied with her life.

HEALTH AND HUMAN BEHAVIOR

Susan had a medical problem. Her coronary arteries had occluded (narrowed), and she developed a thrombus (blood clot) in one of the arteries. As a result she developed permanent muscle damage in her heart. Is that all there is to it? We think there is more.

This book is about health and human behavior, two concepts we believe are inseparable. Consider the many relationships in the case of Susan. First, we must consider the reasons Susan got sick in the first place. Heart attack rates differ for men and women. At 54,

Susan was young to be struck with this problem. One of the lessons we will learn in this book is that we also know less about the risk factors for women because most studies are based only on men (Cotton, 1992). What we do know suggests that Susan's behavior placed her at risk for heart disease. Her father had died of a heart attack at age 53. Susan was slightly overweight and had high blood pressure. Although she was aware of this problem, she avoided doctors and did not use medications. Furthermore, Susan smoked cigarettes and had a diet that emphasized fatty foods. She exercised rarely (the tennis game was the first outing in 5 months), and she exposed herself to high levels of stress at work.

Once the heart attack began, several behavioral factors came into play. For example, there was a delay in seeking help. Tom did not want to take command when his mother was apparently very sick. Susan failed to call the paramedics because she worried about the embarrassment of the ambulance coming to her house for what may be a false alarm. Once at the hospital, many psychological and behavioral issues were raised. The family reacted emotionally to Susan's crisis, and Susan reacted to the loss of personal control. Susan was required to make a complex decision about surgery without fully understanding the range of potential benefits and consequences. The doctors, nurses, and technicians required Susan to act in a role she did not enjoy or feel prepared for. She was angry, afraid, and grateful all at the same time. Susan's illness required her to change her life, and her rehabilitation helped her learn new ways of living. These required changes in behavior, adaptation, and new learning.

Susan's case is not unusual: it is like cases affecting thousands of people every day. This book is about health and about human behavior. It is about the prevention of illnesses, such as the one suffered by Susan. It is also about the role of behavior in the treatment of these problems and the psychological process of adaptation to illness. Furthermore, it is about the role of behavioral interventions in the rehabilitation process. Many people are going to have problems like the one Susan experienced. We hope to help you understand how to prevent these problems. When prevention has failed (as it did in Susan's case), studies of human behavior may help guide us toward an understanding of better treatment approaches and new ways to help people adapt to the consequences of their health problems.

THE AGE OF CHRONIC ILLNESS

Soon we will mark the end of the twentieth century. And what a century it has been! Take a minute to think about all the advances in health and health care. Not just one, but many revolutions have taken place. In 1900, 15 percent of the babies born in the United States did not live to celebrate their first birthday. Physicians in the nineteenth century had accepted as the will of God that one of each six children would be sacrificed to early death. Today, 99 percent of the children born alive survive to at least their first birthday. At the beginning of the century the life expectancy was barely more than 50 years. The major causes of death were infectious diseases such as pneumonia and tuberculosis. Today, new drugs have removed the chances of dying of many diseases, and inoculations prevent others from ever developing. Those born in 1990 enjoy a life expectancy of at least 75 years, and probably much longer. However, there are still significant challenges to the health of American citizens and those in other parts of the world. Despite the advances, we still have a long way to go.

The enemies of the modern physician have changed. There are still plenty of microbes to fight. Even the old nemesis, tuberculosis, which was all but extinct a few years ago, has resurfaced as a major health problem of the

1990s. However, due to advances in medical therapy, microorganisms are no longer major causes of death. Most people in your generation will succumb to "lifestyle illness." These are associated with health habits such as diet, exercise, alcohol, and tobacco use and risk-taking behavior that leads to injuries. For example, cigarette smoking kills an estimated 390,000 people per year. Each evening the news reports horrifying stories about deaths due to murder, fires, heroin addiction, and suicide. However, as you will learn later in this book, cigarettes kill more people each year than all of these problems combined.

The Centers for Disease Control estimate that at least half of all premature deaths are related to individual behavior. Susan's health problems, at least in part, can be attributed to some of her personal habits. It is our thesis that medical science must put more emphasis on the study of behaviors related to health in order to improve the health of the population. Much of this book is devoted to demonstrating that we can significantly increase the life expectancy by teaching people to exercise, use less alcohol, modify their diets, practice safe sex, and take steps to prevent accidents. More than ever before, today's youth can have control over their own health.

Understanding health presents many unanswered questions. When exposed to the same illness, for example, why do some people get sick and others remain healthy? Are some people more prone to certain illness? What role does stress play in staying healthy? Questions about behavioral causes of illness and health are the central focus of this book. The relationship between health and behavior is no longer controversial. In fact, nearly all modern medical schools include instruction in behavioral science. Furthermore, behavioral science is now well represented in biomedical research. However, these are new developments. The relationship between health and behavior has only recently grown to the point

that it has attracted university courses and full-length textbooks.

MODELS OF MEDICAL CARE

Most of us are familiar with the traditional medical model. When we get sick, we go to a doctor to find out what is wrong and to have the problem "repaired." Some have suggested that getting medical care is like going to a skilled mechanic. When your car is not running well, a specialist will perform diagnostic tests, identify the problem, and offer the repair (Friedman & DiMatteo, 1989). In medicine, the process is very complex. As a result, the mechanics need to be highly trained. During the last 50 years medicine and surgery have become extremely technical fields that require extensive training. Medical specialists go through extensive certification and review in order to ensure that the standards of care are high and uniform.

Traditional medicine has become very good at the identification and repair of biological problems using surgery or medicines. One of the major accomplishments of traditional medicine is the reduction of deaths from infectious diseases. Today people rarely die of diseases that were feared just a few years ago, like plague or tuberculosis. Instead, most of the modern challenges in the industrialized world are chronic illnesses. A chronic illness is one that lasts over the course of time, like the serious heart disease suffered by Susan. These illnesses require people to adapt and modify their lifestyles.

The new era of medical problems requires a whole new approach to health care. The best way to deal with chronic illnesses—such as cancer, diabetes, arthritis, and heart disease—is to prevent them from ever developing. The traditional medical model is not well suited to prevention because there is no problem to diagnose and fix. Once chronic problems develop, the affected person must learn to change habits, to cope with pain and disability, and to obtain support from other people. The traditional medical model has never been well suited for training people to manage stress, to cope with illness, or to comply with the advice of a health care provider. For example, in Susan's case, her doctors were well prepared to inject clot-breaking drugs, to perform bypass surgery, and to prescribe medications. However, the system did not prevent Susan's problems, nor was the medical care system well equipped to teach Susan how to live with her disability, to overcome the associated depression, and to integrate the complex regimen of medical care into her lifestyle.

An alternative to the medical model is clearly needed. Perhaps the best candidate is the biopsychosocial model. This model recognizes that health is determined by many different influences. Some of them are biological. Many diseases are caused by microorganisms, deficiencies in the immune system, and problems with specific organ systems. However, the model leaves room for other determinants of health, including psychological factors such as behaviors, thoughts, and feelings. Social factors—such as the influences of organizations, culture, and other people—also affect the course of an illness or its prevention. The term *biopsychosocial* recognizes the influence of biological, psychological, and social factors (Engel, 1977). Throughout this book we will be referring to all three influences upon health.

Consider this abstract example of the differences between the medical model and the biopsychosocial model. Suppose you are commuting across town to meet your mother. When you are one-half hour late, your mother begins to worry. What might be the reasons for this tardiness? One set of explanations focuses on your car. Is it out of gas? Is the engine operating properly? These explanations might be analogous to those of the medical model, which seeks to identify the problems in the machine (body) and fix them. However, there are many other reasons why you are late. You might have been detained by a friend, you might not be motivated to get there on time, or you could have been caught in traffic. Whether the reason was that you were out of gas or you were caught in traffic, the end result is the same—you are late. In this analogy, being out of gas is like a biological problem, while the other explanations are psychological, social, or environmental. The medical model would only consider your being out of gas, while the biopsychosocial model asks about all of the reasons. For the biopsychosocial model, the question is more complex than getting your car across town; it extends to getting yourself across town through traffic.

THE CHANGING FACE OF HEALTH CARE

Health care is the biggest industry in the United States and in most westernized countries. Twelve dollars out of each one hundred spent are devoted to health care. These health care expenses were not so extreme just a few years ago. There are many reasons why health care has become so expensive. One reason is that the population is getting older, and older people are more likely to develop chronic, expensive medical conditions. Another reason is that new technologies have been developed, and these new technologies are expensive. A third reason is that we may simply use too many services, including many that are not necessary.

In the 1990s medicine has had to come face to face with some of its failures. For example, little can be done to cure many of the chronic diseases. In some cases in which a treatment is judged "effective," the actual benefit may be small. For example, chemotherapy for metastatic lung cancer is judged to be clinically effective. However, the treatment extends life expectancy by only about 6 weeks (Goodwin, 1992). After years of neglect, the medical establishment has now come to recognize that most of health care should be devoted to improving the quality of life. Measures of life quality are now used in studies of most new medicines and surgeries. The old era of medicine was limited to defined biological processes. The new era of medicine seeks to help the whole person.

BEYOND MEDICAL CARE

We often think of health and medical care as closely associated. When illness strikes, the care of a doctor is sought. Yet health is influenced by many factors, of which medical care is only a small contributor. Think about your own health and the health of people in your family. Many factors contribute to your activity level, your vitality, and your resistance to illness. These include genetic factors, chronic illness, physique, physical fitness, dietary influences, and many others. Figure 1-1 suggests the proportion of total health status that is influenced by different factors. Although it is difficult to sort out the exact percentage attributable to each influence, many experts

place the proportion devoted to medical care at about 10 percent. That leaves about 90 percent attributable to other factors.

When we think of health, it is interesting that so much attention is devoted to medical treatment. For example, politicians promote better health for all people. However, their plan for obtaining better health typically stops at payments to doctors and hospitals. An important thesis of this book is that your health is much more influenced by you and your behaviors than by what your doctor does to you (McKinlay, McKinlay, & Beaglehole, 1989). This represents another point of departure between the medical and the biopsychosocial models.

The medical model and the biopsychosocial model each attempt to improve health. But what exactly is health? Now let us turn to definitions of some of the key concepts used in this book.

SOME BASIC DEFINITIONS

What Is Health?

Health is a highly cherished state of being. Health status can be among our most important assets or liabilities. The importance of health is almost universally recognized. Some years ago, for example, social psychologist Milton Rokeach (1973) developed a study of values. The study required people to rank in order various states of being, such as wealth, power, etc. Rokeach had originally planned to use health as one of these states. However, there was no variability with regard to health. Everybody ranked health first. In other words, nearly everyone values health more than any other personal asset.

Since we find health so valuable and important, it might be assumed that we have a clear understanding of the concept. Not so! Scholars have debated about the definition of health for centuries. Many people have written about

FIGURE 1-1
Estimated contributions of behavior, medical care, genetics, and other factors to health status.

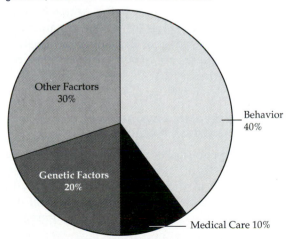

Other Facrtors 30%

Genetic Factors 20%

Behavior 40%

Medical Care 10%

health. Perhaps the most influential definition of health was offered by the World Health Organization (WHO) upon its founding in 1948. The WHO defined health as "a complete state of physical, mental, and social well-being and not merely the absence of disease or infirmity" (World Health Organization, 1948).

The WHO definition of health broke new ground for several reasons. First, it separated itself from traditional definitions, which define health in "negative terms." Many previous definitions of health had emphasized that "health is not being sick" or that "health is the absence of disease." The WHO definition emphasized that health is not just the absence of disease or infirmity.

A second very important aspect of this definition is the recognition of the various dimensions of health status, including physical, mental, and social aspects. Previous definitions of health had emphasized only the physical components. The WHO was widely applauded for also including mental health and happiness as part of its definition. The meaning of *social health* has been more difficult to interpret. The WHO never defined what social well-being was, and various authors have provided different interpretations of social health. Some have focused on social support, which may be an important influence on both physical and mental health (see Chapter 7). Others have suggested that social well-being describes the ability to perform a social role, such as holding a job, participating in social activities, and being a productive member of society. This is also closely associated with physical and mental functioning (Kaplan, 1992).

Some people feel that the WHO definition also included political and social considerations. For example, social well-being might require the elimination of poverty and the freedom to live in a society with social justice. This makes the definition of *health* very broad because achieving health requires political and social reform, as well as improved health care and hygiene.

What Is Psychology?

Virtually every university has a psychology department. Psychology is a required course at most of the institutions. Yet definitions of *psychology* have been constantly changing over the last century. In 1890, William James defined psychology as the science of mental life. James emphasized feelings, desires, cognitions, and reasoning. In 1919, John B. Watson advanced an important behavioral definition of psychology. He suggested that psychology was the division of natural science that used human behavior as its subject matter. Human behavior emphasized observable events or statements. Most textbooks now define psychology as the scientific study of behavior and mental processes (Atkinson, Atkinson, Smith, & Bem, 1990). This definition emphasizes both the science of observable behavior as well as the science of mental processes. These mental processes include perception, memory, and information processing. Thus, psychologists study observable behavior and also apply scientific methods to learn how people and other organisms acquire knowledge, solve problems, and make decisions. *Behavior* is typically defined as activities of a living organism that can be observed, either by another organism or by special instruments. Behaviors can include verbal statements about subjective experiences and symptoms.

What Is Health Psychology and Behavioral Medicine?

Health psychology is the term for a variety of topics related to the interface between psychology and medicine. The Division of Health Psychology of the American Psychological Association defined its specialty as the aggregate of the specific educational, scientific, and professional contributions of the discipline of psychology to the promotion and maintenance of health, the prevention and treatment of illness, and the identification of the etiologic and diagnostic correlates of health, illness, and related dysfunction (Matarazzo, 1980, p. 815).

Most of this book will describe collaborative efforts between behavioral scientists and other participants in health care. The collaboration between physicians and behavioral scientists is not a new phenomenon. As early as the turn of the century, some psychologists were involved in medical education (Franz, 1913). However, in recent years, the number of psychologists participating in direct health care, in collaboration with physicians, and in medical education has dramatically increased. Today, more than 5 percent of the members of the American Psychological Association are on the faculties of medical schools, and combinations of psychologists and medical doctors often work as teams on research and on treatment plans for individual patients.

By the mid-1970s, the importance of behavior in health problems was widely acknowledged and the need for many different specialists to collaborate on biopsychosocial problems came to the attention of several professional societies and government agencies. In February of 1977, Yale University and the National Heart, Lung, and Blood Institute of the National Institutes of Health sponsored a conference to define the emerging discipline of behavioral medicine. The definition they agreed upon was:

> Behavioral medicine is the field concerned with the development of behavioral-science, knowledge, and techniques relevant to the understanding of physical health and illness and the application of this knowledge and these techniques to prevention, diagnosis, treatment, and rehabilitation. Psychosis, neurosis, and substance abuse are included only insofar as they

contribute to physical disorders as an end-point (Schwartz & Weiss, 1977).

Several characteristics of this definition are particularly important. First, the definition recognizes the need for collaboration between physicians, biomedical scientists, and behavioral scientists. Second, the definition stresses the application of behavioral knowledge to problems in physical health, which has not traditionally been within the domain of psychology. Third, the definition excludes the more traditional topics of clinical-abnormal psychology and psychosis, neurosis, and substance abuse. However, in recent years, behavioral medicine specialists have reintroduced the notion of substance abuse into their definition, although they study traditional psychological problems only insofar as they contribute to physical health. Although not specified in the definition, the Yale conference emphasized that research and practice in behavioral medicine should be a collaborative effort between physicians and behavioral scientists. Efforts of psychologists without medical collaborators, or by physicians without behavioral collaborators, were seen to have less potential. Furthermore, the conference participants expressed concern that the status of medical and behavioral collaborators be "equal," with neither participant taking the dominant role. In contrast to health psychology, which emphasizes work done by psychologists, behavioral medicine emphasizes work that is collaborative between biomedical and behavioral scientists.

Throughout this book, we will refer to aspects of behavioral medicine and health psychology. The simple way to distinguish these related fields is to remember that *behavioral medicine* is a collaboration of behavioral and medical scientists to improve health, and that *health psychology* is the contribution of psychologists to this process. Many of the studies we describe are related to prevention. Prevention can be divided into two aspects: primary and secondary. *Primary prevention* is the prevention of the problem before it develops. Thus, the primary prevention of heart disease starts with people who have no symptoms or characteristics of the disease, and the effort is directed to preventing these disease characteristics from becoming established. In *secondary prevention* we begin with a population at risk and develop efforts to prevent the condition from becoming worse or developing into more serious problems. Finally, we will describe behavioral approaches and *tertiary care*, which deals with the treatment of established conditions. Box 1-1 shows three levels of prevention as they relate to problems associated with high blood pressure.

Health Psychology and Its Relationship to Other Fields of Study

Specialists in different fields of study use different terms to describe the study of health and human behavior. Psychologists often prefer the term *health psychology*. Health psychology is a diverse field. Within psychology, health psychology overlaps with virtually all of the other specialty areas. For example, health psychology is an empirical science that depends upon research methodologies derived from statistics, experimental psychology, and

psychometrics. Since health psychology often involves changing health behaviors, there is a significant overlap with social, clinical, and community psychology. Many studies in health psychology focus on cognitive processes. Thus, health psychology overlaps with cognitive psychology. In addition, the biological nature of health requires that health psychology overlap considerably with physiology, physiological psychology, and neuroscience. Since many studies in health psychology involve children or study the development of habits, health psychology also overlaps with developmental psychology. At the other end of the aging continuum, health psychology also overlaps with the study of aging (gerontology). Many problems in aging are also problems in health or adaptation. As you can see, learning about health psychology also means learning a little bit about other specialty areas within the general field of psychology. For example, a health psychologist might want to modify eating patterns of older adults who are at risk for heart disease. To accomplish this, he or she must know about older adult nutrition, social influence (social psychology), and behavioral intervention strategies.

To understand health psychology, it is important to gain an appreciation of the work of other disciplines that contribute to behavioral medicine. For example, this book repeatedly makes reference to basic principles of

---

BOX 1·1

THREE LEVELS OF PREVENTION

Level	When used	Example
Primary	For completely well people	Controlling weight to prevent high blood pressure
Secondary	For people with risks for illness (i.e., high blood pressure)	Using medicine to lower blood pressure.
Tertiary	For people with developed disease (i.e., heart disease resulting from high blood pressure)	Rehabilitation to prevent the condition from getting worse

biology, physiology, anatomy, and medicine. These principles are required in order to understand the basics of the disease process. The chapters in the book also reference recent research from important health-related fields such as nutrition, nursing, physical education, public health, and health education. In addition, we draw upon works in basic social science fields such as sociology and economics. It is because health is such a broad concept that understanding health requires a broad perspective. Although we touch on many fields involved in behavioral medicine, the focus of this book is on health psychology, or the application of psychological methods and principles to the study of health.

A BRIEF HISTORY

Perhaps the most important theme in health psychology is that health and behavior are related. Philosophers have speculated on this connection for centuries. The Bible (both New and Old Testaments) makes repeated references to the health consequences of some dietary practices (Martin, 1988). By the fourth century, Hippocrates had written extensively about health practices and the influences upon health outcomes.

In Chapter 6 we describe the emerging field of psychoneuroimmunology. Psychoneuroimmunologists study the effect of psychological events, including the appraisal of stress, upon functioning of the immune system. The roots of psychoneuroimmunology actually date back several centuries to the French philosopher René Descartes, who discussed mind-body relationships in the seventeenth century (1662). Descartes stimulated philosophers to believe in a mind-body dualism. This means that the mind and the body are separate and do not affect one another. For Descartes the mind was spiritual and the body physical. They were related but did not influence one another. It was not until the mid-nineteenth century that

the prominent physician Claude Bernard changed some opinions by arguing that psychological states did affect bodily processes. These ideas led to the development of psychosomatic medicine in the twentieth century. The term *psychosomatic* actually means mind-body and is derived from *psyche* (mind) and *somate* (body).

Although widely recognized as important, the formal study of health psychology has developed rather slowly. Several events have had an important influence. One of these was the 1977 conference convened by the National Institutes of Health. The organizers of the conference included Stephen Weiss, a research administrator for the National Institutes of Health, and Neil Miller, an eminent psychologist from Yale University. The product of the conference was the definition of behavioral medicine. Over the years, this conference has been acknowledged as having given birth to a new field of study. Weiss and Miller have both been titled "the father of behavioral medicine."

The first major textbook using the title *Health Psychology* was published in 1979 (Stone et al., 1979). The publication of this book was important because the thick volume indicated the amount of scientific evidence that had accumulated. Yet the scientific basis for health psychology was scattered throughout dozens of scientific journals and many books. Although this remains true today, there are now several specialized publications which focus exclusively on health psychology and related areas. For example, *Health Psychology* is a scientific journal that has been published since 1982. The *Journal of Behavioral Medicine* has been published since 1978. Today, it is common to find scientific articles relevant to health psychology published in the *Journal of the American Medical Association*, the *American Journal of Public Health*, *Pediatrics*, and many others.

Another important factor in the development of health psychology was a report published by the Institutes of Medicine of the National Academy of Sciences in 1982. The National Academy of Sciences is a federally sponsored organization designed to provide scientific and technical advice to the President and Congress. Membership in the academy is by election, and participation is extremely exclusive. Thus, the academy includes the most respected scientists in America, and the group is among the most prestigious scientific assemblies in the world. The Institute of Medicine is the aspect of the academy that deals with medicine, health, and health care.

In the 1982 report, the Institute of Medicine explored the relationship between health and behavior. Upon review, members of the institute estimated that as many as 50 percent of all chronic diseases can be traced to individual behaviors, such as smoking, diet, and lack of exercise (Hamberg, Elliott, & Parron, 1982). Similar conclusions have been reached by a variety of European investigators and institutes. The World Health Organization has also expressed considerable interest in individual behavior in relation to the development of chronic disease. In 1987 the commission, headed by former President Jimmy Carter, published an important monograph entitled "Closing the Gap: The Burden of Unnecessary Illness" (Amler & Doll, 1987). The monograph summarized the conclusions of a group of distinguished experts. They concluded that approximately two-thirds of all deaths could be delayed through preventive measures and changes in lifestyle. It was estimated that 1.2 million lives and 8.4 million years of life could be saved each year.

Numerous other reports and documents have underscored these same conclusions. For example, the American Heart Association and the National Heart, Lung, and Blood Institutes of the National Institutes of Health have each emphasized that behavioral change is required to prevent deaths from coronary heart disease. The American Cancer Society and National Cancer Institute have emphasized that many cancers may be preventable through modification of cigarette smoking habits and dietary patterns. The American Diabetes Association underscores the importance of diet and exercise in the management of diabetes. And the list goes on.

THE CONTEMPORARY SCENE: HEALTHY PEOPLE 2000

One of the repeated features in this book is the discussion of the Health Promotion and Disease Prevention Objectives for the United States, Year 2000. These objectives represent the best judgments of health professionals about the highest priorities for health in the United States. The objectives are used to guide the establishment of new health programs as well as research priorities.

In 1979, the United States Department of Health, Education, and Welfare released the report, "Healthy People: The Surgeon General's Report on Health Promotion and Disease Prevention." A year later it published "Promoting Health/Preventing Disease: Objectives for the Nation," which created an agenda and a list of objectives for the year 1990. Many of these objectives were met. In 1991, the Department of Health and Human Services released a new document: "Healthy People 2000." This important report provided a set of guidelines for the new century. It included not only reductions in preventable deaths and disability but also a new concept: quality of life. The goals for the year 2000 do more than direct us to live longer. Now they also direct us to live better.

The goals for the year 2000 are complex. By that time, the United States will be a different country than it was in 1991, when the report was created. For example, by the end of this decade, the U.S. population will be about 270 million people, representing a growth of about 7 percent. In addition, the population will be older, with a median age of 36 years compared with 29 years in 1975. It is estimated that those over 65 will constitute 18 percent of the population (compared with 13 percent in 1950). Furthermore, the oldest old—those over 85 years of age—will increase by 30 percent. Despite growth in the number of older people, the number of children will actually decline by about 1 million (from 18 million to 17 million).

Other demographics of the population will also change. Whites will become a smaller proportion of the total population. It is estimated that they will decline from 76 to 72 percent by the year 2000. In their place will be many rapidly growing groups. Latinos, for example, who were 8 percent of the population in 1990, are estimated to make up 11.3 percent of the population by the year 2000. Because the demographics will be changing, the work force will change. There will be fewer young people coming into the job market. On the other hand, there will be substantial numbers of older people who may continue on in the work force. However, because of the significant numbers of older people, jobs that involve helping those who are dependent will be more in demand. What are the implications of these changes for health problems? What impact will these changes have upon the health care system, upon you, or upon your family? We hope to provide you with some answers in the following chapters.

PLANNING FOR THE NEXT CENTURY

Much of this book is directed toward finding solutions to the health problems we will need to face in the year 2000. We have stated the relevant objectives for improving the health of the population at the beginning of most chapters. Each of the chapters provides information on how we can utilize what we currently know to help plan for tomorrow's health problems. Table 1-1 summarizes the progress toward the 1990 goals as evaluated in 1987. For example, in 1980, the goal was to reduce infant death rates by 35 percent. By 1987, a 28 percent reduction had been realized. Reduction in child deaths by 20 percent was the goal stated in 1980. By 1987, an actual reduction of 21 percent had been achieved. As the table shows, progress toward the 1990 goals was very good.

Table 1-2 shows a variety of health conditions, their effect upon society, interventions that might be used to avoid the problems, and the cost to society of not preventing these problems. For example, heart disease is apparent in 7 million Americans, causes about a half million deaths per year, and results in a quarter million open heart surgeries.

TABLE 1-1

PROGRESS TOWARD 1990 LIFE STAGE GOALS—1987

Life stage	1990 target*	1987 status
Infants	35% lower death rate	28% lower
Children	20% lower death rate	21% lower
Adolescents/young adults	20% lower death rate	13% lower
Adults	25% lower death rate	21% lower
Older adults	20% fewer days of restricted activity	17% lower

* Relative to baseline (1977 data).
Source: Health, United States, 1989 and Prevention Profile

TABLE 1-2

COSTS OF TREATMENT FOR SELECTED PREVENTABLE CONDITIONS

Condition	Overall magnitude	Avoidable intervention*	Cost per patient†
Heart disease	7 million with coronary artery disease 500,000 deaths/yr 284,000 bypass procedures/yr	Coronary bypass surgery	$ 30,000
Cancer	1 million new cases/yr 510,000 deaths/yr	Lung cancer treatment	$ 29,000
		Cervical cancer treatment	$ 28,000
Stroke	600,000 strokes/yr 150,000 deaths/yr	Hemiplegia treatment and rehabilitation	$ 22,000
Injuries	2.3 million hospitalizations/yr 142,500 deaths/yr 177,000 persons with spinal cord injuries in the United States	Quadriplegia treatment and rehabilitation	$570,000 (lifetime)
		Hip fracture treatment and rehabilitation	$ 40,000
		Severe head injury treatment and rehabilitation	$310,000
HIV infection	1–1.5 million infected 118,000 AIDS cases (as of Jan. 1990)	AIDS treatment	$ 75,000 (lifetime)
Alcoholism	18.5 million abuse alcohol 105,000 alcohol-related deaths/yr	Liver transplant	$250,000
Drug abuse	Regular users: 1–3 million, cocaine; 900,000, IV drugs; 500,000, heroin Drug-exposed babies: 375,000	Treatment of drug-affected baby	$ 63,000 (5 years)
Low-birth-weight baby	260,000 LBWB born/yr 23,000 deaths/yr	Neonatal intensive care for LBWB	$ 10,000
Inadequate immunization	Lacking basic immunization series: 20–30%, aged 2 and younger; 3%, aged 6 and older	Congenital rubella syndrome treatment	$354,000 (lifetime)

* Examples (other interventions may apply).
† Representative first-year costs, except as noted. Not indicated are nonmedical costs, such as lost productivity to society.
Source: "Healthy People 2000," p. 5.

There are 1 million new cases of cancer each year, and nearly one-half million cancer deaths. Many of these cancers are preventable simply by reducing or eliminating cigarette smoking or increasing the rate at which people use cancer screening tests. There are 18.5 million Americans who abuse alcohol, and there are over 100,000 alcohol-related deaths each year. Examining Table 1-2 suggests that we can do a lot to reduce the burden of illness through preventive efforts. Simple changes in behavior may have a substantial impact not only on the health of our nation but also on the cost of health care.

While prevention is important, behavioral scientists can also improve the treatment and rehabilitation of existing diseases. In Chapter 4 we will explore the problem of health care costs. Many of the chapters in this book describe methods that can be used to prevent illness, help people cope with illness, or reduce the burden of suffering. The health objectives for the year 2000 help organize our thinking for what needs to be done to improve the health of the whole population.

HEALTH, BEHAVIOR, AND YOU

Preserving your own health and the health of the population will require the acquisition of new information and the development of new skills. The study of health and human behavior should be relevant to your own life in several ways. First, many of the studies described in this book may help direct you toward a healthier lifestyle. There are many messages about healthy eating, exercise patterns, safe sex, and avoidance of risky exposures. Some of these many messages seem obvious. However, surveys continue to show that many people are either confused or misinformed about important health risk factors. In one recent study on risks of cancer, for example, respondents rated the risks of getting bruised as more likely to cause cancer than smoking cigarettes (Loehrer, Greger, Weinberger, Musick, Miller, Nichols, Bryan, Higgs, & Brock, 1991). In fact, there is no established evidence that bruises cause cancer, and there is enormous evidence that cigarette smoking is the most important risk factor for several types of cancer. Information alone will help you keep informed, and you can pass the information on to friends and family.

Beyond simply offering facts, we hope to provide a framework for thinking about health issues. Today health information is everywhere. You might get health advice from your mother, your doctor, your friends, and the mass media. But how do you sort it all out? One of the purposes of this book is to make

you a better consumer of this information. Although information is valuable, it is typically not enough. Nearly all smokers, for example, know that smoking is bad for them. Most people who are overweight want to lose the extra pounds. The challenge is in finding methods for successfully changing behavior. Many of the chapters in this book review the latest methods for helping people make important changes in health behaviors.

Finally, we hope the book will encourage you to consider a career relevant to health and human behavior. We are now at a crossroads. A new field has been created, and demands for all sorts of new services have been defined. The new generation will see new physicians who know more about human behavior than their predecessors. We will need freshly trained behavioral scientists who understand issues in health care. Also needed will be specialists in nutrition and in exercise sciences who will be able to develop and evaluate new programs in prevention. We will also need skilled and empathic clinical psychologists and social workers to assist with the heavy burden associated with chronic illness. Hopefully, this course will stimulate awareness of many career options. This may be a field in which you can make a difference. Some of the training needed for these new professions will be discussed in the final chapter of the book.

We believe that the study of health and human behavior is highly relevant to the lives of contemporary college students. In order to emphasize some of these issues, the chapters have three types of boxes that highlight topics of particular importance or interest. Sometimes the boxes describe a specific study and discuss its implications for health psychology. Sometimes the boxes explain an area of research or summarize several studies on one topic. These boxes are meant both to inform you and to challenge you to think creatively about how you would study or intervene on current health problems. The boxes bring special attention to the concerns of women and ethnic minorities, and they explain some of the most influential recent studies on health and human behavior.

"Focus on Women" addresses some of the differences between women and men in health behaviors or health problems. Many health researchers and policymakers have needed to be reminded that, until recently, most studies in health used only men as subjects. There are many reasons for this common practice, but the result is that we have limited knowledge about the health of half the population. In these boxes we identify current studies and issues relating to women's health.

"Focus on Diversity" addresses ethnic and racial differences and similarities regarding health and behavior. American society is becoming increasingly diverse, and health researchers are challenged not only to understand how race and ethnicity affect disease outcomes but also to develop appropriate methods for improving the health of each segment of the population. An influential five-volume government report on the health of minority populations in the United States documented that most minority groups have higher death and disability rates than Caucasians. Many of these differences are believed to be due to poverty, which is more common among minorities, than to true racial or ethnic differences. Nevertheless, one of the three overriding goals of the year 2000 national health promotion and disease prevention objectives is to "reduce the health disparities among Americans." In recognition of the importance of this goal, we hope the "Focus on Diversity" boxes improve your understanding of the health needs of our diverse population.

"Focus on Research" boxes typically describe one study in detail. The authors chose a particular study from the 1990s for each chapter because it illustrates a creative approach to improving health, shows a novel approach to studying an important topic, or demonstrates that surprising results can lead to new understandings. We hope these boxes also show that research can be fascinating, sort of like a mystery story. Even if you do not plan to become a researcher, you will always be a research consumer through newspapers and television, and so it is useful to have a positive attitude about research.

Behavioral medicine and health psychology are fast-growing and rapidly changing areas. In a very few years, behavioral scientists have made important contributions to the improvement of health and health care. National and international leaders are calling for increased input from psychologists and other behavioral scientists. Medical researchers and practitioners are seeking out collaboration with behavioral scientists. Yet we are just beginning to make progress in this field. Research needs to be improved. There are many opportunities, and young investigators are needed to provide new ideas and energy. People now in college must become the next generation of leaders. Someday you or someone in your class may develop programs or conduct studies that will be taught to future classes. As you read this book, not only think about how you can apply some of the information to improving your own health but also challenge yourself to think of improvements in the studies and programs about which you are learning.

KEY TERMS

WHO. World Health Organization. This international group attempts to achieve equity in health for all people in the world.

Health. A complete state of physical, mental, and social well-being and not merely the absense of disease or infirmity (WHO definition).

Psychology. The scientific study of behavior and mental processes.

Health psychology. The aggregate of the specific educational, scientific, and professional contributions of the discipline of psychology, the promotion and maintenance of health, the prevention and treatment of illness, and the identification of the etiologic and diagnostic correlates of health, illness, and related dysfunction (Matarazzo, 1980, p. 185).

Behavioral medicine. A multidisciplinary field concerned with the development of behavioral-science knowledge and techniques relative to the understanding of physical health and illness and the application of this knowledge and these techniques to prevention, diagnosis, treatment, and rehabilitation.

"Healthy People 2000." An influential government report that set forth the health promotion and disease prevention objectives for the year 2000.

CHAPTER 2

Behavioral Epidemiology

John, like many of his peers, wakes up each morning, goes for a 3-mile run, and returns home to a breakfast of fresh orange juice and oat bran. In the evenings, John eats salad, but avoids red meat. He drinks a moderate amount of white wine, but avoids drinking too much. John is proud of his lifestyle because he knows that it will help prevent heart disease. But how does he know this? John is only 27 years old and has no medical signs of heart ailment. If he does develop heart disease, it may not affect him for 40 years.

The popular media often state that "doctors know that a high-fat diet and lack of exercise may cause heart disease." Yet how did doctors come to know this? Clinical experience in medicine rarely allows a doctor to follow the same people throughout their life span. Further-more, some authors have challenged the belief that heart disease can be prevented (Moore, 1989; Muldoon & Manuck, 1992). How do we decide what is true? In most cases we learn about risks from epidemiologists, who are scientists devoted to the study of health determinants. This science provides much of the foundation for preventive medicine and preventive health care. Few doctors are actually involved in epidemiological research, but many pay close attention to the findings of epidemiological studies. In this chapter we will provide an introductory overview of this important science. We hope this will provide some foundation for you to interpret epidemiological findings.

WHAT IS EPIDEMIOLOGY?

Epidemiology is the study of the determinants and distribution of disease. Epidemiologists (scientists who study epidemiology) measure disease and then attempt to relate the development of diseases to characteristics of people and the environments in which they live. The word *epidemiology* is derived from Greek. The Greek word *epi* translates to "among," while the Greek word *demos* means "people." *Logos* indicates a scholarly discipline The stem *ology* means "the study of." *Epidemiology*, then, is the study of what happens among people. For as long as there has been recorded history, people have been interested in what causes disease. It has been obvious, for example, that diseases are not equally distributed within populations of people. Some people are much more at risk for certain problems than others.

Traditionally, epidemiologists have been primarily interested in infectious diseases. For example, people who live in close contact are most likely to get similar illnesses or to be "infected" by one another. Ancient doctors also recognized that people who became ill from certain diseases, and subsequently recovered, seldom got the same disease again. Thus, the notions of communicability of diseases and of immunity were known many years before specific microorganisms and antibodies were understood. Epidemiologic history was made by Sir John Snow, who studied cholera in London in the mid-nineteenth century. Cholera is a horrible disease that causes severe diarrhea and eventually kills its victims through dehydration. Snow systematically studied those who developed cholera and those who did not. His detective-like investigation demonstrated that those who obtained their drinking water from a particular source were more likely to develop cholera. Thus, he was able to link a specific environmental factor to the development of the disease (Snow, 1855). This occurred many years before the specific organism that causes cholera was identified.

It is common to think of epidemics as major changes in infectious disease rates. For example, we are experiencing a serious epidemic of acquired immune deficiency syndrome (AIDS). Yet there are other epidemics that are less dramatic. For instance, we are also experiencing a major epidemic of coronary heart disease (CHD) in the United States. In 1900, heart disease accounted for about 45 percent of all deaths, while infectious diseases, such as influenza and tuberculosis, accounted for nearly 25 percent of all deaths. In the 1980s, cardiovascular (heart and circulatory system) diseases caused more than 70 percent of all deaths while the effect of influenza and tuberculosis had been reduced to less than 5 percent. The days when infectious diseases were the major killers in the industrialized world appear to be over. AIDS, although rapidly increasing in incidence, still accounts for a very small percentage of all deaths. Today, the major challenge is from chronic illnesses. The leading causes of death include heart disease, cancer, stroke, chronic obstructive lung disease, and diabetes. Each of these may be associated with a long period of disability. In addition, personal habits and health behaviors may be associated with both the development and the maintenance of these conditions (Kaplan, 1985). Table

BOX 2·1

HEALTH OBJECTIVES FOR THE YEAR 2000

In the National Health Promotion and Disease Prevention Objectives for the Year 2000, three overall objectives were proposed. These were (1) to increase the span of healthy life for Americans. Healthy life is a combination of life expectancy and quality of life. Americans currently lose the equivalent of about 11.7 years of life because of diseases and disabilities. These might be called "dysfunctional years." The figure below shows the dysfunctional years lost.

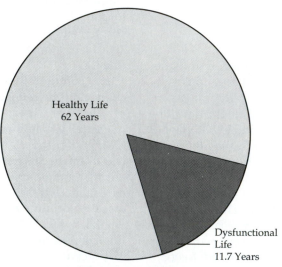

Healthy Life
62 Years

Dysfunctional
Life
11.7 Years

Life Expectancy 73.7 Years

Years of healthy life as a proportion of life expectancy, U.S. population (1980). (From National Vital Statistics System and National Health Interview Survey, CDC.)

(2) To reduce health disparity among Americans. Currently there are substantial differences between whites and various minority groups in several measures of health. For example, the life expectancy in 1988 for white Americans was 75.6 years, while it was only 69.4 years for blacks. This difference has not changed much in recent years (see figure on page 23).

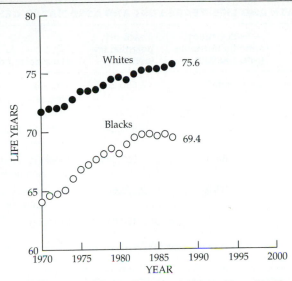

Life expectancy at birth, blacks and whites. (From *Health, United States, 1989 and Prevention Profile.*)

(3) To achieve preventive services for all Americans. Currently, low-income people, Hispanics, and black Americans are significantly less likely to have a source of primary care.

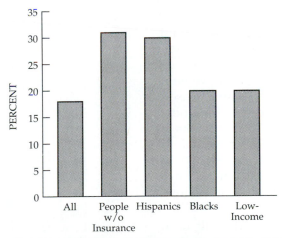

Percentage of people who lack a source of primary care (1986). (From Robert Wood Johnson Foundation.)

TABLE 2-1

TOP FIVE CAUSES OF DEATH AND LIFE-YEARS LOST AND ASSOCIATED BEHAVIORAL VARIABLES

Rank as cause of death	Cause*	1985 cause† specific mortality (rate/100,000)	Years of†, ‡ potential life lost	Behavioral correlate	Reference
1	Diseases of the heart	325.0	1,600,265	Smoking, high-fat diet, sedentary lifestyle	Anderson et al., 1987
2	Cancer	191.7	1,813,245	Smoking, high-fat/ low-fiber diet	Willett & MacMahon, 1984
3	Cerebrovascular disease	64.0	253,044	Smoking, high-fat diet, high-sodium diet	Dawber, 1980
4	Unintentional injuries	38.6	2,235,064	Alcohol use, failure to use seatbelts	Sleet, 1984
5	Chronic obstructive pulmonary disease	31.2	129,815	Smoking	Kaplan, Ries, & Atkins, 1985

* According to the ICD ninth revision codes.
† Data from *Mortality and Morbidity Weekly Report*, 36(15), Table V, April 24, 1987, p. 235.
‡ Based on assumed 65-year life expectancy and excludes death prior to 1 year of age (Kaplan, 1988).

2-1 summarizes some of these causes of death and the behaviors associated with them. In the following sections, we will explore some of the relationships between health behaviors and health outcomes.

It is important to consider the relative importance of different risk factors and different causes of death. Figure 2-1 summarizes six major causes of death and gives the relative numbers of cases in each category. Heart disease is clearly the leading cause of death in the United States, with an estimated 565,755 deaths in 1980. That same year, stroke accounted for another 170,225 deaths; cancer, 414,214; diabetes mellitus, over 304,000; and chronic obstructive pulmonary disease (COPD), over 50,000.

Big numbers are sometimes difficult to interpret. So in order to place these into context, we graphed the major causes of death and also included homicides and Lyme disease (see Figure 2-2). Homicides are included because we all fear being murdered and many people ac-

FIGURE 2-1

United States deaths from selected causes expressed as a percentage of all deaths. (From "Healthy People, Report of the U.S. Surgeon General," 1979.)

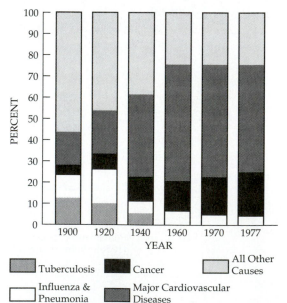

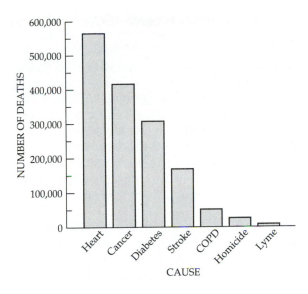

Estimated number of deaths from heart disease, cancer, diabetes, stroke, COPD, and homicide. Lyme disease data are cases, not deaths.

knowledge that they practice particular behaviors in order to avoid being a murder victim. Yet murder is a relatively less common cause of death, with about 23,000 cases reported each year. In fact, deaths from suicide in 1980 (26,689) were more common than murders. Lyme disease, an arthritis-like condition caused by bites from deer ticks, has been the latest reason for serious concern and public panic. Currently many products are marketed to help you prevent being a victim of Lyme disease, and significant numbers of people avoid outdoor activities for fear of becoming infected. Yet there were only about 5000 cases of Lyme disease in the United States in 1988. Figure 2-2 shows the total number of cases of Lyme disease and not the total number of deaths, as it does for the other diseases. As you can see, Lyme disease is very rare in comparison to heart disease, cancer, diabetes, and stroke.

We are not suggesting that murder and Lyme disease are unimportant. In fact, we urge you to engage in behaviors that will prevent them. We often make changes in our behaviors to avoid these dramatic problems because the linkage between our activities and these outcomes is obvious. However, there are similar linkages between behaviors and each of the other major causes of death. In some cases, altering behavior may have substantial effects upon causes of death in the United States and throughout the world. For example, we might have a major impact upon world health by changing cigarette smoking behavior (Peto, 1990).

BEHAVIORAL EPIDEMIOLOGY

We use the term *behavioral epidemiology* to describe the study of individual behaviors and habits in relation to health outcomes. Wise observers have been aware of the relationship between lifestyle and health for many centuries. This is evidenced by the following statement from Hippocrates in approximately 400 B.C.:

> Whoever wishes to investigate medicine properly, should proceed thus: . . . and the mode in which the inhabitants live, and what are their pursuits, whether they are fond of drinking and eating to excess, and given to indolence, and are fond of exercise and labor, and not given to excess eating and drinking.

Despite the long-standing suspicion about the detrimental influence of unhealthy habits, most systematic studies have been reported only within the last 25 years. These studies suggest significant associations between lifestyle variables and cancer, coronary heart disease, and other major causes of death. It has been less than 30 years since the surgeon general released the first report on smoking and health (U.S. Department of Health, Education, and Welfare, 1964). The report summarized evidence on the detrimental effects of cigarette smoking. During the last 25 years, the evidence that cigarette smoking is harmful has mushroomed. There are now several thousand published studies documenting the health consequences of cigarette use (United States Office of Smoking and Health, 1990).

In recognition of these relationships, the Institutes of Medicine of the National Academy of Sciences (1982) implicated the role of individual behavior in the cause and maintenance of many disease states. We will explore some of these linkages in more detail. First, however, it will be important to review the methodologies used to establish them.

EPIDEMIOLOGIC METHODOLOGY

Epidemiologists and social scientists use very similar research methodologies. The methodologies used by epidemiologists can be divided into two broad categories: descriptive and inferential. *Descriptive epidemiology* refers to the descripton of health outcomes and their determinants in terms of person, place, and time. *Inferential epidemiology* uses statistical methods to estimate characteristics of a population on the basis of a sample.

Person variables include the age of members of the population, their sex, and other characteristics including their racial or ethnic origin, marital status, and socioeconomic status. Person variables are sometimes referred to as *host* variables because some diseases may develop more in those with particular biologic or social characteristics. Breast cancer, for example, occurs more commonly in women with a family history of similar problems.

Place variables are also important in descriptive epidemiology. We know that certain problems are more common in some regions of the country than in others. For example, in studies of Lyme disease, which is a musculoskeletal problem associated with a bite by a specific deer tick, the original epidemiologic studies identified a preponderance of cases in Lyme, Connecticut. It was noted that people on one side of a river were much more likely to develop the problem than those who lived on the other side. Thus, place was associated with greater likelihood of exposure. We know that place is associated with a variety of different problems. For instance, people who live in the sunbelt have much higher chances of developing skin cancer than those who live in areas with less sun exposure. Multiple sclerosis becomes more common with greater distance from the equator.

Time is also an important consideration in descriptive epidemiology. Rapid changes in the rate of death are also very important from an epidemiologic standpoint. For example, the rapid increase in the number of persons infected with and succumbing to AIDS is a matter of major concern. AIDS is still not a major cause of death. Yet the rate of increase suggests that this condition is becoming a very serious public health problem. Epidemiologists often want to know about the duration between exposure to an infectious agent and the eventual outcome. The duration between exposure to the human immune deficiency virus (HIV) and development of clinical AIDS may be several years. For other diseases the duration may be even longer. Cigarette smoking may take 20 to 30 years to cause chronic obstructive pulmonary disease, and overexposure to saturated fat in the diet could take several decades before it has an impact on any health outcome. In order to understand these linkages, very long term studies are required.

EPIDEMIOLOGIC MEASURES

A variety of epidemiologic measures are commonly used in behavioral research. Epidemiologic studies typically focus on outcomes expressed as *morbidity* (illness) and *mortality* (death). Morbidity and mortality are usually reported in rates. These rates are divided into two major types: incidence and prevalence. *Incidence* refers to the rate at which new cases are occurring. Incidence is defined as the number of new cases that occur within a specific population within a defined time interval. Typically, the incidence rate is expressed per 1000 in the population. Conceptually it is:

$$\frac{\text{Incidence rate}}{\text{per 1000}} = \frac{\text{new cases per unit of time}}{\text{persons exposed or at risk per unit time} \times 1000}$$

Prevalence rates describe the number of diagnosed cases at a particular point in time.

$$\frac{\text{Prevalence rate}}{\text{per 1000}} = \frac{\text{cases at specific time point}}{\text{persons in population at specific time point} \times 1000}$$

Prevalence rate is equal to the incidence rate times the duration of the disease. For example, if the average duration of dementia is 5 years and its incidence is 3 per 1000 per year, the prevalence would be 15 per 1000. Figure 2-3 shows the incidence of heart disease and AIDS between 1980 and 1988. As the figure shows, AIDS has a low prevalence because it accounts for few deaths (in relation to heart disease). However, AIDS has a very rapid rate of increasing incidence—suggesting the seriousness of the epidemic. Conversely, heart disease has a decreasing incidence, but a very high prevalence.

Virtually all research designs common to clinical and experimental research are used in behavioral epidemiology. In this section we will provide a brief overview of observational and experimental studies. Observational studies do not attempt to manipulate variables in a systematic fashion. Instead, inferences are made on the basis of an ongoing series of observations. Some of the most common obser-

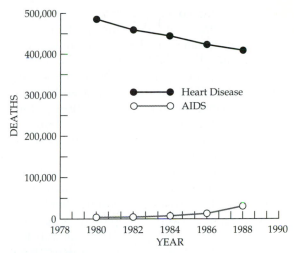

FIGURE 2-3

Incidence and prevalence of mortality due to heart disease and AIDS, U.S.A., 1980–1988.

vational studies include the cohort study, the panel study, and the case-control study.

Cohort Study

In a cohort study, groups of people who share some common characteristics are followed over the course of time. These studies, which are often prospective, resample the same population of individuals on repeated occasions. However, the exact participants in the study may not be the same on repeated observations.

Panel Study

A panel study is similar to a cohort study. However, the panel study has the stricter requirement that the exact same individuals who were in the original sample are followed at each repeated assessment. An example of a panel study was conducted by Jessor and Jessor (1977). These investigators were interested in alcohol, drug abuse, and deviant behavior among college students. A group of students were evaluated during their freshman year of college in 1969. This same group was restudied in 1970, 1971, 1972 and 1973. The investigators were able to report, for example, that marijuana use increased between the freshman and junior years in college. However, it leveled off during the senior year.

Cohort and panel studies are considered to be longitudinal designs. *Longitudinal studies* make inferences about changes over the course of time. The most respected epidemiologic studies use the prospective longitudinal panel study design. A variety of epidemiologic studies have considered both behavioral and biologic predispositions toward coronary heart disease. For example, the Framingham Heart Study began with 5127 participants who had no visible signs of heart disease. Each participant was given a physical examination and a detailed interview, including lifestyle and demographic characteristics, and was then followed every other year.

Epidemiologists typically evaluate risk factors in terms of ratios. For example, suppose that 30 percent of all smokers and 24 percent of all nonsmokers died from a fatal heart attack in a population-based study. Then: $\frac{0.30}{0.24} = 1.25$.

Thus, smoking increased the risk of a fatal heart attack 25 percent over that due to all other risk factors combined. The *relative risk*, in this example, is a measure of the importance of smoking as a cause for a fatal heart attack.

Cross-sectional studies differ from longitudinal studies in that they examine different groups of individuals at the same point in time. To make inferences about drug use in college, for example, the cross-sectional method would require sampling of each current class. Then, freshmen could be compared with sophomores, juniors, and seniors. These individuals would not be members of the same class or birth cohort.

Case-Control Study

This methodology compares a group of people with a diagnosed disease (cases) with one or more groups that have not been given the same diagnosis. Case-control studies are typically retrospective because they make inferences about events that have caused currently diagnosed cases. Longitudinal studies are often prospective and have the advantage of documenting antecedents of new cases.

In observational studies variables that are uncontrolled through the experimental design are often adjusted for using statistical methods. Randomized clinical traits and quasi experiments are covered in the next section.

Experimental Studies

In contrast to observational studies in which important variables are not controlled, experimental studies typically involve the systematic manipulation of variables. Illnesses have natural histories, and in most instances their course fluctuates considerably without treatment. One of the difficulties in determining the effects of an intervention is that the intervention may occur at a crisis time. For example, patients with an illness might seek care on days when they are most sick. If the illness is likely to get better on its own (as in the case of most common illnesses), any treatment will appear to have "worked." A control group can help sort out the effect of treatment from other factors. In this way, a group receiving the intervention under study is compared with the control group that does not receive treatment to determine whether there are differences attributable to the intervention.

It is widely accepted among medical and biobehavioral scientists that a control or comparison group is required to establish causal inference. In some cases, investigators are willing to accept "quasi-experimental" data in which an *ad hoc* control is used, or where there is a stable baseline of observations prior to an intervention. However, several authors have argued that an experiment characterized by a single observation, an intervention, and a second observation is virtually impossible to interpret from a causal perspective.

Bias occurs when the design of a study does not ensure an impartial assessment of the treatment. For experiments using control groups, random assignment to treatment and control conditions is very desirable. Simply stated, randomized clinical trials remove several sources of bias. The value of randomized clinical trials has been emphasized by Sacks, Chalmers, and Smith (1982), who reviewed six therapies for which approximately equal numbers of randomized clinical trials and nonrandomized trials have been reported in the literature. They found that 79 percent of the studies in which patients were not randomly assigned to groups reported that the therapy was better than the control regimen. In contrast, the same therapies were found to be effective in only 20 percent of the studies in which patients had been randomly assigned to the treatment or control condition. In a related review, Chalmers and his colleagues (1983) analyzed 145 scientific reports which were divided into three categories: those in which the randomization process was blinded, those in which the randomization was unblinded, and those in which assignment to treatment or control was by a nonrandom process. *Blinding* refers to the process of keeping investigators ignorant of the treatment assignments. Review of these studies suggested that there was a systematic relationship between the rigor of the experimental design and the probability of finding a treatment benefit. There was a significant treatment benefit in 58 percent of the studies in which the subjects were not randomly assigned. The same benefit was observed in 24 percent of the unblinded randomized studies and in approximately 9 percent of the blinded randomized studies.

In summary, there are many sources of bias in studies that do not use control groups, and the end result is frequently an overestimate of the effects of the therapy under study. These biases are reduced in experimental studies, but the rigor of the experimental design is systematically related to the chances of not finding a treatment benefit. Valid scientific inferences must be built upon a solid experimental foundation.

MAJOR EPIDEMIOLOGIC STUDIES

Much of what we know about behavioral risk factors comes from a limited number of major epidemiologic investigations. There are several major studies that have been conducted in the United States, Canada, Europe, and Australia. To provide a flavor of these studies, we will review three of the major investigations: the Framingham Heart Study, the Alameda County Population Study, and the Stanford Three- and Five-Community Studies. These studies will be mentioned repeatedly throughout the rest of the book because they provide some of the basic justifications for behavioral interventions.

Framingham Heart Study

The Framingham Heart Study is the oldest and perhaps best known population study in the United States. In 1948, a group of medical researchers entered the average New England town of Framingham, Massachusetts (population about 68,000) to begin one of the largest and most important epidemiologic studies in the history of medicine. Framingham is an average Massachusetts town, not far from Boston. In fact, it is along the course of the

Boston Marathon. The purpose of the Framingham Heart Study was to determine the causes of stroke and heart failure. Before the Framingham Study, most investigations of heart disease had been retrospective. *Retrospective* studies start with a group of people who have already developed heart trouble and then look into their pasts to determine what they had in common. In contrast, the researchers in the Framingham Study started with healthy people and attempted to predict which ones would eventually die of heart and circulatory problems. This approach is called *prospective* and is considered to produce superior and more convincing scientific data than the retrospective method. The study began by identifying every other man and woman in Framingham between the ages of 30 and 60 who had no signs of heart disease. In the beginning there were 5127 participants. Each time a new subject was enrolled, he or she was given a thorough physical exam and a detailed interview about lifestyle. The subjects were remeasured every 2 years.

Within a few decades, the picture of the "heart disease prone" individual began to emerge, because many of the Framingham subjects had suffered heart attacks or strokes. Some of the predictors of heart disease were identified as beyond the subject's control, such as age (older people are more prone), sex (males are more prone), certain diseases such as diabetes, and race (blacks are more prone). However, a major finding of the study was that some of the best predictors of heart disease and early death are direct consequences of our own behavior. These predictors of heart disease include smoking, obesity, high cholesterol level (perhaps associated with a high animal fat diet), physical inactivity, and possibly excessive tension and stress.

The Framingham Heart Study has been very important in establishing that some risk factors for heart disease are *mutable*, or subject to change. Thus, much of the current practice of

preventive medicine was launched. Risk factors were identified, and important recommendations for behavior change were offered. The Framingham Heart Study has continued to follow the original group of participants. In addition, the study has been expanded to include the offspring of the original participants and, more recently, their grandchildren. Literally hundreds of scientific papers have been based on observations from this important New England community.

Alameda County Study

The Alameda County Study originally identified 8300 adults who lived in 4735 households. Eighty-six percent of the eligible adults completed questionnaires, and these 6928 individuals have been followed by the investigators for 25 years. The study began in 1965, and by the mid-1970s, a variety of interesting findings began to emerge. For example, a series of important analyses (Belloc & Breslow, 1972; Breslow & Enstrom, 1980; Kaplan, 1985; Kaplan, Lazarus, Cohen, & Lew, 1991; Wingard, Berkman, & Brand, 1982) demonstrated that health habits were a major predictor of survival for the residents of this urban California community. The specific predictors of surviving (not dying early) included not smoking cigarettes, using alcohol in moderation, being average weight, moderate leisure time physical activity, and obtaining 7 to 9 hours of sleep each night. In some of the analyses the investigators simply counted the number of good health habits the participants engaged in. They found systematic relationships between the number of these activities and both morbidity (illness) and mortality (early death). For example, those who engaged in zero of these practices were 3.11 times more likely to die of heart disease than those who engaged in five of the activities.

The Alameda County Study also broke new ground by demonstrating the relationship between social support and health outcomes. Those who were more "socially connected" had significantly greater chances of survival than those who were less connected. We will discuss this particular issue in more detail in Chapter 7.

The Stanford Three-Community Study

The Framingham Heart Study and the Alameda County Study are each prospective *observational* studies. Another approach to epidemiology has sometimes been called *experimental epidemiology*. Studies in experimental epidemiology attempt to manipulate risk factors within free-living populations. Several years ago a group at Stanford University headed by cardiologist John Farquhar and psychologist Nathan Maccoby began heroic experiments designed to evaluate changes in health behavior within entire communities. They found three small farming communities in California that had approximately equal distributions of ethnic groups, income levels, and average risks of heart disease. One community—Tracy, California—served as a control group. A survey of health habits and cardiac risk factors was conducted there each year between 1972 and 1975. A second community—Gilroy, California—was also studied for the same 4 years. However, during the second 2 years of the study, residents of this town were exposed to mass media campaigns designed to change their smoking habits, their consumption of animal fats, and their exercise patterns. The media campaign consisted of 50 television commercials, 3 hours of television programming, several hours of radio programming and 100 radio spots, a newspaper column that appeared weekly in the local paper, newspaper advertisements, billboards, direct mail information, calendars, and several other advertising gimmicks (Maccoby et al., 1985).

The third community, Watsonville, also received the intensive media campaign. In addition, individuals who were at high risk for heart disease were identified, and $\frac{2}{3}$ of these potential heart victims were given intensive individualized instruction. The instruction was based on well-determined methods of behavior modification and social learning theory. The methods included self-observation, modeling, and token reinforcement (Meyer et al., 1980).

The study demonstrated that mass media can be successfully used to change behavior when the media campaigns are based on the scientific principles of social and clinical psychology. Figures 2-4 and 2-5 summarize the findings for the three-community study. The control group showed the greatest continued

FIGURE 2-4

Percentage of change from baseline (0) in knowledge of cardiovascular disease risk factors after the three annual follow-up surveys. (From Meyer, A. J., Nash, J. D., McAlister, A. L., Maccoby, N., and Farquhar, J. W. Skills training in cardiovascular health education campaign. *Journal of Consulting and Clinical Psychology* 48. Copyright 1980 by the American Psychological Association. Reprinted by permission of the publisher and author.)

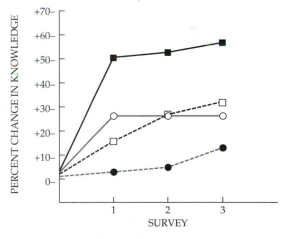

- ● Tracy Control
- ▢ Gilroy Media Only
- ○ Watsonville Media Only
- ■ Watsonville Intensive Instruction

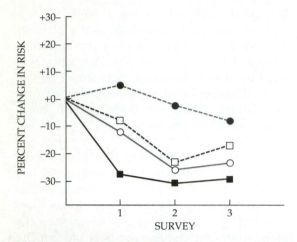

● Tracy Control
□ Gilroy Media Only
○ Watsonville Media Only
■ Watsonville Intensive Instruction

FIGURE 2-5

Percentage of change from baseline (0) in risk of cardiovascular disease after the three annual follow-up surveys. (From Meyer, A. J., Nash, J. D., McAlister, A. L., Maccoby, N., and Farquhar, J. W. Skills training in cardiovascular health education campaign. *Journal of Consulting and Clinical Psychology* 48. Copyright 1980 by the American Psychological Association. Reprinted by permission of the publisher and author.)

risk for heart disease and the least change in knowledge about heart disease over the course of the 3 follow-up years. The media-only condition, which was used in Gilroy, might be considered the same as the campaign given for those residents in Watsonville who did not get individualized counseling. As the figures show, these groups were quite similar in change of heart risk factors and in knowledge about heart disease. The most impressive changes in heart risk factors and knowledge gain were obtained for the group receiving both media exposure and intensive counseling. Overall, the results are quite impressive: they demonstrate that psychological methods can be used on a large scale to reduce the threat of heart disease (Maccoby et al., 1985).

We will discuss the Stanford Study in more detail in Chapter 18. Suffice it to say, however, that epidemiologic studies include both observation and, in some cases, manipulation of experimental variables.

PERSON, PLACE, AND TIME IN EPIDEMIOLOGICAL STUDIES

Epidemiologists are interested in the influences of person, place, and time upon health outcomes. Most epidemiologic studies involve all three components. In the next few sections, we will consider studies that focus primarily on person, time, or place.

Person

As an example of the person variable, sex differences in morbidity and mortality will be considered in Box 2-2, "Focus on Women."

Place

One example of the importance of place concerns the relationship between sunlight exposure and the development of cancer. One group of researchers believes that exposure to sunlight may be helpful in preventing certain cancers. For example, they have demonstrated that skin cancers are more common in regions of the world where people are exposed to more ultraviolet light from the sun. However, sunlight is also an important source of vitamin D, and some cancers may be related to deficiencies in this important vitamin. They suggest that vitamin D does play an important role in colon and breast cancer. One of their hypotheses is that the high levels of pollutants in the air that cause haze block ultraviolet light and may result in vitamin D deficiencies. In one study they examined the relationships between sulfur dioxide and other components of air pollution that block sunlight in 20 Canadian cities. They found significant relationships between the presence of this type of air pollution and the development of colon cancer in both men and women as well as significant relationships between the pollutants and breast cancer in women. Mortality rates for cancer not believed to be associated with vitamin D were not associated with these levels of aerosols (Gorham, Garland & Garland, 1989).

In conclusion, place may be very important because people in some areas have toxic exposures. These might be exposures to contaminants in the air, difficult weather, water systems, or other environmental factors. The studies described above suggest that air pollution may block sunlight. This can ultimately result in increased risk of cancers of the breast and colon (Garland, Garland & Gorham, 1991).

Another example of a place variable concerns cancer epidemics. There has been some controversy as to whether certain cancers are caused by radiation exposure. One study evaluated men who worked at the Oakridge National Laboratory, a U.S. Department of Energy Research Facility in Oakridge, Tennessee. Workers at this facility are exposed to higher levels of radioactive material than people in the general population. Overall, workers at this facility tend to be very healthy in comparison to the U.S. population. Although it was previously believed that radiation exposure had only small effects, recent evidence suggests that excesses in leukemia deaths occur among those exposed to higher dosages of radiation at work (Wing et al., 1991). Place of work as well as place of residence may have a substantial impact on who develops certain illnesses.

Time

Many illnesses develop slowly. Thus, the epidemiologist must consider time in addition to person and place variables. The epidemiology of heart disease is a good example. Heart disease may develop slowly over the course of time, and behavioral variables have been shown to be a major contributing cause. Before we consider the time issue, it will be necessary to give an overview of heart disease epidemiology.

It has been estimated that 6 million Americans have coronary heart disease and that an additional 2 million have cerebrovascular disease (problems with blood flow to the brain). Furthermore, about 58 million people have high blood pressure (National Heart, Lung, & Blood Institute, 1985). In the United States, there are about 4000 heart attacks every day. If you spend 1 minute reading this paragraph, about three people will have had heart attacks while you are reading. Prospective epidemiologic studies have identified a variety of major risk factors for coronary heart disease and stroke. These will be reviewed in more detail in Chapter 10. Some of these risk factors are difficult to do anything about. For example, men die of heart disease more often than women, particularly in the younger age categories. Blacks are more likely than whites to have high blood pressure and to eventually die of heart disease (National Center for Health Statistics, 1985). Family history is also an important predictor of death due to heart disease. Those with family histories of heart attack or stroke are more likely to develop these problems themselves.

Although many risk factors are difficult to do something about, epidemiologic studies have demonstrated that most of the risk factors for heart disease are under our control. These risk factors include cigarette smoking, cholesterol, obesity, and high blood pressure. Some studies have tried to compare the population attributable risk relevant to four risk factors for heart disease. Among these, high blood pressure is the most important risk factor, followed by cigarette smoking. High blood pressure may be the cause of 30 percent of all cardiovascular deaths. It has been estimated that $\frac{1}{2}$ of those suffering a first heart attack and $\frac{2}{3}$ of

BOX 2-2

FOCUS ON WOMEN

Women live longer than men (Wingard, 1984). Today the life expectancy for a female is 78.3 years, while the equivalent life expectancy for men is about 71.3 years. Epidemiologists and health psychologists have been very interested in why women survive longer. Is it because women are biologically superior? Or could it be that women have healthier lifestyles? The answers to these questions have intrigued and, in fact, puzzled many interested scholars.

Figure 2-6 summarizes the ratios of mortality for men and women across different age ranges. The ratio is formed by taking the age- and sex-specific death rates for males and dividing them by these same statistics for females. The rate is the mortality rate per 100,000 people in the population. As the figure suggests, the ratio is greater than 1 at each age. Thus, for those under 1 year of age, the ratio is 1.26, suggesting that even within the first year of life 1.26 males die for each female that dies. The peak point is during late adolescence and early adulthood. Between the ages of 15 and 24, 3.1 males die for each female that dies. Then, the ratio tails off as a function of age. Yet even in the 85-and-over age category 1.27 males die for each female that dies.

Epidemiologists might consider sex to be a "person variable." However, place is also important. For in-

stance, the sex differential in mortality is not constant across locations in the world. Women do live longer in most developed countries. In Finland, for example, women have an 8.5-year advantage. However, in developing countries there may be no advantage for females. In fact, females may have a shorter life expectancy, as evidenced by the 3-year male advantage in India (Waldron, 1983).

The sex differential may also be influenced by time variables. For example, the survival advantage of women may be a more recent phenomenon. Figure 2-7 shows the sex mortality ratio in the United States estimated during different decades. As the figure indicates, the differences between males and females in mortality rate have increased successively from 1900 through 1980. The figure also shows differences in the different age categories. The largest increase has occurred for those between the ages of 15 and 24 and for those between 55 and 64. It is not entirely clear what accounts for these differences. However, in the 15 to 24 age category the differences may reflect a decrease in the number of females who die of complications of pregnancy and childbirth. In the later age category the differences may reflect the increase in the number of men who die of coronary heart disease.

Another explanation for the differences is that men and women die from different diseases. Men may make themselves susceptible to a variety of diseases or problems that cause early death. Figure 2-8 summarizes the age-adjusted mortality rates for 12 leading causes of death. The figure identifies differential rates between males and females. Calculating the ratio of male to female deaths suggests that some causes of death are much more common in men than women. The figure presents these in rank order. Concerning homicide, for example, a male is 3.9 times more likely to be victimized than a female. Diabetes, at the other extreme, is an equally common cause of death in males and females. There are seven causes of death for which men are at least twice as likely to die as women. These are homicide, lung cancer, suicide, chronic obstructive pulmonary disease, accidents, cirrhosis of the liver, and diseases of the heart. Each of these is believed to be related to individual behavior. For example, lung cancer and chronic obstructive pulmonary disease are both primarily caused by smoking cigarettes. Homicide, accidents, and cirrhosis of the liver each have a suspicious association with alcohol use. Suicide is a behavioral act, and the relationship between behavior and heart disease has

FIGURE 2-6

Sex ratios for mortality by age (M/F).

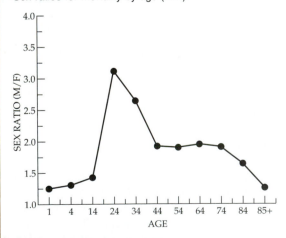

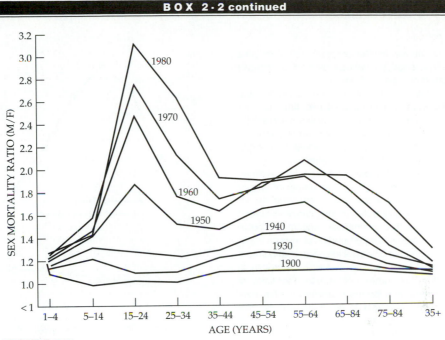

FIGURE 2-7

Sex mortality ratio (M/F) by age, United States, 1900–1980. Based on mortality rates. (From data in Winegard and Cohn 1990.)

FIGURE 2-8

Sex mortality ratios for 13 causes of death, U.S., 1980. (After Wingard & Cohn, 1990, Table 2.)

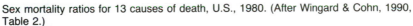

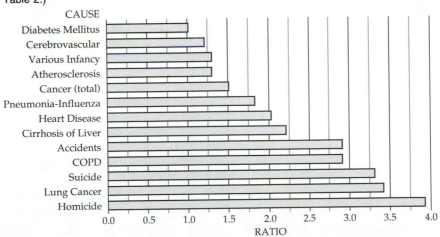

BOX 2·2 continued

been discussed above. In later chapters, we will discuss the relationships between various aspects of lifestyle and these different causes of death.

There are certain areas in which we would expect the sex differential in mortality to decline over time. Cancer of the lung is one important case. Forty years ago smoking cigarettes was relatively uncommon among women. However, campaigns by the tobacco industry have significantly increased the number of women who smoke cigarettes. Overall, the number of smokers has declined in the past few decades, and yet the number of female smokers has gradually increased. There was an increase in the rate of death due to lung cancer between 1950 and 1975. As the commercial suggests, "You've come a long way, baby." The proportion of women experiencing serious chronic diseases associated with smoking has gradually increased to match the increase in smoking rates. Even more unfortunate, the risks of smoking for women may be more severe than for men. In the past, death rates due to heart disease, chronic lung disease, and lung cancer were lower for women than for men. However, this can be attributed to the difference in the number of men and women who smoke cigarettes. Since the number of female smokers has increased greatly, we can expect a big increase in the number of female heart attack and cancer victims. Figure 2-9 shows the male/female ratio in deaths from lung cancer and heart disease between 1950 and 1985. In 1960 there were nearly 7 male deaths from lung cancer for every 1 female death. By 1985 this ratio was down to less than 3 to 1. It was during this period (1960–1985)

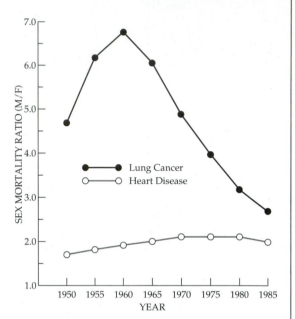

FIGURE 2-9

that the proportion of female smokers increased. Now the number of female smokers is beginning to exceed the number of male smokers. Thus, we may expect habits to explain some decline in the female advantage sometime in the future (Wingard & Cohn, 1990).

those suffering a stroke have high blood pressure (Kannel, Thom, & Hurst, 1986). Several studies have now demonstrated that we can reduce the burden of suffering by controlling high blood pressure. Treatments for high blood pressure (which will be discussed in Chapter 10) depend upon behavior change. Some treatments involve changing long-standing habits such as reducing dietary salt, increasing daily exercise, and reducing weight. Other treatments involve the use of medications. Although substantial evidence suggests that blood pressure can be reduced with medications, compliance with these treatments is

often disturbingly low. In other words, patients simply do not take their medications on a regular basis. Behavioral interventions may be very important in helping people find ways to comply with these difficult medical regimens (Kaplan & Ries, 1992).

In addition to elevated blood pressure, high blood cholesterol is also a major risk factor for death due to heart disease. It is widely believed that "luxury" diets with high percentages of calories from animal fats increase the probability of death from heart disease. Several epidemiologic studies have identified high levels of cholesterol in blood serum as a risk factor for death, and it is assumed that high dietary fat contributes to these high blood cholesterol levels. Thus, the behavior of consuming a high-fat diet may be a risk factor for coronary heart disease. This will be discussed in more detail in Chapter 14.

Perhaps the most important controllable risk factor for heart disease is cigarette smoking. Although smoking is on the decline, more than 30 percent of all adults still smoke cigarettes. As many as 17 percent of all heart disease deaths may be attributed to cigarette smoking. This translates into about 78,000 deaths per year (American Heart Association, 1986). Others have estimated that smoking causes many more deaths. For example, one report suggested that more than 145,000 cardiovascular deaths in 1980 could be attributed to cigarette smoking (White, Tolsma, Haynes, & McGee, 1987). It is important to consider the number of smoking-related heart disease deaths in relation to deaths from other causes. For example, consider deaths due to murder. There are approximately 23,000 per year in the United States, and we have come to think of murder as very common. Thus, we spend much of our resources on more police and stricter laws, and we deal with murderers very harshly. Yet we have been relatively lenient with those who promote and sell cigarettes. Considering only heart disease (just one of the many diseases caused by cigarette smoking), there may be four to eight people who die from cigarette use for each person who dies from murder.

The risk factors for heart disease were almost all identified and confirmed in the major epidemiologic studies. The studies evaluated people's habits while they were healthy. Then the participants were followed over the course of time, and the researchers observed differences in adverse health outcomes among those with the various risk factors. Time is important in these epidemiologic studies because we have witnessed genuine epidemics of heart

---

BOX 2-3

FOCUS ON RESEARCH

Cigarette smoking is one of the major causes of death in the world today. (See Chapters 10, 11, 15.) However, epidemiologists believe that this problem may be more severe in the future. Richard Peto is chair of the World Health Organization Group on Statistical Aspects of Tobacco-Related Mortality. He recently performed an analysis of the expected future changes in mortality as a function of cigarette smoking. The results were shocking.

Today, there are about 3 million deaths per year attributable to cigarette smoking. However, today's rates represent the development of tobacco habits that began many years ago. It may take 15 to 30 years to develop heart disease, cancer, or chronic lung disease associated with cigarette use. In China, for example, there were about 30,000 lung cancer deaths in 1975. The Chinese population will increase four times over by the year 2025. Furthermore, the proportion of men in the Chinese population using cigarettes has increased dramatically. As a result of the increase in smoking, the cancer rates are expected to increase sevenfold. The projection for the year 2025 is that there will be 840,000 lung cancer deaths. This is calculated as current deaths $\times$ growth in population $\times$ increase in cancer death rate ($30,000 \times 4 \times 7 = 840,000$). Those to be killed by tobacco in the year 2025 are already alive today. Examining the use of cigarettes around the world suggests that there have been declines in westernized countries such as the United States and the United Kingdom. However, cigarette smoking is increasing rapidly in the third world. At least $\frac{1}{4}$ of all regular smokers will be killed by lung cancer or by other cigarette-related diseases. In countries such as China, the rate of increase in cigarette use is staggering. There were about 500 billion cigarettes sold to China in 1978. By 1987, this number had increased to 1400 billion, and the rate was rising about 10 percent per year. Projections on a worldwide basis are even more shocking. Without a major reduction in the uptake of cigarette smoking, we might expect more than 10 million deaths per year worldwide after the year 2020 (Peto 1990; Peto et al., 1992).

---

disease in this century. At the turn of the century, heart disease was relatively uncommon. However, there were rapid increases in the numbers of people who died from heart disease over the first half of the century. Since about 1968, the number of people dying of heart disease has been declining. Many believe that these reductions are associated with the identification of heart disease risk factors. The declines coincide with greater awareness of some of the behavioral factors that cause these ailments. Heart disease and its risk factors will be covered in more detail in Chapters 14 to 17.

SUMMARY

In this chapter we have provided an overview of the science of epidemiology. Epidemiology is the basic science that offers the foundation for preventive medicine. It uses the methods of social sciences alongside the techniques of the biological sciences. In recent years epidemiologists have discovered that many of the risk factors for the major causes of death are behavioral. Heart disease may be associated with high dietary fat consumption, physical inactivity, and cigarette smoking. Cancer may be caused by smoking cigarettes and by eating a high-fat and low-fiber diet. Epidemiologists have also shown that women are less at risk for some of the major causes of death and have a longer life expectancy in the western world. Despite advances in modern medicine, there are substantial differences between white and nonwhite populations in the chances of suffering from most of the major diseases.

How does this affect you? The answer may be obvious. Avoid cigarettes, high-fat foods, and other unhealthy activities. Yet once we have identified these problems, implementing the changes is often difficult. Most smokers know that it is bad to smoke, and most adults are aware that they need to avoid junk food. Yet breaking habits is hard. In several of the remaining chapters we will explore how health habits develop and how to use behavioral technologies to modify these habits.

KEY TERMS

Population attributable risk. The proportion of cases of a disease in the entire population that can be attributed to a risk factor.

Cross-sectional study. A study of individuals at a specific point in time. In a cross-sectional study, inferences about the differences between age groups, for example, are based on observations of people of different ages measured at the same point in time.

Case-control study. A study that compares a group of people with a diagnosed disease or problem with one or more groups who do not have the same diagnosis. Typically case-control studies are retrospective.

Experimental study. A study that involves the systematic manipulation of variables. In experimental studies the investigator typically manipulates the variables.

Framingham Heart Study. A major epidemiologic study of the town of Framingham, Massachusetts. This study was one of the first to establish the risk factors for heart disease.

Alameda County Study. The study of adults in a heterogeneous California community. The Alameda County Study has been important in establishing the role of psychosocial variables as risk factors for various illnesses.

The Stanford Three-Community and Five-Community Studies. These studies are examples of quick experimental epidemiology in which interventions to modify risk factors were undertaken and people in established communities were followed over the course of time to determine the effects of the intervention.

CHAPTER 3

Understanding and Changing Health Behaviors

There was a jovial discussion at Victor's party. Everyone was talking about Herman, Victor's friend who had not yet arrived. Herman would be the first to admit that he had unhealthy habits. He smoked cigarettes, drank excessively, and lived on a diet of hamburgers and potato chips. There was considerable speculation about why Herman did this. Jill argued that Herman was simply self-destructive. Margaret speculated that this was the way Herman had been raised and he was simply doing what his parents had done. Jim suggested that Herman did what was pleasurable to him and that, in a sense, the feedback he got from cigarettes and hamburgers was much more pleasurable than he could obtain from carrot sticks and fish.

What determines our health habits? We will explore some of the explanations in this chapter.

THE CHALLENGE OF HEALTH BEHAVIOR CHANGE

Human behavior is one of the greatest mysteries of our world. We are all "experts" in human behavior because we are intimately familiar with it. Yet our ability to understand, predict, and control behavior is still very limited. Science has made so much progress in the physical and biological sciences that we sometimes get the impression that we already know just about everything (or that we soon will). We know so much about outer space that humans have gone to the moon and back, and unmanned probes are exploring beyond our solar system. We have learned many of the secrets of the atom, and this knowledge has allowed us to endanger our own existence. We now understand the secrets of the genetic code, and this ability to create new life forms has raised profound questions of ethics and morality. Our advances in computing and communications technology are so impressive that we often assume further technological progress will soon solve many of the remaining problems of the human race.

This reliance on technological approaches has also been evident in medicine. Rooms full of scanners, lasers, computers, laboratory instruments, and diagnostic aids are supplemented by an amazing variety of vaccines, medications, and drug delivery systems, for almost every possible ailment. Progress in the biomedical sciences has been extraordinary and has resulted in increases in longevity and cures for many diseases.

However, neither biological nor electronic technology has resulted in the elimination of all diseases, and as you learned earlier, the major causes of death are diseases of the heart and blood vessels, cancers, and injuries. Many of the causes of these problems are behaviors, and without a clear understanding of these behavioral causes, great progress in fighting these health problems may be slow. Another result of the reliance on medical technology is that more patients are dissatisfied with their care. Many argue that there is insufficient emphasis in medical school on the doctor-patient relationship, with the result that physicians who are well trained to treat diseases are not as skilled in treating their patients. Patients who are not happy with their care are less likely to follow their doctor's recommendations, so concern with the behavior of health care providers is based on its impact on health outcomes. Thus, even in this technological age,

the behaviors of both patients and health care providers are still important.

Psychologists have just begun to apply their theories and methods of studying human behavior to the field of health behavior. While 100 years of the science of behavior have produced a large body of knowledge for psychology as a whole, it must be admitted that we are still limited in our ability to understand and change health behaviors. There have been many successes that are detailed in later chapters, but much is still to be learned. With continued study we will be better able to answer such questions as:

- Why do some people continue to smoke even after a heart attack or cancer surgery?
- How can we improve adherence to prescribed medications?
- Why do most people not exercise even though they believe it is a healthy thing to do?
- How can a physician most effectively prepare a patient for a stressful medical exam?
- Why do adolescents have unsafe sex despite knowledge that it puts them at risk for AIDS?
- How can we teach children to eat low-fat foods even though they enjoy fatty foods more?
- Why do people under stress often try to cope by abusing alcohol, when this usually creates other problems?
- Can we predict which candidates for heart transplants will successfully adjust to having a new heart?
- How can we control the expensive and often self-injurious behavior of continually seeking medical care for nonexistent medical problems?

You can see from this short list that health psychologists are called upon to deal with difficult problems that have no easy or obvious solutions. Health psychology must deal with the behavior of patients and health care pro-

BOX 3·1

HEALTH OBJECTIVES FOR THE YEAR 2000

Behavior Change and Health Objectives

Behavior change is required to meet most of the year 2000 health objectives for the nation. The many agencies and experts who developed the objectives realized that many health problems will not improve unless behaviors change. There are 22 priority areas, and objectives in all of them call for some type of behavior change. In most cases, the behavior of individual citizens is targeted. Individual behavior change is most evident in the *health promotion* objectives:

1. Physical activity and fitness
2. Nutrition
3. Tobacco
4. Alcohol and other drugs
5. Family planning
6. Mental health and mental disorders
7. Violent and abusive behavior
8. Educational and community-based programs

This list reflects the consensus of health professionals about individual behaviors that are most important to the health and well-being of the population. Most of these topics are addressed in chapters or major sections in this book, so that after reading it you should have a good understanding about why these behaviors are important and how to go about changing them to improve health.

It is not only individual behaviors that are important. "Healthy People 2000" emphasizes that behaviors are performed in a social context. This means that the behavior of other people is also important. Of particular importance are the behaviors of people who make policies that affect our health. Individuals and policymakers at various levels of government, as well as in industry, share responsibility for meeting the *health protection* objectives. Those topics are:

9. Unintentional injuries
10. Occupational safety and health
11. Environmental health
12. Food and drug safety
13. Oral health

In all of these cases, the individual needs to regulate his or her own behavior to reduce the risk of injuries, to follow safety guidelines at work, to practice oral hygiene, etc. However, the actions of policymakers can work either for or against the actions of the individual. Although most people are not aware of it, the government has been steadily improving the safety of roads and highways through engineering changes. Before the individual had the choice of wearing seat belts, government and industry had to work together to put them in cars.

Even though air bags are becoming more widely available now, the auto industry fought against them for over 20 years, and this policy has cost the lives of many people.

Employers are responsible for the safety of workplaces, industry and government must work together to protect the environment and the food supply, and local government decisions about fluoridating the water supply affect oral health. In the health protection area, the behavior of government and industry officials is of interest, in addition to individual actions.

Regarding *preventive services,* individuals share responsibility with health professionals to improve health in the following areas:

14. Maternal and infant health
15. Heart disease and stroke
16. Cancer
17. Diabetes and chronic disabling conditions
18. HIV infection
19. Sexually transmitted diseases
20. Immunization and infectious diseases
21. Clinical preventive services

Many of the behaviors in the health promotion section are relevant to these health problems, so individuals have a responsibility to change their behaviors so as to reduce risk. However, for the millions of people with these problems, health professionals must provide quality services. Thus, the behavior of health professionals is targeted in this section. The health care system is struggling with ways of using limited resources to have the greatest impact on the health of the population. When physicians and other professionals prescribe an effective treatment, it is usually up to the patient to comply with that treatment.

The final priority area is *surveillance and data systems,* and it is targeted to government officials who are responsible for funding and collecting national health information. This priority will help determine whether the other health objectives are being met.

As you can see, "Healthy People 2000" is full of behavioral goals and objectives. However, there are very few statements about what specific methods can be used to change the behaviors of individual citizens from diverse backgrounds, health professionals, business executives, government officials, and lawmakers. This chapter describes theories and methods of behavior change that apply to people from all of these groups. As you read the chapter, consider how you can apply what you are learning to your own behavior as well as the behavior of these other groups.

viders, the healthy and the sick, children and adults, well-educated and illiterate individuals. The behaviors of concern range from common behaviors such as eating, exercise, and talking to friends, to specialized behaviors such as keeping medical appointments, submitting to painful tests, and taking care of sick relatives. Some health behaviors occur under supervision in the hospital, clinic, or doctor's office. Other behaviors must be performed without assistance at home, at work, and at school. Some health behaviors are performed only once, while others must be continued for a lifetime. Some behaviors make you feel better, while others make you feel worse. Given the diversity in health behaviors, it is not surprising that no single theory or model has been shown to explain all behaviors. No one approach has been shown to be effective for changing all behaviors. However, several theories have been useful in explaining some behaviors, and the next section of this chapter describes the major theories of health behavior.

RESPONDENT AND OPERANT LEARNING

Both respondent and operant learning emphasize environmental events and do not consider cognitive variables. These are not theories or models in the usual sense. They were not developed by a theoretician as a guide to further research and conceptualization. Rather, these "theories" are the result of many years of careful research on animals and humans. On the basis of these thousands of studies, basic principles of learning have been summarized, and these are what we now refer to as respondent and operant learning theories. While most of the early research was conducted on mice, rats, and pigeons, the principles apply well to human behavior. Since health behaviors are simply a subset of the general category of "be-

havior," these principles are useful in understanding health behaviors as well.

Principles of Respondent Learning

As you recall from introductory psychology, respondent conditioning was discovered by the great Russian physiologist Ivan Pavlov (1927). Pavlov was studying the process of digestion that begins with salivation. He was conducting experiments in which he placed meat powder on a dog's tongue. Since salivation occurred every time, he called this an unconditioned response, or reflex. It can be diagramed like this:

UNCONDITIONED   UNCONDITIONED
STIMULUS $\longrightarrow$ RESPONSE
(food)   (salivation)

With repeated trials he began to observe an annoying phenomenon. Soon the dog would salivate just before the meat was placed in its mouth. Then the dog would salivate when it saw the food, then when the technician came near, and then at the sight of the technician. Even though this odd response was interfering with his experiments, Pavlov's curiosity was aroused. He began to study this new problem. By repeatedly sounding a bell just before placing the food in the dog's mouth, Pavlov found that the sound of the bell would soon come to elicit the salivation response. This new association between the bell and salivation was called a *conditioned response*, because Pavlov had to condition the dog to respond to the bell. The response is the same, but it occurs in the presence of a new stimulus.

CONDITIONED   CONDITIONED
STIMULUS $\longrightarrow$ RESPONSE
(bell)   (salivation)

This effect can be extended by additional pairings. For example, the bell could be paired with a picture, so that the picture then elicited salivation. Respondent conditioning can become complex, and in some situations it may be difficult to trace how a stimulus came to be associated with a response. Pairings can also take place "by accident." If Pavlov's technician always turned on the light in the dog's room before presenting any stimuli, then the light would become a new conditioned stimulus.

An unconditioned stimulus will always elicit the response, but there are relatively few unconditioned stimuli in nature. Some of the reflexive or unconditioned stimulus-response associations are:

WARMTH $\longrightarrow$ PERSPIRATION

INGESTION OF CERTAIN CHEMICALS $\longrightarrow$ VOMITING

LOUD NOISE $\longrightarrow$ STARTLE

IRRITATION OF EYES $\longrightarrow$ TEARS

TOUCH HOT SURFACE $\longrightarrow$ MUSCLE CONTRACTION

Conditioned stimuli will not continue to elicit the conditioned response unless they are paired with the unconditioned stimulus at least occasionally. If several soundings of the bell are not followed by food, the dog will no longer salivate following the sound of the bell. This is called the *extinction* of the conditioned response. If the bell is again followed by food, even once, the bell will again elicit salivation, at least for a while. This shows that the conditioning is reversible and that repeated changes in the environment will continue to influence behavior.

Respondent conditioning plays a role in many health problems, and several therapeutic approaches are based on the principles of respondent learning. Here are some examples of how knowledge of respondent conditioning helps improve understanding of a variety of health problems.

CASE 1

When Fred was a teenager, his mother remarried. Fred's stepfather yelled at him often and sometimes hit him. Part of Fred's physiological stress response in this situation was secreting gastric acid. Thus, threats (UCS) produced gastric acid secretion (UCR). Soon Fred became upset whenever he was around his stepfather, and his stomach became upset even when his stepfather was not yelling at him. The sight of his stepfather had become a CS. As the threats from the stepfather continued, interactions with other male authority figures, such as teachers, stimulated the stomach upset. Before he graduated from high school, Fred was diagnosed as having bleeding ulcers caused by frequent excessive gastric acid secretion.

This case illustrates the limitations of the biomedical model. The typical medical treatment in a case such as this would be to prescribe a bland diet and medication to soothe the stomach lining. However, without treating the social and behavioral roots of the problem, any medical therapy is likely to be only partially effective.

CASE 2

Gwen is like most smokers. She started while in high school and smokes about 20 cigarettes per day. Last New Year's eve she made a resolution to quit smoking, and the next day she did quit. She struggled through 5 or 6 days of withdrawal, only to discover that the cravings were still nagging at her. After every meal she found herself wanting a smoke. Every time she got into her car, she had strong cravings to smoke. During her coffee breaks she spent most of her time thinking about how good a cigarette would taste. After only 3 weeks of abstinence she went back to smoking because she did not think she could tolerate a lifetime of unsatisfied craving.

While the addictive properties of nicotine are known to be a major factor in making it difficult to quit smoking, respondent conditioning makes it difficult to stay quit. Nicotine stimulates the release of adrenaline that produces a mild feeling of exhilaration. The UCS of inhaling tobacco smoke is paired with almost every other activity a smoker does: getting out of bed, eating, working, relaxing, driving, talking, and making love. Thus, a multitude of CS's are developed, and these are remembered after someone like Gwen quits smoking. These CS's trigger memories of smoking and remind the ex-smoker what they used to feel like when they smoked. When you consider that the average smoker smokes about 7300 cigarettes a year, you can see that with this many learning trials the CS→CR connections become very strong.

CASE 3

Marcia is a 20-year-old college student with a weight problem. She gradually became overweight during adolescence, but she cannot attribute it all to genetics. Her parents are normal weight, and she was a lean child. Marcia spent most of her childhood being cared for by her grandmother, and her grandmother tended to feel guilty that she had not been affectionate enough with Marcia's mother in the past. To make sure that Marcia felt loved, her grandmother was constantly holding her, talking and singing to her, and giving her all the cookies and cake she wanted. All through childhood Marcia was being told what a beautiful, sweet child she was, as she was comfortably sitting in her grandmother's lap eating delicious cookies. When Marcia was 12, her grandmother died. Marcia's mother was very career-oriented and not accustomed to spending much time with her children. When Marcia was at home, she began to feel a bit lonely and empty. She found that she could feel much better by eating sweet snacks. She began eating more and more sweets, and while away from home at college, she spent even more time eating sweets. Her obesity was getting worse and worse.

In this case, affection was the UCS that produced the warm, pleasant feelings (UCR). Her grandmother repeatedly paired her affection with snacks, so that the snacks (CS) by themselves elicited the warm feelings. In this case the respondent learning did not extinguish even though the affection and the sweets had not been paired in years. This is because Marcia could recall the grandmother's affection, so they were paired strongly in her mind.

A study by Birch, Zimmerman, and Hind (1980) documented this very phenomenon. Preschool children were given a variety of foods to choose from, so their preferences could be determined. Then some of the children were given specific foods as rewards, and they were paired with praise from an adult. No matter what food was given as the reward, in later testing the preference score for that food increased. Even carrots came to be a preferred food when they were paired with praise. This study showed that food acquires personal meaning based upon our experiences with it. Might this approach be used to increase children's enjoyment of nutrient-rich but unexciting foods like vegetables?

Operant Learning

The principles of operant learning state that behaviors are controlled by their consequences, or environmental events that follow the behavior. Events that precede the behavior, called *antecedent stimuli*, also control behavior, but they are less powerful. Respondent conditioning cannot produce new behavior; it can only alter the conditions under which existing behavior will be emitted. Operant learning can be used to teach new types of behavior, as well as to increase or decrease the frequency, duration, and intensity of behavior. This makes operant learning an extremely powerful approach to behavior change. As you will see throughout this book, operant conditioning in its many variations has been successful in improving diverse health behaviors. The field of operant learning is in large part the creation of B. F. Skinner, who conducted hundreds of experiments that demonstrated the principles and who wrote numerous books to summarize the findings (Skinner, 1938; 1953).

Environmental stimuli that affect behavior are classified as being either "positive" or "negative." These classifications are not based on whether we enjoy them or not. Rather, stimuli are classified based on their effects on behavior. Behaviors that are followed by positive stimuli (reinforcers) are increased or strengthened. Behaviors that are followed by negative stimuli (punishers) are decreased or weakened. Sometimes our preconceptions are in conflict with the observed effects of the consequences. We might expect that a child would find a spanking to be a negative event. However, a child that is starved for attention might behave in such a way to ensure a spanking, so in this case a spanking would be a positive consequence.

There are four techniques for modifying operant behavior, and all of these techniques are important in understanding and changing health behaviors (see Table 3-1).

Positive reinforcement occurs when the behavior is followed by a stimulus that increases the probability that the behavior will be repeated. In the classic operant experiment a hungry pigeon presses a lever, a pellet of food is dropped into the cage, and the bird presses the lever again. Positive reinforcement is a powerful influence on human behavior as well. We go to work, and soon after that we are given money. The payment makes it quite likely that we will continue to go to work. If the work were not quickly and reliably followed by money, many of us would not be likely to repeat the behavior for very long. An essential quality of positive reinforcement is that the reinforcement is contingent upon the behavior. That means the positive reinforcement is available if and only if the behavior is performed. Noncontingent reinforcement is ineffective. If I pay you whether or not you go to work, the money will do nothing to increase the regularity of your working.

Positive reinforcement can take many forms. Primary reinforcers are those that are biologically necessary. Food, water, air, and sex are considered primary reinforcers. We will work very hard to earn these reinforcers, because either we or the species would be in jeopardy without them. A very thirsty person will do just about anything necessary to get water. At times it seems that college men will perform many complicated "rituals" for long periods of time in the hope of being reinforced (or rewarded) with the affections of a female student. All other types of reinforcement are termed *conditioned reinforcers*, because we have to learn to value them. Money is a particularly good conditioned reinforcer because it is associated with, and can be redeemed for, many other reinforcing stimuli. Also, most people do not become satiated with money; it continues

TABLE 3-1		
OUTLINE OF OPERANT BEHAVIOR CHANGE METHODS		
	Behavior increases	**Behavior decreases**
APPLY STIMULUS	positive reinforcement	punishment
REMOVE STIMULUS	negative reinforcement	extinction time out from reinforcement response cost

to be reinforcing. Social reinforcement controls many of our actions, because the expressed opinions and praise of others are so important to us. This reliance on social reinforcement is proper in that it helps us live together. If the acts of others were not reinforcing, we would have no incentive to please others, and our society would certainly be even more cruel and violent than it is today.

Since positive reinforcement is such a powerful influence on behavior, it is no wonder its effects are seen often in health psychology. Many times the effects are positive. When an obese friend of yours loses weight, you comment on how good he or she looks and encourage him or her to keep working at it. This is positive social reinforcement at its best. Mothers praise children for eating healthy foods. Your physician praises you for taking your prescribed medications as ordered. However, positive reinforcement can also increase "unhealthy" behaviors. Every time a smoker takes a puff of a cigarette, a small burst of nicotine is delivered directly to the brain. That burst of nicotine is a mild but frequent reinforcer that is largely responsible for making smoking such an addictive habit. When a family member is sick and in pain, other members of the family usually do favors for the patient. When the pain becomes long-term, this reinforcement of helpless and sedentary behavior becomes detrimental to the patient, who stops doing anything for him or herself. You can probably think of examples of how some of your own health behaviors are controlled by positive reinforcement.

Positive reinforcement is unique among behavior change methods in its ability to create new behaviors. This is often accomplished by shaping. *Shaping* is the positive reinforcement of successive approximations of the desired response. In the laboratory the pigeon must press the lever before lever pressing can be increased or decreased. The experimenter shapes the response of lever pressing by giving a pellet when the pigeon faces the lever, then when the pigeon steps toward the lever, and then when the pigeon stands near the lever and pecks, until the pigeon finally presses the lever. In the laboratory very complex behaviors are shaped, but shaping is commonly used with developing human behavior as well. No one expected you to write perfectly when you first started school. You were initially reinforced for holding the pencil correctly, then for making a straight line or a circle, then for making a letter, then for writing a word, a sentence, and so on. Teachers typically use praise, gold stars, notes in red pencil, and good grades to reinforce this behavior.

Teenagers are usually shaped into becoming smokers. A smoking friend or sibling will offer you a puff, and when you take one, they will express approval. Then they suggest that you hold the cigarette and take several puffs, and they signal their approval for that accomplishment. Step by step you smoke a whole cigarette, buy a pack, and adopt a brand as "your own." While the smoking habit does not always start out with social reinforcement, many teens would not start smoking by themselves, because the first few cigarettes are not reinforcing. Of course, shaping is also used to develop new "healthy" behaviors. An injured person with a new artificial leg is shaped very gradually to put on the leg, stand on it, take a step with help, take a step without help, walk a little bit, and so on. Shaping is a very versatile and powerful tool for health psychologists.

Negative reinforcement is another method of increasing behavior. Many people confuse this term with "punishment," but they are quite different. In *negative reinforcement* the behavior is reinforced by removing or terminating an aversive stimulus. Thus, behaviors that terminate an aversive event are likely to be repeated because they allow us to escape from unpleasant situations. When you start your car, you have to fasten your seat belt to escape the buzzing or beeping sound your car makes. This is an example of negative reinforcement for the health-protecting behavior of buckling up. Social negative reinforcement is very common. If you want Chinese food for dinner, but your group of friends wants pizza, they will often nag you until you agree to have pizza. In this case, you escape from the whining of your friends by agreeing with them. Negative reinforcement is another reason why it is so hard to stop smoking, drinking, or using drugs. When you stop smoking, for example, you experience a mild but very irritating and persistent withdrawal reaction. The only way to escape from that unpleasant feeling is to smoke. Thus, smoking is increased by negative reinforcement.

To review, operant behavior can be increased by positive reinforcement or negative reinforcement. In positive reinforcement, the behavior is followed by a pleasant stimulus. In negative reinforcement, the behavior is followed by termination of an unpleasant stimulus.

Punishment is the presentation of an aversive stimulus following the behavior, and the effect is to decrease that behavior. Remember that punishment is defined by its effect on behavior, not by whether we consider it aversive. While you might expect criticism and yelling of a parent to be aversive, a child who is usually ignored by the parents might find the yelling to be very reinforcing. One person's poison is another's delicacy.

The effectiveness of punishment depends on its immediacy and frequency. Punishment must closely follow the behavior to effectively decrease it. Punishing children immediately after a fight sends a clear message. However, the much delayed aversive health consequences of alcohol abuse are not very effective at reducing that behavior. If punishment is inconsistently applied, its effectiveness is greatly reduced. Unless you are given a ticket every time you speed, then ticketing is un-

likely to control your fast driving. If you did receive a citation every time you went over the speed limit, be assured that your driving speed would decrease noticeably.

We sometimes experience punishment after some health-related behaviors, but it is easy to see that the punishment is rarely effective. When an overweight friend orders a piece of chocolate cake for dessert at a restaurant, someone at the table is likely to make a punishing comment like, "It doesn't look like you're sticking to that diet of yours." A common response to that type of situation is for the struggling dieter to have subsequent pieces of cake when concerned friends are not around. This illustrates that punishment is very good at teaching us under what conditions we are likely to be punished and when we are "safe" to behave in the way we want. Thus, we learn to drive fast when no police are around, and we slow down when we see flashing blue lights. Another problem with punishment is that there are frequently undesirable side effects. Punishment tends to elicit emotions such as anger and sadness that interfere with any behavioral improvements. Going back to the dieter, the social punishment is more likely to stimulate an angry response ("Just leave me alone"), a depressive response ("I'm so ashamed that you are seeing me fail in my diet"), or an avoidance response ("I'll just leave you perfect people to yourselves") than any kind of constructive behavior.

Punishment is often not very effective because it must be applied immediately and consistently, it has negative side effects, its effects are usually transitory, and it does nothing to shape alternative behaviors. There are also ethical problems with punishment. Many people correctly object to such coercive and unpleasant methods unless the ends clearly justify the means. For these reasons, most experts in behavior modification resort to punishment only in carefully selected situations, usually when there is no apparent alternative for decreasing self-injurious behavior. A preferred method of decreasing an undesirable behavior is to positively reinforce an incompatible alternative behavior. Rather than relying on punishing people who are caught drinking and driving, the new approach is to teach people who are drinking to ask for rides and to teach nondrinkers to offer rides to those who have been drinking.

In some cases, however, society has judged it appropriate to resort to punishment to decrease certain behaviors, and in many cases health behaviors are controlled through punishment. The punishment is dictated by laws. Familiar examples are laws governing drinking and driving, the purchase of alcohol by minors, and the use of seat belts and child safety seats. While the use of punishment, or the threat of punishment, is frequently used to protect the public health, health psychologists are actively working to develop more positive approaches to decreasing unhealthy behaviors.

Extinction refers to the withholding of reinforcement, and this results in decreases in behavior. Behavior that fails to produce reinforcement does not persist for very long. If your employer stops paying you (removal of reinforcement), you will soon stop going to work. In health psychology, extinction is often used in rehabilitating chronic pain patients. Family members often reinforce the patient's requests by doing services and favors that promote further helplessness. A therapeutic approach based on extinction would include instructing family members to ignore the requests. Initially, the patient is likely to increase the behavior by making more requests to test the family members or by making louder requests. With continued extinction the patient will cease making requests, because he or she will get the idea that they are not going to be reinforced. After some time of doing things for him or herself, the patient will typically try a few more requests, and this is called *spon-*

taneous recovery. If these requests are not reinforced, the requesting will very quickly extinguish again.

Do not get the idea that this is an example of a cruel therapy in which family members are encouraged to be insensitive to a suffering patient. As you will find out later, having the chronic pain patient become self-sufficient once again is a major goal of the treatment, and despite superficial appearances, the approach is not only effective but also compassionate.

Whereas extinction is the removal of reinforcement from one behavior, *time out* from reinforcement is the elimination of the opportunity to earn any reinforcement. After the behavior one wishes to decrease, the subject is removed from the reinforcing environment for a brief period of time. This method is most often used with children and psychiatric patients, because their environments can be controlled with some degree of ease. For example, a child who is having a tantrum is placed in a chair facing a wall or a plain room for 1 minute or less. Time out is finished when the desired behavior is displayed (i.e., end of tantrum). This method decreases the undesired behavior very rapidly and is most effectively paired with the reinforcement of alternative behaviors.

Response cost is the forfeiture of positive reinforcers contingent upon the undesired behavior. "Sin taxes" are an example of response cost. The idea is that high taxes on tobacco and alcohol will decrease their use. Thus, the response cost occurs when you purchase tobacco or alcohol and you forfeit money, which (as was discussed earlier) is a powerful positive reinforcer. Other examples of response cost that are designed to influence health-related behaviors are higher insurance rates for drunk drivers and smokers.

The different types of consequences that control operant learning have been discussed in some detail. Because these are both strong influences over health behaviors and the basis

BOX 3-2

FOCUS ON DIVERSITY

Health Behaviors in U.S. Latinos

Since most of the research conducted on health behaviors of the U.S. population has been conducted on Caucasians, most of what we know about health behaviors and how to go about changing them may pertain only to whites. A number of studies in the past 10 years have examined health behaviors of African Americans, but very little is known about the behavior of U.S. Latinos. In recognition of the growth of the Latino population and the general lack of information about their health, a major study was undertaken in the 1980s called the Hispanic Health and Nutrition Examination Survey (HHANES). Over 3300 Mexican Americans from the Southwest, 900 Cuban Americans from the Miami area, and 1200 Puerto Ricans from New York City were studied.

This study could not escape the fact that many Latinos are living in poverty. About 30 percent had incomes less than $10,000 per year, and about 25 percent had less than 7 years of education. Thus, it is difficult to separate characteristics of Latinos from the effects of poverty. The economic and educational differences also make it difficult to compare this group with other U.S. samples. Nevertheless, the survey produced some interesting findings.

Over 40 percent of the men smoked cigarettes, compared with about 25 percent of the women. Over 70 percent of the men reported using alcohol, and this rate was double the rate of women's alcohol use. One indicator of dietary quality was the frequency of eating "junk foods." About 70 percent of U.S. Latinos said that they eat junk food daily; the rate was somewhat lower for Mexican Americans. These results suggest that U.S. Latinos are regularly engaging in behaviors that are harmful to their health. Subsequent research needs to determine whether the principles of behavior change that have been developed with other populations will be similarly effective with Latinos.

U.S. Latinos are a very diverse group. Not only do they differ by country of origin, but they differ by how much general American culture they have adopted. The term *acculturation* is used to describe whether Latinos use English and identify with the American culture or whether they use the Spanish language and retain their ethnic identification. In the HHANES study, acculturation was related to the health behaviors. For both males and females, those who lived a more American lifestyle reported more alcohol use. For the Mexican American group only, the more Americanized group had lower-quality diets. Finally, there was a tendency for more acculturated women to smoke more.

It appears that exposure to the U.S. culture affects the health behavior of Latinos. Unfortunately, whenever a relationship was found, those Latinos living an American lifestyle had less healthy habits. Hopefully, U.S. Latinos will benefit from programs designed to improve health behavior of the entire population. Special efforts will be needed to reach those who speak mainly Spanish and who are not in the mainstream communication channels.

Source: Marks, G., Garcia, M., & Solis, J. M. (1990). Health risk behaviors of Hispanics in the United States. Findings from HHANES, 1982–1984. *American Journal of Public Health, 80* (Suppl.), 20–26.

for many effective therapeutic and preventive approaches, it is important to have a clear understanding of operant learning. While behavior modification based on operant learning can be very effective, one major limitation must be kept in mind. That limitation is that health professionals often do not have control over the consequences that in turn control behavior. Physicians and health policymakers rarely have control over the primary, social, and other conditioned reinforcers that influence health behaviors. When these reinforcers can be controlled, the results can be dramatic. Governmental laws and insurance policies are examples of operant approaches to behavior change, even if they rely on aversive methods. As friends, acquaintances, and family members, we control many reinforcers, so we can all be effective agents of change. Those who control the controlling consequences must remember their obligation to use their influence for the good of others and not for exploitation.

One final note on operant learning. While consequences are the most powerful behavioral controls, antecedent stimuli can also affect behavior. This is referred to as *stimulus control* of behavior. Antecedent stimuli can indicate whether reinforcement is or is not available for a particular behavior. The presence of a police officer produces stimulus control of speeding, because it signals that punishment may be contingent upon the behavior. The presence of family members may stimulate helplessness in a chronic pain patient because it signals that they will reinforce the requests. Antecedent stimuli can be altered to increase the probability of behavior regardless of the consequences that may or may not follow. People who are trying to start a program of regular exercise are taught to schedule a time for exercise, to lay out exercise clothes the night before, and to put up reminders around the house. This approach to arranging antecedent stimuli can increase the probability of exercise behavior, but this method is usually not as effective as consequence control.

SOCIAL COGNITIVE THEORY

Social cognitive theory is an updated version of social learning theory, both of which were articulated by Albert Bandura (1977; 1986). Bandura is a psychologist who was dissatisfied with respondent and operant learning theories. He felt that while these theories generated more useful concepts and effective behavior change methods than previous theories, there were two major problems with them. First, respondent and operant learning theories only studied the effects of environmental events on behavior. This can be diagramed as:

$$ENVIRONMENT \longrightarrow BEHAVIOR$$

Bandura believed that this formulation ignored the obvious fact that animals, and especially humans in the real world, influence their environments. This is done in a number of ways. In the United States we voters institute the laws that spell out the contingencies of reinforcement to which we are then subject. On a more personal level, if your roommate criticizes you for not cleaning up after yourself in the kitchen, you have several choices in how you respond. If you start cleaning up in the kitchen, then this is an example of negative reinforcement, since you are avoiding the aversive stimulus of the criticism. However, if you tell your roommate that he or she had better be quiet about your kitchen cleaning until he or she starts cleaning up the bedroom, then you are influencing your social environment. Bandura calls this principle *reciprocal determinism* because each factor can influence the other. In social cognitive theory, causation goes both ways:

$$ENVIRONMENT \longleftrightarrow BEHAVIOR$$

Bandura's other main complaint with other learning theories was that cognitive processes were a taboo topic. Other learning theories assumed that cognitions, or thoughts, were merely a side effect of contingencies of reinforcement, and besides, thoughts are difficult to measure. However, Bandura conducted many studies demonstrating that people can learn many things and alter their behavior in many ways without ever being reinforced.

You probably read about his famous Bobo doll studies in social psychology. Children who watched a videotape of other children hitting a Bobo doll punching bag acted aggressively toward the doll and other children when they were in a room with the doll. Children who did not watch the aggressive video showed generally peaceful behavior. This study and many others showed that learning requires neither reinforcement nor practice, although both are helpful. We learn many important things by observing others, such as how to carry on a simple conversation, how to drive, how to smoke cigarettes, and how to order in a restaurant. Children learn virtually everything by watching their parents and peers, and we all continue to learn by watching friends and movies and by reading. Through his studies of modeling, Bandura became convinced that *vicarious* learning, or learning through observation, is an important method of acquiring information and skills. Moreover, vicarious learning requires cognitive activity, so cognitions must be an important aspect of any comprehensive theory of human behavior. Thus, a third factor was added to the theory. It was termed *personal variables* because this category included not only cognitions but emotions, physiological processes, and other internal variables. The principle of reciprocal determinism still applies.

DIAGRAM OF SOCIAL COGNITIVE THEORY

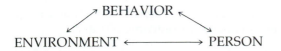

Two cognitive processes that Bandura feels are especially influential over behavior are outcome efficacy expectations and self-efficacy expectations (Bandura, 1977). *Outcome expectations* are one's belief that a behavior will produce a specified effect. For example, if you believe that taking a prescribed medication will reduce your pain or that exercise will help you lose weight, then you have high outcome efficacy since you believe that the behavior will produce the outcome. *Self-efficacy* is your belief in your ability or your competence to perform the behavior. Can you remember to take the medication, and can you discipline yourself to exercise regularly? While you may have high outcome efficacy for the medication, you may have low self-efficacy that you can take such a large pill.

Self-efficacy beliefs vary according to the situation. A smoker who is trying to quit may feel very confident (have high self-efficacy) that he or she can refrain from smoking in a business conference where no one else is smoking. This same smoker may have very low self-efficacy about his or her ability to abstain from smoking later that evening after a few drinks in a smoky bar. Therefore, it makes no sense to ask whether a person has high or low self-efficacy. You must ask whether a person has high or low self-efficacy for a specific behavior in a specific situation. Self-efficacy that is assessed in this way is a very good predictor of behavior. Again, using a smoking example, Condiotte and Lichtenstein (1981) asked smokers who had just completed a smoking cessation program about their confidence in the length of time they could stay abstinent and their confidence to abstain in a number of situations. The subjects' confidence or self-efficacy ratings predicted very well not only how long they actually stayed off cigarettes but also in what situations they were most likely to return to smoking. Some smokers anticipated that they would have a hard time refraining from smoking when under stress, while others identified being with smokers as a high-risk situation. Thus, self-efficacy is a useful concept for understanding and predicting behavior. Bandura argues that self-efficacy plays a central role in human behavior and is the type of cognition that is most closely linked to behavior (Bandura, 1986).

Social cognitive theory has been very useful because it has generated many new methods of behavior change. These methods incorporate modeling as a way of teaching new behaviors, and cognitive modification procedures have opened up whole new fields of therapy. These methods are now widely used in health psychology. The self-directed behavior change approach that is described in detail later in this chapter is largely based on Bandura's social cognitive theory.

THE HEALTH BELIEF MODEL

The health belief model is the oldest and most widely used model specifically developed to explain health behavior. As the name implies, this model focuses almost exclusively on cognitive influences on behaviors. It was originally developed by Rosenstock in 1966 to explain preventive health behaviors such as checkups and immunizations. It has since been further developed by Becker (1974) and applied to several areas of health psychology including sick-role behavior, adherence to medical regimens, and health promotion behaviors.

There are four major types of beliefs that influence the likelihood of taking action that is relevant to a given disease or condition. A simple version of the model is diagrammed in Figure 3-1.

The perceived susceptibility of disease X refers to the subjective probability that "I" could get the disease. One of the main goals of AIDS prevention campaigns is to convince people that they are at risk, so they will be motivated to take precautions to prevent AIDS.

The perceived seriousness of the disease may or may not be related to the actual sever-

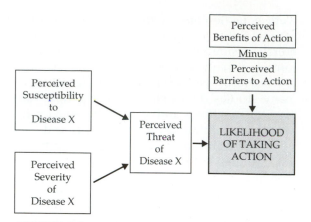

FIGURE 3-1

Diagram of the health belief model.

ity of the disease. The model states that the perceived severity is much more influential on behavior than the actual severity of the disease, which may be measured in mortality rate.

Susceptibility and severity combine to form the overall perceived threat of disease. If "I" feel susceptible to a serious disease, such as cancer, then I should be more motivated to take action because the level of threat is high. If I do not feel that I am at risk for a less severe disease such as the flu, then I am unlikely to take action because I perceive the threat as minimal.

Beliefs about the required preventive or therapeutic behaviors also influence their probability of occurrence. The perceived benefits of the behavior generally refer to how effective the behavior is in producing a health benefit. Behaviors like taking a pain medication are likely to be perceived as very effective, since they have a noticeable immediate effect. Behaviors like eating fiber to reduce the risk of colon cancer may be perceived as less effective, because the effect is long-term and the data supporting the effectiveness are not conclusive. Perceived benefit is similar to Bandura's concept of outcome efficacy.

Perceived barriers to the behavior also influence action. The behavior may not be feasible because it takes too much time or effort. Spending an hour per day relaxing to control hypertension may be perceived as not feasible. Another barrier could be lack of availability of the behavior. For example, a medication to control a serious illness may be too expensive, or physical therapists may not live in a patient's rural area.

The perceived benefits and perceived barriers must be considered together in a cost-benefits analysis. A difficult behavior, like self-injection, may be performed routinely by a diabetic whose life depends on it. However, self-injections of vitamins may not be adhered to when the benefits are not obvious. When the benefits of the behavior outweigh the costs, in the mind of a given patient, then the likelihood of action is increased.

The perception of threat of the condition or disease is then combined with the perception of the behavior to yield the likelihood of action. Thus, the highest likelihood of action occurs when the perceived threat of the disease is high and the perceived benefits of the health behavior outweigh the barriers. The health belief model is very appealing because it deals with beliefs that are directly related to the health behavior. It has generated a great deal of research in many areas, and it has served as the basis for many health education programs, especially mass media campaigns.

Research based on the health belief model has yielded mixed results. When the model is used to predict the types of behavior for which it was originally developed, the results tend to support the model. Cummings and colleagues (1979) studied immunization to swine flu and found that each of the four major health beliefs —susceptibility, severity, benefits, and barriers—predicted actual immunization. However, when more complex behaviors are studied, the health belief model is often not supported. A good example is smoking acquisition in adolescents. In general, beliefs about the severity of smoking-related disease and the benefits of smoking do not predict which adolescents will start smoking. Intervention programs, based on the health belief model, that teach the hazards of smoking have changed attitudes, but they have not reduced smoking acquisition (Flay, 1985). Another study with diabetic teenagers produced an unexpected result. Those with the best adherence to their complex regimen had high levels of perceived benefits, but they perceived a *low* threat of the disease (Bond, Aiken & Somerville, 1992).

The health belief model continues to be used frequently by health psychologists and others who are studying the behaviors for which it is most applicable (Rosenstock, 1990).

THE THEORY OF REASONED ACTION

The theory of reasoned action was developed by social psychologists Icek Ajzen and Martin Fishbein (1980) and was designed to explain all human behavior that is under voluntary control. Thus, it is a general theory of behavior that has been applied extensively in the health field. A major assumption in the theory is that people are usually rational and make predictable use of the information available to them. The main parts of the theory are outlined in Figure 3-2.

The theory states that intentions are the most immediate influence on behavior. Thus, if a person intends to perform a behavior, then it is likely he or she will do so. If the person does not intend to perform the behavior, then the behavior is unlikely to be performed. You can see that the theory does emphasize rational causes of behavior. This part of the theory is basically common sense, but Ajzen and Fishbein have also tackled the problem of what influences intentions.

Intentions are influenced by attitudes and subjective norms. In this case *attitudes* consist

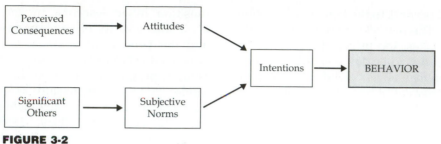

FIGURE 3-2
Diagram of the theory of reasoned action.

of good or bad feelings about the specific behavior in question. More specifically, these attitudes refer to people's feelings about themselves performing the behavior. Their attitudes about someone else doing the behavior may be very different from their feelings about themselves performing the behavior, so this is a key distinction.

Subjective norms are the person's perceptions of social influences about performing the behavior. If one feels that most people smoke and most of their friends want them to smoke, then they will probably perceive there is a norm that favors smoking.

Intentions regarding a behavior are jointly determined by attitudes and subjective norms. Thus, the theory predicts that a person is most likely to perform a behavior when he or she feels good about performing the behavior and feels social pressure to perform the behavior.

Ajzen and Fishbein go one step further and hypothesize that attitudes are determined by the most prominent beliefs about what would happen as a consequence of the behavior. It is only the most easily remembered consequences that really affect attitudes. Therefore, if a person's first thought when they see someone smoking is "Smoking makes you look cool," then this is the belief that will determine their attitude about smoking. It does not matter so much that they also believe smoking will cause cancer and heart disease. That belief may not come to mind easily, and the person

may believe that it is "other people" who will get those diseases if they smoke.

Subjective norms are affected mainly by pressures from significant others. *Significant others* are those whom we are motivated to please. Thus, if someone feels that their family, all of their friends, and their physician do not want them to smoke, the opinions of these significant others will have a major impact on perceptions of social pressures to smoke or not to smoke.

As with most theories, the theorists continue to develop their ideas, and both Fishbein and Ajzen have made revisions. Ajzen (1985) added the concept of "perceived control" as a third influence on intentions besides attitudes and subjective norms. He indicates that intentions to perform a behavior will become stronger when people perceive that they have personal control over the behavior. Thus, a smoker who perceives that he or she can control the behavior is expected to have stronger intentions to quit than a smoker who does not feel that he or she can control that behavior. By including this variable, Ajzen recognizes that there are degrees of voluntary control. Since the original theory was designed to explain only "voluntary" behavior, Ajzen (1985) proposes to change the name to the "theory of planned behavior."

The theory of reasoned action has been used to predict several health behaviors, including smoking and exercise, and it has received some support (Carter, 1990). It is rarely used to guide the development of therapeutic or preventive interventions. However, some ideas for interventions may be derived from the model. On the basis of this theory, social psychologists Olson and Zanna (1987) developed recommendations for designing more effective interventions to promote exercise. These intervention recommendations now need to be tested against recommendations that can be derived from other theories.

THE COMMUNICATION-BEHAVIOR CHANGE MODEL

The communication-behavior change model was developed by social psychologist and communication expert William McGuire (1981). This model is meant to be useful in the design of public communication campaigns, and it has been one of the guiding models of several community heart disease prevention programs. The model is based on communication "inputs" and "outputs" that are largely psychological in nature. The output factors describe a theoretical progression of information processing steps that are thought to occur in a person who receives a communication that leads to attitude and behavior change.

The input factors are as follows: (1) source, (2) message, (3) channel, (4) receiver, and (5) destination.

The input factors are manipulated in the public communication campaign in order to have the desired effect on the audience's health attitudes and behaviors. If you imagine that you have been called upon to design a communication campaign to promote seat belt use, then you may see that the list of input factors can help you design the program. The *source* is usually thought of as the person or group from whom the message is perceived as coming. In choosing the source or spokesperson for your seat belt campaign you must consider how credible they are and how the intended audience will be able to relate to him or her. The gender, age, racial group, social status, and attractiveness of the source can all influence dramatically how the audience responds to the campaign.

Message factors include what is said as well as how it is said. This is obviously a critical part of the campaign design, and a great deal of research has been conducted on issues such as whether to use a positive appeal ("Buckle your seat belt") or a negative appeal ("If you don't buckle your seat belt, you may die"). Speed of delivery, length of message, and tone of voice can all affect the receiver.

The *channel* is the medium through which the message is transmitted. One has to consider not only such questions as the cost and number of people reached by television versus newspaper ads versus direct mail but also the fact that some channels are more effective for simple rather than complex messages.

The *receiver* refers to the intended target audience. Communicators need to know the age, likes and dislikes, and habits of the target group, in this case people who do not use seat belts. For example, what radio stations do people who do not wear seat belts usually listen to when they are driving? Creating demographic and psychological profiles of audience segments helps develop more effective communications.

The *destination* is the intended outcome of the communication. In this case we are targeting long-term change in the use of seat belts rather than a short-term change in buying habits or a shift in attitudes.

McGuire's (1981) model specifies a 12-step sequence of events that must occur between exposure to the communication and long-term changes in behavior. The output factors are as follows:

1. Exposure to the communication
2. Attending to it
3. Liking, becoming interested in it

4. Comprehending it (learning what)
5. Skill acquisition (learning how)
6. Yielding to it (attitude change)
7. Memory storage of content or agreement, or both
8. Information search and retrieval
9. Deciding on basis of retrieval
10. Behaving in accord with decision
11. Reinforcement of desired acts
12. Postbehavioral consolidating (maintenance)

This sequence can help you think about what effects your communication is intended to produce in the audience. These steps are based on general ideas about the relationship between perceptions, attitudes, and behaviors rather than specific data confirming this sequences of steps. However, the model is logical and can be helpful in designing the communication strategy. The target person must be exposed to the message, must pay attention to it, and must become involved enough in it to understand what the message is. In a society in which everyone is bombarded with messages over every conceivable channel, it is no easy task just to get someone's attention. When skills are being taught, such as how to shop for healthy foods, there is an extra step in the sequence. Once the message is comprehended, it must create an inclination to change, and this attitude change must be stored in memory and retrieved when there is an opportunity to act on that attitude change. When the opportunity arises, one must decide to change behavior and try out the new behavior. For example, when someone who sees the seat belt television ad gets in the car, the object is to induce him or her to remember the message and then buckle the seat belt. Finally, the change must be somehow reinforced so that it is maintained.

Communication campaign designers must consider how each input factor may affect each output factor. This can be complicated, because one input component may have unex-

pected effects. For example, having music in your radio ad may have the positive effect of grabbing the listener's attention, but it may have the negative effect of distracting the listener so much that comprehension of the message is reduced. The communication-behavior change model shows that designing a public communication campaign is a demanding process, but it also assists the designer in thinking through the entire process to maximize the effectiveness of the communication. The model also helps explain why creating behavior change through the media is so difficult. Even after you attract the receiver's attention, there are 10 more changes that must be accomplished before the final outcome of a stable new habit is achieved.

THE PRECEDE-PROCEED MODEL

The PRECEDE model was developed by Lawrence Green to assist health educators in conducting a thorough evaluation of all factors that may be involved in planning a communitywide health program. The original PRECEDE model (Green, Kreuter, Deeds & Partridge, 1980) was recently expanded and named the PRECEDE-PROCEED model (Green & Kreuter, 1991), because it now deals more fully with the implementation and evaluation of health programs. The model shows what steps must *precede* the initiation of a program, then provides guidance on how to *proceed* with implementing the program. It has been used to plan health programs on local, national, and international scales. The PRECEDE-PROCEED model is similar to McGuire's communication-behavior change model in that both are meant to be used in designing programs to change the behavior of large groups of people.

Following the PRECEDE-PROCEED model ensures that planners consider exactly what outcomes will be of most benefit to the community. This is certainly preferable to just choosing the health problems the planners are most interested in. The model insists that planners first decide why they want to have a program, and then move on to answer how they are going to create that change. There are five phases in the PRECEDE portion and four phases in the PROCEED portion of the model. The model is diagramed in Figure 3-3.

Phase 1 is social diagnosis. The quality of life of the target population is assessed as well as the major problems that concern the people. Successful programs tend to deal directly or indirectly with the issues that the people are most concerned with and therefore are motivated to change.

Phase 2 is epidemiological diagnosis. What health problems are most related to current concerns? Epidemiologic data may need to be collected to identify the major causes of morbidity and mortality in this population. Then,

scarce resources should be devoted to the important health problems.

Phase 3 is behavioral and environmental diagnosis. The behaviors and environmental factors that are related to the major health problems must be identified. Environmental factors are often beyond the control of a given individual, but factors such as lack of low-fat foods can be important to consider in a dietary change program. Since the intervention programs will be designed to change these behaviors and environmental conditions, the assessments should be as specific as possible. Different behaviors and environmental factors should be prioritized, because it will not be possible to target each important factor.

Phase 4 is educational diagnosis. Green has proposed three factors that health education programs must consider to produce behavior

FIGURE 3-3

The PRECEDE-PROCEED model for health promotion planning and evaluation. (From *Health Promotion Planning: An Educational and Environmental Approach* by Lawrence W. Green and Marshall W. Kreuter by permission of Mayfield Publishing Company. Copyright © 1991 Mayfield Publishing Company.)

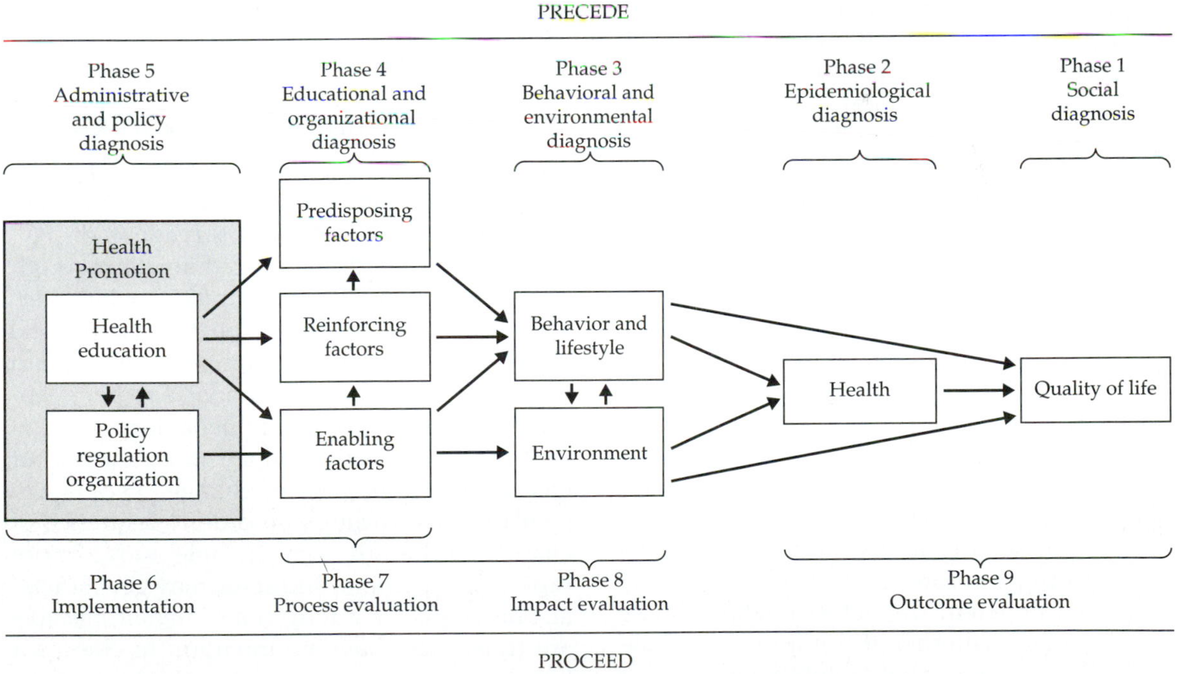

change. *Predisposing factors* increase or decrease the motivation for change. Cognitive variables such as attitudes, beliefs, and values can affect motivation to change. *Enabling factors* are usually thought of as barriers to change created by societal forces or systems. Examples include limited facilities, lack of income or health insurance, advertisement or promotion of unhealthful behaviors, and restrictive laws. *Reinforcing factors* are usually social feedback that encourages or discourages behavior change. The educational diagnosis consists of identifying those predisposing, enabling, and reinforcing factors that have the most direct effects on the target behaviors. These factors should be prioritized, and the intervention should be designed to impact the most important factors identified in the evaluation process.

Phase 5 is administrative diagnosis. Steps 1 through 4 lead to the design of the targeted intervention program. In step 5 the realities of resources, time constraints, and abilities are assessed. The health education program that is needed must be reconciled to the availability and limitations of these administrative considerations. Inevitably, limited resources require that only the intervention components with the highest priority, based on likelihood of success or cost-effectiveness, can be implemented.

Phases 6 through 9 concern the implementation and evaluation of the intervention. Implementation of the program (phase 6) is easy to write, but it is always much more difficult to do in the real world. Changing health behaviors requires educating people, working with people in diverse disciplines, working with organizations that may not be interested in improving health, and trying to stay within a budget. Process evaluation (phase 7) determines whether the intervention changed the predisposing, reinforcing, and enabling factors that were targeted. Impact evaluation (phase 8) determines whether the important behavioral and environmental factors were success-

fully altered. Finally, outcome evaluation (phase 9) determines whether the population experienced improved health and quality of life as a result of the intervention. These evaluations are both difficult and costly to do, and many programs are never adequately evaluated. However, this model describes an ideal approach to evaluation.

This model is particularly useful because it forces planners to deal with the logistics, or realities, of conducting a health behavior change program, as well as the theories of behavior change. Most of the theories developed by psychologists assist planners in developing behavior change procedures, but they do not provide guidance on how to implement or evaluate those procedures. McGuire's model provides suggestions about how to sequence a media campaign, and the PRECEDE-PROCEED model gives a framework for putting all the elements of the program together in a way that can be delivered to a large number of people at a realistic cost. In developing health behavior change programs, many psychologists and others draw on more than one of these models.

THE TRANSTHEORETICAL MODEL

The transtheoretical model was developed by psychologists James Prochaska and Carlo DiClemente (1984). In their observations of psychotherapy, people appeared to go through similar stages of change no matter what therapy was being applied. The transtheoretical model was developed to describe and explain these changes, and the model has been applied to a variety of health behaviors.

It has two basic dimensions: stages of change and processes of change. People appear to move through an orderly sequence of change, although some people move more rapidly than others, and some may get "stuck" at one stage for a long time. *Precontemplators* are those who have no intention to change a behavior, and *contemplators* are thinking about making a change. In the *action* phase, the person is involved in changing the behavior, and in the *maintenance* phase, they have been successful in sustaining a change. The stages of change can be easily measured with a questionnaire.

There are a number of processes of change that can be used in altering a wide variety of behaviors. Some of the processes are more applicable at certain stages of change. For example, consciousness-raising is more appropriate for precontemplators, and self-reevaluation and self-liberation may be particularly well suited for contemplators. For those in the action phase, contingency management (that is, reinforcement), helping relationships, and stimulus control may be helpful; but these same processes may be appropriate in the maintenance phase as well.

This model not only implies that different intervention approaches are needed for people at different stages of change but also suggests which processes are most important at each stage. This is a very promising aspect of the model, but it has not been fully tested.

The transtheoretical model has been shown to be useful in studying several health behaviors. The model has been studied most extensively in smoking cessation (DiClemente, Prochaska, Fairhurst, Velicer, Velasquez, & Rossi, 1991). However, the stages of change concept has also been found to be related to exercise (Marcus, Selby, Niaura, & Rossi, 1992), alcohol treatment (DiClemente & Hughes, 1990), weight control (O'Connell & Velicer, 1988), and mammography (Rakowski, Dube, Marcus, Prochaska, Velicer, & Abrams, 1992). The transtheoretical model is currently being studied regarding AIDS-related behaviors.

CONCLUDING THOUGHTS ON MODELS

When trying to understand health behavior or design a program to change the health behav-

ior of an individual or group, it is useful to have a theoretical model as a starting point. Numerous models have been described in this chapter. The complexity of health behaviors has spawned other theories and models, including protection motivation theory (Prentice-Dunn and Rogers, 1986), self-regulation theory (Leventhal, Zimmerman, & Gutmann, 1984), relapse prevention theory (Marlatt & Gordon, 1985), the social ecology framework (Stokols, 1992), and social action theory (Ewart, 1991). Theories and models may not represent "truth," but they help organize thinking about a problem. They may help set priorities and prevent the planner from overlooking important factors. There are many existing models of health behavior, and each of them has its advantages and disadvantages. Some are based on research, and others are not. Some are designed primarily to guide the study of individual behavior, and others are designed to aid in the understanding of the behavior of groups or communities. All of the theories and models presented here are in current use by researchers, therapists, and health educators with an interest in health behavior change, so psychologists and others active in the field should at least be acquainted with all of these theories and models.

CHANGING HEALTH BEHAVIORS

Changing health behaviors is perhaps the greatest challenge facing health psychologists. Through the numerous models discussed in this chapter, we have gained some understanding of the many forces that can influence health behaviors. The ultimate test of a model of behavior is whether it can lead to effective methods of behavior change. The key word is *effective*, because if the method does not actually change behavior to an important degree, it is not going to be helpful in preventing or treating health problems. Fortunately, psychologists have developed many methods of behavior change that are moderately effective.

Not only have these successes played a role in improving the health of many people, but behavioral scientists are now valuable members of the health care team because of their expertise in behavior change.

Most of the effective methods of behavior change have their roots in respondent and operant learning theory. Behavior modification approaches to health behavior change have generally been much more effective than other approaches, but they do not always work. Thus, there is much room for improvement in methods of health behavior change, and continued research in this area makes health psychology an exciting and dynamic field.

The next section describes some of the most effective methods of behavior change. These methods will be applied to a great many health problems throughout this book. The focus of this section is on applications of behavioral methods to individual behavior change. The rapidly developing area of applying behavior change methods to entire communities of people is described in Chapter 19.

Self-Directed Behavior Change

The purpose of self-directed behavior change is to provide people with the tools they need to change their own behaviors. This may seem unnecessary, since there is a common belief that if someone really wants to change their actions, they will do it. Maybe there is no need for special techniques. But what about the millions of people every year who make serious New Year's resolutions to change their behavior and then do not follow through? What about the 90 percent of all cigarette smokers who want to quit and have tried several times to quit but who are still smoking? What about the heart attack patients who have been told that exercise is very important for their survival but who fail to exercise regularly? These are just a few of the many cases in which knowledge and motivation are not sufficient to

produce the needed behavior changes. Therefore, special techniques of behavior change are indeed needed to help people succeed.

Self-directed behavior change was developed by behavior modification experts who wanted to teach people with problems how to apply effective reinforcement methods in their own lives. Bandura's social cognitive theory (Bandura, 1986) and social learning theory (Bandura, 1977), with their emphasis on both environmental and cognitive influences on behavior, stimulated the development of the many methods of self-directed behavior change described below.

Matarazzo's concept of behavioral health (1980) emphasizes that we have responsibility for our own health, and we are not really healthy unless our behavior patterns help us decrease risks of disease and injury. Self-directed behavior change provides us with methods to put that responsibility into action. By using these methods we can take control of our own behavior and make healthful changes. If we do not use these methods, we are more likely to fail in our attempts.

Mahoney and Arnkoff (1979) have categorized five types of self-directed behavior change methods. These are often referred to as techniques of self-management, self-regulation, or self-control, but these terms mean the same thing.

1. Self-monitoring
2. Goal specification
3. Stimulus control
4. Self-reinforcement
5. Behavior rehearsal

Several additional methods that have also been found to be effective, social support and behavior contracting, are discussed in this chapter as well.

Self-Monitoring   Self-monitoring involves keeping records of your own behavior. When done carefully, it provides many benefits.

In order to self-monitor, you have to be able

BOX 3·3

PERSONAL APPLICATION

These methods for self-directed behavior change are discussed as they have been applied in health psychology research. It is important to understand their major role in health psychology prevention and treatment programs. However, these methods are also relevant for each student reading this book. You engage in behaviors every day that influence your health. Some of your behavior may reduce your health risk, such as buckling your seat belt and eating and drinking in moderation. If you are like most other people in modern society, you also engage in behaviors that are detrimental to your health. These may include eating a diet that has excessive amounts of fat, exercising irregularly, and spending too much time exposed to the sun. Thus, all of us have health behaviors that we can and should change. The methods of self-directed behavior change discussed in this section can assist you in changing your own personal health behaviors. While reading this section, please think about how you can put these methods into practice in your own life. By learning to change your own health behavior, you will be getting more out of this course than just a grade.

to define and measure the behavior. This is a difficult first step for many people. If you are interested in improving your diet, then you would start out writing down everything you eat and drink. This process may help you further specify the problem behavior, because by looking at your records you could identify particular foods that are unhealthful. Besides common behaviors like diet, smoking, exercise, and practice of relaxation techniques, self-monitoring can be used to keep track of other behaviors and nonbehaviors. A patient with stress-related headaches could monitor episodes of anger. A parent could monitor a diabetic child's insulin doses. A patient with a gastrointestinal disorder may keep track of abdominal pains. Typically, you keep track of the frequency of the behavior in a small notebook, a 3 × 5 card, or a special form. However, simple devices like golf counters can also be helpful.

Self-monitoring helps you become more familiar with your own behavior. Keeping records forces you to pay close attention to the behavior. Although you will already know in a general way what you eat during the day, keeping self-monitoring records may help you become aware of just how many fried foods or sweets you eat. This increased awareness of behavior helps you define the problem.

Self-monitoring provides an initial measure of behavior so that later improvements can be documented. Sometimes it is difficult to know whether you are making progress at changing your behavior, but self-monitoring records allow you to chart your behavior change daily or weekly. This is very reinforcing.

Most important, self-monitoring is used to perform *behavior analysis*, which means identifying the factors that control your behavior. You need to find out what environmental and cognitive events influence you. Therefore, in self-monitoring you do not simply keep track of your behavior. You also monitor the antecedent and consequent events. To identify important antecedents you should record where you were, what you were doing and thinking, and who you were with before the behavior occurred. You may find out, for example, that eating fried foods occurs when you are with friends at a fast-food restaurant and at no other times. This information can be used in devising a behavior change program. To identify consequences, you record what happened just after the behavior. What did you feel or think? What did other people say or do? From this information you can determine what reinforcers are controlling your behavior. For example, if you find that you feel very comfortable after a high-calorie meal, then you can use this new awareness when you are planning to reduce your calorie consumption.

Behavior analysis is not something that automatically happens when you monitor your behavior. You must observe the antecedents, behaviors, and consequences carefully and

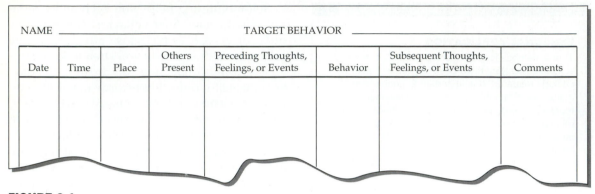

Date	Time	Place	Others Present	Preceding Thoughts, Feelings, or Events	Behavior	Subsequent Thoughts, Feelings, or Events	Comments

NAME _____ TARGET BEHAVIOR _____

FIGURE 3-4
Self-monitoring form.

write them down. Then you review the records to look for patterns of antecedents and consequences that can give you clues about controlling factors. You then use your best judgment about what events are controlling your behavior to develop a behavior change program that is based on behavior analysis.

A final benefit of self-monitoring is that it usually increases motivation to change behavior. Self-monitoring itself is an act of change that encourages people to continue to work on the problem. Very often self-monitoring by itself will produce behavior change, even if you are not trying to change your behavior. For example, smokers who monitor their cigarette smoking usually cut down, and overweight individuals who monitor their eating behavior usually reduce their calories (Nelson, 1977). However, this therapeutic effect of self-monitoring is temporary, so self-monitoring by itself is not a sufficient behavior change program.

An example of a self-monitoring form is shown in Figure 3-4. You can use a form like this in changing your own behavior.

The results of self-monitoring are usually displayed on a graph so that trends over time can be easily seen. Several days or weeks of self-monitoring information are usually collected before trying to modify behavior in

clinical situations. This initial phase is called the *baseline*. On the graph, the baseline is usually distinguished from the treatment phase to highlight behavior changes resulting from the treatment. A typical graph is shown in Figure 3-5. This graph indicates the results of a program to decrease the numer of items eaten in fast-food restaurants. Two weeks of baseline showed that fast foods were eaten frequently. After the program started, fast-food intake decreased steadily for 3 weeks, but the subject

FIGURE 3-5
Graph of program to change fast foods.

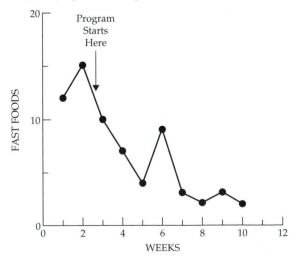

had a temporary setback in week 6. Consumption of fast foods stayed low for the last 4 weeks.

Goal Specification   Self-monitoring prepares you to set behavior change goals, since you know the initial frequency (or duration or intensity) of the behavior, the behavior problem has been clearly defined, and controlling factors have been identified. There are several characteristics that tend to distinguish effective goals, which are those that assist you in making behavior change.

Goals should be specific. Goals such as "to become healthier," "to eat a balanced diet," and "to do what my doctor tells me" are not effective because they do not specify the behavior to be changed or the amount of the change. Goals that can be highly specific are especially likely to be achieved. Here is a very specific goal: "My goal for the next week is to play racquetball at the gym on Monday, Wednesday, and Friday at 8 A.M. with my roommate." This goal demonstrates a highly detailed knowledge of the behavior and its controlling factors. It is defined in terms of *what*, *when*, *where*, and *with whom*. The act of setting a specific goal prepares you in many ways to achieve that goal.

Goals should be realistic. Remember that the principle of shaping from operant learning theory indicates that behavior can be changed gradually. In setting behavior change goals it is usually best to follow this principle, because we tend to find abrupt changes difficult. Let's imagine that you have been eating a lot of salty foods, and you decide one day that to help prevent hypertension you will cut out salt. You will notice that your food tastes very bland, and this bland taste will probably convince you to give up on your health behavior change program. However, if you use the principle of shaping and set realistic goals, you are much more likely to be successful. For example, if you usually put six shakes of salt on

your dinner, begin by cutting back to five shakes. By simply reducing your salt intake a little bit every day, at the end of a few weeks you will be eating very little salt. By changing gradually you do not notice the change in taste very much, because your taste preferences themselves will adjust to the gradual change. The principle of shaping applies to many other health behaviors, such as gradually phasing in a complex medication regimen.

In deciding what a realistic goal is, self-monitoring records are useful. If your baseline self-monitoring indicates that you perform relaxation once per month when the recommended frequency is three times per week, your initial goal should be a small increase over your baseline behavior. Thus, in this case a reasonable goal for the first week would be one time. The goal would increase in subsequent weeks to twice and then three times. By making small improvements you almost guarantee success. That success increases your self-efficacy, so you are further encouraged to keep working at your program. One of the most common mistakes in behavior change is to set overly ambitious goals and, when those goals are not met, to give up.

Goals should be moderately challenging. While small goals seem to be the most effective, it is possible to have goals that are too small. Goals that do not provide some challenge will not lead to changes in your behavior. If your overall goal is to quit smoking, then a realistic initial goal would be to smoke one cigarette per day less than your baseline. If your weekly goal is to smoke one less cigarette per day than the week before, it would take a very long time to get down to zero cigarettes. In this situation the smoker might not be able to notice much progress because the goals would not be challenging enough. Each person must find the proper balance so that the goal is both realistic and challenging.

Goals should focus on behavior change. In health psychology, it is understandable that some patients will want to set goals such as "decreasing the frequency of my headaches" and "reducing my blood pressure." These nonbehavioral goals are not effective because they do not provide any guidance on how to accomplish the ultimate health goal. Behavioral goals tell you exactly what behavior must be changed. An excellent study by Mahoney (1974) illustrated this principle. Obese subjects were randomized to several treatment groups. One group received no treatment, and one group merely self-monitored weight and diet. A third group set weight loss goals, and a fourth group set dietary behavior change goals. The group with the diet goals lost by far the most weight, and the group with only weight loss goals did no better than the control groups.

Goals should be short-term. In the prevention and treatment of most health problems we are concerned with long-term behavior change, but to achieve long-term change, it is usually more effective to set short-term goals since they provide more specific information about what needs to be done now. In a very clever study, Bandura and Simon (1977) randomized obese women into either a control group, a self-monitoring group, a short-term (daily) goals group, or a long-term (weekly) goals group. Since many of the women in the long-term goals group reported that they started setting daily goals on their own, the investigators divided that group according to whether they used short- or long-term goals. The women who actually used short-term goals lost much more weight than the women using long-term goals. When you have a goal for every day, you know very well what needs to be done, and you know that you cannot put it off until tomorrow.

In summary, the very act of setting goals and the kinds of goals you set can be important influences on the overall success of your behavior change program.

Stimulus Control *Stimulus control* is the term given to the set of procedures that seek to alter the antecedent stimuli that control behavior. These antecedent stimuli can be in any one of three environments: physical, social, and private (Mahoney & Arnkoff, 1979). The physical environment consists largely of inanimate objects and includes such characteristics as signs and signals, weather, and other characteristics associated with specific places and times. Just as street signs control our driving behavior, other antecedents control some health behaviors. The social environment is made up of the people around us, and the influence of people on health behavior is very strong. The private environment includes thoughts, feelings, and physiological processes that occur inside of us.

The most common stimulus control techniques for behavior change are associated with changing the physical environment. These techniques are routinely included in programs for weight reduction and smoking cessation. Patients are taught to identify antecedent stimuli through self-monitoring and then to alter those stimuli to remove cues for overeating and smoking. A few common stimulus control methods are listed here.

STIMULUS CONTROL FOR OVEREATING

1. Remove high-calorie foods from your home, and do not purchase others.
2. Eat in restaurants that have a selection of low-calorie dishes.
3. Plan ahead, and write down your grocery shopping list.
4. Use small plates so that the portions look larger.
5. At parties, stand far away from the food table.

STIMULUS CONTROL FOR SMOKING CESSATION

1. Take all cigarettes out of the house.
2. Remove from view all ashtrays and lighters.

3. Do not drink alcohol.
4. After a meal, immediately get up and take a walk.
5. Keep sugarless gum where you used to keep cigarettes.

Controlling the social environment may be more difficult, but it is also very important. Just after quitting smoking it may be necessary to stay away from your smoking friends for several days. Their modeling of smoking will be a powerful cue to join them in your old habit. For the sake of your health you may need to change some of your social habits. A diabetic teenager may have to refuse offers to go out for an evening with friends if that evening includes dinner at a restaurant known for fried foods and abundant desserts. Often the social environment can be altered rather than avoided. The diabetic teen could ask his or her friends to go to a restaurant that serves healthful foods, and this would significantly change the social cues, as well as the physical cues, at the restaurant. A person wanting to start an exercise program could control the social stimuli by exercising at a place with many models for exercise, instead of exercising at home.

Controlling internal stimuli can sometimes be the most difficult, but specific methods have been developed for changing cognitive stimuli. We talk to ourselves almost continually, and this internal dialogue is a major influence on our feelings and actions. Donald Meichenbaum (1977) reasoned that these thoughts could be changed to support our behavior change goals. He developed self-instructional training that teaches people to actively change their self-talk. Often we instruct ourselves to behave in unhealthful ways, although sometimes we are not aware of these instructions. You may see a piece of cheesecake in the bakery and instruct yourself, "That looks good; I think I will have a piece."

With self-instructional training, patients are taught to counter that instruction with one such as, "I have had enough calories today, so I will pass up that cheesecake."

The basic idea of self-instructional training is to identify the thoughts that interfere with your goal and consciously instruct yourself to stick to your goal. Some people rehearse their positive self-instructions several times during the day to maintain a private stimulus environment that is conducive to achieving their health goals. This is a simple but effective method of self-directed behavior change. Here are a few examples:

SELF-DEFEATING THOUGHTS	CONSTRUCTIVE THOUGHTS
It's impossible to live a normal life when you have diabetes.	Every day I will do at least one thing that I enjoy.
I'm too busy to exercise.	I can at least find time for a 15-minute walk every day.
This pain is too much to bear.	The pain is easier to handle when I think about something pleasant.

Self-Reinforcement Since reinforcement strategies are the single most powerful method of behavior change, it is not surprising that psychologists have developed ways for people to learn to reinforce themselves. Self-reinforcement works similarly to the usual type of reinforcement, except that the patient determines the reinforcement contingency and delivers his or her own reinforcement. Self-reinforcement is typically used in the early stages of behavior change. The unhealthful behavior is being reinforced, which is why it has persisted. For example, eating greasy french fries is reinforced by the good taste. If eating french fries is to be successfully decreased, then reinforcement for incompatible behaviors must be introduced. Providing self-reinforcement each day that no french fries are eaten will increase motivation to establish this new behavior. In this case the reinforcement may be saving a small amount of money for a special purpose.

Studies with obese individuals have shown that self-reinforcement, sometimes known as self-reward, is more effective than self-punishment. Mahoney, Moura, and Wade (1973) assigned overweight patients to several groups, but within the self-reinforcement group, subjects were free to choose self-reward or self-punishment, or both. As shown in Figure 3-6, the best results were achieved by those who used self-reward. There was no real benefit of adding self-punishment to self-reward. Thus, it is better to emphasize a positive approach to self-reinforcement, although many people will initially want to try to punish their own unhealthful behavior.

There are many reinforcers that can be self-administered, but the best guideline is probably to use something simple that you enjoy.

Self-reinforcers must still be chosen carefully, especially when dealing with health problems. It seems that when you ask many people "What would be a good reward for going a day without eating in a fast-food restaurant?" the most common responses are "Some chocolate candy" or "A double cheeseburger." For some reason food seems like a great reward, maybe since it is a tangible, primary reinforcer. However, this tendency illustrates just some of the difficulties in choosing self-reinforcers.

It is important for each person to choose his or her own rewards. They cannot be assigned, because the reinforcer must be desirable for the person. He or she must be willing to work for it. This does not mean that everyone chooses an effective reinforcer every time. Frequently, after trying the first choice, the patient will find that it is not effective; but after this trial run most usually have an idea about a reinforcer that would work well for them.

Tangible reinforcers are commonly used. Money is particularly effective when it is put into a fund or piggy bank a little bit at a time. These immediate rewards can be saved up to

FIGURE 3-6

Weight loss with different self-management procedures.

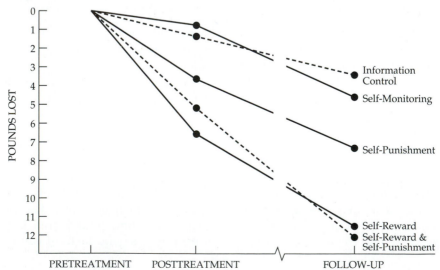

purchase a larger long-term reinforcer. Symbolic rewards are more effective than you might think. In a classic early weight loss study, Bellack (1976) had subjects give themselves letter grades based on their goal achievement for the day. These grades were shown to work at motivating the subjects to lose weight. We all know what valued reinforcers gold stars are for kindergarten children, but few of us would guess that gold stars and progress charts are also effective with adults.

Another type of symbolic reinforcer is our own thoughts. Self praise—such as saying "Good job," "I'm proud of myself for meeting that goal," "This is helping me look good," or "I'm working toward getting healthier"—can also be good reinforcers. Each person can identify a thought or image that would be reinforcing at any particular time. Thoughts have the particular advantages of being positive, convenient to use, highly portable, noncaloric, and (best of all) free.

The best reinforcers, then, are immediate, simple and desirable. They should also be appropriate in that they do not cause other problems. Having an enjoyable martini after sticking to a low-calorie diet for a day is obviously not appropriate. In general, it is better to use something other than food as your self-reinforcer. A more appropriate reward for meeting a diet goal would be to save up for some smaller clothes. An appropriate reinforcer for meeting an exercise goal would be to save up for exercise equipment, to create a picture in your mind of a very fit version of yourself, or to simply tell yourself "Awesome workout."

Social Support Another method of self-directed behavior change is enlisting social support. You can arrange the social environment so that it reinforces you for your goal achievement. This is a very meaningful method of reinforcement, because it comes from people who care for you, and for whom you care.

However, do not expect that when you meet your health goal all of your friends and family will stand in line to congratulate you. Probably not. It is up to you to take responsibility to ask them to help you with your program. Tell them how they can help. Give them suggestions on how to encourage and praise you. There are organized support groups for people with just about every medical problem, and the power of these groups should not be underestimated.

Ask a friend to exercise with you, to stop smoking with you, or to eat a low-fat diet with you. Most of your friends will be willing to help you do something positive for yourself, and participating with you is excellent reinforcement (as well as excellent stimulus control). If they will not participate, they can praise you by saying simple things such as "Looks like you had a good workout" or "You're doing great—it's been 3 days since you had a cigarette." If your buddies do not feel comfortable praising you, they will probably at least refrain from harassing you if you ask them to help. Almost everyone can find at least one person who will help them in their health behavior change program.

There are many studies that demonstrate the power of social support, but the most impressive one was conducted by social psychologist Irving Janis (1983). In this study smokers were randomly assigned to one of three conditions, but all smokers received a structured smoking cessation program. In the first group, subjects talked with a different partner each session, so there was no stable support. In the second group, subjects talked with their partners only in the weekly sessions. In the third group, subjects talked with their partners each day on the telephone to provide one another with support. Not only was the group with the daily support more effective at quitting smoking for 1 year, but these subjects were followed up 10 years later, and subjects in the first two groups were smoking four to five times as much as the subjects in the high support group. Apparently social support not only is effective but can be a long-lasting intervention method as well.

Behavioral Contracting   Once the patient has developed the self-directed behavior change program—taking into consideration results of self-monitoring, goals, stimulus control, self-reinforcement, and social support—it is useful to write down the entire program as a contract. The contract can be simply with oneself, or it can also be signed by a social support person, the physician, or any other interested person. The contract is a symbol of commitment and requires that the program be well enough thought out to be written down. The contract can then serve as a reminder not only of the commitment to better health but also of the behavior change strategy that was worked out.

Contracts can take any form, but Figure 3-7 shows an example of a contract that can be used in just about any situation.

Behavior Rehearsal   The final step in the self-managed behavior change program is to rehearse the new behavior. In a therapy setting, this is usually done as role playing. However, one can conduct behavioral rehearsals without any formal support. All you need to do is try out your new behavior. For behaviors that involve another person, it is useful to practice by yourself first, much the same way as you practice in front of the mirror asking someone for a date. One reason for rehearsing is to become more comfortable with the behavior. Another reason for practicing a health-related behavior is to improve your skills. This can be done by self-criticism or by watching a videotape of yourself. You can also get someone to watch

FIGURE 3-7
A behavioral self-contract.

What is the target behavior? _____

When will this goal be reached? _____

What subgoals need to be reached and when?

	Subgoal	Date
1.	_____	_____
2.	_____	_____
3.	_____	_____

What is my action plan? Specify what, when, where, how, and with whom? What needs to be done to reach the goals?

_____

_____

What my helper will do: _____

Rewards for daily goals or subgoals: _____

Reward for long-term goal: _____

Date _____   Signed: _____

Helper: _____

you and giving gentle and constructive feedback. The most important point is that there is no substitute for behavioral rehearsal.

Are Behavioral Methods Effective?

There are at least two major schools of thought concerning health behavior change. One group maintains that people are motivated to change health habits, because health is so highly valued. Therefore, all that needs to be done is to educate patients about what behaviors they need to change. Heart patients need to be taught the benefits of exercise, and diabetics need to be taught which foods to eat. Then they will make the changes.

The other school of thought says that knowledge is not sufficient to change behavior, and specific behavior change methods need to be used. Even when people are highly motivated to make a change, they often lack the skills. This group points to the high percentage of heart patients who drop out of exercise, the many diabetics who do not follow their diets, and the millions of smokers who want desperately to quit and yet fail to do so.

Which group of dedicated health professionals is more correct? To begin to answer this question, Steven Mazzuca (1982) reviewed the literature to find studies that used interventions based on either didactic, knowledge-based, interventions, or behavioral skill-based programs. He summarized the results of many studies on different types of patients using a procedure called *meta-analysis*. Didactic interventions had an effect on health behavior of 0.26 units, which was not significant. However, behavioral interventions had an effect on health behavior of 0.64, which was significant. This suggests that behavior change programs were more than twice as effective as knowledge-based programs. Mazzuca also looked at the effects on physiological variables, like blood pressure, blood glucose, weight, and blood cholesterol. Again, the results strongly supported the behavioral programs. The effect was 0.18 for didactic programs (not significant) and 0.74 for behavioral programs (highly significant).

The results of this meta-analysis indicate that specific behavior change procedures, like the methods of self-directed behavior change discussed in this chapter, are effective in changing health behaviors and physiological outcomes. It is not enough to educate people about *what* behaviors to change. It is necessary to teach them the skills and provide additional incentives so that they will know *how* to change.

SUMMARY

There are many models and theories used to understand health behaviors. Some of these models are more easily translated into behavior change methods than others, but all models have some value. Behavior change methods based on respondent and operant learning models, as well as social cognitive theory, have been most effectively used to change important health behaviors. Behavioral self-management is the approach used to change a wide variety of health behaviors of individuals. The same skills are sometimes taught using media in programs designed to change the behavior of entire communities. Throughout this book you will see many applications of behavioral self-management. This approach is favored over other methods of behavior change because the person controls his or her own behavior. Self-management is not coercive and does not make people change. For those who want to improve their health, self-management provides them with the tools. The other primary approach to health behavior change is legislative, and punishment is the usual means of enforcing the laws. An example would be strict laws against drunk driving. Sometimes the legislative approach is necessary. Generally self-management is preferable because it enhances rather than restricts people's freedom.

KEY TERMS (AND THE NAMES ASSOCIATED WITH THEM)

Respondent conditioning. This occurs when a stimulus comes to elicit a response because it has been paired with an unconditioned stimulus. (Pavlov)

Operant learning. Behavior that is controlled by its consequences. Positive events that occur after a behavior reinforce or increase the behavior. Negative events that occur after a behavior punish or decrease the behavior. (Skinner)

Shaping. Positive reinforcement of gradual approximations of desired behavior.

Social cognitive theory. A general model of behavior emphasizing the effect of the social environment and cognitions on behavior and the reciprocal effect of behavior on environment and cognition. (Bandura)

Self-efficacy and outcome expectations. Self-efficacy is your belief in your ability to perform a behavior. Outcome expectations are your belief that the behavior will produce desired outcomes. (Bandura)

Health belief model. A model designed to predict health behavior. It proposes that the main influences are perceived susceptibility to disease, perceived threat of disease, perceived benefits of action, and perceived barriers to action. (Rosenstock, Becker, and Maiman)

Theory of reasoned action. Social psychological model of voluntary behavior. Intentions are the most immediate influence on behavior. Intentions are influenced by attitudes and subjective norms, or perceptions of social pressures. Attitudes are determined by beliefs about the consequences of behavior, and subjective norms are affected by the actions of significant others. (Ajzen and Fishbein)

Communication-behavior change model. This model from communication theory describes a sequence of behavior change and the types of input needed to create movement throughout the sequence. Inputs include the source of information, the message to be communicated, the medium of communication, the intended target audience, and the intended outcome of the communication. (McGuire)

PRECEDE-PROCEED model. This model from the health education field describes the steps in planning and evaluating a communitywide health behavior change program. Phases 1 through 5 focus on assessing the social context, epidemiologic data, factors that control the target behavior, health education needs, and administrative factors. Phases 6 through 9 concern implementation and evaluation of the program impact. (Green)

Transtheoretical model. This psychological model states that the stages of change are similar for many health behaviors. At each stage of change, different processes of change, or intervention approaches, are needed (Prochaska and DiClemente).

Self-directed behavior change. Also called self-management, self-regulation, or self-control. People are taught principles and methods of behavior modification so that they can change their own behavior effectively. The key methods are self-monitoring, goal specification, stimulus control, self-reinforcement, and behavior rehearsal. (Mahoney)

CHAPTER 4

The Health Care System

Jean, a 42-year-old divorced woman with three children, had maintained the same weight since high school. When she lost 13 lb over the course of 3 weeks without making any attempt to change her diet or increase her exercise, she had a reason to worry. There are many possible explanations for her weight loss. For example, she had been nervous about her divorce settlement, which was not completely final. There were problems with her children and the adaptation to a new lifestyle. But there were also other explanations that she wanted to think less about. Sudden weight loss may indicate a potentially serious illness such as cancer.

Ordinarily, Jean would have made an appointment with her doctor and gone there directly. However, since the divorce she no longer had adequate health insurance. While trying to make ends meet, she realized that a doctor's exam would set her back $100 and that it is likely a doctor would order a variety of different tests to evaluate her endocrine function. A friend told her that the entire workup could easily run $1000 or more. Over the weeks, Jean convinced herself that she was really OK and that she would wait a little bit longer before seeing a doctor.

How would you react to these circumstances? Using the health care system involves a complex series of decisions. Different people are in different circumstances. Some are totally insured and do not worry about the expense of using health care. Yet other concerns and beliefs about their own health keep them away. Others, like Jean, are inhibited by the financial situation. As we will discover in this chapter, there are somewhere between 32 and 40 million Americans who have no health insurance and a growing number for whom health insurance is inadequate.

In this chapter, we will explore the interface between patients and a complex health system. In addition, we will compare the American health care system with that of other countries. In doing so, we hope to expose some of the strengths and some of the weaknesses in our system of delivering health care. The problems we face in health care delivery are very complex, and we hope you will come to understand some of the major dilemmas we now face.

In addition to problems in gaining access to medical care, patients often fail to obtain benefits from health care because they do not follow the advice of their health care providers. This problem, which is called noncompliance or nonadherence, will be considered in Chapter 5.

WHY PEOPLE USE HEALTH SERVICES

When you are sick, you should see a doctor. But how often? People differ greatly in the likelihood that they will use health services when they are ill. Some people stay away from physicians and ultimately end up in medical trouble because preventable diseases have progressed too far. Conversely, others use medical services too much and expose themselves to unnecessary complications of treatments. In addition, overuse of services leads to the esca-

lation in health care costs. We will return to the cost issue in the next section.

Illness is a concept that we typically relate to objective symptoms and physical signs. *Symptoms* are subjective interpretations of experiences and may not be directly observed. *Signs* describe characteristics of illness that can be observed by others. When people become ill, they interpret their symptoms in an attempt to do something about them. Often people go through a search process in which they attempt to determine whether or not their symptoms are a matter of concern. They may seek information from friends or family, or they may solicit help from others. Although the illness itself may be affected by biological conditions, illness behavior can be affected by a variety of social circumstances. According to social comparison theory, when we are confused about our internal state, we turn to others to help interpret it for us (Kulik & Mahler, 1990). For example, if you have lost weight unexpectedly, you may be uncertain as to whether or not you have a medical problem. You are confused about your physiologic condition. In order to help interpret this, you may talk to a variety of other people as a way of gaining some perspective on the problem. Social comparison theory is a traditional social psychological theory that helps us understand these processes. The stress of an illness creates uncertainty, and this uncertainty may be partially resolved by input from others. Thus, we know from a variety of studies that people first consult friends and relatives before speaking to a doctor.

Early social psychological studies suggested that, when confronted with a stressful situation, people tend to seek affiliation with someone who faces the same stress themselves (Schachter, 1954). This generated the saying "Misery loves miserable company." However, recent research in health psychology has not confirmed these findings. In one study pa-

BOX 4·1

HEALTH OBJECTIVES FOR THE YEAR 2000

In the "Healthy People 2000" report, one of the three overall goals for the United States was to achieve access to preventive services for all Americans. Currently there are large disparities. For example, black women are still significantly less likely to receive prenatal care than white women.

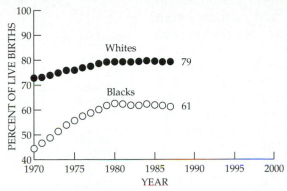

Percentage of pregnant women receiving first trimester prenatal care, blacks and whites. (From National Vital Statistics System, CDC.)

One of the reasons there is unequal access is that there are so many Americans with no health insurance. As the following figure shows, 15 percent of the people (an estimated 37 million) in the United States have no health insurance.

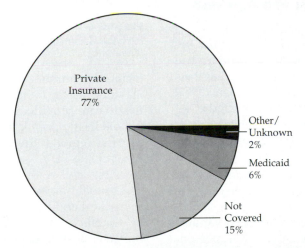

Health insurance coverage for people aged 64 and younger, by type of coverage (1986). Note: Percent distribution approximate due to overlap among categories. (After *Health, United States, 1989* and *Prevention Profile*.)

tients who were about to receive coronary artery bypass surgery were asked if they would like to have a hospital roommate who was also preparing for the surgery or one who had already received it. A significantly larger portion of the patients wanted to be with someone who had already been through the surgery. Furthermore, those who were given rooms in which the roommate had already been through the surgery were less anxious and were able to be released from the hospital sooner than those who were paired with someone who had not yet had the surgery (Kulik & Mahler, 1987). Mechanic (1977) argued that the medical history of the patient is much more complex than the information typically obtained by the physician. History involves lots of experiences, referrals from friends, and interpretations of sensations and events. Physicians who do not attend to this array of information view their role in a rather limited way. These doctors regard their job as requiring the technical aspects of medical care.

MODELS OF HEALTH SERVICE USE

Eventual choice to use health care depends on a variety of different factors. Perhaps the best known conceptual framework for understanding the use of health care services has been presented by Andersen and Newman (1973). The framework is summarized in Figure 4-1. There are three major factors that may determine the use of services: predisposing factors, enabling factors, and illness level.

There are three categories of *predisposing factors*: demographic, social, and belief. Demographic variables include age, sex, marital status, and past illnesses. The social variables include education, race, and other personal characteristics. Belief variables concern values, attitudes, and knowledge.

Enabling factors include personal resources such as income, health insurance, and access to medical care. The enabling component also

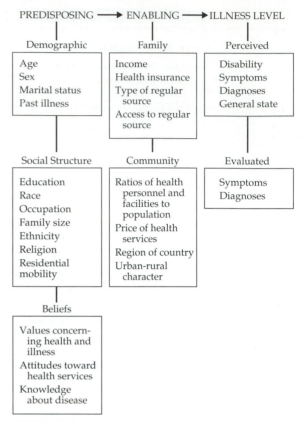

FIGURE 4-1
Individual determinants of health service utilization. (From *Anderson & Newman*, 1973.)

includes community resources. For example, in some areas there are a large number of health care providers relative to the number of people in the population. In other areas, such as rural regions, there are too few doctors to care for the ill.

Illness level is the third component of the conceptual framework. This is often referred to as medical care need. Illness level is the degree of disability, the symptoms experienced, and the general state as perceived by the patient. It also includes a component for the evaluation of illness by a health care provider.

In the following sections we will refer back to this conceptual model as we discuss various components. We will begin by talking about the enabling component and the crisis that we face in providing adequate health insurance and access to health care.

THE HEALTH CARE CRISIS

America is currently facing a health care crisis. The United States may be the only country in the world where a serious medical crisis can result not only in bad health but also in financial collapse. Medical bills are the number one reason for personal bankruptcy in the United States. Most people think of health care costs as what they have to pay out of their own pocket for medical services. Yet what we personally pay is only a small fraction of the total expenditure.

Americans are excessive in their spending on health care. Between 1970 and 1980, infla-

tion-adjusted per capita spending on health care grew by 4 percent per year. Between 1980 and 1986 this trend accelerated toward 4.6 percent per year. Health care costs now constitute more than 13 percent of the gross national product (GNP), and there is concern that this will rise to 15 percent by the year 2000 (Office of the Actuary, 1987). With such great resources devoted to health care, other aspects of the economy will become constrained. In comparison with other industrialized nations, the United States spends significantly more of its GNP on health care. For example, Germany and Japan are each well below 10 percent (Japan is closer to 7 percent). Figure 4-2 summarizes the spending on medical care in relation to other westernized cultures. We currently spend nearly three-quarters of a trillion dollars on health care (1992 estimate =

FIGURE 4-2

Increases in health care expenditures in six western countries. (From *The Economist*, July 6, 1991, p. 4.)

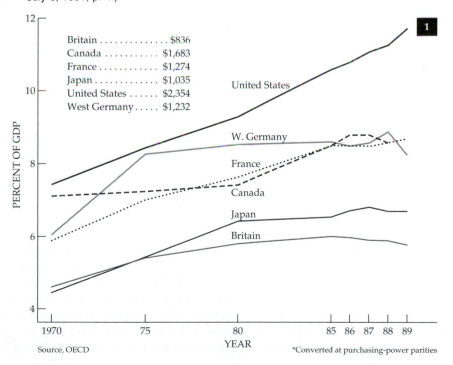

Britain $836
Canada $1,683
France $1,274
Japan $1,035
United States $2,354
West Germany $1,232

Source, OECD   *Converted at purchasing-power parities

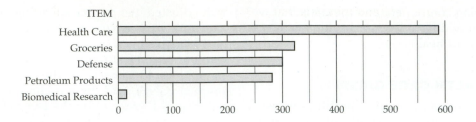

FIGURE 4-3

Comparison of health care spending to expenditures on food, petroleum, and bio-medical research. (From Rekeysers & Company, 1987.)

$800 billion). This exceeds what we spend on food. Figure 4-3 summarizes 1988 expenditures on health care in relation to other sectors of the economy. Food includes both groceries consumed at home and food eaten in restaurants and other establishments. In fact, we spend just over $300 billion on groceries, less than 60 percent of what we spend on health care. It has often been argued that the cost of petroleum products dominates the economy. Yet we spend less than 40 percent on petroleum products of what is invested in health care. In order to anchor the comparison, Figure 4-3 also includes our expenditures on biomedical research. Despite our extensive establishment in the National Institutes on Health (NIH-supported training programs, clinical trials, hospitals, and laboratories), we spend nearly $550 on health care for each dollar invested in research.

THE COST PROBLEM

Health care costs are raging out of control. As noted by Enthoven and Kronick (1989) our health care system provides no budget within which physicians must manage their patients. We currently have no incentives for physicians to use less expensive methods in achieving the same health outcomes for their patients. In fact, it has been suggested that health outcomes do not enter into the equation of patient management and physician reimbursement.

Furthermore, we have a deplorable paradox in that we devote more of our GNP to health care than any other nation and yet we have a substantial portion of our population that cannot get health care because they cannot afford it. In fact, our current system shuts out many of those patients who most need health care services. Over the last 10 years, the number of uninsured has grown, and employers are finding increasingly creative ways to avoid paying for the health care of their employees and their dependents. Recent estimates suggest that between 32 and 40 million Americans have no insurance in either public or private plans (Suleveda & Swartz, 1986).

SMALL AREA VARIATION STUDIES

It is typically assumed that the amount of health service consumed is a reflection of the need for the service. Thus, it would be expected that in demographically equivalent communities the use of specific health care services would be approximately equal. However, Wennberg and his colleagues have shown this not to be the case. Within New England communities with demographically equivalent populations, the variation in the use of some services is substantial (Wennberg, Freeman, & Culp, 1987). For example, women in some communities are 9 times more likely to have a hysterectomy than women with the same characteristics in a bordering commu-

FOCUS ON WOMEN

The current health care crisis may pose particularly difficult problems for women. Women are more likely than men to have no employer-based insurance. Low-income women are sometimes eligible for Medicaid funding. Medicaid is a program run by the states with assistance from the federal government. However, Medicaid recognizes only certain categories. The most common one for women is Aid to Families with Dependent Children (AFDC). This provides health insurance to families with low incomes who also have children. However, it excludes women who do not have children. Among two equally poor women, one with a child and the other child-free, only the woman with a child could get health insurance.

Because of concern about poor prenatal care, most states have now adopted programs that automatically enroll pregnant women into Medicaid. This means that a woman can get insurance if she becomes pregnant. As the health care crisis of the 1990s became more severe, there was an increase in the number of women with serious chronic illnesses reporting that they had become pregnant because it was the only way they could get medical care. These problems highlight the continuing need to seek reform in health care.

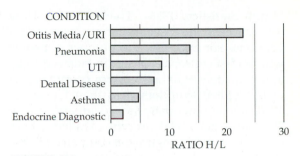

FIGURE 4-4
Variations in the use of selected pediatric services in 16 university/community hospitals. (From Wennberg, 1989.)

nity. Men with the same symptoms are 13 times more likely to have prostate operations in some communities than demographically identical men who live elsewhere (Roos, 1984; Wennberg, 1989). Figure 4-4 shows some of these small area variations.

The figure shows the variation in the use of various procedures to treat children across 16 university or community hospitals serving similar communities. The horizontal axis of the graph is the ratio of highest to lowest use (H/L). This ratio is expected to be 1, since all communities are expected to have about the same demand for these services. As the figure shows, some hospitals may be 23 times more likely to admit children for otitis media (ear infection) or URI (upper respiratory infection). Although need is important, hospitals and doctors may be motivated by other factors when deciding how to treat some problems.

IS MORE BETTER?

One of the basic objectives in health care is to deliver service. Indeed, many policy options are justified because they provide more services. We assume that expenditure is an accomplishment. The more money allocated to a program, the better the expected outcomes. It is often assumed that the states or countries that are achieving the best health outcomes are those spending the most money. Thus, it might be argued, Americans should have the world's best health profile because they spend the most money on health care.

Recently, substantial evidence has emerged suggesting that many unnecessary services are delivered by our health care system. Consider coronary artery bypass surgery. The United States Congress Office of Technology Assessment reported that in France there are 19 such operations per million members of the population. In Austria there are 150 operations per million in the population. In the United States there are nearly 800 operations per million persons (Rimm, 1985). Approximately 200,000 procedures were performed in the United States in 1985, nearly twice as many as had been performed in 1980 (National Center for

Health Statistics, 1986). There are also large differences in the use of other expensive interventions. For example, the number of people with end-stage renal disease is believed to be approximately equal in western countries. Yet in the United Kingdom, less than 1 case per 1000 was on renal dialysis in comparison with 39 cases per 1000 in the United States (Schroeder, 1987). Figure 4-5 compares the use of several medical procedures in the United States, Canada, and Germany. In each case, U.S. usage is significantly greater (Kaplan, 1993). As argued by a variety of analysts, there is no evidence that these regional variations in use of procedures have had substantial effects on health outcomes. They do have systematic effects upon health care costs.

Policy analysts are faced with difficult choices because they hope to maximize health outcomes while maintaining control over costs. Western countries differ in the rate at which health care costs have escalated. The United States now spends over 12 percent of its gross national product on health care, while other countries with high-technology medicine, such as Japan, spend less than 8 percent and Great Britain spends about 6 percent. It is not clear that escalating expenditure has been associated with equal returns in health status. Among countries reporting data to the Organization for Economic Cooperation and Development, the shortest life expectancies for men are in Ireland and the longest are in Greece. Among the reporting nations, Greece paradoxically spends the smallest percentage of its GNP on health care while Ireland spends the most. In fact, there is a rough negative relationship among the reporting nations between expenditures and life expectancy (Sick Health Services, 1988). Studies (reviewed by Voulgaropolous, Schneiderman, & Kaplan, 1989) have shown that many widely used and expensive procedures have essentially no health benefit.

A related question is whether or not we are getting more return for our health care expenditure. Since we are spending more than other countries, we might expect to achieve more in health benefits. We have witnessed a decline in infant mortality and in total mortality since the turn of the century. Yet, as McKinnlay and McKinnlay (1977) have demonstrated, the decline in mortality far exceeds our acceleration in spending on health care. This is illustrated in Figure 4-6. The figure shows declines in several major disease categories. The arrows in

FIGURE 4-5

Procedures/million people. (After *Health Care in the 90s*, Blue Cross, 1990, p. 18—Canada data, 1989; German and U.S. data, 1987.)

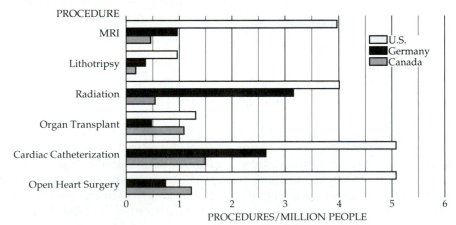

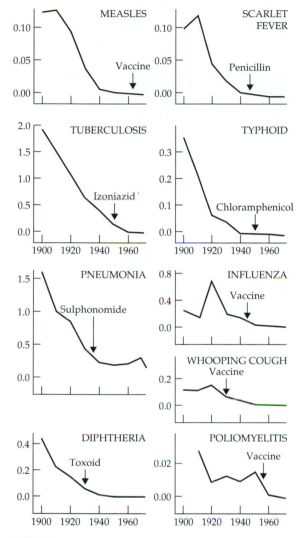

FIGURE 4-6

Rates of selected diseases as a function of time. The arrows mark the point at which medical intervention was introduced. In each case, the intervention was introduced after the epidemic began to decline. (From McKinnlay & McKinnlay, 1977, reproduced with permission.)

the figure mark the point at which the medical intervention to which the decline was attributed was introduced. The treatment in each case was introduced well after the epidemic was apparently getting better on its

own. On the basis of this, the McKinnlays questioned how much of the change in health status could be attributed to expensive medical interventions.

International comparisons show that there is no relationship between per capita expenditure on health care and longevity. Indeed, some analyses of westernized countries demonstrate a significant linear relationship between the number of doctors in the population and the infant mortality rate (see Figure 4-7). In other words, countries with the most doctors are the ones that have the highest death rate among infant children (St. Leger, Cochrane, & Moore, 1978). Indeed, this relationship exists even after adjusting for per capita income in the population.

It is widely argued that health promotion programs will reduce the expense of our current health care system (Pelletier, 1989). This very reasonable argument suggests that health promotion will result in disease prevention. Disease prevention, in turn, will result in reductions in health care costs. Thus, an employer who pays for many coronary artery bypass surgeries might be expected to save money if heart disease can be prevented. However, this line of reasoning assumes that the high number of coronary artery bypass graft surgeries (CABG) is determined by the specific patient need for these operations. As has been suggested, other factors may dominate in the use of this service. For example, the rate of CABG surgery in other countries is a fraction of what it is in the United States, and the number of people who die of heart disease appears to be similar. Other mechanisms for cost control must be considered.

COST CONTAINMENT

Because health care costs have grown out of control, there have been several different efforts to control costs. Since 1980, there have been waves of cost containment strategies rep-

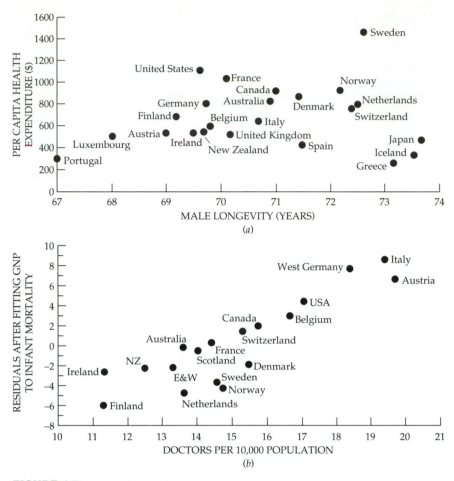

FIGURE 4-7

Relation between infant mortality and doctor population. (From A. St. Leger, A. Cochrane, and F. Moore, "The Anomaly That Wouldn't Go Away," *Lancet II*, 1978: 1153. Reprinted by permission of the publisher.)

resented by various acronyms. Most of these are known as *managed care* plans. More than 60 million Americans are now enrolled in some sort of program that attempts to control costs. These include Health Maintenance Organizations (HMO's) and Preferred Provider Organizations (PPO's). In HMO's an employer typically pays a fixed fee to an HMO, which in turn provides all necessary health care for the employee. These plans may or may not require a copayment from the employee. In PPO's, the employer pays for a specific plan that includes independent health care providers. The independent provider gains the business of all the employees, but in exchange agrees to take a fee fixed by the plan.

Another attempt to control costs involves reimbursements of hospitals by Diagnosis Related Group (DRG). Hospitals are reimbursed for the median length of stay by diagnosis rather than by the actual length of stay associated with a patient. For example, the hospital gets paid a fixed fee for each heart attack patient it cares for, rather than a variable fee based on how long the patient is hospitalized. This has created incentives to move patients out of hospitals more promptly and ultimately to reduce other aspects of costly care. Indeed some cost savings have been realized under these systems. Yet the systems have in and of themselves become extremely complex. DRG's, for example, now allow for a remarkable number of local adjustments, secondary diagnosis adjustments, teaching-related adjustments, etc. Even with these strategies, health care costs have still continued to rise.

The most recent strategy is to control physician fees. Beginning in 1992, a new strategy known as Resource Based Relative Value Scaling (RBRVS) was implemented. The system attempts to define the value of a physician service based on several components, including training required, time required, work required, etc. Under this system, some highly reimbursed procedures may be reimbursed at a lower rate. Conversely, some aspects of primary care, including patient counseling, may be reimbursed at a higher rate (Hsiao et al., 1988). The Congress and the Health Care Financing Administration created a Physicians Payment Review Organization in order to refine the approach. Its impact will take several years to evaluate.

One of the potential problems with RBRVS is that there will be an incentive to increase volume. If a physician receives $100 to do an electrocardiogram and the customary allowable charge is reduced to $50, evidence suggests that he or she will double the volume (Wennberg, 1989). According to this argument, the system will increase the volume of tests but not necessarily decrease total expenditures. Thus, before the system was implemented, another complex system to control volume was added.

IS HEALTH PROMOTION A PROFITABLE HEALTH SERVICE?

Health promotion is the effort to ensure a healthy population through disease prevention and the promotion of healthy lifestyles. Health promotion has now become a major growth industry. Weight control alone may be a multi-billion-dollar per year industry. Health promotion involves not only the use of behavioral interventions but also the use of food and drug interventions. In 1986, 3 of the 10 most widely used drugs in the world (Tenormin, Inderal, & Aldomet) were products to lower blood pressure (Rukeyser & Cooney, 1988).

One of the most important justifications for health promotion programs is that they reduce health care costs. Yet several authors have begun to challenge the cost-effectiveness of prevention or health promotion programs. In an intriguing book, Russell (1986) posed the challenging question, "Is Prevention Better Than Cure?" Weinstein (1986) suggested that the belief in health promotion as a money-saving venture was "naive assumption number one." More recently Warner, Wickizer, Wolfe, and coworkers (1988) examined the conventional wisdom that workplace health promotion programs yield financial dividends for companies. After reviewing the literature, they concluded that most studies published prior to 1986 did conclude that health promotion programs increased profitability. However, these studies tended to use anecdotal evidence for analyses that were seriously flawed in terms of their assumptions or methodology. In fact, they found very little evidence that health promotion programs save money for companies. However, they also found little evidence against this assertion. The difficulty was that few studies had systematically examined the issue. Thus, they recommended healthy skepticism for readers of the literature.

INDUSTRY AND HEALTH OUTCOMES

There is considerable commercial interest in promoting health. Indeed, many products and services are offered because they can enhance health status. Food is one of the most interesting of these commercial interests. Each year, Americans spend about $513 billion on food and beverages (about the same as they spend on health care). About $10 billion is spent on health enhancing activities, such as diet food, health clubs, diet drugs, and weight reduction programs. We spend about $800 million on frozen dinners that may not be nutritious and then devote about $350 million to diet pills and diet powders. Weight Watchers International, one of many weight reduction programs, has had 25 million participants, with 700,000 currently enrolled. The value of the company is estimated to be about $400 million in gross receipts (Rukeyser & Cooney, 1988).

An example of the commercialization of health promotion is provided by the February 13, 1989, issue of *Newsweek*. Each year, *Newsweek* magazine provides a supplement, typically written by physicians, on health promotion. This particular supplement focused on heart health. The supplement included five articles. Adjacent to each page of the supplement was a full-page ad for a commercial product. The table of contents faced an advertisement for Bayer aspirin. Recent evidence has suggested that regular use of aspirin may reduce the probability of a fatal myocardial infarction. However, these same studies show no advantage of aspirin for increasing survival, because reductions in heart attacks are associated with increases in other types of cardiovascular death (Kaplan, 1989).

The first article on heart attack prevention was followed by a two-page advertisement for Kellogg's Oat Bran. The next two-page article on exercise included 2 one-page advertisements, one for Schwin fitness machines (stationary bicycles) and another for Nordic track stationary cross-country machines. The third article was on healthy eating. It was two pages long and was accompanied by two full-page advertisements, one for Metamucil, a bulk laxative which was promoted as a good source of wheat and oat bran, and an advertisement for Miracle Whip, which was promoted as a healthier product than mayonnaise. Then there was an article on exercise, followed by another full-page ad for Kellogg's Oat Bran. This was followed by an article on what to do about a heart attack, accompanied by a full-page ad for Tylenol. The Tylenol ad acknowledged that many people are now taking aspirin to prevent a heart attack. The ad read, "If you are taking aspirin for your heart, you probably shouldn't take aspirin for your headache."

The section ended with a full-page advertisement for Searle Pharmaceuticals. In total, the 20-page supplement included 10 full pages of advertising. Remarkably, the 20-page supplement on prevention of heart attacks devoted only two paragraphs to cigarette smoking, even though cigarette smoking is clearly the most important modifiable risk factor for coronary heart disease. On the back cover of that particular issue of *Newsweek*, somewhat far away from the healthy heart supplement, was a full-page, full-color advertisement for Marlboro cigarattes.

Health promotion specialists have repeatedly questioned why preventive medicine is not widely practiced. One of the major reasons is that it is simply not profitable. Table 4-1 shows the rates for reimbursement for a variety of preventive services relative to the rates of reimbursement for other services which are

TABLE 4·1

COSTS FOR VARIOUS MEDICAL SERVICES

Service	Time required (min)	Charge*
Brief nutrition counseling	15	16.50
Nutrition counseling	45	44.00
Extended clinic visit (Family Medicine)	45	68.50
Influenza vaccination	5	28.00
Electrocardiogram	10	60.50
Flexible sigmoidoscopy	10	129.00
Vasectomy	45	331.25
Cataract surgery	45	2,200.00

* Based on estimates of prevailing rates for San Diego, CA, 1990.

equally time-consuming for doctors. As the table shows, practitioners lose money by offering prevention services. From an economic perspective, there is no incentive for them to engage in preventive care. Although most physicians are well meaning, they are also too busy treating acute problems to attend to prevention needs (Hovell, Kaplan, & Hovell, 1991).

Although there is no incentive for health promotion, the trend toward self-insurance may be appealing. As companies begin to take on more of the burden of health care costs, they develop incentives to prevent disease. If they see a link between preventive services and health outcome, it may be to their advantage to invest in preventive services in order to defer later costs. To date, several factors have prevented this from happening. First, many companies have unstable work forces with high turnover. For example, the fast-food industry expects to turn over nearly all of its employees within a relatively short time frame. Thus, there is no incentive for them to invest in disease prevention because they are spending current resources for an employee who will be insured by someone else at the time the disease develops.

Similarly, most health care costs accrue to the elderly, who are covered for these expenses by Medicare rather than by their specific employer. Some new proposals for universal health insurance, in particular that offered by Enthoven and Kronick (1989; 1991), suggest that employers should contribute to a general fund which would cover not only their employees but also the uninsured. Such a system would create new incentives for the payers (employers) to invest in disease prevention.

COMPARATIVE HEALTH CARE SYSTEMS

Not all countries have the same health care system as the United States. Western countries have traditionally assumed that medical care is good and that greater access is advantageous to citizens. Thus, most countries have developed systems to provide medical care for most people. An interesting set of comparisons is provided by modern and westernized countries: the United States, France, Canada, and England. Although these four countries have similar cultural and economic characteristics, they differ in the way they distribute health care services. France has the oldest national health insurance system in Europe, and it has evolved to cover both public and private hospitals as well as to reimburse private practice physicians. Despite the national health insurance system, private practice has survived very well in France.

In contrast to France, England has a national health insurance system in which hospitals are controlled by the state and physicians are reimbursed through salaries or a flat fee based on the number of patients that they serve. In Canada, hospitals are almost entirely financed by the government; yet physicians are generally reimbursed on the basis of the specific services they provide. The United

---

BOX 4.3

FOCUS ON POLICY

The Medical Care Crisis at the University of California: A Case Study

The University of California is one of the largest employers in the state of California. With 93,000 employees, 19,000 retirees, and more than 100,000 family members, it is one of the largest systems of public education and research in the United States. In 1990 the University spent an estimated $365 million on health benefits for its employees. In 1970 the University made a monthly contribution of $8 for each employee, while the employee contributed 73 percent of the costs of the insurance plan. However, the total cost per employee for health insurance was less than $30 per month. By 1989 the University was paying $276 for each employee, with the employee paying only about 3 percent of the total plan premium. Between 1970 and 1990 the University's total cost for health and welfare insurance for its employees had increased over 3000 percent. Yet it is interesting to consider the employees' contribution. Adjusted for inflation, the 1970 and 1990 employee contributions out of their paychecks were comparable (between $8 and $30 per month). What had really happened was that health insurance costs had gone completely out of control.

Many of the increased costs are accounted for by new medical technologies. However, the higher use of services was also a significant factor. For example, claims by University employees increased 12.5 percent between 1988 and 1989, and the cost of claims for the average employee had jumped 73 percent between 1983 and 1989. The cost of prescription drugs used by employees increased 36 percent in 1987 and 1989. Furthermore, there was a large increase in the number of psychiatric and substance abuse claims.

By 1990, the University had to rethink the options for providing benefits to its employees. Although the University always prided itself on its employee benefits program, it became apparent that it could no longer afford its own programs. To make things worse, the University itself owns and operates five major hospitals and numerous clinics in association with its five medical schools. In fact, the University is one of the major health care providers in the state of California. The system is both part of the cause and a victim of the problem. By 1990, the University needed to inform its employees that big changes were ahead. Although most employers will continue to provide health insurance coverage, the era of unrestricted use of resources had come to an abrupt end. In the 1990s, experimentation with alternative ways for financing employee benefits is likely to be the rule rather than the exception.

States actually has a peculiar system in which there is a mixture of public, private nonprofit, and private for-profit hospitals. Physicians are typically reimbursed on a fee-for-service basis through a variety of different mechanisms. Sometimes they are paid by insurance companies, sometimes they are paid directly by their patients, and sometimes they are paid by the government. In all four countries medicine

went through an expansionary phase in which health planners tried their hardest to build new hospitals, train more doctors, and do everything imaginable for patients. During this era, health planners, hospital administrators, and physicians all got along very well. They had common goals.

By the early 1970s, however, it became apparent that the expansion of health and medi-

BOX 4·4

FOCUS ON DIVERSITY

Allocating Scarce Resources in the State of Oregon

Virtually all states are running out of money to pay for health care. Perhaps the boldest step has been taken by Oregon. Led by State Senator John Kitzhauber, who is also an emergency room physician, Oregon decided to radically alter the way it paid doctors under its Medicaid program. Medicaid is a federal program that provides health insurance for the poor. To be eligible, one needs a low income, less than $5700 for a family of three in most states. The program also covers the blind, the disabled, and families with dependent children. However, it is very difficult for poor women who do not already have children to get any medical services. Medicaid could only afford to cover 200,000 people of an estimated 400,000 people in Oregon who had no health insurance at all. Kitzhauber and his colleagues realized that the Oregon Medicaid program was paying for many expensive services that had questionable impact on health. At the same time, it denied payment for many people who might be helped because the State simply did not have the money. For example, it was possible to get an organ transplant in Oregon even though the surgery may have very little effect on the life expectancy. On the other hand, thousands of pregnant women were unable to get prenatal care, and it has been estimated that 1 in 4 cases of infant death could be prevented with appropriate medical care during pregnancy. Thus, it was felt that it was time to reexamine the whole system.

In response, Oregon passed Senate Bill 27. This bill suggested that services should receive priority for funding based on the likelihood that they actually benefited patients. In February of 1991, Oregon released a prioritization list. Doctors could be paid for services that were high on the list, while they could expect no reimbursement from the State for services that were less likely to benefit people. The proposal became very controversial because, in effect, it involved a form of rationing. People with some illnesses may get services while people in other categories would be denied. However, the designers of the Oregon Plan suggested that there is already rationing. The current system rations people by letting some in and keeping others out. States are unable to pay for all services, and there are arbitrary decisions about who is actually covered. In August of 1992 the U.S. Department of Health and Human Services denied Oregon permission to go forward with its controversial plan. This decision was also very controversial because many people felt that Oregon had proposed the most realistic solution to the health care financing crisis (Kaplan, 1993).

cal care had to be slowed or even stopped. Planners, hospital administrators, and physicians began to do battle with one another. In all four countries, health planners needed to face up to the limitations of contemporary health care. Yet the problems in the different systems began to be apparent when placed under stress. In England, for example, patients began to complain because of inadequate access to doctors. They argued that having the government pay doctors' salaries rather than basing them on fee for services discourages doctors. As a result, the doctors take on shorter hours and are not motivated to go out of their way to help people. In addition, many expensive services are simply not available. In recent years, more and more wealthy English citizens began taking out private health insurance. In the

United States, the major problem has been that the various systems have not been able to work well together. Substantial numbers of people remain medically uninsured.

Canada, although faced with many of the same problems as the United States, seems to have avoided much of the criticism (Rodwin, 1984), and Canada is often cited as the ideal system. However, private doctors in Canada want to use many of the same technologies used in the United States, and small area variation problems are becoming apparent. Increasingly, Canadian citizens are coming to the United States to obtain services that are low priority in the Canadian hospitals (Kaplan, 1993).

In this chapter we have considered the ways that policies and health care systems influence the use of health care services. In the next chapter, we will look at the other extreme. Once patients get into health care, they often decide not to go along with treatment that has been prescribed for them.

SUMMARY

This chapter began with a description of Jean, a woman who is unable to obtain appropriate health care because she is uninsured. It went on to describe why people use health services. Traditional models suggested that there were at least three factors that explained health care use: predisposing factors, enabling factors, and illness level. It has typically been assumed that people use health care because they are sick and need to see a doctor. However, new evidence shows that the health care system itself stimulates usage. For example, doctors in some areas of the country perform many more operations than other doctors in demographically similar communities. In fact, many health care services may be unnecessary and overutilized.

The high use rate for services, coupled with their high costs, has created a major financial

crisis in the United States. America now faces a situation in which there is a paradox of excess and deprivation. Patients who are well insured can gain access to expensive services—even when those services may be unnecessary. At the other extreme, between 32 and 40 million Americans have difficulty obtaining the most basic services. Other countries such as England and the Scandinavian communities have socialized services controlled by their governments. Countries such as Canada and France have systems in which private doctors are reimbursed through a national health insurance system. The United States must now face a variety of complex policy options in order to deal with this situation.

KEY TERMS

Social comparison theory. A social psychological theory suggesting that when people are confused about their internal state, they turn to others in order to interpret the situation.

Predisposing factors. Demographic, social, and belief variables that may influence the utilization of health services.

Enabling factors. Variables such as personal resources, health insurance, or transportation that influence the use of health services.

Illness factors. The degree of disability, symptoms, or perceived health state that may influence the use of health services.

U.S. health care crisis. The United States spends nearly 13 percent of its gross national product (GNP) on health care. This high cost of medical care has created a financial crisis for the entire U.S. economy.

Cost containment. Policies and strategies designed to control health care costs.

Health promotion. The effort to ensure a healthy population through disease prevention and the promotion of healthy lifestyles.

Industrial health promotion. Efforts to promote health and prevent diseases through programs at the work sites.

CHAPTER 5

Compliance with Medical Regimens

Adrian, a second-year college student, was serious about staying healthy. When he got an upper respiratory infection that did not go away after 2 weeks, he went to the college health center. The doctor told him that it was a relatively minor illness and that he would need to take antibiotic medications. The doctor gave Adrian a prescription and told him to take a pill four times each day until all the pills were gone. Adrian assured the doctor that he would do so.

For the first 3 days Adrian religiously swallowed his pills. However, the third day was Saturday, and he was feeling much better. Adrian remembered to take two of his four pills. By Monday he was feeling fine and saw no need to continue taking the medication. Besides, Adrian looked in the medicine cabinet of the apartment he shared with two other students and there were several prescription bottles with half the pills remaining. Two weeks later, when Adrian returned to the health center with a severe cough, he was embarrassed to admit to the doctor that he had neglected the advice to consume all the pills.

The next time you are home, look in your medicine cabinet. Are there leftover medications from the last time you had a prescription? For example, if you were given an antibiotic medication and told to take it for 10 consecutive days, did you actually do it? In fact, failure to follow the advice given by doctors is not uncommon. In this chapter we will explore some of the reasons that people fail to completely comply with the recommendations offered by their health care providers.

Despite major advances in diagnosis and medical therapeutics, patients often do not receive optimal benefit from medical care. While many diseases are preventable or treatable, benefits will accrue only if specific treatment recommendations are followed (Haynes, Taylor, Snow, & Sackett, 1979). Nearly all patient encounters end in advice to the patient. This advice might include scheduling another appointment, filling a prescription and following directions, or adopting a recommended change in behavior such as weight loss or smoking cessation. Noncompliance is the failure to follow such advice. Various authors have described the same process as nonadherence, noncooperation, or patient resistance. We use the terms *compliance, adherence*, and *cooperation* interchangeably. However, many authors emphasize that the term *compliance* stresses that patients should be passive receivers of what doctors tell them to do rather than active participants in decisions about their own care. *Cooperation* implies that doctor and patient are working together as a team. Although this term is preferable, most of the medical literature is referenced under compliance or adherence.

A rapidly growing literature suggests that failure to adhere to therapeutic regimens is a major problem hampering the quality of medical care (Becker, 1985; Becker & Maiman, 1980; DiMatteo & DiNicola, 1982). Published figures suggest that rates of noncompliance vary between 15 and 93 percent, depending on the

---

BOX 5-1

HEALTH OBJECTIVES FOR THE YEAR 2000

The Health Promotion and Disease Prevention Objectives for the Year 2000 did not specifically consider compliance with medical care.

---

patient population and the definition of nonadherence. Most studies indicate that at least 33 percent of all patients fail to adhere to the recommended therapeutic regimen (Becker & Maiman, 1982; Blackwell, 1973; Davis, 1968; Stimson, 1974). Noncompliance rates appear to be much higher among patients with chronic conditions who must undergo long-term therapy (Sackett, 1979; Sackett & Snow, 1979; Stone, 1979). Noncompliance rates are also very high among patients who must comply with regimens involving lifestyle changes, such as changes in physical activity (Becker, 1985; Carmody et al., 1980; Dunbar & Stunkard, 1979).

PHYSICIAN AWARENESS OF THE PROBLEM

Although evidence consistently demonstrates that patient noncompliance is common, many physicians do not appear to appreciate the problem. DiMatteo and DiNicola (1982) reviewed a variety of studies on practitioner awareness. They found that physicians most often overestimated the extent to which their patients cooperated with recommendations. Thus, Caron and Roth (1971) found that 22 out of 27 medical residents overestimated the degree to which their patients complied with a prescribed liquid antacid prescription. The same investigators found that correlations between estimates made by senior faculty physicians and actual patient compliance were near zero. Several studies (i.e., Norell, 1981) have suggested that physicians are typically inaccurate in their estimates of patient compliance and that they generally overestimate correspondence between their orders and patient behavior. These problems raise serious doubts about the validity of physicians' predictions of future patient compliance.

THEORIES ABOUT COMPLIANCE

There are a variety of different theories about why people fail to adhere to advice given to them by their doctors. Perhaps the best-known theory is the health belief model. This model was developed by Rosentock (1974) as an attempt to understand why people failed to use screening tests or to follow the advice of their physicians and other health care providers (Becker, 1974). The health belief model was discussed in Chapter 3. Briefly, the model depends on two major variables: the value an individual places on a particular goal and an individual's belief in the chances that the action taken will lead to that goal (Maiman & Becker, 1974). At least 46 different studies have evaluated the health belief model in relation to compliance. In most of these studies health beliefs were significantly related to compliance. The most common reason for noncompliance was that there were perceived barriers. For example, the appointments were thought of as unpleasant, painful, inconvenient, or too expensive. The second most common reason for noncompliance relates to perceived susceptibility. People do not take preventive action because they simply do not regard themselves as being at risk. The third most common reason for noncompliance concerns the perceived benefits. Patients often do not believe that taking the action will help them. Finally, many studies have considered seriousness of illness. Often, patients do not regard the consequences of noncompliance as something that will harm their health.

Other theories used to describe adherence include the theory of reasoned action and a variety of behavioral theories, including social learning theory (see Chapter 3).

HOW DO WE MEASURE COMPLIANCE?

One of the major problems in studying medication compliance is in obtaining accurate measures of adherence behaviors. There are a variety of different ways that we can evaluate compliance. One is to use the doctors' judgment. However, as noted above, doctors are notoriously poor at determining whether or not their patients have used medications. A second approach is to trust patient's self-reports. Researchers are divided as to whether or not they believe self-reports. When patient reports have been compared to some objective measure of medicine taking, studies have tended to show that patients are accurate when they claim that they have not taken their medication. However, for those who claim that they have used the medication as prescribed, these verbal reports are often not confirmed by objective records (Spector et al., 1986). We will return to the problem of patient self-reporting later in the chapter.

Another approach to evaluating compliance is to use some objective measure. For example, you can count pills, check pharmacy records, or weigh medicine containers that are used to distribute liquid medications. Using these methods requires that you understand exactly how much medicine the doctor had prescribed. There are also a variety of different problems that can lead to inaccurate assessments. For example, medications are often shared by other members of the household, given to friends, or simply dumped out. This is more true for particular types of medications such as tranquilizers and sleeping pills.

A third approach to the measurement of compliance involves biochemical analysis. Some medicines can be followed by examining blood, urine, or other bodily excretions. Sometimes a pharmacist can put a "marker

BOX 5-2

FOCUS ON TECHNOLOGY

Perhaps the major technical breakthrough in monitoring adherence is the Medication Event Monitoring System (MEMS). This new device includes a small microprocessor that is fitted into the lid of a medicine container (see Figure 5-1). The MEMS system is activated each time the bottle cap is opened. Several newer studies have shown that the MEMS system gives more information than pill counts. Sometimes people can take exactly the same number of pills prescribed by the doctor, but they use the medication in an erratic fashion. For instance, they may be told to take the medication four times a day. Evaluation from the MEMS system might show that on some days the patient skipped taking the medication and then made up for it by double-dosing on other days. Following are a variety of patterns of medicine taking observed using the MEMS system.

	MEDICATION EVENTS		
Start of Dose	Dose Interval (Elapsed Time)	Length (Cap Open)	Notes
- - - - - - - - - - - - - - - - 1988 - - - - - - - - - - - - - - -			
Jul 06 14:07	First Dose		« DD
14:08			« DD
Jul 07 - - - - - - No doses - - - - - - - - - - - -			
Jul 08 16:07	2d 01hr 59min		
Jul 09 - - - - - - No doses - - - - - - - - - - - -			
Jul 10 - - - - - - No doses - - - - - - - - - - - -			
Jul 11 - - - - - - No doses - - - - - - - - - - - -			
Jul 12 07:07	3d 15hr 00min	3m	
22:10	15hr 04min		
	00s		

FIGURE 5-1

MEMS™—Electronic compliance monitors.

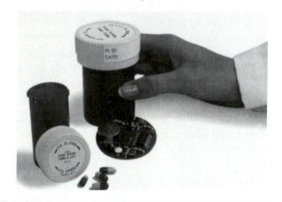

DOSING BY COUNT

Day Distribution

Daily dose count	0	1	PRESC 2	3	4	5	6	7	>7
Number of days	6	3	32	1	0	0	0	0	0
% of total monitored days	14.3%	7.1%	76.2%	2.4%	0.0%	0.0%	0.0%	0.0%	0.0%

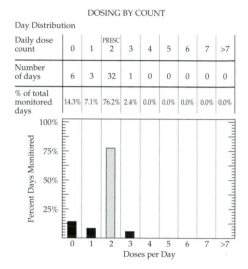

REGIMEN QUANTIFICATION REPORT (RQR)

The MEMS RQR combines the specificity of the patient's real-time dosing record *and* the power of statistical analyses.
It provides:

- dosing events by day and hour
- interdose intervals
- a Calendar Plot of daily doses taken

substance" in the medication. Riboflavin, for example, can be added to medication as a method of tracking its use. There are other biochemical by-products that can be studied. For example, smokers can be detected by studying carbon monoxide in their blood or exhaled breath. Smoking can also be followed using tests for metabolites for nicotine. One of these is called cotinine. Although biochemical measures of compliance are attractive for the sake of accuracy, there are also some problems. For example, these measures often produce misleading findings. For instance, thyocynide, which is often used to evaluate

BOX 5·2 (Continued)

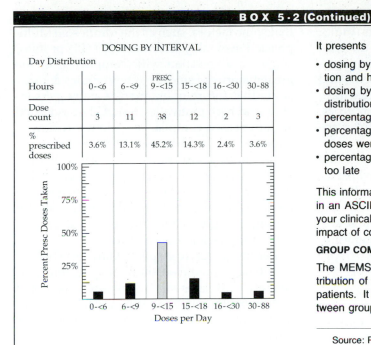

DOSING BY INTERVAL

Day Distribution

Hours	0-<6	6-<9	PRESC 9-<15	15-<18	16-<30	30-88
Dose count	3	11	38	12	2	3
% prescribed doses	3.6%	13.1%	45.2%	14.3%	2.4%	3.6%

It presents

- dosing by count (daily dose count frequency distribution and histogram)
- dosing by interval (dose count by interval frequency distribution and histogram)
- percentage of prescribed doses taken
- percentage of days in which the correct number of doses were taken
- percentage of doses taken on schedule, too early, or too late

This information comes back to you in printed form and in an ASCII format data file which you can merge into your clinical data base. The data help to distinguish the impact of correct versus erratic drug dosing.

GROUP COMPLIANCE ANALYSIS SUMMARY REPORT

The MEMS Group Compliance Report shows the distribution of compliance parameters in entire groups of patients. It allows formal statistical comparisons between groups.

Source: Reprinted courtesy of the APREX Corporation.

---

cigarette smoking, can also be affected by other aspects of the diet. Cabbage, for instance, increases thyocynide concentrations. Cotinine, a commonly used biochemical tracer of cigarette smoking, is so sensitive that it is affected by secondary smoke as well as by cigarette use. For instance, if you are in the room with a smoker, your cotinine level will be affected even though you did not smoke yourself (Rand, 1990).

Explanations for patient noncompliance abound. These can be divided into three categories: patient-related, environment-related, and patient-provider–interaction-related. The most common patient-centered theories hold that patients intentionally resist medical advice in order to reject authority (Appelbaum, 1977), because they misunderstand information (Stone, 1979), or to exert control over the provider (Brehm, 1966). These theories suggest that remedies for patient noncompliance require the patient to change. Yet we have

found essentially no empirical evidence to support the belief that patients fail to comply because of rebelliousness. A second theory holds that the social ecology must be considered because a variety of environmental factors may influence compliance behaviors. These include cultural variables, family or situational variables, and environmental cues. For example, arthritis patients are most likely to miss taking their medications when they have changes in their daily routines (Corish, Richard, & Brown, 1989). According to these formulations, the most efficient way to improve compliance is to alter the patient's environment. Evidence suggests that environmental manipulations, such as reminders, can improve compliance (Haynes, Taylor, & Sackett, 1977). Yet these approaches fail to consider patient experiences with the medications.

The third theory holds that patient noncompliance reflects defects in the patient-provider relationship. Substantial evidence documents deficiencies in information exchange between patients and providers (Inui & Carter, 1985). According to this view, the remedy for noncompliance lies in the improvement of the interactions between patients and providers. This approach suggests that providers must obtain more information from, and provide more information to, their patients.

The compliance literature is enormous, and some excellent reviews have been provided by DiMatteo and DiNicola (1982), and by Taylor, Sackett, and Haynes (1979). In the next sections, we will provide some general observations that have been reported in this literature.

SOCIODEMOGRAPHIC CHARACTERISTICS

The great majority of studies fail to find an association between compliance and patients' sociodemographic characteristics, including age, sex, education, socioeconomic status, occupation, income, marital status, race, ethnic background, religion, and urban versus rural residence (Haynes, 1979). Since these findings are unambiguous and quite consistent, sociodemographic factors will not be considered further. Suffice it to say that there is little evidence that compliance can be consistently predicted from demographic information (Kaplan & Simon, 1990).

PERSONALITY FACTORS

There is also relatively little evidence to suggest that personality factors can be used to predict compliance (Haynes, 1979). In their comprehensive review of compliance with therapeutic and preventive regimens, Haynes, Taylor, Snow, and Sackett (1979) considered 537 original articles. They also considered methodological articles and reviews/commentaries, bringing the total to 853 references. One detailed analysis reviewed psychosocial factors

of patients. Haynes and associates (1979) found that some factors, such as the Minnesota Multiphasic Personality Inventory (MMPI) profiles, show no association with compliance in the great majority of studies. A few studies demonstrate that future orientation, a stable personality, and high motivation tend to be associated with increased compliance. Another review of papers published between 1979 and 1988 confirms these conclusions (Kaplan & Simon, 1990). Traditional measures of personality traits are poor predictors of compliance. On the basis of this, we find little justification for administering psychological tests to screen patients for possible noncompliance.

Recent research in personality psychology might have predicted the failure to find personality correlates of compliance. As noted earlier, clinicians often overestimate their ability to predict compliance. Mischel (1979) has devoted considerable effort to understanding the difficulties of predicting behavior. He states:

> Clinicians, like other scientists and indeed like other ordinary laypeople, easily tend to infer, generalize, and predict too much while observing too little. Moreover, the judgements of clinicians—like everyone else's judgements—are subject to certain systematic bias that can produce serious distortions and oversimplifications in inferences and predictions (p. 740).

Research over the course of the last 25 years has consistently demonstrated that clinical prediction is less accurate than that derived from actuarial models (Dawes, Faust, & Meehl, 1989). One of the major reasons why clinicians are so poor at predicting behavior is that they tend to make their predictions on the basis of personality characteristics. Personality tests usually attempt to determine which "traits" characterize people. These trait explanations ignore variability in the same individuals across diverse situations. Yet very substantial evidence suggests that situational variables account for more variation in compliance than personality traits. For example, Haynes (1979) found that the number of drug treatments, frequency of dosage, and complexity of regimen were predictors of noncompliance. These data suggest that one individual may be compliant in some situations but noncompliant in others. This has been particularly evident when a medical regimen includes several components. Thus, diabetic patients must comply with diet and medical regimens. Patients with coronary heart disease may need to comply with many different medical regimens. Yet studies show that the same patients comply with some of their regimens, but not others. Compliance behaviors are not correlated with one another (Glasgow, McCaul, & Schafer, 1987). Global measures of personality fail to capture these variations. Nevertheless, attempts continue to forecast compliance in accord with personality measures. This problem was so well recognized in the behavioral science literature that Ross (1977) has labeled it "The Fundamental Attributional Error." This is the tendency to underestimate the importance of situations and overestimate the importance of personality traits in predicting future behavior.

At the other extreme, there have been some attempts to describe compliance strictly on the basis of situations. Thus, Moos (1973) has published a series of papers documenting environmental determinants of behavior. The differences between these approaches are characterized by the following simple example. When answering the question, "Why does Mr. Jones fail to take his medication?" trait-oriented analysts would assess Mr. Jones's characteristics. They might use measures of personality, motivation, or personal traits. In contrast, situation-oriented analysts would measure characteristics of Mr. Jones's environment. They might consider where he stores medications, whether his employment facilitates his use of medications, or whether his family supports medication use.

THE RATIONAL PATIENT

Theories of noncompliance vary in their view of patients. Many suggest that patients are rebellious and are attempting to interfere with the good intentions of their doctors. An alternative view is that patients are rational and that they comply with treatment when they perceive a net health benefit. They fail to comply when the consequences of compliance outweigh the expected benefits. Figure 5-2 shows several symptoms that are experienced before and after the use of medicines used to control

FIGURE 5-2

Symptoms in general population, before and after treatment for hypertension. (Adapted from Bulpitt, 1988.)

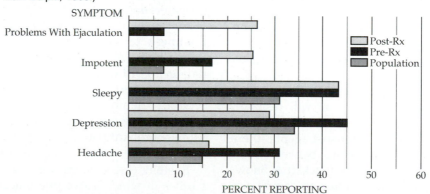

high blood pressure. As the figure shows, after treatment patients are more likely to have troubles with sexual function, sleepiness, and other symptoms. In this decision process, patients may discount future benefits because of current side effects. A corollary of the theory is that treatments that have a short-term effect should evoke better compliance than those for which benefits occur later. Thus, we would expect better compliance with painkillers that provide immediate symptomatic benefit than with antihypertensive therapies that exchange current inconvenience for future benefits (Kaplan & Simon, 1990).

Several previous papers have described the related phenomenon of rational noncompliance (see Becker, 1985). Often, patients adhere to their regimen but fail to obtain the desired health benefit. If the medicine does not work, why take it? If no eventual treatment benefit is expected, and if undesirable side effects are associated with the regimen, noncompliance is rational. Similarly, noncompliance is rational when the patient achieves the desired result despite noncompliance. Patient perceptions must also be considered independent of the empirical health outcomes. The health care provider is only one source of information relevant to a decision to comply. Other input comes from media exposures of medical controversies, contradictions between providers, and word-of-mouth descriptions of adverse reactions (Becker, 1985). With this input, patients may decide that the provider's recommendations are not in their best interest. Noncompliance involves weighting other opinions more than those of the physician in the decision process.

It is generally held that compliance with effective therapeutic regimens will result in better health outcomes. For many situations, such as use of antihypertensive agents, there may be a direct relationship between compliance and health outcome (Sackett & Snow, 1979). However, many studies on compliance fail to consider health outcomes. When health outcomes are evaluated, their correspondence with compliance is not always systematic. Noncompliant patients may improve clinically, while some compliant patients may not benefit from treatment. Furthermore, in addition to yielding benefits, compliance can also increase the probability of side effects (Green, Mullen, & Stainbrook, 1984). In one study, 36 percent of the inpatients in a large tertiary care hospital had some problem caused by the treatment. (Steel et al., 1981). The elderly experienced a sevenfold increase in adverse reactions in comparison with those aged 20 to 29 (Hurwitz, 1969). In England, it has been suggested that 10 percent of admissions to a geriatric unit resulted from undesirable drug side effects (Williamson & Chapin, 1980). Since side effects are often measured differently from benefits, analyses often overlook the consequences of compliance (Kaplan & Anderson, 1988; 1990).

DIRECT EFFECTS OF COMPLIANCE

A corollary of this view of compliance is that patients should continue to comply when their health is improving. Thus, independent of therapeutic efficacy, those who feel better will comply more and those in failing health will comply less. At least some support for this notion comes from studies on the direct effects of compliance. Compliance is often taken into consideration in evaluations of new medicines or therapies. Patients assigned to experimental treatment programs may not always comply with them. When investigators analyze the data in accord with the actual amounts of medication delivered to the patient, these studies typically demonstrate that there is a relationship between compliance and outcome. More compliant patients usually achieve better outcomes than noncompliant patients.

Epstein (1984) identified six experimental studies in which active pharmaceutical agents were tested against placebos. In each of these studies a compliance/noncompliance determination was made. Only half of the studies demonstrated a statistically reliable benefit of the drug in comparison with the placebo. However, five of the six studies demonstrated a main effect of compliance. To achieve this effect, it was necessary for patients in both the treatment and the placebo groups to achieve better health outcomes when compliant. For example, in the Coronary Drug Project (1980) 3789 post-MI patients were randomly assigned to use clofibrate (a drug to lower cholesterol) or a placebo. Patients were followed between 5 and 8.5 years to detect differences in mortality. Compliance was evaluated on the basis of patient interviews and pill counts.

Initial analysis showed no difference in mortality between the clofibrate- and placebo-treated groups. However, early analysis within the clofibrate-treated group showed that those who consumed the medication experienced lower mortality rates than those who failed to comply. When the same analysis was done within the placebo-treated group, the placebo-treated compliers *also* experienced lower mortality rates than the noncompliers (see Figure 5-3). Another example is a study of a drug called HCG that has been used for weight loss. Although, overall, patients using the drug lost more weight than those using a placebo, compliant patients lost more weight than noncompliant patients in both the active drug and the placebo groups (Asher & Harper, 1973; see Figure 5-4).

There are several alternative explanations for these outcomes. First, patients may fail to comply because they are in poorer health to begin with. Thus, the direct effects of compliance may reflect prior differences in health status. A second explanation is that compliance may create the expectation of better health outcomes. Compliance may stimulate other health behaviors which, in turn, result in better health outcomes. Compliance with med-

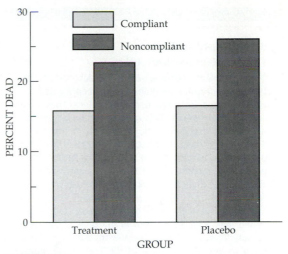

FIGURE 5-3

Direct effects of compliance in coronary drug project. Better outcomes were achieved for compliant patients in both active drug and placebo conditions.

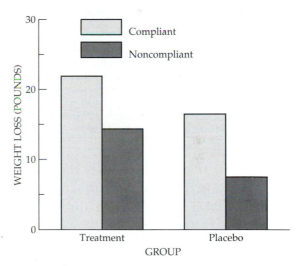

FIGURE 5-4

Direct effects of compliance in HCG Study. Compliance was associated with better outcomes for patients on either active drug or placebo. (Adapted from Asher & Harper, 1973.)

ication may stimulate patients to comply with diet, exercise, and other aspects of their regimen. Patients expect benefits from medica-

BOX 5·3

FOCUS ON RESEARCH

The Beta Blocker Heart Attack Trial

There are some circumstances in which compliance is very important. One of these was recently demonstrated in the Beta Blocker Heart Attack Trial (also known as the b-hat). This experimental study evaluated drugs that affect the beta cells in the heart. These drugs have now become commonly used for people who already had a heart attack and want to prevent a second one. The study clearly demonstrated that the drug works. However, it was also shown that compliance with the medication was related to survival. Noncompliance was defined as taking less than 75 percent of the prescribed medication. Those in this category were 2.6 times more likely to die within 1 year of the end of the study. However, supporting the "direct effects" hypothesis, this increase in death was equally as likely for those taking the beta blocker or a placebo. The confused investigators evaluated several other explanations in a futile attempt to explain this result. For example, the direct effect of compliance could not be accounted for by characteristics of the subjects, such as the race, marital status, or education. Furthermore, it was unrelated to cigarette smoking, high-stress lifestyles, or social isolation. Even more interesting was the absence of a relationship between survival and the severity of the heart attack. All that we are able to conclude is that people who comply seem to achieve better outcomes. Why this happens will be the focus of future research (Horwitz et al., 1990).

BOX 5·4

FOCUS ON DIVERSITY

Adherence with medical regimens is sometimes an even more severe problem for particular populations. The elderly, for example, may experience more problems than other age groups. Adverse drug effects for older people are very common. In one study by the Royal College of Physicians in England it was estimated that about one-quarter of all old people admitted to the hospital are there because of adverse drug effects. Rates of adverse effects of medication may be 3 to 4 times higher for older people than for younger members of our populations (Roth, 1990). There are a variety of different reasons why older people have difficulty with medications. First, some older people may have difficulty understanding and following complex instructions. Although aging by itself is not necessarily related to mental decline, significant numbers of old people do develop cognitive impairments that make it more difficult to follow medical instructions. A second problem is that older people often have difficulty with medicine containers. For example, some older patients have difficulty with child-proof caps or lack the manual dexterity to easily remove them. In one study, it was noted that patients often transferred their medications to other bottles. Then they had to recognize them by the color of the tablets, and this often resulted in confusion and medicine-taking errors (Murray et al., 1986).

A third problem is that older people will sometimes keep bottles of medication and continue to use them even without checking with their doctors. The major difficulty is that substantial numbers of older people take several different medications. In one study, for example, the average person at an outpatient clinic was taking 6.1 medications (German & Klein, 1986). Although older people in the general population may be taking fewer medications, there is still considerable evidence that the elderly typically use several different medications for different health conditions. For example, it is not uncommon for an older person to be taking medication for arthritis, high blood pressure, and gastrointestinal problems. Sometimes these medications are prescribed by different doctors. The different specialists are not aware of what one another is prescribing, and these medications can interact, causing undesirable effects.

tions. When they fail to obtain these benefits, they quit taking the medication and they are often aware of their reasons for doing so. This will happen whether or not the patients are receiving the presumed effective treatment.

IMPROVING SELF-REPORTING OF COMPLIANCE

It is widely asserted that self-report measures of compliance are untrustworthy. The fact that patients overreport compliance to physicians has long been recognized. For example, Hippocrates stated that the physician "should keep aware of the fact that patients often lie when they state that they have taken certain medicines." Several studies reviewed by Gordis (1979) indicate that physician estimates of compliance tend to be artificially high (Wittenberg, Blanchard, McCoy, et al., 1983), and it has been known for a long time that patients also overreport compliance in situations where actual compliance is verified by pill counts (Feinstein, Wood, & Epstein, 1959). As Epstein and Clauss (1982) suggest, studies with objective verification of self-reports show that, when patients actually have taken their medications, they usually report that they have done so. However, patients who have failed to take their medications also tend to report that they have consumed them.

Despite the prevalent skepticism about the reliability of self-reporting, Kaplan and Simon (1990) identified circumstances in which patients were surprisingly accurate in forecasting their own future compliance. In fact, when asked simply and directly, patients were remarkably accurate in describing the likelihood that they will comply. In particular, the situations in which patients accurately self-report are those that they understand clearly and have personally experienced.

An example of accurate self-assessment of compliant behavior is provided in a study by Litt (1985). In this investigation, 110 adolescents beginning an oral contraceptive regimen were asked to indicate whether or not they resembled either of two women described in vignettes. One woman was forgetful, while the other woman was careful and systematic. Among those adolescents who eventually complied with the regimen, 64 percent described themselves as resembling the careful and systematic woman, while only 14 percent of the noncompliant women described themselves in such terms.

Findings from the Litt (1985) study are consistent with current behavioral science theory. At least two lines of theoretically derived evidence support these views. First, there is the concept of *self-efficacy*, which was derived from social learning theory (Bandura, 1982). Self-efficacy is the expectation that an individual can succeed in a defined endeavor. For a complicated regimen of contraceptive use, for example, a high efficacy expectation is a patient's personal belief that the regimen can be successfully completed. This expectation may be independent of beliefs about the efficacy of the medication. The latter independent dimension is known as *outcome expectancy*. In other words, an adolescent female may believe that continuous use of oral contraceptives will decrease the probability of pregnancy. However, she might simultaneously have low expectations that she will successfully adhere to the regimen. Similarly, virtually all smokers know that their habit is harmful and that quitting will enhance their outlook for better health (outcome expectancy). Yet many smokers lack the expectation that they can successfully quit (efficacy expectancy).

Research relevant to self-efficacy theory suggests that specific efficacy expectations are reasonably good predictors of compliance behavior and health outcomes. Thus, Kaplan, Atkins, and Reinsch (1984) demonstrated that the stated expectation to complete a painful exercise regimen by patients with chronic obstructive pulmonary disease (COPD) accurately forecast persistence with the regimen and performance on laboratory exercise tests. Patients randomly assigned to a treatment designed to increase compliance also significantly increased efficacy expectations in comparison with patients randomly assigned to control groups.

A related study evaluated self-efficacy theory in relation to compliance with a complex regimen for adults on hemodialysis. Actual fluid intake compliance can be reliably measured by means of monitoring body weight between dialysis episodes for the 3 months prior to the study and throughout follow-up periods. Expectations for success were predictive of compliance with the fluid diet (Rosenbaum & Ben-Ari, 1986). Rees (1985) found that compliance with alcohol treatment programs could be predicted from patient expectations of the relationship between improvement and remaining in treatment. In the Litt (1985) study, 75 percent of the adolescents were able to assess themselves accurately in terms of future compliance behavior. A related study demonstrated that joining or not joining a smoking cessation program was predictable from perceived self-efficacy judgments. Joiners were shown to have higher self-efficacy expectations for treatment effectiveness than nonjoiners. These studies also show that those who expect to fail in treatment do indeed experience a greater failure rate. Success in quitting smoking, for example, can be roughly predicted from the expectation that an attempt to quit will succeed (Broad & Hall, 1984; Condiotte & Lichtenstein, 1981). Patients in cardiac rehabilitation programs accurately describe their future inability to walk on a treadmill, despite their physical capability to perform the required tasks (Ewart, Taylor, Reese, & DeBusk, 1983).

Past compliance is perhaps the best predictor of future compliance. Several studies show that noncompliance early in a study is a reliable predictor of later noncompliance. On the other hand, those who comply in defined situations develop expecations for future compliance and continue to comply (Dunbar, 1990). Conversely, patients will be less likely to comply when they discover that treatments cause side effects. Once they have experienced these adverse effects, they might quite accurately forecast that they will avoid treatments that cause them to feel badly. In summary, studies consistently suggest that patients have considerable self-knowledge and that their performance expectations are reasonably good predictors of compliance behavior.

Much of this self-knowledge is acquired through experience. After experiencing side effects or facing difficult physical demands, patients may accurately estimate their chances of staying with a treatment. Self-predictions should be poorest when the demands of the regimen or the side effects of the treatment are unfamiliar.

In summary, there is little evidence that traditional methods of patient assessment can enhance the prediction of compliance. Methods that allow the clinician to infer patient behavior on the basis of psychological tests or clinical impressions have been disappointing because they fail to consider that the same people may respond differently to different demands. However, patients can sometimes predict their own compliance when the questions are direct and clearly stated. The continuing attraction of personality measures for predicting compliance may be a dead end because compliant behaviors are not correlated with one another. Thus, any global approach to personality assessment is unlikely to successfully forecast these different behaviors. On the other hand, simple self-reports of expectations to perform compliant behaviors have been overlooked. Current evidence and theory suggest that patients may be remarkably accurate in identifying situations in which they will comply or fail to comply. Compliance may be highest when patients expect that the benefits of the treatment outweigh the consequences and when they believe that they can perform the behaviors required by the regimen. These expectations are more accurate when patients have some experience with the medication or behavioral regimen (Kaplan & Simon, 1990).

SUMMARY

In addition to problems in gaining access to health care, patients also fail to achieve many of the benefits of health care because they do not follow the recommendations of their providers. Noncompliance with health care is common and may occur in at least one-third of all cases. Some estimates suggest that rates of noncompliance are as high as 93 percent. The reasons for noncompliance are not fully understood. However, there is very little evidence that personality or demographic variables are good predictors of noncompliant behavior. Furthermore, physicians are very poor at predicting which of their patients are compliant or noncompliant.

One explanation for noncompliance is that patients are making conscious decisions about whether or not they feel the treatment will benefit them. When they feel that treatment is helpful, compliance is likely. On the other hand, noncompliance occurs when patients feel that the treatment does not work or that the side effects of treatment outweigh the benefits. New approaches to assessment that consider the patient's appraisal of the expected benefit of treatment may enhance the prediction of compliance behavior.

KEY TERMS

Compliance. The act of following the advice of a physician or health care worker.

Noncompliance. Failure to follow advice provided by a physician or health care provider.

Adherence. A term used interchangeably with compliance.

Nonadherence. A term used interchangeably with noncompliance.

Direct effects of compliance. The observation that compliant patients achieve better health outcomes whether or not they are taking an active medication.

Medication Event Monitoring System (MEMS). A small microprocessor in the cap of a medicine container used to monitor compliance.

Life Stress

CHAPTER 6

Stress and Coping

Joan, a junior behavioral science major, had to work to support herself while taking a full load at college. When midterms came, she studied until the wee hours of the morning after getting home from work at 10 P.M. It was difficult for Joan to prepare for her examinations and meet the deadlines for the term papers that her professors demanded of her. The crowning blow came when she always seemed to come down with a cold or some other infection at this time. She attributed the illness to the stress she was under. But was it the stress that Joan experienced that brought on this illness, or was her cold brought on by some other change in her health behavior, such as the sleep deprivation that she experienced at this time?

Many people have accepted the common wisdom that stress is the major cause of common health problems. However, despite much study, there are many unanswered questions about stress. What is stress? How do we measure it? What is the evidence that stress has an impact on the health of an individual? What are the physical and psychological conse-

quences of stress? Why do some individuals seem to thrive in stressful situations while others suffer physically and psychologically? In this chapter we will explore these and other questions.

It is difficult to separate psychological from biological causes of disease states. For example, alcoholism is a physiological addiction

103

BOX 6·1

HEALTH OBJECTIVES FOR THE YEAR 2000

1. Reduce to less than 35 percent the proportion of people aged 18 and older who experienced adverse health effects from stress within the past year (1985 baseline: 42.6 percent).

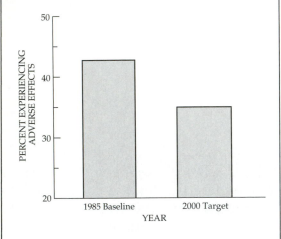

2. Reduce to no more than 5 percent the proportion of people aged 18 and older who report experiencing significant levels of stress but do not take steps to reduce or control their stress (1985 baseline: 21 percent).

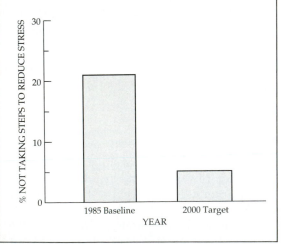

which may be exacerbated by exposure to stressful situations. Anorexia is a behavioral eating problem that may result from some physiological imbalance of the hypothalamus or may result from psychological stress that an individual undergoes. Finally, some individuals who experience depression may suffer from some biochemical imbalance, which in some cases may be of genetic origin. Or the origins of depression for some may be the result of experiencing some stressful situation. Many viruses that we contract are considered stress-related. For example, Epstein-Barr virus (EBV) is almost ubiquitous in our society. Approximately 85 percent of the population in the United States carry EBV. Some people are exposed to and contract EBV and show no symptomatology, only to have symptoms express themselves months or years later. One explanation for the sudden expression of the EBV virus that has found some support is that prior to its expression the host had been exposed to stressful life events.

DEFINITION OF STRESS

One of the most difficult problems in the stress field has been defining exactly what stress is. The story of different approaches to its definition is interesting itself. The term *stress* has been used in the English language for centuries to describe human experience. Early definitions used stress to refer to "hardship, straits, adversity or affliction" (Onions, 1933). Later definitions borrowed from physics and engineering give a physical perspective (Hinkle, 1974). Thus terms such as *stress*, *strain*, and *load* were used in defining stress.

Stress, or the stress experience, can be considered from at least two perspectives. First, stress can be viewed as a trigger for a response. In this sense it may be thought of as a cause. When stress is used in this way, it is commonly called a *stressor*. Second, stress can be thought of as an effect, in which case it is

FOCUS ON RESEARCH

Sheldon Cohen, from Carnegie-Mellon University, intentionally exposed a group of individuals to viruses responsible for the common cold and studied how psychological stress contributed to actually contracting a clinical cold (Cohen et al., 1991). Healthy subjects were given nasal drops containing one of five rhinoviruses responsible for colds or saline drops. Individuals were assigned a psychological-stress score based on the number of major stressful life events that they reported during the past year, the degree they felt that current demands exceeded their ability to cope, and an index of how psychologically distressed they currently felt. Eighty-two percent of the subjects who received a virus and 19 percent of those who received saline drops became infected as indicated by laboratory tests for the virus. Those who became infected after exposure to the saline probably became infected through transmission from infected subjects in the same apartments. Interestingly, infection rates increased from 74 percent among those who received the lowest psychological-stress score to 90 percent among those with the highest stress scores. Furthermore, not everyone who was infected exhibited a clinical cold, that is, experienced a stuffy head, runny nose, chest congestion, or other symptoms. Of those exposed to virus 38 percent experienced a clinical cold, while none of those who received saline experienced cold symptoms. Stress again was a significant predictor of who would become ill. The percentage of individuals who contracted clinical colds increased from 27 percent among individuals who had a low psychological-stress score to 47 percent among those who had the highest stress score. Even after the investigators examined factors such as diet, exercise, and personality factors, psychological stress continued to play a major role in determining who would experience a cold.

called a *stress response*. The stress response is made up of a relatively stereotypic set of psychological and biological patterns.

In reality neither stressors nor the stress response exists in isolation. Rather, both feed back on each other to produce the stress experience. The idea that stress exists only when there is a stress response has lead to concern about potential circularity in thinking by some researchers. That is, if there is a stress response, there must be a stressor and vice versa. For many researchers, this circularity is intentional, since the stress experience is made up of both stressors and the stress response. It is useful for discussion purposes to separate the two parts of the stress experience.

In this chapter, when we refer to stress, we focus on the stressor end of the equation. Baum et al. (1981) have defined stress as a "process in which environmental events or forces, called stressors, threaten an organism's existence and well-being." Other investigators have defined stress as a condition in which there is a marked discrepancy between the demands made on an individual and the individual's ability to respond to those demands (e.g., Caplan, 1981). Lazarus and Folkman (1984) have provided what is widely regarded as the best definition to date: Stress is "a particular relationship between the person and the environment that is appraised by the person as taxing or exceeding his or her resources and endangering his or her well-being." This definition emphasizes that stress refers to a "taxing relationship" between the person and the environment. When a person is unable to deal with that relationship, he or she may experience a reduction in physical and psychological well-being. Stressful life events are those external events that make adaptive demands on a person. Individuals may successfully adapt to those demands or not. When they fail to adapt, the end result may be physical or psychological illness, or both.

What constitutes a stressor? Virtually any stimulus that makes demands on an organism requiring adaptation or adjustment can be termed a stressor. These stimuli can include heat, cold, joy, sorrow, exercise, drugs, lack of sleep, nutrition, fear, anger, frustration, noise, crowding, or change in any of these conditions. Obviously some of these stimuli are much easier to study than others, because they are observable. It is also important to note that this list includes events that have both negative and positive consequences. Positive experiences, like negative ones, may require adjustment and result in biological changes commonly associated with exposure to events that have negative consequences.

Dohrenwend and Dohrenwend (1984) distinguish between stressful life events and personal dispositions. They suggest that stressful life events are by definition those events that are proximate rather than distant in time. Thus the death of a parent is a stressful life event if it occurs in the recent past, but is considered a personal disposition when it occurred in the distant past when the subject was a child. The early death is important to understanding current illness episodes only insofar as it is internalized in some way.

There is much individual variability in which specific events elicit a stress response (one person's meat is another person's poison). One cannot assume that exposure to the same stimulus will always result in a stress response in every, or even the same, individual. Why do people respond differently to stressors? Some potential moderators of this relationship, including coping behavior and social support, will be discussed in this chapter.

FOCUS ON THE STRESS RESPONSE

For at least four centuries the term *stress* has been used in the English language to describe human experience. As stated above, Onions (1933) noted that in the seventeenth century stress was defined as "hardship, straits, adversity or affliction." During the eighteenth and nineteenth centuries the focus or definition of stress changed to a "force, pressure, strain or strong effort" acting on an individuals "organs or mental powers" (Hinkle, 1974). As Hinkle pointed out, this definition focuses on how external pressures (stresses) affect an individual.

It was not until the early twentieth century that the hypothesis that stress could lead to physical illness was put forth. Sir William Osler (1910), who has been called the "Father of Epidemiology," argued that businessmen who were "living an intense life, absorbed in work, devoted to pleasures, passionately devoted to home" were predisposed to angina pectoris. By the 1930s Walter Cannon (1932) had described his physiologic studies of the "flight-or-fight" reaction in terms of stress. However, it was not until the late 1930s and early 1940s that the first serious attempt to link stress to illness was attempted by Hans Selye.

Selye (1956; 1980), the "Father of Modern Stress Research," conducted his initial work during the late 1930s. In his practice he noticed that regardless of the type of disorder being examined, patients often complained of diffuse joint and muscle pain, disturbance of the intestines with loss of appetite, and loss of weight, among other symptoms. Selye moved from these clinical observations into the laboratory and was able to reproduce these symptoms in rats by introducing them to diverse damaging or "alarming" agents. These agents included injections of a wide variety of toxic agents such as bacterial infections, trauma, heat or cold, and psychological stimuli. He argued that a degree of nonspecific damage to the organism is superimposed on the specific damage of any disease. Selye made a third observation that some nonspecific curative measures such as rest, eating soft foods, and medical treatments such as shock therapy and blood letting often reduced symptoms in patients with a wide variety of illness.

From these observations Selye hypothesized that organisms exhibited a general nonspecific reaction pattern in response to threat of damage that permitted the body to mobilize against these threats, and he proposed a general theory of stress to explain this response. He called this pattern of exposure to stressors the *general adaptation syndrome* (GAS).

Selye's reasoning for naming the phenomena GAS included the following. It is "general" since it is produced by a variety of stressors that, in his view, have a general effect on many systems of the body. It is "adaptive" because it triggers the defenses and begins the restorative process. It is a "syndrome" because all of its components tend to occur together as a pattern.

Selye (1980) viewed stress in terms of a nonspecific adaptive response of the body to any agent or situation. He posited that the body responds in a relatively constant way regardless of the type of stimulus (stressor), while the degree of response varies as a function of the strength of the demand for adjustment. The same general bodily response can be elicited by pleasant or unpleasant stimuli. The nonspecific response that Selye proposed is really quite specific. The GAS is the general bodily reaction to nonspecific demands. The GAS evolves through three stages: (1) the alarm reaction, (2) resistance, and (3) exhaustion. Table 6-1 outlines the behavioral and physiologic responses to stressors that organisms pass through according to the GAS stages.

TABLE 6·1

ORGANISMIC RESPONSES TO STRESSORS ACCORDING TO THE GAS STAGES

Stage 1: alarm reaction

Physiologic response
   Enlargement of adrenal cortex
   Enlargement of the lymphatic system
   Increase in hormone levels, such as epinephrine, leading to high physiological arousal

Behavioral response
   Increased sensitivity to changes in stressor intensity
   Increased susceptibility to illness

   If stage 1 is prolonged, the organism moves into stage 2.

Stage 2: resistance

Physiologic response
   Shrinkage of adrenal cortex
   Lymph nodes return to normal size.
   High hormone levels continue.
   The parasympathetic branch of the autonomic nervous system attempts to counteract the high arousal.

Behavioral response
   Sensitivity to stress is increased.
   Individual attempts to endure the stressor and resist further debilitating effects.

   If the organism continues to be exposed to intense stress, hormonal depletion may ensue, leading to stage 3.

Stage 3: exhaustion

Physiologic response
   Lymphatic structures become enlarged or dysfunctional, or both.
   Hormone levels are further increased or maintained at high levels.
   Adaptive hormones are depleted.

Behavioral response
   Resistance to stressors (including the original one) is reduced.
   The individual often becomes depressed.
   The individual becomes physically ill and may die if the severe stress continues.

The first stage of the GAS was termed the *alarm* stage by Selye. For example, if an organism is exposed to electrical shock, the system responds initially with alarm. If the stressor is physical, as in the case of more severe shock, there may be signs of injury. In the case of psychological stress or less severe physical stress, there may be no outward signs of injury. The alarm stage is characterized by the mobilization of glucoids and adrenaline, which quickly energize the body. However, in time, the body's reserves of these chemicals become depleted, leading to fatigue. At this point the organism enters the second stage of the GAS, termed *resistance*. The body's response during the resistance stage is in opposition to its response during the alarm stage. During this phase, an organism's glucose release drops off and its immune function kicks in. Finally, the organism under chronic stress reaches a state of *exhaustion*, wherein the cellular response, immune functions, and energy are overwhelmed. Exhaustion may lead to death if stress continues.

According to this model, the weakest link in the body's defenses breaks first, and that weakened system is then susceptible to problems. In the case of immune system failure, cancer may result. In the case of the cardiovascular system, there may be heart failure. Stressors may combine to trigger or aggravate these systems. For example, starvation results in the release of glucose, which may alter the circulating pattern and decrease leucocyte responses.

It is important to understand that, according to Selye, stress is a state within the organism. Since this stress state is inferred from physiologic and pathologic changes, it is not the stimulus itself that is stressful but rather the response to the stimuli within the organism that identifies it as stressful. It is this response that triggers physiological and, in some cases, pathological changes. This thinking is somewhat circular; i.e., a stimulus is stressful if there is a physiological response and vice versa. This has led some researchers to distinguish between stressors and the stress response.

FOCUS ON STRESSORS

Stressors are defined as any stimulus that requires the organism to adapt or adjust. This adaptation or adjustment is termed the *stress response* (again note the circularity). Since most models of stress include a feedback or interaction between the stress response and the stressor, this circularity is intentional. For example, if an individual is given adrenaline and put in a situation where there are environmental cues for anxiety—i.e., other individuals who are present appear to be anxious—that person is likely to "feel" anxious as well. On the other hand, that same individual given adrenaline in the presence of happy people often reports feeling happy too.

Different individuals respond to potentially stressful situations in different ways. The same stimuli may evoke a stress response in one individual but not in another. In fact, a particular stimulus may elicit a stress response one time but not at another time in a single individual. This suggests that there may exist some individual differences or mediating variables that may explain this phenomenon.

Individual differences in functioning in the face of severe stress have been studied by a number of researchers. For example, the distinguishing characteristics of survivors of the Nazi concentration camps have been examined by several investigators (e.g., Bettelheim, 1943; Dimsdale, 1974). Interest in individual differences is cited as one of the key recent developments responsible for the current interest in stress and coping (Lazarus & Folkman, 1984). Coping behaviors and how they may mediate the stress-strain relationship are discussed later in this chapter.

FOCUS ON LIFE EVENTS

In contrast to focusing on the stress response, a number of investigators have attempted to identify and quantify potential stressors or, as they are often called, *life events*. The first large-scale attempt at identifying stressors was conducted by Holmes and Rahe (1967). Their Social Readjustment Rating Scale (SRRS) contains items which range from those that are quite stressful (e.g., "death of a spouse," "divorce," and "marital separation") to those least stressful (e.g., "vacation," "minor violations of the law"). This scale was developed by identifying potentially stressful situations. Subjects then rated the average degree of readjustment necessary for each event, the length of time necessary for that adjustment, and the severity of these events. In the original study, the event of marriage acted as the anchor point for the rating of each other event. Thus, subjects rated if the adjustment required for a particular event was more or less intense and prolonged than that required for marriage, which was arbitrarily assigned the value of 500. Interestingly, good rating agreement was reported for various subgroups—including age, sex, and social class—who classified these events. Using the resulting scale, life events study participants indicate which stressful life events they have experienced during the preceding 6 months or 1 year. The weights assigned to those items endorsed are totaled, and a risk of illness is then assigned.

Using the SRRS, Rahe studied 2500 officers and enlisted men on three Navy ships. He found that 30 percent of the men with the highest life change scores had 90 percent more illness during the first month of the cruise when compared with the 30 percent of the men with the lowest scores. This pattern held true for all 6 months of the cruise. Interestingly, this study does not take into account possible differences in perception about the stressors that were reported. As was pointed out above, for some people one of these events might be much more stressful than for another. For example, the event of "pregnancy" does not take into account if it was wanted and anticipated or unwanted and unanticipated. The list of SRRS events has also been criticized for not being comprehensive and for being overly simplistic, failing to take into account feelings about changes that have taken place. In addition, some of the items on the scale may be confounded with the outcome. For example, the sixth most stressful event on the scale is "personal injury or illness." It might not come as a surprise to find that people who endorse this item are more likely to have been ill than people who do not endorse it. If one were predicting depression using the SRRS, "sexual difficulties," "sleep problems," and "eating problems" are all hallmark symptoms, while many other items such as "increased arguments with family or friends" may be indicative as well. Thus it should come as no surprise that symptoms predict symptoms, one of the difficulties involved with attempting to separate cause and effect in stress research.

Pearlin and Schooler (1978) identified the general stressors that individuals who were engaging in ordinary daily pursuits had undergone. They asked 2300 people living in Chicago aged 18 to 65 what stressors they had experienced during their day-to-day lives. Table 6-2 gives a sample of the types of events that were identified. Most of the items listed here should come as no surprise to most of us.

Sarason and colleagues (1978) introduced the carefully constructed Life Experiences Survey (LES), which merits note. The LES is a 57-item self-report measure on which individuals first indicate events that have occurred in their lives. The events were chosen on the basis of having occurred most frequently in the general population. The LES contains the refinement of having subjects rate separately the desirability (positive or negative) and impact (positive or negative) at the time of occurrence

---

TABLE 6-2

EXAMPLES OF LIFE EVENTS IDENTIFIED BY A NORMATIVE SAMPLE OF 2300 INDIVIDUALS LIVING IN CHICAGO

Event category	Specific event
Marital	Nonacceptance by spouse
	Give-and-take not reciprocated
	Role expectation frustration
Parental	Not following parental behavior standards
	Not following parental aspirations and values
	Not respecting parents' role
Economics	Insufficient funds
Occupation	Inadequately rewarded
	Noxious work environment
	Depersonalized work environment
	Work overload

---

of each of the events they experienced during the past year. Ratings for each item are obtained on a 7-point scale ranging from extremely negative (-3) to extremely positive ($+3$). Summing the impact rating on those events rated as positive yields a positive change score. A negative change score is calculated by summing the impact ratings that are negative. Sarason's associates report, as have others, that negative change is the best predictor of health change and other outcomes of interest. For example the negative LES score was found to be related $-.38$ to grade-point average and $+.46$ with trait anxiety among a group of university students. Thus, more life happenings rated as negative related to lower grade-point averages and more anxiety. Table 6-3 presents the LES scale.

There is some evidence that different groups of people experience differing numbers of life events. Goldberg and Comstock (1980) found that younger individuals tended to experience more life events compared with older individuals. Those under 30 years of age reported almost 3 times the number of stressful events compared with individuals older than 30. They also found that married and widowed

people reported fewer life events when compared with single, separated, and divorced individuals. Goldberg and Comstock also reported that women tended to accumulate more life change scores when compared with men. Some studies suggest that poorer individuals experience more life events compared with people who are more affluent, while other studies find no relationship.

While life events scales have generated much research and interest in the popular press, they have been criticized by a number of researchers on a number of grounds. First, it may be difficult to identify which events an individual experienced were truly stressful. The context in which an event occurs and the characteristics of the individual, such as those discussed above, may change an individual's perception of a particular event. In addition, the time that has elapsed since an event has occurred may change the perception or impact of a stressor, as more or less coping effort is directed at that event. In addition, the degree of success or failure that an individual experiences in dealing with an event may change the recalled characteristics of an event. This has led to the development of weighting schemes

---

TABLE 6·3

THE LIFE EXPERIENCES SURVEY. SUBJECTS INDICATE WHICH EVENTS THEY HAVE EXPERIENCED DURING THE LAST YEAR AND RATE EACH EVENT'S IMPACT ON THEIR LIFE. RATINGS ARE MADE ON THE FOLLOWING SCALE:

Key:
−3	**Extremely negative**
−2	**Moderately negative**
−1	**Slightly negative**
0	**No impact**
+1	**Slightly positive**
+2	**Moderately positive**
+3	**Extremely positive**

1. Marriage
2. Detention in jail or comparable institution
3. Death of spouse
4. Major change in sleeping habits (much more or much less sleep)
5. Death of close family member:
   a. mother
   b. father
   c. brother
   d. sister
   e. grandmother
   f. grandfather
   g. spouse
   h. other (WHO? _____)
6. Major change in eating habits (much more or much less food intake)
7. Foreclosure on mortgage or loan
8. Death of a close friend
9. Outstanding personal achievement
10 Minor law violations (traffic tickets, disturbing the peace, etc.)
11. MALES: Wife/girlfriend's pregnancy
12. FEMALES: Pregnancy
13. Changed work situation (different work responsibility, major change in working conditions, working hours, etc.)
14. New job
15. Serious illness or injury of close family member:
   a. mother
   b. father
   c. brother
   d. sister
   e. grandmother
   f. grandfather
   g. spouse
   h. other (WHO? _____)
16. Sexual difficulties
17. Trouble with employer (in danger of losing job, being suspended, demoted, etc.)
18. Trouble with in-laws
19. Financial status a lot worse off

(continued)

TABLE 6-3 (continued)

20. Family members much less close
21. Gaining a new family member (through birth, adoption, moving in, etc.)
22. Change of residence
23. Marital separation from mate (due to conflict)
24. Major change in church activities (increased or decreased attendance)
25. Marital reconciliation with mate
26. Increase in number of arguments with spouse
27. Change in spouse's work outside the home (beginning work, ceasing work, change to a new job, etc.)
28. Major change in usual type and/or amount of recreation
29. Borrowing more than $15,000 (buying home, business, etc.)
30. Borrowing less than $15,000 (buying car, TV, getting school loans, etc.)
31. Being fired from job
32. MALE: Wife/girlfriend having abortion
33. FEMALE: Having abortion
34. Major personal illness or injury
35. Major change in social activities, e.g., parties, movies, visiting, etc. (increased or decreased participation)
36. Major change in living conditions of family (building new home, remodeling, deterioration of home, neighborhood, etc.)
37. Divorce
38. Serious injury or illness of close friend
39. Retirement from work
40. Son or daughter leaving home (due to marriage, college, etc.)
41. Ending of formal schooling
42. Separation from spouse for two weeks or more (due to work, travel, etc.)
43. Engagement
44. Breaking up with girlfriend or boyfriend
45. Leaving home for the first time
46. Reconciliation with girlfriend or boyfriend
47. Parents split up (divorce or separated)
Other recent experiences which had an impact on your life. List and rate.
48.
49.
50.
Section 2: Students only
51. Beginning a new school experience at a higher academic level (college, graduate school, professional school, etc.)
52. Changing to a new school at same academic level (undergraduate, graduate, etc.)
53. Academic probation
54. Being dismissed from dormitory or other residence
55. Failing an important exam
56. Changing a major
57. Failing a course
58. Dropping a course
59. Joining a fraternity/sorority
60. Financial problems concerning school (in danger of not having sufficient money to continue)

Source: Sarason, I. G., Johnson, J. H., and Siegal, J. M., *Journal of Consulting and Clinical Psychology, 46*(5), 1978, pp. 932–946, with permission.

in an attempt to take some of these factors into account. Some researchers have suggested that weighting events for their desirability adds little or nothing to the prediction of health outcomes. Another issue that some research has been directed at is the impact of positive events. In general researchers have found that good events, such as receiving a promotion, are not related to health change.

Many of the events that people experience are more minor or even positive in nature. This observation lead Kanner and colleagues (1981) to develop the Hassles and Uplifts Scale. Examples of items that are included in this scale are listed in Table 6-4. In a study of 100 middle-aged individuals studied monthly for 10 months, Kanner and her colleagues found that scores on the Uplift Scale were more strongly related to psychological distress than life events scores for women, but not for men. More current research has found more mixed findings in this regard.

Some of the problems that have plagued life events investigators have been addressed through the development of the Bedford College Interview for Life Events and Difficulties developed by Brown and his colleagues (Brown & Harris, 1978). Unlike the Holmes and Rahe–type scales, the responsibility of rating events lies with trained raters blind to the re-

---

TABLE 6-4

THE 10 MOST FREQUENT HASSLES AND UPLIFTS SCALE ITEMS REPORTED BY 100 MIDDLE-AGED ADULTS. THE PERCENT OF TIME CHECKED IS THE MEAN PERCENTAGE OF PEOPLE WHO ENDORSED THAT ITEM EACH MONTH.

Item	% of time checked
Hassles	
1. Concerns about weight	52.4
2. Health of a family member	48.1
3. Rising prices of common goods	43.7
4. Home maintenance	42.8
5. Too many things to do	38.6
6. Misplacing or losing things	38.1
7. Yard work or outside home maintenance	38.1
8. Property, investment, or taxes	37.6
9. Crime	37.1
10. Physical appearance	35.9
Uplifts	
1. Relating well with your spouse or lover	76.3
2. Relating well with friends	74.4
3. Completing a task	73.3
4. Feeling healthy	72.7
5. Getting enough sleep	69.7
6. Eating out	68.4
7. Meeting your responsibilities	68.1
8. Visiting, phoning, or writing someone	67.7
9. Spending time with family	66.7
10. Home (inside) pleasing you	65.5

Source: From A. D. Kanner, J. C. Coyne, C. Schaeter, and Lazarus, *Journal of Behavioral Medicine,* 1981, *4* 1–39. Used by permission of Plenum Publishing Corporation.

spondents' condition. In this way the circularity of including subjective ratings of already distressed individuals, or the contamination of successful versus unsuccessful coping, is removed. In addition, this interview procedure is not limited by a list of possible events. The event's contextual meaning defines the circumstances surrounding the event and eliminates consideration of the individual's reaction to that event. For example, the death of a loved one may be identified as being desirable by a subject when a lingering illness has preceded the death. This is true despite the fact that there has been a significant loss. By using contextual ratings, all of this information can be considered simultaneously. Good reliability of ratings by trained judges have been reported by Brown and Harris (1978) and by Ndetei and Vadher (1981).

BOX 6-3

FOCUS ON WOMEN
Gender Differences in Life Events

Do men or women experience more life stress? Do more men or women believe that their health is effected by stress? In general, women report experiencing more stressful life events than men. Silverman, Eicher, and Williams (1987) reported on data collected in the National Health Promotion and Disease Prevention Questionnaire. Twenty-three percent of the women and 18 percent of the men reported experiencing a lot of stress in a 2-week period. These figures imply that nearly 20 million women and 14 milion men report "a lot" of stress in their lives. In addition, as they grow older, this discrepancy grows even greater. Women over the age of 65 are twice as likely to report a lot of stress in their lives compared with men. In addition, more women (49 percent) than men (38 percent) believe that stress had "a lot" or "some" effect on their health. Still, more than half of the total population thought that stress had hardly any or no effect on their health. Women also reported being more likely to seek help for personal or emotional problems when they were stressed. These findings suggest that we may need to create different intervention strategies for men and women.

The use of contextual ratings focuses attention on objective aspects of the event. Other investigators have argued that it is the individual's perception of an event that is important. Lazarus and associates (1985) have advocated a focus on the perceptual aspect of life stress, while Dohrenwend and colleagues (1985) have argued for a focus on the exact environmental context of the stressor. While this debate has not been resolved, it is probable that both perspectives should be included in analysis of the stress process.

It is clear that the qualification of stressful events remains one of the major challenges in the field of life events research. A number of discussions of the measurement of events exist in the literature. The interested reader is directed to Brown (1989), Paykel (1983), and Evans (1991).

MODELS OF STRESS

Almost any model of stress that one can imagine has been proposed at one time or another. For example, Dohrenwend and Dohrenwend (1984) provided a lucid description of six hypothesized models that have been suggested for describing the relationships between stressful life events, personal dispositions, and social conditions. One of the earliest models concerns the direct effects of undergoing stress, such as that experienced by concentration camp victims and individuals who have been in combat. Sometimes referred to as the "victimization hypothesis," this model underlies much of the early work in this field (e.g., Holmes & Masuda, 1974).

Later models posit that life events may illicit a perception of stress, which in the presence of some environmental pathogen (e.g., a virus) or some physiological vulnerability to some disorder (e.g., heart disease) leads to illness. This model has been referred to as the "stress-strain hypothesis." Further refinements suggest that personal dispositions and social situations may moderate, or may add to the impact of, stressful life events.

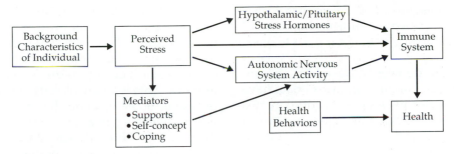

FIGURE 6-1
Biopsychosocial stress model.

There is published evidence that each of these models has merit. In fact, it is likely that there is some truth to all of them and that the relationship between stressful life events and health is complex, with the environment and personal predispositions and characteristics feeding back on each other. In this case, reality is probably quite complex, depending on multiple factors interacting with each other to produce health change. The model that we present in Figure 6-1 depicts the complexity of the potential relationships between health and stress. This may be called the biopsychosocial model of stress and health.

LIFE EVENTS AND THE PREDICTION OF ILLNESS

In this section we briefly present examples of studies which have used stress (here we define *stress* as the experience of stressful life events) to predict a range of physical and psychological disorders. Now the readers might ask themself, "Do specific features of life events and individual vulnerability factors differ in different disorders?" There are currently scores of papers relating life events to various illnesses, ranging from physical illness (such as appendicitis, multiple sclerosis, hypertension, and cancer) to psychological illness (such as depression, anxiety, and schizophrenia). Here we provide a flavor of the findings in stress research in a few examples of illness. The reader who would like to delve into this

area in more detail is referred to Brown and Harris (1989), one detailed presentation of this area.

Multiple Sclerosis

MS is a progressive neurological disease which typically has its onset between the ages of 20 to 40. More women than men (60 percent versus 40 percent) are afflicted. Early symptoms include complaints of fatigue, clumsiness, visual disturbance, weakness of limbs, and numbness or tingling in parts of the body. As the disease progresses, more pronounced symptoms occur, such as paralysis, loss of vision, and loss of control of the bowel and bladder. Approximately 10 percent of all patients die within 15 years, and the mean survival time has been estimated at 30 years. The typical course of the disease is intermittent, with repeated attacks over time.

Almost from the time that MS was first identified in the early 1800s, emotional factors and stressful life events were implicated in the onset and exacerbation of symptoms (see Grant et al., 1989, for a review of this literature). Interestingly, although case studies (considered by most to be weak evidence) suggested a relationship between stressful life events and the onset of MS, two controlled studies (Pratt, 1951; Antonovsky et al., 1968) found no relationship. This is in contrast to other positive findings by Warren and associates (1982) and Grant and colleagues (1989).

Grant and colleagues (1989) found that 77 percent of the patients studied experienced marked life adversity in the year prior to onset of symptoms.

Do stressful life events cause MS? The answer is still forthcoming. Studies to date have utilized retrospective designs. In addition, it is clear that since MS has some tendency to run in families, there is some vulnerability to it. To further complicate the picture, the risk for contracting MS is highest in the temperate and northern climates, and lowest in the tropics. However, if an individual moves to the tropics before the age of 15, the risk is reduced, suggesting that there is some agent that individuals are exposed to which increases risk. Still, some researchers (e.g., Grant et al., 1989) suggest that findings in life events are consistent with the idea that events may precipitate symptoms of MS in the biologically vulnerable individual.

Myocardial Infarction

Research in this area illustrates how stress may have multiple pathways, some of which are indirect to affect health. Jenkins (1967) pointed out that there are two important categories of socioenvironmental stressors that may effect coronary heart disease. The first are those that relate through behaviors such as smoking and drinking, behaviors which may be used by individuals to "control" their stress response. That is, individuals undergoing stress may smoke or drink more. Research investigating this possibility is less frequent compared with the second stress category, stress that creates sustained long-term arousal of the autonomic nervous system. The autonomic nervous system is where the interpretive process occurs between experience of stress and cardiovascular response.

Note that both of these stress categories potentially require long periods of exposure in order to have their effects on the cardiovascular system. This has led some writers

(e.g., Jenkins, 1967) to conclude that the study of life events as a causal agent is likely to be unfruitful. Thus most researchers have focused on the question of determining if life events may trigger a myocardial infarction (MI) in individuals who are already physically predisposed. Some evidence has been presented which suggests that acute stress can trigger an MI (Connolly, 1976; Parkes, Benjamin, & Fitzgerald, 1969). However, perhaps the larger, more difficult question is, "Does stress contribute to the development of cardiovascular disease."

A Swedish study of 9097 male construction workers over a 12- to 15-month period, a relatively short period in terms of heart disease, has yielded mixed results. In one report (Theorell et al., 1975), overall life change scores did not predict subsequent diagnosis of coronary heart disease. However, feelings of chronic overload at work did predict MI; 19 percent of those with MI reported feeling overloaded, compared with 9 percent of the rest of the men. Another study compared 380 German male patients who had had their first MI with 180 other individuals (Siegrest et al., 1982). They found that 31 percent of the MI patients were exposed to three or more "critical negative life events" (most important, chronic work load) compared with 14 percent in the comparison group. This study's modest stress effect yielded a population attributable risk of 20 percent, a rate that is similar to that reported by Neilson et al. (1989). These findings should be considered carefully since most of the reports of stress were obtained retrospectively, a design problem discussed later in this chapter.

Cancer

Cancer is really a multitude of more than 100 diseases which are characterized by malfunctioning DNA, causing rapid cell growth and proliferation. These growths may displace normal organs and sap the body of vital resources.

Much research has focused on identifying the cancer-prone person, either from the perspective of genetics or personality. Some of this work has been reviewed by Temoshok (1991). But is cancer stress-related? Work with animals suggests that experiencing uncontrolled stressors is associated with increased risk of cancer. Visintainer, Seligman, and Vopicelli (1983) implanted rats with cancer cells. Half the rats were exposed to inescapable shock and half remained in their cage. More rats who had been exposed to the shock grew tumors compared with those who had not. Among humans, Jones et al. (1989) and others have reported that the loss of a loved one is related to higher incidence of cancer. In addition, a review by Sklar and Anisman (1981) cites a substantial literature to support the notion that cancer growth may be significantly augmented by stress and sense of helplessness. The mechanism for this increase in risk is being explored through stress-related changes in the immune system discussed below.

Infections

Cohen and Williamson (1991) have provided a scholarly review of the literature dealing with the role of stress in infectious disease. Behavioral medicine researchers interested in the role that psychological factors play in human diseases have primarily focused on coronary heart disease and cancer, while neglecting infectious diseases. Some, but not all, individuals who are exposed to infectious agents (i.e., microorganisms or parasites such as viruses, bacteria, and mycoplasma) develop clinical disease. Cohen and Williamson present three models to explain relationships between stress and infectious disease. The first model suggests that stress alters one's susceptibility to infection through changes in immune function or changes in health behaviors (e.g., unsafe sex practices could increase exposure to infectious agents). The second model suggests that stress may alter the course or severity of infec-

tious disease, or both, through physiological changes, changes in health practices, or failure to comply with medical regimens. Finally, the third model suggests that stress may influence the various stages and timing of individuals' health behavior, for example recognizing and acting on symptoms. This paper points out that to date most research has focused on establishing a relation between stress and infectious disease and it is time to test these models.

The literature reviewed by these authors suggests that stress is associated with increases in illness behaviors and *may be* associated (i.e., the evidence is less convincing but provocative) with increased onset and reactivation of verified infectious diseases such as upper respiratory infections, herpes virus infections, and bacterial infections. Cohen and Williamson suggest that future studies of stress and disease need to detail the timing between stress and infection, consider how chronic the stressors experienced are, and detail how the body translates stress (i.e., study the biological pathways) into disease relationships.

Depression

Psychologists and psychiatrists have long believed that clinical depression can be provoked by stressful life events in the environment. However, evidence for this relationship has been questioned for a number of reasons. For example, a number of studies of depressed patients indicate that, compared with normative samples, the depressives give uniformly higher ratings for the stressfulness of events (Grant et al., 1976; Schless et al., 1979). Thus, it is possible that a negative cognitive set influences a subject's ratings of event stressfulness and may contaminate the association between depression and events.

Brown and his colleagues' work in England supports the idea that there is an association between the report of recent severely threatening life events and the subsequent onset of psychiatric disorders, nearly always associated with depression, in a sample of women drawn from the general population (Brown & Harris, 1978). Their work indicated that loss events (i.e., deaths) more often preceded depression. Other researchers support the finding that life events often precede the onset of depressive episodes (e.g., Jacobs et al., 1974; Lloyd, 1980). However, the variance contributed by life stressors to the prediction of depressive recurrence is quite modest compared with that contributed by personal history of depression (Warheit, 1979). It may be that people with different depressive disorders may respond differently to stressful life events (Hirscheld & Cross, 1982).

Some researchers have suggested that some subsets of patients (i.e., those who have a genetic loading) may be more vulnerable to the effects of stress. Akiskal and McKinney (1973) proposed a study that took into account biological factors, psychological factors, and stress. Some clinicians distinguish between *reactive* depressions (that is, depressions that are precipitated by happenings in the environment) and *endogenous* depressions (those depressive episodes that are not linked to events in the environment). The challenge in this area is that no one has yet identified a biological marker of endogenous depression. Thus researchers use clinical symptoms to infer the origin of the depression. The discerning reader will appreciate the potential problems with this approach. Monroe and associates (1985) found that diverse types of life events preceding entry into treatment for depression significantly predicted the course of disorder for endogenous, but not for nonendogenous, depression over a 9-month period.

How are environmental experiences translated into health change? In the next section we consider how the organism responds to stress.

THE STRESS RESPONSE

The stress response is made up of a complex interaction among physiological activities, cognitive processes, and behavioral responses. Figure 6-1 illustrates how the physiological component of the stress response works. In essence the stress response activates the sympathetic and parasympathetic branches of the autonomic nervous system. In and of themselves, these responses may affect some health outcomes such as cardiopulmonary functions. They do not, however, explain changes in individual susceptibility to other disorders such as viruses or tumors. To understand how stress may impact on these other disorders it is necessary to turn to a relatively new field of study focusing on the impact of stress and other psychological processes on the immune system. This area of study is known as *psychoneuroimmunology*. Some discussion of this area is contained in Chapter 12 on AIDS.

A central premise underlying the observed association between life adversity and health status is that stress exerts a suppressive effect on immune functioning. Studies from several laboratories have shown that a variety of stressors affect the immune response in animals as well as humans (Borysenko & Borysenko, 1982; Palmblad, 1981).

The immune system is made up of cells, tissues, and organs that connect to each other through the bloodstream and lymphatic system. In Figure 6-2 we can see the various parts of the body that make up this system.

Two types of immunological reaction have been described: humoral and cellular. Humoral reactions, which are faster-acting, involve the release of immunoglobulins (antibodies) to neutralize bacterial toxins and to aid phagocytosis (i.e., removal of cell debris). Cellular immunity, on the other hand, acts more slowly and is responsible for the body's defense against cancer cells, viruses, and bac-

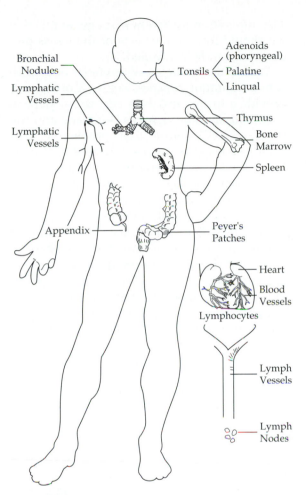

Bronchial Nodules

Lymphatic Vessels

Lymphatic Vessels

Tonsils

Adenoids (phoryngeal)
Palatine
Linqual

Thymus

Bone Marrow

Spleen

Appendix

Peyer's Patches

Heart

Blood Vessels

Lymphocytes

Lymph Vessels

Lymph Nodes

FIGURE 6-2

The immune system is composed of cells, tissues, and organs that are connected by blood and lymphatic vessels, making it an extensive network. (From Cooper, E. L. *Stress, Immunity and Aging.* New York: Marcel Dekker, Inc., 1984, with permission.)

teria. Cellular immunity is made up of two major cell types, T- and B-lymphocytes. T-cells include helper cells, which tell the system to turn on in the face of a virus (for example), and suppressor cells, which tell the system to slow down.

A number of cellular immune parameters have been found to be effected by stress. A study by Kiecolt-Glaser and colleagues (1984) assessed several immune parameters in 75 first-year medical students 1 month before final examinations and again at the start of final examinations. The authors found that immune cell activity was significantly lower after the test when compared with before the test. In another study (Kiecolt-Glaser et al., 1987), immune status was assessed in 38 married and 38 separated or divorced women. Poor marital quality in the married group and shorter separation time in the second group were associated with poorer functioning of several immune measures. In our own work (McNaughton et al., 1990), we compared the immune status of 12 highly stressed elderly women with that of 12 matched nonstressed women. For the women in the high-stress group, the immune systems seemed to be less activated. These findings indicate that the immune system's ability to respond to foreign invaders was reduced. In addition to the association between increased stress and reduction in immune function, we found that depressed mood and dissatisfaction with social supports were related to immune "suppression," whereas using problem-focused coping was associated with better immune functioning.

A cautionary note: This is a young field, and not all studies in this area have reported consistent findings. For example, in animals, acute stress has been associated with diminished immunocompetence, while chronic stress has been associated with enhanced immunocompetence (Monjan, 1981; Sklar & Anisman, 1981). It is clear that more studies are needed in this area.

How people perceive stress, how they cope with stress, and how their social environment affects their reaction to stress may in part explain discrepant findings in the area of psychoneuroimmunology. In fact, inadequate coping in the face of marked adversity is often part of the definition of stress (Plaut & Friedman,

1981). Such researchers argue that stressful events will induce a "stress response" only if the organism cannot, or believes that it cannot, cope with the adversity. Thus, an organism's coping attempts may be an important variable in the stress-health relationship (Antonovsky, 1974; Locke et al., 1984; Seligman, 1975; Vitaliano et al., 1987).

Dorian and colleagues (1982) demonstrated that examination stress may be more immunosuppressing among individuals who react with much more anxiety compared with those who do not. In a longitudinal study of patients with metastatic breast cancer, Derogatis (1979) found that long-term survivors appeared to be more able to externalize their negative feelings and psychological distress through the expression of anger, hostility, anxiety, and sadness. Short-term survivors tended to be those individuals whose coping styles involved suppression or denial of effect or psychological distress. Although there were no significant differences in various measures of disease status at baseline, short-term survivors had a mean of 407 days of chemotherapy versus 181 days in the long-term survivors group.

Relaxation training can affect the immune system. Kiecolt-Glaser and colleagues (1985) found that relaxation training was associated with increased immune activity in an elderly population. The ability to relax may be conceptualized as an adaptive coping strategy in response to life adversity.

There is also a substantial body of literature which suggests that stress hormones, such as catecholamines and corticosteroids, are not always secreted in response to stress. Rather, in situations where coping opportunities may be reduced, such as uncontrollable or ambiguous situations, more of these stress hormones are released compared with responses to controlled situations (Mason, 1975; Selye, 1956; Weiss et al., 1980). This suggests that coping may have its most important effects when individuals experience uncontrollable situations.

The implication for stress management is that we should focus on aspects of the stress process that can be controlled.

We discuss the deleterious effects of depression on immune function below. Coping may provide a further link between stress, depression, and immune changes. Vitaliano and colleagues (1987) found that problem-focused coping styles were inversely related to depression, while wishful-thinking coping styles were positively related to depression. Thus, if stress is moderated by coping—which in turn impacts an individual's affective status, which in turn impacts their immune status—another link in the stress-strain model can be made.

In the animal research discussed above, Sklar and Anisman (1981) infected two groups of mice with tumor cells, subjected the groups to either escapable or inescapable shock, and found that tumor growth was significantly faster in the inescapable shock group. This difference was found despite the fact that equal amounts of total shock were administered to each group. Again this shows that uncontrolled stress is more dangerous. Laudenslager and colleagues (1983) investigated whether this difference was immune-modulated. As predicted, in the inescapable shock group, lymphocyte response to two different types of mitogen stimulation was suppressed. These results, as well as the findings reported above that some types of stress may enhance immune functioning while others act to suppress it, help to illustrate the complexity of this type of research.

SOCIAL SUPPORT, DISEASE, AND IMMUNE STATUS

Detailed discussion of social support appears in Chapter 7. Here we limit ourselves to discussion of findings relating social support to immune functioning. In a study of 256 healthy adults, Thomas and colleagues (1985) found that women, but not men, with higher scores on a social interaction scale had better immune functioning. Medical students who were more lonely were found to have reduced immune functioning (Kiecolt-Glaser, 1984).

Animal models of stress, utilizing maternal separation and social isolation, have also yielded hormonal and immune effects. In a study by Gisler (1974), mice that were isolated and restrained in test tubes had increased plasma corticosteroid levels (a stress hormone) and an associated decrease in immune reactivity. Similarly, Laudenslager and colleagues (1985) studied the influence of early maternal and peer separation in monkeys and found that those with early separation experiences had significantly reduced immune function.

As in the stress and coping literature, research on the effects of social support on immune functioning and disease processes is in its infancy. It is exciting to see that lines of evidence exist that suggest a pathway between social support and health outcomes. Thus, we find correlations between measures of social support and stress hormone levels (Henry & Stevens, 1977; Kiecolt-Glaser et al., 1984a), between social supports and immune measures (Kiecolt-Glaser et al., 1984a; Kiecolt-Glaser, et al., 1984b), and between social support and morbidity and mortality (Berkman & Syme, 1979; House et al., 1988). This suggests that poor social support networks lead to an increase in glucocorticoids, which suppresses immune function, which in turn affects an individual's susceptibility to disease and mortality.

DEPRESSION, DISEASE, AND IMMUNE FUNCTION

The final pathway between psychological stress and immune response that we consider is depression. Early observations of autoimmune diseases suggested that emotions might affect the immune system. For example, Solomon and Moos (1964) found that emotional

conflict predicted faster onset and a worse course for people with rheumatoid arthritis. The authors reported that, despite similar genetic predisposition, a control group of women who were not depressed or socially isolated remained free of the disease.

A great deal about stress, depression, and immune function has been learned by studying people who have just experienced the death of a close family member. This is consistently rated as one of the most stressful events that people can experience. Most people who have experienced a loss have at least a temporary episode of depression during the grieving process. After it was found that grieving people had immune system alterations (Bartrop et al., 1977), it became important to find out whether it was the event or the depressive response that caused the immune effects. Schleifer and colleagues (1983) found immune changes only in widows who were also depressed, suggesting that depression was the most important factor. However, Irwin and coworkers (1990) found that both bereavement and depression led to a state of immune suppression.

In summary, the data from these studies suggest that stress either directly or indirectly through changes in affective status may increase an organism's vulnerability to certain diseases by means of exerting an immunosuppressive effect. It should be kept in mind, however, that the clinical importance of laboratory measures of "immune suppression" has not been directly demonstrated. That is, immune suppression does not always lead to illness.

OTHER PHYSIOLOGIC INDICATORS OF STRESS

The body communicates the stress response to the immune system through two major pathways, the neuroendocrine and the catecholamine systems. The neuroendocrine system is made up of the hypothalamus and the pituitary glands, which release several stress hormones including cortisol, adrenocorticotropic hormone (ACTH), growth hormone, and beta endorphin. Individuals who are under stress release more of these substances. In turn, more of these stress hormones decrease immune activity.

The catecholamine system excretes the stress hormones adrenaline and noradrenaline. These hormones have their major action on the cardiovascular system. Thus, the individual under stress secretes more of these hormones, which have the effect of driving up heart rate and blood pressure. Alzheimer's disease caregivers have increased activity of the catecholamine system and increased blood pressure (Irwin et al., 1991). Prolonged increases in blood pressure may lead to hypertension. In addition, these increases in catecholamines appear to reduce immune responsiveness, increasing the deleterious effects on the immune system.

Figure 6-3 presents a schematic representation of the role of the three biological systems we have discussed: the immune, neuroendocrine, and catecholamine systems.

Each of the systems listed above responds in a characteristic way when an organism is stressed. When an organism is stressed, the catecholamine system first kicks into action. Increases in catecholamine system activity result in increased metabolic activity. This metabolic activity is obviously quite useful in stressful situations that may require fight or flight. To date, most studies have focused on the catecholamines without reference to the

neuroendocrine and immune systems, and vice versa. We know, however, that all three systems interact in concert in response to stress. For example, as norepinephrine increases, so does the neuroendocrine hormone cortisol, while the immune system activity declines. The exact details of the mechanism through which psychological distress is linked to changes in immunity have not been fully explored, although the autonomic nervous system and the neuroendocrine appear to serve as a major communication link between the brain and the immune system (Livnat et al., 1985).

STRESS AND APPRAISAL

The extent of a person's reaction to stressful events depends on the degree to which a situation is perceived as stressful or threatening. Lazarus and Folkman (1984) provide a lucid discussion of primary versus secondary appraisal. Figure 6-4 provides a schematic of the appraisal process. Primary appraisal occurs when a person is exposed to a potential stressor. When exposed to the situation, the person makes a decision regarding the potential positive, neutral, or negative consequences of that situation and the harm it has already caused or may cause. For example, for the individual who has already found a new job, being laid off may be appraised as neutral or mildly negative and causes little harm. In contrast, the primary appraisal of being laid off for the individual who has no job prospects would be extremely negative and could potentially cause much financial harm.

Once primary appraisals of potentially stressful events have occurred, individuals engage in secondary appraisal. At this time they assess whether they have adequate resources and the ability to cope with that situation. Stress occurs when individuals experience an imbalance between primary and secondary appraisal of a situation. For example, people who

FIGURE 6-3

Schematic of three biological systems' effect on health.

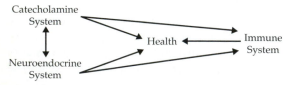

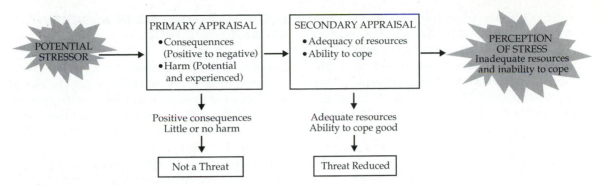

FIGURE 6-4
Stress appraisal of situations.

are laid off but who have large bank accounts and believe that they will be able to find new work do not experience much stress compared with those whose secondary appraisal is that they are not up to the task at hand.

STRESS AND COPING

The term *coping* has been used in many ways by various stress researchers. The different usages of the word reflect conceptual differences. From the psychoanalytic approach coping is sometimes regarded as a subcategory of defense. To complicate the issue, terms such as *coping mechanisms, coping skills, coping resources, coping strategies, coping styles,* and *coping traits* are sometimes used interchangeably, although they appear to express different ideas. One of the clearer definitions of coping has been provided by Lazarus and Folkman (1984). They define coping as "constantly changing cognitive and behavioral efforts to manage specific external and/or internal demands that are appraised as taxing or exceeding the resources of the person" (p. 178). Basically, coping is our attempt to change a stressor or a stress response.

Lazarus and colleagues have suggested that coping responses be seen as representing two primary categories: problem-focused coping

and emotion-focused coping (Cohen & Lazarus, 1979; Folkman & Lazarus, 1980; Lazarus, 1981). Problem-focused coping has been characterized as the taking of focused action either to eliminate a problem or to change a situation. Emotion-focused coping, on the other hand, represents mitigating efforts to modify one's emotional functioning in the face of a stressful situation, without attempting to change the stressor directly. For example, in the case of our layoff, the problem-focused component of coping might consist of applying for a job, while the emotion-focused component might consist of not taking it personally, thus protecting one's sense of self-worth. As can be seen, many if not all events require both categories of coping. However, the balance of emotion- and problem-focused coping changes depending on the demands of the situation.

Despite this distinction, McCrae and Costa (1986) point out that coping behaviors are simply categories of behavior in response to stressful events. The question is, "Which are adaptive and which are maladaptive?" Lazarus and Folkman (1984) make the case that the effectiveness of a coping strategy depends on the situation. There are frequent examples of researchers who assert that some coping responses are inherently superior to others. For example, in the introduction to a report on adaptive coping in adulthood, Irion and Blanchard-Fields (1987) expressed the common bias that "effective copers distort reality less frequently," and that distortion and denial are "more ineffective coping mechanisms." This may be true, and there is almost automatic agreement with such statements. However, even denial probably cannot be considered either maladaptive or adaptive without answering the questions, "In which person?" "In what situation?" For example, some concentration camp victims who denied the hopelessness of their situation fared better than their counterparts who gave up.

A number of studies have attempted to identify the most effective way of coping with a situation. For example, parents of surviving children with cancer reported that they coped moderately well by relying on information seeking, problem solving, help seeking, maintaining emotional balance, religion, being optimistic, denying, and accepting (Barbarin & Chesler, 1986). Therefore, a wide variety of coping methods may be adaptive in a given situation.

Understanding coping behaviors is complicated by the idea that coping is a changing process that unfolds as the individual encounters a specific situation which itself changes. This approach to understanding coping is different from others which view coping as a stable trait of a person. At best, coping trait measures have had modest predictive value of actual coping processes (Cohen & Lazarus, 1973; Kaloupek et al., 1984). It appears that coping is more complex than is represented by simple trait measures. As events change, individuals' coping efforts change to meet demands. In turn, as the individual copes with the event, the event changes, leading to reappraisal of the situation. New coping efforts must continue until the stressful event is no longer a threat.

LOGICAL PROBLEMS IN ASSESSING STRESS RESEARCH

Experiencing life events may or may not have a negative impact on physical or psychological well-being of groups or individuals. In spite of a large body of literature supporting this view, the public and most behavioral scientists persist in assuming that exposure to "stressors," retirement for example, leads to negative health outcome. In a review of the literature on the impact of retirement on the health of individuals, Smith et al. (1992, 475–502) concluded that retirement does not increase the risk of either death or a deterioration in health. In fact, it has been suggested that retirement may have beneficial effects on some existing medical conditions (Ekerdt et al., 1983). In this section we use the case of retirement to explore some of the reasons why, even in the face of hard evidence, there is a dogmatic acceptance of the idea that a stressor (e.g., retirement) leads to poor health.

Why does the idea that retirement causes illness and death persist in popular lore? Ekerdt (1987) provided a detailed set of answers to this question. First, provocative anecdotes about retirement, based on both popular and clinical observations, reach an enormous audience through the mass media. Consequently, an event will seem to occur more frequently or appear more plausible to the extent that people can easily imagine it (Tversky & Kahneman, 1982). Ekerdt (1987) pointed to the news about the death of football coach Paul "Bear" Bryant of the University of Alabama, who died of a heart attack 37 days after his retirement. To the casual observer the retirement might be viewed as having "caused" his death. For example, one can imagine hearing such statements as: "Sports meant everything to him; he shouldn't have retired," etc. The truth is that Bear Bryant had been ill for 3 years and retired because of his ill health. Since anecdotes such as that about Bear Bryant are mentioned in headlines while happy stories of individuals experiencing a healthy retirement are not considered newsworthy (precisely because they are too common), we form the erroneous conclusion that retirement is often associated with premature death.

The second reason why the idea that retirement causes illness and death persists is that people tend to seek order and attempt to bring understanding in their lives. Since retirement is frequently considered a milestone, individuals will often consider its connection with other dimensions of life. For example, when asked about any life events that might have preceded illness, people often attribute causality to a single, important, vivid, and recent event (Brim & Ryff, 1980), such as retirement. In prospective studies that obviate such a bias, however, retirement per se does not appear to predict ill health. The literature provides a common pattern of retrospectively finding support for the linkage between stress and health outcomes while finding little or weak associations between stress and health outcomes when careful prospective designs are utilized.

Other reasons the idea that retirement causes illness and death persists include the fact that some individuals have a prejudice against retirement, which stems from our culture's celebration of work as the major source of self-worth, self-esteem, identity, and personal fulfillment. This may lead individuals to have a difficult time imagining a truly healthy life without being employed. In addition, there sometimes exists an assumption that retirement must have some effect because it is of such great importance that it is anticipated by many individuals for decades. Any event as significant as that might be thought to have astounding effects. These are but a few reasons for the persistence of the unsupported generalization that retirement is harmful to health.

The example of retirement as a precursor of ill health is only one illustration that could be considered. Researchers and readers should not necessarily expect that there will exist a relationship between life events and ill health. In one 3-year prospective study of the effects of life events and previous symptoms on current symptom levels, psychiatric patients and nonpatients reported on life events and symptoms every 2 months on 18 occasions. The best predictor of current symptom level was level of previous symptoms, or as the provocative title of the paper suggests: Life events do not predict symptoms; symptoms predict symptoms (Grant et al, 1987). It is wise, therefore, in efforts to relate changes in the social environment to health, to first consider the possible contribution of antecedent symptom level to health outcome.

A common criticism of life events research is that the amount of variance in health change "explained" by life events is invariably low, usually in the range of 10 percent (Craig & Brown, 1984). This has suggested to some researchers that life events have no clinical significance (e.g., Andrews & Tennant, 1978). Craig and Brown (1984) pointed out the flaw in this logic using the example of lung cancer and smoking, where less than 1 percent of the variance in lung cancer prevalence is accounted for by heavy smoking. This apparently puzzling fact is explained by two factors: first, most lung cancer victims are not heavy smokers; and second, most heavy smokers do not have lung cancer. Since there are more individuals in the second group than the first, using a two-way measure of association (i.e., variance accounted for) leads the reader to an invalid conclusion. Using this logic, epidemiologists utilize "attributable risk" percent, which is the proportion of the disorder that can be attributed to the experience of a risk factor. Most studies of life events have failed to conceptualize life events as a risk factor, with the notable exception of Paykel (1978) and Brown and Harris (1978). Craig and Brown (1984) found that the attributable risk of life events ranged from a low of 20 percent for myocardial infarction to 83 percent for death from lung cancer, with a mean of 43 percent for the 13 studies they reviewed.

Finally, in any discussion of limitations of life events research, it is important to stress the importance of prospective rather than cross-sectional or retrospective designs. Antecedent-consequent relationships cannot be inferred with any degree of confidence from cross-sectional designs and can only be suggested by retrospective studies. Typical sources of error that are magnified by such designs include selective memory, denial of certain events, and overreporting to justify a current illness (Rabkin & Streuning, 1976). An example of how conclusions can change when appropriate designs are utilized is provided by Grant and associates (1982). They found that only about one-third of the subjects that they studied could be grouped together in such a way to fit the model of life events preceding symptoms. An additional 14 percent of the subjects tended to be unresponsive to events. This group may represent those individuals who are coping well with (or denying) events. The largest group of subjects was characterized as having patterns of events and symptoms that were not coherent; i.e., events occurred but symptoms did not necessarily follow. In fact, no more than 20 percent of the variance in symptoms is typically reported in studies of life events and symptoms. These findings stress the need to consider the possibility that occurrence of life events may not necessarily lead to changes in symptoms in most people. It is likely that progress in life events research will require finding methods of identifying that group of individuals who show a strong relationship between events and symptoms.

STRESS AS A PERFORMANCE ENHANCER

Lennart Levi (1922) called stress the common feature in the reactions of the living organism to all stimuli which tend to disturb the dynamic homeostasis of the psychological, biochemical, and physiological processes. When most of us think of stress, we usually think of its negative connotations. "I'm stressed out by exams," or "Traffic jams and long lines make me stressed," or "Work is too stressful." This view, however, does not fully express the entire potential spectrum of stress effects.

In some cases stress may actually improve performance. For example, the stress of worrying about a test may motivate a person to study, or the stress of competing in a big game may help a person perform at peak level, or the stress of a crisis may allow or force a person to make an immediate decision about something. However, as we all have experienced, too much stress can become incapacitating. This is the feeling of becoming "unglued" or being unable to cope further. Freeman (1940) demonstrated that there is an optimum activation level for quick reaction, although the performance of individuals was extremely variable at the highest levels. The relationship between stress and performance may be thought of as following an inverted U-shaped function, as indicated in Figure 6-5. This relationship implies that at intermediate levels, stress may cause arousal, focus attention, and improve performance. At high levels, stress may interfere with a person's ability to respond through overstimulation. Perhaps more surprising is that some minimal amount of stress may be necessary for an individual to exhibit optimal performance.

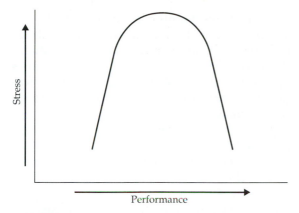

FIGURE 6-5
Relationship between stress and performance.

STRESS AND POSITIVE HEALTH OUTCOMES

Most of the research in the area of stress has been directed at understanding the negative impact that stress has on health. There is currently little evidence that stress can enhance health. However, Cohen and Hoberman (1983) have suggested that life events which subjects appraise as being positive may buffer the individual from the stress experience. In addition, Cousins (1976) provides anecdotal evidence that positive psychological states (e.g., laughter during humorous movies) may produce positive health outcomes. Karasek and associates (1982) reported that individuals who successfully coped with challenging or stressful situations may experience physiological growth. In addition, there is some evidence from the animal literature which indicates that rats who are chronically stressed initially show a decline in immune function, which over time gradually recovers to levels above baseline, and finally drops back to baseline. There may be some health benefit to having a "super activated" immune system during recovery. The idea that stress may provide some health bene-

fit is only weakly supported by current research. However, by focusing solely on the negative side of the equation we may be missing some exciting relationships.

WHO STAYS HEALTHY UNDER STRESS?

It is clear that many individuals remain healthy in the face of what most would agree is a stressful stimuli. In order to identify personality characteristics of those hardy individuals, Kobasa (1979) studied managers from a large metropolitan public utility. She first identified two groups of individuals, both of whom were under stress. One group had high levels of illness; the other group was more healthy. All subjects were male, had good incomes, and had stable family environments. Both groups were administered a battery of questionnaires, including measures of alienation from self, perceived control, and tendency to seek novelty and challenge. The high-stress low-illness subjects were less alienated from self, believed they were in control, were more interested in novel experience, were more oriented toward achievement, showed more endurance, and perceived less threat in personal, financial, and interpersonal areas than the high-stress high-illness group. From this work she developed the Hardiness Questionnaire (Maddi & Kobasa, 1984).

Other investigators have also found hardiness to be important in health outcome. Solomon and colleagues (1987) compared long-term AIDS survivors with those who succumbed more rapidly. They found that the survivors scored significantly higher on Kobasa's control scale than those who had died. Incidentally, survivors also reported using more problem-solving help from others than subjects who died, indicating that survivors tended to utilize social support more effectively. Temoshok and associates (1988) found that HIV-positive men who scored lower on the Hardiness Questionnaire, particularly the control scale, showed more neuropsychological impairment than those with higher hardiness scores. These results were interpreted to indicate that persons who coped more adaptively had fewer symptoms associated with HIV infection.

Though the work in this area is limited, it is intriguing. If the findings show further substantiation, it may lead to stress inoculation training programs. To date, stress intervention programs have been developed primarily on the basis of data focusing on behaviors associated with poor health outcomes. It will be interesting to see if focusing on the opposite side of the coin will result in more effective programs.

MANAGEMENT OF STRESS

In a world filled with tension and anxiety, management of stress has become one of psychology's major goals. A number of techniques have been found to be useful in reducing subjective distress. Here we briefly review three methods that are commonly used by clinicians: biofeedback, relaxation, and cognitive therapy. These three methods represent a sampling of the methods used in this area and are not exhaustive.

Biofeedback systems operate by detecting changes in the biology of the person and, by means of visual and auditory signals, providing feedback to the patient of those changes. The patient uses this immediate information to engage in different strategies, by trial and error, to make these signals change in the desired direction. With this biofeedback as a guide the patient learns how to control the biological system from where it originates. With repeated training the patient is gradually weaned away from the feedback and, having learned how to recognize and control the subtle internal events associated with that feedback, can maintain control.

Biofeedback training focuses on biological systems that are beyond conscious control and have been operating in a maladaptive fashion. By maladaptive we mean that the system is operating in a range that impairs the performance of individuals or contributes to stress-related disease.

There are three stages to biofeedback training (Budzynski, & Stoyva, 1984). The first stage is *awareness* of the maladaptive response. During this stage the person learns that certain responses, both thoughts and bodily events, can influence the target response. In the second stage the individual is guided by the biofeedback signal to *control* that response. Finally, in the third stage the individual learns to *transfer* that learned control to everyday situations that previously provoked that maladaptive response.

For example, to teach someone to relax they are first attached to a device that measures surface electromyographic (EMG) activity, and provides them with an auditory and visual feedback (an objective indicator of relaxation). With repeated exposure patients learn to be aware of when they are or are not relaxed and to control the maladaptive response in the laboratory. Gradually they learn to use these techniques in real-world settings which had previously caused tension. This method works best with patients who seem to be unable to relax even when they consciously attempt to do so. These individuals seem to be relatively unaware of the stress that they are experiencing and their tension level. Without development of an awareness of this tension, they are often unsuccessful in their attempts to relax. Biofeedback has been used to treat a range of problems including anxiety, tension headaches, temporomandibular joint (TMJ) problems, tinnitus, muscle rehabilitation, and a variety of pain syndromes.

Deep relaxation can be achieved through ''progressive relaxation training'' (PRT), biofeedback, hypnosis, or other forms of therapy.

Deep relaxation therapy involves training individuals to relax in the presence of a feared stimulus. This provides the individual with a way of reducing autonomic arousal. Once this has been accomplished, individuals are more able to tolerate fear-provoking stimuli, and learn alternative and more adaptive responses to such stimuli (for example, rational cognitions, described below), which may forestall or eliminate subsequent detrimental autonomic arousal.

PRT attempts to indirectly reduce the autonomic arousal components of anxiety by altering one of its manifestations, i.e., musculoskeletal tension. As muscoloskeletal tension is reduced, other correlates of autonomic activity, such as heart rate and blood pressure, also drop. It is not clear if the drop in these other autonomic indicators is actually due to PRT or to the individual developing a set of voluntary skills that are utilized more centrally and thus prevent arousal from becoming problematic.

This type of therapy is useful in individuals who have been conditioned to overarousal through a series of unfortunate learning experiences. For example, an individual may become overaroused repeatedly from exposure to a noxious stimulus such as examinations. PRT will not, however, be effective if the fundamental problem involves a reaction to punishment brought about by a lack of social skills or the presence of maladaptive cognitive habits (e.g., "I am not as smart as these people, thus I will do poorly on this examination"), or both.

In PRT individuals are first provided with a rationale for its usefulness. Following this explanation they are taught to first tense and then relax each of 16 muscle groups that include the whole body (e.g., the dominant hand and forearm, the neck, the nondominant foot, etc.). Once the individuls have learned to quickly relax all muscle groups, they are asked to achieve relaxation by merely recalling the

sensations associated with the release of tension when in real-life situations. At the same time the individuals are learning to deal with stress through PRT, they are usually exposed to an integrated approach to dealing with their problems.

Techniques such as PRT have been utilized in treating a variety of physical problems including headache (e.g., Brown, 1984), cancer (Holland et al, 1991). and arthritis (Parker et al, 1989).

Cognitive approaches to stress attempt to change the way one thinks about the nature of a situation, or their cognitive set to that situation. The accuracy of one's cognitions about one's self and the environment in which one behaves appears to play a role in how stressful a situation is judged to be and how one is able to cope with stressful events (Beck, 1976; Ellis & Grieger, 1977). Beck maintains that systematic negative distortions about the future, self, and others cause many of the components of depression, one extreme outcome of experiencing negative life events. In this theory dysfunctional attitudes consist of excessively rigid rules of a contractual nature, such as the belief that one's self-worth is dependent upon achieving impossibly perfectionistic goals or upon *always* having others' approval. According to Beck, when a person endorses these views and is then exposed to a stressor, the individual may become vulnerable to a stress response such as depression. Albert Ellis specified 11 irrational beliefs, such as overly high expectations for oneself and demand for unconditional approval by everyone in one's environment. These beliefs are considered irrational because they are not based on reality and can harm health and psychological well-being.

Cognitive approaches to stress involve teaching individuals to evaluate their primary appraisal of a potentially stressful situation from automatically being noxious to being more accurate. This judgment takes into account the amount and probabilities of damage inherent in the threat, and the coping resources available to the individual that can be mobilized to reduce that threat. These responses are to a large degree automatic and are prone to considerable error; thus two individuals faced with similar situations and with similar coping mechanisms available may respond in different manners. The individuals' cognitive structuring of a situation is in this view responsible for mobilizing them to action. If this mobilization persists beyond what the individual views as realistic demands, they may experience a stress reaction.

The cognitive approach to the treatment of stress reaction focuses on how individuals think about potentially stressful situations. They are encouraged to examine the internal factors which contribute to the stress response. From the cognitive perspective these factors include thoughts, impulses, and feelings. The individuals are taught to identify the meanings they have assigned to events that are connected to both activation of behavior and effect. Cognitive techniques—such as identifying what are termed automatic thoughts, recognizing and correcting cognitive distortions and identifying broad beliefs and assumptions which are in some cases irrational and underlie how a particular event is thought about—are used to clarify problems. Individuals are taught to increase their objectivity and perspective about their perception of events that occur in their lives. This process of analysis of specific stressors and cognitive changes results in the modification of habitual cognitive errors which lead to misclassification of events as threatening.

Cognitive therapeutic techniques have been utilized in the field of health, including the areas of health promotion and disease prevention, detection, and treatment. Specific applications of cognitive stress management interventions have been developed for chronic illnesses such as asthma (Bartlett, 1983), rheu-matoid arthritis (Parker, Frank, Beck, et al., 1987), and peptic ulcer (Hoffman et al., 1982). In addition, this approach has been used in various pain management programs, including the pain associated with cancer (Fishman & Loscalzo, 1987) and back pain (Cinciripini & Floreen, 1982).

Other stress management interventions which are utilized but will not be discussed here include aerobic exercise training, mental imagery, and social support enrichment. These and other programs which utilize various combinations of these techniques would require a book unto themselves.

SUMMARY

By now the reader should realize that stress is a complicated, multifaceted construct that has been approached from many perspectives by a host of researchers. In this short space it is impossible to be comprehensive in our coverage of the stress area. Rather, we have chosen to use the "cafeteria" approach, which we hope will stimulate further discussion and reading in this area. Much excitement has been generated by research in the areas tracing the effects of stress on immunology. Once again it should be emphasized that a single study relating a stressful life experience to changes in the CNS and immune system and finally to health change remains to be conducted. We have much research, which taken together provides strong evidence that this model is at least true in some cases. However, it is the wise reader who takes this model with a grain of salt.

KEY TERMS

Stressor. Any stimuli that makes demands on an organism requiring adaptation or adjustment.

Stress responses. A relatively stereotypic set of psychological and biological patterns that organisms exhibit in response to exposure to a stressor.

General adaptation syndrome (GAS). A general, nonspecific reaction pattern organisms exhibit in response to threat of damage that permits the body to mobilize against these threats.

Life events. Potential stressors that occur in the environment, measured by observation, checklists, and interviews.

Social Readjustment Rating Scale (SRRS). A much-used life events scale which was developed in an attempt to quantify the amount of stress an individual had been exposed to.

Hassles and Uplifts Scale. Life events scale that focuses on minor or positive events, or both.

Bedford College Interview for Life Events and Difficulties. A life events interview developed in an attempt to remove subjective idiosyncratic responses. Trained raters, blind to the respondents' condition, evaluate stressfulness of events.

Stress response. A complex interaction among physiological activities, cognitive processes, and behavioral responses.

Psychoneuroimmunology. Field of study focusing on the impact of stress and other psychological processes on the immune system.

Catecholamines. Hormones that are indicative of sympatho-adrenomedullary system (SAS) activity, which is activated when undergoing stress.

Coping. The constantly changing cognitive and behavioral efforts that individuals make in attempts to manage specific external and/or internal demands that they have appraised as taxing or exceeding their resources.

Hardiness Questionnaire. A questionnaire which attempts to identify individuals who stay healthy in the face of stress.

CHAPTER 7

Social Support

When Mrs. Stevens died, Mr. Stevens became with-drawn, depressed, and absentminded. Although his own health had always been excellent, Mr. Stevens now began to go downhill. He died within 2 years of his wife's demise. Can we attribute the problems Mr. Stevens experienced with his physical health to the loss of a spouse? A growing body of research suggests that loss of a family member can have important consequences for the elderly, particularly elderly men (Siegel & Kuykendall, 1990). For example, widowed men and those who do not belong to a church or temple become significantly more depressed upon the loss of a nonspousal family member than men who have a wife or are more socially connected.

We know that exposure to disease can increase the chances of poor health outcomes. But can the social environment also be related to poor health outcomes? A growing body of evidence suggests that social support may be an important determinant of health outcomes. In this chapter, we consider the relationship between social support and physical health. We will briefly review the epidemiologic data linking social support to mortality. Then we

will discuss the evidence that social support is relevant to self-care and health outcomes in chronic disease conditions. The review will consider evidence that social support enhances health outcomes and the contrary evidence that social relationships prolong and reinforce physical dysfunction.

Social support has been defined in several different ways. In some epidemiological studies, social support is defined as the number of

BOX 7·1

HEALTH OBJECTIVES FOR THE YEAR 2000

The National Health Promotion and Disease Prevention Objectives for the Year 2000 did not specifically include social support. However, the document suggested that social isolation is a major risk factor for reduced functional independence in older people. Social isolation may also be a risk factor for depression and suicide among the elderly. Although no specific objectives were stated, the report urges community networks to be set up in order to help older adults maintain independence. The report also urged primary care providers to learn about available community support resources and to refer their patients to them (p. 26).

social contacts maintained by a person or the extensiveness of a social network. More recent studies on social support emphasize the perception of belonging. Cobb (1976), defined social support as the perceived belonging to a social network of communication and mutual obligation. People in the perceived social network are those whom we can rely on and who we know value, care about, or love us. Social support is present to the extent that we perceive belonging to the network of communication and mutual obligation.

Just a few years ago, most textbooks gave little mention to social support. However, social support has become a very active area for research investigation in the last decade. As a result, we decided to devote an entire chapter to an exploration of the social support construct.

THE EPIDEMIOLOGY OF SOCIAL NETWORKS AND HEALTH OUTCOMES

Epidemiology is the study of the determinants and distribution of disease (see Chapter 2). The hallmark of epidemiological methodology is the prospective/longitudinal cohort study. Major investigations, such as the Framingham Heart Study, attempted to establish prospective predictors of mortality in a random sample from the general population. For example, the Framingham Study began with 5127 participants who had no visible signs of heart disease. Each participant was given a physical examination and a detailed interview that included lifestyle and demographic characteristics. Then each participant was followed every other year (Kannel, 1987). Other major epidemiologic investigations have used similar methodologies.

Most epidemiologic studies were started some years ago before formal measures of social support had been developed. Nevertheless, simple measures of social network appeared to be predictive of health outcomes in a variety of studies. The Alameda County Population Monitoring Study demonstrated that a simple measure of social network was a significant predictor of longevity. The measure included marital status, number of close family and friends, church membership, and group membership. Men with weak social networks were nearly 2.5 times as likely to die within a defined time period than men with extensive networks. Women benefited even more from established social networks (Berkman & Breslow, 1983).

Similar results were obtained in Tecumseh, Michigan, where 2754 men and women were studied. In this investigation, men who were married, who attended church, and who participated in voluntary organizations and community activities were significantly less likely to die within a 10-year period than men who were disconnected. The Tecumseh Study did not show similar relationships for women (House et al., 1982). In contrast to the findings of Berkman and Breslow (1983) and House and colleagues (1982), in the Durham County, North Carolina, Study (Blazer, 1982) no consistent pattern of increased mortality rates was associated with a progressive decrease in social support. Rather, there appears to be a threshold effect in which only those individuals, either male or female, who were at the extreme end of the continuum in terms of the least amount of social support had increased mortality rates. In a study of residents of Evans County, Georgia, those with the fewest ties were at increased risk for mortality. The findings reported were significant for older white males only and not for black individuals and white females (Schoenbach et al., 1986).

Several studies have suggested that the combination of high stress and low social support is a particularly strong predictor of negative outcome. For example, 142 women in the Framingham Heart Study who had more cardiovascular disease worked in clerical roles and had emotionally nonsupportive spouses (Haynes & Feinleib, 1980). A study of Swedish workers revealed that cardiovascular disease was excessive for workers who had low social support, perceived their jobs to be stressful, and felt that they had little control over their work environment (Welin et al., 1985). In one study of survivors of myocardial infarction, survivors were classified according to social isolation and stress and then followed prospectively. Those who experienced low stress and were socially connected had one-fourth the rate of mortality in comparison with those who were under high stress and were isolated (Ruberman et al., 1984). Despite these strong results, some studies have also failed to show a relationship between social support and health outcomes (Cohen & Syme, 1985).

It is difficult to make comparisons across these studies. Different studies used different definitions of heart disease. Some of them used myocardial infarction (heart attack), some used mortality, and some used less objective diagnoses, such as self-reported chest pain. Populations varied greatly from study to study, as did definitions of social support. The measures of social support were usually crude. In some of the studies, they merely record the presence of a spouse or participation in group activities. In addition, the degree of satisfac-

tion associated with these relationships was often not considered. Nevertheless, these studies generally show an association between social relationships and longevity (Davidson & Shumaker, 1987). These findings have intrigued epidemiologists and supported the notion that friends and family are health assets. Yet the epidemiological studies provide few clues about why social relationships enhance health (Ruberman, 1992).

It is important to emphasize that epidemiologic studies use different measures than psychological investigations. Support is usually the number of social contacts, and "health" is most often survival or mortality. Yet epidemiologic studies provide the basis for many arguments that social support protects against illness. However, the relationship between network size and mortality is not necessarily related to the association between social support satisfaction and disability. At best, the epidemiologic studies have stimulated interest in the relationship between social support and health. Yet epidemiological data provide only a very small piece of the puzzle. To follow up on the suggestive evidence from epidemiological studies, we need to focus on a wider array of health outcomes and learn more about the nature of social interactions among people.

HOW IS SOCIAL SUPPORT MEASURED?

Although definitions vary, most measures of social support include tangible components, such as financial assistance or physical aid, and intangible components, such as encouragement and guidance. Heitzmann and Kaplan (1988) reviewed the literature on the assessment of social support. They identified at least 23 different measurement techniques. Most of the measures had suitable reliability. However, only about half of the measures had any evidence of *validity*, defined as the correlation between the measures of social support and well-defined criterion measures. This was particularly problematic for studies concerning the relationship of social support to health, because there are few well-validated measures of health status.

Some would question why health measures should be used as validity criteria for measures of social support. The rationale is that social support interventions are justified on the basis of their presumed relationships to health out-comes. Authors repeatedly evoke the social support–health outcome connection in discussions of either direct effects or buffering models. It is the evidence for these support-health relationshisp that we examine here.

Table 7-1 provides a summary of scales used as validity criteria for social support measures. The left-hand column of the table lists the social support scale. The next column gives the

---

TABLE 7·1

SUMMARY OF SCALES USED AS VALIDITY CRITERIA FOR SOCIAL SUPPORT MEASURES

Social support scale	Validity criterion	Nature of criterion measure	Correlation
Norbeck Social Support Questionnaire; Norbeck (1981)	SSQ; Schaffer et al. (1981)	Social support scale	−.03 to .56
Personal Resource Questionnaire (PRQ); Brandt and Weinert (1981)	Family integration measure	Social support scale	.21 to .44
Arizona Social Support Interview Schedule (ASSIS); Barrera (1981a)	Inventory of Socially Supportive Behaviors (ISSB); Barrera (1981b)	Social support measure	.42 (network size)
Interpersonal Support Evaluation Schedule (ISES); Cohen et al. (1985)	Psychiatric and physical symptoms	Symptom checklists	−.60 with measures of psychiatric symptoms; −.39 with measures of physical symptomatology
Social Relationship Scale (SRS); McFarlane et al. (1981)	Clinician reports	Clinical judgment	Specific correlations not reported
Interview Schedule for Social Interaction (ISSI); Henderson et al. (1980)	Eysenck Personality Inventory (EPI)	Personality test	Modest correlation
Social Support Questionnaire (SSQ); Sarason et al. (1983)	Multiple Affect Adjective Checklist (MAACL) and EPI	Adjective checklist and personality test	−.43 between SSQ-S and MAACL; −.37 between SSQ-S and EPI (for women)
Social Support Scale (SSS); Lin et al. (1979)	Psychiatric symptoms	Symptom checklist	.36
Perceived Social Support from Friends (PSS-Fr); Procidano & Heller (1983)	Psychiatric symptomatology	Symptom checklist	Modest negative correlation with psychiatric symptoms
Work Relationship Index (WRI); Billings & Moos (1982)	Personal functioning	Personality measure	−.33 for men; −.15 for women
Diabetes Family Behavior Checklist (DFBC); Schafer et al. (1984)	Adherence with diabetes regimen	Adherence behavior	Significant negative correlations w/ changes in three categories of adherence to diabetic regimen

Source: Heitzmann and Kaplan, 1988.

measure the scale was validated against, and the remaining columns describe the nature of the criterion measure and the association. In the Heitzmann and Kaplan review, 11 of 23 measures were validated against some external criterion. In 3 of the studies, measures were validated against other social support measures. In another 3, they were validated against symptom checklists. In 3 studies, the measures were validated against personality tests. One study validated the social support scales against clinical judgments, and in one case social support was validated against self-reported measures of behaviors.

Inspection of Table 7-1 suggests that social support measures have rarely been validated against widely accepted measures of health status. Most often, when validity data are presented, mental health measures are used as the outcome. For example, McFarlane and co-workers (1981) validated their social relationship scale against clinical judgments. Henderson and associates (1980) found modest correlations between their interview schedule

for social interaction and the Eysenck Personality Inventory. Sarason and colleagues (1983) found substantial correlations between their social support questionnaire and the Multiple Affect Adjective Checklist. Some of the studies used psychiatric symptoms as validity criteria (Cohen et al., 1985; Lin et al., 1979; Procidano & Heller, 1983). A few studies have used adherence behaviors as an outcome (Schafer et al., 1986).

As Table 7-1 suggests, the "health" variables have been inconsistent across studies of social support and health. In order to clearly understand the relationship between social support and health, it is always important to consider how both support and health are defined and measured.

An example of a commonly used social support measure is shown in Table 7-2. The table displays the Social Support Questionnaire (SSQ). This measure allows the user to determine both the size of the social support network and the perceived quality of the relationships (Sarason, Sarason, & Pierce, 1990).

TABLE 7·2

SOCIAL SUPPORT QUESTIONNAIRE (SSQ)

NAME: _____

STUDENT NUMBER: _____

AGE: _____ SEX: _____ DATE: _____

CLASS IN SCHOOL: Freshman   Sophomore   Junior   Senior   Graduate

Instructions:

The following questions ask about people in your environment who provide you with help or support. Each question has two parts. For the first part, list all the people you know, excluding yourself, whom you can count on for help or support in the manner described. Give the person's initials and their relationship to you (see example). *Do not list more than one person next to each of the letters beneath the question.*

For the second part, circle how *satisfied* you are with the overall support you have.

If you have no support for a question, check the words "No one," but still rate your level of satisfaction. Do not list more than nine persons per question.

Please answer all questions as best you can. All your responses will be kept confidential.

T A B L E   7 · 2 (continued)

EXAMPLE

Ex. Who do you know whom you can trust with information that could get you in trouble?

No one | 1) T.N. (brother) | 4) T.N. (father) | 7)
| 2) L.M. (friend) | 5) L.M. (employer) | 8)
| 3) R.S. (friend) | 6) | 9)

How Satisfied?

6-very satisfied	5-faily satisfied	4-a little satisfied	3-a little dissatisfied	2-fairly dissatisfied	1-very dissatisfied

1. Whom can you really count on to be dependable when you need help?

No one | 1) | 4) | 7)
| 2) | 5) | 8)
| 3) | 6) | 9)

2. How Satisfied?

6-very satisfied	5-fairly satisfied	4-a little satisfied	3-a little dissatisfied	2-fairly dissatisfied	1-very dissatisfied

3. Whom can you really count on to help you feel more relaxed when you are under pressure or tense?

No one | 1) | 4) | 7)
| 2) | 5) | 8)
| 3) | 6) | 9)

4. How Satisfied?

6-very satisfied	5-fairly satisfied	4-a little satisfied	3-a little dissatisfied	2-fairly dissatisfied	1-very dissatisfied

5. Who accepts you totally, including both your worst and your best points?

No one | 1) | 4) | 7)
| 2) | 5) | 8)
| 3) | 6) | 9)

6. How Satisfied?

6-very satisfied	5-fairly satisfied	4-a little satisfied	3-a little dissatisfied	2-fairly dissatisfied	1-very dissatisfied

7. Whom can you really count on to care about you, regardless of what is happening to you?

No one | 1) | 4) | 7)
| 2) | 5) | 8)
| 3) | 6) | 9)

8. How Satisfied?

6-very satisfied	5-fairly satisfied	4-a little satisfied	3-a little dissatisfied	2-fairly dissatisfied	1-very dissatisfied

9. Whom can you really count on to help you feel better when you are feeling generally down-in-the-dumps?

No one | 1) | 4) | 7)
| 2) | 5) | 8)
| 3) | 6) | 9)

(continued)

TABLE 7-2 (continued)					

10. How Satisfied?

6-very satisfied	5-fairly satisfied	4-a little satisfied	3-a little dissatisfied	2-fairly dissatisfied	1-very dissatisfied

11. Whom can you count on to console you when you are very upset?

No one
1)	4)	7)
2)	5)	8)
3)	6)	9)

12. How Satisfied?

6-very satisfied	5-fairly satisfied	4-a little satisfied	3-a little dissatisfied	2-fairly dissatisfied	1-very dissatisfied

Source: Reproduced courtesy of Irwin G. Sarason.

HOW CAN SOCIAL RELATIONSHIPS IMPACT UPON HEALTH OUTCOMES?

Health is a much broader concept than mortality, or absence thereof, as observed in epidemiological studies. The World Health Organization defines health as a complete state of physical, social, and mental well-being. This includes absence of a disability, freedom from symptoms, and a general state of wellness. A wide variety of studies identify a relationship between social support, coping, and physical disability (Wallston et al., 1983). For example, family, friends, and other social contacts can ease the emotional stress resulting from injuries incurred in automobile accidents (Porrit, 1979). Burn victims experience higher self-esteem and general life satisfaction if they have support from friends and family (Davidson, Bowden, & Tholen, 1979). For patients with kidney disease, those with support from spouses and cohesive families experience higher morale and fewer changes in social functioning during hemodialysis than those with less support (Dimond, 1979). Finlayson (1976) has reported that males experience better outcomes following heart attacks if they have support from their spouses. Box 7-2 gives an example of how social support may be related to increased survival for women with

BOX 7-2

FOCUS ON WOMEN

Breast cancer is one of the leading causes of death for women (see Chapter 11). Although there are many studies evaluating the effects of medical treatment upon victims of breast cancer, the determinants of survival are not clearly understood. Social support may be an important predictor of outcome for these women. One study evaluated 133 women after they had received the diagnosis of breast cancer. Shortly after diagnosis, data on the treatment were obtained from medical records, and information about the women's social support network was assessed using questionnaires. As expected, the stage of the disease was a significant predictor of survival. Those women with more advanced disease were less likely to survive. In addition, the number of supportive persons in the woman's life was also a significant predictor. The variables that were associated with longer survival included the number of supportive persons the woman associated with, whether or not the woman worked, and whether she was married. In addition, the extent of contact with friends and the size of the network were important predictors. Women who had more and deeper friendships and those who worked outside the home tended to survive the cancer for a longer period of time. Newer research is beginning to study this phenomenon in more detail. In particular, investigators want to figure out what it is about friendships that helps people survive a serious disease like breast cancer (Waxler-Morrison, Hislop, Mears, & Can, 1991).

breast cancer. Without reviewing the literature in detail, suffice it to say that a wide variety of studies suggest a social support–health outcome connection. Yet, less well described are the complex relationships between adaptations to chronic illness, self-care, and the social environment. In the following sections, we will explore some of these issues in relation to specific chronic illnesses.

Causal Modeling

The relationship between social support and mortality is indeed impressive. However, the relationships are primarily correlational. There are at least three rival explanations for the association between the presence of social relationships and health. First, there is the assumed explanation that the correlation between social support and disease is causal: high support protects against illness. The second explanation is that individuals who are sick drive away their social support system. This suggests that early illness causes changes in social support. A third explanation is that a third variable such as social class, personality, and so on, causes both poor social support and poor health outcomes. We will review the latter two alternatives first and then return to the theme that social support protects against disease.

Illness Causes Disruption in Social Support

Illness can cause modifications in the support environment. Asthma, cancer, and other diseases are common reasons for alterations in family interactions. For example, heart patients may be victimized by family members and friends. These potential supporters may feel uncomfortable interacting with someone who is impaired (Wortman & Dunkel-Schetter, 1979). Disturbance in marital relationships often follows diagnosis and treatment of serious conditions such as heart disease. Spouses may be overly concerned, or the family may shy away from emotional involvement with someone who is not likely to survive. Although it is possible that illness causes low social support, we will present evidence that the more likely direction of causation is that low support causes illness.

Third Variable Explanations

An alternative explanation for the association between social relationships and mortality from heart disease involves third variables, of which a variety have been postulated. For example, poverty and social class are remarkably strong predictors of death from coronary heart disease (Kaplan, 1985). Individuals of lower socioeconomic status may be subjected to demanding and unrewarding work situations in which they have little control over their environment. These situations have been postulated as predictive of illnesses such as coronary heart disease (Karasek, Baker, Marxer, Ahlbom, & Theorell, 1981). In addition, evidence suggests that low-income families are exposed to greater levels of environmental insult. For instance, National Center for Health Statistics data reveal a relationship between blood lead levels and family income, race, and degree of urbanization (Mahaffey, Annest, Roberts, & Murphy, 1982). Living in these difficult circumstances may cause disruptions in social support and may independently cause heart disease.

A related third variable explanation is that those with better social support also have healthier lifestyles. The Alameda County Study identified a variety of health practices as predictive of coronary heart disease mortality (Bellock & Breslow, 1972). It is possible that those with poor health habits have difficulty obtaining social support, and these health habits independently predict mortality.

Finally, Type A behavior (see Chapter 18) has been postulated as a third variable that may explain the association between social relationships and health outcomes. Individuals with Type A personalities are difficult to get along with. They are temperamental, reactive, and impatient. Since Type A personality is believed to independently predict heart disease, it seems plausible that a difficult personality could cause both poor social interaction and risk for mortality.

Some evidence refutes each of these third variable explanations. Although the literature on kin relationships and socioeconomic status is a rich one (Stack, 1984), there is not convincing evidence that low socioeconomic status individuals have poorer social support than high socioeconomic status individuals. In both the Evans County and the Tecumseh, Michigan, studies, low-income black participants were well integrated into stable rural communities. Social support scores for these groups tended to be very high despite their elevated risk for coronary heart disease (House, Robbins, & Metzner, 1982; Schoenbach, Kaplan, Fredman, & Kleinbaum, 1986). Furthermore, studies that make statistical corrections for socioeconomic status suggest that the gradient of association between close relationships and mortality exists even when socioeconomic status is statistically controlled.

Similar data have been presented for the effects of health habits. Virtually all of the studies described above had statistical controls for smoking, dietary fat, obesity, etc. The Alameda County Study (Bellock & Breslow, 1972) systematically controlled for health habits, and yet still found the association between personal relationships and mortality. Type A behavior seems an unlikely third variable at this point. For many years, Type A behavior was believed to be a significant risk factor for coronary heart disease. The behavioral medicine literature began focusing on correlates of the Type A behavior pattern and ignoring a rising tide of evidence that Type A behavior was not related to mortality. The Multiple Risk Factors Intervention Trial (MRFIT) failed to show any association between Type A behavior pattern and mortality. Most recently, Ragland and Brand (1988) found that individuals with Type A personalities actually had a better chance of surviving a myocardial infarction than members of the cohort who were Type B's.

Third variable explanations cannot be ruled out. Indeed, we have considered only a few of the many potential third variables that could explain the association between personal relationships and mortality. However, we find little current evidence to support the third variable explanations most commonly postulated in the literature. Since this is not an area of experimental investigation, it is difficult, if not impossible, to rule out third variable explanations.

Low Social Support Causes Mortality

Upon review, we suggest that there is a causal relationship between social support and mortality. Epidemiologists do not often use experimental data, so these studies rarely establish causal relationships in a definitive manner. Instead, they use a variety of criteria to estimate the plausibility of causal interpretation. These criteria include temporality, strength of association, consistency, gradient, and biological plausibility.

Temporality Temporality occurs when the suspected cause precedes the outcome. In studies that prospectively evaluate the relationship, the measurement of social support occurred prior to the coronary heart disease event. Particularly in the case of mortality, it is impossible for the outcome to precede the measurement of social relationships.

Strength The strength of association (or correlation) between social support and outcomes varies from study to study. For example, some studies show that those with poor social support have significantly shorter life expectancies than those with more people in their social network, while other studies indicate that social support has only modest impacts upon health. However, the strength is typically within the range of other risk factors for heart disease or other health outcomes. The health consequences of living alone, for example, may be as predictive of early death as having moderately elevated cholesterol.

Consistency The association between social relationships and mortality is consistent across studies. The effects have been shown for urban and rural populations as well as for men and women. They have also been observed in several western cultures. However, not all studies demonstrate the effect for men and women within the same cohort (Berkman, 1986). The direction of effect has been consistent across studies. There appear to be no studies in which availability of social relationships is associated with increased mortality.

Gradient For some (but not all) biologic outcomes, there is a gradient between the exposure to the risk factor and likelihood of the outcome. For example, as the number of cigarettes smoked increases, so do the chances of death from cancer or from heart disease. There is also a systematic relationship between serum cholesterol and mortality, and a similar relationship between blood pressure and death from heart disease. In addition, there is some evidence for this type of gradient effect for social contacts. Several of the studies (Berkman & Syme, 1979; Blazer, 1982; House et al., 1982; Schoenbach et al., 1986; Welin et al., 1985) obtained a systematic relationship between number and frequency of social contacts and mortality. This relationship is not as well established for perceived quality of social support.

Biological Plausibility The argument that a risk factor causes a health outcome must include some reasonable biological explanation for the association. Although there are few studies of this problem, preliminary evidence identifies relationships between social factors and blood flow as well as activities of hormones relevant to stress. These studies have been suggested by analyses of human data and confirmed with animal models (Manuck, Kaplan, Adams, & Clarkson, 1988). Other lines of research demonstrate the impact of loneliness upon immune function (Keicolt-Glaser, Garner, Speicher, Penn, Holliday, & Glaser, 1984).

In summary, there are at least three alternative causal models to explain the relationship between social support and health outcomes. The observational nature of epidemiological data does not allow a definitive choice between the alternative explanations. However, we believe that current data support the notion that social support is protective against coronary heart disease.

THEORIES OF HOW SOCIAL SUPPORT AFFECTS HEALTH

The mechanism whereby close relationships protect against illness is not well understood. Cohen and Syme (1985) identified at least two rival explanations for this relationship. Two models, the main-effects model and the stress-buffering model, differ in their views of the importance of stress. The *stress-buffering model* assumes that stress leads to poor health outcomes and that social relationships buffer the impact of stress. The *main-effects model* assumes that social relationships influence health outcomes and stress is only one of several factors that impact upon health.

The Main-Effects Model

The main-effects model suggests that stress is not the only important variable influencing health outcomes. Instead, social relationships enhance health and well-being independently of stress. There are a variety of ways that social relationships may directly affect health outcomes. One is through support for health-promoting behaviors. Social relationships influence behaviors, and these behaviors in turn promote desirable health outcomes. Another interpretation is that social involvement provides identity and sources of positive self-evaluation. This may enhance the perception of control and mastery and reduce the experience of anxiety (Thoits, 1985). Reduction in anxiety, helplessness, and despair may result in enhanced health outcomes. For example, consider how stressful it is to stand up in front of class to give a speech. Yet with the right help from your family and friends, you can get guidance and practice that will eventually help you feel more comfortable in front of the audience. A graphic summary of the main-effects model is shown in Figure 7-1.

Considering some of the research linking social support directly to health behaviors, Kaplan and Toshima (1990) reviewed the literature on the relationship between social support and health for chronically ill adults. They found the associations between social relationships and health outcomes to be very

mixed. Some studies showed a positive benefit of social support, some showed that social relationships were associated with poorer health outcomes, and some studies were neutral. However, studies indicating a positive benefit of social support tended to use outcome measures of health behaviors, such as compliance with antihypertensive medications or compliance with a complex regimen for diabetic patients. Other studies have shown that supportive partners may help prevent relapse in smoking cessation programs or may be associated with improved outcomes in weight loss programs (Brownell, Heckerman, Westlake, Hayes, & Monit, 1978; Dubbert & Wilson, 1984). In fact, averaged over all studies in the literature, people are significantly more likely to lose weight if they participate in programs with a partner (usually a spouse) than if they participate alone (Black, Gleser, & Kooyers, 1990).

The main-effects model is a compelling explanation for the relationship between social support and health outcomes. Substantial evidence suggests that behaviors are predictive of mortality from cardiovascular disease (Kaplan & Stamler, 1983). Furthermore, health habits aggregate within families (Patterson, Kaplan, Sallis, & Nader, 1987), and it seems reasonable that health outcomes will be enhanced by any support. However, studies on the relationship between support and health behaviors have not always been consistent (Malott, Glasgow, O'Neill, & Klesges, 1984).

Studies demonstrating the relationship between support of behaviors and health habits have suggested that behaviors of the supportive person are specific rather than general. In other words, members of the support environment may reinforce specific health habits rather than being generally supportive. For example, Sallis, Grossman, Pinski, Patterson, and Nader (1987) found that specific social support items correlated with diet and exercise behaviors. However, a general measure of so-

FIGURE 7-1

Graphic summary of the main-effects model of social support.

THE MAIN EFFECTS MODEL

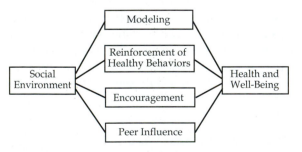

The social environment influences health outcomes through a variety of processes including modeling, reinforcement, encouragement, and peer influence.

cial support was unrelated to either the support for specific health behaviors or an enactment of those behaviors. Schafer, McCaul, and Glasgow (1986) also found that adherence to a diabetic regimen was related to specific rather than generalized aspects of social support. Box 7-3 gives an example of the relationship between social support and cigarette smoking in an African American community.

Although the main-effects model appears to be a plausible explanation for the relationship between social support and health outcomes, several lines of evidence challenge it. First, not all studies on social support and health outcomes are consistent (Kaplan & Toshima, 1990). Furthermore, the epidemiologic studies linking close relationships to mortality tend to show that the association is with social connectedness (network size) rather than satisfaction

with relationships. There is little evidence that specific emotional support for making life changes, stopping smoking, and the like, is related to outcomes.

Perhaps the most important challenge to the main-effects model is that major epidemiologic studies use statistical methods to remove the effects of other health habits. Thus, to the extent that health habits can be measured, they are controlled in the analysis. The effect of social support remains even after the habits of those in the social network are removed. In summary, the main-effects model does appear plausible, and social support may influence important health behaviors. However, there are also reasons to doubt that it will fully explain the association between close relationships and health outcomes.

The Stress-Buffering Model

Perhaps the leading model used to describe the protective effects of social support is the stress-buffering model. Proponents of this model assume that psychological stress has pathogenic effects. Cohen and Syme (1985) described two different ways the model may work. First, social support may intervene in the pathway between the stressful event and the receiver. Members of the social environment may help reinterpret the event or minimize its response by aiding in coping. The second point at which social support may effect stress is between the response to the stress and the outcome. Members of the support environment might help tranquilize the stressed individual or facilitate helpful behaviors such as medicine compliance, personal hygiene, sufficient rest, and so on.

Cohen and Syme (1985) made an important distinction between structural and functional perspectives on support. *Functionalists* consider the functions of close relationships. For example, functionalists measure whether interpersonal relationships serve certain func-

---

BOX 7·3

FOCUS ON DIVERSITY

Cigarette smoking is a major cause of cancer and other illnesses. Thus, there are extensive public health efforts directed toward the reduction of cigarette use. Nevertheless, African Americans continue to use cigarettes at high rates, and researchers hope to determine why cigarette use remains higher among African Americans than among other groups in society. One study evaluated smoking patterns in 1137 African American adults in San Francisco and Oakland, California. The study inquired about social networks and the emotional aspects of smoking, as well as the effects of stress upon cigarette use.

The study revealed that the prevalence of smoking was nearly 42 percent in these communities of African Americans. Those who reported high levels of stress in their lives were more likely to smoke than those who reported low levels of stress. For women, those with poor social networks were significantly more likely to smoke than women who had more social relationships. This relationship did not hold for men. In fact, men lacking emotional support from friends or family were actually less likely to smoke than men with more complex social networks (Romano, Bloom, & Syme, 1991).

tions, provide affection, or support specific behaviors. *Structuralists* focus on the existence of interconnections and generally measure characteristics of network size. Different researchers have tended to choose either a functional or a structural approach to their investigations. Most of the research on the buffering model is in the functionalist tradition.

There are several lines of evidence that question the buffering model as the most plausible explanation for the support-mortality relationship. One of the most important challenges is that the stress-mortality connection for heart disease is not necessarily clear. At least two different models have been proposed to suggest that stress causes death due to heart disease. One model argues that stress affects biochemical processes associated with the disease. For example, Dimsdale (1985) has argued that psychological stress can increase blood cholesterol. Cholesterol, in turn, is a well-documented risk factor for heart disease. However, not all studies support the stress-cholesterol hypothesis. Indeed, Dimsdale (1985) acknowledged that there are inconsistencies in the data. Niaura and colleagues (1988) failed to show that accountants under tremendous stress at tax time had any rise in serum lipids. Similarly, the relationship between stress and blood pressure has been variable across studies (Haynes & Matthews, 1988). The stress-buffering model is shown graphically in Figure 7-2. As the figure shows, high stress in combination with good social support does not lead to illness. The pathway to illness is through the combination of high stress and low support.

Another argument favoring a stress–heart disease relationship is centered on the stress-prone Type A personality. The Type A personality describes a hard-driving, impatient person who may be prone to heart disease (see Chapter 18). The original evidence for the relationship between Type A behavior and heart

THE STRESS BUFFERING MODEL

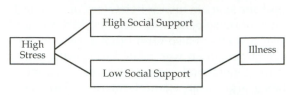

The essential components for stress to cause illness are high stress and low social support. When there is high stress and high social support, the impact of stress is absorbed or "buffered."

FIGURE 7-2
Graphic illustration of the stress-buffering model.

disease comes from a prospective study known as the Western Collaborative Group Study. This investigation followed 3154 healthy men for 8.5 years. Those who were categorized as Type A were almost twice as likely to have coronary artery disease in comparison with those who were classified in the more relaxed Type B pattern. This relationship existed even with controls for other risk factors (Rosenman, Brand, Jenkins, Friedman, Straus, & Wurm, 1975). The other major line of evidence for the Type A hypothesis came from coronary angiography studies. At least three different groups found that those with Type A personalities had more occlusions of their arteries (Blumenthal, Williams, Kong, Shanberg, & Thompson, 1978; Frank, Heller, Kornfeld, Sporn, & Weiss, 1978).

Unfortunately, the Type A hypothesis has fallen into disfavor in recent years. A detailed review of Type A research suggested that studies published after 1977 were much less likely to find a detrimental effect of Type A behavior and that cross-sectional studies are more likely to find the effect than prospective studies (Booth-Kewley & Friedman, 1987). Perhaps the most damaging data were published in a recent study suggesting that those with Type A personality patterns were more likely to survive a myocardial infarction than those with Type B pattern (Ragland & Brand, 1988). Interestingly, this analysis used the same data set that was previously analyzed to support the Type A hypothesis. As Dimsdale (1988) suggested, "This is a topsy-turvy career for a risk factor" (p. 110).

The Type A studies bring into question the real role of stress as a predictor of coronary heart disease. Indeed, the stress-mortality hypothesis is not consistently documented in the literature. If stress does not serve as the major variable causing mortality, then the buffering hypothesis is difficult to embrace. A newer study of Swedish men provides a different slant on the complex relationships between Type A personality, support, and death from heart disease. In this 10-year prospective study Type A men were no more likely to die than Type B men. However, there was a significant relationship between social support and death only for the Type A participants. Previous studies had shown that Type A men do reduce their risks of dying when they participate in Type A modification programs. One explanation for this benefit is that the programs improve support (Orth-Gomer & Unden, 1990).

Most epidemiologic studies supporting the social support–mortality relationship have not been designed to test the buffering hypothesis. Indeed, buffering has not consistently been supported when attempts have been made to evaluate it (Reed et al,. 1983).

We do not wish to suggest that both the main-effects and stress-buffering explanations can be ruled out. However, we do believe more complex models may be required to explain the data. One such approach is a modified main-effects model that considers the functional effects of social environment. The social environment may have either positive or negative effects upon health behavior (Kaplan & Toshima, 1990). However, we would expect that close, caring relationships would play a stronger role in reinforcing health behavior and in enhancing use of the health care system. At the other extreme, social isolation

might contribute to disconnection with services, poor nutrition, and inadequate response to emergencies. The available data may allow comparisons between isolation and nonisolation. Newer, richer data sets will be required to separate positive from negative influences for those with some social network.

IS SOCIAL SUPPORT IMPORTANT RELATIVE TO OTHER RISK FACTORS?

It is not likely that either the main-effects or the stress-buffering model will be found to be correct for all circumstances. In fact, there is support for each of them in some studies. In addition, there are a variety of other studies that simply show interesting relationships between both the positive and the negative effects of social support. Kaplan and Toshima (1990) emphasize main effects. However, they focus more specifically on the impact of social environment upon health and refer to this as a *functional-effects model*, which is more specific than the descriptions of main effects (Cohen & Wills, 1985; Thoits, 1985).

Although social support may be a risk factor, we still must ask whether it is as important as other risk factors such as diet or cigarette smoking. This issue has been best studied in relation to heart disease. Table 7-3 summarizes the strength of association across the various studies considering social support. Table 7-4 presents risk ratios across studies of traditional risk factors. As the table suggests, low social support is a risk factor, and the strength of this risk factor is comparable to most other established risk factors.

Given the emerging evidence that social support is a risk factor for health outcomes and cardiovascular disease in particular, it is unfortunate that relatively few researchers have systematically investigated this relationship. Intervention at this level may prove to be as profitable as existing preventive measures aimed at dietary modification or stress reduc-

TABLE 7·3

STRENGTH OF ASSOCIATION ACROSS STUDIES

Study	N	SS measure	Finding
Alameda County*†‡	6928	Marital status/satisfaction Contacts w/ family/friends. Church attendance. Social affiliations.	↑ SS associated with ↑ longevity. Males with ↑ SS 2.3x and females with ↑ ↑ SS 2.8x more likely to survive nine years.
Tecumseh Study*†‡	2754	Marital status. # of visits w/ family/friends. # of pleasurable activities. Church attendance. Voluntary organizations. Leisure activities.	↑ SS associated with marital status, voluntary rates in activities predicted survival rates in males. For females, only church attendance significantly associated with survival.
Durham County†‡	331	Marital status. # of living children. # of siblings. Frequency of interaction. Perception of support.	↑ SS associated with ↓ mortality risk over a 30-month period. Those who perceived their environment to be adequate were 3.4x as likely to survive 30 months.
Evans County*‡	2059	Marital status. # of relative families nearby. # of relative families seen often. # of close friends. # of close neighbors. Church attendance. Spare time in church activities.	Social network variable was modestly predictive of survival. This effect was most pronounced among white males. The social network effect for white females, black males, and black females was not significant.
Japanese-American Men in San Francisco*†‡	3809	Marital status. Church attendance. Membership in organizations.	↑ SS associated with ↑ survival rates. Those with ↑ SS 1.94x more likely to survive.
Japanese-American Men in Hawaii*†‡	7639	Proximity of parents and in-laws. Marital status. # of children. # in household Social activities. Church attendance. Social organizations. Discuss problems with coworkers.	Examined incidence and prevalence data. Closer social relationships correlated with angina pectoris. Those men reporting more intimate social contacts were 1.5 times more likely to suffer from a non-fatal myocardial infarction.
Framingham Study*†	142	Non-supportive boss.	Only female clerical workers were studied. ↓ SS (non-supportive bosses) associated with ↑ cardiovascular disease.

TABLE 7-3 (continued)

STRENGTH OF ASSOCIATION ACROSS STUDIES

Study	N	SS measure	Finding
Israeli Ischemic Study*†	10,000	Family difficulties. Wife's love and support.	Only male civil service workers were studied. Males with ↓ SS from wives 1.8x more likely to have angina pectoris in anxiety provoking situations. Family difficulties were an important predictor of angina pectoris.
Gothenburg Study*†	989	Marital status. # of persons in home. Social activities.	Studied males only. ↑ SS was associated with ↓ mortality.
Swedish National Mortality Registry Study*	17,433	# in social network.	The risk ratio for being in the lower tertile as compared to the upper two tertiles was 1.34. This was a significant correlate of mortality.
Beta Blocker Heart Attack Trial*	2323	Communication with family and relatives. Social relatedness. Occurrence of life crises. Reaction to life crises.	Studied male MI survivors. ↑ stress and ↑ social isolation associated with 4 to 5 times the increased risk of death over a 3-year period.

Source: Atkins, C.J., et al., "The Epidemiology of Cardiovascular Disease," in Jones and Perlman, *Advances in Personal Relationships.*

* *Adjusted for age, SES, cigarette smoking, health status, body mass, physical activity.*

† *Adjusted for physical helath indices (serum cholesterol, serum glucose, blood pressure), alcohol consumption.*

‡ *Adjusted for other factors (e.g., family history, life satisfaction, use of preventive services, stressful life events, anxiety, race, symptoms of major depressive disorder, occupation, employment status).*

tion. The risk ratios for traditional coronary heart disease risk factors are rarely over 3.0. (See Chapter 2 for a discussion of the meaning of risk ratios). A ratio of 3.0 suggests that those with the risk factor have about 3 times greater risk of dying than those without the risk factor. Indeed, cigarette smoking, the largest controllable risk for coronary heart disease, nearly always has a mortality ratio less than 2.0. In other words, smokers are about twice as likely to die of heart disease than nonsmokers over periods of about 10 years. In comparison with other risk factors, the strength of association for mortality among the socially isolated is at least as much as it is for those who have other risk factors.

It is interesting to consider the strength of association for social support in relation to variables that the public perceives as major risks for coronary heart disease. For example, there is a strong relationship between serum cholesterol and mortality, although the relationship between diet and serum cholesterol has been difficult to demonstrate (Stallones, 1983). Because of these findings, sources ranging from the American Heart Association to the popular media consistently advise adults to lower their dietary intake of cholesterol in order to avoid death by heart disease. Stallones (1983) points out that the risk ratio for comparing those who eat high levels of dietary cholesterol with those who eat low levels is very near 1.0. In contrast,

TABLE 7-4

RELATIVE RISK RATIOS OF COMMON RISK FACTORS FOR CARDIOVASCULAR DISEASE

Risk Factor	Definition	Ratio	Reference
Cigarette smoking	None vs. 1.5–24/day	1.58	Doll & Peto, 1976
	None vs. 20/day	1.70	Pooling Project, 1978
	None vs. 1.5–24/day	2.20	Doll et al. 1980
	Never vs. 1 ever	1.90	Wingard, 1982
LDL cholesterol	Increase of 20 mg/dl	1.07	MRFIF, (UC group), 1986
	Increase of 20 mg/dl	1.13	MRFIF, (SI group), 1986
	Lowest vs. highest quintile	1.29	MRFIF, (UC group), 1986
	Lowest vs. highest quintile	1.51	MRFIF, (SI group), 1986
HDL cholesterol	Increase in 5 mg/dl	1.00	MRFIF, (UC group), 1986
	Increase in 5 mg/dl	0.97	MRFIF, (SI group), 1986
	Lowest vs. highest quintile	0.98	MRFIF, (UC group), 1986
	Lowest vs. highest quintile	0.84	MRFIF, (SI group), 1986
Body mass index	Increase in 5 kg/m^2	1.14	MRFIF, (UC group), 1986
	Increase in 5 kg/m^2	1.02	MRFIF, (SI group), 1986
	Lowest vs. highest quintile	1.09	MRFIF, (UC group), 1986
	Lowest vs. highest quintile	1.18	MRFIF, (SI group), 1986
	Under (9.9%) vs. over (29.9%)	1.20	Wingard et al., 1982
Alcohol consumption	None vs. 1 drink/day	1.00	Dyer et al., 1980
	None vs. 2–3 drinks/day	0.90	Dyer et al., 1980
	None vs. 4–5 drinks/day	0.70	Dyer et al., 1980
	None vs. 6+ drinks/day	2.00	Dyer et al., 1980
	None vs. 0–29 oz./month	1.00	Stason et al., 1976
	None vs. 30+ oz./month	0.70	Stason et al., 1976
	High (>45 drinks) vs. low	1.50	Wingard, 1982
Physical activity	Inactive vs. active	1.40	Wingard, 1982
Contacts with friends	Few vs. many	1.70	Wingard, 1982

Source: Atkins, C.J., et al., "The Epidemiology of Cardiovascular Disease," in Jones and Perlman, *Advances in Personal Relationships.*

the studies on social relationships consistently show risk ratios above 2.0. Despite these findings, popular discussions of risk factors for heart disease rarely, if ever, mention social support.

SOCIAL SUPPORT IN CHRONIC ILLNESS

The chronically ill may have a greater than average need for various forms of social support. For example, a person who is no longer able to meet certain responsibilities within the home may need more help from caregivers and housekeepers. Although the chronically ill may experience needs for many kinds of social support, they may encounter difficulties obtaining adequate support. Chronic illnesses may produce feelings of alienation and estrangement from family members and friends. Frequently, misconceptions about the infectious nature of a condition can reduce the amount of available support. For example, diseases such as AIDS may discourage contact with others. In the following sections, we will review the impact of social relationships on a variety of health outcomes. This section will focus more on main or functional effects of social relationships, since Chapter 6 on stress discussed some of the stress-buffering findings.

Asthma

Asthma is the leading cause of activity limitation and disability for children (Newacheck, Halfon, & Budetti, 1986). According to 1982 data, asthma accounted for 190,000 hospitalizations for children under the age of 15, with an average length of stay of 3.9 days (Cropp, 1985). It has been estimated that asthma is the major cause of time lost from school due to a chronic illness. Asthmatic children account for between 20 and 25 percent of all school days lost because of a chronic condition (Evans, et al., 1990).

The role of the family in asthma has been a topic of considerable speculation. For many years, psychiatrists and pediatricians were misled by early psychoanalytic interpretations of the asthma syndrome. For example, French and Alexander (1941) believed that asthma represented the incompatible conflict between maternal attachment and sexual genital wishes. Furthermore, they suggested that asthmatic wheezing was the suppressed cry and solicitation of the mother. Although there is no systematic evidence supporting the psychoanalytic models, these ideas had a substantial impact upon pediatricians for many years (Creer, 1982; Renne & Creer, 1985).

Negative Functional Effects   Several psychoanalysts have suggested that maternal-child relationships are atypical when the child is asthmatic. Sandler (1965) went so far as to suggest that mothers of asthmatic children remove love in order to maintain discipline. However, systematic studies evaluating the relationship between asthmatic children and their parents have consistently failed to show any atypical relationship between asthmatic children and their mothers (Gauthier et al.,

1978). Some residential treatment programs for asthmatic children are based on the belief that parental overconcern is bad for asthmatic children. In other words, they ascribed poor outcomes to negative functional effects. More than 60 years ago, Peshkin (1930) stimulated residential treatment programs by presenting some evidence from a self-selected group of 41 children with severe asthma. He argued that 23 of the 25 children who were separated from their parents experienced improvements, while no improvement was observed in 16 children who remained with their parents. Peshkin went so far as to advocate "parentectomy," the planned separation of child from parent, as a treatment for asthma.

Unfortunately, the data did not clearly support parental separation as the best treatment for asthma. There was some evidence that separated children were well behaved in residential treatment centers. However, over the course of years, behavioral problems within the centers became more common (Creer, Ipacs, & Creer, 1983). Renne and Creer (1985) argued that some patients in early residential treatment centers were from first generation Jewish families and may have used asthmatic symptoms to manipulate their parents. However, the benefits of parental separation were not clear. In one systematic study, Purcell and colleagues (1969) separated parents and children for 2 weeks. The results suggested that separation helped children with emotional precipitants for asthmatic problems but had little effect on children with no emotional precipitants. Even for those who benefited, the strength of the effect was relatively weak.

Positive Functional Effects   Improvements in behavioral observation techniques have facilitated our understanding of families with asthmatic children. Recent studies have suggested that some families overattend to the asthmatic child while giving less attention to other family members (Creer & Leung, 1982). These observation systems often lead to systematic interventions that help not only the asthmatic child but other siblings as well.

The benefits of family therapy have received some support in recent years (Lask & Matthew, 1979; Liebman et al., 1974). In the families of children with severe asthma, studies have uncovered dysfunctional family relations (Liebman et al., 1976). The goal of family therapy is to improve family function, such that the parents, the asthmatic child, and siblings are better able to manage symptoms at home, reduce exposure to precipitous factors, and positively impact the physiological manifestations of the disease. In a controlled study of 20 severe, chronic asthmatics, ages 6 to 15, Gustafsson and coworkers (1986) demonstrated that family therapy which consisted of psychological and educational components produced functional improvements in the children when comparison with a group that did not receive family therapy. Over a $3\frac{1}{2}$-year period, improvements were evaluated by the percent of predicted peak expiratory flow (a measure of pulmonary function), compliance to medications, and a general pediatric assessment, as well as significant reductions in beta-2 agonist and steroid usage and functionally impaired days (e.g., staying home from school and restrictions in activities). There were also reductions in hospitalizations and emergency room visits, but these findings were not statistically significant. Although the sample size was small, family therapy seems to improve severe bronchial asthma in children. The findings support the notion that overinvolved parents are actually "harmful" to the asthmatic child. Through education involving instruction techniques and breathing exercises, as well as an understanding of the role asthmatic symptoms play in the family system, the support network was modified, and the result was a positive influence on the disease state.

In summary, family influences upon asthma in children have been the source of study and speculation for over 60 years. The findings suggest that the family unit, a child's primary source of social support, significantly impacts the asthmatic child. The most common belief is that parents harm asthmatic children and may even provoke asthmatic symptomatology through overprotection and overconcern. These findings would support the negative functional-effects model. It is interesting that there are very few studies on the positive role of social support for children with asthma. Supportive families may be important in promoting health behaviors and medication compliance. The Gustafsson study suggests that the negative family influence can be modified to a more positive one through therapy. Future work should investigate the benefits as well as the consequences of parental involvement with asthmatic children.

Coronary Heart Disease

Heart disease remains the major cause of death and disability in the western world (see Chapter 10). There are many types of heart disease, and adaptations to differing manifestations of disease may require different coping skills. Two common types of heart disease, myocardial infarction (MI) and cardiac arrest, have an abrupt onset and typically require hospitalization. Patients who have ongoing heart disease may require one of two types of traumatic intervention: (1) coronary artery bypass surgery, a procedure that involves the revascularization of the coronary arteries; and (2) coronary angioplasty, which involves the dilation of coronary arteries. Other patients have serious heart disease which is manifested through symptomatic angina pectoris. This typically involves severe chest pain and may require hospitalization if it becomes frequent, severe, or unstable. In general, heart procedures are stressful and often require a period of adaptation and rehabilitation followed by other lifestyle changes.

Although patients are commonly hospitalized for heart disease, a critical period occurs after hospital discharge. A coronary event often creates considerable fear and anxiety. When released from the hospital to the home, the families may not be fully equipped to cope with the uncertainties and stresses of these conditions. It has been suggested that supportive environments will enhance health outcomes following a cardiac event (Davidson & Shumaker, 1987).

Negative Functional Effects Several studies have provided support for the negative functional-effects model, which suggests that the involvement of supportive, but overconcerned, family members may lead to poorer health outcomes. In one study, congestive heart failure patients who were not working, 3, 6, or 9 months posthospitalization were reported to have more overprotective families than those patients who resumed working during the same time period (Lewis, 1966). Garrity (1973) studied first-time MI patients and found that the more concerned the patient's family was, the fewer hours the patient worked at a job, independent of the severity of the heart attack. These findings suggest that the patients' families, though concerned, are interfering with the recovery. Furthermore, the actions of family members may actually be harming the patient by not allowing him or her to exercise and strengthen the heart muscle/tissue. Presumably the family members are supportive and want to see recovery. However, their personal beliefs about the frailty of the patient may lead to the reinforcement of sedentary behaviors.

Positive Functional Effects Positive social influences have also been documented. Significant others in the support environment may encourage adherence to the medical regimen and the adoption of appropriate health behaviors. A related positive functional-effect is through modeling. Members of the support environment may model appropriate coping skills as well as health behaviors (Pearlin & Aneshensel, 1986). Thus, if a network member makes these changes at the same time, outcomes may be enhanced through mutual encouragement, mutual modeling, and a reduction in the perceived difficulty of making the changes. Another mechanism accounting for the benefits of social support is the stress-buffering channel. Adaptation may be facilitated by having network members absorb some of the stress.

Some studies have confirmed the positive functional effects of a social support network. An intervention study with hypertensive patients (Caplan et al., 1976) found that lectures alone did little to help patients achieve controlled blood pressure (see Box 7-4 for two examples of positive effects of social support). However, lectures in conjunction with social support and encouragement were significantly more effective. Social support has also been found to aid in the maintenance of desirable health behaviors, such as weight loss, in patients who have had heart attacks (Finnegan & Suler, 1984). In addition, dropout rates from coronary heart disease (CHD) rehabilitation and intervention programs were also shown to be correlated with the amount of perceived social support in female hypertensive patients (Williams et al., 1985). Thus, perceived social support may present or reduce attrition in such programs.

Miller and associates (1985) examined specific prescriptive factors (diet, medication, exercise, smoking cessation, and other lifestyle changes) leading to optimal health functioning in patients who had experienced a heart attack. They found that adherence to medical regimens after recovery from an initial attack is generally low, but varies according to the prescription component. Those behaviors requiring minimal lifestyle changes, such as taking medication, were more readily adopted. Conversely, there was poorer compliance with prescriptions involving more intense lifestyle alterations, such as changing dietary patterns or participating in a regular exercise program. Of particular interest was the finding that attitudes and perceived beliefs of significant others toward the prescriptive components were strong correlates of actual regimen adherence. These findings parallel those found in the diabetes compliance literature.

There is also some evidence for the buffering model, suggesting a link between social isolation and mortality in the CHD patient. Ruberman and colleagues (1984) reported that mortality from myocardial infarction was associated with social isolation and high levels of stress. In fact, these two factors increased the risk of mortality more than 4 times in males who had had a heart attack.

In summary, social support has been suggested as an important variable in adaptation to cardiovascular disease (Davidson & Shumaker, 1987). Several mechanisms have been proposed to account for the effects of social support networks on health outcomes. Of these mechanisms, the stress-buffering model and the "positive" functional-effects model have received considerable attention in the research literature. However, to date, few empirical studies have addressed the contribution of overconcerned spouses and family members in the reinforcement of maladaptive or inappropriate behaviors that ultimately lead to decreased health outcomes.

Back Pain

Nearly 80 percent of all Americans experience disabling back pain at some point in their life (see Chapter 9). Back pain affects all social classes, men, and women, and is common in both industrialized and developing nations. Disability associated with back pain affects nearly every family in the country (Nachenson, 1976; National Center for Health Statistics, 1977). Back disorders are the most com-

---

BOX 7·4

FOCUS ON RESEARCH

Can Solitude Be Hazardous to Your Health?

The 1990 census revealed several interesting new trends. One of them was that 12 percent of all American adults, or nearly 22.6 million people, live alone. This is an increase of 7 percent, or nearly 10.8 million adults, since 1970. The negative and positive effects of this trend toward living alone have been debated. On the one hand, quiet and independence might lead to more relaxation and less stress. On the other hand, there appear to be significant health benefits associated with the availability of supportive relationships.

Several recent studies have emphasized this point. In one study of 1234 heart attack patients living alone nearly twice were as likely as others to suffer a second heart attack. Furthermore, patients living alone were significantly more likely to die within 6 months. The effects of living alone were comparable to other risk factors for heart attack, including previous damage to the heart muscle and disturbance in heart rhythm. In other words, living alone is a warning sign for future problems, just as is damage to the heart muscle.

One of the interesting findings in the study was that divorce or death of a spouse was not a significant predictor of second heart attacks or death. Among those who had been divorced or widowed, more than half were living with someone else at the time of the study (Case et al., 1992).

In a related study of 1368 male and female heart patients, the combination of insufficient social contact and low income was a very strong predictor of death from heart disease. One significant factor was income. Patients with an annual income of less than $10,000 were significantly more likely to succumb to heart disease than those with incomes greater than $40,000. In addition, however, being socially isolated made the impact of low income more severe Williams et al., 1992).

With the consistency of these findings, the debate now becomes focused on the reasons for a relationship between social isolation and death from heart disease. There are at least two explanations for these findings. The first explanation is that the availability of a support person makes it more likely that patients will follow medical advice. For example, they may be more likely to take medications, stay with their diet, or stop smoking. The other explanation is that the availability of other people helps mitigate the impact of stress upon everyday living (see text).

mon cause of disability for people under the age of 45 (National Center for Health Statistics, 1977). The impact of low back pain on the economy is remarkable. Nearly $14 billion is spent annually on the treatment of back pain, and $9 billion is spent on compensation to the afflicted (Akeson & Murphy, 1977). In some industries, the incidence of low back pain is about 50 per 1000 workers per year, and heavy industries lose about 1400 workdays per 1000 workers each year. Although most episodes of back pain spontaneously heal within about 2 weeks, there is an increasing incidence of chronic back pain. *Chronic pain* is defined as pain that lasts for 6 months or more.

Clinical approaches to the management of back pain emphasize different patterns of interaction between patients and their support network. Physical therapy approaches, including back schools, often emphasize reassurance from spouse and family. In contrast, behavioral approaches often require modification of the social environment. These approaches will be considered in more detail.

Negative Functional Effects According to operant approaches to pain management, individuals experiencing pain engage in pain behaviors. *Pain behaviors* might include changes in physical activity, reduction or avoidance of work, frequent use of pain medications, and communication of pain through facial expression. The operant model suggests that these natural behaviors, which are responses to acute pain, may be strengthened through reinforcement. Over the course of time, they may have reinforcing consequences, including attention from a spouse or friend, avoidance of undesirable tasks, and use of narcotic drugs.

A variety of intervention programs based on operant principles have been described in the literature. Of particular interest is the role of social support network members in the management of chronic pain. There are three basic "family" treatment approaches being used in multimodal treatment centers. The *transac-*

tional approach promotes awareness of the ways in which patients use pain for psychological gain. In this approach, the goal of therapy is to get the patient to discontinue his or her manipulative behavior. A *systems theory approach* assumes that certain types of social support network systems are organized in such a way that the patient's sick role behavior maintains the homeostatic balance. Therapy focuses on changing the structure of network organizations such that the patient no longer needs to play the sick role. Finally, in the *behavioral approach*, supportive network members are trained to praise and encourage well behavior, such as walking and exercise, while minimizing the attention directed toward pain behaviors. Although many pain programs employ methods from several different "family" treatment approaches, most programs emphasize these behavioral techniques.

Several reports suggest that these programs are efficacious (Roberts & Reinhardt, 1980). In one study, pain patients were led to believe that they were being observed by either their spouse or a ward clerk. For those with a solicitous spouse, pain was rated significantly higher when a patient believed that the spouse was observing. The treatment was designed to extinguish these responses. It has been argued that cooperation between spouses and family members is required to make this treatment work. Inpatient treatment is used when families do not cooperate; however, generalization outside the hospital may be difficult when the spouse is not an agent in the treatment (Keefe & Gill, 1986). Several follow-up studies from pain treatment programs indicate that social support involvement in treatment is essential to long-term success. In one study (Hudgens, 1979), 24 families who completed a behaviorally oriented program were assessed 6 months to 2 years following treatment. The results showed that five of the six patients who had not maintained treatment gains did not have adequate social supports at the time of follow-up.

Most studies indicate that family or supportive network members can contribute to the maintenance and treatment of pain behaviors. It appears that when family members are appropriately supportive and have learned not to reinforce pain behaviors, pain patients have a higher likelihood of long-term success. In summary, these studies demonstrate that it is possible to impact the social support network system in a way which promotes the functional relief of pain.

The pain literature provides clear support of the negative functional-effects model. In a majority of cases, it appears that the concerned, caring, supportive family member often reinforces pain behavior, by doing tasks for the patient when they grimace and moan, or by allowing the patient to remain largely sedentary. As a result, the patient is reinforced for not getting well. Thus, the chronic pain patient often remains disabled and unable to cope with the pain.

Positive Functional Effects It is interesting that coping with pain has been described as analogous to coping with stress. Some investigators believe that cognitive factors similar to those that help individuals cope with stress may be particularly helpful for coping with pain (Turk & Redy, 1986). In other words, pain is conceptualized as stress. According to these models, supportive interactions, availability of a confidant, and general warmth and acceptance may help rather than inhibit pain tolerance. To date, there have been few systematic studies that compare the efficacy of interventions contrasting supportive versus operant approaches to the management of pain. The few controlled studies evaluating the operant approach suggest that these interventions are superior to no treatment or to supportive relaxation interventions (Linton & Gotestam, 1985). As with other chronic illnesses, there is some conflict between advocates of supportive care and advocates of approaches that modify inter-

personal relationships within the support network. On the other hand, studies of patients with chronic painful conditions such as rheumatoid arthritis (see Chapter 8) demonstrate benefits of social support. For example, one study demonstrated that quality of social relationships helped explain family functioning and depression among women with rheumatoid arthritis, beyond what could be accounted for by the level of illness (Goodenow, Reisine, & Grady, 1990).

SUMMARY

The effects of social support upon various health outcomes may be complex. The availability of a support network is clearly linked to positive health outcomes in epidemiologic studies. There are many conflicts in the literature about the benefits and consequences of supportive social relationships.

How might we interpret some of the complex interactions between social support and health outcomes? Presently, few studies have addressed the role of social support for the chronically ill. Several directions for future research should be considered. (1) There is a major movement to create support groups for the physically ill. These support groups are typically directed by lay leaders. Groups are prevalent for patients ranging from cancer, to chronic lung disease, to arthritis. Systematic evaluation of the risk and the potential benefits should be undertaken. (2) There is evidence from a variety of studies that social support enhances mental health outcomes. On the other hand, family studies within chronic disease conditions often suggest that family members must be retrained to avoid overconcern and the reinforcement of sick-role behaviors. Little research has attempted to separate the benefits versus risks of unconditional love and concern from family members. (3) Many current interventions imply that we understand the impact of family interactions upon health behaviors. At present, however, there are few systematic studies, such as those on asthma reported by Creer and associates, documenting the relationship between interaction patterns, health behaviors, and health outcomes.

How might we synthesize the results of these studies? First, we must carefully evaluate the role of caring and concern. According to the stress-buffering model, genuine family concern may help chronically ill patients cope with difficult illnesses. On the other hand, evidence supporting the negative functional-effects model suggests that caring and concern might reinforce behaviors that are not compatible with optimum functioning. The positive functional-effects model emphasizes that caring family members may have a positive effect, but only if they reinforce appropriate health behaviors. To date, very few studies have attempted to separate these functions.

The results of these studies should not be interpreted negatively with regard to intervention. Indeed, several studies have suggested that social support interventions may actually enhance health outcomes. Functional-effects models suggest that successful interventions are those that turn negative social influences into positive ones. In cases where family members reinforce sick-role behaviors, behavioral interventions might result in supportive interactions that ultimately improve the patient's functioning (Roberts & Reinhardt, 1980).

KEY TERMS

Social support. The effect of social relationships upon health outcomes. Social support is defined either by the number of social contacts or by the satisfaction with social relationships.

Social Support Questionnaire. A commonly used measure of social support that quantifies both size of social network and perceived quality of social relationships.

Third variable explanation. In relation to social support, the theory that observed associations between social relationships and health outcomes are caused by a third variable, such as social class or personality.

Temporality. In determining causal relationships, temporality requires that the measure (in this case, a social support) be taken before the undesirable health outcome develops.

Consistency. The requirement that the association between social relationships and outcomes be consistent over time and studies.

Gradient. The requirement that greater levels of the predictor variable (that is, social support) be related to better levels of health status.

Biological plausibility. The requirement that relationships between social support and outcomes make sense according to biological theories.

Main-effects model. The theory that social support directly affects health outcomes.

Stress-buffering model. The theory that social support absorbs the impact of stress. This theory predicts that the relationship between social support and health outcome should occur only for those under high levels of stress.

Functional effects. The impact of social support upon health outcomes can be either negative or positive. Negative effects suggest that members of the social environment detour positive health behaviors, while positive functional effects suggest that social contacts reinforce positive health behaviors.

Chronic Illnesses

CHAPTER 8

Pain and Arthritis

Martin knew he was in trouble as soon as he awoke. Just attempting to sit up left him in severe pain. The back is in the middle of the body, and for Martin, the back pain spread everywhere. Martin had been a successful construction worker. In high school, he had been an All-City football player and a hurdler on the track team. Martin went to a doctor, who gave him muscle relaxant medication and told him to stay in bed for 3 days. That helped some, but within a few days the pain was once again unbearable. After that, Martin saw a whole series of different doctors. An orthopedic surgeon did several tests and suggested that surgery may be necessary. A chiropractor told Martin that his back was out of alignment and performed a series of manipulations. All of this seemed to provide some benefit, but ultimately the pain continued. Eventually, Martin had back surgery, but the operation did not leave him cured.

Unable to work construction jobs, Martin began to get depressed. Once an active person, the back pain forced him to be inactive and he gained weight. His relationships with other people were also affected. Martin became dependent on his wife to take care of him, and his wife began to get angry and resentful. What began as a physical injury was taking on important psychological dimensions The pain now dominated Martin's life.

Pain is fundamentally connected with life. If we were unable to experience pain, we would have a great deal of difficulty surviving. Pain is a basic danger signal informing the body to behave differently in order to avoid further injury. Pain is probably the most common and most universal symptom of disease. Nearly half of all patients who visit physicians have the primary complaint of pain. Expenditures on pain treatments are astronomical. For example, as a society, we spend many billions of dollars annually on the treatment of low back pain and lose more than 100 million workdays each year because of pain complaints. Treatment for acute pain is also very expensive. Indeed, pain remedies such as aspirin and Tylenol are among the most commonly consumed products in the western world. Nearly all households keep these products on hand.

Evaluation of pain is very difficult because pain is a perception rather than a sensation. A variety of psychological characteristics influence the extent to which pain is experienced and interpreted. Professional football players, for example, may be battered without mercy during a contest, often leaving the field with many body parts swollen and bleeding. Yet they are frequently unaware of these injuries. Conversely, others with only very minor injuries can become more severely disabled. In this chapter we explore the notion of pain. Unfortunately, the topic is very complex, and a thorough discussion would require several volumes. We will touch on the major issues in pain research and then devote attention to chronic pain problems associated with musculoskeletal disorders.

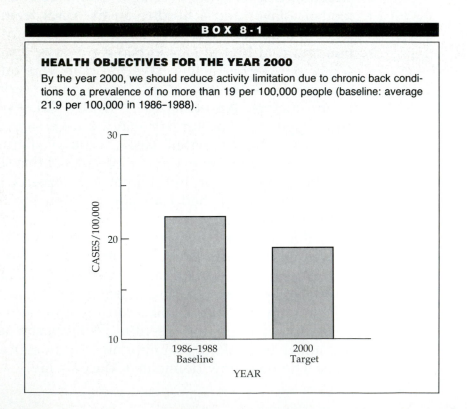

BOX 8·1

HEALTH OBJECTIVES FOR THE YEAR 2000

By the year 2000, we should reduce activity limitation due to chronic back conditions to a prevalence of no more than 19 per 100,000 people (baseline: average 21.9 per 100,000 in 1986–1988).

PAIN VERSUS NOCICEPTION

Understanding pain requires several important distinctions. Although there are many competing definitions of pain, we prefer that offered by Chapman and Bonica (1985). They define *pain* as "an emotionally disabling sensory discomfort typically associated with tissue injury" (p. 4). The definition emphasizes that pain is an emotionally disturbing event, that it is sensory in nature, and that it is typically *although not always* associated with tissue injury. There are, for example, cases in which tissue injury heals but the pain response continues. The distinction between acute and chronic pain is important. *Acute pain* is typically associated with an active disease state or a traumatic injury. When the damaged area heals, the pain typically goes away. Acute pain serves as an important signal identifying that there is damage. With this information, behavior change can be initiated so that further injury might be avoided. Sometimes pain persists even after injuries have healed. This is usually referred to as *chronic pain*. Chapman and Bonica (1985) identify three types of chronic pain: (1) pain that lasts after the normal feeling of a disease or an injury; (2) pain associated with a chronic medical condition, such as a degenerative disease or a neurological condition; or (3) pain that develops and persists in the absence of identifiable organic problem.

It is now widely recognized that there are at least two important components to the pain responses. One component is physiological or sensory, while the other psychological (Bonica, 1991; Maciewicz & Martin, 1987; Rudy & Turk, 1991). Most medical management of pain is based on the understanding of sensory physiology. Stimulation of pain receptors and the neuroelectrical communication of pain stimulation are very well studied. The process of receiving sensory information is known as *nociception*. Sensory stimulation activates nerve endings within the skin, the underlying tissue, or the viscera. These signals are conducted to the dorsal horn of the spinal cord, where they are directed to appropriate centers in the brain. Axons of nociceptive neurons terminate in several different centers in the brain stem and thalamus. Within the brain, nociceptive stimulation is received and acted upon. In addition, there are descending pain pathways in which messages from the central nervous system are conveyed back to the originating tissues. Neurochemical events can modulate nociceptive stimulation along these pathways. A variety of medicines can be used to block nociceptive stimulation and may affect either the brain itself or the communication of information along these pathways. A variety of different receptors receive sensory information, and some of these are shown in Figure 8-1.

FIGURE 8-1

The pain receptors. There are a variety of sensory receptors. Various receptors within the skin receive nociceptive information. A few of them include Meissner's Corpuscle (*a*), Krause's end bulb (*b*), Ruffin's end organ (*c*), Pacinian Corpuscle (*d*), bear nerve endings from the cornea of the eye (*e*), and Merkel's Disk, which is sensitive to touch (*f*). (From Bainbridge and Menzie, 1925.)

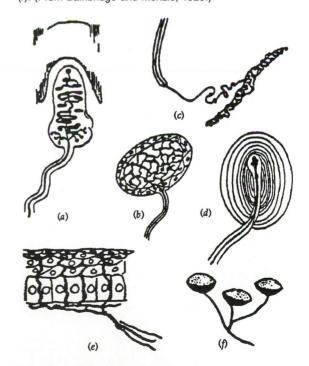

Another important distinction is between pain and suffering. This distinction is particularly apparent for those who have chronic back pain (Fordyce, 1988). Some studies suggest that 85 percent of those who injure their backs should regain normal function within a few days (Anderson, Svensson, & Anders, 1983). The definition of pain is different from that of nociception. Pain is defined as the perception of sensation arising from nociception. The connection between pain and nociception is not always clear. For example, there are some conditions, such as the phantom limb syndrome, in which pain is experienced in the absence of nociception. The condition occurs when patients with limb amputations report pain arising from the amputated arm or leg. Conversely, there are other situations, such as those experienced by professional athletes, in which there is substantial sensory input without any awareness that there is a problem (see Figure 8-2).

Suffering is an emotional response. It is sometimes triggered by nociception, while in other cases it results from other nondesirable events including threat, fear, or the loss of a loved one. This state of distress is not directly connected to a physiological event but can be observed in behaviors that are characteristic of suffering. These include crying, certain facial expressions, and depression.

A final dimension is *pain behavior*. These are behaviors that are observable when pain is experienced. Examples of pain behaviors are facial grimacing, limping, or vocal moans and groans. Most often, pain behaviors occur naturally in response to nociception. Thus, when stuck with a pin, a person may exhibit a pain behavior, including a facial grimace or a yell. Someone who has injured a back may show this behavior each time he or she attempts to stand up or walk. However, pain behaviors can be modified, as can other behaviors. Thus, a spouse who attends to an injured husband

FIGURE 8-2
The experience of pain involves a cognitive component. Sometimes people can experience significant tissue injury without any awareness that they are in pain. (Tropham/ The Image Works.)

may reinforce pain behaviors. She might attend to him more or bring more things to him. With reinforcement, pain behaviors can become autonomous. In other words, behaviors continue in the absence of initial pain stimulation. (Loeser, 1980). Box 8-2 considers whether different ethnic or cultural groups respond differently to pain terms.

In summary, the experience of pain is complex. Traditionally, physicians have focused on nociception. However, there is more to the pain experience than sensory stimulation. It is now well established that pain has a psychological component. In addition, pain behavior

BOX 8·2

FOCUS ON DIVERSITY

Pain, at least in part, may be determined by cultural experience. But do people from different ethnic or racial groups experience pain differently? In one study pain terms commonly used by Hispanics, Native Americans, blacks, and whites were studied. The participants in the study were asked to rate the intensity of terms such as *pain, ache*, and *hurt*. When they had completed this task, they were given copies of the McGill pain questionnaire and asked to choose the words that, for them, represented pain, ache, and hurt. All four groups rated pain as the most intense experience. All four groups also ranked hurt as the second most intense and ache as the least. These studies suggest that the conceptualization of pain is similar among people of Hispanic, Native American, African American, and white backgrounds (Gaston-Johnasson, Albert, Fagon, & Zimmerman, 1990).

may be distinct from pain experience. Acute pain is different from chronic pain, and the two must be thought of in different ways.

CURRENT MODELS OF PAIN

Traditional models of pain have been inadequate. Those that emphasize nociception cannot explain why there are wide difference in complaints among patients who have the same injury. Furthermore, when drugs are given to block pain stimulation, some patients continue to experience pain. For example, studies on dental pain show that some patients experience pain even though the relevant nerves have been completely anesthetized.

Within the last 30 years, there have been substantial changes in pain theories. Many of these developments have been inspired by Ronald Melzack and his colleagues in Canada. Melzack and Wall (1982) separated pain into three different dimensions: (1) sensory-discriminative, (2) emotional-motivational, and (3) central.

Melzack has proposed a theory of pain that has stimulated considerable interest and debate. According to his gate control theory, nociceptive stimulation is carried by small, slow fibers that enter the dorsal horn of the spinal cord; then other cells transmit the impulses from the spinal cord up to the brain. These fibers are called T-cells (not to be confused with t-cells in the immune system). The T-cells can be located in a specific area of the spinal cord, known as the substantial gelatinosa. These fibers can have an impact on the smaller fibers that carry the nociceptive stimulation. In some cases they can inhibit the communication of stimulation, while in other cases they can allow stimulation to be communicated into the central nervous system. For example, large fibers can prohibit the impulses from the small fibers from ever communicating with the brain. In this way, the large fibers create a hypothetical "gate" that can open or close the system to nociceptive stimulation. According to the theory, the gate can sometimes be overwhelmed by a large number of small activated fibers. In other words, the greater the level of nociceptive stimulation, the less adequate the gate in blocking the communication of this information (see Figure 8-3).

The gate control theory has generated considerable research interest and many practical applications. For example, electrical devices that stimulate the large fibers have been commercially produced. The devices are known as transdermal electrical nerve stimulators (TENS). Pain patients have used TENS devices to stimulate the segment of the spinal cord that receives input from the injured area. For example, if a person experiences pain in the legs, electrical stimulation of the spinal cord in the area that receives input from the legs would be used. Psychological and emotional states can also influence the large fibers that open and close the gate. The gate control theory has generated substantial interest, although many

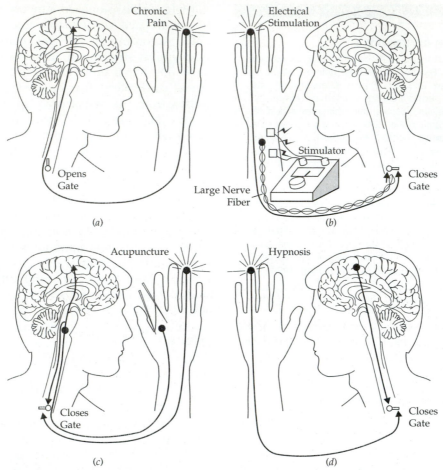

FIGURE 8-3

The gate control theory of pain. Painful stimulation is first received by pain receptors and then communicated to the brain through the dorsal horn of the spinal cord. However, for the stimulation to reach the brain, it must go through a "gate." When the gate is open, the sensory stimulation goes directly to the brain (a). A variety of techniques might be used to close the gate. These include electrical stimulation to the skin (b), acupuncture (c), and techniques that close the gate but originate from the brain, such as hypnosis (d). (From Gazzaniga, Steen, and Volpe, *Functional Neuroscience*, p. 211.)

aspects still remain to be experimentally tested. Currently, it is the most commonly advanced theory to explain variations in pain (Melzack & Wall, 1983).

EPIDEMIOLOGY

Chronic pain is remarkably common. Virtually all people experience some pain on a regular basis. Those with neurological conditions that prevent them from experiencing pain are much more prone to serious injury and early death. In addition to acute "warning signal" pain, substantial numbers of people experience pain continuously. It has been estimated that chronic pain affects as many as 80 million Americans and that 31 million suffer from chronic low back pain. In the United States more than 50 million people are partially or totally disabled by pain for at least a few days each month. Pain results in the loss of more than 100 million workdays each year (Bonica, 1980). These estimates exclude the treatment of chronic pain–causing conditions. It has been estimated that nearly 80 percent of all adults will experience back pain that limits their function sometime during their lives. Figure 8-4 shows the economic impact of three musculo-skeletal problems (to be defined below). Direct costs include the cost of medical care and time lost from work. Indirect costs might include income lost when a person leaves work to care for a sick family member. As the figure shows, the economic costs of these problems are stag-gering. Back pain alone may cost society over $17 billion per year in direct and indirect costs!

It will not be possible to discuss all the pain syndromes within this chapter. Instead we will devote most attention to arthritis and mus-culoskeletal problems, which are the most common causes of chronic pain. After intro-ducing these diseases, we will review the psy-chological correlates of pain and discuss pain treatment.

FIGURE 8-4

Estimated costs of arthritis. (From McDuffie, Carter Cen-ter, 1984.)

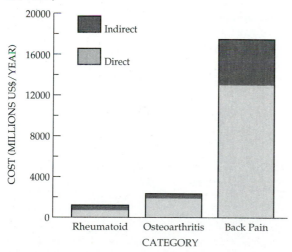

ARTHRITIS AND MUSCULOSKELETAL DISORDERS

Technically, *arthritis* is defined as inflamma-tion of a joint. However, the term has been used much more generally and now describes any damage to a joint that produces pain. The term has also been extended to include symp-toms that arise from injuries in tissues near the joints where no specific damage to the joint itself is evident.

"Arthritis and rheumatism" include a wide variety of disorders affecting the peripheral joints (e.g., knees, ankles, finger joints), the spine, the soft tissues surrounding joints (tendons, ligaments, capsules), and the con-nective tissues of the body. These structures and tissues may be affected by congenital anomalies, metabolic or biochemical abnor-malities, infections, inflammatory conditions, or cancer. Certain rheumatic disorders occur more commonly in the young (inflammatory arthritis), in women (connective tissue dis-eases such as lupus erythematosis and rheu-matoid arthritis), in men (gout, ankylosis spondylitis), or in the aged (osteoarthritis).

Arthritis is the major cause of functional limitations in most western countries. In the United States arthritis accounts for about 50 percent of all disabilities. Data from the Health and Nutrition Examination Survey (HANES) indicate that nearly a third of the population is affected by some type of swelling in their joints, limitation in their motion, or pain when they move. Seventeen percent of the American population (about 37 million people) report that they have arthritis (Cun-ningham & Kelsey, 1984).

Historically, the nonfatal nature of arthritis and related conditions has made it difficult to assess and express "outcome" of these disor-ders. Recent improvement in outcome mea-sures have helped portray the impact of arthritis upon function, disability, and quality of life. Data have indicated that over 21 percent of the population reporting musculoskeletal symptoms experience moderate or severe restrictions of activity. Eighteen percent of these patients have a change in their job status (Cunningham & Kelsey, 1984). In one study, 60 percent of the patients with rheumatoid arthritis (RA) were considered disabled (Yelin et al., 1980). Meenan reported that persons with RA who are able to work earned only 50 percent of their expected income, and 63 percent experienced major psychosocial changes as a result of their disease (Meenan et al., 1981).

Arthritis is a troubling condition for several reasons. As noted above, it has an enormous impact upon disability and ultimately takes a substantial toll in terms of human suffering. Furthermore, the exact causes of many of the arthritic conditions are still poorly understood. Research is actively attempting to identify what causes these diseases. Perhaps most concerning is that there are no known treatments that will completely cure these conditions. Patients with arthritis may benefit from treatment but must learn to cope with pain and disability which are likely to last the rest of their lives.

The term *arthritis* is used to refer to several different distinct musculoskeletal problems. These include osteoarthritis, rheumatoid arthritis, juvenile arthritis, systemic lupus, gout, ankylosis spondylitis, fibrositis, and psoriatic arthritis. These are among the more common rheumatic diseases. Indeed, there are nearly 100 other rheumatic conditions, although many are more rare.

OSTEOARTHRITIS

The most common type of arthritis results from a wearing out of the joints. This condition produces aching and swelling and is most common in the hips, knees, spine, and fingers. The ends of bones are typically covered by cartilage. Softer tissue absorbs shock and aids in the biomechanics of walking and other movements. Degeneration in the cartilage may disrupt these normal movements and ultimately might result in changes in the ends of the bone. Sometimes small bony spurs known as *osteophytes* develop (see Figure 8-5). The exact causes of osteoarthritis are unknown. However, the condition is clearly associated

FIGURE 8-5

Cartilage degeneration characteristic of osteoarthritis. In osteoarthritis, the cartilage at the end of the bone degenerates or wears out. As a result, the soft plating at the end of bones is no longer available, and hard bones rub against one another. This might result in changes in the bone structure and significant chronic pain. (From Fries, J. F., *Arthritis*, Menlo Park, Calif., Addison-Wesley, p. 55.)

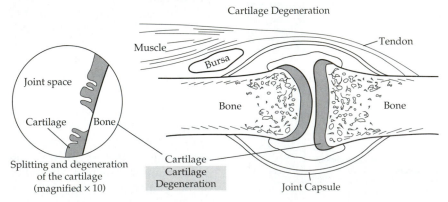

with age: the older you are, the more likely you are to develop this condition. In fact, nearly half of the elderly experience some type of osteoarthritis.

It has also been suggested that strain on weight-bearing joints may produce this problem as a function of overuse. Osteoarthritis is more common in the hip and knee. Obesity has been suggested as an important risk factor. People who suffer from osteoarthritis may be in good health otherwise. The condition does not cause general infection. However, osteoarthritis is a common cause of disability. It has been estimated that nearly 16 million Americans suffer from this condition. By self-report, about 3 times as many women as men report osteoarthritis. However, studies of joint x-rays suggest that men and women are approximately equally affected (Maurer, 1979). This suggests that women may be more likely to report symptoms and dysfunction than men.

RHEUMATOID ARTHRITIS

Rheumatoid arthritis is a chronic condition that may cause major disability over the course of time. Rheumatoid arthritis is systemic, meaning that it is a problem that affects the body systems in general rather than a specific joint. Rheumatoid arthritis causes pain and swelling in the synovial membranes, or linings of the joint. This often causes enlarged red areas around the joints. The infection is typically symmetrical. This means that if it affects a joint on the left side of the body, it will affect the same joint on the right side. The major affected area in rheumatoid arthritis is the synovial membrane. This membrane creates synovial fluid, which is a substance that lubricates joints. In rheumatoid arthritis, this membrane becomes inflamed, red, and very tender. Unfortunately, rheumatoid arthritis is a chronic disease and may sometimes lead to disabling symptoms. It affects an estimated 2.1 million people in the United States and is about twice as common in women as it is in men. Although RA can start at any time, it typically begins in the forties or fifties.

Rheumatoid arthritis usually begins with swelling and pain in one or more joints. Physicians begin to suspect the problem if the swelling and pain have lasted more than 6 weeks. Any joint can be affected, but wrists and knuckles are almost always involved. Other joints likely to be affected are the knees and the joints of the ball of the foot. On the hands, the joints at the end of the fingers are typically spared, while those in the middle of the finger are more commonly involved (see Figure 8-6). A variety of laboratory tests help confirm the diagnosis of RA. One of these is the latex rheumatoid factor test. Many patients with RA have an elevated level of a substance known as rheumatoid factor circulating in their blood. This factor is higher in RA patients than in nonaffected people. However, the test is not perfect. For example, other diseases cause elevation in rheumatoid factor, and some patients with no disease also have an elevation. A related test is the erythrocyte sedimentation rate (ESR). The sedimentation rates tend to be higher when there is a lot of inflammation. Blood is collected and allowed to settle in a test tube for 1 hour. The distance that it settles in this period defines the sedimentation rate. If it settles slowly, there is probably some inflammation. This test can provide information on how active the infection is. X-rays are often used for patients with arthritis. These pictures identify the extent to which bone and cartilage are affected.

RA is a mysterious disease because its cause is unknown. Furthermore, the condition is cyclic. Patients go through cycles in which the disease goes into remission and they feel much better. However, the symptoms typically come back, often without warning.

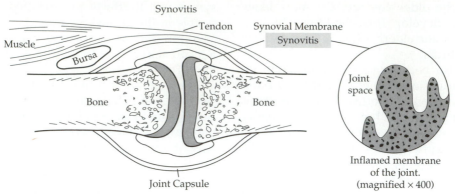

FIGURE 8-6
In rheumatoid arthritis, the synovial membrane of the joint becomes inflamed (synovitis). This typically happens on both sides of the body, and the joint becomes red, warm, and painful. (From Fries, J. F., *Arthritis*, Menlo Park, Calif., Addison-Wesley, 1979, p. 16.)

SYSTEMIC LUPUS

Perhaps the most life-threatening of the common rheumatic diseases is systemic lupus. This condition begins with high fevers, rashes, and hair loss, and may eventually result in kidney dysfunction. Systemic lupus affects approximately 131,000 Americans. It is 8 times as common in women as it is in men. This condition, most commonly referred to as *lupus*, is considered a musculoskeletal disease. However, it also affects the nervous system, the skin, the kidneys, the lungs, the heart, and the blood-forming organs.

There are two common forms of lupus: one type, *discoid*, is most often limited to problems in the skin. However, the other form, *systemic lupus*, is the one that develops into a rheumatic disease. The causes of systemic lupus are unknown. It is suspected that there may be a genetic disposition toward this condition. Other theories suggest that a virus may activate a genetic predisposition. As noted earlier, the condition occurs 8 times more frequently in women than in men. Some of the psychological effects of lupus for women are discussed in Box 8-3. Lupus also occurs more often in black, Asian, and Native American groups than among whites.

Lupus is an autoimmune disease. The immune system typically attacks potentially harmful bacteria for viruses by creating antibodies. In autoimmune diseases the system

---

BOX 8-3

FOCUS ON WOMEN

Lupus and rheumatoid arthritis affect women significantly more than men. Several studies have attempted to identify variables associated with illness severity among women. One study evaluated the relationship between illness and perceived health status, self-esteem, and body image among women with rheumatoid arthritis and lupus, and women who were healthy. In addition, the study evaluated the fears of women with rheumatoid arthritis and lupus.

Several authors have speculated that women who have chronic illnesses suffer problems in self-image and self-esteem. However, this study demonstrated that self-esteem differences between healthy women and those affected by these illnesses were not statistically significant. Although women with lupus tended to have slightly lower scores on measures of body image, differences between arthritis patients and healthy controls were not significant. Other studies have suggested that women with arthritis or lupus do not necessarily experience significant psychological problems with self-esteem (Cromwell & Schmidt, 1990).

somehow gets the wrong message and begins turning against one's own body tissue. For some reason, the system attacks healthy tissues rather than the invading organisms.

Those affected by lupus may experience fever, weakness, and substantial weight loss. Often they develop a skin rash on their face, neck, and arms. The pattern of the skin rash is symmetrical. When it appears on the face, it might appear in a butterfly pattern and is sometimes described as the butterfly rash. Early signs of the condition also include pain in the major joints, including hands, wrists, elbows, knees, and ankles. People complain of general muscle aches, loss of appetite, and sometimes nausea and vomiting. Like RA, lupus can go into remission without treatment. This can sometimes confuse patients, who incorrectly attribute the remission to recent behavior or dietary changes.

The diagnosis of lupus typically involves evaluation of the red cells and blood platelets (cells that control bleeding). A newer test attempts to determine a specific antinuclear antibody (ANA) that is characteristic of most patients with lupus.

FIBROSITIS

Fibrositis—also known as fibromyalgia, nonarticular rhematism, or muscular rheumatism— is one of the most interesting musculoskeletal disorders. For many years, rheumatologists denied that this condition existed and often referred to it as a psychosomatic problem. In most rheumatic diseases, it is possible to identify some specific physiologic problem, such as swelling, damage to a joint, or an abnormality in a blood test. With fibrositis, there appears to be no identifiable damage to joints, muscles, ligaments, or tendons.

Fibrositis is associated with specific tender points. People affected by this problem experience pain in identifiable areas (see Figure 8-7). The pain appears to come from the muscles themselves or from the points at which liga-

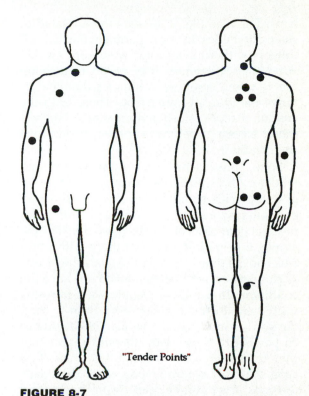

"Tender Points"

FIGURE 8-7

In the fibrositis syndrome, no blood or x-ray tests are abnormal. However, affected individuals are tender in response to pressure in specific areas, as shown here. (Reprinted from the booklet entitled "Fibromyalgia," copyright 1989. Used by permission of the Arthritis Foundation.

ments attach muscles to bones. The most common symptom of fibrositis is pain. Most people describe this pain as aching, stiffness, and tenderness near the joints or muscles. The condition seems to affect both men and women. There are no specific laboratory tests that can be used to evaluate fibrositis. Instead, the diagnosis is made by locating specific tender points near the shoulders, back, and other parts of the body that are often affected. Since there are no specific tests for this condition, it is also difficult to estimate how commonly it occurs. Many people who complain to their doctors of these problems may be told that nothing is wrong with them. However, fibrositis is associated with certain other problems. For example, it appears to be related to sleep difficulties. In one experiment normal volunteers without symptoms were kept awake. After this experience, they began to develop the pain and soreness in muscles that characterize the fibrositis syndrome. Those with the condition report sleep abnormalities. Furthermore, sleeping medications seem to improve the condition.

Some physicians have even questioned whether fibrositis exists, because it cannot be detected with standard medical tests. However, the syndrome is associated with high medical care costs and high disability. For example, one study found that those with fibrositis had 3.4 times as many hospital admissions in comparison with peers who do not have the condition. In addition, people with fibrositis visit their doctor 3 times more than a comparison group (Kathey et al., 1986). About 35 percent of those with fibrositis report that they have been sickly most of their lives. This type of report is rare among other rheumatic diseases. For example, those with rheumatoid arthritis rarely report this problem (Kirmayer et al., 1988). This does suggest that the fibrositis syndrome is associated with adopting the sick role. Fibrositis is often seen as a psychological problem. Clearly psychological distress plays an important role. Yet it is unclear whether sleep disturbance is the cause of fibrositis or the result. Patients with fibrositis are often depressed, and yet it is unknown whether they are depressed because they are in a chronic state of pain, misery, or disability, or whether their psychological state causes the condition, (Hench & Mitler, 1986). These issues contribute to the mystery associated with the disease.

OTHER RHEUMATIC DISEASES

Some of the other rheumatic diseases include *juvenile arthritis*, which is a severe disease affecting as many as 71,000 young Americans. This condition is probably an autoimmune problem that begins in childhood. It affects 6 times as many girls as boys. The symptoms include high fever, rash, and pain in many joints. *Gout* is another common rheumatic disease affecting about 1 million Americans. This condition is 4 times as common in men as it is in women. Gout is associated with a specific biochemical abnormality that causes swelling of the large toe. This often spreads to other joints and can result in sudden and often very severe pain. *Ankylosis spondylitis* results in the loss of the movement of the back, legs, collar bone, and other joints near the spinal column. It is characterized by an abnormal curvature of the spine and may result in the development of lung and heart problems. This condition affects 318,000 Americans. Ankylosis spondylitis is twice as common in men as it is in women. *Psoriatic arthritis* affects 160,000 Americans. This condition, which occurs in a small percentage of the people who have the skin problem psoriasis, involves inflammation and stiffness in both sides of the body, particularly in the small joints of the hands. It also affects elbows and hips.

THE IMPACT OF ARTHRITIS ON BEHAVIOR

Musculoskeletal problems may cause more disability than any other medical conditions. Kelsey and her associates (1979) have analyzed data from the National Health and Nutrition Examination Survey (NHNES) in order to evaluate how much arthritis impacts upon the daily lives of people in society. The impact is substantial. Musculoskeletal conditions are the leading cause of activity impairment, resulting in the loss of ability to perform activities of daily living. This finding is true for both men and women, and it is characteristic in each aspect of the age distribution. Musculoskeletal conditions are the second leading cause of physician office visits, the third most common reason for surgery, and the fourth most common reason listed for a hospital visit. The economic burden for musculoskeletal diseases varies but the HANES data suggest that it may be in excess of $20 billion per year (Cunningham, Kelsey, 1984).

Not everyone is affected the same way by arthritis. However, more than a fifth of those who report musculoskeletal symptoms experience moderate or severe restriction in activity, and 18 percent need to change jobs because of their illness (Cunningham & Kelsey, 1984). Rheumatoid arthritis is more severe than osteoarthritis. In the rheumatoid category 60 percent of those affected are considered disabled (Yelin, Meenan, Nevitt, & Epstein, 1980). Meenan (1980) has reported that RA has even more severe impacts. Those able to work earn only about 50 percent of their expected income, and 63 percent report some psychological problems such as depression.

THE MEASUREMENT OF CLINICAL OUTCOMES IN ARTHRITIS

Arthritis is not a condition that can be easily measured. In contrast to some medical conditions like cuts on the skin or enlargement of a specific organ, arthritis often affects many joints at the same time. Tugwell and Bombardier (1982) argued that clinical outcomes in arthritis are measured by the "eight D's." The eight D's include disease activity, distress, death, disadvantages/drug effects, disability,

dysfunction, disharmony, and dissatisfaction.

As Deyo (1988) has suggested, outcome measures in studies of rheumatology have been difficult to evaluate. Clinical measures often include joint tenderness, grip strength, and joint circumference. Some studies have shown that the reliability of these measures is often poor (Buchanan, 1982). Laboratory measures are also often difficult to evaluate. Fries (1983) questions the relevance and reliability of a variety of traditional outcome measures, ranging from laboratory measures of erythrocyte sedimentation rate (ESR), latex fixation titer, and hemoglobin. In addition, Fries suggested that traditional clinical measures such as grip strength, walking time, and patient global assessment are merely surrogates for true outcome in arthritis. The real outcomes are disability, physical discomfort, and financial impact. It has been asserted that only pain and functional outcomes are meaningful to the patients. Patients strive for extended life expectancy and for improved function during the years they are alive. Laboratory findings may be predictive of this dysfunction and are only important for that reason. As demonstrated by McCarty (1979), RA patients may develop serological abnormalities that do not precisely coincide with joint inflammation.

Table 8-1 summarizes the discrepancies between laboratory and clinical outcomes for RA patients participating in a trial of plasma-

TABLE 8-1

LABORATORY VERSUS CLINICAL OUTCOMES IN A TRIAL OF PLASMAPHERESIS (TRUE THERAPY VERSUS SHAM THERAPY) FOR RHEUMATOID ARTHRITIS

Laboratory measures		Clinical measures	
Tests	Significance of advantage for true plasmapheresis	Test	Significance of advantage for true plasmapheresis
ESR	$P = .001$	Subjective improvement	NS
IgM	$P = .045$	No. active joints	NS
Complement (C_3)	$P = .005$	Grip strength	NS
Rheumatoid factor	$P = .01$	Walking time	NS

ESR = erythrocyte sedimentation rate; IgM = Immunoglobin M; NS = not significant.
Source: Deyo, 1988.

pheresis, which is a method of filtering undesirable factors from the blood of arthritis patients. Although biochemical measures tended to change significantly as a function of the treatment, clinical measures remained unchanged in the sham-treated group. Patients with arthritis are concerned about pain, symptoms, and dysfunction. There is a growing consensus that patient health status or quality of life is the most important outcome in health care. Furthermore, there is a growing consensus that these outcomes can be measured using questionnaires (Bergner et al., 1981; Kaplan & Anderson, 1988; Meenen & Pincus, 1987). In the following sections we will explore the development of clinical outcome measures in arthritis.

HISTORICAL APPROACHES

The American Rheumatism Association has promoted functional assessment for many years. By 1949, they had introduced a simple scale for the classification of patients with arthritis. The scale is summarized in Table 8-2. This scale has been used extensively in clinical studies and patient care. It has been shown to have moderate negative correlations with grip strength and positive correlation with ESR and x-rays (Deyo et al., 1983).

TABLE 8·2

SUMMARY OF THE AMERICAN RHEUMATISM ASSOCIATION (ARA) FUNCTIONAL CLASSIFICATION SYSTEM

I.   Complete functional capacity with the ability to carry on all usual duties without handicaps.

II. Functional capacity adequate to conduct normal activities despite handicap of discomfort or limited mobility of one or more joints.

III. Functional capacity adequate to perform only little or none of the duties of the usual occupation or self-care.

IV. Largely or wholly incapacitated, with patient bedridden or confined to wheelchair, permitting little or no self-care.

However, the scale has well-known drawbacks. The major problem is that the four categories are limited. Several studies have demonstrated that over half the patients with RA are in functional class II (Cooperating Clinics of the American Rheumatism Association, 1965; Meenan et al., 1981). Deyo (1988) has criticized the ambiguity of the terms used in the classification system. For example, there is no definition of *normal activities* or *usual duties*.

The major difficulty with the ARA scale is its restricted range and consequent difficulty in making fine distinctions. For example, in Deyo's (1983) study, some patients were followed over the course of time and rated to be unchanged between the beginning of the study and the follow-up. Correlations between scores on these two occasions are expected to be high, but were shown to be zero for the ARA scale. Thus, the ARA scale is far too crude to use as an outcome measure in clinical trials. In 1991 the ARA revised its scale, but even the revision makes only crude distinctions.

An alternative to the ARA scales is based on the argument that the major outcomes in health care involve combinations of mortality and morbidity. Mortality is clearly of importance in health care, and many treatments are evaluated in terms of their ability to reduce deaths. However, rheumatic diseases often produce years of dysfunction rather than death. Therefore, it seems reasonable that the major benefits of health care can be evaluated in terms of their effects upon combined indexes of morbidity and mortality (Kaplan & Anderson, 1990). In the following sections, we will provide a brief overview of health status and quality of life measurement.

ARTHRITIS-SPECIFIC MEASURES

Most health-related quality-of-life measures developed before 1980 or so were designed for use with any disease. Recently, some investigators promoted disease-specific quality-of-life measures. This is usually done by combining a general measure with disease-specific measures. Nowhere is there a better example of this interplay than in research on rheumatoid arthritis. Investigators studying new treatments for arthritis have developed a whole series of quality-of-life measures that apply only to patients with arthritis. This field was reviewed in a special issue of the *Journal of Rheumatology* in 1982. Most of the new scales have been adapted from Activities of Daily Living (Katz et al., 1970) or other functional status measures (Kaplan et al., 1976; Kaplan & Bush, 1982), but they typically include a series of items that specifically measure the impact of arthritis upon daily functioning.

ARTHRITIS IMPACT MEASUREMENT SCALE (AIMS)

One example of a quality-of-life measure specific for arthritis is the Arthritis Impact Measurement Scale (AIMS). The AIMS is a health index designed at the Multi-purpose Arthritis Center at Boston University. It is intended to measure physical health and social well-being for patients with rheumatoid arthritis (Meenan, 1982). The resultant scale includes 67 items, with questions about functioning, health perceptions, morbidity, and demographics (Meenan, 1982). The AIMS contains scales for mobility, physical activity, social activity, activities of daily living, depression and anxiety, and arthritis-related symptoms. In effect, it is an adaptation of a general health index developed by Bush and colleagues (see Kaplan et al., 1976; 1978), with a series of items designed to tap more specifically the effect of arthritis upon functioning and the quality of life. Factor analysis of the AIMS has produced three subscales: physical function, psychological function, and pain. Most current applications of the AIMS use composite scores for these three areas.

The psychometric properties of the AIMS were evaluated in a study involving 625 patients with rheumatoid disease. Alpha reliabilities were found to be acceptable ($> .7$) for the various subscales, and the mean test-retest correlation was .87. In order to assess validity, the investigators correlated AIMS scores with physician ratings of health status, and these correlations were found to be highly significant. In addition, AIMS subscores were found to have convergent and discriminant validity when correlated with specific measures used in rheumatology research. For example, the physical activity portion of the AIMS correlated more highly with walking time than with grip strength. A dexterity scale of the AIMS was significantly correlated with grip strength but did not correlate significantly with walking time. In summary, the AIMS is one of several well-documented quality-of-life measures used exclusively for arthritis research.

HEALTH ASSESSMENT QUESTIONNAIRE (HAQ)

Another commonly used arthritis-specific measure is the Stanford Health Assessment Questionnaire (HAQ), which includes 20 questions grouped into eight categories. The questions concern various components of activities of daily living, ranging from dressing, cutting meat, walking outside, and turning faucets on and off, to doing chores such as vacuuming or yard work. Patients are asked to self-report whether or not they can do the activity using the following four-point scale:

0—without any difficulty
1—with some difficulty
2—with much difficulty
3—unable to do

In eight categories of the HAQ, patients note whether or not they required help from another person or from an assistive device. Use of an assistive device is automatically scored as 2, i.e., equivalent to performing the activity with much difficulty. Recently, the HAQ was modified to include scales to assess patient satisfaction with their capacity to perform the eight selected activities. Studies with this new version, termed the Modified Stanford Health Assessment Questionnaire (MHAQ), have demonstrated a modest correlation between dissatisfaction and disability. However, a substantial number of patients report satisfaction with their health status even though they have some limitations (Pincus et al., 1983).

PSYCHOLOGICAL ISSUES IN PAIN AND ARTHRITIS

As noted in the last section, there are many different types of arthritis. In fact, more than 100 different types exist. Yet the most common conditions are osteoarthritis and rheumatoid arthritis. There are no medical cures for these conditions. Thus, it is important that people with these conditions learn to function as best as possible, given their condition. There are many controversies concerning how patients with arthritis should take care of themselves. One of the controversies concerns exercise. For years, it was believed that exercise was bad for people with arthritis. However, newer evidence suggests that exercise is healthy for a joint. In fact, some evidence suggests that cartilage and the synovial membrane take up fluid like a sponge during exercise periods. Thus, if joints are not exercised, the cartilage may actually decay.

We know much less than we should about psychological problems associated with arthritis and chronic pain. In part, this may be because most earlier investigations were attempts to identify a "rheumatoid personality" (Actenberg-Lawlis, 1982). These early studies hypothesized that people with musculoskeletal problems had a certain personality profile. Searches for the arthritic personality

have not produced consistent results. What seems to be more profitable are studies on how patients cope with chronic pain and disability.

Mechanic (1977) has identified at least five different resources that patients can use in order to successfully adapt to chronic illness. These are economic, skills and ability, psychological, social, and motivational. Baker (1981) showed how these resources can be used for patients with rheumatoid arthritis. Economic resources are required for patients to use the medical care system and cope with potential loss of income. Skills and abilities are required in order for patients to adapt to the condition. Often this may involve some vocational training so that a person can find a job appropriate for someone with limitations in manual dexterity or mobility. Psychological support appears to be very important in the adaptation to any chronic illness. A variety of studies (Lorig & Holman, 1989) have demonstrated that self-help groups bolster self-esteem and promote adaptation to illness. As we will suggest later in the chapter, support must be appropriate. Social support is needed in order to adapt to the condition. However, families can sometimes reinforce the wrong behaviors—ultimately resulting in negative rather than positive influences (see Chapter 7). Finally, motivation is extremely important. Successfully dealing with a chronic illness requires energy. Patients must comply with medications and engage in difficult and sometimes strenuous activities.

CHRONIC PAIN AND DEPRESSION

Chronic pain and arthritis are frequently accompanied by depression. Some studies suggest that this relationship is a very strong one (Kazis, Meenan, & Anderson, 1983), while others suggest that the relationship exists but that it is weaker (Keefe, Wilkins, Cook, et al., 1986). Some people believe that there is an association between the experience of chronic pain and "learned helplessness." The learned helplessness model suggests that the organism learns to be helpless as a function of random feedback. In early experiments, Seligman (1975) placed healthy dogs in a box and forced them to wait on an electrified floor while they received electric shocks on a random schedule. Later, the situation was changed, and the dogs were allowed to escape the shock by jumping over a hurdle. Normally, dogs can easily learn how to make this escape in a very short time. However, dogs that were exposed to random shock over which they had no personal control seemed unable to learn how to get away. Instead, they just laid on the shock grid and took the punishment.

Many experiments with humans have produced similar results. Subjects who have been put in situations over which they have no control seem unable to learn new responses. For example, suppose that you are in an experiment in which you are attempting to solve a series of hard problems. The only information you have about whether or not you are doing the task correctly comes from feedback you are getting from the experimenter. The experimenter, however, does not really pay attention to what you are doing. Instead, he or she randomly tells you that you are solving the problem correctly or incorrectly. Experiments have shown that this sort of treatment results in (1) the inability to perform well on new problems, (2) lack of motivation to continue responding, and (3) depression. This syndrome has become known as *learned helplessness*. It has been suggested that rheumatoid arthritis creates learned helplessness. Activities patients engage in may or may not lead to better outcomes. In addition, the symptoms of disease may be cyclic or may come and go on a random schedule.

One of the major consequences of learned helplessness is depression. Several studies have demonstrated that depression is common in patients with arthritis. In one recent study, 106 patients with rheumatoid arthritis were given a measure that evaluated their degree of learned helplessness. The study used mathematical models that test the relationship between variables. It is suggested that helplessness is actually a function of disease severity and that helplessness, in turn, causes depression. However, the relationship between disease severity and depression was nonsignificant. In other words, helplessness mediates the relationship between being sick and feeling depressed. Those patients who were severely ill but did not feel helpless did not develop depression (Smith, Peck, & Ward, 1990) (see Figure 8-8).

The learned helplessness model suggests that those who have active coping strategies may be better able to adapt to the illness and avoid debilitating depression. In one study, researchers evaluated the coping strategies as well as depression in 287 patients with rheu-

FIGURE 8-8

Causal model of relationship among helplessness, illness severity, and depression. Helplessness mediates relationship between illness and depression. (From Smith, Peck, & Ward, *Health Psychology* 9(4), 1990: 377–389.)

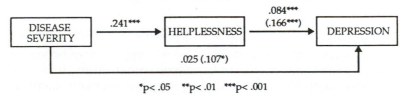

BOX 8·4

CONTENT OF 11 ITEMS, USED TO ASSESS PASSIVE COPING STRATEGIES
Strategy

Wishing doctor would prescribe better pain medication
Thinking the pain is wearing one down
Telling others how much the pain hurts
Praying for relief
Restricting social activities
Depending on others for help with daily tasks
Thinking one cannot do anything to cope with the pain
Taking medication for purposes of immediate pain relief
Calling a doctor or nurse
Focusing on the location and intensity of the pain
Suppressing angry, depressed or frustrated feelings

Source: Adapted from Brown et al., 1989.

---

matoid arthritis. The coping strategies were divided into active and passive. In order to evaluate these, the researchers gave an 11-item scale that evaluated passive coping strategies for pain management (see Box 8-4). The measure asks about taking medications, depending on others, restricting activity, suppressing anger, and so on. It also deals with coping strategies such as staying busy or active, ignoring pain, and the like. Depression and functional ability were also assessed. The results suggested that depression could be predicted from the amount of reported pain and a passive coping strategy. Those who experience the most depression over the course of time are also the patients who used passive pain coping strategies. There was a significant interaction between coping strategies, pain, and depression. This means that when *not* in pain, those with high and low passive coping scores experienced about the same level of depression. However, when confronted with acute pain, those who were passive copers experienced significantly more depression (Brown, Nicassio, & Wallston, 1989) (see Figure 8-9).

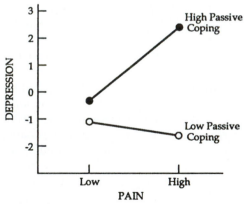

FIGURE 8-9
Relationship between coping, pain, and depression. At low levels of pain, those with high and low passive coping scores experience about the same level of depression. When in acute pain, however, those with passive coping strategies experienced more pain. (From Brown, Nicassio, and Wallston, 1989, p. 654.)

SOCIAL SUPPORT IN ARTHRITIS

Social support may be very important for patients with arthritis. It has been suggested that a supportive enviornment may help patients cope with chronic pain and adapt to the condition. Lorig has developed extensive programs for patient education in which social support is a major factor (Holman & Lorig, 1992). Other evidence suggests that social support may provide a moderating influence that results in a better functioning immune system (Kiecot, Glaser, & Glaser, 1989).

The effects of social support upon health outcome were reviewed in detail in Chapter 7, and a section of that chapter reviewed the role of social support in the treatment pain. Research suggests that social relationships can have either positive or negative effects on the ability to cope with pain. For example, a caring spouse can reinforce pain behavior and increase the chances that a patient will stay in bed or miss work. Thus some treatments train spouses to ignore (not reinforce) pain behavior. In other cases, family members can provide positive support and assist in care. This type of support often results in better health outcomes (Flor, Turk, & Rudy, 1989).

Another interesting issue is the correspondence between the support patients feel they receive and the support providers feel they offer. In one study (Brenner, Williamson, & Melamed, 1989), rheumatoid arthritis patients and their spouses were asked about 21 different behaviors that might be regarded as supportive. These behaviors might include getting the patient medication, expressing sympathy, taking over job duties, or even ignoring the person when they exhibit pain behaviors. Each spouse was then asked whether or not the different behaviors were supportive or unsupportive.

Although there were many consistencies in the reports of these behaviors, there were also many inconsistencies. Both spouses agreed that certain behaviors were supportive. These include solicitous activities (such as getting medication or helping the patient rest). On the other hand, distracting behaviors, such as engaging the patient in a discussion about something else to distract from pain or encouraging the patient to work on a hobby, were not

consistently viewed as supportive. Finally, punishing behaviors, such as expressing frustration, were consistently regarded as unsupportive.

These findings suggest that communication between spouses is sometimes poor. Even when the non-ill spouse wants to be helpful by engaging the patient in distracting conversation, their efforts might be regarded as unsupportive and unhelpful. Some of the supportive behaviors are difficult to interpret. For example, the husband who takes over his wife's job duties may be trying to help but might also interfere with developing her own self-confidence and chances for rehabilitation. Some of the complexities in evaluating social relationships and social support are discussed in more detail in Chapter 7.

TREATMENT OF CHRONIC PAIN

The treatment of pain in arthritis is a multi-billion-dollar industry. Pain treatments are the very core of medical treatment. Indeed, many of the first medicines were designed to relieve pain. Historically, people have tried a variety of different remedies to relieve pain. These include crocodile dung, teeth of swine, hooves of asses, spermatic fluid of frogs, eunich's fat, lozenges of dried vipers, oil derived from ants, earthworms, spiders, hair, human perspiration, and mosses scraped from the skull of a victim of violent death (in Turk, Michenbaum, & Genest, 1983). Although modern remedies for pain are less disgusting, we still do not have the ultimate treatments. There are medications that will completely alleviate pain, but most of them have serious side effects. It has been suggested that when a treatment works, most practitioners apply the same method. When there is no cure or remedy for a condition, there is a lot of variability in what is tried. Wennberg (1989) has suggested that there is more variability in the treatment of chronic pain than there is for any other medical condition.

Various theoretical models have been used to develop treatments for chronic pain. The treatments depend on the conceptualization of pain. One important approach to pain is the operant view. This is best represented in the writings of Fordyce (1976). According to this view of pain, there is an initial response to pain stimulation (nociception) that produces certain behaviors. These pain behaviors might include avoidance of work, staying in bed, and verbal descriptions of pain. In addition, pain behaviors might include taking medications. Initially, these pain behaviors are a response to pain stimulation. However, according to the principles of learning, behaviors can be strengthened through reinforcement. If pain behavior is reinforced or followed by positive consequences, its probability will increase in the future. Suppose, for example, that a man injures his back. This injury results in pain behaviors, including staying in bed, grimacing, and complaining of pain. The man's wife responds by paying more attention to him, taking over some of his household chores, and expressing empathy and concern. According to the operant view of pain behavior, these activities act as reinforcement and increase the probability that the man will continue to emit pain behaviors, even after there is no physiologic pain stimulation.

The operant approach to pain requires that activities be reinforced and that pain behaviors be extinguished. Thus, families might be taught to ignore pain behaviors, but to provide reinforcement for functional activity or "well behaviors." A variety of reports suggest that these treatments are effective (Fordyce, 1989; Keefe et al., 1987). There have been a variety of different criticisms of the operant approach. One of the main criticisms is that it interferes with the patient's social support network. Indeed, family members are taught to be less sympathetic to pain complaints. A related criticism is that the operant approach does not take into consideration the objective experience of pain. Cognitive factors may be very important

in maintaining pain behaviors and pain responses.

A cognitive-behavioral approach to pain takes into consideration both cognitive and behavioral approaches. Turk and his colleagues (Turk, Michenbaum, & Genest, 1983) have suggested that cognitive factors play an important role in pain and pain behavior. For example, cognitive factors influence coping with painful stimulation. They determine how people respond to symptoms and whether or not they decide to use medical services or medications. Some people believe that cognitive coping responses are also related to activities of the immune system. Thus, thoughts may actually affect the disease process. In contrast to the operant approach to pain management in which the patient's environment is modified, the cognitive-behavioral approach makes the patient play a central role. Their role is to control cognitions (thoughts, beliefs, and expectations) which might in turn influence their actions and capabilities of coping with painful stimulation. In some of his earlier studies, Turk (1986) demonstrated that individuals have very different responses to painful stimulation. For example, a common laboratory analog of clinical pain is called the *cold pressor test*. In this test situation, subjects are asked to put their hand in cold water. After a few minutes, this experience can be very painful. It would be unethical to allow people to keep their hand immersed in this cold water for more than about 5 minutes.

In Turk's study, some participants placed their hand in the water only briefly, while others left it in the entire 5 minutes. Interviews with the participants suggested that those who were able to cope with these stimulations for 5 minutes used cognitive strategies. They might have talked to themselves in productive ways ("I can take the pain"), or they might have used diversion strategies, like thinking about something else. For example, successful copers might imagine that it was a hot day on the beach and that they are jumping into cold water. Those who were unable to keep their hand in the water were more likely to say to themselves "I am not going to put up with this!" or "This bothers me."

Part of the rationale for the cognitive-behavioral intervention is to train patients to use cognitive coping strategies that are realistic but characteristic of good coping responses. The interventions actually use the technology of behavior modification to implement these changes in cognition. The cognitive-behavioral intervention involves five components. These include (1) the reconceptualization of cognitions for thoughts about pain, (2) the monitoring of thoughts (patients record their feelings and the actions they take when they experience pain, and are also taught to recognize the relationships between their thoughts, feelings, actions, and pain responses), (3) belief in control (patients are taught that they can perform the necessary behaviors that are required to effectively deal with the pain), (4) principles of reinforcement, to alter the way the patients think, feel, and respond to painful stimulations and to their environment, and (5) relapse prevention, since after some patients learn to master their pain, they often relapse. In this final stage the patients are told to identify factors that may contribute to their eventual relapse.

Turk, Michenbaum, and Genest (1983) teach a variety of different techniques to achieve these objectives. One of the most important is relaxation training. Under controlled circumstances, the participants learn to relax muscles. In addition, they are given a variety of different cognitive strategies. These might involve imagining that they are experiencing something incompatible with pain, like relaxing on the beach or experiencing a very cool sensation. They are also taught cognitive reappraisal, which means that they reinterpret painful stimulations. They might learn to say to themselves statements such as "This bothers me but I will be able to deal with it. Just relax—it will be OK." Some of the strategies

involve focusing on the physical environment, while others involve mental distraction or imagining that they are somewhere else. The exact techniques that are used might vary from patient to patient.

Several studies have demonstrated that these techniques are effective for helping people deal with both acute and chronic pain. For example, Kaplan, Atkins, and Lenhard (1982) studied cognitive-behavioral interventions to help patients cope with sigmoidoscopy. Sigmoidoscopy is a common medical screening test used to diagnose cancers of the rectum and sigmoid colon. The test is embarrassing and uncomfortable, and many people avoid it altogether. In this experiment, patients were taught cognitive-behavioral interventions prior to the exam. The results suggested that in comparison with a control group, those in the intervention portion were better able to cope with the test. In addition, the test was about half as long in duration, suggesting that the more relaxed patients facilitated completion of the tests by the physician. In a related study, Kaplan, Metzger, and Jablecki (1983) trained patients to cope with a painful electromyelograph examination. This examination requires a series of painful electric shocks followed by the insertion of fine needles in order to evaluate diseases of the nervous system. Those in an experimental condition receiving cognitive-behavioral training exhibited fewer pain behaviors during the test than those in a control group.

Turk and his colleagues have demonstrated that cognitive-behavioral interventions are also effective for chronic pain. If that is so, they might also be effective for helping patients cope with arthritis. Although very few studies have addressed this issue, those that have been published have produced promising results. For example, Keefe and his colleagues (1987) considered the rationale for using cognitive-behavioral interventions in osteoarthritis. They measured sense of control and cognitive style in a group of patients with this condition. They found that those who felt they had poor control over their pain also had greater functional limitations. Although cause and effect was not clearly established by the study, it did provide some suggestive evidence that cognitive factors are related to functional limitations.

One of the challenges is to determine whether changes in this cognitive pattern resulted in better outcomes. This has been evaluated in one study by Bradley, Young, and their associates (1987). These researchers randomly assigned 53 rheumatoid arthritis patients to one of four conditions: biofeedback, cognitive-behavioral group therapy, structured social support, or a no-treatment control group. Only those in the cognitive-behavior group demonstrated a significant improvement in their disease activity. This improvement was recorded on a rating scale completed by the patient's physician. The cognitive-behavior group also showed a significant decrease in pain behaviors. However, the benefits were not well maintained over the course of time.

Calfas, Kaplan, and Ingram (1992) have also evaluated cognitive-behavioral interventions for patients with osteoarthritis (OA). They randomly assigned 40 OA patients to one of two groups: (1) cognitive-behavior modification or (2) education control. Those in the education control group heard a series of lectures about arthritis and had the opportunity to talk with distinguished experts in the field. However, they did not learn the specific techniques designed to help them cope with pain. At the 2-month follow-up, those in the cognitive-behavioral condition showed significant improvement in functioning and health-related quality of life.

UNPROVEN REMEDIES

Patients who suffer from chronic pain and arthritis often become desperate in their search for a cure. Arthritis providers have expressed great concern about the use of unproven and unconventional remedies among those who suffer from musculoskeletal problems. In 1980, it was estimated that the national costs for unorthodox treatment usage was nearly $1 billion (Brown, Spitz, & Fries, 1980). The Arthritis Foundation has estimated that this number is actually $2 billion (Arthritis Foundation, 1983), and the American Medical Association has estimated that the cost of all unconventional remedies in health care exceeds $10 billion annually. An advertisement for an unconventional remedy is shown in Figure 8-10.

Virtually all studies agree that large numbers of patients use unconventional remedies.

FIGURE 8-10
Example of advertisements promoting various remedies for arthritis. (Courtesy Arthritis Foundation.)

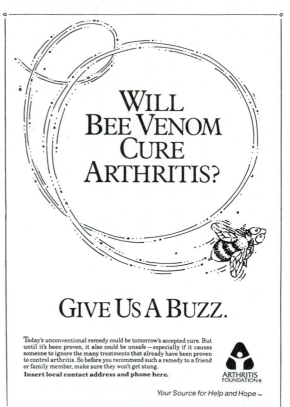

Various studies have suggested that as many as 90 percent of those who have been diagnosed with arthritis use these remedies (Duffy, 1987; Kushner, 1985). A study of patients at Stanford University demonstrated that about 45 percent of the arthritis patients used copper bracelets; while other remedies, including special diets (fish or cod-liver oil, alfalfa seeds, herbs, and the like), are commonly used. Studies from the United States are consistent with similar reports from the United Kingdom (Higham & Jayson, 1982) and from Australia (Worsley & Crawford, 1984). The types of treatments used by patients with arthritis are wide-ranging. They include dietary interventions. However, the diets vary considerably. Some of the interventions involve increases in the intake of fish, while others involve decreases in fish consumption. Some diets recommend increased consumption of red meats, while others recommend decreased consumption of these meats. A variety of vitamins have been proposed, including calcium and multi-purpose vitamins. It is of interest that some of the dietary interventions may have a scientific basis. For years, arthritis providers assumed that all of these dietary recommendations were "quackery." However, recent evidence suggests that some of the diets involving fish oils may actually have benefit to arthritis patients and work on known biological mechanisms (Panush, 1991).

Other remedies include bed rest, exercise, prayer, relaxation, and hot baths. Exotic remedies include dimethyl sulfoxide (DMSO), WD40 sprayed directly on joints, and injections of urine. Some patients use jewelry such as copper bracelets and special rings. Liniments, ointments, and lotions are also commonly employed.

The exact prevalence rate for the use of remedies is less clear. Most studies suggest that virtually all patients use unconventional remedies. However, many rheumatologists, critical of nonphysicians offering treatment, have lumped all nonconventional remedies together. In one recent study, the prevalence of unconventional remedy use in a metropolitan community was evaluated. In this study, a telephone survey was used to identify a random sample of the population who suffered from arthritis or musculoskeletal problems. Three hundred eighty-two individuals were identified. Among these 84 percent had used an unconventional remedy in the last 6 months. However, most of the individuals had used inexpensive and harmless remedies such as exercise, prayer, and relaxation. In fact, those who had used these cognitive or behavioral strategies (exercise, relaxation, prayer) felt that they had benefited from them.

A much smaller number had used exotic remedies, such as urine injections and DSMO. Among those using the peculiar remedies, very few felt that they had received a benefit, and most had discontinued a peculiar treatment after only a short trial (Cronan, Kaplan, Posner, et al., 1990). Although unconventional remedy use is widespread, these findings suggest that the most popular remedies are neither harmful nor expensive. It is unclear whether use of these unconventional remedies is actually a major problem: the remedies seem to be inexpensive and not particularly damaging. Some observers believe that unconventional remedy use represents "normative behavior." In other words, when afflicted by a medical problem, it may be appropriate to continue trying different treatments until something useful is found. Much of the difficulty is that the traditional remedies, like the nontraditional ones, have not provided a cure for the disease. Use of unconventional remedies is likely to continue at a high rate.

SUMMARY

Pain is a common result of most medical conditions. The traditional view of pain has been that it reflects the specific stimulation of nerves. However, recent evidence suggests that pain is much more complex and almost certainly involves a strong psychological component. Important distinctions include that between acute pain, which might be associated with an active disease or traumatic injury, and chronic pain, which persists after injuries are expected to have healed. Operant psychologists have focused on pain behaviors, which are observable responses to pain stimulation. Reinforcement of pain behaviors might establish these behaviors in the absence of pain stimulation. Modern views of pain, including the gate control theory, separate dimensions of pain into sensory-discriminative, emotional-motivational, and central aspects.

Pain causes a significant amount of disability in our society. One of the major causes of chronic pain is arthritis. In this chapter, we considered several important forms of arthritis including rheumatoid arthritis, which is an autoimmune disease, and osteoarthritis, which is a condition associated with the degeneration of joints.

Behavioral scientists have made significant contributions to the measurement of pain and pain conditions such as arthritis. In addition, there have been significant studies of the association between chronic pain and psychological outcomes such as depression and disability.

Behavioral treatments for chronic pain include operant approaches that extinguish pain behavior, cognitive-behavioral approaches that train patients to cope with pain, and social support groups. For those who fail to gain benefit from treatment, unconventional remedy use is common.

KEY TERMS

Nociception. The process of receiving sensory information from pain receptors.

Pain. An emotional, disabling sensory discomfort typically associated with tissue injury.

Pain behaviors. Observable responses to pain stimulation, including facial grimace, limping, and vocalizations.

Gate control theory of pain. A theory that divides the pain process into three components: sensory-discriminative, emotional-motivational, and central.

Arthritis. A group of diseases associated with inflammation of joints.

Osteoarthritis. The most common form of arthritis associated with degeneration of cartilage between joints.

Rheumatoid arthritis. The more severe form of arthritis believed to be the result of an autoimmune process.

Systemic lupus. A general systemic autoimmune disease that causes symptoms of pain in the joints. However, lupus can be a very serious disease resulting in damage to a variety of organ systems.

Fibrositis. A mysterious musculoskeletal disease associated with aching, stiffness, and tenderness near joins or muscles. Fibrositis is associated with sleep problems, but there is no known diagnostic test for it.

Gout. A disease associated with swelling of the large toe. This condition spreads to other joints and is associated with severe pain. Gout is understood in terms of a specific biochemical abnormality.

Arthritis Impact Measurement Scale (AIMS). A measure of health status specific to arthritis. The AIMS measures a variety of behavioral impacts of rheumatic diseases.

Health Assessment Questionnaire (HAQ). A measure similar to the AIMS that evaluates the functional effects of arthritis.

Cognitive-behavioral therapy. A treatment approach that combines cognitive and behavioral principles. The treatment has been used successfully for the treatment of chronic pain and arthritis.

Unproven remedies. A variety of unproven remedies are known to be used by arthritis patients. However, dangerous remedies appear to be used less frequently than has previously been reported in the literature.

CHAPTER 9

Diabetes

Susan was a happy 11-year-old. She was active and very healthy. However, 4 months before her twelfth birthday she developed an unusually strong appetite. In addition, she was thirsty almost all the time, and she needed to go to the bathroom much more often than ever before. In fact, she needed to get up several times each night in order to urinate. Despite her strong appetite, she was losing weight. When she complained of being drowsy and nauseated, Susan's mother realized it was time to take her to the doctor.

Upon examination and some special tests, Susan learned that she had insulin-dependent diabetes mellitus (IDDM). Had it gone untreated, she would have died. With treatment, she will live a relatively normal life. However, her condition is chronic. She will need to take insulin injections for the rest of her life. In addition, she will need to watch her diet, modify her activities, and be on the lookout for a variety of problems. Although doctors and nurses can oversee treatment, the most important treatment specialists will be Susan and her family, who will be responsible for administering most of the care. Personal behavior and the proper care of diabetes cannot be separated. In this chapter we will review diabetes mellitus and discuss the relationship between behavior and diabetes care.

BOX 9-1

HEALTH OBJECTIVES FOR THE YEAR 2000

1. To reduce diabetes-related deaths to no more than 34 per 100,000 people (1986 baseline: 38 per 100,000).

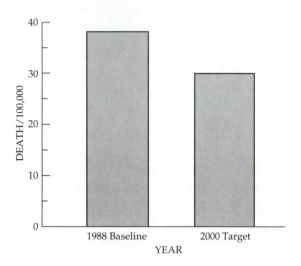

2. To reduce the percentage of overweight people to a prevalence of no more than 20 percent among those aged 20 and older, and no more than 15 percent among adolescents aged 12 through 19 (baseline: 26 percent for those aged 20 and older, and 15 percent for adolescents aged 12 through 19).

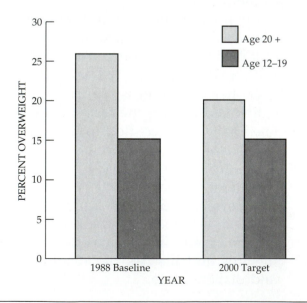

Diabetes mellitus is a major medical, personal, and public health problem. *Diabetes* is a chronic disease associated with abnormally high levels of glucose (sugars) in the blood. A rise in glucose occurs when foods are consumed. Glucose from blood is an energy source for cells and tissues throughout the body. However, utilization of glucose requires a hormone, insulin, that allows the glucose to be used. Diabetes occurs when the body does not make enough insulin or when cells cannot make use of the available insulin. Later in the chapter we will discuss the pathophysiology of diabetes in more detail. It has been estimated that 5.5 million people in the United States have diabetes. In addition, it has been estimated that at least an equally large number of people have the disease but have not been diagnosed. Thus, as many as 11 million people may suffer from these conditions (American Diabetes Association, 1986). Each year approximately one-half million new cases of diabetes are diagnosed (Harris, 1985). Diabetes is the seventh leading cause of death in the United States. Each year approximately 130,000 deaths are directly attributable to the disease, while many other deaths are associated with the complications of diabetes (Centers for Disease Control, 1988).

PATHOPHYSIOLOGY

Many different factors may cause the onset of diabetes, and its course and prognosis vary among individuals. The term *diabetes mellitus* actually covers several separate and distinct conditions. The two most common forms of diabetes mellitus are Type I, or insulin-dependent diabetes mellitus (IDDM), and Type II, non-insulin-dependent diabetes mellitus (NIDDM). Insulin-dependent diabetes (Type I) is considered to be the most severe form, and individuals in this subclass require insulin injections to preserve life. Those with non-insulin-dependent diabetes mellitus (Type II) may use insulin to correct their high blood glucose levels but do not require an external source of insulin in order to survive. NIDDM is clearly the most common type of diabetes, although we typically think of a diabetic patient as one who requires insulin. Type I diabetes is a relatively rare form of the condition, accounting for only about 10 percent of all cases. About 90 percent of those with diabetes are in the NIDDM category. Among these, 60 to 90 percent are overweight (Herman, Teutsch, & Geiss, 1988), and some evidence suggests that weight loss can be of substantial benefit to these individuals (Wing, 1989). Thus, the American Diabetes Association (1984) now recommends diet and exercise as the primary interventions for the control of NIDDM. In other words, they recommend that patients be given a serious trial of behavioral intervention before they are exposed to drug treatment.

Type I and Type II diabetes are very different diseases. In each case, environmental factors acting in concert with genetic susceptibility may be important precursors. There is substantial evidence that Type I diabetes has a genetic component. People with certain genetic markers for human leukocyte antigens (HLA's) are at increased risk for developing Type I diabetes. Siblings of children with IDDM are at increased risk of developing the condition. In fact, the chances are 7 times the rate in the general population (Harris, 1985). However, if the condition was truly genetic, we would expect perfect concordance, or correspondence, in identical twins. Yet only between 20 and 50 percent of the identical twins of those with IDDM actually develop the disease.

It seems most likely that IDDM is an autoimmune disease. The immune system (see Chapter 12) has at least two distinct functions. The first function is to identify harmful pathogens, and the second function is to seek out and destroy these harmful invaders. Implicit in the first function is the ability to separate cells that are "self" from those that are "nonself." In other words, the system must separate cells that it needs for its own survival from those that might be potentially harmful. An autoimmune disease occurs when the system fails to distinguish the self from the nonself functions. Although there is still some debate, evidence suggests that Type I diabetes is associated with the destruction of the cells that produce insulin. Insulin is produced by beta cells in the pancreas.

One compelling theory is that genetically predisposed individuals have had an inflammatory response to certain infections. These infections might result from common viruses such as mumps, measles, and the like. The infection may cause the insulin to leak out of the cells. Then antibodies are produced in response to the excess insulin. The autoimmune response fails to recognize the insulin, and the antibodies come to destroy the beta cells. As a result, insulin secretion decreases and eventually ceases altogether. The viruses-autoimmune theory may explain why there are a greater number of new cases of Type I diabetes during the winter months (Rossini, Mordeis, & Handlar, 1989). Other evidence for this theory is provided by studies showing that drugs which suppress the immune response may reverse some recent cases (Stiler et al., 1984).

Although there is little evidence that psychological factors contribute to the development of diabetes, at least one group of researchers believes that psychological factors affect the immune process, leaving a person vulnerable to diabetes. McClelland, Patel, Brown, and Kelner (1991) showed that diabetic patients who had recently experienced the loss of a loved one had increases of helper-induced T-cells (see Chapter 12) when reminded of the loss in a laboratory experiment comparing them with subjects suffering from other diseases. Theoretically this heightened immune response could be related to the autoimmune deficiency seen in IDDM.

Regulation of Blood Sugar

Diabetes is a problem in glucose or energy metabolism. The human body uses two fuels for energy: glucose and oxygen. Glucose serves as a fuel for most of the tissues and organs of the body. It is delivered to cells of various organs through the blood. The food that you eat is absorbed in the intestines, and sugars are extracted for circulation in the blood. These blood sugars, or glucose, eventually become the energy supply. However, sugars cannot get out of the blood by themselves. In order to gain entry into the cells, they need the help of a hormone known as *insulin*. Many have suggested that the role of insulin is that of a key which opens shut cells (see Figure 9-1). Without the presence of insulin, glucose cannot gain entry and continues to build up in the blood.

FIGURE 9-1

Lock and key hypothesis. (Reprinted with permission from Harris and Rossini, *Diabetes Spectrum*, 2(3): p. 196, 1989. Copyright © 1989 by the American Diabetes Association, Inc.) Within the circle of the lock are three regions, each analogous to the tumbler in a real lock. The three tumblers discussed in the review are the environment, genetic factors, and cell biological factors that contribute to the development of autoimmune IDDM. At the center of the lock is the pancreatic β-cell, which is destroyed in IDDM. A comprehensive understanding of the pathogenesis of IDDM will require an understanding of all the tumblers. Only when they are all in alignment will the key turn—unlocking, as it were, our understanding of the process of autoimmune β-cell destruction.

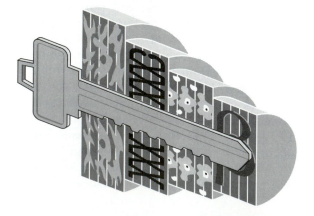

Physiologists have documented that the rise of blood glucose following a meal stimulates insulin release from the pancreas, which is the organ that produces insulin (shown in Figure 9-2). People with diabetes have difficulty either producing insulin or utilizing it. Since insulin cannot get from the blood to the cells, it builds up to very high levels within the circulatory system. At the same time, cells receive no energy and begin to starve.

The glucose system is *homeostatic*. Homeostatic systems are self-balancing. The body attempts to maintain blood glucose at a relatively constant level. If a person does not eat food, insulin secretions stimulate release of stored glucose from the liver. The normally functioning person makes a series of internal adjustments that result in relatively steady levels of blood glucose throughout the day. In the absence of appropriate levels of insulin, or when insulin receptors are defective, blood sugar levels rise. At the same time, hungry cells starve and begin to burn other fuels as an energy source. When cells burn fat as an energy source, they release ketones as a metabolic by-product. These ketones can be released into the blood and can cause the blood to become acidic. Severe cases of this problem are known as *ketoacidosis* (implying that the blood has become acidic from ketones). Severe ketoacidosis can result in coma and death. The kidneys separate elements that are retained in the blood supply and waste products that are eliminated in urine. When the blood sugar gets to a very high level, it may reach a point where the kidneys can no longer

FIGURE 9-2

Schematic representation of the anatomy of the pancreas. Inset: Arrangement of the various cell types in a typical islet of Langerhans. (From West, J. B., Ed., *Physiological Basis of Medical Practice*, 11th ed. Baltimore, Williams & Wilkins, 1985, p. 819.)

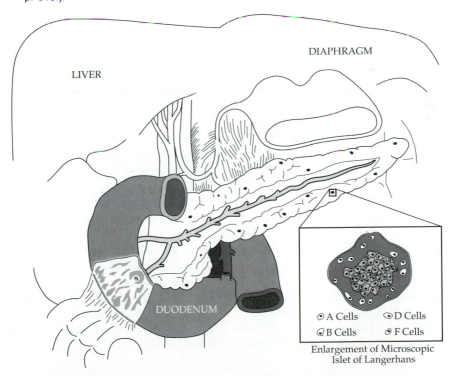

⊙ A Cells   ⊙ D Cells
⊙ B Cells   ⊙ F Cells

Enlargement of Microscopic
Islet of Langerhans

process it. As a result, some of the sugar "spills" into the urine. Thus, elevated levels of sugar in urine are sometimes an indicator of diabetes.

For those with Type II diabetes, the picture is the opposite. Several decades ago, a test was developed to measure how much insulin the body produced. Until this time, it was believed that those with Type II diabetes had difficulty producing insulin, as did those with insulin-dependent diabetes (Type I). However, the new tests demonstrated that those with NIDDM actually had higher levels of insulin in response to sugar ingestion than controls who did not have diabetes. This condition is known as *hyperinsulinemia* because it is associated with overproduction (hyper) of insulin (insulinemia). A variety of researchers have demonstrated that hyperinsulin may be associated with obesity; in fact, the amount of excess body weight is related to the degree of hyperinsulinemia (Bagdade et al., 1967). In other words, evidence suggests that Type II diabetes might be associated with too much rather than too little insulin. Some of the more recent studies suggest that Type II diabetes is associated with insulin resistance, which results when cells that process insulin do not function properly.

The reasons for insulin resistance are not known. However, it has been suggested that insulin resistance is an adaptive response to hyperinsulinemia. Some of the newer studies also suggest that Type II diabetes is heterogeneous. In other words, different people have the conditions for different reasons. Some people may overproduce insulin, some may produce about average amounts, and some may actually underproduce it. Some people may have problems with insulin receptors, while others may not (Davidson, 1986).

Insulin was discovered and used in the treatment of diabetes more than 65 years ago. The discovery of insulin led many observers to believe that diabetes had a cure. However, the physiological replacement of insulin has not provided the ultimate answer to the treatment of diabetes (Zinman, 1991). It is important to emphasize that without insulin, patients with insulin-dependent diabetes have less than a 2-year life expectancy. However, the use of insulin does create some problems. These include hypoglycemia (low blood sugar), skin reactions, weight gain, and other related problems.

The Complications of Diabetes

It may be inappropriate to think of diabetes as a disease. Rather, it is an abnormality in metabolic control. Poor metabolic control over a long period of time is a health concern because it is associated with breakdowns in nearly every system within the body. In June 1980, the National Diabetes Advisory Board convened a census conference. The conference identified some of the major complications of diabetes and offered recommendations on how they should be managed. Some of the major complications are heart disease, nephropathy, blindness, amputations of the feet and toes, and perinatal mortality and morbidity (Ross, Bernstein, & Rifkin, 1983). It must be noted that these are only a few of the many serious complications of the condition.

Heart Disease Heart disease is a serious threat for patients with diabetes. A variety of studies have demonstrated that diabetic patients are at a greater risk of developing atherosclerosis than nondiabetics of the same age. This condition restricts blood flow to the heart and is associated with a greater probability of heart attack and stroke. These relationships have been observed consistently for Type I diabetics (Eaton, 1979; Ganda, 1980), and evidence suggests that Type II diabetic patients are also at greater risk of developing cardiovascular problems (Stamler & Stamler, 1979; West, 1978).

Nephropathy *Nephropathy*, or kidney disease, may develop in approximately half of all Type I diabetic patients and in a significant number of Type II patients. Diabetic patients are 17 times more likely to develop kidney disease than age-matched members of the general population (National Diabetes Data Group, 1979). The most common form of diabetic nephropathy involves the thickening of membranes that line the glomeruli. The glomeruli are small organs within the kidney which have an important filtering function. They sort elements that are retained by the blood and waste products that are eliminated as urine. Diseases of these organs can reduce the efficiency with which these functions are performed. Thus, the thickening of the glomeruli may result in the accumulation of waste products in the blood and elimination of essential blood components such as protein.

Eye Problems Diabetic patients are very much at risk of developing serious complications of the eye. Today diabetes is the major cause of blindness in the world. Diabetic patients are 25 times more likely to develop blindness than age-matched members of the general population. The cause of vision complications in diabetic patients is usually *retinopathy*, which is a problem with the small blood vessels in the retina. In this condition, the walls of small blood vessels become weak. As a result, the vessels can balloon out and break, leaking in blood to the vitreous humor, or center area of the eye.

Approximately 85 percent of all patients with diabetes develop retinopathy within 25 years after the onset of their condition. In most cases, retinopathy will cause only minor problems or temporary vision disturbances. Minor hemorrhage in the eye may block vision or produce black spots inside the eye. However, when this blood is absorbed, only small scarring remains, and this scarring has little impact upon vision. In about 20 percent of the cases,

there is a large hemorrhage or a series of small hemorrhages within the same eye. This can cause detachment of the retina or larger-scale destruction of retinal tissue and permanent blindness. Patients with this complication may benefit from *photocoagulation therapy*, which uses a laser beam to cauterize small blood vessels or to repair the detached retina. Established scar tissue in the vitreous area can be removed with a newer surgical technique known as *vitrectomy*. This surgery has been successful in restoring vision in many cases.

Amputations of Lower Extremities Diabetes is the major condition necessitating amputations of lower extremities. In diabetic populations, the probability of therapeutic amputation is 15 times greater than in the general population. Diabetic complications account for 45 percent of all lower extremity amputations with an age-adjusted rate of 59.7/10,000 (amputations/diabetic individuals) (Most & Sinnock, 1983). The reason these amputations are necessary is that diabetes can cause severe circulatory problems. As a result, blood flow to the extremities is often restricted. Small lesions on the foot can lead to gangrene, and in many cases, areas affected by gangrene must be removed. In order to avoid these problems, the diabetic patient must take very good care of his or her feet. This involves self-inspection, good hygiene, and the avoidance of behaviors which are associated with vascular diseases. Cigarette smoking is particularly dangerous in that it is known to cause restrictions in blood flow. Similarly, hypertension and weight should be vigorously managed.

Neuropathy *Neuropathy* is disease of the nervous system. Diabetes is known to cause a variety of forms of neuropathy. In the peripheral nervous system this is manifested by dysfunction in motor movements of the fingers, toes, arms, and legs. Patients often report tingling sensations in the extremities and difficulty with some muscular movements. Neuropathy in the autonomic nervous system often causes greater concern. As a result of these conditions, approximately 50 percent of all diabetic males eventually become organically impotent and may lose partial control over important body functions such as urination. In severe cases, there is difficulty with the regulation of basic autonomic function, such as blood pressure and heart rate.

Perinatal Mortality and Morbidity A diabetic condition can cause severe problems in pregnancy. Expectant diabetic mothers may find that their diabetes is exacerbated by the pregnancy. Some forms of diabetes are apparent only during pregnancy. If not well managed, diabetic mothers are more likely to give birth prematurely, to have stillborns, or to have deformed children. Thus, aggressive management of diabetes during pregnancy is essential.

All of these problems can be exacerbated by specific behavioral patterns. For example, the probability of complications in the diabetic mother may be increased if she smokes cigarettes or if she does not follow her dietary regimen.

EPIDEMIOLOGY

Diabetes is associated with a number of identifiable risk factors. Age, for example, is an important factor. Type I diabetes typically develops during childhood, with the greatest number of cases beginning between the ages of 10 and 14 (LaPorte, Fishbein, & Drash, et al., 1981) (see Figure 9-3). In contrast, Type II, or NIDDM, typically starts in adulthood and increases substantially as a function of age.

Figure 9-4 summarizes the estimates of the number of people with diabetes taken from the National Health and Nutrition Examination Survey. This is an important study because it

FIGURE 9-3
Age at onset of IDDM for white males and females. (Reprinted with permission from LaPorte et al., *Diabetes* 30:281, 1981. Copyright 1981 by American Diabetes Association, Inc.)

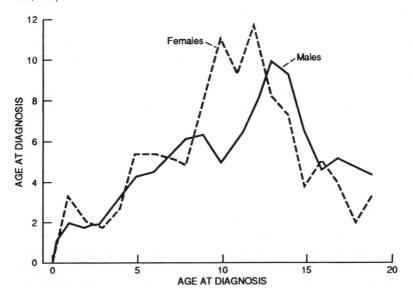

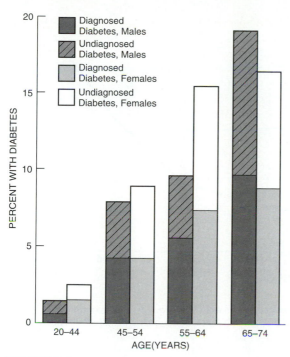

FIGURE 9-4

Percentage of U.S. population aged 20 to 74 years with diabetes from HNAMES II, 1976–1980. (From Harris, M. I., Haiden, W. C., Knowlar, U. C., & Bennett, P. H. (1987). Prevalence of diabetes and impaired glucose tolerance and plasma glucose levels in U.S. population age 20–74 yr. *Diabetes*, 36, 523–534. Reproduced by permission of the author and the American Diabetes Association, Inc.)

took a random sample of American residents, rather than a sample of those who had come to doctors. Half of the people (5901) were given an oral glucose tolerance test to evaluate diabetes. All the people were asked if they had ever been told by a doctor that they had diabetes. Using this method it was possible to estimate both the number of people who have diabetes and the proportion who were formerly unaware of the condition. As the figure demonstrates, nearly half of those who meet the criteria for diabetes were unaware of their condition (upper half of each bar). In addition, the figure demonstrates that the chance of having diabetes dramatically increases as a func-

tion of age. Males and females are equally likely to develop Type I diabetes. However, women are more likely to develop Type II diabetes than men (Harris et al., 1987, Harris, 1991).

Whites are slightly more likely than nonwhite groups to develop Type I diabetes (Herman et al., 1987). For Type II diabetes, nonwhite groups are particularly at risk. For example, Hispanics are 3 times as likely to develop NIDDM in comparison with their Caucasian non-Hispanic counterparts, and Native Americans are nearly 11 times more likely to develop the problem (Harris, 1985).

From a behavioral perspective, two of the risk factors for diabetes are of particular importance. These are obesity and inactivity.

Obesity is not associated with IDDM. However, the association between obesity and NIDDM is impressive (see Figure 9-5). Between 60 and 90 percent of all the adults with NIDDM are overweight. Brothers and sisters of diabetic patients are 3 times as likely to develop the problem themselves if they are overweight when compared with their nonobese siblings (Herman et al., 1988). Substantial evidence now suggests that glucose tolerance does return to normal with weight loss for patients with NIDDM (Wing, 1989).

Physical inactivity may be an issue for both Type I and Type II diabetes. Although exercise cannot "cure" diabetes, regular activity may help maintain glucose control. In addition, regular exercise may help in weight regulation. We will return to the issues of diet and exercise in a later section of this chapter.

Controversies about Treatment

Patients with non-insulin-dependent diabetes mellitus (NIDDM) are faced with a complex and perhaps ambiguous set of treatment alternatives that include the use of insulin therapy, prescription of oral agents, diabetic diets and weight loss, and patient education. The choice

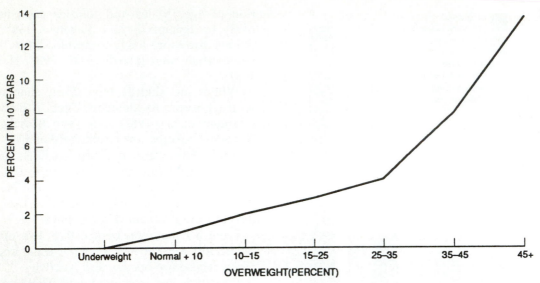

FIGURE 9-5

Age-adjusted 10-year incidence of diagnosis of diabetes related to percent overweight at initial examination. (From *Diabetes in America*, National Data Group, U.S. Dept. of Health and Human Services, NIH Publication No. 85-1468, August 1985, pp. IV–19.)

among these alternatives is complex because the costs, risks, and benefits of the alternatives have not been well defined.

The UGDP Controversy

Substantial epidemiologic data suggest that prolonged elevated blood glucose levels are correlated with complications in a variety of organ systems (Ross, Bernstein, & Rifkin, 1983). However, the assumption that reductions in blood glucose are associated with reductions in the probability of these complications has been more difficult to demonstrate in humans. The best available evidence, the large and controversial University Group Diabetes Program (UGDP), was a cooperative randomized clinical trial involving 12 medical centers. A total of 823 patients were randomly assigned to one of five treatment groups. Two groups received insulin injections, one on a variable dosage schedule and the other on a standard dosage schedule. The third group received tolbutamide, a drug taken by mouth to

reduce blood sugar (oral hypoglycemic), while the fourth group received a placebo. The fifth group, which was assigned to take a second drug, was discontinued after complications were observed early in the study. All groups were given a special diet.

After 8 years, the mortality status of 818 of the original 823 patients was determined. Those randomly assigned to receive tolbutamide had a significantly *increased* probability of death due to cardiovascular diseases in comparison with the placebo group. The two insulin groups did not differ significantly from the placebo group. The UGDP study touched off a variety of controversies. Various authors suggested that there were methodological flaws associated with the randomization, the dependability of the outcome measures, the uniformity of protocols across centers, and a variety of decisions that were made throughout the project (Feinstein, 1971; Kilo, Miller, & Williamson, 1971; Schor, 1980). By 1971, statisticians were calling for moratoriums on reanalysis of the UGDP data. Indeed, when the

BOX 9·2

FOCUS ON DIVERSITY

There are about 1.5 million persons of Native American heritage currently living in the United States. Until 1930, diabetes was rarely observed among North American Indians. However, the situation has changed rather dramatically in the last 50 years. Particularly in some tribes, diabetes has reached epidemic proportions. The Pima tribes provide an example of a population in which diabetes has become unusually common. It has been estimated that about half of the Pimas who are age 35 or older currently have diabetes. That is the highest rate known for any population. In the Pimas, and in other Native American groups, the development of diabetes appears to occur simultaneously with obesity. It is possible that some groups are genetically predisposed toward diseases such as diabetes. However, the expression of the illness may occur only if the person is overweight. In the Pimas, the combination of having one parent with diabetes and becoming overweight appears to be a good predictor of developing the problem. Figure 9-6 shows the relationship between a body mass index and the incidence of diabetes among the Pimas. Body mass index is a measure of obesity. The figure shows that as body mass increases, so does the number of cases of diabetes. Unfortunately, the incidence of diabetic complications among the Pima Indians is also quite high. Thus, it is important to develop programs to control weight for members of several Native American groups (Sievers & Fischer, 1985).

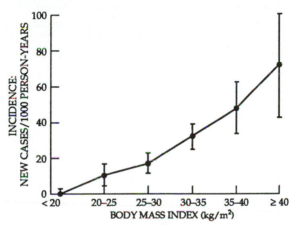

FIGURE 9-6

Age-sex adjusted incidence rates (with 95 percent confidence intervals, i.e., $\pm$ 1.96 standard errors) for diabetes in Pima Indians, by body mass index. (From Knowler, W. C., Pettit, D. J., Savage, P. J., and Bennett, P. H. Diabetes incidence in Pima Indians: Contributions of obesity and parental diabetes. *Am. J. Epidemiol.* 113(2):149, 1981.)

final results were published in 1982, most observers had already made up their minds about the credibility of the study. To this day the study's merits and problems are still debated. Most diabetes specialists have discounted the UGDP results, and some new evidence has raised questions about the original results. Initially, the sales of oral hypoglycemic drugs fell sharply after the publication of the UGDP data. However, the use of these drugs has sharply increased since 1980. By 1986, they accounted for about 1 percent of all prescriptions, or about 21.5 million orders (Kennedy, Piper, & Baum, 1988). Many of the recent prescriptions for oral hypoglycemic medications are for newer and different products that were not evaluated in the UGDP study. Although the newer agents are more effective in reducing blood sugar, their value in reducing complications remains to be demonstrated. Thus controversy remains in most aspects of diabetes care.

Choices among treatment alternatives are complex. The benefits of each treatment alternative are not definitively established. Although each alternative may be associated with side effects, few studies have measured these side effects or have provided systematic guidelines for evaluating benefits versus side effects. The target of treatment is typically improved glucose tolerance. Yet we cannot say with certainty that improved glucose tolerance, particularly for the marginally affected NIDDM patient, will result in less mortality or morbidity, or better quality of life. Modern treatments are often a nuisance for patients, yet the literature rarely documents patient attitudes toward their care or patient preferences for alternatives.

The Patient's Role

Clinical articles often make the paternalistic assumption that physicians are entitled to make treatment decisions for their patients. Despite a growing consensus that patients should be involved in decisions affecting their health care (Schneiderman & Arras, 1985), recent studies suggest that patients rarely report being advised of their options regarding surgical procedures (Wennberg, 1989). This failure to inform is all the more indefensible in diabetes care because many interventions affect quality of life in addition to life expectancy. Determining potential benefit requires the integration of patient utilities and the assessment of various outcomes weighted by their probabilities.

Patient Factors in Diabetes

The published literature tells us remarkably little about patient preferences for different treatment modalities. Many studies have attempted to predict compliance among NIDDM patients. Yet these studies tend to focus on demographic and personality characteristics used to "diagnose" the noncomplier. Little consideration is given to the effect of the treatment on the patients and their lifestyles. For example, a recent paper concerning insulin-dependent diabetes mellitus (IDDM) patients evaluated discontinuation of continuous subcutaneous insulin-infusion (CSII) therapy. The authors focused on demographic characteristics, mental illness, and cigarette smoking, all of which were poor predictors of dropping out of treatment. However, the most common reason for terminating treatment was that it was uncomfortable, that it caused irritation, or that there was an infection at the infusion site (Gwinn, Bailey, & Mecklenburg, 1988). Several studies have reported that patients are more likely to drop out of treatment if they have poor outcomes (Kaplan & Atkins, 1987). Being "noncompliant" might mean that the treatment is not working or that it is creating new problems. It is interesting that there is essentially no literature evaluating the nuisance factor of using oral medications. A computer literature search crossing oral compounds with patient compliance revealed only five articles published in the last 20 years.

Social learning theory suggests that situational factors play a more important role in determining compliance behavior than dispositional or demographic characteristics. Social environment and specific health beliefs may be good predictors of compliance (Wilson, Ary, Biglan, Glasgow, Toobert, & Campbell, 1985). Other studies have demonstrated that diabetic adults deviate from their regimen when it becomes a nuisance. Open-ended questions suggest that common reasons for dietary nonadherence include eating out in restaurants or being in social situations where food offers are difficult to refuse (Ary, Toobert, Wilson, & Glasgow, 1986).

Occasional change in regimen may have

FOCUS ON RESEARCH

One of the major problems for young people with diabetes is the feeling that they have little control over their environment. The expectation that rewards and punishments are independent of one's own behavior is known as *learned helplessness* (see Chapter 8). Many young people with diabetes may believe that they have little control over their lives. In one study 50 males and 30 females (ages 10 to 16) completed measures of learned helplessness and depression. In addition, detailed evaluations of diet and compliance with the diabetic regimen were taken. A careful study of blood chemistry measures was made to evaluate the control of diabetes.

The results of the study demonstrated that learned helplessness was associated with poor control of diabetes. In addition, those who felt that outcomes were unrelated to their own behavior were also significantly more depressed. The careful study of the behaviors showed that those who exercised, followed their eating plan, and used insulin (as suggested by their physicians) achieved better control of their diabetes than those who did not adhere to these recommendations. Control of diabetes was unrelated to age, level of physiological development, sex, duration of illness, or socioeconomic status. Overall, the results of the study suggest that learned helplessness is associated with depression and poor control of diabetes. Furthermore, the young people who followed the regimen carefully appeared to achieve better outcomes (Kuttner, Delamater, & Santiago, 1990).

dent diabetes mellitus were asked to describe their requests. There was a significant correlation between the perceived fulfillment of these requests and perceived health status, and a nonsignificant trend suggesting a relationship between request fulfillment and better biochemical control of diabetes (Uhlmann, Inui, Percoraro, & Carter, 1988). In another experimental study, Greenfield and associates (Greenfield, Kaplan, Ware, et al., 1988) randomly assigned NIDDM patients to a control condition or to a 20-minute session designed to improve information seeking during physician encounters. In comparison with controls, those experiencing the intervention were twice as effective in eliciting information from their physician and eventually achieved lower blood sugar values. The study showed that patients can productively contribute to therapeutic decision making and that the time has come to involve patients more actively in the treatment decision process. It is worth noting that even a small bit of help can make a difference once the patient gets access. For example, for those who have made commitments to change their diets, a single session with a dietitian can produce significant benefits (Stetson, Vints, Gregory, & Schlunndt, 1991).

TREATMENT

Behavioral interventions are important in the treatment of both Type I and Type II diabetes.

Behavioral Interventions in Type I Diabetes

A diagnosis of diabetes is truly disruptive. Patients with Type I diabetes must follow a complex regimen of diet, exercise, and insulin injections. Failure to follow this very complicated set of prescriptions can result in increased risk of complications, symptoms, and, in severe cases, even death. For people with diabetes, an ordinary day might involve repeated pricks with needles in order to draw

other consequences. For example, diabetic patients are not allowed to operate commercial motor vehicles if they take insulin. They may gain commercial certification if their condition is stabilized by either diet or a combination of diet and oral hypoglycemic drugs (Federal Register, 1987). A diabetic adult can get a commercial pilots license if his or her condition is controlled by diet. Yet use of insulin or oral medications is grounds for disqualification (Krall, Entmacher, & Drury, 1985).

There are now a few published examples of patient co-participation in the decision process. In one study, adults with insulin-depen-

small blood samples for glucose tests, a series of insulin injections, and adjustments of diet and exercise in order to keep blood glucose balanced. Too much insulin may result in hypoglycemia, or overcorrection. This may cause dizziness, tiredness, and in more serious cases unconsciousness. On the other hand, failure to take enough insulin may result in hyperglycemia. This can cause other symptoms, including excessive thirst, dizziness, and in more severe cases ketoacidosis, coma, and even death. Exercise is useful because it functions like an injection of insulin. Yet too much exercise may result in hypoglycemia. Various foods can increase blood glucose, sometimes in an unpredictable way. Thus, the daily lives of people with diabetes are very complex and involve a wide variety of activities designed to keep blood glucose levels normal.

Rigorous self-care is difficult for diabetic individuals of any age. However, it is a particular challenge for adolescents who are desirous of the care-free lifestyle typified by their peers. IDDM teenagers often violate their self-care protocols because they are unable to resist peer influence.

Most educational programs for young people with diabetes emphasize factual knowledge about the disease process. However, correlations between factual knowledge and diabetes control are often disappointing (Marquis & Ware, 1979). Many IDDM teenagers apparently know how to control their condition but lack the skill or desire to implement these behaviors. The failure of educational programs might be considered analogous to research on smoking prevention (see Chapter 16). Traditional smoking education programs that emphasize facts about cigarette smoking and its health consequences often show the expected changes in knowledge and attitudes about cigarette use. However, these programs have not typically resulted in reductions in smoking behavior.

In contrast to educational approaches, recent efforts derived from social learning theory have produced more impressive results. These programs emphasize peer modeling, peer communication, and immediate and primary social consequences of smoking. These peer programs have also been successful in modifying resistance to peer influence in other areas. Social skills interventions have been successfully applied to help IDDM teenagers avoid peer influence.

In one study, 21 IDDM teenagers were recruited for a summer camp. They were divided into two groups. During a diabetes summer school, one group participated in daily social learning exercises designed to improve social skills and the ability to resist peer influence. The second group spent an equal amount of time learning medical facts about diabetes care. Four months after the intervention, blood tests showed that those in the social skills group were in significantly better control of their diabetes than those assigned to the control group. A variety of variables were significantly correlated with good control of diabetes. These included the subject's self-reported compliance with their diabetic regimen and attitudes toward self-care. In other words, those who reported that they regularly checked their blood glucose and took their insulin on a regular basis were also in better control of their diabetes. In addition, those teenagers who had more positive outcomes and attitudes about the disease were also in better control. However, the study produced some surprising findings. One of them was that social skills and satisfaction with social networks were actually correlates of *poor* control, rather than good control. Those teenagers who were most integrated with their social group were not doing as well with their diabetes as those who were more socially competent. This suggests that teens who are deeply involved with their peers and act just like them do not do as well with their diabetes care (Kaplan, Chadwick, & Shimmel, 1985).

Consistency   The diabetic regimen is very demanding. It may require weight control, monitoring of blood tests, taking medications, keeping doctor appointments, and so on. Traditionally, people felt that there were "good patients," who did all of these things, and other patients who could not be relied upon. Indeed many caretakers still view patients in these simple terms. However, studies have demonstrated that people are not consistent in the way they deal with their diabetic regimens. For example, Orne and Binik (1989) studied 227 diabetic patients and observed that there was a surprisingly poor correspondence between compliance with various aspects of the diabetic regimen. Patients complied with some aspects but failed to comply with many others.

Similar results were reported by Glasgow, Toobert, Riddle, and their colleagues (1989). These investigators wanted to predict three different behaviors required of diabetic patients: diet, exercise, and glucose testing. They found that different variables predicted different aspects of the regimen. Patients viewed diet and exercise as important but extremely difficult to achieve. Blood glucose testing, in contrast, was seen as easier to achieve but as having fewer benefits. The study identified two distinct aspects of diabetes self-care. One aspect is medically related (taking insulin or blood glucose), while the other aspect focuses more on lifestyle. Currently, most diabetes education programs are built on medical aspects. However, the lifestyle variables may be equally if not more important to the control of this condition. Furthermore, this study demonstrated that demographic variables (age, marital status, and the like) gave very little information about adherence to diet, exercise, or blood glucose testing. Many doctors focus on these variables, despite their relatively low

levels of importance in predicting behaviors. Conversely, social learning variables, which focus on the environmental influences, were considered much more important. These findings suggest that the diabetes programs of the future should emphasize social influences upon diabetes self-care and upon barriers to performing the behaviors required to control the condition. For example, it may be more important to teach teenage diabetics to cope with tempting food offers from friends than to understand how insulin works.

Home Glucose Monitoring   One of the recent advances in diabetes care involves home glucose monitoring. Until recently, diabetic patients got little individualized daily feedback about their blood glucose control. It used to be common for people to test urine for acid levels and ketones. Yet this technology was very crude and provided relatively poor feedback. Different people have different thresholds for spilling by-products into the urine. Thus, some people could be in poor control of their diabetes without necessarily having it reflected in the tests. The breakthrough was the development of small monitors that can be carried by patients. Using these monitors, the patient can prick his or her own finger several times per day. With just one drop of blood, they can get an accurate estimate of their blood sugar level. Knowing this information allows them to make on-the-spot adjustments of their insulin and diet plans.

Originally, there was tremendous enthusiasm about these new methods. Indeed, they have very substantial potential for helping patients with diabetes. Yet, more behavioral research needs to be done to achieve the potential for these methods. Some studies have produced discouraging results. For example, Wing and colleagues (1986) did not observe a consistent relationship between home glucose monitoring and patient outcomes. Perhaps this is because home glucose monitoring may be a problem for patients. In one study, Mazze and colleagues (1984) found that nearly three-fourths of the patients asked to keep self-monitoring records of blood glucose failed to report the values accurately. Many studies have reported problems with compliance. This innovative aspect of care may create significant burdens without producing benefits. Psychological studies that compare compliance with the accurate use of these devices may help us understand how to gain the most from this technology.

Newer technological developments have improved techniques for monitoring blood glucose. One new device includes memory microprocessor chips. Using this device, the monitor actually remembers various blood glucose values. In one study, 30 patients were randomly assigned to use these new meters. Half of the teenage subjects were given contracts than enforced regular use of the monitor. The others were not given the contracts. The adolescents who had not signed contracts declined sharply in their use of the meters over a 16-week period. However, those who had signed the contracts maintained their level of blood glucose monitoring. Both groups showed moderate improvement in the control of their diabetes. Thus, blood glucose monitoring by itself could not explain these improvements. In addition, those who used their monitor regularly did not show improvements in overall compliance in comparison with those not assigned to the meters. These data further suggest that the various pieces of behavior required to manage diabetes may be independent of one another. Those who regularly monitor their blood glucose and understand how they are doing may still not be making the correct behavioral changes to manage their condition (Wysocki, Green, & Huxtable, 1989).

Family Variables The diagnosis of a child with diabetes would be expected to have a substantial impact upon families. Imagine what happens when an ordinary healthy child all of a sudden has a life-threatening illness. Managing the condition, particularly for younger children, involves a concerted effort for everyone in the environment. It is commonly believed that marital dissatisfaction is much more common among parents whose children are in trouble (Christensen et al., 1983). In one study, La Greca and her associates (1991) found that family cohesion and diabetes-specific family support were related to adherence to the diabetic regimen among 74 IDDM adolescents between the ages of 10 and 19.

Hanson and colleagues (1989) evaluated control of diabetes in 94 intact families in which an adolescent had NIDDM. The initial analysis showed that those adolescents in better control of their illness came from families with higher cohesion, flexibility, and marital satisfaction. However, more detailed statistical analysis revealed that other variables may account for this relationship. In particular, the duration of the illness seemed to explain much of the results. Among those adolescents who had been diagnosed relatively recently, family variables did predict control of the condition. However, duration of illness was ultimately the best predictor of how well the children were doing. These results suggest that family variables can help us understand some of the mystery of diabetes control. However, duration of the illness is also very important. Furthermore, duration of illness can have an impact on family relationships. The stress of dealing with a complex medical problem can create family frictions in otherwise stable units.

Mood and Diabetes Diabetes, like most other chronic diseases, is often associated with depression (Gill, 1991). To some extent, this depression may be associated with dysfunction caused by the illness. Yet variations in blood sugar may be associated with variations in mood. For people without diabetes, the blood sugar level is kept within a fairly tight range, typically between 80 and 120 mg/dl of blood. For people with diabetes, the ranges can vary greatly. Thus, on the average day, a person with IDDM may experience blood sugar levels much lower and much higher than the nondiabetic person. Researchers have become interested in whether these variations in blood glucose are associated with variations in mood and symptoms.

In one study, Gonder-Frederick, Cox, Bobbitt, and Pennebaker (1989) intensively studied 34 adults with IDDM. Four times each day these adult subjects completed a mood and symptom checklist and measured their blood glucose. The symptom checklist included both positive and negative mood states. The investigators found that blood glucose levels and mood were systematically related for the majority of the participants. However, different individuals experienced different moods when their blood sugars were high or low. On average, low levels of blood glucose were associated with negative mood states, such as nervousness. On the other hand, positive mood states were more likely to be associated with high blood glucose values. Nevertheless some of the participants reported negative moods such as anger and sadness when blood sugar levels were high. These findings suggest that some of the variations in mood, observed among diabetic patients, might be explained by changes in their blood glucose levels. In a related study the same group of investigators was unable to improve awareness of blood glucose even with intensive training. The training did not reduce fear (Cox et al., 1991). Thus new clinical approaches are still needed.

Behavioral Interventions in Type II Diabetes

The controversies surrounding the use of medications for NIDDM patients have stimulated more interest in behavioral treatments. In the next sections, we will consider diet and exercise interventions in more detail.

Exercise The value of exercise for diabetes and diabetic care has been recognized for centuries (Skyler, 1979). Some time ago, the Kroc Foundation held a conference on diabetes and exercise (Vranic, Horbath, & Wahren, 1979). The conclusion of the conference suggested that exercise may be of great importance for those with diabetes. For example, inactivity may be associated with relative resistance to insulin and increased glucose tolerance. Increased exercise appears to increase sensitivity to insulin (Horton 1992). However, there may be some complications of increased exercise. For example, for patients with IDDM, increased exercise may also increase the risk of hypoglycemia. Thus, in the insulin-dependent patient, there must be a careful balance between food intake, insulin treatment, and exercise (Henry & Edelman, 1992).

These risks are greatly decreased in the Type II diabetic patient because these patients rarely, if ever, experience serious consequences of hypoglycemia. Several lines of evidence suggest that exercise may be valuable in the treatment of people with Type II diabetes (Ackerman, 1992). For example, the major objective of many treatments is to lower weight. In studies designed to compare the value of diet and exercise on weight control, it has been reported that combinations of exercise and diet produce more and longer lasting weight loss than either approach alone (Dahlkoetter, Callahan, & Linton, 1979; Henry & Edelman, 1992). Exercise may contribute significantly to weight loss because increased activity may lead to changes in the metabolic rate (Thompson et al., 1982).

Diet Nutritional management has long been a core ingredient of diabetes care. Control of blood glucose requires a balance between energy expenditure (exercise) and energy sources (food). In the normal person, the metabolic equilibrium is maintained through the regular secretions of insulin and other hormones. However, in the diabetic patient, insulin or insulin utilization is abnormal, and therapeutic approaches are necessary to maintain blood glucose levels. The relationship between diet and diabetes control is discussed in virtually every publication on diabetes care. Determining just exactly what diabetic patients should eat, however, has been somewhat more confusing. There are some specific characteristics of diet which may be very important to those with Type II diabetes. For example, studies have shown that diets high in complex carbohydrate and fiber will increase glucose tolerance.

Until recently, patients with diabetes were advised to eat a high-fat, low-carbohydrate diet. However, recent evidence has demonstrated that diets high in complex carbohydrate and fiber reduce blood sugar levels and improve the control of NIDDM (Anderson et al, 1991). Both the American Diabetes Association (Arky, Wiley-Rosette, & ElVeheri, 1982) and the British Diabetic Association (Nutrition Subcommittee of the British Diabetic Association, 1982) have issued guidelines recommending that dietary carbohydrates be increased to 50 percent or more of all calories consumed, and that fat in the diet be reduced to 35 percent or below. In addition to recommendations for content changes, total reductions in calories are also being recommended. Reductions in weight and body fat may produce very significant benefits for NIDDM patients. Even those who lose 7 to 10 lb may receive substantial benefits as witnessed by their blood tests (Arky, 1978). Yet most treatment programs are difficult to evaluate because they make changes in what people eat at the same time they reduce the number of calories. Thus, it is very difficult to tell if benefits result from reducing calories or from changing the composition of the diet. Some studies have shown that traditional wisdom about dietary composition

may not be correct. For example, ice cream is high in sugar. Yet eating ice cream may not dramatically increase the blood sugar levels of people with diabetes (Henry & Crapo, 1991).

Perhaps the most serious limitation of a dietary intervention approach is the likelihood that people will be unable to maintain lower weight over the course of time. West (1978) suggested that less than 15 percent of all diabetic patients achieve long-term weight reduction. In fact, relatively few studies have actually demonstrated that people can lose weight and keep the weight off over the course of time.

Developing Behavioral Programs

In the preceding sections, we have suggested that behavioral factors play an important role in Type II diabetes. Patients who take good care of themselves may have a higher probability of living normal lives without complications of cardiovascular disease, neuropathy, nephropathy, and retinopathy. Conversely, those who take poor care of themselves may be exposed to greater risks of these frightening conditions and might expect a shorter life of poorer quality. Diabetic patient education typically emphasizes these issues. Yet few diabetes manuals recognize the potential of behavioral interventions for the management of these conditions (Gill, 1991).

As the evidence reviewed above suggests, Type II diabetic patients benefit from controlled dieting, exercise, and stress reduction. These are essential components of successful weight control programs. Methods that have been used and evaluated for weight loss may be of value for the management of Type II diabetes. Several authors have suggested that reduction of obesity will result in enhanced insulin utilization (Ireland et al., 1980). Since the patient with Type II diabetes may return to normal insulin secretion and proper functioning of insulin receptors, it has been suggested that control of obesity and long-term compliance with diet and exercise programs may offer a "cure" for some patients. By 1979, the American Diabetes Association (ADA) issued a policy statement suggesting that diet is the first-line treatment and that oral drugs for lowering blood sugar should be considered only if diet therapy fails (ADA, 1979). Even ads for oral hypoglycemic drugs note that diet and exercise should be used before graduating to pharmaceutical treatments. With this in mind, let us consider the value of behavioral programs for the management of obesity.

Approximately 30 percent of all American women and 15 percent of all American men are obese. Obesity is defined as weighing more than 120 percent of desired weight (Abraham & Johnson, 1979). The consequences of being overweight are severe because obesity is associated with increased risk of heart disease (National Academy of Science, 1980), Type II diabetes, and a variety of other chronic diseases (Thorn, 1970). In addition to chronic disease problems, being overweight is associated with many undesirable social situations, including difficulties in sexual function, inability to travel and participate in athletic activities, and greater difficulty in entering certain occupational fields (Ferguson & Birchler, 1978).

Obesity appears to be caused by a variety of factors, including a hereditary predisposition (Stunkard, Harris, Pedersen, & McClearn, 1990), the influence of the endocrine system on the shape a body takes, and the influence of prenatal or childhood nutrition on the number of fat cells (Charney et al., 1976; Ravelli et al., 1976). However, despite the physiologic predisposition to gain weight, the development of obesity is a complex interaction of physiological and psychological events (Rodin, 1978). Furthermore, there is extensive evidence that behavioral programs can be successfully used for a variety of individuals despite their physiological predisposition (Rodin, 1978; Stunkard, 1979).

In 1962, Ferster, Nurnberger, and Levitt published a detailed analysis of the behavioral control of eating. This early paper outlined the relationship between eating and reinforcement. Building on this early effort, many behavior therapists developed programs to help individuals shed unwanted pounds. Within the last few years there has been a surge of interest in weight reduction programs, and commercial programs using behavioral methods have been quite successful. National programs such as Weight Watchers, run primarily by paraprofessionals, use a group behavioral format and see about 400,000 individuals each week (Stunkard, 1979).

The elements of at least one successful behavior modification strategy for weight loss include (1) describing the behavior to be controlled, (2) identifying the stimuli which typically occur prior to eating, (3) employing behavioral methods for controlling eating behavior, and (4) changing the consequences of eating (Stunkard, 1979) (see Table 9-1). The appropriate application of behavior therapy requires appropriate behavioral assessment. The best results are obtained when the package is tailored to fit the characteristics of a particular client (Wolpe, 1981).

A variety of studies have evaluated the value of behavior modification programs specifically designed for Type II diabetic patients. Rainwater and colleagues (1983) found that Type II diabetic patients assigned to a behavior modification program lost more weight than a group given conventional treatment. Urine sugar and fasting blood glucose values also declined in comparison with a baseline established in the treatment group. However, patients were not randomly assigned to the two groups, and the experimental subjects were more overweight prior to the treatment. Box 9-4 investigates the role of some family issues in weight loss programs for people with diabetes.

Another study evaluated the effects of various behavior modification techniques for the

---

TABLE 9·1

STEPS IN THE DEVELOPMENT OF A STRATEGY FOR WEIGHT REDUCTION

Step	Example
Describe the behavior to be controlled	Ask clients to keep records of what they eat, under what circumstances they eat, who they were with, how they felt before and after eating.
Identify the stimuli which precede eating	Focus attention on characteristics of situations associated with eating. For example, does the client eat while cooking, does he or she eat at a particular location in the house, is the setting of the table a cue for food consumption?
Employ behavior methods for eating control	There are many behavioral methods for regulating food intake. Examples include asking clients to count each mouthful of food, put down their eating utensils after each third mouthful of food, and avoid "distracting" activities such as watching TV while eating.
Change the consequences of eating	Develop methods whereby clients are rewarded for complying with the program. Points can be awarded for accurate record keeping, counting chews, etc. The client might agree to wait until they have accumulated a certain number of points before they will treat themselves to a desired activity such as going to a movie.

Based upon the University of Pennsylvania program described by Stunkard (1979).
Source: Saccuzzo, D.P., Kaplan, R.M. *Clinical Psychology*, 1984, p. 289.

---

management of Type II diabetes. In comparison with patients in an attention control group and those in a no-treatment control group, those experiencing behavioral programs lost more weight and significantly reduced their requirements for medication. Changes in a measure of blood sugar were nonsignificant, but in the expected direction (Heitzmann et al., 1988).

In another study Rabkin, Boyko, Wilson, and Streja (1983) reported a randomized trial comparing individual nutritional counseling with behavior modification for the control of Type II diabetes. Those who had nutritional counseling lost more weight than those in the behavior modification group. There were no differences between the groups for cholesterol or for fasting blood glucose. However, the study had many methodological problems. For example, those who had nutritional counseling were given individual attention, while the behavior modification subjects were seen in groups. From the description, the nutritional counseling appearaed to use behavior modifi-

cation techniques. It included a review of eating habits, an individual meal plan, social support, and reinforcement of principles previously taught. Conversely, the behavior modification group sessions were offered by a nutritionist and began with a discussion of the pathophysiology of diabetes. The authors stressed that "the patient's eating habits were not assessed nor was an individualized meal plan established" (p. 51). On the basis of this study, it appears inappropriate to conclude that behavior modification is less effective than nutritional counseling.

It should be noted that the enthusiasm for behavioral interventions for weight loss has recently waned in some circles. Foreyt and colleagues (1981) have painted a rather gloomy picture of the long-term success rate after a review of all studies reporting 1-year follow-up data. Brownell (1982) carefully reviewed the complexities of evaluating behavioral approaches to weight loss. Despite some skepticism, behavior modification methods, particularly some of the newer approaches, remain

BOX 9-4

FOCUS ON WOMEN

Dealing with NIDDM often requires participation of family members. Yet it is not clear that husbands and wives are equally supportive in helping their spouses deal with diabetes. In one study, 49 obese diabetic patients participated in a program designed to achieve weight reduction. Each of the participants had an obese spouse. In some cases the spouse had diabetes, while in other cases they did not. The subjects were randomly assigned to participate in the program by themselves or with their spouse. For those participating alone, the spouse came only to measurement sessions. In the couple participation group, both spouses participated in a 20-week program designed to achieve weight loss and the control of diabetes. Considering men and women together, the two groups were equally effective at achieving weight loss as evaluated after the program and 1 year later. However, there was a difference between men and women. Women actually did significantly better when they participated with their spouses. Conversely, men did better when they were in the program by themselves. Family-based approaches may be valuable for women but not for men (Wing, Marcos, Epstein, & Jawad, 1991) (see Figure 9-7).

FIGURE 9-7

Weight of male and female patients in the *together* (T) and *alone* (A) conditions after adjusting for weight at baseline. (FU = follow up. Male T, n = 8; male A, n = 10; female T, n = 12; female A, n = 13.) (*Source:* Wing et al., 1991.)

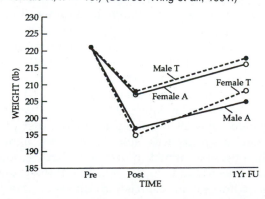

the best established techniques for achieving long-term weight control (Brownell, 1982).

Although there are an enormous number of studies on the effects of diet upon weight, there are fewer systematic studies evaluating the effects of exercise. A review of research on exercise and its effects on obesity does demonstrate that exercise has a very promising effect, particularly when combined with diet (Dahlkoetter et al., 1979). Thus, there is a strong rationale for using exercise as a method for controlling weight. As noted above, there is also convincing evidence that exercise has beneficial effects on the regulation of blood glucose for patients with diabetes. The major problem with exercise is that adherence to exercise programs tends to be poor.

Several groups have studied the effects of behavioral diet and exercise programs for NIDDM patients. In a series of reports, Kaplan and colleagues have evaluated the effects of these programs on cholesterol levels (Kaplan et al., 1985), quality of life (Kaplan et al., 1987), and cost-effectiveness (Kaplan et al., 1988). In one study, they randomly assigned 76 volunteer patients to one of four programs: diet, exercise, diet plus exercise, or an education control group. Each program required the patients to participate in 10 weekly meetings. Detailed evaluations were completed prior to the program and after 3, 6, 12, and 18 months. The evaluations included various psychosocial measures, measures of quality of life, and a variety of blood tests designed to assess diabetes control.

Figure 9-8 shows the weight reduction in the various groups over the course of 6 months. When reevaluated at 18 months, the combination of diet and exercise had achieved the greatest reductions in the blood chemistry measures of diabetes control. The diet plus exercise group was also the one that showed the greatest improvement in measures of quality of life. Interestingly, however, these findings did not exactly parallel the benefit in

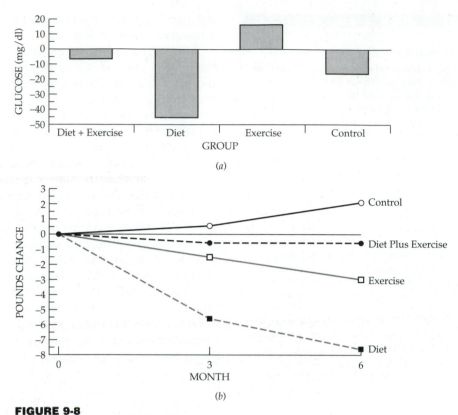

FIGURE 9-8

Blood glucose change (*a*) and weight loss (*b*) at 6 months by group. (From Hartwell, Kaplan, & Wallace, *Behavior Therapy*, 1986, pp. 454, 455.)

weight loss. Results from a similar research program at the University of Pittsburgh have been reported by Wing and colleagues (Wing, 1989). Patients in these studies have been successful in achieving weight losses in the range of 20 to 30 lb over the course of 1 year. In order to achieve this level of weight loss, it is necessary to have very intensive contact, with at least 20 weekly meetings. In addition, the best results have been obtained when the therapists are given specialized training in behavior modification and are assisted by physicians, exercise physiologists, and nutritionists.

Good programs offer formal exercise "prescriptions" and, in some cases, diets that severely restrict calories. Some of the studies demonstrate that even modest weight loss can produce long-term benefits for some patients (Wing et al., 1987). For example, those who lost 15 lb achieved significant improvements in their diabetes 1 year later. In another study, Wing and colleagues compared diet only with diet plus exercise. They found that those in the diet-only group lost an average of about 12 lb, while those in the diet plus exercise group achieved a weight loss of over 20 lb. When followed 1 year later, both groups had regained some of the weight, but the diet plus exercise group was still significantly lighter than those assigned to diet only. Both groups had lower blood glucose levels. But those participating in the exercise group were able to reduce their use of medications more substantially. In addition, the level of self-reported exercise was associated with the amount of weight loss and the level of improvement in blood tests. This study, then, suggests that diet plus exercise is probably the best approach for NIDDM patients (Wing, Epstein, Paternostro-Bayles, et al., 1988).

Clearly we have a long way to go in developing behavioral programs for the management of diabetes. These issues were recently reviewed by Goodall and Halford (1991). They cautioned that too few studies have long-term follow-up. Unfortunately, those studies that follow up patients for a longer period of time are less likely to show significant benefits of treatment. Future programs for patients with diabetes may need to include booster sessions to make sure the treatment lasts over the course of time. Another issue raised by Goodall and Halford is that statistically significant improvements may not translate into significant improvements in diabetes control. In fact, short-term benefits associated with weight loss may mean very little if the patients regain the weight. Furthermore, changes in weight may not be associated with changes in control of blood sugar. The behavioral management of diabetes remains a very important area for investigation. We hope future research continues to investigate these problems.

SUMMARY

Diabetes is a serious public health problem. The term *diabetes mellitus* actually describes several different medical conditions. Type I, or insulin-dependent diabetes mellitus (IDDM), results from the inability to make the hormone insulin. Living with this condition requires adjustment in diet and exercise. It also involves a complex program of regular insulin injections, frequent self-testing, and self-examination. Behavioral scientists have contributed to a variety of programs to improve the quality of life for these patients.

Non-insulin-dependent diabetes (NIDDM), or Type II, may be a completely different type of disease. It usually starts later in life and is often associated with obesity. Evidence suggests that patients who lose weight often gain better control of this condition. Prudent self-care, diet, exercise, and compliance with treatment may be the keys to a longer life without complications.

The involvement of behavioral scientists in diabetes care is a relatively recent development. At present, studies are few and unanswered questions are many. We expect research in this area to continue and to produce important new developments for the future.

KEY TERMS

Insulin-dependent diabetes mellitus (IDDM). A serious form of diabetes in which the cells that produce insulin die. Those diagnosed with insulin-dependent diabetes mellitus cannot survive without supplemental injections of insulin. Also known as Type I diabetes.

Non-insulin-dependent diabetes mellitus (NIDDM). The most common form of diabetes. Individuals with this condition do not depend on insulin for survival, although they do have glucose intolerance. Also known as Type II diabetes.

Diabetes. A problem with glucose or energy metabolism. Glucose is one of two major energy sources in the human body.

Nephropathy. A kidney disease, often associated with diabetes.

Neuropathy. Disease of the nervous system, often associated with diabetes.

UGDP study. A controversial epidemiological study suggesting that oral medication either is not effective or may produce damage for patients with NIDDM.

Home glucose monitoring. Home blood tests that can be used to evaluate current blood glucose status.

CHAPTER 10

Cardiovascular Diseases

Mary Jensen was awakened by the phone early in the morning. Her husband answered and then gave the phone to her. She was told that her older brother had just been admitted to the hospital because they thought he had a heart attack. He was 55 years old. This news triggered an avalanche of thoughts and concerns. She immediately recalled that her father had died suddenly of a heart attack at age 61. She wondered whether her brother would survive, and if he did, what kind of limitations would he have to live with? Would he be bedridden? What were his chances for a second episode?

Then concerns about herself started to surface. Would she be next? What is it like to have a heart attack? Is there anything she can do to prevent a heart attack, or is her fate sealed by her family history? All of the information on smoking, blood pressure, cholesterol, fatty diets, Type A behavior, and exercise that she was vaguely aware of from television and newspapers suddenly took on new importance. She realized that she was confused about what heart disease is and what causes it, but she vowed that she would pay more attention so that she could help her brother and herself survive this disease.

In this chapter we hope to answer your questions about heart disease and to help you understand the role of behavior in the prevention and treatment of heart disease and the other related diseases of the cardiovascular system.

As you learned in Chapter 2, cardiovascular diseases are the major causes of death and disability in the United States and most industrialized nations. More than 50 percent of the people who die each year die from some form of heart disease, so you can see that it is important to learn about heart disease, its causes, its treatment, and its prevention. Heart disease is a major concern of each individual because we all have it (more about that later). Cardiovascular disease has been a field in which health psychologists have been especially active and have made significant contributions. In this chapter we hope to give you a sense of the excitement shared by many health psychologists who are involved in research and practice related to reducing the epidemic of cardiovascular diseases in the industrialized world. This excitement is stimulated by the fruitful collaboration among many types of health professionals, the progress that has been made in understanding and controlling this disease, and the continuing opportunities to make important contributions.

WHAT IS CARDIOVASCULAR DISEASE?

Cardiovascular disease is actually a group of diseases with essential elements in common. There are three main categories.

1. *Coronary artery disease* results when the small arteries that supply blood to the heart muscle itself become blocked. There are three types of coronary artery disease.

a. *Primary cardiac arrest* occurs when the normal rhythmic beating of the heart is disturbed. The heart muscle flutters instead of beating regularly, with the result that blood is not pumped throughout the body. This condition often leads to sudden death before lifesaving techniques can be applied. There are often no warning signs prior to cardiac arrest, and in 25 percent of the patients, their first symptom of cardiovascular disease is sudden death.

b. *A myocardial infarction* is commonly called a ''heart attack.'' It is referred to by health professionals as an ''MI'' and indicates a blockage in a coronary artery that cuts off the blood supply to a part of the heart. That part of the heart then dies. Whether the patient lives or dies depends on the amount of heart muscle that dies as well as promptness and quality of medical care. MI's are usually both frightening and painful. A person can tell if he or she is having an MI because there will usually be pain and intense pressure in the chest. Many people describe it as feeling like ''an elephant is standing on my chest.'' The pain often radiates to the left shoulder and upper arm. Many people become sweaty, dizzy, or nauseous, and some lose consciousness. The pain can last for many minutes, but sometimes it will fade away even if the patient receives no medical attention. Physicians confirm the occurrence of an MI by looking for characteristic patterns on the electrocardiogram and by looking for the presence of specific enzymes in the blood that are released after damage to the heart muscle.

c. *Angina pectoris* is severe pain in the chest caused by a restricted flow of blood in the coronary arteries. When the heart muscle cannot get enough oxygen, the patient experiences *ischemic pain* that is similar to, but not usually as severe as, MI pain. There will be pain in the chest that often radiates to the left shoulder. Since physical exertion increases the need of the heart for oxygen, many patients have angina pectoris upon exertion and thus must limit their physical activity. Angina pectoris is not fatal in itself, but it can signal the onset of an MI, which may become fatal.

2. *Cerebrovascular disease* is commonly referred to as ''stroke.'' Health professionals

B O X   1 0 · 1

HEALTH OBJECTIVES FOR CARDIOVASCULAR DISEASES FOR THE YEAR 2000

Reduce coronary heart disease deaths to no more than 100 per 100,000 people (age-adjusted baseline: 135 per 100,000 in 1987).

GOAL FOR CORONARY HEART DISEASE DEATHS

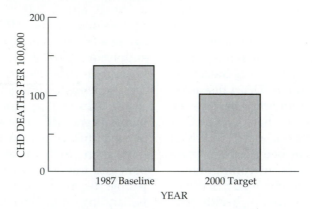

Reduce stroke deaths to no more than 20 per 100,000 people (age-adjusted baseline: 30.3 per 100,000 in 1987).

YEAR 2000 GOAL FOR DEATHS FROM STROKE

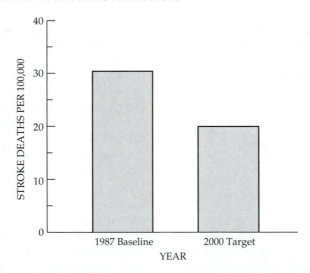

usually use the initials "CVA," which is an abbreviation for "cerebrovascular accident." A CVA occurs when the blood flow to a part of the brain is disturbed through either a blockage in an artery in the brain or a leak or breakage in a cerebral artery. A part of the brain then dies. The consequences of a CVA vary dramatically, depending upon which part of the brain is affected. There may be disturbances in speech or other language functions, motor abilities, sensation and perception, emotional responses, or cognitive processes. Often the deficits caused by CVA's are confined to one hemisphere of the brain, so the patient is unable to move, for example, the left leg. Because the brain is a very adaptable organ, patients are often able to regain some function with time and therapy. However, CVA's are often fatal, and cerebrovascular disease is the third leading cause of death in the United States.

3. *Peripheral artery disease* is pain or loss of function in the arms or legs that is the result of reduced blood flow in the extremities. This causes tissue to die or to otherwise suffer from lack of oxygen. While peripheral artery disease itself is rarely fatal, it often restricts use of the affected limb and can lead to the need for amputation.

Epidemiology of Cardiovascular Diseases

Figure 10-1 shows that about half of all deaths in the United States are caused by CVD. The human and economic toll is truly staggering. Over 900,000 people per year die from CVD in the United States alone; that is about one death every 32 seconds. About 200,000 of those deaths are people of working age, below 65. Not only is CVD the number one killer of Americans, but it is the number one cause of disability days from hospital stays and work

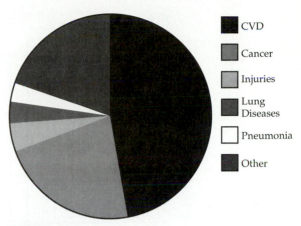

FIGURE 10-1

Causes of death in the U.S., 1985. (From American Heart Association, *Heart Facts, 1988.*)

loss. It is estimated that the costs to society of CVD—including medications, health professional services, hospital and nursing home services, and lost productivity due to death and disability—amount to over $80 billion per year (American Heart Association, AHA, 1988).

A great deal is known about who suffers from CVD, and here are some of the more important facts.

• Men are twice as likely to die from heart disease as women until women reach menopause, and then the death rates are about equal.

• CVD mortality rates are about equal for white and black men, but black women have higher risk than white women. Mortality rates for Latinos appear to be slightly lower than those for whites, and CVD mortality rates for Asian Americans are the lowest of all. Death rates by ethnic groups in the United States are shown in Figure 10-2 (Frerichs, Chapman, & Maes, 1984).

• Poor people are more likely to die from CVD, regardless of race, than those from high socioeconomic groups.

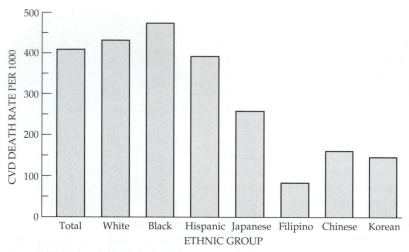

FIGURE 10-2
CVD death rate per 1000, L.A. County, 1980. (Data from Frerichs et al., 1984.)

- The good news is presented in Figure 10-3. While we are still experiencing an epidemic of CVD, the mortality rates have declined dramatically since the middle 1960s. (The large jump in the late 1960s is due to a change in the definition of CVD.) All race and sex groups have experienced a decline in CVD rates, but the timing of the decline was not the same for all groups. For example, populations with higher levels of income, education, and occupational status started the decline earlier than other groups (Wing, Barnett, Casper, & Tyroler, 1992). The cause of the decline is still a matter of spirited debate, with one group arguing that healthful changes in lifestyle have produced the decline. The other group insists that improvements in medical care—such as early diagnosis, better drug therapy, and availability of coronary care units—have reduced the toll.
- As shown in Figure 10-4, CVD mortality rates differ dramatically by country. These international comparisons have provided

important clues about the causes of CVD and will be discussed in a later section.

Pathophysiology of Cardiovascular Diseases

Even though the different cardiovascular diseases described above have their own separate characteristics and appear to be different diseases, they are all manifestations of the same disease. Atherosclerosis is the disease that causes coronary artery disease, cerebrovascular disease, and peripheral artery disease. *Atherosclerosis* is the buildup of a complex tissue called *plaque* in the inner wall of the arteries. Over a period of many years the plaque accumulates until the buildup becomes so thick that it interferes with the flow of blood through the artery. If the flow of blood is totally blocked by the plaque itself or by a blood clot that plugs up the remaining open part of the artery, then the patient will experience one of the manifestations of CVD. If the blocked artery is in the heart, the patient will have

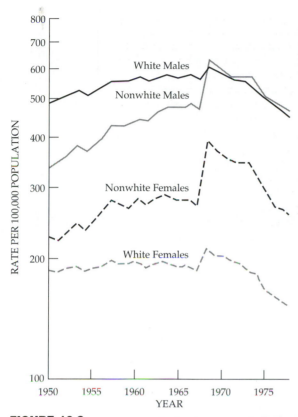

FIGURE 10-3

Death rates for coronary heart disease by sex and color. Ages 35 to 74: United States, 1950–1978. (From National Center for Health Statistics: Vital Statistics of the United States.)

angina pectoris or an MI. (The causes of primary cardiac arrest are somewhat more complex than this.) If the blocked artery is in the brain, the result is a CVA. If the blocked artery is in the arm or leg, then there will be severe peripheral artery disease.

The stages of the development of atherosclerotic plaques are illustrated in Figure 10-5. The artery wall starts out smooth and clean. At the next stage, fatty streaks can be found, which are made up of fat and cholesterol. While these are not dangerous, they are the foundation upon which the plaque develops.

In the next stage the plaque becomes harder and more complex as calcium, fibrous tissue, and more fat and cholesterol are added. This process continues until eventually the plaque is so large that blood flow is interrupted.

We usually think of CVD as a problem for old people, and most of us have lost a grandparent or other older relative to heart disease. However, MI's are fairly common in 50-year-olds, and in some cases people in their forties have MI's. People with rare genetic disorders can have MI's during their teens, so this is not a disease that affects only the elderly. In fact, Figure 10-5 clearly shows that atherosclerosis begins in childhood. Fatty streaks are found in young children (Strong, 1983), and advanced plaques are commonly seen in the coronary arteries of young adults. It takes decades for the plaques to build up to the extent that CVD manifests itself with clinical symptoms, but the disease itself begins during childhood and continues throughout life.

Virtually everyone reading this chapter, even the 19-year-old university student, has cardiovascular disease right now. We do not point this out to alarm you, and you should not be overly concerned, because you are at no immediate risk. However, like just about everyone else in the industrialized countries, your risk for CVD will increase. In a society where half the people die from heart disease, it is wise for everyone to be concerned about his or her own risk.

One bright spot is that CVD is not an inevitable result of living. While CVD is epidemic in some countries, it is unknown in others. Look at Figure 10-4 and notice that the CVD mortality rate is much higher in the United States than in Japan, for example. During the Vietnamese war autopsy studies were conducted on both American and Asian soldiers who were killed in battle. Almost all of the young Americans had advanced fibrous plaques, but very few of the young Asians had

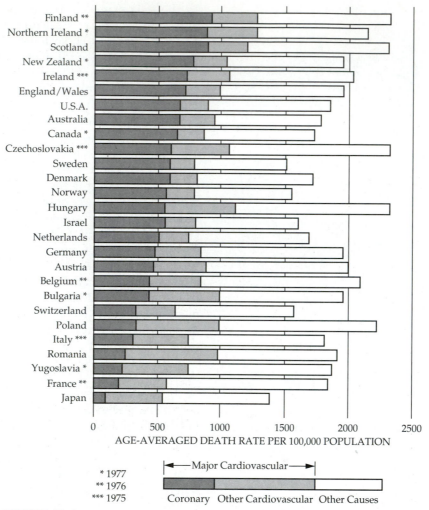

FIGURE 10-4

Death rates for all causes of death for ischemic heart disease and for other major cardiovascular diseases: men aged 35 to 74, by country. (From Working Group on Arteriosclerosis of the National Heart, Lung and Blood Institute, 1981b, p. 514, with permission.)

these plaques (McNamara, Molot, Stremple, et al., 1971). Does this finding mean that some racial groups are genetically protected from CVD? Or does it mean that lifestyle and environmental differences affect the development of atherosclerosis? This gets us into the question of what causes CVD.

Etiology of Cardiovascular Diseases

Through years of careful study, health scientists have discovered the major causes of CVD. For years they grappled with the question of whether heart disease was primarily genetic or whether it was caused by some kind of ac-

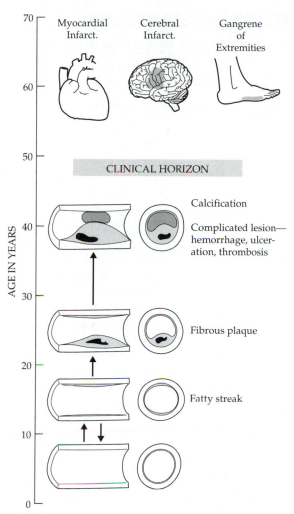

FIGURE 10-5

Diagram of the natural history of atherosclerosis. (Slightly modified and reproduced with permission from McGill, H. C., Jr., Greer, J. C., Strong, J. P.: Natural history of human atherosclerotic lesions. In Sandler, M., & Bourne, G. H., Eds.: *Atherosclerosis and Its Origin*, New York, Academic Press, 1963.)

into consideration, most psychologists are more interested in the behavioral and environmental causes, because these are the domain of psychology. Some of the strongest early evidence that CVD was influenced by nongenetic causes came from international migration studies.

The most famous migration research was the Ni-Hon-San study (Worth, Kato, Rhoads, et al., 1975). It began as part of the investigation of the effects of radiation on the survivors of the atom bomb blasts that leveled Hiroshima and Nagasaki at the end of World War II. Large groups of Japanese men were studied in Japan, in Hawaii, and in San Francisco. Since all of the men had similar Japanese genetic heritages, differences observed in CVD death rates could not be due to the effects of genes. The men were examined periodically, and the cause of death was recorded up until 1970. In each of the three age groups studied, two important findings emerged. An example of the results is shown in Table 10-1.

There was a clear pattern for deaths from coronary artery disease to increase and for cerebrovascular disease to decrease as Japanese men moved from Japan to Hawaii to California. This evidence was interpreted as indicating that behavior and environment played an important role in the development of CVD. The Japanese diet is very different from the typical American diet. The typical Japanese diet is high in fish, rice, and pickled foods, and low in fat. Pickled foods and common condiments, like soy sauce, are very salty. Many studies have linked this kind of high-sodium diet to high blood pressure, which increases the risk of stroke. This probably explains the high rate of strokes found in Japan.

The American diet is very high in animal fat and cholesterol, but it is lower in sodium than the Japanese diet. The Japanese men in California adopted an American style of diet, so they should be expected to increase their risk of coronary artery disease but to decrease their

quired characterstics. As is usually the case in controversies of this kind, the answer is that both nature and nurture are important. As geneticists like to say, "The best way to lower your risk of CVD is to choose the right parents." While the genetic causes must be taken

TABLE 10·1

CARDIOVASCULAR DISEASE MORTALITY IN JAPANESE MEN LIVING IN JAPAN, HAWAII, OR CALIFORNIA

Cause of death at ages 55–59	Mortality (%)		
	Japan	Hawaii	California
Coronary artery disease	1.4	1.7	4.8
Cerebrovascular disease	1.5	0.9	0.5

risk of stroke. The Japanese men in Hawaii had a diet that was partly Japanese and partly American, so their CVD rates should be in between. The results fit the predictions exactly, so the search was on to firmly establish what physiological, behavioral, and environmental characteristics led to CVD.

One study conducted in the United States has been more fruitful in confirming the factors that cause CVD than any other. About 3000 residents of the small town of Framingham, Massachusetts, began having thorough medical examinations every 2 years in the early 1950s. Not only have the investigators continued to follow the original subjects to study the development of many diseases, but the children and even the grandchildren of the subjects are participating in important medical studies. Much of what we know about the causes of CVD is a result of the dedication of these subjects and the many scientists who have studied them (Dawber, 1980).

Several risk factors for CVD have been identified. A *risk factor* is a characteristic of a person that increases the likelihood that he or she will suffer from manifestations of a disease, CVD in this case. The major risk factors for CVD are summarized in Figure 10-6. Several risk factors either are genetic or cannot be changed. These include age, sex, coronary anatomy, and inherited aspects of lipid and glucose metabolism. Therefore, as you age, your risk increases. Men are at greater risk for CVD than women, at least until the menopause. Some hearts and coronary arteries are more prone to CVD than others. Lipid metabolism refers to how fat and cholesterol are used, transported, and stored in the body; and there are a number of rare genetic disorders that can greatly increase one's risk of CVD. There appears to be a genetic predisposition to develop disorders of glucose metabolism, and these disorders may become manifest as diabetes mellitus. While diabetes mellitus is a serious disease in itself, it is also a risk factor for CVD.

Other risk factors have received more attention in the medical and popular literature because they are subject to change. These risk factors are the targets of CVD treatment and prevention programs. Only the most well documented risk factors are discussed in this book. The three physiological risk factors that are known to cause atherosclerosis are high blood cholesterol, high blood pressure, and obesity. There are also three behavioral risk factors that are known to either directly affect risk for CVD or influence the physiological risk factors. You are probably already aware that those behaviors are cigarette smoking, diet, and physical activity. Type A behavior has also been identified as a risk factor for CVD, but the research evidence supporting this is much weaker than that for the other risk factors. The psychological research on the etiology, treat-

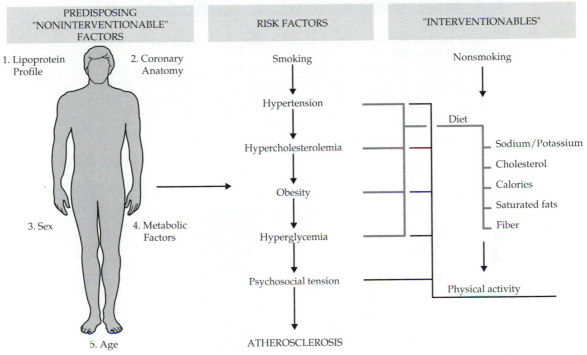

FIGURE 10-6
Multifactorial concept of the development of atherosclerosis and suggested means of intervention.

ment, and prevention of each risk factor will be presented in several chapters. Blood cholesterol and blood pressure are discussed here.

BLOOD CHOLESTEROL AND LIPOPROTEINS

Cholesterol is a waxy substance that is a part of the cell walls in animal cells. It is necessary for the manufacture of sexual and other hormones. Cholesterol is essential to life, but in excess quantities, it can threaten life. *Hypercholesterolemia*, or high levels of cholesterol in the blood, is one of the strongest risk factors for CVD. The amount of research data supporting this is quite overwhelming, and three examples of classic epidemiologic studies are briefly presented.

The first is the Seven Countries Study, which began in the 1950s. Middle-aged men from Japan, Greece, Yugoslavia, Italy, the Netherlands, the United States, and Finland had their blood cholesterol measured, and the CVD mortality and morbidity in these populations were also measured. In general, countries with the highest cholesterol levels also had the highest CVD rates (Keys, 1970). These results show that blood cholesterol and CVD are correlated, but the findings do not prove that there is a causal relationship.

The Framingham Study (Dawber, 1980) provided stronger evidence. Blood cholesterol was measured at the initial examination, along with many other variables, and CVD mortality and morbidity were studied continuously over more than 20 years. The Framingham Study

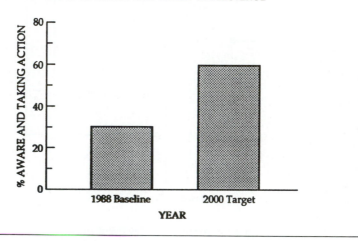

HEALTH OBJECTIVES RELATED TO BLOOD CHOLESTEROL FOR THE YEAR 2000

Increase to at least 60 percent the proportion of adults with high blood cholesterol who are aware of their condition and are taking action to reduce their blood cholesterol to recommended levels (baseline: 11 percent of all people aged 18 and older, and thus an estimated 30 percent of the people with high blood cholesterol, were aware that their blood cholesterol was high in 1988).

% OF ADULTS ACTING TO LOWER HIGH BLOOD CHOLESTEROL

showed that those people with high blood cholesterol levels were more likely to suffer from CVD than those with low cholesterol levels at nearly every year of follow-up. Cholesterol predicted CVD in every subgroup: young and old, men and women, fat and thin, smokers and nonsmokers. The relationship between serum cholesterol and CVD mortality is shown in Figure 10-7. Because the high cholesterol was present before the CVD, it was not possible that CVD caused the high cholesterol. However, it was still possible that both cholesterol and CVD are affected by a common third factor, so the causal relationship was still not definitely established.

To provide the conclusive evidence of this very important relationship, a controlled experiment was undertaken. The Lipid Research Clinics Program (1984) is the most expensive

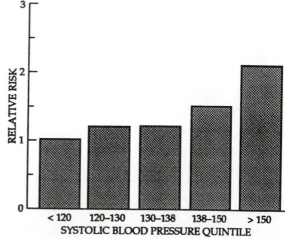

FIGURE 10-7

Standardized incidence ratio for experience of sudden cardiac death or first myocardial infarction in middle-aged men, categorized according to initial level of serum cholesterol. (Adapted from The Pooling Project, 1978).

medical study ever conducted (it cost more than $150 million over 10 years). Over 3000 men with high cholesterol were randomized to receive either the cholesterol-lowering drug cholestyramine or a similar placebo. This was a *double-blind study*, which means that neither the patients nor the experimenters knew whether they were taking the actual drug or the placebo. Both groups received dietary counseling and regular cholesterol tests over a 7-year period.

Psychologists were involved in developing counseling methods to enhance adherence to the medication schedule. This was a crucial part of the Lipid Research Clinics Study because cholestyramine is not a pill. It is a packet of sandy-type granules that taste bad and cause upset stomach and excess gas. This drug had to be mixed with liquid and taken up to six times per day. While it is very unpleasant to take, it is effective at lowering cholesterol. The success of the study depended on subjects being faithful to their medication regimens. With the intensive counseling, the adherence rate was very good, and the study produced clear results.

The medication group lowered their blood cholesterol about 9 percent more than the placebo group. This resulted in a 23 percent decrease in deaths from CVD. Thus, for every 1 percent decrease in cholesterol, there was about a 2 percent decrease in CVD risk. This study, reported in 1981, provided the conclusive evidence that blood cholesterol is one cause of cardiovascular disease and, furthermore, that lowering cholesterol will reduce risk of CVD.

What Are Lipoproteins?

The cholesterol story begins to get complicated now. Cholesterol is needed by every cell in the body, but since it is waxy, it cannot become dissolved in the blood and travel in the blood-stream to all the cells. It needs to be carried, and the name of the transport system is the *lipoproteins*. Lipoproteins are used to carry cholesterol and fats (i.e., lipids) throughout the body. Protein molecules surround the cholesterol and fat, and since proteins can travel freely in the blood, the cholesterol and fat go along for the ride. There are three major types of lipoproteins, and each of them is quite distinct.

1. Low-density lipoprotein (LDL) particles carry most of the cholesterol. LDL has been identified as the lipoprotein that is most responsible for atherosclerosis. The current thinking is that LDL delivers cholesterol and fat to the walls of the arteries, so the more LDL you have, the faster your atherosclerotic plaques will build up.
2. High-density lipoprotein (HDL) particles are less numerous. HDL appears to have the opposite function from LDL. HDL seems to carry cholesterol and fat away from the artery wall. Therefore, the more HDL you have, the slower your plaques will build up and the lower your risk of CVD will be. Thus, HDL is often referred to as the "good cholesterol."
3. Very-low-density lipoproteins (VLDL) contain very little cholesterol but large amounts of fat. VLDL does not seem to affect CVD very much one way or the other.

Triglycerides are fats in the blood that are not attached to proteins. Triglycerides are usually thought of as being unrelated to atherosclerosis, but new studies are showing that if they are very high, they can increase risk of CVD.

To understand risk of CVD it is necessary to study the different types of lipoproteins. When most people go to their physician for a checkup, they are likely to get a report of their total cholesterol only. Since total cholesterol is the sum of cholesterol carried by LDL, HDL, and VLDL, you can see that the information the report provides is not very specific. If you have a mildly elevated total cholesterol, it matters very much whether the excess is in LDL or HDL.

Etiology of Hypercholesterolemia

The wide variability in serum cholesterol levels has led to a search for causes of hypercholesterolemia. Several important causes have been found.

1. Genetic factors. It is well known that genetic influences are important. Familial hypercholesterolemia is a rare and dramatic genetic disorder that can produce cholesterol levels ranging from 300 up to 1000 mg/dl. Average adult values in the United States are about 220 mg/dl, and those with 240 mg/dl are at significantly increased risk. Familial hypercholesterolemic patients develop cholesterol deposits around their eyes and joints, and in severe cases they have heart attacks while still in their teens. Even in the general population you will inherit the tendency to have high or low cholesterol from your parents, in much the same way that you inherit the tendency to be tall or short. As with heart disease itself, there are many nongenetic factors (Feinleib, 1983).

2. Dietary cholesterol and fats. The foods we eat influence the levels of serum cholesterol and lipoproteins. LDL is increased by dietary cholesterol, particularly by dietary saturated fats. Equivalent amounts of saturated fat will increase LDL about 3 times as much as dietary cholesterol (Fraser, 1986). Foods rich in these nutrients include high-fat dairy products— such as milk, cheese, and ice cream—plus red meats and processed meat products. While saturated fats increase LDL, polyunsaturated fats and monounsaturated fats decrease LDL. Commonly used foods with monounsaturated fats include fish (not shellfish), olive oil, peanuts, nuts, and avocados (Trevisan, et al., 1990).

3. Obesity. Excess body fat is associated with high LDL and low HDL levels. These levels change as one loses weight. This effect on lipoproteins is one reason why obesity is such a health-damaging condition (Hubert, 1986). Similar correlations between obesity and lipoproteins have been found in children aged 5 to 17 (Kikuchi, et al., 1992).

4. Age. In industrialized nations, total cholesterol and LDL levels increase with age. In more "primitive" societies where CVD is rare, the age-related increase is not seen (Dawber, 1980).

5. Gender. Women tend to have HDL levels that are 10 to 15 percent higher than those of men, and this is thought to be one reason why women have lower CVD rates. However, for both women and men, HDL is protective from CVD death (Jacobs, Mebane, Bangdiwala, Criqui, & Tyroler, 1990). Women tend to have LDL levels that are slighly lower than men's (Gorden, Castelli, Hjortland, et al. 1977).

6. Exercise. HDL can be increased substantially with regular vigorous exercise, although exercise has little or no impact on LDL (Haskell, 1984).

7. Cigarette smoking. Cigarette smoking decreases HDL to a small degree, although the mechanism is not known (Criqui, Wallace, Heiss, et al., 1980).

8. Female hormone use. Oral contraceptives may increase cholesterol levels, but estrogen taken after menopause increases HDL.

9. Alcohol. Moderate alcohol consumption increases HDL. However, before you take this finding as a good reason to increase your drinking, you should know about the Stanford Alcohol Study (Haskell, Carmargo, Williams, et al., 1984). Sedentary men were assigned to either abstain from alcohol or have about two drinks per day. The results showed that moderate alcohol consumption increased HDL, but there was a catch. There are several subcategories of HDL, and HDL-2 has been shown to be

the protective type. Exercise increases HDL-2 and has small effects on HDL-3. However, in the Stanford Study, alcohol increased only HDL-3, suggesting that drinking alcohol will not protect you from CVD. In addition, alcohol greatly increases levels of triglycerides and has a number of other health-damaging effects.

10. Race. In the Framingham study the total cholesterol/HDL ratio was the best predictor of CVD mortality. Thus, racial differences in the TC/HDL ratio were examined in a large representative sample of the United States. Whites consistently had higher values than blacks. This means that black men and women had a more favorable lipid ratio than whites (Linn et al., 1991). However, in a study of preschool children, blacks had higher total cholesterol levels than whites, Latinos, or Native Americans (Freedman, Lee, Byers, Kuester, & Sell, 1992).

Treatment and Prevention of Hypercholesterolemia

Since the publication of the Lipid Research Clinics Study results, there has been an increased interest in the prevention and treatment of hypercholesterolemia. A National Cholesterol Education Program (NCEP) has been initiated by the National Heart, Lung, and Blood Institute to stimulate and coordinate such efforts. One of the first tasks of the NCEP was to provide guidelines for physicians on defining and treating hypercholesterolemia (The Expert Panel, 1988). The guidelines for

defining hypercholesterolemia in adults are presented in Table 10-2.

Treatment always begins with a 3- to 6-month trial of diet modification. The dietary approach to cholesterol control is detailed in Chapter 14. If diet alone is not effective, then medication can be used. There are several types of cholesterol-lowering medications, in addition to cholestyramine, that have been shown to be effective, at least in the short-term. Several of them have unpleasant side effects, and the long-term safety of some medications is not known at this time. There are several aspects of the treatment of hypercholesterolemia that are of particular relevance to health psychologists and that are important health psychology research topics.

1. What is the best way to train physicians to screen, diagnose, and treat hypercholesterolemics according to the NCEP guidelines?
2. What effective behavioral or other intervention methods can be used to help patients follow the NCEP dietary guidelines?
3. What effective methods can be used to help patients adhere to their medication regimens?

Serum Cholesterol in Children

Just as U.S. adults have high serum cholesterol levels compared with other societies, so do U.S. children. The consequences of high serum cholesterol in children appear to be the

TABLE 10·2		
NATIONAL CHOLESTEROL EDUCATION PROGRAM GUIDELINES FOR THE TREATMENT OF HYPERCHOLESTEROLEMIA		
Recommended level	200 mg/dl TC	130 mg/dl LDL
Moderate risk	200–240 mg/dl TC	130–160 mg/dl LDL
High risk	>240 mg/dl TC	>160 mg/dl LDL

BOX 10·3

THE NATIONAL CHOLESTEROL EDUCATION PROGRAM

One of the most ambitious health behavior change programs in the United States is being organized by the National Cholesterol Education Program (NCEP). The primary purpose of the National Heart, Lung, and Blood Institute is to conduct research that will aid in the fight against heart and lung diseases. However, the Institute goes beyond research at times to apply what we have learned about reducing disease. The NCEP is a major effort to use research findings to improve the health of the population. Three teams of respected medical and behavioral scientists produced three types of reports that serve as blueprints for the NCEP. The Adult Treatment Panel's report is discussed in this chapter. Two reports of the expert panels, "Population Strategies for Blood Cholesterol Reduction" and "Blood Cholesterol Levels in Children and Adolescents," are outlined here.

The expert panel on population strategies recognized that high CVD rates occur in adults with total cholesterol levels greater than 240 mg/dl. However, the greatest number of cases of CVD occur in Americans with total cholesterol less than 240 mg/dl. If the attention was focused on just those at highest risk, many preventable deaths would be ignored. Thus, the population strategy is to lower the blood cholesterol level of individuals *and* to reduce the average cholesterol level in the population. Cholesterol lowering is to be achieved through dietary change. Dietary behaviors are influenced by many factors, so a variety of recommendations are needed to target these different influences. Here is a sample of the recommendations:

The following guidelines are recommended for the general population: less than 10 percent of all calories from saturated fat, less than 30 percent of all calories from total fat, less than 300 mg of cholesterol per day.

The guidelines are also recommended for special groups, such as women, the elderly, children older than 2 years, and diverse cultural groups.

Health professionals should adopt these guidelines and advocate them to their patients.

The food industry should design, promote, and distribute good-tasting foods that follow the recommendations.

Government agencies should consistently promote these recommendations and should standardize food labeling policies.

Health education curricula at all levels should teach how to meet these recommendations.

The mass media should provide information on these recommendations through news, entertainment, and advertising policies and programs.

Public screening for blood cholesterol should be done only when adhering to high standards of quality.

The expert panel's report entitled "Blood Cholesterol Levels in Children and Adolescents" provided recommendations for children with high cholesterol levels and for the general population of children (NCEP Expert Panel on Blood Cholesterol Levels in Children and Adolescents, 1992). The panel concluded that blood cholesterol is important in children because the process of atherosclerosis begins in childhood and is affected by blood cholesterol levels. The same recommendations for dietary fat and cholesterol are proposed for adults and children older than about 2 years. The rapid growth for infants from birth to 2 years requires a higher percentage of fat. Energy (calories) intake should be sufficient to allow normal growth and development.

The recommendations for the population approach include the following changes from the previous list:

Schools should serve meals that are consistent with the recommendations and encourage the selection of healthful meals.

Schools should teach students at all levels about healthful eating patterns, including the understanding and use of food labels.

The recommendations for the individual approach for high-risk children and adolescents include the following:

Children with high cholesterol levels should be detected through selective screening of those with a family history of premature cardiovascular disease or at least one parent with high blood cholesterol. The panel did not recommend cholesterol screening for all children because:

a. not all young people with high cholesterol levels will also have high levels in adulthood
b. too many children would be inappropriately labeled as "diseased"
c. detection and treatment in early adulthood is sufficient for many who will be missed by selective screening
d. identification of too many high-cholesterol children could lead to overuse of cholesterol-lowering drugs

Individualized treatment is based on levels of LDL cholesterol, not total cholesterol.

A two-step diet therapy program is recommended. The first step is the same as the population strategy recommendations. In the second step, saturated fats are less than 7 percent of all calories, and dietary cholesterol is limited to 200 mg a day.

For children 10 years and older in whom diet is not effective, drug therapy is permitted. The two recommended drugs are cholestyramine (the drug used in the Lipid Research Clinics trial) and nicotinic acid (a B vitamin). These drugs are considered generally safe for older children, although they are recommended only for those with the highest LDL-cholesterol levels.

same as in adults. The landmark Bogalusa, Louisiana Heart Study has been researching CVD risk factors in children for over 20 years (Berenson, 1980). Some of the children they studied several years ago have died of accidents, homicide, suicide, and other non-CVD causes. These investigators were able to autopsy the teenagers and young adults and examine their coronary arteries. They found that the young adults with the most fatty streaks in their coronary arteries (a precursor of plaques) had high LDL levels when they were much younger children (Newman, Freedman, Voors, et al., 1986). This study suggests that it is dangerous to have high serum cholesterol as a child because it speeds up the process of atherosclerosis. This type of finding has produced a movement to prevent the development of high serum cholesterol in children through programs of diet modification.

Can Blood Cholesterol Be Too Low?

While it is well known that high blood cholesterol increases risk of CVD, there has been increased concern recently over the possibility of health risks if blood cholesterol is too low. Both epidemiologic studies and cholesterol reduction experiments have found low levels of blood cholesterol to be associated with higher death rates. Risk, in some studies, starts to increase when blood cholesterol is below about 160 mg/dl. Muldoon and Manuck (1992) have reviewed this issue and identified three specific conditions that may be associated with low blood cholesterol: cancer, hemorrhagic stroke, and nonillness causes such as accidents, violence, and suicides.

Many epidemiologic studies have measured blood cholesterol and documented cancer mortality some years later. Seven studies found no association between blood cholesterol and cancer mortality, while five studies found higher cancer death rates in those with low cholesterol levels. This is not strong evidence of a connection. This connection is further ques-

tioned because some studies have found that blood cholesterol may decline up to 10 years before cancer is diagnosed, and cancer itself may cause low cholesterol. Thus, it is possible that cancer causes low cholesterol rather than low cholesterol causes cancer.

Hemorrhagic stroke refers to bleeding inside the brain, and this can be a devastating condition. In Japan, where stroke rates are very high, the risk of hemorrhagic stroke increases as blood cholesterol decreases. This trend has also been seen in a few studies in the United States. Further support for this association was provided by a natural experiment in Japan. Since 1960 a community has been studied as the people naturally changed from their low-protein, low-fat Asian diet to a richer western-style diet. Serum cholesterol increased, but stroke rates dropped by 60 percent. However, dietary sodium could have also decreased. It has been hypothesized that dietary fat may strengthen small blood vessels in the brain, but this has yet to be proven. Although there are not many studies, there is a consistent link between hemorrhagic stroke and low blood cholesterol.

Perhaps the most intriguing connection is between low blood cholesterol and violent deaths. In China, which has generally low levels of blood cholesterol, those with the lowest cholesterols were more likely to die of nonillness causes, such as suicide, violence, and accidents. Several studies have shown people with a variety of behavioral disorders have low blood cholesterol levels: violent criminals, criminals with histories of suicide attempts and alcohol-related violence, depressed patients, and patients with mania. However, serum cholesterol was no different in aggressive versus nonaggressive children. The most alarming evidence comes from randomized studies of diet and/or drugs to lower high cholesterol. When the results of several studies are combined, subjects in the treated groups had a 75 percent higher risk for violent death than those in the control groups. While both diet and drug treatments have been tied to higher rates of violent death, not all studies show this trend.

These findings that low cholesterol levels may be associated with non-CHD (coronary heart disease) causes of death are both surprising and disturbing. There are several possible mechanisms by which low cholesterol may increase risk.

Because the walls of all animal cells are composed of lipids and cholesterol, changes in the blood levels of fat and cholesterol could affect the cell walls. Although it appears that changes in dietary fat do affect the cell walls, it is unknown whether these changes affect cancer growth, bleeding in the brain, or violent behaviors.

Prostaglandins are compounds that affect a great many bodily processes, such as communication between cells, cell replication, constriction of blood vesels, and immune function. Dietary fat has been shown to influence the synthesis of prostaglandins. Although they are a potential mechanism of health risks associated with low blood cholesterol, there is no evidence to support or refute this hypothesis.

There is some evidence that reduced fat diets affect the brain and behavior. For example, monkeys fed a low-fat diet were more aggressive than those fed a high-fat diet. The neurotransmitter serotonin is both reduced by low-fat diets and known to be lower in violent criminals, impulsive fire-setters, and suicide attempters. Thus, serotonin is a plausible mechanism by which low-fat diets or low blood cholesterol could increase risk for deaths by impulsive means such as suicide, violence, and accidents.

In summary, the evidence that low blood cholesterol increases risk for cancer, hemorrhagic stroke, or nonillness causes is interesting but not definitive. Muldoon and Manuck (1992) conclude that the safety of long-term cholesterol reduction is not established and needs further study. For those who already have low blood cholesterols, for example, meeting the current guidelines of less than 200 mg/dl, there is probably little reason to reduce it much further. However, the benefits of blood cholesterol reduction for those with established heart disease are so great, they are likely to offset any increased risk in non-CHD mortality. These questions about low cholesterol are just starting to be taken seriously, but they may be very important. Health psychologists and other health researchers will be working hard to understand this puzzling issue.

Summary

The amount of cholesterol in the blood is a very strong predictor of CVD. Cholesterol is carried in the blood by lipoproteins, and there are three major types. LDL encourages atherosclerosis, HDL discourages the buildup of plaques, and VLDL does not seem to have much impact. Cholesterol is a major ingredient in the plaques that build up inside arteries and lead to CVD. Cholesterol is affected mainly by genetics and diet; but exercise, obesity, and alcohol intake also play a role. Hypercholesterolemia is the condition of having a cholesterol level that is too high. The National Cholesterol Education Program has defined safe levels of cholesterol for adults and children. Treatment of hypercholesterolemia begins with a low-fat diet and progresses to medications if diet change is not effective. Health psychologists are involved in issues such as training health care providers to follow the guidelines, improving adherence to low-fat diets, and improving adherence to cholesterol-reducing medications.

BLOOD PRESSURE

Blood pressure is the force the blood exerts on the walls of the arteries as it is pumped throughout the body. Like atmospheric pres-

BOX 10·4

FOCUS ON DIVERSITY
CVD Risk Factors among Asian Americans

U.S. immigration from Asia has increased dramatically since the 1960s, but there is surprisingly little health information available on Asian Americans. A previous study found that Asians in California have lower total mortality and lower CVD mortality rates than blacks, whites, and Latinos. However, within the numerous Asian groups, there were different rates of CVD. A recent study of 13,031 Asian Americans who were examined at a northern California Health Maintenance Organization between 1978 and 1985 sheds light on CVD risk factors among Asian American groups. The study included about 6000 Chinese, 4000 Filipinos, 1700 Japanese, and 1200 others. Most of the Japanese Americans, less than half the Chinese Americans, and less than 10 percent of the Filipino Americans were born in the United States.

After statistically adjusting for education and marital status, risk factors were compared across groups. Chinese men and women were more likely to be obese than all others. Filipino men and women had the highest blood pressures. Japanese women had higher total blood cholesterol than the other Asian groups. Chinese men smoked less than other Asian men, and Japanese women smoked more than other Asian women.

CVD risk factors differed according to country of birth. Asian men born in the United States were more likely to be obese than those born in Asia, but among women this was true only for "other" Asians. In general, men born in the United States were *less* likely to be smokers. Except for Japanese women, women born in the United States were much *more* likely to smoke and to consume at least a pack a day. In other words, Asians born in the United States are more likely to have U.S. lifestyles than those born in Asia.

The authors suggest that smoking rates are lower for U.S.-born men because they have been influenced by the antismoking campaign. Why was the smoking pattern for women different? The authors suggest that, except for the Japanese, smoking is not accepted for women in many Asian nations. The more liberal attitude about women smoking in the United States may explain the higher rates in women born in the United States. This acceptance may balance the effect of the antismoking campaign on women. These findings led the authors to call for the development of more antismoking education, specifically for Asian American women.

Although blood cholesterol levels are generally lower in Asia, country of birth was not related to blood cholesterol in this sample of Asians. This may suggest that Asians rapidly adopt a high-fat American diet that accounts for the relatively high cholesterol levels in all groups. These data can be used to set priorities for health promotion programs. Obesity programs are needed for Asian American men, antismoking programs are needed for Asian American women, hypertension programs are needed for Filipino American men and women, and cholesterol reduction programs are needed for all Asian Americans (Klatsky & Armstrong, 1991).

BOX 10-5

HEALTH OBJECTIVES FOR HIGH BLOOD PRESSURE FOR THE YEAR 2000

Increase to at least 90 percent the proportion of people with high blood pressure who are taking action to help control their blood pressure (baseline: 79 percent of aware hypertensives aged 18 and older were taking action to control their blood pressure in 1985).

GOAL FOR TAKING ACTION TO CONTROL HYPERTENSION

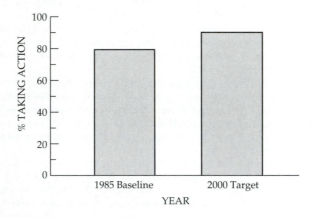

Decrease salt and sodium intake so that at least 65 percent of all home meal preparers cook foods without adding salt, at least 80 percent of all people avoid using salt at the table, and at least 40 percent of all adults regularly purchase foods with modified or reduced levels of sodium (baseline: 54 percent of all women aged 19 through 50 who served as the main meal preparer did not use salt in food preparation, and 68 percent of women aged 19 through 50 did not use salt at the table in 1985; 20 percent of all people aged 18 and older regularly purchased foods with reduced salt and sodium content in 1988).

sure, blood pressure is measured in millimeters of mercury (mmHg). Two blood pressures are usually discussed. *Systolic* blood pressure is the higher of the two. It corresponds to the pressure created when the heart pumps a pulse of blood. Systolic blood pressure is the force of the leading edge of that pulse. In between pulses or heart beats the pressure is lower. This is known as *diastolic* blood pressure. When a health professional or a machine in a shopping mall takes your blood pressure, it is always reported as systolic/diastolic.

Blood pressure is constantly changing. With every beat of your heart a systolic and a diastolic blood pressure are created, so in a 24-hour period you will have over 100,000 blood pressures! Because blood pressure changes so much, it is not possible to summarize all of your blood pressures. Thus, health researchers and health care professionals usually estimate your "average" blood pressure when you are at rest. Even though blood pressure changes moment by moment, this average resting blood pressure is very useful. Most of the work on blood pressure described in this section is based on this average. There is also considerable interest in variations in blood pressure, especially blood pressure responses to stress. This aspect is also discussed in this chapter.

Hypertension is high blood pressure, and it is a major risk factor for CVD. Studies conducted all over the world have consistently shown that people with high blood pressure are at more than twice the risk of having coronary artery disease as people with low blood pressure. This relationship applies for men and women of all ages and races, and is illustrated with data from several large studies in Figure 10-8. One question often arises: "Is systolic or diastolic blood pressure more important?" While some studies show systolic blood pressure to be a better predictor of CVD and some studies suggest the importance of diastolic blood pressure, the overall conclusion is that both blood pressures are related to risk.

Hypertension is an even stronger risk factor for stroke. In the Framingham Study hypertensive men were 8 times as likely and hypertensive women were 7 times as likely to suffer a stroke as their normotensive counterparts.

FIGURE 10-8

Standardized incidence ratio for occurrence of sudden cardiac death or first myocardial infarction in middle-aged men, categorized according to initial level of systolic blood pressure. (Adapted from the Pooling Project, 1978).

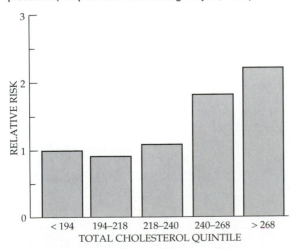

There are standard definitions for the diagnosis of hypertension in adults, and the criteria from the Joint National Committee on Detection, Evaluation, and Treatment of High Blood Pressure (1984) are shown in Table 10-3.

The shortcoming of the diagnostic criteria is that, in reality, there is no dividing line between safe and risky blood pressures. The higher the blood pressure the higher the risk, and the lower the blood pressure the lower the risk. It may be falsely reassuring to tell a person with a systolic blood pressure of 139 mmHg that they have "normal" blood pressure, when they would be termed "borderline high" if the blood pressure was just 1 mmHg higher. Nevertheless, practicing physicians find diagnostic criteria useful for classifying people, so they will continue to be used and debated.

Because blood pressure is so variable, it is difficult to obtain an estimate of the resting level. In practice, multiple readings are taken over a period of time. Practicing physicians usually take two or three readings each visit, and repeat this over two or three visits before confirming a diagnosis of hypertension. There is a phenomenon known as "white coat hypertension," in which blood pressures taken in the medical clinic are higher than those taken at home or in other settings. White coat hyper-

TABLE 10-3

DEFINITIONS OF HIGH BLOOD PRESSURE

Systolic blood pressure (mmHg)	
<140	Normal
140–159	Borderline high
≥160	High

Diastolic blood pressure (mmHg)	
<85	Normal
85–89	High normal
90–104	Mild hypertension
105–114	Moderate hypertension
≥115	Severe hypertension

tension is believed to occur because people are worried about what the physician will find, and this worry tends to result in increased blood pressure. Because of this problem, many people with suspected hypertension are asked to purchase home blood pressure kits and monitor themselves on a regular basis. This monitoring has been found in itself to be therapeutic, and psychologists have devised biofeedback approaches using these simple devices that appear to be quite effective (Engel, Glasgow, & Gaarder, 1983).

It is known that high blood pressure accelerates the atherosclerotic process, but the exact processes are active areas of continuing study. Hypertension has a variety of negative health effects, in addition to its role in CVD. Persistent, uncontrolled hypertension can lead to kidney disease, sexual impotence in men, and pathological changes in the heart muscle itself. It is estimated that hypertension is responsible for about 20 percent of all deaths from the nine most deadly chronic diseases (Hahn, Teusch, Rothenberg, & Marks, 1990).

Epidemiology

High blood pressure is a very common risk factor, but as is the case with the other risk factors, it is not evenly distributed throughout the population. If diastolic blood pressure of 90 mmHg or higher is used as the criterion, then about 25 percent of the adults in the United States are classified as hypertensive. However, the prevalence of hypertension has declined in recent years owing to efforts in detection and treatment (American Heart Association, AHA, 1988).

Some of the most striking features of the hypertension epidemic are shown in Figures 10-9 and 10-10, which are the results of a large study of the U.S. population (Fraser, 1986). The most obvious finding is that blood pressure increases with age. While this is characteristic of blood pressures in the industrialized world, there are many societies in which blood

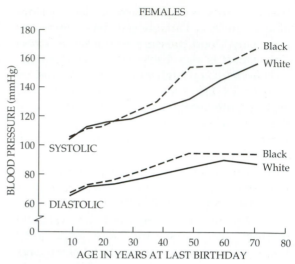

FIGURE 10-9

Mean systolic and diastolic blood pressure of white and black females 7 to 74 years, by age: United States, 1971–1974. (From National Health Survey, U.S. Dept. of Housing, Education and Welfare, 1978.)

FIGURE 10-10

Mean systolic and diastolic blood pressure of white and black males 7 to 74 years, by age: United States, 1971–1974. (From National Health Survey. U.S. Dept. of Housing, Education and Welfare, 1978.)

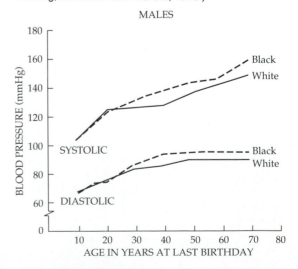

pressure does not increase with age. Joossens (1973) and Page (1980) documented that native societies in many countries showed no age-related increases in blood pressure: the Carajas from Brazil, the Murapins from New Guinea, the Kung from Botswana, the Pukapukas from the Cook Islands, Aborigines from Australia, people from the Himalayas, Eskimos, several tribes of Native Americans, and various African tribes.

Men tend to have higher blood pressures than women, although this difference is not as clear in blacks. Figures 10-9 and 10-10 show that blacks have consistently higher blood pressures than whites, and the epidemic of hypertension among blacks in the United States has been a major concern of health professionals. At least part of the race differences can be attributed to the generally lower socioeconomic levels of blacks, since lower socioeconomic groups of any race tend to have higher blood pressures than more advantaged groups.

Etiology

Elevated blood pressure is sometimes the result of other medical problems such as kidney dysfunction, endocrine disorders, pregnancy, oral contraceptive use, and malformations of the aorta. If physiological causes are found, the term *secondary hypertension* is used to describe the elevated blood pressure. In 80 to 90 percent of the cases no physiological cause can be found, so most cases are diagnosed as *essential hypertension*, which means that there is no known cause.

In fact, many "causes" of essential hypertension have been identified. While hypertension is itself a risk factor for CVD, there are several risk factors for hypertension. Some of these are of particular interest to health psychologists.

1. Genetics. It has been repeatedly shown that children of hypertensives are at high risk for developing hypertension. While the hu-

man studies do not often separate the genetic from the environmental influences, animal studies have demonstrated that there is a modest genetic contribution to elevated blood pressure.

2. Obesity. The accumulation of fat in the body is accompanied by additional blood vessels to nourish the fat tissues. Thus, obesity strains the heart and tends to increase blood pressure. Because obesity is so common in our culture, it is a major contributor to high blood pressure. This relationship between obesity and blood pressure is seen in both adults and children. However, reductions in body fat are accompanied by decreases in blood pressure, so weight reduction is a common recommendation for controlling hypertension (Hovell, 1982).

3. Alcohol. Consumption of more than two alcoholic drinks per day tends to increase blood pressure, although one drink per day is associated with slightly lower blood pressures when compared with nondrinkers (Criqui, 1987). Moderate alcohol intake is rarely recommended to abstainers because of the medical and social problems that occur when drinking becomes excessive.

4. Dietary sodium. Sodium is one of several dietary factors that influence blood pressure. Excessive sodium in the diet often causes retention of fluid in the body. The excess fluid leads to increased blood pressure. Populations with low sodium intakes—such as the Yanomamo and Xingu Indians of Brazil, and rural populations from Kenya and Papua, New Guinea—have virtually no hypertension (Carvalho, Baruzzi, Howard, et al., 1989). Societies with high sodium intakes tend to have high rates of hypertension. For example, the Japanese eat very large amounts of sodium, and they have one of the highest rates of hypertension and stroke in the world (MacGregor, 1983).

Sodium in the diet comes from a variety of sources. About one-third is from food products, although processed foods have much higher sodium contents than foods in their natural state. Table 10-4 dramatically shows how processing can increase the sodium content of foods. About one-third of the sodium in the typical American diet is added as salt during cooking, and about one-third is added by the consumer at the table. Thus, most Americans eat about 10 g of sodium, which is about 20 times the amount required by the body. Although the taste for salt develops during childhood, taste preferences can be changed through gradual reductions in salt. After the reductions, processed foods that were once enjoyed suddenly taste too salty.

The American Heart Association (AHA) has recommended an intake of sodium that is less than 3 g per day, although this level is still far above the body's requirements. This level could be attained by a gradual elimination of added salt at the table, by decreasing by half the amount of salt added during cooking, and by substituting fresh foods for processed food products.

Some health authorities question the recommendation to decrease sodium consumption because it has been shown that salt restriction does not lower blood pressure in everyone. Only about one-third of the population is "so-

TABLE 10-4

THE SODIUM CONTENT OF SOME AMERICAN FOODS (1000 mg SODIUM = 44 mEq SODIUM)

Comparable foods with either low or high sodium content

Low	High
Shredded wheat: 1 mg/oz	Corn flakes: 305 mg/oz
Green beans, fresh: 5 mg/cup	Green beans, canned: 925 mg/cup
Orange juice: 2 mg/cup	Tomato juice: 640 mg/cup
Turkey, roasted: 70 mg/3 oz	Turkey dinner: 1735 mg
Ground beef: 57 mg/3 oz	Frankfurter, beef: 425 mg each
Pork, uncooked: 65 mg/3 oz	Bacon, uncooked: 1400 mg/3 oz

Some foods with very high sodium content

Catsup, one tbsp: 156 mg
Olive, one: 165 mg
Cinnamon roll, one: 630 mg
Soup (chicken noodle), one cup: 1050 mg
Dill pickle, one large: 1928 mg

Sodium content of some fast foods

Kentucky Fried Chicken
  3 pieces of chicken,
  mashed potatoes, and gravy,
  cole slaw, and roll: 2285 mg
McDonald's Big Mac: 962 mg
Burger King Whopper: 909 mg
Dairy Queen Chili Dog: 939 mg
Taco Bell Enchirito: 1175 mg

Source: From Kaplan and Shamler, 1983.
Note: mEq = milliequivalents.

dium sensitive,'' meaning that their blood pressure goes down when they eat less salt. Sodium restriction clearly reduces blood pressure in hypertensives, but the effect on normotensives is usually quite modest. The AHA counters that sodium-sensitive people do not know who they are, so the advice cannot be limited to only a high-risk group. In addition, there are no risks of lowering sodium, so a general change in the population would produce a small degree of benefit that would be widely shared. Reducing sodium intake is not a hardship because tastes adjust with time. As the public becomes more informed about the risks of a high-sodium intake, the consumption of sodium is decreasing every year.

5. Dietary potassium. Sodium and potassium work together in the body, but they have different effects on blood pressure. Potassium tends to decrease blood pressure, so it counteracts some of the blood pressure–raising effects of sodium. The increased use of processed foods has led to a decrease in potassium, because potassium is found primarily in fresh fruits and vegetables. As you might have guessed, the consumption of potassium is low in the United States, but it can be increased simply by eating a couple more servings of fresh fruits and vegetables every day.

6. Dietary calcium. Calcium is a very important mineral. It is involved in bone development and the transmission of neural impulses, and it also affects blood pressure. Calcium deficiencies are quite common, especially in women, since some foods block the use of calcium. Increasing the intake of calcium has been recommended, because several studies have shown that people with high calcium intakes have lower blood pressures (McCarron, Morris, Henry, & Stanton, 1984.) Dairy products, especially yogurt and cottage cheese, are particularly good sources of calcium, and it is important to eat some dairy products every day. Since nonfat dairy products have as much calcium as the high-fat varieties, it is preferable to choose the nonfat products.

7. Physical activity. Regular vigorous physical activity such as jogging, aerobic dancing, and swimming lower blood pressure to an important degree in hypertensives and to a lesser degree in normotensives (Tipton, 1991). A 20-year study found that college men who continued to be physically active throughout their adult years were half as likely to be hypertensive as their peers who were sedentary (Paffenbarger, Wing, Hyde, & Jung, 1983).

8. Psychosocial variables. It has been known for a long time that psychological variables affect blood pressures. Various ''hypertensive personality'' patterns have been proposed over the years, and the most well known was put forth by Alexander in 1939. Alexander hypothesized that hypertensives were characterized by difficulties in the expression of hostility, resentment, rage, rebellion, and dependency. The research based on the psychosomatic theories has tended to confirm the relationship between hypertension and anger, as shown in Diamond's (1982) review of this topic. In one study, patients recorded their blood pressures four times per day and also rated their feelings of anger and anxiety (Whitehead, Blackwell, DeSilva, & Robinson, 1977). When they felt either angry or anxious, their blood presures (BP's) tended to be higher than when they were feeling calm.

While the research shows that anger and anxiety play a role in hypertension, the strength of the association is not clear. Studies have not been conducted to determine whether controlling excess anger and anxiety will aid in the prevention or treatment of hypertension. Nevertheless, this is a fertile area for psychological investigation.

While acute emotional stress can produce short-term elevations in blood pressure, the effects of chronic stress are less clear. Many studies show that people who abandon a traditional or ''primitive'' lifestyle and move to a westernized city tend to develop hypertension. However, these studies rarely consider changes in diet or body weight. When upward socioeconomic mobility is thwarted, there is some evidence that blood pressure increases. Surprisingly, those with the highest perceived job stress tend to have the lowest blood pressures. This could be explained by the familiarity of the job situation and habituation of the blood pressure to job stress (Mustacchi, 1990). Partly because stress is so complex, it is difficult to demonstrate associations between psychosocial demands and chronic hypertension.

9. Cardiovascular reactivity. Most biomedical reserach on hypertension has involved measures of resting blood pressure. However,

---

BOX 10·6

FOCUS ON WOMEN

Gender Differences in Blood Pressure Responses to Stress

It is well known that women have lower rates of CVD morbidity and mortality, at least until the menopause. However, the mechanisms by which women are protected from CVD are not well understood. It is accepted that female hormones, particularly estrogen, reduce CVD risk in women, but other mechanisms are suspected. For example, women have lower total blood cholesterol and higher HDL cholesterol on average. They also have lower resting blood pressures. As we learn more about the apparent risks of exaggerated blood pressure response to behavioral stressors, it is important to determine whether there are gender differences in blood pressure reactivity.

Karen Matthews and Catherine Stoney identified some studies suggesting that women had less blood pressure response to stress than men. However, those studies had some methodological problems. Thus, Matthews and Stoney conducted a study of gender differences in blood pressure reactivity. They also included children in the study so that it could be determined at what age gender differences emerge, if they exist at all.

Over 200 children (aged 7 to 18) and 200 adults participated in a laboratory study. Blood pressures were taken with an automated device. Each subject participated in three mildly stressful tasks. The first involved serial subtractions (older subjects were given more difficult numbers to subtract). The second task was mirror tracing. Subjects traced the outline of a star by watching themselves in a mirror. A buzzer sounded when they went outside the lines. The third task required subjects to grip a dynamometer at 30 percent of their maximal strength for $2\frac{1}{2}$ minutes.

Because resting blood pressure and obesity level are known to affect responses to stress, these variables were statistically adjusted in the analyses. Men had larger systolic blood pressure responses to the stressors than women, and boys had significantly larger responses than girls. Men also had larger diastolic blood pressure responses than women, but boys and girls did not differ on diastolic response. Overall, adults had higher systolic and diastolic blood pressure responses than children.

These results confirm that females have less blood pressure response to behavioral stressors than males, and this difference is partially evident during childhood. The pattern of blood pressure response could explain some of the gender differences in premature cardiovascular disease. In addition to several other mechanisms of protection, females' blood pressures are less reactive to stress, and this appears to be an adaptive characteristic that appears early in life. Maybe a follow-up study will determine whether this gender difference is due to psychological or physiological factors (Matthews & Stoney, 1988).

it has been known since the 1960s that blood pressure can vary more than 100 mmHg during the course of the day (Bevan, Honour, & Stott, 1969). Psychologists have become very interested in exploring the causes, consequences, and mechanisms of those blood pressure variations.

Psychologists David S. Krantz and Stephen B. Manuck (1984) wrote an influential article that summarized the research on cardiovascular reactivity, particularly BP reactions to stress. Early studies indicated that BP reactivity to stress in childhood predicted the development of hypertension years later. E. A. Hines, a physician, used the cold pressor task, a painful experience in which the hand is immersed in ice water for 1 or 2 minutes (Hines, 1936). Some studies have found that BP reactivity predicts hypertension up to 45 years later, but other studies have found it not to predict at all (Sallis, Dimsdale, & Caine, 1988). While we do not know whether BP reactivity is a good marker for risk of hypertension, we do know that BP reactivity is greater in young people with a family history of hypertension (Light, 1981).

One of the most important studies in the area of BP reactivity is by Ancel Keys and colleagues (Keys et al., 1971). Keys was a pioneer in the identification of risk factors for CVD. In one study he evaluated possible risk factors in a large group of middle-aged men. One measure he included was the BP response to the cold pressor task. The subjects were followed up 23 years later to evaluate the predictors of CVD mortality. Surprisingly, the most powerful predictor was the BP reactivity to the cold pressor task, and it was a stronger risk factor than resting BP, smoking, and cholesterol level.

Results showing that BP reactivity predicts hypertension and CVD mortality have led to an explosion of studies in this area. Current research is trying to answer such questions as:

- Why do some people have large reactions to stress while others react very little?

- What are the physiological mechanisms that link BP reactivity with negative health outcomes?
- What is the importance of the type of stressor?
- Can BP hyperreactivity be controlled?

There are many examples in science of how a technological advance has opened up whole new fields of study. The telescope was a critical invention for astronomers, and the microscope allowed microbiology to come into existence. For researchers in the area of cardiovascular reactivity, the development of ambulatory BP monitors is something of a revolution. The new devices weigh less than a pound and automatically pump up a cuff at predetermined intervals. The monitors interfere very little with the person's ongoing activities, and people adjust quickly to the periodic pressure on their arms. Now it is possible to study physiological changes in real time in almost any setting. This new methodology has the potential to vastly increase our understanding of the effects of stress, emotions, and the physical and social environments on cardiovascular functioning.

Ambulatory BP monitors have been used to study several important topics. For example, family history is known to be a risk factor for hypertension, but studies sometimes find no differences in resting blood pressure levels at the clinic or laboratory among young people with and without family histories of hypertension. Fredrikson, Robson, and Ljungdell (1991) were interested in whether young people at risk due to family history had high-risk patterns of blood pressure during their usual days and nights. Fifteen young adults with a family history and fifteen without a family history were monitored. In the laboratory, there were no differences in resting blood pressures, but those with a family history were more reactive to stress. They had higher daytime blood pressures, but the BP levels were not different at night.

If an investigator is interested in studying

the effects of stress on blood pressure, then it is essential that the person wearing the monitor encounter some stress. Two studies illustrate different approaches to this issue. Goldstein, Jamner, and Shapiro (1992) recruited male paramedics to wear the ambulatory monitors. Paramedics routinely encounter life-or-death situations that put them under a great deal of stress. Thus, they are an excellent group to study. They were monitored on workdays and nonworkdays. Average BP's did not differ between days, but there were differences in specific situations. BP's were 10 mmHg higher while in the ambulance on workdays than while in the car on nonworkdays. Similarly, BP's were significantly higher at the scene of the emergency and at the hospital than during nonworkday activities.

Students are another group that predictably undergo the stress of examinations. Sausen, Lovallo, Pincomb, and Wilson (1992) monitored a group of medical students on 2 days. Lecture days were considered low stress, and exam days were considered high stress. As expected, systolic BP's were much higher (about 12 to 15 mmHg) during the exam than during the lecture. After the exam, the BP's fell quickly back to normal. However, the systolic BP before the exam was as high as during the exam, so the anticipation of the stressful event was itself very stressful. These studies are just beginning to explore the potential of ambulatory blood pressure monitors.

Prevention and Treatment of Hypertension

Recommendations for preventing hypertension usually include weight control, reduction of dietary sodium, moderate alcohol intake, regular exercise, and stress management. Preventive approaches are just beginning to be studied, but the treatment of hypertension has been heavily researched and is very effective.

The first step of treatment is detection. Since hypertension is such a common and dangerous condition with no noticeable symptoms, detection programs are a high priority. You have probably seen hypertension screenings at shopping centers, fairs, and other public places. Screenings are also held at work sites, churches, and schools. The goal of screening programs is to find people who may have high blood pressure but do not know about it. Those potential hypertensives who are detected are referred to their physician for more definite diagnosis and treatment if necessary. It is now standard practice for physicians to take BP readings during every clinic visit so that hypertension can be caught early and treated before there are serious medical complications.

The primary treatment of hypertension is drug therapy. There are several classes of medications that are effective in reducing BP, and they are among the most commonly prescribed drugs in the world. While these medications are usually effective, patients frequently experience unpleasant side effects. Diuretics are taken by millions of hypertensives, but one side effect is that they increase blood cholesterol, and this offsets some of the risk-reducing effects. These drugs often cause impotence in men. Beta blockers affect the sympathetic nervous system and produce persistent feelings of lethargy. Calcium channel blockers and ACE inhibitors are newer classes of drugs that do not have the side effects of the older antihypertensives, but they are quite expensive.

Since hypertension is a chronic condition, drug therapy is often required for a lifetime. Patients may be prescribed two or three drugs that must be taken several times per day. Not surprisingly, many patients have a great deal of difficulty adhering to their prescribed regimens. Since it is so important for hypertensives to take their medications regularly, health psychologists have been very active in helping patients stick to their regimens. Prom-

BOX 10·7

FOCUS ON RESEARCH

Do Stressful Laboratory Tasks Tell Us Anything about the Real World?

People who have exaggerated blood pressure reactions to laboratory tasks, such as the cold pressor, may be at risk for developing hypertension and cardiovascular diseases. Investigators have developed a large number of mildly stressful tasks and used them to study blood pressure reactivity. For example, video games, mental arithmetic, mirror tracing, isometric handgrip, exercise, reaction time tasks, and forehead cold pressor have all been reported. What do these mostly unfamiliar tasks tell us about how people react to stress in everyday life? There is an assumption on the part of most researchers that if laboratory stressors predict future disease, they must tell us something about how people usually react to stress. What does the research tell us?

Two approaches have been used to study whether blood pressure reactivity generalizes from the laboratory to real life. The first approach uses ambulatory blood pressure monitors. These small computers are very light and are worn on a belt. They automatically take blood pressures every few minutes. Just a few studies have examined the amount of variation in blood pressure during an entire day in relation to response to laboratory tasks. Pickering and Gerin (1990) reviewed these studies and concluded that there was not much evidence of generalization of laboratory tasks. However, besides important problems in measuring blood pressure throughout the day, it may be unreasonable to expect a very crude measure of blood pressure changes during the day to be related to responses to specific laboratory stressors. What if nothing stressful happened during the day? What if many stressful events happened to some people and not to others? Relying on the chance events of the day may be a serious limitation of this approach.

Matthews, Manuck, and Saab (1986) hypothesized that a better way to test generalizabilty would be to see if stress reactions in the laboratory predicted blood pressure changes to an identified stressor in everyday life. They cleverly selected a stressful event that was powerful and predictable so that they would know in advance when and where to monitor blood pressure. Subjects were 23 tenth-grade students who were required to present a 5-minute speech in English class. Giving a speech in class is almost universally stressful, but it is a naturally occurring event.

In the laboratory, students had their blood pressures monitored as they did mental arithmetic, mirror tracing, and handgrip tasks. In general, those adolescents with the highest blood pressure responses to the laboratory tasks also had the largest blood pressure increases before, during, and after their speech in class. Just to make sure the blood pressure responses during the speech were related to the specific stressor, the researchers also monitored the students during the same class when they did not have to give a speech. On these control days, blood pressures were much lower and were unrelated to laboratory reactivity tasks. Thus, it appears from this study that blood pressure reactions to laboratory tasks do reflect responses to naturally occurring events (Matthews, Manuck, & Saab, 1986; Pickering & Gerin, 1990).

ising strategies emphasize behavioral self-management and improvement of social support for adherence (Dunbar-Jacob, Dwyer, & Dunning, 1991).

Because drug therapy is expensive, produces frequent side effects, and is not always effective, and because some people would rather not take medications of any kind, there is a need for nondrug treatments of hypertension. Many factors influence BP, so there are many different approaches to reducing it without medications. Psychologists, physicians, and other health care professionals have incorporated several nondrug treatments into their daily practice, while other treatments are still being researched. The primary nondrug treatments fall into four categories: relaxation therapy, biofeedback therapy, dietary therapy, and exercise therapy.

Relaxation Therapies Relaxation therapies have been applied to the problem of hypertension because it is believed that increased muscle tension and sympathetic nervous system activity contribute to elevated BP. Thus, it follows that decreasing muscle tension and sympathetic activity should reduce BP. There are numerous procedures that have been developed to create a state of relaxation, and they have been applied to a wide variety of medical and psychological disorders (Lichstein, 1988). Meditation as a means of quieting the body and mind has been practiced extensively in Asia for centuries, and modern studies have shown that meditation produces changes in many physiological indicators, including BP (Lichstein, 1988). Herbert Benson (1975) developed a secular version of transcendental meditation that consists of sitting quietly for 20 minutes twice each day and silently repeating the word *one*. In some studies this procedure has produced important reductions in BP, but in other studies it has not (Blanchard, Martin, & Dubbert, 1988).

Autogenic training is a relaxation method that was developed in Germany and is used widely in Europe. Typically the treatment consists of patients reclining in a quiet room and silently repeating phases indicating that they are calm and that each part of the body in turn is becoming "warm and heavy." Since warmth and heaviness in the limbs are feelings associated with relaxed states, autogenic training is based in part on self-suggestion. Many studies have indicated that autogenic training can lower BP (Lichstein, 1988). A recent study of the treatment of mild hypertensives was conducted collaboratively by American and Soviet scientists (Blanchard, Khramelashvili, McCoy et al., 1988). The average reduction in diastolic BP was 8.5 mmHg at both sites. Only the Soviets achieved significant reductions in systolic BP (12.8 mmHg). One year after treatment 75 percent of the Soviet patients had diastolic BP's in the normal range (<90), while 24 percent of the American patients achieved normal BP's. This study indicates that autogenic training can be clinically effective in reducing hypertension.

Progressive relaxation, as originally developed by Edmund Jacobsen, consisted of about 100 sessions of tensing and relaxing each muscle group in the body. Joseph Wolpe popularized a much briefer program that could be completed in 6 to 8 weeks, although the tensing-relaxing exercises have been retained in all later versions of progressive relaxation (Lichstein, 1988). The effectiveness of this technique in reducing elevated blood pressure has been shown in dozens of studies. One of the most influential was conducted by Taylor and colleagues (Taylor, Farquhar, Nelson, & Agras, 1977). Thirty-one patients who were on medication but remained hypertensive were randomly assigned to one of three treatments: (a) brief progressive relaxation (about five sessions), (b) an equal number of sessions of supportive psychotherapy, and (c) medication only. The results are shown in Figure 10-11. After treatment the patients who received progressive relaxation decreased systolic BP by 13.6 mmHg and diastolic BP by 4.9 mmHg. Blood pressures changed very little in the

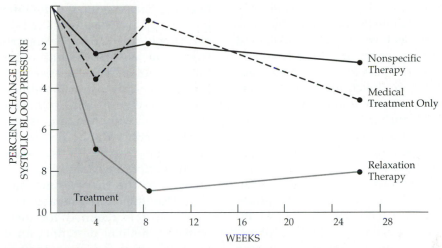

FIGURE 10-11

Percent systolic blood pressure change for relaxation therapy (+ medical treatment), non-specific therapy (+ medical treatment), and medical treatment only, from before to after treatment and including a 6-month follow-up. The latter point includes data for only eight patients in each group. The pretreatment reading is after at least 2 months' medical care, including pharmacotherapy. (From Taylor, C. B., Farquahar, J. W., Nelson, E., & Agras, S. Relaxation Therapy and High Blood Pressure. *Archives of General Psychiatry, 34,* 1977, p. 341.)

other two groups. After 6 months the progressive relaxation group had maintained their BP reductions, and the average BP's were in the normal range. This study showed that the relaxation was responsible for the treatment success. Supportive psychotherapy, which was intended as a placebo, had no effect on blood pressure.

In general, relaxation therapies are effective in lowering BP (Jacob, Chesney, Williams, Ding, & Shapiro, 1991). Relaxation is most effective in patients who need help the most, that is, in those with the highest BP's. Relaxation is particularly effective for patients who are not controlled by medication, so it is an effective adjunct (or additional) treatment of hypertension. While relaxation therapies can produce clinically meaningful BP reductions in a relatively short treatment length of five sessions, these treatments are not used very often in practice. A few physicians will refer hypertensives for relaxation therapy, but health

psychologists have not been able to make relaxation a standard treatment. One major problem seems to be that even five relaxation sessions create a substantial increased cost in both time and money. Continued work is needed to make relaxation therapy a more cost-effective treatment for hypertension.

Biofeedback Therapies It is very difficult to exert voluntary control over blood pressure since you cannot feel it. *Biofeedback* uses technology to make you aware of bodily processes of which you were previously unaware. Thus, using BP feedback to control hypertension is an appealing idea. A procedure was developed in the late 1960s in which a BP cuff was inflated to the approximate level of the systolic BP and left at a constant level for about 1 minute. Patients listened for their blood pressure sounds through a stethoscope and tried to make them disappear, which meant that they were making their BP decrease. After each trial the cuff deflated and they rested. When they lowered their BP below the first level, the pressure in the cuff was lowered by 2 mmHg, and the patient tried again to make the Korotkoff sounds disappear. In several laboratory studies this method of direct BP feedback was unreliable. Some studies found an effect, but others did not (Blanchard, Martin, & Dubbert, 1988). However, psychologist Bernard Engel and others adapted this method so that patients could use it while taking their own BP's at home (Glasgow, Gaardner, & Engel, 1982). Neither direct BP feedback nor relaxation therapy alone was very effective, but when BP feedback at home was combined with progressive relaxation training, impressive decreases of 13.2/10.2 mmHg were found. While direct BP feedback is rarely used as a treatment for hypertension, the home-based application seems promising and does not require expensive equipment.

Thermal biofeedback has been found to be effective for treating migraine headaches and other disorders, and it has also been applied to hypertension. Patients are instructed to try to warm their hands, and they are provided with feedback of their hand temperature. Hand warming is believed to decrease sympathetic nervous system activity. You may notice that when you are calm, your hands tend to be warm; and when you are nervous, they may become cold. Decreased sympathetic activity also leads to dilation of the blood vessels, which will reduce BP. Although no controlled studies have been conducted, uncontrolled studies by Edward Blanchard (reviewed in Blanchard, Martin, & Dubbert, 1988) have shown modest decreases, especially in diastolic BP in patients who have undergone thermal biofeedback training.

Biofeedback for hypertension is not well developed, and with the fairly consistent effectiveness of the simpler relaxation therapies, it seems unlikely that biofeedback will become a frequently used clinical treatment for hypertension.

Dietary Treatment of Hypertension Two types of dietary treatments are recommended very frequently for hypertensives: calorie restriction for weight loss and sodium restriction (often coupled with increases in potassium). Dietary treatments are sometimes used as the sole intervention and sometimes used in combination with medications. Dietitians have been directing these diet interventions for many years, and health psychologists have recently gotten involved, largely because adherence to the diet recommendations is so poor that their effectiveness was limited. A team effort is required for dietary therapy, with the dietitian designing an effective diet that is nutritionally adequate and the psychologist designing a behavioral strategy to improve adherence.

For the millions of overweight hypertensives, weight loss is a very effective method of lowering BP. It has been determined from a review of many studies that for every 1 kg (2.2 lb) of weight loss there is a 2-mmHg fall in systolic BP and a 1-mmHg fall in diastolic BP (Hovell, 1982). A study by Wing and colleagues (Wing et al., 1984) investigated the effects of a behavioral weight loss program on overweight hypertensives. At the end of the 8-week treatment the average weight loss was 4.4 kg (9.6 lb), and BP's decreased 13.9/7.7 mmHg. Of course, the major problem with obesity treatments is that the weight is usually regained, and the BP rises accordingly.

Sodium-restricted diets can also decrease BP in hypertensives. While sodium is measured by weight in milligrams (mg), its chemical activity in the body is reflected more by measuring sodium in milliequivalents (mEq). One teaspoon of salt contains about 100 mEq of sodium, and the average U.S. diet has 100 to 250 mEq per day. In the Wing study (1984) mentioned above, hypertensives were assigned to either the weight loss treatment or the sodium restriction treatment. After 8 weeks, the sodium restriction group reduced their sodium intake from 169 to 108 mEq per day.

While that is a sizable decrease, it was far from the goal of 70 mEq per day. Nevertheless, significant BP reductions were found, averaging 6.2/4.1 mmHg. For many patients with mild hypertension these reductions would place them in a normal BP range. It should be noted that the BP reductions from sodium restriction were only about half as large as those from weight reduction.

Low sodium and weight reduction diets are clearly effective in reducing BP in hypertensives, but psychologists need to contribute more studies on improving long-term maintenance of the dietary changes.

Exercise Treatment of Hypertension On the basis of epidemiologic evidence that regular vigorous activity inhibits the development of hypertension, exercise has been used as a non-drug treatment. In some cases, exercise can

have a dramatic impact on BP, as shown in Figure 10-12. Martin, Dubbert, and Cushman (1990) conducted a study to determine whether exercise, and not some other related factor, accounted for the BP decreases. Twenty-seven males with mild hypertension were assigned to receive either a vigorous exercise program or a mild "stretching" exercise program that was not expected to have any effect on BP. The stretching condition was a placebo that controlled for expectation of improvement and amount of contact with therapists. The exercise program consisted of walking, jogging, or cycling for 30 minutes, four times per week, for 10 weeks. At the end of treatment, the BP's of the stretching group increased slightly, but the BP's of the exercise group decreased 9.6/6.4 mmHg. Just to make sure that the effect was real, the vigorous exercise program was offered to the placebo condi-

FIGURE 10-12

Diastolic blood pressure as a function of aerobic exercise for Subject 2. Random-zero readings are indicated by an open circle. (From Dubbert, P. M., Martin, J. E., Zimering, R. T., Burkett, P. A., Lake, M., & Cushman, W. C. Behavioral Control of Mild Hypertension with Aerobic Exercise: Two Case Studies. *Behavior Therapy, 15*, 1984, p. 377.)

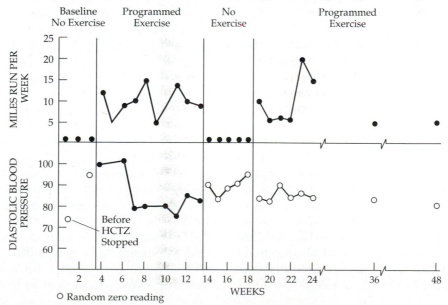

tion subjects. After undergoing the exercise therapy their BP's decreased 7.2/8.1 mmHg. This study is an excellent demonstration that regular exercise can contribute to the treatment of hypertension. However, some studies fail to find any effect of exercise on mild hypertension (Blumenthal, Siegel, & Appelbaum,1991).

Exercise is thought to lower BP partially by reducing body fat and partially by reducing the level of catecholamines (for example, adrenaline) in the body. Since catecholamines are increased during times of stress, health psychologists are very interested in this mechanism. Researchers at the Institute for Aerobics Research studied this hypothesis in a group of 56 hypertensives (Duncan et al., 1985). Half of the subjects were classified as hyperadrenergic, meaning that they had high levels of catecholamines, and half were normoadrenergic. Both groups received 16 weeks of vigorous exercise therapy, and a control group of hypertensives received no exercise. After 16 weeks, the BP's of the controls had increased. Among those who were exercising, the hyperadrenergic subjects experienced a larger decrease in BP than the normoadrenergic subjects. The more the catecholamines dropped, the greater the decrease in BP. This finding suggests that exercise does lower BP by reducing catecholamines. The study also suggests that exercise may be helpful in stress management.

Prevention of Hypertension Early prevention of hypertension is encouraged by teaching children the dietary and physical activity practices that will lead to normal weight and blood pressure. The long-term studies that would be needed to show that intervention in childhood prevents the development of hypertension in adulthood have not been conducted. However, another approach to prevention is to detect high-risk individuals in early adulthood and initiate an aggressive behavior-change program with this identified group.

A hypertension prevention program was carried out for over 5 years in men and women with high-normal resting blood pressures (Stamler et al., 1989). The rationale for this study was that decades of use of antihypertensive drugs can have many negative side effects. Therefore, it is important to develop effective nonpharmacologic interventions to prevent the development of hypertension in hypertension-prone people. The subjects were between 30 and 44 years of age and had diastolic blood pressures between 80 and 89 mmHg. Over 200 subjects were randomly assigned to either the control group, which was monitored every 6 months, or the lifestyle intervention program. The targets of the behavioral intervention were diet, weight, alcohol, and physical activity. Intensive individual sessions were held with both trained physicians and nutrition counselors. Frequency of sessions varied from biweekly to quarterly, depending on the needs of the patient. Family members were involved in the program, and group counseling sessions were used periodically for specific purposes, such as weight control. Printed materials were developed to support the counseling.

Blood pressures were taken every 6 months at both work sites and physician offices. Diet was assessed by food intake diaries. There were very few dropouts, and 87 percent of the participants were in the study at least 4 years. The intervention was effective in reducing the incidence of hypertension. Over the 5 years of the study, 9 percent of the intervention subjects and 19 percent of the control subjects developed definite hypertension. The behavior-change intervention was successful in producing changes in the other targeted behaviors and risk factors. The results are summarized in Table 10-5.

The resting pulse was used as a crude indicator of physical activity and fitness, but there was no significant group difference on that measure. However, at year 2, treadmill exer-

TABLE 10-5

FIVE-YEAR CHANGES IN THE HYPERTENSION PREVENTION PROGRAM

Variable	Intervention	Control	p value
Weight (kg)	−2.0	+0.8	.001
Sodium intake	−25%	−6%	.001
Alcohol intake	−33%	−24%	ns
Resting pulse	−2.6 bpm	−2.2 bpm	ns
Calorie intake	−30%	−12%	.001

cise tests were conducted, and the significant differences found there suggested that intervention subjects had increased their physical activity. These results over a 5-year period are impressive and indicate than an intensive behavior-change program conducted in the physician's office can prevent the development of hypertension in high-risk adults. This study is encouraging for those who would like to see behavior-change programs of this type become a standard form of medical practice. Widespread adoption of effective programs like this could reduce reliance on antihypertensive drugs. The primary disadvantage of this program is likely to be its high cost due to the frequent and prolonged individual counseling.

Summary

Blood pressure is strongly related to risk of CVD, but the mechanisms by which it increases risk are not known. A diagnosis of borderline high blood pressure is made when the readings are 140/90 mmHg or greater, but it is important to remember that the lower the blood pressure, the lower the risk of CVD. *Essential hypertension* is the name given to most cases of high blood pressure. There are many factors in the etiology of essential hypertension. In addition to a strong genetic component, obesity, exercise, and consumption of sodium, potassium, calcium, and other minerals affect blood pressure. Blood pressure is a

sensitive indicator of psychological stress, and studies of blood pressure reactivity to stress have become a major field in health psychology and behavioral medicine. Level of blood pressure reactivity predicts future development of hypertension, so reactivity appears to be an early marker of risk. Although medications are the primary means of treating hypertension, nonpharmacologic (or behavioral) treatments can also be effective. Dietary change, exercise, weight loss, and relaxation treatments have all been found to lower blood pressure in hypertensives. These same methods can be applied to prevent the development of hypertension in high-risk adults.

BEHAVIORAL TREATMENT OF CARDIOVASCULAR DISEASES

Changes in diet, smoking, physical activity, and other behaviors are effective in improving the pattern of lipoproteins and reducing blood pressure. Thus behavior change is the focus of CVD prevention programs. After clinical signs of CVD have been detected—such as angina, myocardial infarction, or stroke—treatment usually involves both medication and behavior change. Most of the time only modest changes in health behaviors are seen, even when patients are put into formal cardiac rehabilitation programs. Although these programs are effective in extending the life of CVD patients, when compared with patients in no program (O'Connor, Buring, Yusuf, et al., 1989), some people believe that behavior change can have even more dramatic effects on heart disease.

For a long time it was believed that the hard, crusty buildup of plaques in the arteries could not be reversed, but recent animal and human studies have shown that it is possible to cause the plaque to shrink by vigorous treatments. A multidisciplinary team led by physician Dean Ornish conducted a study to find out whether atherosclerosis could be reversed by behavioral changes only. The Lifestyle

Heart Trial (Ornish et al., 1990) is a unique study because of the comprehensiveness of the behavioral changes. Patients with severe heart disease were recruited into the program. Most of them had already had at least one heart attack. About 40 patients were randomly assigned to the intervention or control groups. Control subjects received the usual medical care. The experimental subjects took part in a program that radically changed their lifestyles.

The study began with a weekend retreat to introduce subjects and their spouses to the program and to each other. For the next year they were expected to attend group meetings for 4 hours twice a week. As you can see, this required a major commitment. Subjects were placed on a vegetarian diet with very low fat content (10 percent of all calories). To make it easier for subjects to stick with the diet, meals were served at group meetings, cooking lessons were given, and free meals were available to take home. Caffeine was eliminated, and alcohol was restricted to two drinks per day. Several relaxation and yoga exercises were taught in the group sessions, and subjects were instructed to practice relaxation and meditation at least 1 hour each day. Moderate levels of regular exercise were prescribed and were practiced at group sessions. Of course, smokers were helped to stop smoking. Since no other program has promoted such comprehensive behavior changes, there was a great deal of interest in learning the results.

Experimental subjects adhered to the diet very well. They reduced their percentage of calories from fat from 31 percent at baseline to 7 percent during the intervention; the control group did not change. The experimental group increased exercise from 11 minutes per day to 38 minutes per day; the control group did not change. Experimental subjects increased their stress management time from 5 minutes per day to 82 minutes per day. The changes in risk factors after 1 year were very impressive and were larger than the effects of most drug treat-

ments. LDL cholesterol fell by 37 percent, while most diet interventions produce only 10 to 15 percent declines. Many patients achieved total blood cholesterols below 150 mg/dl, and this is in a population with severe heart disease! Systolic blood pressure fell from 134 to 127 mmHg. As expected with such a drastic change in diet and physical activity, average weights decreased from 200 lb to 178 lb in the experimental group, while the control group increased in weight.

The main point of the study was to determine whether lifestyle changes had any effect on the clinical status of the patients. Here again, the results were impressive. Angina pain decreased 91 percent in the experimental group, but it increased 165 percent in the control group. The progression of atherosclerosis in the arteries supplying blood to the heart was studied by computer-aided angiography, which is a state-of-the-art procedure. Angiograms made at baseline and 1-year posttest were used to track changes in specific locations on the arteries. The amount of blockage decreased in 18 of the 22 experimental subjects, and those who adhered best to the program had much more reversal. In contrast, the amount of blockage in the arteries increased in 10 of the 19 control subjects, decreased in 8, and did not change in 1.

This is the first study to show that a comprehensive program of behavior change can lead to actual reversal of artery blockage due to atherosclerosis. This should be good news to heart disease patients, because dramatic changes were documented in just 1 year. These results raise a question about whether similar behavior changes could prevent or greatly slow the development of heart disease in the first place. Many people may be frustrated by the thought that vegetarian diets and 1 hour per day of relaxation may be needed to treat heart disease. However, the regimen recommended in this study has similarities to the lifestyles of people in "primitive" cultures who have very low rates of heart disease. We are going to have to decide whether eating our high-fat diets and living in a high-stress culture are worth what we have to pay in heart disease and a shorter life.

SUMMARY

Cardiovascular diseases (CVD) kill more people in the United States and other industrialized nations than any other cause. Atherosclerosis refers to the buildup of plaque in the inside of arteries. All forms of CVD—including myocardial infarctions (heart attacks), cerebrovascular accidents (strokes), and peripheral vascular disease—are caused by atherosclerosis. The disease begins early in life and is influenced by many factors. In addition to genetics, the main physiological risk factors are lipoproteins, blood pressure, obesity, and diabetes. The main behavioral risk factors are smoking, diet, and physical activity. The complex etiology of CVD means that there is no easy cure. However, the important contributions of behavior mean that people can make changes to improve the health of their hearts.

This chapter explained the different types of lipoproteins and their different effects on CVD. LDL is affected mostly by dietary change, while HDL is affected by physical activity and alcohol. Both resting blood pressure and reactivity to stress appear to be important in the etiology of CVD. Numerous methods are available for the prevention and treatment of hypertension, but no method of reducing blood pressure reactivity has yet been documented.

The topic of CVD has relevance for every reader of this book. CVD is a large field in health psychology and behavioral medicine because it is such a common disease. We hope that this chapter has informed you about the role of individual behavior in the development of CVD. We also hope this chapter has stimulated you to think about what you may do to alter your lipoproteins and blood pressure, and thus reduce your own risk.

KEY TERMS

Cardiovascular diseases (CVD). A collection of related diseases of the heart and blood vessels that includes heart attacks, strokes, and peripheral artery disease.

Atherosclerosis. The common cause of virtually all forms of CVD. It is the buildup of cholesterol and other tissues on the inside of arteries that eventually leads to a blockage of the blood vessel.

Myocardial infarction (MI, also known as a "heart attack"). When an artery that supplies blood to the heart muscle is blocked, part of the heart dies.

Angina pectoris. Severe pain in the chest, resulting from a lack of blood and oxygen to the heart muscle.

Cerebrovascular accident (CVA, also known as a "stroke"). When an artery that supplies blood to the brain is blocked, part of the brain dies.

Peripheral artery disease (PAD). When an artery that supplies blood to the legs or arms is blocked, part of the extremity dies.

Cholesterol. A waxy substance that is part of every animal cell. High levels of cholesterol in the blood promote atherosclerosis and increase risk of CVD.

Lipoproteins. Combinations of proteins and cholesterol that transport cholesterol in the blood. Different lipoproteins have different functions: LDL increases risk of CVD, HDL decreases risk of CVD, and VLDL has no major effect on CVD.

Hypercholesterolemia. The condition of having excessive cholesterol in the blood. Recommended levels are below 200 mg/dl for adults. The condition may be due to genes or diet.

Framingham Study. About 3000 residents of Framingham, Massachusetts were studied over a period of 30 years. This research identified most of the major risk factors of CVD.

Lipid Research Clinics Study. This large study proved that decreasing cholesterol caused a decrease in CVD mortality in high-risk men. For every 1 percent of cholesterol reduction, there was a 2 percent reduction in mortality.

Bogalusa Heart Study. A study in Bogalusa, Louisiana, that identified risk factors of CVD in children.

Blood pressure (BP). The force blood exerts on the walls of arteries as it is pumped by the heart. This CVD risk factor is measured in millimeters of mercury (mmHg). The top number indicates systolic blood pressure, and the bottom number is diastolic. A recommended level for adults is 120/80.

Hypertension. A condition of having high blood pressure, that is, greater than 140/90. It does *not* mean that someone is tense or anxious.

Sodium restriction. Reducing sodium in the diet as a method of treating hypertension.

Cardiovascular reactivity. Blood pressure increases in response to psychological and physical stress. High levels of reactivity indicate that one may be at risk of developing hypertension or CVD.

Relaxation therapy. Producing a calm state can be an effective treatment of hypertension. Methods of relaxing include meditation, autogenic training, and progressive muscle relaxation.

Biofeedback. Using technology to make you aware of your own physiology. When you can get feedback from your body, you are sometimes able to control physiological processes such as blood pressure. Hypertension has been treated with direct blood pressure feedback as well as feedback on hand temperature.

Nonpharmacologic therapy. Any treatment for a medical condition that does not use drugs. Nonpharmacologic therapy for hypercholesterolemia includes low-fat diet and weight loss. Nonpharmacologic therapy for hypertension includes diet change, exercise, relaxation, and weight loss.

Lifestyle heart trial. This study tested a radical behavior change intervention with severe heart disease patients. Not only did the program change behavior, but plaques in the arteries regressed.

CHAPTER 11

Cancer

Visits to the hospital were very painful for Sharon. Her father was 62 years old when he was diagnosed with small cell cancer of the lung. At first she was very angry, blaming her father for his own disease. Sharon's father had smoked cigarettes for over 45 years, and the first question everyone asked when they found out he had lung cancer was, "Did he smoke?" It made Sharon furious that people became so unsympathetic if they were able to place blame on the victim.

Once beyond that, Sharon noticed a new dimension in her relationship with her father. He had undergone a lot since the diagnosis. Surgery removed portions of his left lung, and the recovery was miserable. Then, a series of chemotherapy sessions weakened him and caused him to lose his hair. Despite the fact that he was losing his battle to cancer, Sharon discovered a whole new relationship with her father. The illness had caused him to forget about his job, his cars, and all the other possessions that had come to dominate his life. For the first time, Sharon felt that her father wanted to know about her as an adult and to discover what it meant to be a family. In this chapter we will explore cancer—what it is, how it can be prevented, and how people cope with the disease and the uncertainties it brings into their lives.

What does cancer mean to you? For many people cancer is the most feared disease. In fact, in many parts of the world patients are never told the name of their disease. Even in modern westernized societies many cancer victims deny they have the disease. Obituaries for cancer victims often state that the person "died after a long illness," failing to acknowledge that cancer was the cause of death. Many people still believe that cancer is a death sentence. Furthermore, they fear that the diagnosis of cancer will change the way people relate to them—ultimately making the cancer victim a social outcast.

Is this fear of cancer well-founded? Clearly, cancer is a very serious diagnosis. In 1992, about 1 million people were diagnosed as having it. Yet the chances of surviving cancer have improved dramatically. In the early 1900s, very few cancer patients survived more than a few years. By 1930, only about 20 percent of those treated for cancer were still alive 5 years later. But by the 1940s, survival had improved to 25 percent; and by 1960, it had increased to 33 percent. Today, about 40 percent of those diagnosed with cancer survive 5 years. Furthermore, we must take into consideration the age at which people get cancer. Cancer occurs most commonly in elderly people, who have a lower chance of surviving 5 years. Taking a normal life expectancy into consideration and the probability of dying from other causes (such as heart disease, accidents, and the like), it is estimated that about half of those diagnosed with cancer will survive 5 years (American Cancer Society, 1992). These improvements in cancer survival led Vincent DeVita, the former director of the National Cancer Institute, to. suggest that cancer is one of the most curable diseases in the western world (DeVita & Kershner, 1980).

Despite major advances in cancer treatment, cancer remains a huge public health problem. In the past 50 years there has been approximately a 250 percent increase in the number of people who die from cancer (De-

BOX 11·1

Objectives for the Year 2000/Health

By the year 2000, we should:

1. Reduce the rise in cancer deaths to no more than 130 per 100,000 people (1987 baseline: 133).

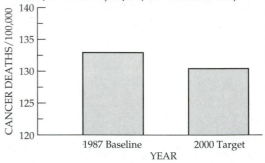

2. Increase clinical breast exams and mammography every 2 years to at least 60 percent of all women aged 50 and over (1987 baseline: 25 percent).

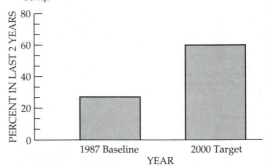

3. Increase Pap tests every 1 to 3 years to at least 85 percent of all women aged 18 and older (1987 baseline: 75 percent).

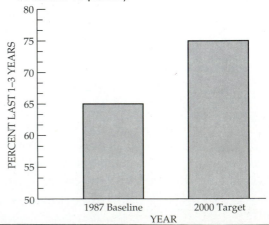

vesa & Schneiderman, 1977). The American Cancer Society estimates that about 514,000 die of cancer each year in the United States. This translates into nearly 1400 deaths per day, or about 1 death every 61 seconds (American Cancer Society, 1992). Cancer is the second leading cause of death in the United States and accounts for approximately 21 percent of all mortality. The prevalence of cancer is also high: an estimated one-third of all Americans born today will develop some form of this disease (American Cancer Society, 1985). In addition to the high death rate, cancer is responsible for staggering costs to society in terms of medical treatment, employment absenteeism, and reductions in quality of life (Mor, 1992).

WHAT IS CANCER?

The American Cancer Society defines cancer as "a large group of diseases characterized by uncontrolled growth and spread of abnormal cells" (p. 3). Cancer is a complicated disease because it can affect almost any organ system. Cancerous growths in different parts of the body are associated with different treatments and different chances of surviving. Some cancers, such as common cancers of the skin, pose very little threat to life. Other cancers, such as those of the liver, are associated with very poor chances of survival.

The terminology associated with cancer is complex. The common theme among cancers is that they result from recurrent injuries to specific cells that occur over an extended period of time (Fries & Vickery, 1990). When cells grow into masses of tissues, they are called *tumors*. Some of these tumors are *benign*, meaning that they are not made up of cancer cells. *Malignant* tumors are cancerous. When the cells are injured, cell division is required in the normal healing process. However, when the cells are injured repeatedly, the chances of an error in cell division increase. When the normal processes that halt cell division break

down, cells may begin dividing out of control. This is referred to as the *malignant process*.

The immune system is typically capable of destroying malignant cells. However, for a variety of reasons, the immune system may become less effective. For example, as people age, their immune systems become less effective. Malignant cells may grow out of check and may begin interfering with the function of tissues or organs. The term *metastasize* refers to spread of the malignant cells to other parts of the body. Many cancers involve solid tumors. However, others are softer. For example, *leukemias* are cancers of the blood, while *lymphomas* are cancers of the lymph system. Most cancers are localized, meaning that they stay near their original site. When cancers metastasize, they are spread to other parts of the body through the blood or lymph systems. Sometimes the metastasis is regional. This means that the cancer stays within one region of the body because the cancer cells are trapped in lymph nodes. However, if regional cancer is not treated, the cancer cells will spread throughout the body and advanced cancer will develop. Advanced cancer typically results in death.

EPIDEMIOLOGY

Table 11-1 and Figure 11-1 summarize the estimated new cases of cancer and the cause of death for men and women in 1990. The incidence of most cancers is declining or staying relatively steady. This can be seen graphically in Figure 11-2. The figure shows changes in the rate of death per 100,000 in the population between the years 1930 and 1986. As you can see, the rates for most cancers are not changing much. Some cancers, such as cancer of the uterus and cancer of the stomach, have declined significantly, particularly in the years prior to 1970. The most striking feature of Figure 11-2 is the significant increase in lung cancer. As the figure shows, lung cancer steadily increased between the years 1930 and 1986. It has been estimated that about 85 percent of

TABLE 11·1

ESTIMATED NEW CASES OF CANCER AND THE CAUSE OF DEATH FOR MEN AND WOMEN IN 1990

	Estimated new cases			Estimated deaths		
	Total	Male	Female	Total	Male	Female
All sites	1,040,000*	520,000*	520,000*	510,000	270,000	240,000
Buccal cavity & pharynx **(ORAL)**	30,500	20,400	10,100	8,350	5,575	2,775
Lip	3,600	3,100	500	100	75	25
Tongue	6,100	3,900	2,200	1,950	1,300	650
Mouth	11,500	6,900	4,600	2,500	1,500	1,000
Pharynx	9,300	6,500	2,800	3,800	2,700	1,100
Digestive organs	236,800	121,300	115,500	122,900	64,600	58,300
Esophagus	10,600	7,400	3,200	9,500	7,000	2,500
Stomach	23,200	13,900	9,300	13,700	8,300	5,400
Small intestine	2,800	1,500	1,300	900	500	400
Large intestine ⎱ **(COLON-RECTUM)**	110,000	52,000	58,000	53,300	26,000	27,300
Rectum ⎰	45,000	24,000	21,000	7,600	4,000	3,600
Liver & biliary passages	14,600	7,700	6,900	11,900	6,200	5,700
Pancreas	28,100	13,600	14,500	25,000	12,100	12,900
Other & unspecified digestive	2,500	1,200	1,300	1,000	500	500
Respiratory system	173,700	115,000	58,700	147,100	95,900	51,200
Larynx	12,300	10,000	2,300	3,750	3,000	750
LUNG	157,000	102,000	55,000	142,000	92,000	50,000
Other & unspecified respiratory	4,400	3,000	1,400	1,350	900	450
Bone	2,100	1,200	900	1,100	600	500
Connective tissue	5,700	3,000	2,700	3,100	1,500	1,600
SKIN	27,600†	14,800†	12,800†	8,800§	5,700	3,100
BREAST	150,900‡	900‡	150,000‡	44,300	300	44,000
Genital organs	185,000‡	113,100	71,900‡	54,100	30,600	23,500
Cervix uteri ⎱ **(UTERUS)**	13,500‡	—	13,500‡	6,000	—	6,000
Corpus, endometrium ⎰	33,000	—	33,000	4,000	—	4,000
Ovary	20,500	—	20,500	12,400	—	12,400
Other & unspecified genital, female	4,900	—	4,900	1,100	—	1,100
Prostate	106,000	106,000	—	30,000	30,000	—
Testis	5,900	5,900	—	350	350	—
Other & unspecified genital, male	1,200	1,200	—	250	250	—

lung cancers are attributable to cigarette smoking. In fact, it has been suggested that excluding cancers associated with cigarette smoking, cancer rates either remained steady or declined.

By reviewing Table 11-1, you will notice that cancers occur in many different systems. Thus, cancer is not a single disease, but rather a family of different diseases that occur in different parts of the body. The causes of the different cancers are not the same, and this makes cancer a particularly difficult problem to get a grasp on. Table 11-1 does show that some cancers are more common than others, and we will focus on these more common cancers in our discussions. Lung cancer, for example,

TABLE 11-1 Continued

	Estimated new cases			Estimated deaths		
	Total	Male	Female	Total	Male	Female
Urinary organs	73,000	51,000	22,000	20,000	12,600	7,400
Bladder	49,000	36,000	13,000	9,700	6,500	3,200
Kidney & other urinary	24,000	15,000	9,000	10,300	6,100	4,200
Eye	1,700	900	800	300	150	150
Brain & central nervous system	15,600	8,500	7,100	11,100	6,000	5,100
Endocrine glands	13,600	4,000	9,600	1,750	775	975
Thyroid	12,100	3,200	8,900	1,025	375	650
Other endocrine	1,500	800	700	725	400	325
Leukemia	27,800	15,700	12,100	18,100	9,800	8,300
Lymphocytic leukemia	11,600	6,700	4,900	5,200	3,000	2,200
Granulocytic leukemia	11,500	6,300	5,200	7,600	4,000	3,600
Other & unspecified leukemia	4,700	2,700	2,000	5,300	2,800	2,500
Other blood & lumph tissues	54,800	28,900	25,900	28,700	14,900	13,800
Hodgkin's disease	7,400	4,200	3,200	1,600	1,000	600
Non-Hodgkin's lymphomas	35,600	18,600	17,000	18,200	9,500	8,700
Multiple myeloma	11,800	6,100	5,700	8,900	4,400	4,500
All other & unspecified sites	41,200	21,300	19,900	40,300	21,000	19,300

Note: The estimates of new cancer cases are offered as a rough guide and should not be regarded as definitive. Especially note that year-to-year changes may only represent improvements in the basic data. ACS six major sites appear in boldface caps.

* Carcinoma in situ and nonmelanoma skin cancers are not included in totals. Carcinoma in situ of the uterine cervix accounts for more than 50,000 new cases annually, carcinoma in situ of the female breast accounts for about 15,000 new cases annually, and melanoma carcinoma in situ accounts for about 5,000 new cases annually. Overall, about 100,000 new cases of carcinoma in situ of all sites of cancer are diagnosed each year. Nonmelanoma skin cancer accounts for about 600,000 new cases annually.

† Malenoma only.   ‡ Invasive cancer only.   § Melanoma 6,300; other skin 2,500.

INCIDENCE ESTIMATES ARE BASED ON RATES FROM NCI SEER PROGRAM 1984–86.

Source: American Cancer Society 1991.

is the most common cause of cancer death among men, accounting for an estimated 92,000 deaths in 1990. Considering men and women, lung cancer accounts for about 142,000 deaths per year. Cigarette smoking is clearly the predominant risk factor in the development of lung cancer, although there are other causes, including occupational exposures and exposure to radon gas. However, the number of cases caused by these exposures is relatively small in comparison with cases caused by the use of cigarettes.

Breast cancer is the most common cause of cancer death among women. An estimated 150,000 new cases of breast cancer will develop in the United States during 1990. About 1 in 10 women will develop breast cancer sometime during her life. Breast cancer does occur in men, although it is relatively rare. Perhaps more alarming is the rate at which breast cancer is increasing. New evidence suggests that breast cancer has been increasing about 1 percent per year since the early 1970s.

Breast cancer is a treatable disease. Although there are over 150,000 new cases per year, there are only about 43,000 deaths. Thirty years ago the 5-year survival for localized breast cancer was 78 percent. Today it

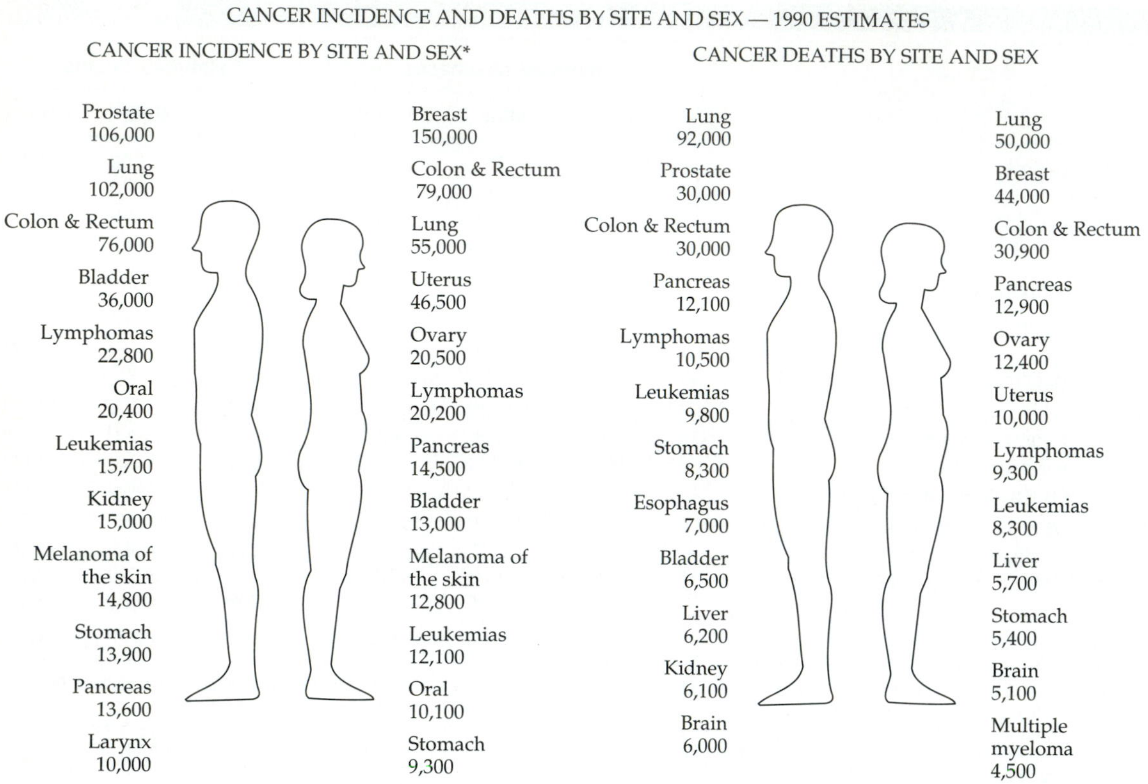

CANCER INCIDENCE AND DEATHS BY SITE AND SEX — 1990 ESTIMATES

CANCER INCIDENCE BY SITE AND SEX*

CANCER DEATHS BY SITE AND SEX

Prostate 106,000	Breast 150,000	Lung 92,000	Lung 50,000
Lung 102,000	Colon & Rectum 79,000	Prostate 30,000	Breast 44,000
Colon & Rectum 76,000	Lung 55,000	Colon & Rectum 30,000	Colon & Rectum 30,900
Bladder 36,000	Uterus 46,500	Pancreas 12,100	Pancreas 12,900
Lymphomas 22,800	Ovary 20,500	Lymphomas 10,500	Ovary 12,400
Oral 20,400	Lymphomas 20,200	Leukemias 9,800	Uterus 10,000
Leukemias 15,700	Pancreas 14,500	Stomach 8,300	Lymphomas 9,300
Kidney 15,000	Bladder 13,000	Esophagus 7,000	Leukemias 8,300
Melanoma of the skin 14,800	Melanoma of the skin 12,800	Bladder 6,500	Liver 5,700
Stomach 13,900	Leukemias 12,100	Liver 6,200	Stomach 5,400
Pancreas 13,600	Oral 10,100	Kidney 6,100	Brain 5,100
Larynx 10,000	Stomach 9,300	Brain 6,000	Multiple myeloma 4,500

*Excluding nonmelanoma skin cancer and carcinoma in situ.

FIGURE 11-1

Cancer incidence by site and sex in 1990. (From American Cancer Society, 1991. Reprinted with permission.)

is 90 percent. Women who have breast cancer detected in situ (localized to the initial tumor) have nearly a 100 percent survival rate.

The risk factors for breast cancer are not clearly understood. However, being over age 50 and having a personal or family history of breast cancer are known to increase the odds. Also, women who have never had children or women who have had their first child after the age of 30 are at increased risk. As we will see later (in the section on diet), there is some suggestive evidence that diets rich in animal fats may also cause breast cancer. We will spend more time on breast cancer in this chap-

ter because there are behavioral issues at each phase of this disease. Breast cancer may be preventable through appropriate diet. Once the disease has developed, the behavior of obtaining early cancer screening through breast self-examination, clinical examination, and mammography might significantly increase the chances that a woman will survive. For those who are unfortunate enough not to have their cancers detected, behavioral factors are important in coping with the disease, obtaining appropriate treatment, and dealing with the side effects of cancer treatment. We will examine each of these issues in this chapter.

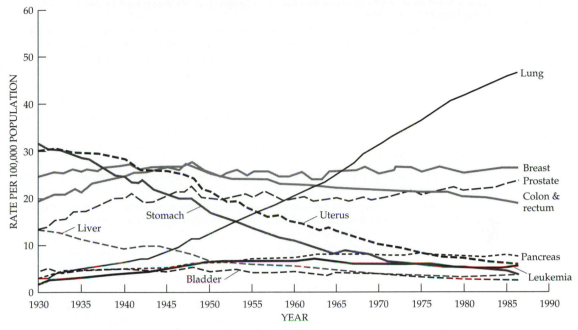

CANCER DEATH RATES* BY SITE, UNITED STATES, 1930–86

*Rate for the population standardized for age on the 1970 US population.
 Sources of data: National Center for Health Statistics and Bureau of the Census, United States.
 Note: Rates are for both sexes combined except breast and uterus (female population only) and prostate (male population only).

FIGURE 11-2
Changes in the cancer death per 100,000 in population between the years 1930 and 1986. (From American Cancer Society, 1991. Reprinted with permission.)

SELECTED FACTORS BELIEVED TO INCREASE RISK FOR CANCER

Diet and Cancer

Although genetic factors are important in determining who gets cancer, environmental factors are also significant contributors as cancer causes (Doll & Peto, 1981; Wynder & Gori, 1977) (see Table 11-2). Of the environmental variables, nutrition may be one of the most important factors. Results from a combination of epidemiological and experimental animal studies have indicated specific nutrients that may function as cancer-causing factors (carcinogens) or as substances that protect against cancer (anticarcinogens) (Wynder & Gori, 1977). For example, a high intake of fat has been associated with higher rates of breast, colon, rectum, uterus, and prostate cancer, whereas a higher intake of dietary fiber has been associated with lower rates of colon and rectal cancers (Greenwald & Sondik, 1986).

Although the specific biochemical reasons why these nutrients are important in cancer prevention are not well understood (Wynder & Gori, 1977), the general body of evidence has stimulated nutritional recommendations for cancer prevention by the National Cancer Institute (NCI), the National Research Council, and the American Cancer Society. The NCI recommendations have been compatible with, although not identical with, the United States

TABLE 11·2

HOW TO LOWER YOUR CANCER RISK

Prevention

Primary prevention refers to steps that might be taken to avoid those factors that might lead to the development of cancer

Smoking	Cigarette smoking is responsible for 85% of lung cancer cases among men and 75% among women—about 83% overall. Smoking accounts for about 30% of all cancer deaths. Those who smoke two or more packs of cigarettes a day have lung cancer mortality rates 15 to 25 times greater than nonsmokers.
Sunlight	Almost all of the more than 600,000 cases of nonmelanoma skin cancer diagnosed each year in the U.S. are considered to be sun-related. Recent epidemiologic evidence shows that sun exposure is a major factor in the development of melanoma and that the incidence increases for those living near the equator.
Alcohol	Oral cancer and cancers of the larynx, throat, esophagus, and liver occur more frequently among heavy drinkers of alcohol.
Smokeless tobacco	Use of chewing tobacco or snuff increases risk of cancer of the mouth, larynx, throat, and esophagus and is highly habit-forming.
Estrogen	For mature women, estrogen treatment to control menopausal symptoms increases risk of endometrial cancer. Use of estrogen by menopausal women needs careful discussion by the woman and her physician.
Radiation	Excessive exposure to ionizing radiation can increase cancer risk. Most medical and dental x-rays are adjusted to deliver the lowest dose possible without sacrificing image quality. Excessive radon exposure in homes may increase risk of lung cancer, especially in cigarette smokers. If levels are found to be too high, remedial actions should be taken.
Occupational hazards	Exposure to several different industrial agents (nickel, chromate, asbestos, vinyl chloride, etc.) increases risk of various cancers. Risk from asbestos is greatly increased when combined with cigarette smoking.
Nutrition	Risk for colon, breast, and uterine cancers increases in obese people. High-fat diets may contribute to the development of cancers of the breast, colon, and prostate. High-fiber foods may help reduce risk of colon cancer. A varied diet containing plenty of vegetables and fruits rich in vitamins A and C may reduce risk for a wide range of cancers. Salt-cured, smoked, and nitrite-cured foods have been linked to esophageal and stomach cancer. The heavy use of alcohol, especially when accompanied by cigarette smoking or chewing tobacco, increases risk of cancers of the mouth, larynx, throat, esophagus, and liver. (See above.)

Secondary prevention refers to steps to be taken to diagnose a cancer or precursor as early as possible after it has developed

Colorectal tests	The American Cancer Society recommends three tests for the early detection of colon and rectum cancer in people without symptoms. The digital rectal examination, performed by a physician during an office visit, should be performed every year after the age of 40; the stool blood test is recommended every year after 50; and the proctosigmoidoscopy examination should be carried out every 3 to 5 years, based on the advice of a physician.
Pap test	For cervical cancer, women who are or have been sexually active, or have reached age 18 years, should have an annual Pap test and pelvic examination. After a women has had three or more consecutive satisfactory normal annual examinations, the Pap test may be performed less frequently at the discretion of her physician.
Breast cancer detection	The American Cancer Society recommends the monthly practice of breast self-examination (BSE) by women 20 years and older as a routine good health habit. Physical examination of the breast should be done every three years from ages 20–40 and then every year. The ACS recommends a mammogram every year for asymptomatic women age 50 and over, and a baseline mammogram between ages 35 and 39. Women 40 to 49 should have mammography every 1–2 years, depending on physical and mammographic findings.

Source: Cancer Facts and Figures 1990, American Cancer Society, 1991.

Department of Agriculture (USDA) Dietary Guidelines for Americans—including avoidance of high-fat diets, eating adequate fiber, and drinking moderate amounts of alcohol—and with the American Heart Association's recommendation to reduce dietary fat. The goals for daily fat and fiber intake for the year 2000 are 25 percent of all daily calories and 20 to 30 g a day, respectively. Results from two dietary intervention studies suggest that a reduced fat and an increased fiber diet may be complementary in terms of subjects maintaining mean baseline levels of total energy intake. Thus, long-term adherence to the combination of these recommendations may be higher than adherence to each recommendation alone (Maugh, 1982). The 1982 report issued by the Committee on Diet (1983) National Research Council estimated that U.S. cancer

incidence could be reduced by one-third if these and other nutritional recommendations are adopted.

Much of our current thinking was stimulated by an important study by Doll and Peto (1981), two well-known British epidemiologists. These investigators developed quantitative estimates of the impact of various risk factors on cancer mortality. The most important risk factor for all cancer mortality was diet. This is shown most dramatically in Figure 11-3, which sketches the relationship between dietary fat consumption in different countries and the chances of getting breast cancer. As the figure shows, countries with high-fat diets are also the ones in which breast cancer is most common. Doll and Peto estimated that 35 percent of all cancer deaths might be attributable to food consumption. There is considerable

FIGURE 11-3

The relationship between dietary fat consumption in different countries and the chances of getting breast cancer. (From Transactions and Studies of the College of Physicians of Philadelphia. Reprinted with permission.)

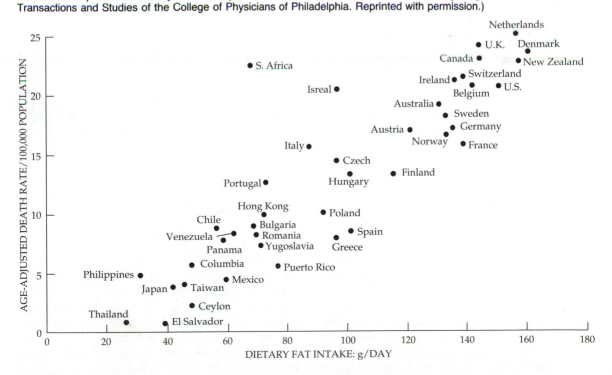

debate about the extent to which diet affects cancer mortality. Doll and Peto suggested that the acceptable range was 10 to 70 percent. The 35 percent estimate is approximately midrange. Wynder and Gori (1977) estimate that 40 percent of all cancer in males and 57 percent of all cancer in females may be associated with diet. Despite the "softness" in these estimates, it is also suggested from several epidemiologic studies that diet is a major risk factor. Although we are still awaiting conclusive evidence that modification in diet causes reductions in cancer mortality, the evidence seems compelling enough that health promotion programs should be undertaken at this point. The Committee on Diet, Nutrition, and Cancer of the National Research Council (1983) also raised questions about the exact linkages between diet and cancer. Nevertheless, they found significant evidence to implicate diet, in particular dietary fat, as a cause for cancer.

Cigarette Smoking

It has now been one-quarter of a century since the publication of the surgeon general's first report entitled "Smoking and Health: Report of the Advisory Committee to the Surgeon General of the United States" (Bright-See & Levy, 1985). Twenty-five years ago there was strong evidence for the detrimental effects of cigarette smoking. Current evidence on the health consequences of cigarette smoking now leaves no doubt that cigarettes cause premature deaths. According to the American Cancer Society 400,000 people died of causes attributable to cigarette smoking in 1992. This represents one-fifth of all deaths in the United States (Maugh, 1982). Many of our public health programs are directed toward preventing the most feared types of death. Enormous amounts of public attention are devoted to AIDS, cocaine, heroin, homicide, and suicide. However, it is important to emphasize that the impact of cigarette smoking far exceeds that for any of these other causes of death. In fact,

cigarette smoking causes more premature deaths than the combination of AIDS, cocaine, heroin, alcohol, fire, automobile accidents, homicide, and suicide (Warner et al., 1988). Thirty percent of all cancer deaths are caused by cigarette smoking, as are twenty-one percent of all cases of death resulting from coronary heart disease. An overwhelming 82 percent of all deaths from chronic obstructive pulmonary disease (chronic bronchitis and emphysema) are also attributable to cigarette smoking. Finally, stroke is another disabling disease closely linked to the use of cigarettes.

The epidemic of deaths associated with cigarette use is directly traceable to investments by tobacco companies in advertising. Groups are targeted, and advertising material is directed toward them. There is substantial evidence that cigarette smoking rates increase in these targeted groups. Women, for example, are a major new target of cigarette advertising, and lung cancer is now a major cause of death for women. Twenty-five years ago, lung cancer was a relatively uncommon disease in women. Over the last 25 years, lung cancer rates for nonsmoking women have remained very constant at about 12 per 100,000 women. For smoking women, lung cancer death rates rose from 23.9 per 100,000 to 130.4 per 100,000 (Kaplan, 1989). Lung cancer alone is the major factor affecting the increasing rate of deaths from cancer. In fact, age-adjusted cancer death rates would be falling, and we would have a declining rate of cancer death if it were not for cigarette smoking.

On the basis of quantitative estimates from Doll and Peto (1981), cigarette smoking accounts for 30 percent of all cancer deaths. In their analysis, Doll and Peto suggested that the range of acceptable estimates for cigarette smoking was 25 to 40 percent. Despite the "softness" in these estimates, several epidemiologic studies suggest that cigarette smoking and diet are the major risk factors for cancer. Figure 11-4 shows the best estimates of proportions of cancer deaths attributable to various

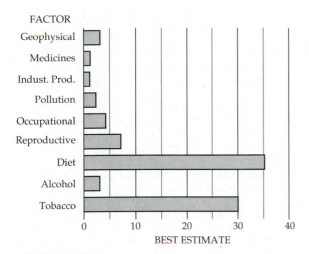

FIGURE 11-4

Best estimates of cancer cause factors. (After Doll & Peto, 1981.)

risk factors according to a detailed study by Doll and Peto (1981). As the figure shows, cigarettes and diet are the most important risk factors. Indeed, these two habits account for more cancers than environmental exposures, medicines, industrial product, or occupational exposures.

In a variety of reports, the National Cancer Institute has identified tobacco use and dietary variables as the major controllable risk factors for cancer. They have suggested major efforts to prevent cancer deaths attributable to tobacco, diet, and exposure to other carcinogens. In Chapters 14, 16, and 19, we will discuss dietary programs, smoking programs, and issues in evaluating health promotion programs.

CANCER SCREENING: THE CASE OF MAMMOGRAPHY

There is substantial evidence that we could reduce the number of women who die of breast cancer if we could increase the use of cancer screening tests. The American Cancer Society and the National Cancer Institute have found that mammography can reveal cancers that are too small to be felt by most experi-

enced examiners. Mammography is x-ray examination of the breast tissue. The technique uses a very low level of radiation and is very safe. Both the National Cancer Institute and the American Cancer Society have recommended mammography for women over age 50, as have a variety of organizations. Nevertheless, many women do not obtain mammograms according to their recommended schedules (Hayward, Shapiro, Freeman, & Corey, 1988).

Since mammograms can be so helpful, why do women not get them? In one recent national survey sponsored by the National Cancer Institute, several explanations were explored. Combining seven different surveys of women between the ages of 50 and 74 without breast cancer, it was noted that 90 percent of the non-Hispanic women had a regular source of medical care. However, only between 25 and 41 percent had had a mammogram within the past year. The women listed a variety of reasons for not obtaining this screening test. The most common reason was that they did not think they needed it. The next most common reason was that the woman's doctor had not suggested it. Very few women cited costs or the effects of radiation as the reasons they had not pursued this test (NCI Breast Cancer Screening Consortium, 1990).

One of the curious problems about the use of mammography is that the women who need it most may be least interested. In one study of 1163 women in eastern North Carolina, about 25 percent of the women in their thirties had had a mammogram and 34 percent intended to have one in the coming year. However, women in their thirties are at relatively low risk for breast cancer. Only 45 to 52 percent of the women in their forties, fifties, and sixties had ever had a mammogram, and only 37 percent of the women over 70 had had one. These older women are at the highest risk for developing breast cancer. Worry and attitudes about breast cancer were related to the likelihood of

BOX 11-2

FOCUS ON WOMEN

The Mammography Controversy

Medical tests are not unlike psychological tests. They have validity and reliability and can be assessed in relation to younger (less than age 50) outcomes. One interesting controversy involves the use of mammography to screen women for breast cancer. Mammography has clearly been shown to be a valuable medical test for women age 50 and older. However, there is some controversy concerning its use for women who are less than 50. The reason for this controversy is related to the base rates, and the false positive, and the false negatives.

Breast cancer is very much related to age. Although the American Cancer Society argues that 1 in 9 women will develop breast cancer, these tumors are much more common among older women than among younger women (see Figure 11-5). For women in their twenties, breast cancer is an extremely rare disease. In fact, 100,000 mammograms would have to be performed in order to find one woman with breast cancer. This suggests that for younger women the base rate for breast cancer is very low (1 per 100,000). This has become somewhat of a controversy because the popular media has lodged a campaign attempting to increase the use of mammography for all women. If we pay for mammography from public funds, and the cost of a mammogram is $100, that would mean it would cost about $10 million to detect one case. Of course, any investment would be worth it if lives were saved. However, analyses of studies of breast cancer suggest that the rare case of breast cancer detected in young women has no better chance of survival than a case left undetected. However, this is a matter of considerable debate in the medical community.

The related concern for performing mammography in younger women is that breast tissue is denser than it is in older women. As a result, there are a significant number of false positives in younger women. A false positive is when the test suggests something suspicious when, indeed, there is not a problem. It has been estimated that one younger woman in three who gets repeated mammograms will have a false positive that requires further medical tests or biopsies (Miller, 1991).

What does this tell us? Clearly mammography has been shown to be a valuable medical test for older women. For younger women, those in their twenties and early thirties, the picture may be different. There is a very low base rate for the problem, and there are significant risks of false positive tests. Of course, women with risk factors for breast cancer, such as those with a strong family history of the condition, may still benefit from routine screening.

FIGURE 11-5

Age-specific breast cancer annual incidence. (After Sondic, 1988.)

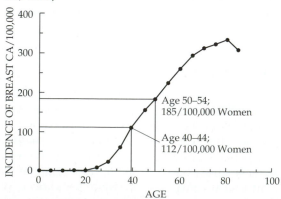

getting a mammogram. The studies show that young women were more worried about breast cancer than older women and that younger women were more likely to obtain the service. Overall, the study suggested that the use of mammography may be excessive among younger women but may be underutilized among older women (Harris, Fletcher, Gonzales, et al., 1991).

One of the reasons that mammography is rarely performed is that physicians often do not recommend it. However, behavioral procedures can sometimes be used to increase the rate at which important tests are ordered. Sometimes, this is as simple as providing reminders or cues to the doctors. In one study, three different approaches to prompting physicians were studied: no prompting, nurse-staff–initiated prompting, and computerized prompting. The results of the study suggested that prompting works. The use of mammography went from 4 to 33 percent. However, whether a human prompter (a nurse) or a machine prompter (a computer) was used made little difference. The advantage of the computer system is that it prompted the doctor more often. The key to success is to have the prompts done regularly. The doctors did not generalize the use of these tests to patients not enrolled in the study (Harris, O'Malley, Fletcher, & Knight, 1990).

CANCER TREATMENT PSYCHOLOGICAL ISSUES

Cancer treatment is not simple. A wide variety of therapies are used to attack tumors. Somewhat sarcastically, it has been suggested that cancer treatments are designed to cut, burn, and poison. Cutting therapies involve surgical removal of tumors. Burning therapies involve radiation, while poisoning therapies include chemotherapy, hormonal therapy, and immunotherapy. Unfortunately, cancer requires strong treatment. Surgery often causes new physical or cosmetic problems. Chemotherapy

and radiation therapy typically require doses that create other side effects. Radiation therapy, for example, is administered to about 350,000 individuals each year. These treatments do cause significant side effects including hair loss, sterility, nausea, vomiting, fatigue, and diarrhea. However, anxiety about these side effects may make the whole experience even worse. Studies have demonstrated that many patients experience classically conditioned anticipatory symptoms (Andrykowski & Gregg, 1992; Burish & Jenkins, 1992; Carey & Burish, 1988). Without treatment, these psychological reactions to radiation therapy may last as long as 3 months after therapy is over (Redd, Silberfarb, Anderson, et al., 1991).

Because new treatments are more effective, patients are living with cancer a longer time. Yet cancer and its treatments affect many important aspects of life including physical functioning, psychological functioning, sexual functioning, family relationships, and vocational functioning (Ganz, 1992). Various theoretical models have been developed to explain the coping process. One of the best-known models divides the coping process into three components: problems specification, response enumeration, and response evaluation. The model attempts to move away from descriptions of emotional distress and focus instead on the documentation of problems (specification), the identification of potential responses (enumeration), and the assessment of the interventions that might be most beneficial (evaluation) (Ganz, 1990).

In order to evaluate problems of cancer patients, a variety of scales have been developed. Perhaps one of the most important measurement instruments is the Cancer Inventory of Problem Situations (CIPS). This measure lists problems commonly encountered by cancer patients. In the early phases of development, 100 cancer patients and significant others in their lives were carefully interviewed. This process led to the identification of 142 items.

Some of these items had been on the original questionnaire and others were added after reviews by professionals. For example, new items were added to cover pain, pain medications, relationships with family, and other areas. Not all items apply to all patients. For example, some items refer to chemotherapy and are appropriate only for those undergoing treatment.

The final version of the CIPS was developed on the basis of statistical procedures and included 31 subscales grouped into five major categories: physical, psychosocial, medical interaction, marital, and sexual problems. Table 11-3 summarizes these scales. Physical problems include ambulation (walking), participating in recreation, performing normal activities of daily living (such as bathing, dressing, walking, and the like), difficulties with work, pain, weight loss, and the requirement for special clothing. Psychosocial problems involve difficulty in communicating, anxiety, distress, worry, and so on. The medical interaction problems involve obtaining the appropriate in-

---

TABLE 11-3

THE CIPS 31 SUBSCALES GROUPED INTO FIVE MAJOR CATEGORIES: PHYSICAL, PSYCHOSOCIAL, MEDICAL INTERACTION, MARITAL, AND SEXUAL PROBLEMS

Subscale and factors	Number of items	Sample item
Physical	26	
Ambulation	4	I have difficulty walking and/or moving around.
Recreational activities	4	I do not engage in the recreational activities that I used to.
Activities of daily living	4	I have difficulty doing household chores.
Difficulty working	2	I find that cancer or its treatments interfere with my ability to work.
Pain	4	I frequently have pain.
Weight loss	5	I cannot gain weight.
Clothing	3	I find that my clothes do not fit.
Pyschosocial	44	
Psychological distress	6	I frequently feel anxious.
Worry	4	I worry about whether the cancer is progressing.
Anxiety in medical situations	6	I become nervous when I am waiting to see the doctor.
Cognitive problems	3	I have difficulty thinking clearly.
Body image	3	I am uncomfortable with the changes in my body.
At-work concerns	5	I have difficulty talking to my boss about the cancer.
Difficulty communicating with friends/relatives	7	I do not know what to say to friends or relatives.
Friends/relatives difficulty interacting	7	I find that my friends or relatives do not visit often enough.
Interaction with children	3	I have difficulty helping my children talk about my illness.
Medical interaction	11	
Problems obtaining information from medical team	3	I find that doctors don't explain what they are doing to me.
Difficulty communicating with medical team	6	I have difficulty asking doctors questions.
Control of medical team	2	I would like to have more control over what the doctors do to me.

formation from the doctor or medical providers, difficulty in communicating with the medical team, and the ability to control medical providers. The marital problems involve a variety of concerns about interaction with partners, communication, neglect, and overprotection. Sexual problems include changes in sexual interest or sexual difficulties created by cancer or its treatment. Finally, there are a variety of miscellaneous measures such as problems caused by the chemotherapy or radiation therapy, problems in coping with the regimen, and economic barriers in obtaining the appropriate treatment.

A variety of studies have shown that the CIPS is substantially correlated with other measures. For example, measures of physical, psychosocial, and medical interactions are highly correlated with the Karnofsky performance status measure, which is a general method used to assess the severity of cancer. In addition, the CIPS is correlated with general measures of psychological and physical symptoms (Schag, Henrich, Aadlend, & Ganz, 1990).

TABLE 11-3 (continued)

THE CIPS 31 SUBSCALES GROUPED INTO FIVE MAJOR CATEGORIES: PHYSICAL, PSYCHOSOCIAL, MEDICAL INTERACTION, MARITAL, AND SEXUAL PROBLEMS

Subscale and factors	Number of items	Sample item
Marital	18	
Communication with partner	6	My partner and I have difficulty talking about our fears.
Affection with partner	4	I do not feel like embracing, kissing, or caressing my partner.
Interaction with partner	4	My partner and I are upset with each other more often than usual.
Overprotection by partner	2	My partner won't let me do activities that I am capable of doing.
Neglect of care by partner	2	My partner does not take care of me enough.
Sexual	8	
Sex interest	4	I am not interested in having sex.
Sexual dysfunction	4	I have difficulty becoming sexually aroused.
Miscellaneous subscales		
Chemotherapy-related problems	9	I feel nauseated after I receive chemotherapy.
Radiation-related problems	3	I feel fatigued after my radiation treatments.
Dating	5	I have difficulty telling a date about the cancer or its treatments.
Compliance	4	I sometimes don't show up for my doctor's appointment.
Economic barriers	4	I have financial problems.
Miscellaneous items	7	
Ostomy		
Bladder control		
Frequent diarrhea		
Prosthesis		
Too much weight gain		
Diagnostic procedures painful		
Transportation		

Source: Schag et al., 1990, *Health Psychology, 9*(1), 92–93.

BOX 11-3

FOCUS ON DIVERSITY

An Example of Current Needs: Health Care Access in Hispanic Women

Hispanic Americans are the second largest minority group in the United States. Currently, more than 7 percent of the U.S. population is Hispanic. Census data suggest that the Hispanic population includes people of various origins, including Mexican (60.6 percent), Puerto Rican (15.1 percent), Cuban (6.1 percent), Central and South American (10.2 percent), and "Other" (8 percent). There has been an enormous increase in the Hispanic population within the last decade. Between 1980 and 1985, the rate of growth of the Hispanic population was more than 5 times that in the total population (Bureau of the Census, 1985). Nearly one-half of the 16.9 million Hispanic Americans live in just two states: Texas and California. Furthermore, the Hispanic population is largely concentrated in cities, with 90 percent living in major urban areas.

Nearly 20 percent of the population of California is Hispanic in origin. Hispanic Californians tend to be young (median age 25) and poor. Less than one-half have graduated from high school, and the unemployment rate among Hispanics is 50 percent higher than that in the general population (Bureau of the Census, 1985).

Hispanic ethnicity is not routinely reported in state and local morbidity and mortality data. Therefore, it is difficult to define excess mortality and morbidity. However, data from the National Center for Health Statistics suggest that the risk of death from any cause under the age of 45 is 1.5 times higher for Mexican-born males than for white non-Hispanics (USDHHS, 1985). Nearly 1 in 5 Hispanic Americans has no regular source of health care (USDHHS, 1985). Among Hispanic groups, the percentage of persons with no physician contacts during the year preceding study by the National Health Interview Survey was highest among Mexican-Americans (Trevino & Moss, 1984). The same data source suggested that 17.4 percent of Mexican-Americans older than 4 years of age have never received dental care, while the comparable figure for white non-Hispanics was 2.5 percent. In 1982, more than 1 in 5 Hispanic participants in a public opinion survey reported that they had difficulty in gaining access to medical care. This included needing service but not finding it, being refused care, or having major financial problems due to illness. In the same study, only 13 percent of the white non-Hispanics reported the same difficulty (Anderson et al., 1986).

Special Populations: Cancer Screening in Hispanic Women

The 1985 National Health Interview Survey compared Hispanic and non-Hispanic women, ages 30 to 34, with regard to knowledge about the benefits of breast self-examination. Hispanic women were less likely to know the benefits of these self-exams. Similarly, Hispanic participants in the survey were less likely to have heard about the fetal alcohol syndrome or to be aware that dental sealants may help prevent tooth decay. Hispanic participants in the survey were less likely to have a smoke detector in their home or to engage in healthy behaviors such as regular exercise or abstinence from alcohol. These data suggest that health promotion messages are not reaching the Hispanic population.

In summary, data from a variety of sources suggest that many members of the Hispanic community are in need of health promotion services. Hispanic Americans may have approximately equal life expectancies but are at greater risk for early mortality associated with preventable deaths. Thus, we believe that the Hispanic community is an appropriate target for specialized cancer prevention efforts. As an example, we will consider the case of cancer reduction among Hispanic women. Cancers may be reduced by lowering dietary fat, and increasing the rate of usage of mammography and Pap smear tests.

Risk reduction goals for the year 2000 included the reduction of dietary fat to no more than 30 percent of all calories and average saturated fat intake to no more than 10 percent of all calories among people aged 2 and older. The objectives also included increasing the average intake of dietary fiber and complex carbohydrates in the diets of adults to five or more servings of vegetables and fruits and to 6 or more daily servings of grain products and legumes, to provide between 20 and 30 g of daily dietary fiber.

BOX 11·3 (continued)

The health status objectives might be achieved through the increased use of screening tests. One of the health objectives for the year 2000 is to increase to at least 80 percent the proportion of women age 40 or older who have ever received a clinical breast examination and a mammogram (see Figure 11-6). The baseline for this measure was 36 percent in 1987. However, among Hispanic women only 20 percent had ever had a clinical breast examination and a mammogram. The health objective for the year 2000 for Hispanic women is 60 percent rather than the national goal of 80 percent.

A related objective is to increase to at least 60 percent the proportion of women aged 50 and older who had received a clinical breast examination and a mammogram within the preceding year. Although the national baseline in 1987 was 19 percent, the rate among Hispanic women was only 6 percent. The objective for the year 2000 is to increase this number to 50 percent for the Hispanic subgroup. Since breast cancer is the leading cause of cancer death among women, early detection and treatment are essential (Werteimer et al., 1986). Results of recent studies place Hispanic women in the highest risk category for failing to be screened by mammography. In an analysis of a random sample survey from six towns, demographic factors were shown to be associated with the failure to obtain mammography. These factors included not having a regular physician, restricted social interaction, unemployment, and low income. Among religious groups, Catholics were less likely to receive mammography than Protestants or Jews.

Low health knowledge was also associated with failure to get a mammogram (Zapka et al., 1989). The impact of these factors upon low socioeconomic status (SES) women was demonstrated in a study by Farley and Flannery (1989). These investigators used the Connecticut Tumor Registry to determine time of diagnosis. They demonstrated that low SES women with breast cancer were less likely than higher SES women to have their breast tumors diagnosed at an early stage. These findings strongly support aggressive approaches to stimulate early screening for low SES women.

The health objectives for the year 2000 will be challenging for Hispanic women. For example, the proportion of women who have received a clinical breast examination and a mammogram in the last year must increase from 6 to 50 percent, while the percentage of women who have ever received these examinations must increase from 20 to 60 percent. However, we feel that these are worthy goals. Evidence suggests that mortality due to breast cancer can be

FIGURE 11-6

Current use of clinical breast exam and mammogram and objective for the year 2000.

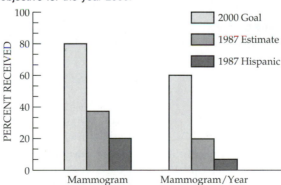

B O X 11 - 3 (continued)

reduced by 30 percent if women obtain mammography and clinical breast examinations. These data come from the cancer control supplement to the 1987 National Health Interview Survey. In this survey, women eligible for mammography reported a variety of reasons for not using it. These include "Did not need it," "Doctors did not recommend it," and the belief that there was a risk of radiation exposure. In low-income women, cost is also an important barrier.

The value of regular Pap smears has been demonstrated in several analyses. Some evidence suggests that Pap smears may be effective for reducing mortality from cancers of the uterine cervix by as much as 75 percent. In most communities, there has been a substantial increase in the use of Pap smear tests. However, the 1987 National Health Interview Survey demonstrated that low-income women were significantly less likely to obtain Pap smears. In fact, Hispanic women have the lowest probability of ever having received a Pap smear (59 percent) or of having received a Pap smear within the preceding year (44 percent) (Figure 11-7).

Currently, we are poorly equipped to meet these challenges. In order to develop better interventions for the future, we must learn more about Hispanic culture. Furthermore, it will be essential to involve the Hispanic community as the major players in health promotion efforts. Finally, it will be crucial to find answers to difficult problem of financing health care for the poor.

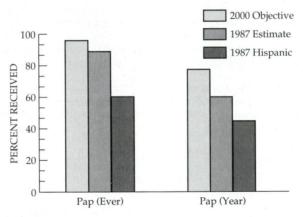

FIGURE 11-7
2000 objective and current use of pap smear and objective for the year 2000.

COPING WITH CANCER

Certainly, the diagnosis of cancer is bad news. There have been a variety of studies summarizing psychological distress in cancer patients. Unfortunately, these studies use different methods for selecting patients and different tests to evaluate psychological concerns. However, studies consistently suggest that cancer patients exhibit elevated levels of depression, and some studies also show increased levels of anxiety (Ganz, 1992), although few studies have shown that the diagnosis of cancer leads to psychopathology. For example, about 25 percent of hospitalized cancer patients have depressive symptoms, but only about 5 percent are severely depressed (Massie & Holland, 1990). This 5 percent figure is about the same as would be expected in the general population (Lansky et al., 1985). A large study on the psychological aspects of breast cancer (Bloom, 1987) also found no differences in psyhopathology between women undergoing mastectomy (breast removal), those receiving other surgical procedures, and normal controls in the community. The mastectomy patients initially reported more psychosocial distress, but these problems became less apparent as the women were followed for a longer period of time. Thus, the literature suggests that the initial diagnosis of cancer is highly distressing and that cancer patients may experience more depression and problems in daily functioning than their peers who do not have cancer. However, there is little evidence that cancer causes major psychopathology (Dunkel-Schetter, Feinstein, Taylor, & Falke, 1992).

Despite cancer being a serious threat, some evidence suggests that facing a serious illness may actually help clarify events in people's lives. For example, research indicates that normal mental functioning involves positive bias about the self and the ability to control events in the world. Furthermore, many people are characterized by very optimistic assessments about the future. These optimistic views of the world are maintained even in the face of very negative information, such as the diagnosis of cancer. Negative information may be processed differently from positive information. However, people are able to maintain a positive outlook while still taking advantage of the negative information they receive (Taylor & Lobel, 1989). In one study, 55 men and women with a variety of different cancers were interviewed about their life experiences. The interviews covered personal activities and priorities, personal relationships, views of the self, views of the world, and outlooks toward the future. The cancer patients had outlooks about evenly split between positive and negative for beliefs about the self, the world, and the future. However, these cancer patients had been forced to think more deeply about their priorities because they were threatened with a limited life expectancy. The study showed that in terms of personal priorities and relationships with other people, the cancer experience made the patients more positive (Taylor, 1990).

Although cancer may not cause psychopathology, it clearly causes distress. In fact, measures of psychological distress due to cancer have been created. One of these is known as the Illness Distress Scale (IDS). This brief measure evaluates physical and emotional responses to illness. Physical manifestations of cancer appear to be the most distressing to patients. In one study of over 400 cancer patients, younger patients and those who were not married were more likely to be distressed by their illness than older patients. There appear to be at least four different dimensions of stress related to cancer. These are (1) loss of meaning, (2) concerns about the physical illness, (3) concerns about medical treatment, and (4) social isolation (Noyes, Kathol, Debelius-Enemark, et al., 1990).

Cancer may also affect the patient's self-concept. Studies of self-concept in adults have been somewhat difficult because various authors have defined self-concept differently. Furthermore, self concept is sometimes used as a predictor of poor outcomes in cancer, while in other studies the focus is on how cancer can change self-concept (Curbow, Somerfield, Legro, & Sonnega, 1990). Some of the most challenging issues concern children with cancer. Although we often consider children to be the most psychologically vulnerable to chronic illness, some studies suggest that children are relatively hardy. One study involved 56 children between the ages of 5 and 12 who had all been diagnosed with cancer. They were compared with healthy children who did not have cancer. The children were evaluated on the self-perception profile, and a variety of other measures were used to assess their social adjustment. Ratings were also obtained from their parents and teachers. Although the cancer patients recorded more social isolation, there were actually relatively few differences between children with cancer and matched children who did not have the disease (Spirito, Stark, Cobiella, et al., 1990).

Another study of 8- to 18-year-olds observed children in the classroom and did oberve some differences between cancer patients and nonpatients. Although major differences in behavior were not common, the investigators did notice that children with cancer were less sociable and less likely to demonstrate leadership. In addition, the cancer victims were more socially isolated (Noll, Bukowski, Rogosch, LeRoy, & Kulkarni, 1990). Sometimes the psychological impact of cancer is more difficult on parents than on children. For example, Hughes and Lieberman (1990) studied 18 parents of children with cancer. They discovered that 13 of them suffered symptoms of anxiety. Among these 13, 6 had serious enough anxiety that they needed further psychiatric attention. At least a third of the parents had difficulty in communication with staff, friends, and spouses.

At the adult level, isolation among cancer patients is also common. In fact, it has been reported that cancer patients frequently become depressed (Massie & Holland, 1991, 1992). Although this depression is not "psychopathology," it often requires treatment with psychotherapy or medications. Psychologists often play an important role in identifying this depression, helping with its treatment, or providing training for oncologists or oncology nurses on how to deal with cancer patients (Meyerowitz, Heinrich, & Schag, 1989).

DEALING WITH CANCER TREATMENT—THE CASE OF ADJUVANT CHEMOTHERAPY FOR BREAST CANCER

There are many alternative approaches to the treatment of breast cancer. The choice of treatment usually reflects the preferences of the woman with consultation from her physician. The major treatments are lumpectomy, which is the removal of the tumor without the removal of other breast tissue, and mastectomy, or the surgical removal of the entire breast. Other alternatives include radiation therapy to destroy the tumor with radioactivity or chemotherapy to destroy the tumor with toxic substances. Many women are concerned about mastectomy because the surgery alters their appearance. However, new procedures for breast reconstruction have produced better cosmetic results.

Because breast cancer is a serious problem, combinations of approaches are often used. For example, some women will have a lumpectomy to remove the cancerous breast tumor. However, there is still the threat that there are "microtumors" that escaped the initial evaluation. Thus, even after the breast tumor is removed, oncologists typically recommend adjuvant chemotherapy. A 1985 conference suggested that chemotherapy should be used after lumpectomy or mastectomy, and this recommendation was reinforced with a "clinical alert" by the National Cancer Institute in 1988 (NCI, 1988). Many oncologists now recommend adjuvant chemotherapy for all women who have had a breast tumor (Ingle, 1990).

Although adjuvant chemotherapy may be helpful, it has some serious side effects. One of the most serious ones is *emesis*, which is the medical term for vomiting. Women receiving chemotherapy may experience such severe nausea and vomiting that they need to be hospitalized. Uncontrollable vomiting can leave a woman so dehydrated that she needs infusions of fluids just to survive.

Behavioral methods may make important contributions to the control of nausea and vomiting for patients undergoing cancer chemotherapy. One of the common problems for chemotherapy patients is anticipatory nausea and vomiting. In Chapter 3 we discussed basic models of classical and operant conditioning. Anticipatory nausea and vomiting might be the result of classical conditioning (Redd et al., 1991). The cytotoxic drugs used in chemotherapy suppress the immune system and also cause these unpleasant side effects. Thus, the drugs serve as a conditioned stimulus (CS). Infusion of the drugs is paired with the actual drug delivery. The preparation for the drug delivery serves as the unconditioned stimulus (UCS). Vomiting is the unconditioned response to the drug. Over repeated trials, the drug infusion and preparation can produce nausea and vomiting prior to drug delivery (conditioned response, or CR). Several studies have demonstrated the effects of anticipatory nausea. In fact, there is even evidence that the patients develop nausea in response to hospital stimuli years after they have completed their chemotherapy (Cella, Pratt, & Holland, 1986). In addition to anticipatory nausea, there is also evidence that aspects of immune function are classically conditioned. Since cytotoxic drugs reduce immunity, there is now evidence that preparation for drug delivery also suppresses immune functioning (Bovbjerg, Redd, Maier, et al., 1990).

The evidence that some aspects of nausea and vomiting are classically conditioned suggests that learning models may be valuable in designing treatments to help reduce these problems. Several studies have demonstrated the value of behavioral interventions. For example, Redd and Andrykowski (1982) demonstrated that behavioral interventions based on the principles of learning theory can help control nausea and vomiting associated with chemotherapy. Furthermore, hypnosis may also be valuable in controlling anticipatory vomiting (Redd, Andersen, & Minagawa, 1982).

Although behavioral treatment may help reduce side effects of medication, more controversial studies consider the role of psychotherapy in the treatment of cancer. For example, the wellness communities started by Harold Benjamin in Santa Monica, California, promote the idea that positive attitudes are useful in the recovery from cancer. Fox (1989)

reported that depression may lower immune function. Thus, avoiding depression might enhance immunity and aid in the resistance to cancer.

One of the most influential studies was reported in 1989 in the British Medical Journal *Lancet* (Spiegel, Bloom, Kraemer & Gottheil, 1989). In this study, 86 women with metastatic breast cancer were followed over the course of time. The women were randomly assigned to participate in a support group or in a control group that did not receive the social support. Those in the support groups survived an average of 36.6 months, while those in the control group survived an average of only 18.9 months. The treatment consisted of weekly 90-minute group therapy sessions led by a psychiatrist or a social worker. The group leaders were all women who themselves had previously experienced breast cancer. The women in these groups became very involved, visiting one another in the hospital and aiding in the coping process. Those in the therapy group experienced less anxiety, depression, and pain. Newer studies are beginning to examine the effects of these treatments on immune functioning (Bovbjerg, 1991). Another recent study showed adjuvant psychotherapy can reduce depression in cancer patients and make them more functional (Greer et al., 1992). Although this is a very new area of investigation, we feel it deserves greater attention in future studies.

SUMMARY

Each year about one million Americans are diagnosed with cancer. It was previously believed that the diagnosis of cancer was a death sentence. Although progress in the treatment of cancer has created a growing number of cancer survivors, cancer is still a very significant disease causing premature deaths in about one-half million Americans each year. Risk factors for cancer include dietary practices, cigarette smoking, and environmental exposures. Substantial evidence suggests that many cancers are avoidable through behavioral changes. Another way to reduce the impact of cancer is to increase the use of cancer screening tests, which might include mammography and Pap smears. These tests are used too infrequently among low-income and minority populations.

Once cancer develops, a variety of behavioral interventions may aid in coping with the disease as well as with the cancer therapy. Chemotherapy for cancer causes significant side effects which may be reduced with behavioral interventions. Because of the importance of behavioral factors in cancer prevention, diagnosis, and treatment, many cancer centers now include active behavioral scientists.

KEY TERMS

Tumor. A mass of tissues.
Benign tumor. A tumor that is not cancerous.
Malignant tumor. A tumor that is cancerous.
Metastasize. The spread of cancer cells away from the original site to other parts of the body.
Leukemias. Cancers of the blood.
Lymphomas. Cancers of the lymph system.
Carcinogens. Factors that cause cancer.
Anticarcinogens. Factors or substances that protect against cancer.
Chemotherapy. A variety of cancer treatments that involve chemical agents designed to attack tumors or affect the immune system.
Side effects. Effects of treatments that are not direct therapeutic benefits.

CHAPTER 12

The Acquired Immune Deficiency Syndrome (AIDS)

John, a healthy psychology graduate student, enjoyed the southern California lifestyle. He went to the beach, participated in athletics, and attended his share of parties. In 1984, John first started worrying about AIDS. He lived a gay lifestyle and had been exposed to a variety of partners. Although he felt fine, John took the AIDS screening test when it first became available. What he learned was devastating. John had become infected with the human immunodeficiency virus (HIV), and he realized that difficult times may be ahead. Despite a strong spirit and the close support of his many friends, John eventually became weaker. He developed a serious episode of pneumonia in 1988 but recovered and did well after that. He took new treatments for AIDS, but found he was unable to tolerate them because of side effects. In 1990, John died of complications of the AIDS infection. All agreed that at 36 years of age, John was a victim of one of our most serious contemporary tragedies.

In this chapter we will explore the complications of the human immunodeficiency virus and the associated disease, acquired immunodeficiency syndrome (AIDS). We will explore the biology of AIDS in some detail and then talk about psychological issues relevant to this very serious disease.

The acquired immune deficiency syndrome

BOX 12·1

HEALTH OBJECTIVES FOR THE YEAR 2000

1. To confine annual incidence of diagnosed AIDS cases to no more than 98,000 (baseline: 44,000 in 1989).

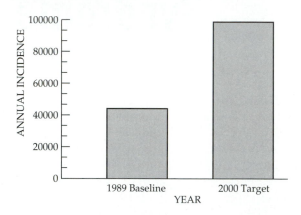

2. To increase to at least 95 percent the proportion of schools that have age-appropriate HIV education curriculum for students in the fourth through twelfth grade, preferably as part of quality school health education (baseline: 66 percent of all school districts had some course, but only 5 percent required education each year in 1989).

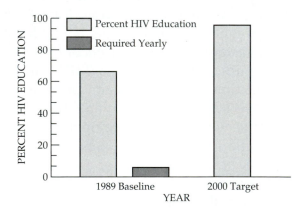

3. To increase to at least 90 percent the proportion of cities with populations over 100,000 that have outreach programs to contact drug abusers and deliver HIV reduction messages (no baseline available).

(AIDS) has directly affected millions of people worldwide and indirectly affects virtually all of us. The human immunodeficiency virus (HIV), a retrovirus of the human T-cell leukemia/lymphoma line, reduces the immune systems' ability to recognize and destroy infectious agents that it is usually able to deal with. As HIV disease progresses, an overall loss in immunocompetence leaves HIV-infected individuals susceptible to a variety of opportunistic infections. When they experience specific illnesses, such as pneumocystis carinii pneumonia, they are classified by physicians as having AIDS, the terminal stage of HIV illness. In this chapter, as is common in the literature and popular press, we will use the terms *AIDS* and *HIV infection* synonymously unless otherwise specified. However, one should keep in mind that AIDS has a special meaning among those who are HIV-infected. The spread of AIDS may be the most serious infectious disease epidemic of modern times (Kelly & Lawrence, 1988). Several characteristics of the AIDS epidemic and unique actions of HIV create increased problems and fears for both the public and health professionals. There are as many as 1.5 million people who are infected with the HIV virus in the United States alone. First, since most individuals remain "healthy" for many years after they have contracted the virus, they may be unaware that they are infected. This is true even though they carry the virus—that is, they are HIV positive—and can spread the disease to others. Second, the behaviors that are responsible for transmission of HIV (for example, engaging in unprotected sex and sharing intravenous needles) are quite difficult to modify. In this chapter we will explore the epidemiology of this disease both here in the United States and worldwide, discuss how one contracts the AIDS virus, examine its clinical course, see how it attacks its victim's body, review what treatments are currently available and possible future developments in that area,

find out how we can protect ourselves and stop its spread, and discuss the social implications of this disease.

THE HISTORY OF AIDS

The first cases of AIDS were reported in June of 1981 in the Los Angeles area when five young homosexual men contracted an extremely rare type of pneumonia called *pneumocystis carinii pneumonia* (PCP) (Heyward & Curran, 1988). Prior to that time this type of infection had been seen only in individuals whose immune systems were profoundly impaired, either because of some genetic defect or because they were undergoing cancer treatments with powerful immunosuppressive drugs. At the same time that these cases of PCP appeared, the U.S. Centers for Disease Control (CDC) received reports of 26 cases of Kaposi's sarcoma, a relatively rare form of cancer that was usually seen in elderly men or again in patients who were taking immunosuppressive drugs. Once again these cases occurred in homosexual men, and later some of these individuals also contracted PCP. Finally, clinicians and epidemiologists began noting increases in two diseases that were again usually associated with impaired immune functioning. The first was a condition characterized by enlarged lymph nodes called *chronic lymphadenopathy*; the second was a rare form of malignant cancer called *lymphoma*. In 1982 this collection of physical problems became known as *acquired immunodeficiency syndrome*, or AIDS.

How was this disease spread? Through the use of case-control studies, it was determined that the factor that distinguished homosexuals who had the disease from those who did not was the number of sexual contacts they reported having. Another study of the pattern of the spread of the disease determined that 20 percent of the initial AIDS cases were connected through common sexual contacts. This

---

BOX 12·2

FOCUS ON RESEARCH

As we found in Chapter 6, stress and depression can reduce the ability of the immune system to function. Many people with HIV believe that by avoiding stress they can extend their lives. Researchers have set out to examine this possibility. Rabkin and colleagues (1991) evaluated the extent to which psychosocial stress and depression were related to changes in immune status among HIV-positive homosexual men. They found that HIV-positive men who were depressed or distressed (or who reported more life stressors) had no greater immunosuppression than others who were not. Why should this be so, since previous studies with non-HIV-infected individuals have found relationships between these variables and immune changes? Rabkin suggests four reasons why her group failed to find the expected relationships. First, individuals participating in her project were not very depressed or distressed. Second, she may not have studied these individuals long enough to see health changes. Third, her study was limited to individuals who were, for the most part, early in the disease process. Finally, we have to consider the possibility that there is no relationship between depression, stress, and immune status. Despite these early negative results, Rabkin recommended the conservative position of waiting for more data before we make unwarranted recommendations to people with HIV.

---

his heterosexual as well as homosexual partners. Later that year it was also recognized that people from central Africa and Haiti were at increased risk for contracting AIDS. These data demonstrated that the extent of homosexual transmission of the disease might vary from country to country.

The isolation of the infectious agent (the HIV virus) was accomplished by Luc Montagnier at the Pasteur Institute in Paris and by Robert C. Gallo and his colleagues at the National Cancer Institute. Soon after the isolation of HIV a laboratory test was developed to detect the antibodies to HIV in human blood. A positive reaction to this test indicated that an individual was infected with the virus. This made it possible to detect HIV in people who were otherwise without symptoms, and to confirm the diagnosis in individuals who showed indications of having AIDS. This also made it possible to determine the incidence and prevalence of HIV in various populations. Finally, this allowed blood to be screened in order to avoid spreading HIV through transfusions.

THE EPIDEMIOLOGY OF AIDS

AIDS in the United States

Exact figures of the number of individuals infected with the HIV virus remain difficult to obtain, since most individuals are asymptomatic for several years after infection and do not seek medical attention until they become ill. It is clear that a startlingly high number of Americans are already infected with the virus, and the numbers continue to climb. It has been estimated by the CDC that between 1 and 2 million Americans are currently HIV positive (CDC, 1992). Through December 1991, 206,392 active AIDS cases among adults or adolescents and approximately 133,232 AIDS deaths have been recorded by the CDC in the United States. Almost 2 million new AIDS cases can

pattern was not likely to have occurred by chance. Finally, in 1982, a number of cases of AIDS were described in individuals who had received blood transfusions. Among those cases, at least two cases of AIDS were documented in instances where the blood donor had subsequently died of AIDS. This information, taken together, provided convincing evidence that AIDS was transmitted by some agent, which at that time was still not identified, through blood and sexual contact.

Soon thereafter, in 1983, it was determined that intravenous (IV) drug abusers and their heterosexual partners were at risk of contracting AIDS. This information demonstrated that an infected man could transmit the disease to

be expected worldwide by the mid-1990s. The current leading cause of death among IV drug users and hemophiliacs is AIDS. Barring a dramatic breakthrough in treatment, it is projected that more than 60,000 Americans will die of AIDS during 1992. The number of deaths from AIDS during this 12-month period alone will exceed the total number of deaths from AIDS in this country from the beginning of the epidemic through 1988. In 1992 it has been projected that 172,000 AIDS patients will require medical care at a cost of from $5 to $13 billion (Public Health Reports, 1988).

Prevalence denotes that proportion of a population which is currently infected; it is usually expressed as cases per 1000 or per 10,000, or it may be written as a percentage (e.g., 0.4 percent, or 4 cases per 1000). *Incidence* denotes the rate of occurrence of new cases of infection per unit of time, usually per year. The possibility of conducting a national probability sample of seroprevalence by the CDC's National Center for Health Statistics is under discussion. The CDC has estimated the seroprevalence rates among four groups: 12.6 million blood donors, 1.25 million military recruits, 8668 hospital patients, and 25,000 job corps applicants (CDC, 1987) (see Figure 12-1). As can be seen, HIV prevalence among blood donors was an order of magnitude lower, 2 per 10,000, compared with the other three groups, in which the prevalence is in the range of 10 to 30 per 10,000.

The estimates that are discussed here should not be interpreted to mean that this is necessarily the true national (or the perfect) estimate of prevalence for these groups, since each group has particular sampling problems associated with it. For example, military recruits come from particular age and socioeconomic strata, and people who report homosexual or drug use are barred from enlistment. Similarly, individuals who apply for the job corps are disadvantaged 16- to 21-year-olds. Hospital patients are older and sicker than the general population. Finally, blood donors are

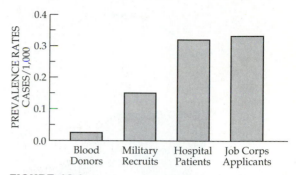

FIGURE 12-1

Seroprevalence among four groups during 1987.

not representative of the general population because individuals who are at high risk of HIV infection have been asked not to donate blood. Thus, the true prevalence of HIV in the general population remains unknown.

Since it appears that most, if not all, individuals with HIV infection will develop AIDS, the morbidity and mortality rates will continue to rise over the next few years. More than 85 percent of the patients diagnosed with AIDS since 1985 have already died (Heyward & Curran, 1988).

What are the characteristics of the typical AIDS patient in the United States today? He is probably homosexual or bisexual and white. Figure 12-2 shows the breakdown of all AIDS patients by risk group. As can be seen from this figure, as of 1988, 63 percent of the total number of infected individuals were either homosexual or bisexual, and an additional 19 percent were heterosexual IV drug abusers. Homosexual or bisexual men and IV drug abusers taken together account for 89 percent of the AIDS cases in 1988.

Hemophiliacs and people with other coagulation disorders and those who were recipients of blood or blood-product transfusions together make up about 4 percent of the AIDS cases. There are indications that the likelihood of infection among hemophiliacs is correlated with the severity of the disorder; that is, HIV

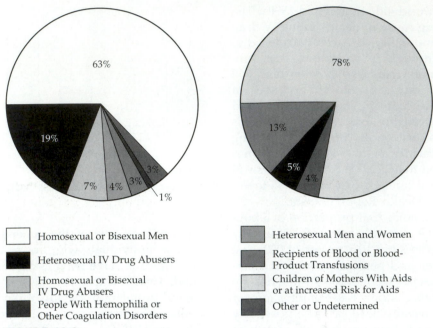

Homosexual or Bisexual Men

Heterosexual IV Drug Abusers

Homosexual or Bisexual
IV Drug Abusers

People With Hemophilia or
Other Coagulation Disorders

Heterosexual Men and Women

Recipients of Blood or Blood-
Product Transfusions

Children of Mothers With Aids
or at increased Risk for Aids

Other or Undetermined

FIGURE 12-2

Population groups accounting for the adult (left) and pediatric (right) cases of AIDS as of July 4, 1988, are indicated by these pie charts. As can be seen, homosexual or bisexual men and IV drug abusers together account for 89 percent of all adult cases. More than three-fourths of the children with AIDS acquire the disease from a mother who either had AIDS or was a member of the group at increased risk for AIDS.

prevalence rates have been 70 percent for hemophilia A and 35 percent for hemophilia B (Heyward & Curran, 1988). Given the improved HIV screening techniques in the United States today, the incidence of HIV among hemophiliacs should drop in the next few years.

Among the 4 percent of AIDS cases attributed to heterosexual transmission, about 61 percent of these individuals report previous sexual contact with a person who was found to be infected with HIV or was in a known risk group. The remaining 39 percent were born in other countries where heterosexual contact is known to be the major means of HIV transmission. The majority of those infected heterosexually are female (71 percent). It appears that male-to-female transmission of the virus is

easier than female-to-male, although the risk is not trivial for female-to-male contacts. Another explanation for the gender difference is that the pool of potentially infectable males is reduced since so many males are already infected by other means.

The number of women with HIV is steadily increasing. The CDC reported that from November 1989 through October 1990, women accounted for 11 percent of all AIDS cases in the United States (CDC, 1991). Compared with the previous year, the diagnosed cases of AIDS increased 29 percent among women versus 18 percent among men. The CDC projects that AIDS will be one of the five leading causes of death among women in 1991 (Chu et al., 1990). Although black and Hispanic women make up 19 percent of the U.S. female population, they represent 72 percent of all U.S. women with AIDS. In one year alone (1988) the death rate from AIDS was 9 times greater among minority women compared with white women (Chu et al., 1990). The differences in HIV rates between ethnic groups may reflect the higher use of intravenous drugs by minority women and their sex partners. Most women with AIDS (85 percent) are of childbearing age—that is, between 15 and 44—and were probably infected when they were teenagers. Parenthetically, many women do not discover that they are infected until they become ill or their child becomes infected prenatally. In addition, many HIV-positive women are of lower socioeconomic status and use public health care and social services, which may increase the costs of management in this population.

Among female prostitutes, HIV prevalence has been estimated to be 0 to 45 percent, depending on the area sampled. In large inner-city areas where drug use is common—such as New York City, Miami, and Detroit—the rate of infection is much higher than in rural and suburban areas. Among female prostitutes who are also drug users, the HIV infection rate is 3 to 4 times higher than among non-IV drug users. The rate of infection is twice as high among black and Hispanic prostitues when compared with others.

As can be seen from Figure 12-3, most individuals with AIDS are white, although a comparison with the racial makeup of the United States as a whole indicates that a disproportionate percentage of blacks and Hispanics are infected. Since one of the groups among whom HIV infection is growing fastest is IV drug users, and the majority of IV drug users are of minority races, we can expect to see this discrepancy grow even larger.

Children are the fastest-growing group of AIDS patients (Heyward & Curran, 1988). There was a 114 percent increase of AIDS cases in children under 13 years of age in 1987 alone.

FIGURE 12-3

Racial and ethnic classification of the adult AIDS cases shows a disproportionate fraction of them are among blacks and Hispanics. The figures reflect the higher reported rates of AIDS in black and Hispanic IV drug abusers and their sex partners.

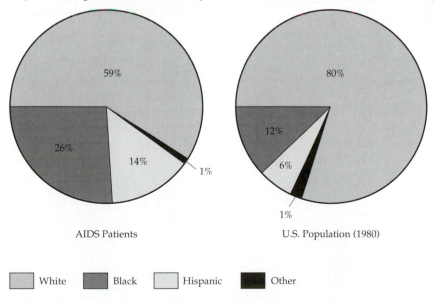

AIDS Patients

U.S. Population (1980)

White   Black   Hispanic   Other

The majority (78 percent) of these children acquired HIV before, during, or soon after birth. Most of their mothers were IV drug users. About 19 percent of HIV children acquired the disease through contaminated blood products, and in approximately 4 percent of the cases, the means of infection is unknown or through some means other than contaminated blood.

The Worldwide AIDS Epidemic

Most of the people infected with HIV live outside the United States, perhaps 9 million out of the estimated 10 million people infected with the virus (Mann et al., 1988). How these victims become infected varies by region. There appear to be three major AIDS infection pat-terns worldwide. Although these patterns may change over time, an understanding of them illustrates the complexity of transmission of HIV disease. The first pattern is primarily seen among homosexual men and IV drug users and includes the regions indicated in Figure 12-4. These regions include North and South America, Western Europe, Scandinavia, Australia, and New Zealand. In the second pattern the number of males and females infected is about equal, and the virus appears to be primarily heterosexually transmitted. This pattern is seen in Africa, the Caribbean, and some of South America. The third pattern of exposure is through contact with pattern 1 and 2 regions. In this last group there are relatively few cases of AIDS. Pattern 3 regions currently

FIGURE 12-4

Three infection patterns of the AIDS virus are apparent worldwide. Pattern I is found in North and South America, Western Europe, Scandinavia, Australia, and New Zealand. In these areas about 90 percent of the cases are homosexual males or users of intravenous drugs. Pattern II is found in Africa, the Caribbean, and some areas of South America; the primary mode of transmission in these regions is heterosexual sex, and the number of infected females and males is approximately equal. Pattern III is typical of Eastern Europe, North Africa, the Middle East, Asia, and the Pacific (excluding Australia and New Zealand); there are relatively few cases, and most of them have had contact with pattern-I or pattern-II countries.

Pattern I
Pattern II
Pattern III or not Reporting
HIV-2

include Eastern Europe, North Africa, the Middle East, Asia, and the Pacific.

Africa has the biggest HIV problem of all the continents. As can be seen in the illustration, all three patterns of transmission are present in Africa. It has been estimated that between 5 and 20 percent of all sexually active individuals are infected with HIV in some urban areas of Zaire, Rwanda, Tanzania, Uganda, and Zambia (Mann et al., 1988). In the next few years the already high mortality rates in these regions may double or triple as a result of the HIV epidemic.

The patterns of HIV infection reported in this section may provide some guidance in targeting interventions to specific groups. We emphasize, however, that prevalence data which have been reported are crude estimates and are subject to selection bias. These biases include samples gathered on homosexual men recruited at clinics for sexually transmitted diseases (STD's). This sampling strategy will result in a higher estimate of HIV in the general homosexual population because the sampled men were being treated for STD's, whose mode of transmission parallels that of HIV. Similarly, determining HIV prevalence from samples of individuals who have come to donate blood will probably result in an underestimation of HIV prevalence since most high-risk individuals presumably avoid donating blood. These last caveats are meant only as cautionary notes and do not totally negate the value of the available prevalence figures.

HOW DOES ONE CONTRACT AIDS?

The HIV virus is transmitted through sexual contact, through exposure to blood and blood products, and from mother to child during the prenatal period. In the United States most of the sexual transmission of HIV has occurred in homosexual men, although this picture is changing. The risk of infection increases as the number of partners increases and the fre-

quency with which an individual is the receptive partner during intercourse. It also appears that contracting sexually transmitted diseases which cause ulcers on the genitalia and anus (such as syphilis and genital herpes) may increase the probability of contracting AIDS. Prompt treatment of these venereal diseases may slow the spread of HIV among sexually active men and women. Recent information indicates that there has been a dramatic decrease in the new cases of infection in homosexual populations.

Heterosexual transmission of HIV appears to be on the increase. Most transmission occurs during vaginal intercourse. One study found that from 10 to 70 percent of the partners of HIV-infected individuals have themselves become infected. It is unclear why some individuals are infected while others are not. It may be that those with HIV are more or less infectious over time or that there are some biological factors which protect some individuals. Although not guaranteeing that one will not contract the virus, condoms do provide some protection against HIV.

Blood transfusions with HIV-contaminated blood are likely to result in transmission of the HIV virus. Between 89 and 100 percent of the recipients of contaminated blood have contracted HIV. Fortunately, screening of blood in the United States has made this mode of transmission extremely rare, although this remains a serious problem in other parts of the world.

Shooting galleries are rooms where drug addicts go to purchase and inject drugs. In this environment hypodermic needles are in short supply and are shared among many individuals. Unfortunately, HIV is also transmitted through the injection of minute amounts of infected blood on the dirty needle. IV drug users have become the second largest group of persons who have developed AIDS in the United States and in Western Europe (Des Jarlais et al., 1990). Cleaning needles with common bleach kills the virus and eliminates the danger of transmission. Bleach does, however, reduce the length of time that a hypodermic needle is useful, since it causes the rubber portions of the plunger to deteriorate. Unfortunately, IV drug users find it difficult to obtain hypodermic needles since they fall under the controlled substance act. Thus, addicts are driven to share needles, and in order to prolong the life of the hypodermics that they do have, they may be unwilling to use bleach. The CDC has reported that HIV is now spreading most rapidly among IV drug users. In addition, since most of these individuals are sexually active, they may then spread the virus to their sexual partners. Individuals who are under the influence of cocaine and its derivatives appear to be at increased risk of infection. This may be due to the prolongation of the sexual act, which increases the chances of tearing or abrasions and thus gives easier access of the host's bloodstream to the virus. It may also be due to the lack of inhibitions when individuals are under the influence of cocaine, which increases the chances of engaging in high-risk sexual behaviors. Through whatever means, the use of cocaine, and perhaps other drugs, appears to increase the chances of contracting HIV.

Infected mothers can transmit HIV to their unborn or newborn children. It is presently uncertain whether the infection of babies occurs in the uterus of HIV-positive mothers or through feeding infected breast milk to the newborn. It is difficult to determine exactly when these infants become infected, since they have their mothers' antibodies circulating in their blood for as long as 12 months after birth and these antibodies will be HIV positive in the infected mother. During 1988, a 114 percent increase, compared with the previous 12-month period, was seen. Most of the pediatric cases were related to IV drug use of the mother or her sexual partner, while a smaller percentage (19 percent) of cases were related to hemophilia or blood transfusions (Heyward & Curran, 1988).

Other methods of becoming infected with HIV include accidental puncture with contaminated materials, such as needles. This method of transmission is relatively rare but does occasionally occur among health care workers. A number of studies indicate that the probability of becoming infected after a puncture with contaminated blood products is very small.

While it is certainly not impossible that one will become infected with the virus, the good news is that for most individuals it is improbable. Taking proper precautions during sexual intercourse, curtailing the numer of sexual partners, using clean needles, and using proper precautions when handling blood products reduce the chances of contracting HIV to almost nothing.

For health professionals in the behavioral fields, it is important to remember that HIV is spread through engaging in specific *behaviors*. Until vaccines are developed, prevention of the spread of HIV must rely on behavior change. The challenge of the 1990s is to develop effective programs to promote safer sex and halt the use of infected needles among IV drug abusers.

WHAT IS THE CLINICAL COURSE OF HIV DISEASE?

The Immune System

In order to understand AIDS it is necessary to first have some understanding of the immune system. The immune system is made up of the thymus, spleen, and a number of different types of cells called *lymphocytes*. Lymphocytes are found in lympahatic vessels, lymph nodes, intestines, tonsils, and the appendix. The lymphatic system is made up of vessels similar to blood vessels that drain excess fluids out of body tissues and convey these fluids back into the veins. Lymph nodes are highly organized collections of lymphocytes located along the extensive system of lymphatic vessels.

The function of the immune system is to protect the body from invasion by viruses, bacteria (termed *pathogens*), or other abnormal cells that sometimes appear in the body, such as cancer cells. The way the immune system accomplishes this protection is by recognizing self from nonself cells, that is, by checking the surface of cells for molecules called *antigens*. These antigens are molecules that differ from those that are recognized as self and are, therefore, probably harmful to the self. The immune system "learns" what is self and nonself during early development. The immune system can be stimulated to recognize and be prepared to kill specific viruses like polio by administering vaccines. It can also be retrained, as is done when a person is desensitized for some allergy by injecting the material that they are allergic to in small doses many times.

The immune system can make a number of different errors. One such error is to make too extreme a response, such as occurs with the shock caused by a violent allergic attack. On the other extreme, the immune system can underrespond, which may result in infections. In other cases the immune system becomes confused and responds to normal cells in the body as if they were invaders. Such is the case with rheumatoid arthritis, where the immune system begins to attack normal healthy tissue in the joints.

When someone contracts the HIV virus, the virus attaches and enters cells in the host's body, usually CD4 helper/inducer T-cell lymphocytes. The CD4 lymphocytes are white blood cells that tell our immune system to "turn on" because there is a foreign invader, termed a *foreign antigen*, in the body. HIV multiples in the body when these CD4 cells replicate in response to contact with a cold virus, for example, which is the immune system's normal response. Thus the life cycle of HIV consists of a series of steps in which it uses the host's own cells to reproduce enormous numbers of new viruses. As more and more CD4 cells become infected, the immune system becomes unable to respond to infectious agents. Individuals die, therefore, from other infec-

tions that the body is no longer able to fight off, not from the HIV virus itself.

It should be noted that despite the importance of the destruction of CD4 lymphocytes in HIV infection, HIV infects a number of other cells including macrophages, skin, lymph nodes, and endothelial cells of the brain. Thus, the picture of the infection is more complicated than can be presented here.

Development and Progression of AIDS

What happens when someone is infected with the HIV virus? When an individual is exposed to the virus, they may or may not experience mild flu-like symptoms which last a couple of days. With or without these symptoms three stages of infection seem to follow. During the first 12 to 18 months after seroconversion, when the virus invades the body, the number of CD4-positive cells rapidly declines by about one-third. Figure 12-5 illustrates the three stages of decline in CD4 cell number in HIV-infected individuals. In the normal healthy individual there are about 1100 cells per volume of blood. This number drops to about 700 cells during this initial period of infection. Most people remain healthy during this time, although they are infectious at any time after they have contracted the virus. In general, as the number of CD4 cells goes down, the number of opportunistic infections that an individual experiences goes up. Opportunistic infections are ones that occur because the immune system has broken down. It is these opportunistic infections that are responsible for death in HIV-infected individuals. In the second stage of infection there follows a prolonged period, which may range from 3 to 7 years or more, during which the number of CD4 cells drops relatively slowly, in the range of about 80 cells per year. As was true during the initial stage of infection, individuals may appear to be perfectly healthy during this time, although as always they can spread the virus to others any time after they are infected. Dur-

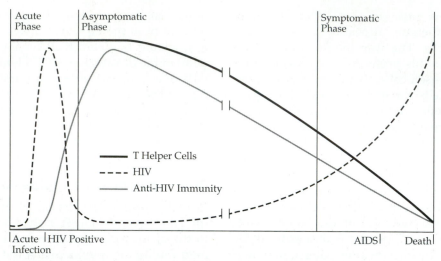

FIGURE 12-5
The national history of HIV infection. (From Ostrow, D. G. *Psychiatric Aspects of Human Immunodeficiency Virus Infection*, The Upjohn Company, 1990, with permission.)

ing the third and final stage of infection, in the 2-year period before AIDS develops, a second accelerated period of CD4 depletion occurs. During this time the number of CD4 cells may decline from 400 or 500 to less than 200 at the time of AIDS diagnosis. It should be noted that there appears to be considerable variation in the pattern of decline among individual patients. This suggests that natural defenses are partially successful in slowing the disease process. Ultimately, however, the body loses the battle, and opportunistic infections and tumors which define AIDS overwhelm the body.

It is clear that HIV disease progresses at different rates in different people. For some, the initial latency period immediately following infection may be brief; while for others, the symptoms that mark disease progression may not appear for several years. The median time from seroconversion to first AIDS-defining event appears to be 8 to 9 years. A recent study of individuals with known dates of seroconversion (Lifson et al., 1989) found that 4 percent of that population developed AIDS within 3 years of infection, 10 percent within 4 years,

15 percent within 5 years, 25 percent within 6 years, 34 percent within 7 years, 39 percent within 8 years, and 43 percent within 9 years. Most individuals do not know when they became infected. Mayers and colleagues (1989) reported that 43 percent of undated HIV-positive individuals showed significant disease progression during a 2-year period. The worst-case picture was presented by Lui and coworkers (1988), who predict that nearly all people who are infected with HIV will eventually develop AIDS. The use of AIDS treatments such as azidothymidine (AZT) may have an effect on these rates. Cox and colleagues (1990) and Schechter and associates (1989) all demonstrated that AZT had little effect on progression to AIDS during the first 4 to 5 years of infection. Craib's group, however, projected that about half (28 percent) as many individuals will progress to AIDS when treated with AZT. The length of time to develop full-blown AIDS may also be lengthened to about 12 years. Few studies have been able to document the date of seroconversion, however; so the true rate and relative risk factors for progres-

sion from asymptomatic infection to AIDS remain in doubt.

DETECTION OF HIV

The most common method of detecting whether an individual has contracted the virus or for screening of donated blood is through the detection of antibodies to HIV. Antibodies do not develop immediately after infection but appear in the vast majority of infected persons within 3 to 6 months. Thus, a negative test for HIV antibody does not exclude recently acquired infection. Children of infected mothers, however, normally acquire antibodies from their mother while in the uterus, regardless of whether or not they are infected. This is problematic since the antibodies persist for over a year. Thus other techniques may be needed to determine the HIV status in this group.

The standard method of detecting antibodies is termed ELISA, which stands for enzyme-linked immunosorbent assay. Repeated positive ELISA tests are strong evidence of HIV infection for those in AIDS risk groups. In persons at low risk of HIV infection, however, even repeated positive tests can be inaccurate. In those cases, and even for those in high-risk groups, confirmation is made by utilizing more sensitive techniques, which are also more complex and expensive. The most common technique is called *western blotting* and measures antibodies to each specific protein of the virus. Infected persons usually have antibodies to multiple HIV proteins. It is also possible to grow HIV in vitro. This technique is used around the world for research but not for routine clinical purposes. Recently a technique for multiplying small fragments of DNA or RNA, called the *polymerase chain reaction* (PCR), has improved the sensitivity of detection of HIV nucleic acids by roughly a million times. PCR allows very small amounts of latent virus to be detected months or even years before antibodies are detectable. The detection of anti-

bodies and other signs of HIV infection has become increasingly accurate, simple, and inexpensive.

STAGES OF AIDS DISEASE

One of the complications that exist in the study of AIDS is characterizing the stage of progression of individuals who have the HIV virus. To be precise, an individual has AIDS only when he or she has exhibited one of the AIDS-defining infections. HIV causes a predictable, progressive decline of immune function that enables normally benign organisms to flourish destructively in patients. AIDS is just one late manifestation of the process of the HIV virus. It is important to understand the progress of the disease for a number of reasons. First, and probably most important, it enables the patient to receive optimal medical care. For example, the medicine Retrovir, also known as azidothymidine (AZT), has been shown to prolong life in patients who have been infected with HIV. The pace of progression of HIV infection varies widely among patients and is difficult to predict. It appears that there may be a number of cofactors involved in this variability, including repeated reinfection with the virus and perhaps psychological factors (discussed below). The time between infection and AIDS varies between 1 and 10 years, with an estimated average time of 7 to 8 years. The risk of developing AIDS appears to increase with each year of infection. It is not clear yet, however, if all or only some individuals who are infected with HIV will develop AIDS at some point.

The most general terminology that is used to describe the stage of illness of HIV-positive individuals is to refer to those people who have been infected with HIV (that is, show antibodies for HIV) but are healthy and exhibit no symptoms of the disease as *HIV positive*, or *seropositive*. Being HIV positive clearly increases the risk that an individual will develop

AIDS. However, being seropositive does not tell when the disease will become evident or what kinds of health changes may precede the development of AIDS. An intermediate stage between HIV positive and AIDS has been called *AIDS-related complex* (ARC). At this stage some physical symptoms exist but not the most severe. Finally, *AIDS* refers to the full-blown manifestation of the disease, which includes severe immunosuppression and the presence of certain severe opportunistic infections such as pneumocystis carinii pneumonia (PCP), or tumors such as Kaposi's sarcoma (KS). This scheme is quite general; thus researchers have struggled to design a finer staging system.

Two other major classification schemes exist for characterizing individuals with HIV. The first was developed at the U.S. Centers for Disease Control (CDC) and is called the CDC classification. There are four CDC classes based primarily on the types of infections that individuals have. Although widely used, the problem with the CDC scheme is that these groupings are not prognostic of disease progression nor do they reflect the severity of the disease. The value of the system, on the other hand, is that it provides a hierarchy of classification; that is, patients are not reclassified to lower levels if their symptoms resolve. However, progression of AIDS does not always follow a well-defined path. Some patients develop one infection before another, while others do not.

The other major classification scheme for HIV infection was developed at the Walter Reed Army Medical Center. Using this scheme, as the disease progresses, the patient moves through six stages of infection. This method takes into account the number of CD4 cells present in the individual, our best prognostic indicator of disease progression, as well as the impairment in cell-mediated immunity. This impairment is determined by injecting foreign proteins under the skin, like allergy tests. When there is no swelling in response to these proteins, cell-mediated immunity has broken down to the point where a number of infections may begin to appear. These opportunistic infections define AIDS. It is these infections that actually lead to death among HIV patients.

NERVOUS SYSTEM INFECTIONS

The implications of nervous system infections for the development of interventions and for the HIV-infected person are great. If an individual is unable to think clearly or make plans for the future, we need to design interventions that take this into account. If problems with thinking occur early in the course of infection, some individuals may lose their jobs. The military has taken the conservative stance of not allowing HIV-positive individuals to fly airplanes and work in other complex jobs. For someone who is HIV positive but feels fine, the stakes are great. It is for this reason that such controversy accompanies each report of cognitive problems associated with HIV. In this section we review the evidence that HIV impacts the thought processes of HIV-positive individuals.

The infections of the central nervous system (CNS) associated with HIV infection have received much attention in recent years (Grant & Heaton, 1990; Gulevich & Wiley, 1991). Neurological findings can include subtle alterations in cognitive function, such as in memory and judgment. The central nervous system can be impacted by HIV infection in several ways. A primary neurological disorder of the brain results when HIV enters the brain and causes cognitive, behavioral, and neurological abnormalities, which in their worst stages have been termed the *AIDS dementia complex* (ADC). ADC is characterized by a gradual loss of precision in both thought and motion. In the end, some people are unable to walk or communicate effectively. It has been estimated that about one-third of all AIDS and ARC patients will develop at least mild ADC, and perhaps another quarter may have subclinical findings.

Secondary neurological disorders result from the opportunistic infections that attack the brain. The most common infectious agents of the CNS are cytomegalovirus (CMV) and herpes simplex virus, but other agents also contribute to this disorder (Grant & Heaton, 1990). As the stage of illness progresses, cognitive disorders can have both primary and secondary causes. The stage of illness at which one is able to detect cognitive dysfunction, and the severity, is currently being actively debated and studied.

Depression and anxiety are commonly seen in patients with HIV infections (Atkinson et al., 1989). For example, early in the course of infection about 20 percent of all HIV patients display generalized anxiety. The percentage of those individuals demonstrating generalized anxiety increases to as much as one-third. Depression is seen in about 15 percent of HIV-infected individuals. This increased rate of depression may also be reflected in increased suicide rates, although this topic remains in debate. These neurological and psychiatric findings underscore the importance of conceptualizing HIV infection in neurobehavioral as well as immunologic virologic terms.

The sources of depression in HIV-positive people may be due to the action of the virus itself, other factors in the environment, or a combination of both the virus and environmental factors. For example, bereavement is commonly seen among gay men. Martin (1988) found that 27 percent of a community sample of New York City gay men suffered from bereavement. One-third of the bereaved men suffered multiple losses. Martin found a direct relationship between the number of bereavements and symptoms of increased psychological distress. These symptoms included demoralization, sleep problems, increased

sedative use, increased recreational drug use, and the increased use of psychological services. Surprisingly, Martin found that statistically controlling for HIV status of the bereaved person did not change the observed relationships.

Persons with AIDS are at increased risk of developing dementia and neuropsychological deficit short of dementia. About one-third of AIDS patients may become demented (Price & Brew, 1988), and another third will manifest more subtle neurocognitive disturbance (Grant et al., 1987; Grant & Heaton, 1990; Perry & Jacobsen, 1986; Perry et al., 1989). Persons earlier in the course of illness can also have neurocognitive impairment (Grant et al., 1987; Perry et al., 1989), although how early such changes might be seen remains a matter of controversy (Grant & Atkinson, 1990; Janssen et al., 1988; McArthur et al., 1989).

AIDS THERAPIES

HIV contains genetic codes for both structural components of the virus and multiple regulatory elements which control the rate of viral replication. Two steps in the HIV life cycle are currently being exploited to try to stop its course. Treatments are aimed at the crucial first step of attachment of the virus to its host cell. AZT, the only licensed drug at the time of the writing of this chapter, acts by terminating growing DNA chains, which interferes with reverse transcription, a crucial step in the life cycle of the virus. The use of AZT has been shown to extend the lives of AIDS patients, decrease the rate and severity of opportunistic infections, and reverse some neurological symptoms. The disadvantage of AZT is that the virus may become resistant to the drug after prolonged exposure. Thus, the treatment may become ineffective after a year or so. In addition, some patients cannot tolerate the drug. It is clear that AZT is not the cure-all for AIDS.

A host of other drugs are currently in various stages of development. Since, at the time of this writing, no other drugs are in widespread use, we will not review them now. We hope that by the time the next edition of this text comes out, we will be able to report on these drugs.

PHARMACEUTICAL PRODUCTS, BUREAUCRACY, AND THE TREATMENT OF AIDS

In the United States, the Food and Drug Administration (FDA) is responsible for licensing new pharmaceutical products. The FDA requires that new products undergo rigorous testing for safety and efficacy. This process typically takes several years, because both side effects and benefits of drug treatments may not be obvious at first. The treatment of AIDS has stimulated some early examination of these policies. On the one hand, there are serious consequences to releasing drugs prematurely. People may be severely damaged or even killed as a result of these medications. On the other hand, AIDS may be a universally fatal disease. In other words, patients may have no other chance of surviving, and their only hope is the experimental drugs. Activist groups, including San Francisco's Project Inform, believe that patients should be given the right to decide whether the benefits of an unproven but potentially effective drug outweigh the risks for people suffering from this fatal illness. These activists have challenged the FDA's authority to go through their usual drug-testing process. As a result of these interventions, some new AIDS drugs have been given advance approval (Wachter, 1992).

The issues in drug approval for AIDS are very challenging. On the one hand, some people may suffer severely because unproven drugs may turn out to be harmful. On the other hand, the slow drug approval process has created some challenging ethical prob-

lems. For example, for several years the FDA approved only one drug (Zidovudine, or AZT) for the treatment of AIDS. During that time only one company (Burroughs Welcome Co.) was able to market the drug. Without competition, the profits are considerable, with the ultimate result that the cost of medication is the most expensive component of AIDS treatment. New drugs for the treatment of AIDS have come along slowly. For example, two new drugs (Ganciclovir and Foscarnet) are now licensed for the treatment of one AIDS complication in the eye. Each of these drugs is remarkably expensive, with Foscarnet being roughly 3 times the price of drugs previously available for AIDS treatment. Although these drugs appear to extend life expectancy for AIDS patients, they create many serious side effects including seizures, kidney failure, fevers, and rashes. Substantial numbers of patients are unable to comply with the treatment.

The AIDS epidemic has pushed the current system to the limit. As a result of the crisis, the FDA has been forced to take a new look at its own procedures. Still the benefits of new AIDS drugs are unknown. In effect, they are very expensive products that may extend life for a brief period of time. It is still uncertain whether quality of life will suffer as a function of exposure to these new medications (Hirsch, 1992).

AIDS VACCINES

History has shown that the best way to combat any disease is to prevent it from happening. Several vaccines are currently being tested, but despite massive amounts of funding and worker-hours directed at the development of vaccines, it is not clear when they will become available for dissemination. Matthews and Bolognesi (1988) list three particular problems that have slowed the development of an AIDS vaccine. The first is the life cycle of HIV itself. The virus can "hide" in cells, installing itself in the genes of the host and protecting itself behind its own coat. Second, unlike polio and other diseases which have all but been eradicated by vaccines, there is no animal model on which tests can be ethically made. Finally, it is difficult to get a clinical trial under way due to ethical concerns, costs, and scientific uncertainties. In order to conduct clinical trials it is necessary to first show some efficacy in the test tube before humans can begin to receive the drug. There are various stages of clinical trials, including phase I trials, which usually involve a small number of patients and are designed to establish toxicity, maximum tolerated dose, and (in the case of treatments) the drug's mechanism of action in the body. Phase II and phase III trials involve larger numbers of people and are designed to assess the effectiveness of the vaccine. These time-consuming, laborious steps are necessary to protect the individual and ensure the effectiveness of the vaccine.

Vaccines are designed to introduce harmless antigens to the immune system so that the immune system can learn and remember what the antigen looks like. In this way, when it next encounters that antigen, it will not be caught unaware and will be able to quickly identify and destroy that invader. Unfortunately, HIV invades the same cells that vaccines need to activate: CD4 cells and macrophages. In fact, as was noted above, the macrophage may actually spread HIV to CD4 cells when they are communicating about potential pathogens. HIV vaccines must, therefore, stop the spread of HIV before it becomes part of CD4 and macrophages.

At least four types of vaccines are currently under development. The most common ones are made up of subunits of the HIV virus along with the envelope which covers the virus; these are genetically engineered or synthesized in the laboratory. Another method is to insert a gene for an HIV protein among the genes of a harmless virus and introduce that

virus to the system. Then there are the *antiidotype vaccines*. These consist of antibodies carrying an internal image of the CD4 receptor which are meant to evoke another set of antibodies that look like CD4 and compete with them for binding to HIV. Finally, while whole, killed HIV has been deemed too risky for inoculating people who have not been previously exposed to HIV, the Salk Institute for Biological Studies has begun trials among HIV+ individuals with whole HIV virus that has been inactivated with the genetic material removed.

While no definitive answers are close at hand, it is remarkable that so many potential vaccines are being tested after so short a period since the virus was discovered. The payoff for the human race is great, and the potential laurels for the individuals who solve the puzzle are also great.

SOCIAL IMPLICATIONS

In addition to medical treatment for HIV opportunistic infections, health professionals must keep in mind that a number of other issues need to be addressed in preterminal patients. Major problems include relief of pain, dealing with anxiety and depression, entering and interfacing with the medical establishment (including astronomically high medical bills), compliance with treatment regimens, utilizing available emotional and physical support, family problems such as estrangement, and finally dealing with wills, power of attorney, and funeral plans. The typical AIDS patient today is homosexual and relatively young. Community support for these individuals in the form of support groups and political activism is relatively well developed. We are, however, faced with the reality that the demographics of infection are changing. As more women, IV drug users, and heterosexual individuals become infected, the need to create specialized support groups and the like will become more urgent. One challenge of behavioral scientists is to work to improve the quality of life for all AIDS patients.

SOCIAL ISSUES RELEVANT TO HIV INFECTION

AIDS has affected disenfranchised groups. Initially, most cases were among homosexual males. In 1987 about 70 percent of all Americans with AIDS were gay men. As a result, much of the original activism regarding AIDS was lead by gay male groups. However, by 1992, there was a relative decline in new cases among gay males and a significant increase among intravenous drug users, people of color, and women. Initially, AIDS activist groups, such as ACT UP, focused almost exclusively on issues relevant to the gay community. However, with the changing nature of the epidemic, many groups began to emphasize the overwhelming social problems related to the other high-risk groups. These problems include poverty, racism, violence, drug abuse, and access to health care. AIDS activists began dividing into at least two groups: those who wanted to emphasize issues for homosexual men, and those with a broader social agenda. In addition, activists became divided over tactics. Some groups wanted to work within the system to encourage the biomedical community to develop new drug treatments. Other groups took a distinctively antiestablishment position, at some points calling for disruption in scientific meetings and more aggressive advocacy for greater allocation of resources to AIDS patients (Wachter, 1992).

PROTECTING OURSELVES AND OTHERS FROM HIV INFECTION

Even though one is not a member of a *high-risk* group, there is still *some risk* of contracting the virus if one engages in high-risk activities. It is therefore important for everyone to know what the activities are that increase the risk of HIV infection. In addition, it is imperative to replace these activities with low-risk behaviors; knowing what to do but engaging in unsafe practices anyway is no better than not knowing anything at all. Surveys show that high-risk behaviors can be modified by education. It appears that the rate of HIV infection in the homosexual community has leveled off. It is imperative to implement effective prevention strategies to reduce misplaced fear about how HIV is spread and stop the spread in other groups.

High-risk sexual practices include any unprotected sexual intercourse with an HIV-infected partner. Vaginal, anal, and oral intercourse are all considered unsafe. The relative risk of infection is probably highest for the receptive partner of anal intercourse. The risk of infection is *lowered* during any type of intercourse through the use of condoms, particularly those lubricated with a virucidal spermicide. We say "lowered" since there is a danger of breakage and leakage with condoms.

While abstinence may be the safest way to avoid the virus, most adults find this solution unacceptable. Mutually monogamous relationships are one way to ensure no exposure to the virus. One should keep in mind, however, that antibodies to the virus may take months to develop, and the use of a condom is advisable to ensure safety. Other safe forms of sexual activity include touching, massaging, hugging, dry kissing, and masturbation, if no cuts or open sores exist.

Sharing of needles by intravenous drug users is a highly dangerous activity that may transmit the HIV virus. IV drug users who are HIV positive may transmit the virus to their heterosexual partners, male or female. Women partners may then infect their unborn or newborn children. In addition, these women may transmit the virus to other male partners. This is especially problematic when the female is a prostitute who may have many partners. The potential for sexually active non-drug-using heterosexuals to acquire and transmit HIV, such as on university campuses, is very real.

Finally, the risk of HIV infection from contaminated blood products during transfusions has been reduced to essentially zero in developed countries. This may not be true in undeveloped countries where the screening of donors and their blood has not, often because of costs, become standard procedure.

LEGAL NEEDLE BUYING

One of the major controversies surrounding the AIDS epidemic for IV drug users concerns the use of sterile syringes. On the one hand, it is argued that we should do everything possible to discourage IV drug use. On the other hand, it is known that many IV drug users become infected through needle sharing. In France, laws were passed to liberalize the regulation of syringe purchases. When this happened, the rate of needle sharing declined. Conversely, when the police in Edinburgh, Scotland, had a crackdown on the supply of legally available syringes, the rate of HIV infection among IV users systematically increased.

Several states in the United States have no laws against purchasing syringes. Missouri is one of them. A recent study evaluated the ease with which syringes could be purchased there by IV drug users. When researchers went to various drugstores in St. Louis in order to purchase syringes, 42 percent of the stores either refused to sell the syringes or packaged them in a way that placed them out of reach for most IV drug users. For example, many stores would sell syringes only in packages of 100. Several of the pharmacies stated that they would sell syringes only to specific customers or that they were specifically concerned about offering syringes to IV drug users. These results suggest that the difficulty in obtaining clean syringes in more than simply a legal issue (Compton, Cottler, Decker, et al., 1992).

ALCOHOL AND THE SPREAD OF HIV

Does the use of alcohol affect sexual practices that people engage in? "Candy is dandy, but Liquor is quicker"; from Ogden Nash's viewpoint alcohol is a common accompaniment to sexual behavior of all types (Leiblaum & Rosen, 1984). Findings from several large-scale surveys have documented our society's widespread belief that alcohol is an aphrodisiac with disinhibiting properties (Rosen, 1991). From Macbeth's porter's point of view, "It provokes the desire, but takes away the performance" (Shakespeare). This contrasting belief has been repeatedly supported by research. Chronic alcohol consumption has potentially deleterious and disruptive effects on all aspects of sexual functioning (Schiavi, 1990).

But does the use of alcohol affect sexual permissiveness and promiscuity? From *The Canterbury Tales* we learn that "women have no defense against wine as lechers know from experience" (Chaucer). Interestingly, from a physiologic point of view, females have reduced vaginal blood flow with increased alcohol consumption. However, despite these findings, women, as well as men, have repeatedly reported increased subjective arousal accompanying the use of alcohol. Interestingly, even when no alcohol has been consumed but the individual believes that he or she has been imbibing, there is an increase in subjective reports of arousal. With increased dosages, performance of both men and women decreases. To date there is no experimental evidence that women are unable to suppress sexual arousal when they have used alcohol.

Might the use of alcohol affect an individual's ability to practice safe sex? Recent research findings show that the combination of alcohol (or drugs) with sexual activity results in a higher likelihood of high-risk sex (Coates, Stall, & Hoff, 1990). One study attempted to predict whether individuals engaged in high-risk sex by comparing the combination of drugs and sexual activity, perception of social support, years engaged in sexual activity, and perception of difficulty in modifying sexual behavior (Siegel et al., 1989). They found that the most powerful predictor of engaging in high-risk sex was whether individuals combined drugs with sex. Thus, AIDS prevention programs that are developed should focus on drugs and alcohol in order to increase their effectiveness.

COPING WITH AIDS

How do people cope with the threat of having AIDS? The study of psychosocial factors among HIV-positive individuals is in its infancy. Only six studies of coping behavior have been published to date. They find that the use of avoidant coping—that is, avoiding thinking about or behaving in direct response to the illness—is related to greater depression and anxiety, lower self-esteem, and less perceived social support (Nicholson & Long, 1990; Wolf et al., 1991). Engaging in this type of coping may result in delays in seeking treatment. In contrast, active behavioral coping—that is, mobilizing energies to deal directly with the illness—is related to better mood, increased self-esteem, and increased perceived social support.

Do people who have HIV differ from people who have other major illnesses? Viney and colleagues (1989) compared the emotional reactions of men who have HIV with a matched sample of men with other major illnesses, including diabetes, epilepsy, multiple sclerosis, and coronary conditions. They found that these groups reacted in similar ways to their illnesses. Compared with healthy people, both the HIV and the other illness groups were more angry, anxious, depressed, and felt helpless. In contrast to these more negative findings, ill individuals who expressed more enjoyment of life—that is, endorsed more

statements such as "I enjoy getting outside"—were less depressed. This expressed enjoyment is seen as a defense against the distressing emotions which are stimulated by illness, or as a spontaneous appreciation of life resulting from effective coping with illness.

SOCIAL SUPPORT AND HIV

Little work has been reported about social support and AIDS. Social support has been shown to be an important variable in studies of stress and morbidity, and may provide some protection against the effects of stress. Reduced perceived social support is related to increased psychological distress, more hopelessness, and more anger among HIV-positive individuals (Zich & Temoshok, 1990). In contrast, turning to others for emotional, informational, and instrumental support is associated with better psychological outcome.

In the gay community, where HIV has had much of its initial impact, grief is a common experience. Individuals who perceive that they have adequate instrumental and emotional support report experiencing less intense symptoms of grief compared with those who feel that they have inadequate supports (Lennon, Martin, & Dean, 1990). This suggests that social support is essential for caretakers of HIV patients.

However, as Zich and Temoshok (1990) pointed out, because of fear or other aspects of reaction to victims, social support may not be as available to HIV-infected individuals as it is to people with other diseases. Several authors have reported that isolation is a major issue among people with AIDS (e.g., Miller, 1990). Zich and Temoshok (1990) found that persons with AIDS who reported more physical symptoms felt that they had less social support available to them and felt more stigmatized by the illness. In studies of people with other serious illnesses, it has been found that individuals often disengage from superficial attachments, maintaining only those relationships that they find important (Kalish, 1985).

Social support may be reduced because the potentially supportive individuals withdraw from the ill person. This may be caused by their own inexperience in dealing with people in life crisis with HIV disease. They may not know what to do or say, or they may have misconceptions about how to deal with people in this new situation. In addition, they may harbor some fear that they are vulnerable to contracting the disease themselves if they come in contact with these patients. Thus, the development of effective interventions to increase social support may need to focus on educating both the patients and their supporters.

PSYCHOIMMUNOLOGIC CONSIDERATIONS IN HIV INFECTION

We have touched on a number of reasons why behavioral scientists should be involved in the study of HIV infections. The first, and foremost, is that until a vaccine or cure for AIDS is found, the only method of controlling the spread of HIV is through behavioral means. Second, the virus invades the brain, which may lead to problems in memory as reviewed above. Third, there are increased rates of psychological problems—including depression, anxiety, and possibly suicide—among HIV patients. A fourth and perhaps less obvious reason that we are involved in the study of this virus is the suggestion that psychological factors may influence the rate of immune function decline among HIV-positive individuals.

What is the importance of understanding psychological factors in individuals infected with HIV? If HIV disease progression was represented by an inexorable linear decline, behavioral scientists would have little to offer in developing ways to modify the course of the illness. The alleviation of anxiety and depression, and dealing with medical cost and deliv-

ery are important issues that are also being dealt with by health professionals, but are not of primary interest here. Fortunately, the course of HIV illness is variable. Although biological determinants obviously modify rates of expressing HIV illness (Goldert et al., 1986; Klatzman & Gluckman, 1986), there is evidence that psychosocial factors also influence immunologic variables. This evidence falls into two areas: (1) immune response to stress (reviewed in Chapter 6) and (2) psychological factors in AIDS outcome.

PSYCHOLOGICAL FACTORS IN OUTCOME OF HIV INFECTION AND ONSET OF AIDS

With regard to psychological factors in onset and outcome of AIDS, Silberstein (1985; p. 137) reported that five of six patients with AIDS and ARC had suffered "major depressive illness between nine months and two years prior to the diagnosis." It was not clear, however, if this depression was the result of brain infections associated with AIDS. Solomon, Temoshok, and colleagues (1987) suggest that men who survived 2 to 8 weeks after diagnosis of AIDS scored higher on the "hardiness" personality scale and reported using more problem-solving social support compared with those who had died (Solomon et al., 1987). Loneliness (see Marangoni & Ickes, 1989, for a review of this construct) also appears to increase the susceptibility of individuals to symptoms of HIV disease (Solomon, Kemeny, & Temoshok, 1991).

Research findings reported at the IVth International Conference on AIDS in Stockholm support the hypothesis that psychosocial factors may be important mediators for the progression of HIV infection. In HIV-positive homosexual men Millon and associates (1988) found, cross-sectionally, that depression and anxiety were related to coping style, which was strongly associated with natural killer cell cytotoxicity. Temoshok and coworkers (1988) reported that more assertive coping, less stress, less emotional distress, and more self-nurturing behaviors were significantly related to the number of CD4 cells, B-cells, CD8 suppressor cells, and natural killer cells in a 6-month follow-up of a group of men diagnosed with ARC. In another study, Joseph and associates (1988) reported that higher levels of depression, anxiety, and global psychological distress were significantly (and consistently over time) associated with subsequent symptom development over a 3-year period. More recent findings reported at the Vth International Conference on AIDS in Montreal again point to the importance of psychosocial factors in HIV illness. Kessler and colleagues (1991) found that increased numbers of stressful life events and distressed mood increased the risk of illness onset in a group of previously asymptomatic homosexual men. Coates and coworkers (1989) reported that sexual practices, but not measures of stress or social support, were related to HIV disease progression.

All of the studies reviewed in the previous paragraph use some immunologic indicator as their outcome. We presume that the changes seen will translate into health changes. That is to say, it is possible that the immune changes observed are too small to translate into disease onset or progression. There are no published studies that relate psychological and immunologic variables to disease outcome. In part this is due to the long period of time between psychological testing and the initiation of disease, progression of the disease, or death.

LIMITING THE SPREAD OF AIDS: HEALTH BEHAVIOR CHANGE

Once HIV infection has occurred, the immune system is unable to eradicate the virus from the body. Since there is currently no cure for AIDS, a large effort must be placed on primary prevention to control the spread of this disease. While information about psychosocial variables and disease progression will likely prove useful, such data have less immediate or widespread impact on society than successful prevention programs. Infection with HIV requires contact with the virus through exposure to bodily fluids, that is, through sexual activity, shared IV drug paraphernalia, and exposure to contaminated blood products. These routes of transmission represent behavior patterns and, as such, are modifiable. The only way we presently have to slow or stop the HIV epidemic is to prevent individuals from coming into contact with the virus. Screening blood products has already virtually eliminated the spread of HIV through this means in the United States. Efforts to modify the other two major routes of transmission, sexual behavior and IV drug use, have only recently been undertaken.

Addictive and pleasurable behaviors are extremely difficult to eliminate. Intravenous use of illicit drugs is a long-standing problem in our society that has resisted prevention efforts and is unlikely to disappear in the near future. Likewise, sexual behaviors are not likely to cease in the near future. Hence, the most practical solution to the problem is to alter or substitute lower-risk behaviors. For example, needles can be cleaned with bleach before they are used, and condoms can be used in sexual intercourse.

How can we change high-risk behaviors that are known to transmit HIV virus and maintain those changes over time? Motivating and sustaining change in risk-associated intimate and addictive behaviors are not easy. There do exist some indications that there have already been changes among homosexual men and IV drug users in response to the AIDS epidemic. Among homosexual and bisexual men there have already been decreases in risk behaviors. Among the IV drug users in New York City there appear to be high levels of awareness and knowledge about AIDS, with increased sterilization of injection equipment and a decrease in the frequency of sharing needles (Des Jarlais, 1987). However, there are wide variations in these changes as a function of group and geographic location.

The National Research Council (Turner et al., 1989) points out two major themes that must be addressed to build effective intervention strategies:

1. For behavior to change, individuals must recognize the problem, be motivated to act, and have the knowledge and skills necessary to perform the action.
2. To increase the likelihood of action, impediments in the social environment must be removed or weakened and inducements for change provided whenever possible.

For behavioral change to take place one must have knowledge; however, information alone is not enough to effect and sustain behavioral change (Emmons et al., 1986; Kelly et al., 1987). It may be that in order to change behavior, knowledge and attitudes need to be modified simultaneously. Even so, the first step is the dissemination of the facts, and it appears that there is still a lot of misinformation among even the highest risk groups. Coates and coworkers (1985) found that some homosexual men believed that they had "fought off the virus," and a high percentage of these individuals continued to practice high-risk sex, thus encouraging the continued spread of the virus. Those individuals who understood the irreversible nature of HIV infection were less likely to engage in high-risk activities. Many believe that today's adolescents may become the future victims of the AIDS epidemic. Unfortunately many adolescents do not understand the mechanism through which infection occurs. They still believe that they can be infected with HIV through casual contact such as shaking hands or simply being near someone with AIDS (DiClemente et al., 1988; Reuben et al., 1988). Misinformation about AIDS has been blamed for a reduction in the number of blood donors. Twenty-six percent of the general population in a nationwide poll indicated that a person could contract AIDS from donating blood.

Various agencies in the public and private sectors have been making considerable efforts to increase public knowledge about AIDS. These efforts, unfortunately, harbor problems. For example, an analysis of 16 educational brochures on AIDS prevention found that, on average, they were written at the reading level of a second-year college student (Hochhauser, 1987). Others have noted that the information disseminated to the public is obscured by the use of unclear language, such as statements indicating that AIDS is transmitted through the "exchange of bodily fluids." This language has lead to confusion about which bodily fluids the brochures are referring to. Information needs to be couched in straightforward language in the idiom of the target population.

Knowledge alone will not motivate behavior change. Unless an individual perceives a personal risk, they are unlikely to change (Joseph et al., 1987). Individuals must be motivated to change their behaviors, to believe that the changes being proposed will do some good, and to perceive that they have a reasonably good chance of making those changes (Emmons et al., 1986; McKusick et al., 1988). Unfortunately, some individuals indicate that it is too late for them to avoid infection (Emmons et al., 1986). Moreover, proposed behavioral changes that conflict with a person's existing beliefs and values are unlikely to be successful (Emmons et al., 1986). Taken together, these factors make the design of successful behavioral intervention programs to modify sexual and drug use exceedingly difficult and challenging.

SUSTAINING BEHAVIORAL CHANGE

Even when the desired behavioral change takes place, it is necessary to maintain that behavior over an individual's lifetime. A single instance of behavior reversal could result in infection of the individual and perhaps transmission to a mate. A number of studies have pointed to high rates of relapse in health behaviors, although a critical review of experimental studies and their methodologies by Green and colleagues (1986) indicates that the problem of relapse has sometimes been overstated.

The major cofactor in relapse of high-risk sexual behavior may be the use of alcohol and other drugs. The combination of alcohol or drugs and sex has been associated with high-risk activities among homosexual and bisexual men (Stall et al., 1986). Apparently, just as the use of alcohol or oher drugs diminishes one's ability to drive or make sound judgments, the use of any psychoactive substance will diminish an individual's ability to use a condom properly (Ostrow, 1990).

BOX 12·3

FOCUS ON WOMEN

There is much evidence suggesting that as the illusion of personal invulnerability goes up, individuals are less likely to engage in preventive or risk-reducing behaviors. People tend to ignore their own risk-increasing behaviors and fail to recognize that others may engage in riskier behaviors (Taylor & Brown, 1988). Weinstein (1984) found that people felt less vulnerable to negative events that they considered to be controllable. Findings from a study by Gerrard and colleagues (1991) suggest that changing a woman's perception of vulnerability to HIV significantly increased perceived risk of HIV infection. Since the vast majority were not using condoms in their sexual encounters, they were taught what the risks were. This review of sexual behavior reminded these women that their sexual behavior increased their risk of HIV infection. This resulted in an increased sense of vulnerability, although this study did not follow up with these women to find out if there was an increase in condom use. However, perceptions of vulnerability have been shown to predict use of preventive behaviors, such as using effective contraception, immunization, and wearing seat belts.

ATTITUDES AND RESPONSES OF SOCIETY

The attitudes of society may affect the speed of response to the HIV epidemic. Cahill (1984) argued that since the epidemic first appeared among individuals who were stigmatized—that is, homosexuals or members of legally proscribed outgroups such as drug addicts—society tended to blame the victims. He contrasted the quick response to Legionnaires' disease and toxic-shock syndrome to the slower response to AIDS. Correct or not, the initial perception of society (which may still persist) was that AIDS was a disease that only infected people who engaged in illegal or immoral activities. This misperception drew attention away from the *behaviors* that are responsible for the spread of HIV, falsely reassuring the majority of the population that they were not in danger of contracting the disease and making it difficult to convince people to modify their behaviors.

Sex is (and always has been) a major theme in all societies. In contrast, it is a legal and moral taboo that is difficult for people (our society in particular) to discuss or display openly. This conundrum leads to debates regarding interventions. For example, should we or should we not teach teenagers about safe sex practices? It is an undeniable fact that some teenagers do experiment with sex. The number of teenagers with HIV is rising (DiClemente, 1990). This suggests the need for interventions among this population. Some argue, however, that teaching teenagers about safe sex practices will increase the amount of promiscuity. DiClemente (1990) provides a discussion of HIV prevention strategies and policy implications among adolescents. In a similar vein, drug use and the sale of IV needles are illegal. Providing clean syringes to IV drug users will stop or slow the spread of HIV in this population but, at the same time, appears to condone the behavior. The legal and moral dilemmas associated with developing effective

BOX 12·4

FOCUS ON RESEARCH

Dying of HIV Infection Versus Hepatitis B

Many doctors and dentists are concerned about treating patients infected with HIV. However, doctors and dentists have cared for patients with the hepatitis B virus for many years. New evidence shows that the annual risk of infection as a result of routine treatment of hepatitis patients is 57 times greater than the risk of becoming infected by a patient with HIV. Furthermore, the chances of a health care worker dying of hepatitis B are 1.7 times greater than the risk of dying from HIV (Capilouto, Weinstein, Hemenway, & Cotton, 1992). In one study subjects were presented with hypothetical scenarios describing situations similar to HIV and hepatitis. If infected by an accidental needle stick from an AIDS patient, the chances of being infected are about 1 in 100. However, for those 1 percent who are infected, the chances of dying of AIDS are assumed to be 100 percent. In the hypothetical scenarios it was suggested that about 20 percent of all people accidentally stuck with a needle taken from a hepatitis B patient will become infected. Among these, about 5 percent will die. Thus, according to the scenarios, the chances of dying from accidental needle stick are about the same for the two diseases (1% × 100% = 1% for AIDS; 20% × 5% for hepatitis B = 1%). Yet in response to the hypothetical scenarios, subjects expressed considerably more concern about being exposed to AIDS than to hepatitis B. In the same experiment some subjects responded to a hypothetical scenario that never mentioned the words *AIDS* or *hepatitis*. Instead, the subjects read about an insect that would infect 1 percent of the people and 100 percent of the infected people would die, or another insect that infected 20 percent of the people with 5 percent of the infected dying. These are the same percentages as AIDS and hepatitis, but without the disease names. Subjects were told that they could avoid one of the two insects, but not both. They were asked to choose which one they would avoid.

The results were almost identical with the AIDS scenario. Although the expected value of death due to exposure to HIV is about equivalent to the expected value of death from hepatitis B, the fear of HIV appears to be greater than the fear of hepatitis. This may be so because the probability of death from AIDS is certain for those who are infected. Even though the chances of being infected are small, the consequences are more serious. Fear of living any length of time infected with a virus for which outcomes are always fatal apparently overrides the fact that the initial chances of being infected are small (Schniederman & Kaplan, 1992).

interventions must also be resolved before the epidemic will be stopped.

SUMMARY

The acquired immune deficiency syndrome is one of the greatest threats to public health in the world today. This condition was unknown before 1980. Now it is projected that 50,000 Americans per year will die of AIDS in the 1990s. With the direction of the epidemic un-certain at the time of this writing, the major risk groups for AIDS are male homosexuals, intravenous drug users, and hemophiliacs. However, recent evidence suggests rapid increases in the infection rate in other groups, including heterosexual women.

HIV damages the immune system, one of the most basic systems of the human body that recognizes foreign invaders and destroys them. HIV infection and AIDS damage the ability of the system to successfully fight off invading antigens. HIV infection probably affects various components of the immune system, including CD4 cells, CD8 cells, and macrophages. Clearer understanding of the nature of the infection has allowed for several screening tests and the possibility of a vaccine.

A variety of behavioral and neuropsychological consequences of AIDS are important. First, anxiety and depression are common among patients with HIV infection. Furthermore, HIV may affect the central nervous system, ultimately resulting in dementia or related problems in thinking, learning, and remembering. AIDS therapy has made some progress in recent years. However, considerably more progress is necessary. For example, the primary current treatment is AZT, which appears to prolong life but may cause a variety of serious side effects.

Prevention is certainly the best approach to the AIDS epidemic. Successful alteration of the epidemic will require changes in health behavior, including the use of condoms, reductions in needle sharing for IV drug users, and improved educational programs about the likelihood of transmitting the virus. A temporary behavior change will not be sufficient. Avoidance of HIV infection may require lifelong patterns of behavior change.

KEY TERMS

Acquired immune deficiency syndrome (AIDS). An acquired disease that destroys the body's capability of fighting off other infections.

Human immunodeficiency virus (HIV). The virus that is responsible for AIDS.

Pneumocystis carinii pneumonia (PCP). A rare type of pneumonia that characterizes the AIDS infection.

Shooting galleries. Rooms where drug addicts go to purchase and inject drugs. These are believed to be responsible for many cases of HIV infection in major cities.

Lymphocyte. Cells of three types: T-cells, B-cells, and natural killer cells. T and B lymphocytes recognize particular risky invaders.

Natural killer cells. Cells that respond in a nonspecific way to invading cells. Natural killer cells kill anything that is not "self."

CD4 lymphocytes. White blood cells that tell the immune system to "turn on" because there is a foreign invader.

Antigen. A foreign invading substance that activates the immune system.

Macrophages. Cells that "clean up" debris in the blood system. Macrophages work by digesting foreign invading substances.

ELISA (enzyme-linked immunosorbent assay). A common test used to determine if a person is infected with HIV.

Western blot measure. A test that measures antibodies to proteins. Persons infected with HIV make specific antibodies that can be detected with this test.

AZT (Azidothymidine). A drug used to treat HIV infection.

CHAPTER 13

Injury, Violence, and Substance Abuse

Television crews were everywhere as south central Los Angeles burned in the spring of 1992. At least 58 people had been killed in rioting, and the evidence of destruction was everywhere. Violence was not new to this area. The incident that touched off the rioting was linked to more violence. Rodney King, a motorist pulled over by the Los Angeles police, had been severely beaten in an episode that was recorded on videotape by a bystander. The African American community was outraged when an all-white jury found the four policemen accused of beating King "not guilty." In part, the police defended themselves by arguing that they were frightened by King and that they were always fearful in areas of Los Angeles dominated by violent street gangs. As we will see in this chapter, unexpected violent deaths and injuries are significant public health problems, and we are making slow progress in finding lasting remedies.

If you are in your twenties or thirties, the greatest risk to your health is the possibility you will be injured. Injury is the most frequent cause of death for young people. Do you know what behaviors put you most at risk for death by injury?

We live in a violent society. Violence occurs at many levels: within families, between

BOX 13-1

HEALTH OBJECTIVES FOR UNINTENTIONAL INJURIES FOR THE YEAR 2000

Reduce deaths caused by unintentional injuries to no more than 29.3 per 100,000 people (age-adjusted baseline: 34.5 per 100,000 in 1987).

YEAR 2000 GOAL FOR INJURY DEATHS

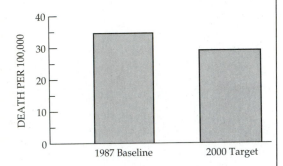

Increase use of occupant protection systems—such as safety belts, inflatable safety restraints, and child safety seats—to at least 85 percent of motor vehicle occupants (baseline: 42 percent in 1988).

YEAR 2000 GOAL FOR USE OF AUTO OCCUPANT PROTECTION

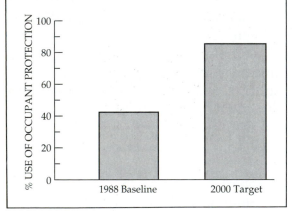

friends, between strangers, and between groups. What is the health impact of violence? What will it take to decrease the impact of violence on our lives?

Everyone must come to grips with alcohol at some time in their life. Even if you do not drink, you will frequently come in contact with people who are drinking. What are the effects of alcohol on health? Is there a safe amount of drinking? Is problem drinking just a fact in our society, or can it be effectively treated and prevented?

Drugs are a national obsession. If you read the newspapers, it is easy to believe that the few people who are not addicted to drugs are victims of drug-related crimes. Drug abuse is a serious social problem, but what are the effects of illicit drugs on health? What approaches to changing this health-related behavior are the most effective?

This chapter deals with behaviors that have caused death and disability for centuries, and they continue to take their toll. Behaviors that place one at risk for injuries, violent actions, and consumption of toxic substances are threats to health all around the world, not just in the United States. Researchers are hard at work trying to understand and control the behaviors that lead to injuries, violence, and substance abuse. This chapter introduces these related topics and highlights some of the promising research that may reduce the health burden of these risky behaviors.

INJURY

Epidemiology

Unintentional injuries are a major cause of morbidity and mortality, but this health problem has been relatively neglected by both medical and behavioral researchers until recently. It is now being more widely recognized that effective injury prevention programs could improve the public health substantially. Behavioral scientists play key roles in this work because almost all injuries have behavioral origins.

Injuries are the fourth leading cause of death in the United States (Committee on Trauma, 1985), but Figure 13-1 shows that injuries account for particularly high percentages

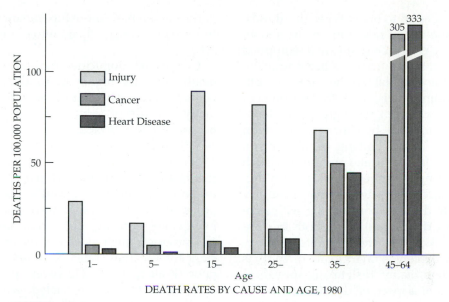

FIGURE 13-1

Injuries in relation to other health problems. (From Committee on Trauma, National Academy Press, 1985.)

of deaths in young people. Injuries are the leading cause of death for Americans below the age of 45. Injury deaths of young children are caused mainly by motor vehicle crashes, drowning, fires, and pedestrian deaths. Teenagers are killed most often by motor vehicle crashes, firearms, and drowning (Committee on Trauma, 1985).

Injuries are a major cause of morbidity as well. About 99 million physician contacts were due to injuries in 1980, compared with 72 million for heart disease (National Center for Health Statistics, 1983). In 1981 Americans spent 144 million days in bed because of injuries (National Center for Health Statistics, 1982). Each year 75,000 Americans suffer brain injuries that leave many disabled for life (Committee on Trauma, 1985). In addition to their impact on health, injuries have a major economic impact by reducing the productivity of workers. The economic impact of all injuries has not been estimated, but the costs of the largest cause of injuries, motor vehicle crashes, were over $36 billion in 1980. These costs are

second only to those of heart disease (Committee on Trauma, 1985).

Developing nations also have a high rate of injuries, yet they lack the resources to treat or prevent them to the extent that is possible in the United States. Injuries have been a major cause of death and disability since the beginning of time, and many of the factors leading to injuries have stayed constant throughout the centuries.

Etiology

Notice that this section does not discuss accidents or motor vehicle accidents. *Accidents* implies that they are random events or that they cannot be prevented. There are identifiable causes for virtually all motor vehicle crashes, and the word *unintentional* distinguishes careless firearm fatalities from murders. Although most injuries are unintentional, they do have specific causes that give us direction for prevention.

A number of risk factors have been identified that are related to many types of injuries. The age differences in risk of injury are shown in Figure 13-1. Young children are ill-equipped to protect themselves from the hazardous environments they inhabit, so they are susceptible to poisoning, falls, and the assaults of others. Older children willingly place themselves at risk of injury by experimenting with their physical skills (climbing or jumping in high places) or failing to take precautions (such as when crossing the street or riding a bicycle). Teenagers place themselves at risk routinely by learning to drive, experimenting with alcohol and other drugs, and doing both in combination. As shown by the high rate of injury fatalities, the perceived invincibility of youth is more myth than reality. Risk taking appears to be a behavioral aspect of development that sometimes leads to death and severe disability.

Among the elderly, falls are a major cause of serious injuries. A study done in Washington State illustrates the financial and human costs of fall-related injuries. More than 5 percent of all hospitalizations for people over 65 were due to injuries from falls. The rate was higher for women and for the older elderly. One reason falls cause such serious problems is that the elderly tend to have osteoporosis. Osteoporosis happens when the calcium dissolves from the bones, leaving them porous and weak. This condition is actually a chronic disease resulting from poor dietary and physical activity habits over many years. The cost of the 7873 fall-related hospitalizations in this one state was over $53 million. This does not include costs after discharge. One of the tragic consequences of these injuries is placement in a nursing facility. Almost half of those with fall-related injuries were discharged to a nursing facility (Alexander, Rivara, & Wolf, 1992).

Males are more than twice as likely as females to have fatal injuries. Males are at higher risk for virtually all unintentional and intentional (homicide and suicide) injuries than females. The major exception is that elderly women have more hip fractures resulting from osteoporosis (Committee on Trauma, 1985).

Except for homicide and suicide, injury death rates are higher in rural areas of the United States. This could be because of the many hazards of farm work, or it could be because of less access to prompt emergency care (Baker, 1984).

Socioeconomic status is an important injury risk factor. Poor people are particularly likely to die from homicide, assaults, pedestrian injuries, and house fires. High-risk occupations, low-quality housing, older cars, and dangerous products such as space heaters are often cited for the high rates of injury among the poor (Waller, 1985). However, psychological and social factors associated with poverty should be considered. Frustration associated with unemployment and many other sources of stress may stimulate aggression that is reflected in the historically high rates of homicide and assault in inner cities. The recent upsurge in drug use and gang activity may increase the risk of injury for the poor, but it is difficult to document these expected effects (Meehan & O'Carroll, 1992).

The use and abuse of drugs, and particularly alcohol, make virtually all types of injury more likely. High percentages of victims of motor vehicle crashes—including drivers, passengers, and pedestrians—have elevated blood alcohol concentrations. The same is true of those killed in falls, drownings, fires, assaults, and suicides (Committee on Trauma, 1985). In a study of emergency room patients, alcohol was found in 56 percent of those injured in assaults, 30 percent of those injured on the road, 22 percent of those injured at home, and 16 percent of those injured on the job (Thum, Wechsler, & Demone, 1973).

Though young children do not drink, alcohol use in the home puts them at risk for injuries. If their mothers are problem drinkers, their risk of injury is doubled. If their fathers are also heavy drinkers, children are at triple the risk of injury than if their parents do not drink (Bijur, Kurzon, Overpeck, & Scheidt, 1992).

Alcohol is the single most important factor in the etiology of the most important cause of injuries: automobile crashes. This relationship is worthy of some attention. The first motor vehicle fatality in the United States occurred in 1899, and alcohol was identified as an important factor in crashes only 4 years later. Currently about half of all fatally injured drivers and one-third of all fatally injured pedestrians have a blood alcohol concentration (BAC) of 0.10 or greater (Waller, 1986).

Waller (1986) summarized a large number of studies which suggested that one or two drinks do not seriously impair most drivers, unless they are teenagers. However, virtually all persons with BACs greater than 0.10 had impaired ability to drive a car. Although five or six alcoholic drinks may be required to raise the BAC to this level, many individuals who are impaired will not appear to be intoxicated, and about 40 percent will pass clinical measures of intoxication commonly used by the police. Most alcohol-related crash fatalities are problem drinkers or alcoholics, not social drinkers. However, even occasional drinkers should not drive if they have had more than one or two drinks.

People below age 25 constitute about 22 percent of the driving population, but they account for 37 percent of car crash fatalities (Waller, 1986). Young people are learning to drive and learning to drink. When they do both in a distracting social situation, the risk of crashes is very high. Risks are higher for young males, presumably because they are most likely to drink and drive as well as engage in more risky driving behaviors in general.

Elderly people are at increased risk for car crashes as well. Although healthy elderly have crash injury rates that are similar to younger adults, many elders have multiple health problems that increase their risk. Difficulty with vision, hearing, cognitive processes, and chronic illnesses can impair driving in unpredictable ways. The elderly also have high rates of pedestrian injuries (Waller, 1986).

There are risk factors that are specific to each type of injury, and a brief discussion of some important behavioral risk factors for different types of injuries will give the reader an idea of the number of opportunities for behavioral scientists to contribute to this field. These examples are taken from Waller's (1985; 1986) excellent reviews.

Driving habits such as excessive speed, reckless driving, and following too close are associated with high crash rates, but the concept of the accident-prone person does not hold up. There is evidence that drivers in fatal crashes are likely to have previous traffic offenses, and those with alcohol-related offenses are likely to have similar offenses in the future. However, being involved in minor crashes (which are the vast majority) at one time does not predict future crashes.

Motorcycle riders are 7 times as likely to die in a crash as car drivers, when adjusted for miles driven. Riding motorcycles is a risky behavior in itself, but wearing helmets and riding with lights on in the daytime are methods for reducing risk of crashes and serious injury. Many riders dislike wearing helmets and exert substantial political power to resist passage of helmet laws in many states.

Alcohol appears to play a role in many private airplane crashes, as well as boating fatalities.

About half of all injury fatalities in the home in persons 15 and older occurred to people who were impaired by alcohol.

Falls are the most common type of injury in the United States. Children have the most falls, but the elderly have the highest death rate from falls. Lack of muscle strength and poor coordination are blamed for many injuries and fatalities from falls. In addition, alcohol was found in 70 percent of the adults who died after falls.

Sixty-four percent of adult fatalities from burns were related to alcohol consumption.

An estimated 365,000 fires each year are due to cigarettes, with a substantial number of fatalities due to falling asleep with a lighted cigarette.

Firearms account for one-fifth of all injury deaths, and this is a uniquely American situation resulting from the easy access to guns. Of the 34,000 firearm deaths, about 1900 are unintentional and occur in the home. In neighborhoods with high crime rates, guns are often left where they are readily available when needed. Even after a gun-related injury, the method of storing the firearm often does not change.

In collisions with motor vehicles, bicycle riders are at fault over 90 percent of the time. Most of these bike riders are children, and this suggests that educational programs may be needed. Reflectors on wheels and pedals are now required in an effort to improve the visibility of bicycles at night.

Winter sports, water sports, and team sports are all associated with different types of injuries. Again, alcohol is a factor in winter sport and water sport injuries, including drowning. Football, baseball, and basketball produce the most injuries, although rates of injury are unknown. The following factors influence injury risk of team sports: (a) physical condition and skill of players, (b) rules of the game, (c) the physical environment, and (d) protective equipment. Downhill snow skiing is also known to be a high-risk activity.

Children are injured in a wide variety of settings. Because they spend so much time at school, it is not surprising that many injuries occur at school. In one study in Colorado, almost 10 percent of children were injured in a single school year. Boys were more likely to be injured than girls at all ages. Injury rates were highest in middle schools and lowest in high schools. The majority of the injuries occurred during sports. Fights also were frequent causes of injuries (Lenaway, Ambler, & Beaudoin, 1992).

Prevention

Many specific educational and behavior-change programs have been proposed for the prevention of injuries. However, policy changes and legislative approaches have been the most common strategies in this area. All of these approaches involve behavior change, including engineering, which requires that design improvements are implemented. Some major programs and proposals are reviewed in this section, along with a few examples of programs that have been carefully evaluated.

An engineering approach to preventing injuries is exemplified by efforts to reduce accidental aspirin overdoses in children in the early 1970s. In addition to putting children's aspirin in bottles too small to hold a lethal dose, child-proof caps were required. Over a 4-year period the number of reported aspirin poisonings decreased 60 percent (Barry, 1975). A wide variety of engineering changes were implemented in the construction of interstate highways beginning in 1969. Skid-resistant pavements, pedestrian and wildlife crossings, bicycle pathways, and median barriers led to a 20 percent reduction in fatality rates per mile traveled, compared with highways built before 1969 (Waller, 1986). When passive approaches to injury prevention can be used—that is, no behavior change is required, as in automobile air bags—the results are usually impressive. However, passive engineering approaches are not often available.

Both legislative and educational approaches require the individual to change behavior. These strategies are often combined, and the results are often disappointing. For example, when motorcycle riders are required by law to

BOX 13-2

FOCUS ON RESEARCH

Understanding Parental Injury Prevention Behaviors

Many steps have been taken to protect children from injury. For example, refrigerators are now designed so that children cannot trap themselves inside. Still, children must count on parents to help them avoid the daily dangers they confront. If a researcher is interested in preventing children's injuries, he or she must at some point study what parents do to protect children. Peterson, Farmer, and Kashani (1990) have conducted a major study of the psychological influences on parents' injury prevention behaviors.

They enlisted a representative sample of 198 parents of children aged 8 to 17. These parents completed a three-part questionnaire about children's safety. The questionnaire evaluated safety behaviors as well as predictors of those behaviors, based on the health belief model. Seven attitudinal factors in the following five categories were expected to be related to the safety behaviors:

1. Susceptibility—probability that the child will have a specific type of injury
2. Competence—*knowledge* about preventing an injury, and *skill* in teaching the child to avoid the injury
3. Responsibility—perception of parental responsibility for preventing an injury versus the school or government
4. Efficacy—belief that injuries are *preventable*, and *effectiveness* of teaching injury prevention skills
5. Cost—the effort involved in performing injury prevention behaviors

Ratings on each of these factors were used to explain whether parents taught their children about these 10 safety-related behaviors:

1. safe after-school activities
2. safe preparation of food
3. safe street crossing
4. safe bicycle riding
5. safe exit from a fire
6. safe treatment of a cut
7. safe treatment of a burn
8. safe way to answer the door
9. safe way to answer the phone
10. safe way to deal with a stranger outside the home

Four of the seven health belief factors were significant correlates of most of the 10 injury prevention behaviors. Knowledge of safety skills, competence to teach safety skills, effort to teach, and the extent to which teaching can prevent injuries were the significant factors.

The health belief factors did not explain other parental behaviors such as putting poison out of reach, putting guns in locked areas, installing a gate on the stairs, and using car seats or seat belts for children.

What do these results teach us about helping parents prevent childhood injuries? If parents knew about safety behaviors, felt competent about teaching those skills, and felt that those skills would be effective, they were more likely to teach safety skills to their children. These results point the way toward programs that focus on safety skills with obvious effectiveness. Parents not only need knowledge but also need to feel competent in teaching the safety skill. Videotape demonstrations—or better yet, supervised practice—would seem to be a promising approach.

Surprisingly, the more effort the teaching required, the more likely parents were to actually do the teaching. Maybe the most important safety behaviors are the most difficult to teach. On the other hand, maybe the parents who have already taught their children know how much effort it really takes.

Because the susceptibility factor was not found to be important, programs designed to increase fears that their children may be injured should not be expected to be effective (Peterson, Farmer & Kashani, 1990).

wear helmets, and the law is strictly enforced, over 90 percent of all riders wear helmets, and morbidity and mortality decline dramatically. When helmet laws are repealed, usually at the insistence of motorcycle riders, half of them stop wearing helmets and motorcycle death rates increase by one-third. Media campaigns to increase helmet use are usually ineffective (Waller, 1986).

Compulsory seat belt laws are more effective, even though they are rarely enforced. Seat belt laws reduce fatalities, but not as much as expected. It is felt that these laws are only partially successful because two high-risk groups, young drivers and drinking drivers, are particularly unlikely to use seat belts, even when required by law (Waller, 1986). It is in situations like this that more effective behavior-change strategies are needed, but it is because of pessimism about the power of behavior change that injury prevention experts have more interest in air bags than education.

Behavioral scientists have just started to develop and test methods of changing safety-related behaviors. There are some promising examples of community-based efforts to prevent injuries in children. One experimental program targeted bicycle helmet use among children in Seattle (Bergman, Rivara, Richards, & Rogers, 1990). This behavior was chosen because most of the 400,000 emergency room visits due to bicycle crashes of children and adolescents involved head injuries. While helmets can reduce head and brain injuries by 85 percent, only about 2 to 3 percent of all children wear helmets when biking. A preliminary survey revealed three major barriers to helmet use: (a) lack of awareness of the benefits, (b) cost of helmets ($40 to $60), and (c) children were reluctant to wear them.

Parent awareness of the risks of bicycle crashes and the effectiveness of helmets was increased by working with physicians, hospitals, and clinics. More important, mass media promotion of the "Head Smart" campaign featured physicians from local hospitals. By working with helmet manufacturers and retailers, helmets were offered for $20 to $25. Children's concerns about "being different" or "being a nerd" were addressed through recruiting local sports celebrities and demonstrations at schools. One method of evaluating the campaign was by observing how many children wore helmets while riding bikes. Observations were made in low-, middle-, and high-income neighborhoods in Seattle and in Portland, which had no special campaign. Observations started in the second year of the program. The

percentage wearing helmets increased from 5 to 16 percent in Seattle. In Portland, which had no program, the increase was only from 1 to 3 percent. The effect of the intervention was substantial, but the vast majority of the bicycle riders are still not wearing helmets. The effect on emergency room visits or severe injuries could not be determined in this study. Nevertheless, this is an example of a well-conceived community behavior-change program that targeted a problem that could not be solved through passive approaches.

Other community-based programs have been reported that were designed to promote several important safety behaviors for children. Encouraging results following school and physician interventions have been reported (Guyer et al., 1989). Injury prevention presents many opportunities for the application of behavior-change principles.

Summary

Unintentional injuries are an important cause of death and disability, especially among the young. Car crashes are the most common cause of injuries. Most people who die in car crashes—whether they are drivers, passengers, or pedestrians—have been drinking. Alcohol plays a role in many types of injuries, but drinking and driving are a particularly deadly combination. Men have more injuries of most types than women, except for elderly women, who have more hip fractures from falls. The most effective methods of injury prevention have involved passive approaches that do not require individual behavior change, for example, improved highway designs and automobile air bags. Laws have been the most common way to attempt to change injury-related behaviors. Some have been successful, such as seat belt laws, while laws requiring motorcycle riders to wear helmets have met with opposition. Educational approaches to behavior change have not been used very much, but a campaign to increase bicycle helmet wearing was partially successful.

VIOLENCE

Violence produces *intentional* injuries, which have different causes than the *unintentional* injuries discussed in the previous section. Violence occurs at a variety of levels, and different disciplines usually take responsibility for studying and controlling violence at each level. Personal violence, or suicide, is the province of mental health workers, because depression is closely linked with this risky behavior. Interpersonal violence is often studied by social psychologists and sociologists, but the control of interpersonal violence is left to the criminal justice system. Wars and group conflict are the domain of political science and governments.

Violent behavior has not been considered to be health-related, even though violence is designed to produce (and creates a great deal of) suffering and death, that is, morbidity and mortality. However, there is a trend for health professionals to become more involved in the study of violence and the search for effective methods of preventing violence and its impact on health. Historically, health professionals were not considered to have expertise in violent behavior, but they were expected to give care to the victims. Emergency room nurses and physicians working in urban neighborhoods are asked to patch up all the gunshot victims that appear every weekend, but they are not asked to help decrease the number of people shot in their communities, because this is the job of the police. Health professionals are no longer content to play such a passive role in this problem. The growth of a multidisciplinary approach to health care and the emphasis on prevention of health problems have led health professionals to recognize that

violence is a health behavior, not just a criminal behavior. The health community shares in the responsibility for reducing the toll of violence.

BOX 13·3

HEALTH OBJECTIVES FOR VIOLENT AND ABUSIVE BEHAVIOR FOR THE YEAR 2000

Reduce homicides to no more than 7.2 per 100,000 people (age-adjusted baseline: 8.5 per 100,000 in 1987).

GOAL FOR HOMICIDE DEATHS

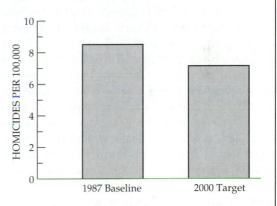

Reverse to less than 25.2 per 1000 the rising incidence of maltreatment of children younger than age 18 (baseline: 25.2 per 1000 in 1986).

Reduce physical abuse directed at women by male partners to no more than 27 per 1000 couples (baseline: 30 per 1000 in 1985).

GOAL FOR ABUSE OF WOMEN

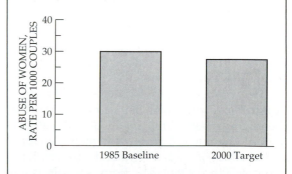

Some major categories of violent behavior are reviewed. The extent of the problem, probable causes, and strategies for prevention are discussed.

Homicide

Homicide is the twelfth leading cause of death for Americans in general, but it is the number one cause of death among African American males aged 14 to 44. This epidemic of violence among these young men is a problem of tremendous importance, but violence affects other groups as well. Homicide rates are high among children aged 3 and under, decrease in middle childhood, and then increase dramatically after age 15, before declining in the mid-thirties (Runyan & Gerken, 1989). Males of both races are twice as likely to be killed as women, but African Americans are much more likely to be killed than whites. The overall homicide rate for Latinos is about $2\frac{1}{2}$ times higher than the rate for non-Hispanic whites (Rosenberg & Mercy, 1992). This apparent difference among ethnic groups is more accurately seen as a reflection of the effects of poverty. When poverty is controlled statistically, the two races have very similar homicide rates (Runyan & Gerken, 1989). This suggests that no easy solution to the problem of homicide in the African American community is likely, because economic, employment, and educational disadvantage play a role in promoting violence.

In 1986 there were at least 22,000 homicide deaths in the United States, and the rate has increased since then (Rosenberg & Mercy, 1992). This homicide rate was the fifth highest in the world, behind Guatemala, Thailand, Puerto Rico, and Brazil. The United States has the highest homicide rate of any developed nation. The rate is 5 times as high as Canada's and 12 times as high as England's (Rosenberg, Stark, & Zahn, 1986). The homicide rate is not decreasing. In the past 25 years, homicide rates for children and adolescents in the United States have doubled (Division of Injury Control, 1990).

Only 4 percent of all homicides are "justifiable" on the basis of self-defense or police action, so the vast majority of homicides are murders. In 40 percent of the cases, the murderer is a friend or acquaintance, and in 15 percent of the cases, the murderer is a family member. Thirteen percent of the murders are committed by strangers, but one-third of the murderers had an unknown relationship to the victim. The vast majority of murders involved people of the same race and sex (Rosenberg & Mercy, 1992). The tendency for murderer and victim to know each other suggests that many murders reflect a breakdown in nonviolent conflict resolution. Easy access to lethal weapons may also play a role in acquaintance and family homicide.

Firearms are used in about 60 percent of all U.S. homicides, and any attempt to reduce homicide rates must take this fact into account. Another 20 percent of all homicides involve knives or other cutting instruments (Rosenberg & Mercy, 1992). Infants and young children are most likely to be killed by beatings from male parents and caretakers. However, by age 12 firearms become the most common means of homicide, and peers are the most common perpetrators (Christoffel, 1990). Firearms appear to be readily available, even to young people. In rural North Carolina, 75 percent of the teens said that they had guns in their homes. In Baltimore, about 50 percent of the males said that they had carried a gun to high school (Runyan & Gerken, 1989). A study of inner-city high schools in five cities indicated that about 6 percent occasionally carried a gun to school, but over 20 percent carried them outside of school. These guns are often used and appear to be creating a climate of fear in the schools. Almost 20 percent of boys said

BOX 13·4

FOCUS ON DIVERSITY

The Toll of Violence in an Inner-City African American Community

It is well known that homicide is a major cause of mortality, especially for young African Americans. Since many experts believe that homicide is just the tip of the iceberg of interpersonal violence, in order to understand the causes of homicide, it is necessary to study the full spectrum of violent acts. It is particularly important to understand violence in inner-city African American communities, because the need for action is so obvious there.

A recent study used emergency room records and death certificates to explore interpersonal violence in a poor inner-city population of about 70,000. Over 97 percent of the population was African American. Almost 2000 interpersonal injuries were seen in local emergency rooms over 1 year. The interpersonal injury rate of 30 people out of every 1000 was less than the rate for injuries from falls, but greater than the rate of injuries from motor vehicle crashes.

In this community of 70,000, 32 males and 9 females died from violence, and most of them were between ages 15 and 39. The highest months for interpersonal violence were in the summer, but firearm injuries were more common in November and December. Interpersonal violence was at its peak for both men and women during the twenties, and rates were very low after age 60.

Almost 300 stabbings were recorded, and 80 percent of the victims were male. There were 75 firearm injuries and 1500 assault injuries treated in emergency rooms. Seven women were treated for rape, although this is an underestimate because the hospitals with rape treatment programs were not in the local area. It was very disturbing that 63 children were treated for abuse during the year.

The magnitude of the violence problem in inner cities was clearly shown in this study. Forty-four percent of all deaths in this community were due to violence. The study also showed that homicides are only a small part of the violence in the homes and on the streets of our cities. Nearly 3 percent of the entire population was treated for the effects of violence during a single year. Children continue to suffer from violence, and because children with a violent past are likely to be violent themselves, there is a need for programs to reduce violence to children. It is hoped that data such as these will motivate people from all sectors of society to make violence prevention a priority in inner-city African American communities (Wishner, Schwarz, Grisso, Holmes, & Sutton, 1991).

they had been shot at, and 85 percent of boys and girls said they often feel afraid in school (Sheley, McGee, & Wright, 1992). Figures such as these highlight the need to take action to reduce the chance that firearms will be used in the heat of argument.

In fact, verbal arguments are the most common circumstances leading to a homicide; almost 40 percent of all murders start that way. About 20 percent of all murders are committed during a felony, such as a robbery or drug-related offense. Brawls, gangs, and prison killings account for another 20 percent, while the circumstances in the remainder are unknown (Rosenberg & Mercy, 1992).

Four types of prevention efforts have been attempted or proposed. The first is increased law enforcement, including more police patrols and tougher penalties for perpetrators. This approach may have some effect in selected situations, such as assaults on the streets; but it is unlikely to affect the most common categories of family and acquaintance homicide, which are not committed by repeat offenders.

The second category is gun control. The logic here is that decreasing the availability of the most lethal and most frequently used weapon will reduce homicide rates. In a recent study, Seattle, Washington, which has no gun control, was compared with nearby Vancouver, Canada, which has strict gun control. The homicide rate was 5 times higher in Seattle, and the difference was due to firearm-related homicides (Sloan, Kellerman, Reay, et al., 1988). Although gun control may be effective, there is significant political opposition, resulting in the current easy access to guns of all types.

The third approach to prevention is educational. Programs targeted to those at high risk of becoming perpetrators or victims of violence have been attempted. One such program targeted elementary school boys who were identified by teachers as being aggressive. The intervention consisted of 12 to 18 group sessions in which the boys learned nonviolent ways to solve social problems and practiced coping with stress nonaggressively. This cognitive-behavioral program produced improved behavior in the classroom and the home but the real test is the long-term effects. After three years, the treated group had less substance abuse and higher self-esteem scores than untreated boys. However, there were no long-term effects on delinquency rates or classroom behavior. These results suggest that intervention may need to continue over several years (Lochman, 1992). Other approaches to reducing aggression that are currently being studied are: training new parents to handle stress better, training high school students to resolve conflicts without violence, discouraging children from playing with guns, and reducing violence on television.

The fourth approach is to change the structure of society. Reducing poverty and the social disintegration and psychological stress that accompany it may be required before large decreases in violence among people will be seen.

Domestic Violence

Domestic violence is usually divided into three categories based on the victim of the abuse: child abuse, spouse abuse, and elderly abuse. Every year, 3 to 4 million women are assaulted in their homes by husbands, former husbands, boyfriends, and lovers (Stark & Flitcraft, 1992). Every year, about 1.6 million children are neglected, physically abused, or sexually abused (Christoffel, 1990). The burden on the health and social service systems created by family violence is enormous.

Spouse Abuse Almost 20 percent of abused women used emergency medical services (Stark & Flitcraft, 1992). Battering is a syndrome of repeated abuse, and battered women usually have multiple physical, emotional, and substance abuse problems. Battered women have a pattern of multiple visits to medical and psychiatric clinics for a variety of complaints, creating a significant use of health resources. Abuse may be the single most frequent cause of serious injury to women, and may account for 3 times the number of visits to health professionals as motor vehicle crashes (Stark & Flitcraft, 1992).

Despite frequent contact with health professionals, battering often goes undetected. It appears that substantial numbers of women admitted to hospitals with injuries are in fact victims of abuse. However, unless specific "trauma histories" are taken, physicians fail to identify the vast majority of cases. One study found that health care providers identified only 1 out of every 25 cases of abuse (Stark & Flitcraft, 1992). However, the medical profession is starting to recognize the seriousness of the problem of violence against women (Council on Scientific Affairs, 1992).

While women are known to use force against men during arguments, battering is almost always done by men to women. Battering is usually not an isolated event, as half the husbands who beat their wives do so at least 3 times per year. Women are more likely to be battered when they have higher educational or occupational status than their partners, or when the man is unemployed or consistently underemployed. The relationship between risk of battering and race and socioeconomic status is not clear. Some studies indicate that poor minority women are most likely to be battered, but other studies show only small differences between economic groups.

Battered women often develop other difficulties. Large percentages of rape victims, female alcoholics, and suicide attempters reported histories of battering. There appears to be a connection to child abuse, in that men who beat women are also likely to beat their children. Unfortunately, it appears that spouse abuse rarely corrects itself (Stark & Flitcraft, 1992). Active prevention and treatment programs are needed to reduce this form of violence.

There are three models often used to explain spousal abuse (Stark & Flitcraft, 1992). The *interpersonal violence model* states that violence occurs when adults lack the skills to respond appropriately to stress and conflict. Lack of interpersonal skills, psychological problems, and personality profile are believed to lead to domestic violence. Although these factors have not been documented to lead to spouse abuse, cognitive-behavioral therapy for victims and skills training programs for batterers have been shown to be effective.

The *family violence model* emphasizes the effect of the norms in American society for using violence to resolve conflict. Conflicts within the family are seen as having high intensity, and violence is even more likely when a family member experienced violence in childhood or is living with the stress of poverty. The clustering of spouse and child abuse in the same family supports the concept that this is a "family" problem, as does the finding that some abused children grow up to be abusive adults.

BOX 13·5

FOCUS ON WOMEN

Date Rape: A Major Threat for College Women

Surprisingly large numbers of college women report that they have been victims of rape. In one study involving 3187 women and 2972 men attending 32 colleges in the United States, over 15 percent of the women reported that they had been rape victims while an additional 12 percent reported being the victim of attempted rape. Perhaps most troubling was the finding that 90 percent of the women who reported being raped were the victims of someone who was an acquaintance. Actually, rape by strangers was relatively uncommon (11 percent), while 53 percent were the victims of either casual dates or steady dates (Koss, Gidycz, & Wisniewski, 1987). Rates of date rape and assault are increasing. Those who were raped by acquaintances are often shocked that someone they know could assault them. When these incidents are reported to the police or medical authorities, the women may be either calm and detached or crying and angry. After the initial emotions subside, they often return and intensify. The victim may seek help for the emotional symptoms without telling the health care provider about the rape.

The long-term effects of rape are similar to other forms of post-traumatic stress disorder. Many types of psychological distress are both common and long-lasting. Suicidal thoughts are extremely common, and almost 20 percent of rape victims report suicide attempts. The consequences of acquaintance rape are as severe as those for stranger rape (Council on Scientific Affairs, 1992).

Victimization has important health consequences for women. Beyond damages that may result from the attack, such as gynecological trauma and risk for sexually transmitted disease, women who experience victimization may be 2.5 times more likely to use physicians' services and outpatient treatment (Koss, Koss, & Woodruff, 1991).

However, most spouse abusers were not subjected to violence when they were children. This model does not lead to specific intervention strategies.

The *gender-politics model* views family violence as one of many examples of male dominance in our society. When men perceive that their access to money, status, or sex is threatened by a woman's actions, then violence is one type of response. Women may stay in abusive relationships because of fear of being alone, and absence of adequate resources makes escape an unattractive option. This model is supported by evidence that arguments about women's traditional responsibilities at home are the most common topics of conflict that lead to abuse. This model leads to recommendations for punishment of male violence, funding for women's shelters, and support for women's economic independence. However, the effectiveness of such approaches has not been documented.

Child Abuse Several decades ago, child abuse was rarely talked about, and abusive parents were assumed to be mentally ill. This attitude changed dramatically in the 1960s and 1970s, when the approach shifted to helping abusive parents become more effective caregivers. Child abuse came to be seen within the context of other family disturbances. The definition of *child abuse* was widened from a focus on physical injury to include child neglect, emotional injury, sexual maltreatment, and deprivation of medical care (Newberger, 1992).

Protecting children from abuse and neglect has become such a high priority issue over the past few decades that all 50 states now have mandatory reporting laws. All professionals who suspect abuse must now report their findings to social service agencies, which investigate the situation and take appropriate action. During the 1980s reports of severe physical abuse did not increase, but the 200 percent increase in reports of sexual abuse reflected growing awareness of this problem.

Fatal child abuse is confined primarily to infants and very young children, and child abuse is the fifth leading cause of death between the ages of 1 and 18 (Newberger, 1992). Nonfatal child abuse tends to continue into adolescence. There are many serious physical and psychological consequences of child abuse. Sexual abuse can lead to sexually transmitted diseases in children, so one may expect that the HIV virus is sometimes transmitted in this manner. Child abuse can lead to injury of every organ system, depending on the form of abuse. Common examples include scalds, burn marks, poisonings, cuts, bruises on the skin and internal organs, brain damage, and malnutrition. Psychological and behavioral outcomes include aggression, language disorders, decreased intellectual functioning, phobias, nightmares, changes in eating and sleeping patterns, abdominal pain, and headaches. Psychological symptoms appear to be more severe when force is used in sexual acts (Newberger, 1992).

Several studies indicate that physical abuse is more common in poor homes, when the mother is young, and when the child was unwanted. Sexual abuse is equally likely in both rich and poor homes. The vast majority of sexual abuse victims are female, and the peak ages of risk are 6 to 7 years and 10 to 12 years. Sexual abuse is more likely when there is discord among parents, when a parent is absent, and when parents are cold and punitive (Christoffel, 1990).

Past approaches to child abuse focused on punishment of abusers, but a human service model is now more common. It is often unclear whether a child should be removed from the home after abuse has been detected. Important strengths of the family may not be readily apparent, and group homes and foster homes are often not ideal nurturing environments. On the other hand, the risk of leaving a child with an abusive family may be great. Child Protective Services workers are typically so overburdened that they do not have the capacity to make a thorough assessment before deciding to remove the child or not. Interventions need to both protect the child and develop support for the family so that the child can be safely returned to an improved family environment. Approaches involving a multidisciplinary team in the hospital, coordination with social services agencies, and systematic follow-up produce shorter hospitalizations, lower cost of treatment, and lower reinjury rates (Newberger et al., 1973).

The most promising method of preventing child abuse is by providing child care aides on a regular basis to high-risk families. Child care aides may be trained volunteers who visit weekly and provide various forms of assistance. They can answer questions about child care, demonstrate how to take care of the baby, provide transportation, and simply be companions. When this service was supplied to single teenage first-time mothers, rates of maltreatment were 75 percent lower than in a control group (Olds, Henderson, Chamberlin, & Tatelbaum, 1986). In addition, emergency room visits were 50 percent lower, mothers with aides did not spank their children, and the mothers felt more positive about their infants. This simple intervention appears to be effective in preventing child abuse.

Educational programs to prevent child abuse have become common in recent years. Most of them teach children how to recognize and protect themselves from sexual abuse. In one study 4-year-olds were taught how to respond to appropriate and inappropriate requests to look at and touch their private parts (Wurtele, 1990). Compared with children in a control group, trained children were better able to correctly identify examples of inappropriate touching and to know effective ways

of preventing abuse. The program did not increase either problem behaviors or fearfulness, as reported by parents and teachers. However, it is not known how effective such programs are in actually reducing sexual victimization.

Elder Abuse   The problem of elder abuse was rarely discussed prior to the 1980s, so this is a new topic on the public agenda. As more and more people live long lives, the maltreatment of the elderly becomes a more important issue. Because of decline in physical or cognitive functioning, or both, many elderly persons depend upon others to meet some of their basic needs. This is not to imply that most older people are frail and senile, because the vast majority function independently throughout their lives. Only about 5 percent of the elderly will ever need to move to a nursing home.

Although definitions of *elder abuse* vary widely, four aspects are usually considered to be part of the problem. Physical violence is clearly abuse. Psychological or emotional abuse, including verbal assault, is also of concern, because of the vulnerability of the elderly. Misuse or theft of the elderly's property or finances is a common and serious problem, and many elders have few resources with which to defend themselves. Finally, intentional failure of a designated caregiver to meet the needs of an elder is considered maltreatment (Pillemer & Frankel, 1992). Many elderly people fall into a gray zone in which they are neglected because there is no identified caregiver, and they are unable to take care of themselves. Elder abuse can take place in a private home or in a nursing home.

As with all forms of abuse, it is impossible to obtain accurate estimates of the incidence of the problem. In 1985 it was estimated that between 51,000 and 186,000 cases of elder abuse were reported to authorities in the United States (Pillemer & Frankel, 1992). By the late 1980s, however, all states had established systems of reporting and responding to elder abuse and neglect.

The causes and outcomes of elder abuse are not yet well known. However, parallels are usually drawn to child abuse. Perpetrators are seen as lacking the ability to resolve conflict nonviolently. The victims tend to be female and vulnerable because of a physical impairment; they usually live with the perpetrator. The concept of *caregiver stress* is sometimes used to explain elder abuse. When children are called on to care for their parents, this represents a reversal of the usual direction of support. As the demands on the caregiver increase, their rewards for taking care of a parent typically decrease. If the caregiver perceives this as an unfair situation and there is no escape, the risk of abuse increases.

Another possible explanation of elder abuse is derived from the finding that abusers are likely to be financially dependent on their victims. An adult offspring or spouse who is dependent on an ill elderly person for income or housing may come to resent their own powerlessness. It may seem unfair that a "weaker" person has that much control over their lives. Dissatisfaction with the situation may lead to abuse.

Both the caregiver stress and financial dependency models have one thing in common. When there is an imbalance of dependency—for example, between a child and a parent—there is a risk of elder abuse. These interpersonal situations may be worsened by socioeconomic deprivation or social isolation (Pillemer & Frankel, 1992).

Few interventions to prevent or respond to elder abuse have been evaluated, but several different types of programs are being implemented around the United States. Mandatory reporting laws have been adopted from the child abuse field, and such laws are on the books in all 50 states. In addition to the problem of different definitions of elder abuse, the laws are not well enforced, and there is a lack of funds for services to victims and abusers.

Some professionals argue that the mandatory reporting laws limit an elderly person's ability to control their own lives and that the laws treat them like children.

Protective service programs for the elderly are again based on the child abuse model. When an elderly person is judged incompetent, a guardian is appointed. Many believe that this approach intrudes on the civil rights of the elderly. When abuse or incompetence is defined too broadly, this has the effect of interfering with family affairs and treating the elder as a child.

If it is assumed that caregiver stress leads to the abuse, the intervention goal is to relieve some of the burden of caregiving. Housekeeping and meal preparation services can give the caregiver a chance to get out of the home for a while. However, this pattern of abuse probably occurs only in a minority of cases.

If it is assumed that the elder is abused by a dependent relative, the approach is similar to that taken with battered women. The perpetrator can be handled by the criminal justice system, and the victim is helped through emergency shelters or periodic social support (Pillemer & Frankel, 1992).

Public recognition of elder abuse is still limited, so both laypeople and health professionals need to increase their awareness of this problem. Elder abuse could be viewed as an outcome of our society's lack of consensus on the role of the elderly in society. Children are often unwilling to assume responsibility for taking care of their parents, but there are limited facilities that provide adequate care for the elderly. Many of the current approaches to elder abuse are not effective because needed support services are underfunded and other approaches take away the elder's personal control over his or her life.

Summary

Until recently, it was largely accepted that violence was the responsibility of the criminal justice system, and the health care system was responsible only for patching up the victims. Because violence has such a major impact on the health care system, public health and behavioral scientists are now working to prevent interpersonal violence. The United States has the highest homicide rate in the world, and murder is the number one cause of death for young African American men. Firearms are used in two-thirds of all murders, and it appears that easy access to firearms is a major factor in the current high murder rate.

The most common forms of domestic violence are men beating their wives and physical and sexual maltreatment of children. Battered women tend to be beaten repeatedly, and they develop a variety of physical and psychological problems that lead to multiple contacts with the health care system. The amount of child abuse has created a continuing overload on the social service system, thus it can deal with only the most serious offenses. Although reports of physical abuse are continuing to be high, the rate appears to be stable. However, during the 1980s reports of child sexual abuse skyrocketed, reflecting increasing public awareness and concern. The focus of current approaches is to try to strengthen the family rather than just punish the abuser. Providing volunteer parenting aides to high-risk families is an effective method of preventing child abuse. A few programs to teach children how to discourage sexual abuse have been reported, but health psychologists are just beginning to get involved in the prevention of interpersonal violence.

Elder abuse came to be recognized as a problem during the 1980s. Elder abuse can include misuse of property and neglect by a caretaker, as well as physical and emotional abuse. The elderly are vulnerable to abuse, and most abusers are relatives. If the elderly person is extremely dependent on the caregiver, or if an offspring or spouse is financially dependent upon the elder, then the risk of abuse seems to be increased. While all 50 states require elder abuse to be reported, current interventions tend to intrude on the rights of elders to make decisions for themselves.

SUBSTANCE ABUSE

The Health Effects of Alcohol

The consumption of alcohol is a behavior with many effects on physical, psychological, and social health. Alcohol use and abuse have been criticized for centuries on a moral and religious basis, but here we examine mainly the health consequences of alcohol consumption. High intakes of alcohol over a long period of time have been associated with morbidity and mortality from the following causes:

- cirrhosis of the liver
- cancers at various sites
- cardiovascular diseases
- motor vehicle crashes
- violence, including suicide and homicide
- other forms of trauma
- birth defects, including mental retardation

It is estimated that 10.5 million U.S. adults are addicted to alcohol, and an additional 7.2 million abuse alcohol. Surveys of high school seniors indicate that about 60 percent reported drinking alcohol in the past 30 days. Total costs of alcohol abuse to the nation were estimated at $128.3 billion in 1986, with this figure including decreased productivity and absences from work. Costs for health care for alcohol-related injuries and illnesses amounted to $16.5 million (U.S. Department of Health and Human Services, 1990). The large number of potentially serious health problems associated with alcohol abuse combines with the large number of problem drinkers to make this a health behavior of serious concern.

One of the most fascinating questions about the alcohol-health relationship is illustrated in Figure 13-2. This shows the risk of dying from all causes at different levels of alcohol consumption. In general, the graph clearly indi-

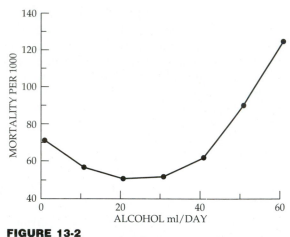

FIGURE 13-2

Mortality from all causes by alcohol. (Data combined from Kagan et al. and Criqui, 1985.)

HEALTH OBJECTIVES FOR ALCOHOL FOR THE YEAR 2000

Reduce deaths caused by alcohol-related motor vehicle crashes to no more than 8.5 per 100,000 people (age-adjusted baseline: 9.8 per 100,000 in 1987).

YEAR 2000 GOAL FOR AUTO CRASH DEATHS

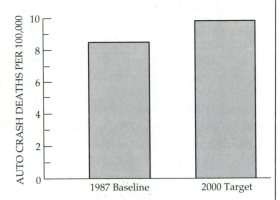

Reduce alcohol consumption by people aged 14 and older to an annual average of no more than 2 gal of ethanol per person (baseline: 2.54 gal of ethanol in 1987).

YEAR 2000 GOAL FOR ALCOHOL USE

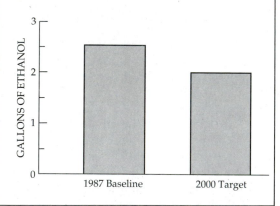

cates that the more alcohol drunk, the higher the risk of dying. The exception is at the lowest levels of use. Nondrinkers are typically found to have higher rates of death than light drinkers. Because the curve dips up at the left, it is called a *J-shaped curve.* The reasons for that J-shape are not known, but there has been a great deal of debate.

One idea is that one or two beers or glasses of wine a night are relaxing and help reduce the stress of the workday. This is a reasonable guess, but it has not been proved. Light drinkers tend to have lower blood pressures and high levels of (protective) HDL cholesterol. It is possible that these apparently beneficial effects of light drinking reduce risk of mortality. While the search for a reason continues, the fact remains that light drinkers live a little longer than teetotalers.

There is a good lesson here in the interpretation of health research. This finding of the apparent benefits of light drinking should not be used as a justification to either take up or continue drinking alcohol. It would be foolish to think of drinking as a health-promoting habit. The protection provided by light drinking is small, especially when compared with the very serious health and social risks of heavy drinking. The widespread abuse of alcohol testifies to the difficulty of controlling intake. You may start out with the intention of being a controlled light drinker, but you probably know of people whose drinking slowly went out of control. If you do not drink, these research results do not provide a reason for starting. If you already drink, these results should encourage you to decrease your intake.

Although alcohol has harmful effects on virtually every system in the body (U.S. Department of Health and Human Services, 1990), it is difficult to accurately estimate the impact of alcohol on the health of the American population. That is because alcohol leads to a number of disorders, and people are diagnosed as having cancer or cardiovascular disease (CVD) rather than alcohol-associated morbidity. Alcohol use itself is underestimated because physicians fail to adequately assess alcohol use and patients underreport their intake (U.S. Department of Health and Human Services, 1990). People who use alcohol regularly also tend to smoke cigarettes and drink coffee (Istvan & Matarazzo, 1984). All of these behaviors are harmful to health, and it is difficult to sort out their effects. Sometimes these behaviors interact. For example, smoking or drinking by themselves are weak risk factors for stomach cancer, but people who drink *and* smoke place themselves at very high risk for developing stomach cancer.

The complexity of alcohol's relationship to health is illustrated by its effects on the cardiovascular system (Criqui, 1985). Heavy drinking can have toxic effects on the heart muscle itself and can cause irregular heart rhythms. Drinkers tend to have higher levels of triglycerides, or fats in the blood, which increases risk. However, high levels of alcohol use are associated with higher levels of (protective) HDL-cholesterol and lower levels of LDL, indicating decreased risk of cardiovascular disease. Risk of hypertension is strongly associated with alcohol intake, and it seems likely that blood pressure is increased during alcohol withdrawal. Alcohol may also affect the tendency to form blood clots. Thus, alcohol has a number of effects on the heart and CVD risk factors. While not all of these effects increase risk, certainly the overall outcome is that drinking, particularly heavy drinking, increases risk of morbidity and mortality from cardiovascular diseases.

Alcohol is toxic to several bodily systems. The liver is severely affected, and cirrhosis of the liver kills many long-term alcohol abusers. Alcohol decreases levels of testosterone in men and disrupts the menstrual cycle in women. Alcohol is a major cause of pregnancy complications and birth defects, so it is essential for women who are pregnant or trying to become pregnant to completely avoid alcohol. Of course, alcohol has detrimental effects on the brain and nervous system, leading to impairments in memory, reasoning, and motor function. Though often not considered, excessive alcohol intake often leads to nutritional problems due to an inadequate diet. Most of these problems are particularly serious among those who have been drinking heavily for years, but adolescents and young adults are affected in similar ways (Arria, Tarter, & Van Thiel, 1991).

The Health Effects of Illicit Drugs

The direct health effects of illicit drugs differ greatly, depending upon the type of drug. Stimulant drugs, such as methamphetamine, are widely abused and often associated with loss of appetite and paranoia. At high doses they can cause convulsions. Although there are reports of cocaine-induced heart failure, this appears to be rare. Heroin overdoses cause death by depressing the respiratory system. Hallucinogens may trigger mental disorders in susceptible individuals. The primary health problem of marijuana use appears to be lung damage caused by long-term heavy smoking. Public health experts point out that very few deaths in the United States are directly caused by illicit drugs. The legal drugs are much more lethal. Tobacco is the most important preventable cause of both death and disability, and alcohol abuse leads to multiple serious health problems. The direct health effects of illicit drugs should be kept in perspective.

On the other hand, the indirect health effects of illicit drugs are worthy of our concern. The costs of drug abuse include lost productivity from work, violence associated with the illegal drug trade, problems arising from drug abuse during pregnancy, risk of injuries, and the costs of drug rehabilitation programs. The billions of dollars spent on law enforcement efforts to apprehend and punish drug abusers and dealers are controversial. The prison population in the United States more than doubled in the 1980s, and much of that increase was due to longer sentences for drug-related crimes. Some policymakers question the wisdom of this costly approach that seems to have had little effect on the use of illicit drugs.

Crack cocaine is a cheap form of this highly addictive drug that became available during the 1980s. A major health problem associated with its use is exposure of the fetus because of the mother's cocaine use. It is estimated that between 100,000 and 250,000 fetuses are exposed to cocaine each year. Cocaine exposure reduces growth in the uterus, increases risk of malformations, and produces abnormalities in the neurological and circulatory systems. Low birthweight leads to numerous complications, and cocaine-exposed newborns stay in the hospital longer and and have much higher medical bills than other infants. Medical, psychological, and behavioral problems are seen during childhood (Phibbs, Bateman, & Schwartz, 1991). Cocaine appears to be highly toxic to babies, so if prevention and treatment programs are not provided, we as a society will be paying the price of this problem for decades to come.

Another important indirect health effect of drug use is increased risk of HIV infection. It is well known that intravenous (IV) drug users infect one another with HIV by sharing contaminated needles. However, heterosexual contact with IV drug users is an important method of HIV transmission. A study of methadone maintenance patients found high rates of risky sexual behaviors. Men were unlikely to use condoms, and women were likely to have unprotected sex with IV drug–using men (Schilling, El-Bassel, Schinke, et al., 1991).

Illicit drugs are commonly used. In 1985, over 60 percent of those aged 18 to 34 reported using some type of illicit drug sometime in their lifetime. Fourteen percent of the teenagers said that they used drugs some time in the past month, with the most common drug being marijuana. Over 20 percent of those aged 18 to 34 used drugs in the past month (Schuster & Kilbey, 1992).

It is often assumed that because most people who are arrested for drug-related crimes are black or Latino that these groups are more likely to use drugs. This is probably an incorrect assumption. In one study, Latino adolescents had higher rates than non-Hispanic whites of marijuana, cocaine, and glue sniffing use. However, when rates were adjusted for school grades and mother's education, the non-Hispanic white youth had higher rates of substance use. Similar to findings for other health behaviors, it appears that socioeconomic factors are more important influences than race or ethnicity (Schinke et al., 1992).

Patterns of Substance Use

There are many patterns of alcohol use; some are strongly associated with negative health outcomes, and some are not. The majority of drinkers are those who are likely to experience no health or social problems as a result of alcohol use and who have little difficulty controlling or stopping their drinking. These are the *social drinkers*. They are at some risk because infrequent episodes of heavy drinking could lead to a car crash.

Alcohol abusers are those who have high-risk patterns of drinking but who are not dependent on alcohol. People in this group may not drink every day, but they occasionally or frequently get drunk. At those times, there is risk of trauma from impaired judgment and motor function, and the high dose of alcohol creates stress on many body systems.

Alcoholics are dependent on alcohol. They experience impaired judgment and associated social problems. The health effects of chronic drinking can be severe, and the physical and psychological dependence on alcohol results in an inability to control drinking. It is the impaired control that defines the important difference between alcohol abusers and alcoholics (U.S. Department of Health and Human Services, 1990). Another common requirement for the diagnosis of alcoholism is alcohol-related health, social, or economic problems.

Because the term *alcoholism* means so many different things to different people, *alcohol addiction* has been suggested as a less ambiguous term (Lawson, 1986). Alcohol is addictive in the classical meaning. With continued use, tolerance develops whereby more alcohol is needed to produce the same effect. Withdrawal symptoms can occur after prolonged heavy alcohol use, and the severity ranges from mild to life-threatening. Withdrawal symptoms include tremor, profuse sweating, muscle cramps, seizures, confusion, and hallucinations (delirium tremens).

Polydrug abuse means that a person abuses more than one substance. People who use or abuse one drug usually abuse additional drugs, although they may have one drug of choice. People who abuse drugs are likely to abuse alcohol as well. Cigarette smoking is also very common in polydrug abusers. Kandel (1978) has described a typical progression of substance use. Many people consider to-

bacco to be the main "gateway" drug that often leads to other substance abuse, but many teenagers begin using alcohol first. After alcohol and cigarettes, the next drug in the progression is usually marijuana. Those who smoke marijuana are very likely to initiate use of other illicit drugs.

Etiology

Similar factors appear to influence the use and abuse of alcohol and other drugs. Most people begin abusing alcohol or drugs before age 21, so etiologic studies focus on teenagers (Schuster & Kilbey, 1992).

1. Anxiety disorders appear to precede substance abuse, so drugs may be taken in an attempt to reduce anxiety.
2. As with smoking, peer behavior is important. If your friends use alcohol or drugs, you probably will too.
3. Teenagers from dysfunctional families or families with other substance abusers are at risk of substance abuse.
4. Young people from low socioeconomic status families are more likely to become substance abusers, although there are clearly many affluent adolescents who develop alcohol and drug problems.
5. Substance abuse among young people is typically part of a pattern of deviant behavior. Alcohol or drug abusers tend to have low grades, are motivated by sensation seeking, tend to be aggressive, and have a history of getting into difficulties with authorities.

There are two major competing models of the origins of alcohol abuse, and they are rarely applied to drug abuse. These dominant models of alcohol abuse suggest two different approaches to prevention and treatment. The *traditional model* views alcoholism as a disease with largely genetic origins (Pattison, Sobell, &

BOX 13·7

FOCUS ON WOMEN

Alcohol and Drug Use in Women

The women's movement has led researchers to question some of their assumptions about substance abuse among females. Most studies have not presented results separately for men and women, thus assuming that substance use is similar in both genders. In the past, researchers complained that it was more difficult to study women: they were harder to follow because their names changed after marriage. However, it is now clear that there are some important biological, psychological, social, and cultural differences related to substance use in women and men.

The most obvious difference is in patterns of substance use. Women are less likely to use and abuse alcohol and illicit drugs. Sixty-one percent of the men reported using alcohol in the past month, compared with 47 percent of the women. Nine percent of the men used an illict drug in the past month, while 6 percent of the women said that they did. Women are less likely to drink alcohol daily, to drink continuously, or to engage in drinking binges.

There appear to be gender differences in the causes and consequences of alcohol and drug use, although there are more studies on alcohol use. Alcoholic women are more likely to have an alcoholic role model in their families of origin or to have an alcoholic spouse. This suggests that women's drinking may be more influenced by social factors. Women are more likely to attribute their alcohol problems to specific stressful events. Very often these are related to crises in reproduction, such as unwanted pregnancy, miscarriage, or failure to become pregnant.

Alcoholic men tend to have antisocial personality disorders, while alcoholic women tend to have affective disorders. There is also much more societal disapproval of alcohol abuse in women. It is seen as more of a character flaw, and this may be related to the depression and guilt experienced by these women.

The most important alcohol-related social consequences for women are disruptions in family life, such as separation and divorce. For men, the most important disruptions are career-related, such as loss of a job.

Women are more likely to have psychiatric treatment, but they are less likely to come into contact with the criminal justice system. Women are said to experience a "telescoping" of medical consequences. This means that it takes less time for health problems to occur. Alcoholic women have rapid development of gynecological, cardiovascular, gastrointestinal, and liver diseases. The effects of drinking on the developing fetus are numerous and serious. The fetal alcohol syndrome includes low birthweight, malformations, and mental retardation. Alcohol-related disruptions of reproductive function can include amenorrhea (failure to menstruate), anovulation, ovarian atrophy, spontaneous abortion, and early menopause. These reproductive changes may be due to alcohol effects on the brain or hormonal systems.

In a study of the causes of mortality in alcoholic women, the most common cause was liver disorders. The average age at death was 45. The next largest category was violence and unintentional injuries, with a mean age of 50. These accounted for 60 percent of the deaths of these alcoholic women.

Women and men in treatment for cocaine abuse have been compared. They were found to be generally similar in their drug habits, although women had been using cocaine for a shorter period. Men spent 3 times as much on cocaine during the previous 6 months (over $9000). More women than men lived with a drug-dependent partner. (It has been found that men tend to influence their female partners to use and abuse drugs.) Similar to findings with alcoholics, women were more likely to be depressed, and only men were diagnosed as having antisocial personalities. Women reported four main reasons for using cocaine: depression, feeling unsociable, family and job pressures, and health problems.

These biological, psychological, social, and cultural differences in drug-abusing women and men are striking. Women are less likely to be substance abusers, but those who are have more adverse health outcomes. Female substance abusers are likely to be depressed, so a combination of services needs to be provided. Hopefully, further research will provide clues on more effective approaches to preventing substance abuse in women (Lex, 1991).

Sobell, 1977). This model is based on the notion that alcoholism is progressive and irreversible. The patient has an uncontrollable compulsion to drink because of genetic or physiological factors largely beyond his or her control. The only reasonable treatment goal in this model is lifelong abstinence; there is no cure, much as an insulin-dependent diabetic can be controlled but not cured. Alcoholics Anonymous is a lifelong treatment approach which emphasizes that alcoholics are unable to control their own drinking. Twin studies have provided data in support of the genetic transmission of some types of alcoholism (Cloninger, Bohman, & Sigvardsson, 1981), but it is clear that having alcoholic parents does not guarantee that the children will become alcoholics.

The *behavioral model* of alcoholism is based on the notion that drinking is a learned behavior under social control (Pattison et al., 1977). In contrast to the disease model which suggests that people are either diagnosable as alcoholics or not, the behavioral model recognizes that drinking habits fall along all points of a broad spectrum. Treatment goals for alcohol addiction may include either abstinence or controlled drinking, because the primary objective is to restore a high level of functioning to the individual. The method of treatment is to provide new skills that can be used to control drinking. The behavioral model emphasizes improving personal control over drinking, instead of teaching that one has no control. There are hundreds of studies documenting both that social and psychological factors influence drinking patterns and that behavioral treatments are effective in achieving both abstinence and controlled drinking (Nathan & Skinstad, 1987). For example, it is clear that the expectation that alcohol will have desirable consequences, especially among unskilled persons in social settings, produces a craving for alcohol (Wilson, 1987). The important influence of expectation was illustrated by Marlatt, Demming, and Reid (1973), who found that the amount consumed was determined not by the *actual* alcohol content but by the *perceived* alcohol content.

Today, the prevailing view is that alcoholism probably results from an interaction of genetic and environmental factors. Genetically susceptible persons appear to develop alcohol problems when there is social pressure or permission to drink, when alcohol is available, and when alcohol fulfills a perceived need of the person. The etiology of alcohol problems is a very active research field which has drawn the interest of both behavioral and biological researchers.

Prevention

The prevention of problem drinking is a well-developed field, but there have been fewer rigorous studies of substance abuse prevention. While special groups such as children from alcoholic families, delinquents, and school dropouts have received targeted prevention programs, most programs have been implemented generally for adolescents in the school setting.

Alcohol education programs often produce important changes in knowledge and attitudes, but they rarely lead to demonstrable changes in drinking behavior (Staulcup, Kenward, & Frigo, 1979). Behaviorally oriented approaches are similar to smoking prevention programs. Here students learn to identify and resist pressures to abuse substances from the media, from adults, and from peers. They specifically practice refusing offers to indulge. It has been common for prevention programs to target cigarettes, alcohol, and drug use (McAlister et al., 1980), because the refusal skills apply to all these substances. In one large study conducted in Los Angeles, over 5000 seventh graders participated in 12 prevention lessons or were part of the control group. The program was successful in reducing the onset of cigarette, alcohol, and marijuana use (Hansen et al., 1988). A follow-up report showed that the program was most successful with delaying cigarette use and that alcohol use was significantly reduced (Graham et al., 1990). The least effects were seen with marijuana. The program was successful for females, but not for males. The program was most effective for Asians and least effective for whites. Success rates for African Americans and Latinos were in between. Because substance use prevention programs are not effective for all groups, improvements are needed.

Another population in need of increased attention by prevention experts is women. It appears that, at the same level of alcohol use, women are more likely than men to experience successful suicide, death from injuries, and cirrhosis of the liver (Hill, 1982). Fortunately, women are less likely to be problem drinkers than men. This may be due to social norms that tolerate more drinking among men than women. For example, prime-time television shows typically portray drinking as more acceptable in men than women (Breed & DeFoe, 1981). Few prevention programs specifically aimed at women have been reported. However, there is substantial interest in targeting pregnant women for alcohol prevention because of the significant damage that alcohol can cause in the fetus. An extensive program to prevent fetal alcohol syndrome was implemented in Seattle (Little, Streissguth, & Guzinski, 1980). The intervention included efforts to educate pregnant women, to inform medical professionals about the program, to improve clinical services for pregnant women, and to access services for fetal alcohol syndrome children. A quasi-experimental evaluation of the project indicated that it was associated with increased knowledge of the public about the harmful effects of maternal alcohol use on the fetus. Most important, there was evidence of decreased alcohol use among pregnant women (Lowman, 1982).

Other approaches to prevention of problem drinking and its consequences include increasing the price of alcoholic beverages. Although it is a basic principle of economics that increased price should lead to reduced consumption, there is considerable controversy about whether alcohol behaves the same way as other consumer goods. The data generally indicate that alcohol consumption is related to price, but the relationship may depend upon the type of beverage (that is, beer, wine, spirits) and the country being studied (Cook, 1981). More research is still needed to determine whether increased alcohol taxes have any effect whatever on rates of problem drinking, drunk driving, and other alcohol-related health problems.

Treatment

A wide variety of treatment approaches for alcoholism and problem drinking have been reported in recent decades, ranging from general alcohol education to Alcoholics Anonymous to classical conditioning to multicomponent behavioral methods. Because the alcohol education approach has generally not been found to be effective, and Alcoholics Anonymous is by its nature difficult to evaluate, behavioral approaches are highlighted here.

The earliest behavioral approaches to treatment of problem drinking attempted to suppress the behavior through conditioning. Pairing electrical shocks with drinking in the treatment setting was found to be ineffective (Wilson, 1978), so this method has been abandoned. However, inducing vomiting when the subject drank was a more promising approach (Lang & Marlatt, 1982). A variation on this treatment is still widely used. It involves taking daily doses of the drug Antabuse (disulfiram), which produces severe discomfort and nausea if alcohol is consumed but is not life-threatening. Antabuse is routinely prescribed for alcoholics as a part of their treatment because it is effective at controlling impulsive drinking. However, compliance with Antabuse is a major difficulty, and the drug does nothing to control the urge to drink.

Conditioning can also be used to teach controlled drinking. In an early study, Mills, Sobell, and Schaefer (1971) shocked the fingers of alcoholics who ordered "straight" drinks, took large gulps of alcohol, or ordered more than three drinks in a laboratory "bar." The alcoholics avoided shocks by ordering three or fewer beer, wine, or mixed drinks, and by sipping instead of gulping. The therapists were attempting to train them in social drinking patterns. However, when the patients were outside the laboratory and away from the shocks, they quickly returned to their usual drinking habits. The realization that it is difficult to generalize treatment gains outside the clinic led to attempts to more directly influence behavior in the real world. One example of this is the Miller study (1975) of 20 severe alcoholics who had been arrested for public drunkenness. For one group, social services—including employment, health care, counseling, free food, and clothing—were made contingent on sobriety. The other group received all the services noncontingently. Sobriety was assessed through unannounced checks of their blood alcohol levels. Miller found that subjects with contingency contracts were arrested less, were employed more, and were more often sober than control subjects. This intensive treatment required very intrusive assessments, but it did suggest that generalizable treatments could be developed if therapists had control over important reinforcers.

It is generally agreed that single approach treatments of problem drinking have both limited applicability and limited effectiveness. Therefore, such methods are rarely used in practice. The dominant psychological approach to problem drinking is based on the observation that drinking is a complex behavior with many influences, and drinking is rarely the only problem that must be addressed. A key element of multicomponent programs based on social learning theory is that drinking is seen as a method of coping with life's problems, so more adaptive means of coping must be learned.

The first step in the skills training approach is a comprehensive assessment, and this starts with gaining an understanding of the drinking behavior. Not only is it important to find out the amount drunk and the length of the drinking problem, but it is esssential to determine the factors that control drinking. What situations increase the urge to drink? What are the client's beliefs about the purpose alcohol serves? What is the motivation to change drinking habits? An assessment of the social situation is critical. Do friends promote drinking, or are they available to help with treatment? To what extent can the spouse or other significant person be involved in the treatment? Occupational, mental health, medical, and legal status must all be considered in devising a treatment approach; so these issues must be carefully evaluated.

An array of treatment options are available, but specific treatments should be chosen to address the problems identified. Medical treatment of serious disorders may be needed before therapy progresses, and treatment for depression or other psychological disorders may be carried out in conjunction with alcohol treatment. Unless detoxification is needed, behavioral therapists prefer to conduct the sessions in an outpatient clinic, because clients are able to practice resisting real-life pressures to drink during the therapy process. It is believed that inpatient treatments do not generalize to the world outside, because it is easy to resist the urge to drink in a hospital setting where there is no alcohol. Many therapists prefer to conduct the treatment with the client and spouse together, and this has been found to be an effective approach (McCrady et al., 1986). A cooperative spouse can be a powerful therapeutic ally.

Some clients may find that progressive relaxation is a more effective coping method than drinking, while others may find that assertiveness training increases their confidence so that they can cope with stressful social situations without drinking. Marital therapy may help relieve some of the stress that leads to drinking, and vocational counseling may be needed to help the client find a more appropriate job or to begin working again. The needs of problem drinkers vary greatly, so a wide range of treatment approaches should be available (Lang & Marlatt, 1982).

As with most health behaviors, the big challenge is to promote long-term maintenance and prevent relapse. Relapse prevention has been the focus of a great deal of alcohol treatment research. Interventions assist people in identifying cues or situations that may lead to relapse and then aid them in developing effective coping strategies. If the client does take a drink, he or she is trained to define it as a *lapse* and to prevent it from becoming a full-blown relapse (Marlatt & Gordon, 1985). For example, a client may identify a situation that provokes anger, such as "My boss criticized me for no reason after I came back to work." The therapist works with the client to recognize this as a high-risk situation and to come up with a constructive coping response. Relaxation, assertiveness, and changing self-statements are applied by the clients to their real-life concerns. This type of problem solving has been found to be effective in reducing drinking (Chaney, O'Leary, & Marlatt, 1978). In a later replication, subjects with relapse prevention training were drinking less and had higher levels of social and emotional functioning 6 months after treatment than a control group (Annis & Davis, 1988). Other approaches to relapse prevention include encouraging clients to develop a positive addiction, such as exercise, meditation, or religion. The spiritual emphasis of Alcoholics Anonymous may serve this purpose.

Many effective treatment methods have been documented in the last few decades. Multicomponent social learning therapies not only are effective but are also helping thousands if not millions of alcoholics every year, although Alcoholics Anonymous remains the most widely used treatment method. Despite this relative success, the majority of people who go through treatment programs will relapse within 1 year. Broader societal trends, such as decreased acceptance of drunk driving and the availability of nonalcoholic beverages at social settings, may aid in the prevention and treatment of problem drinking.

Similar approaches are applied to drug treatment. Professional services are widely available, although it is often reported that the demand for treatment is greater than the ability of programs to deliver it. However, in 1988, more than 834,000 drug abuse clients were treated at 4880 facilities throughout the United States (Schuster & Kilbey, 1992). There are also self-help groups that have developed in a wide variety of settings. For example, a group called the Wharf Rats meets at every Grateful Dead concert to support one another's sobriety. Most groups are patterned after Alcoholics Anonymous. Some of them are Narcotics Anonymous, Cocaine Anonymous, and Marijuana Anonymous.

The largest study of drug treatments was the Treatment Outcome Prospective Study (TOPS). Over 10,000 clients were involved at 37 treatment centers. The outcomes of methadone maintenance, residential treatment, and outpatient treatment were studied. (*Methadone* is used as a substitute for heroin and is dispensed daily at clinics.) All three approaches were effective if clients stayed in them. Those who remained in treatment for 6 to 12 months had good outcomes. For all types of treatment, abstinence rates after 1 year were 40 to 50 percent for heroin, cocaine, and abuse of prescription drugs. Marijuana use was resistant to treatment. Those who stayed in treatment were more likely than others to be employed and less likely to engage in crimes such as assault and robbery up to 5 years after treatment. However, more than one-third of the methadone maintenance patients reentered a program within a year of completing their treatment. This study shows that drug treat-

---

BOX 13·8

FOCUS ON RESEARCH

Alcohol Education for Bartenders

There are many potential approaches for interventions to reduce irresponsible drinking. One obvious site for programs is bars, but they are not well suited for educational purposes. Because drinking establishments are held responsible for the actions of customers who leave their business after drinking, there is incentive for alcohol servers to exert some control over drinking behavior on their premises.

Howard-Pitney and colleagues (1991) reported on a comprehensive program for drinking establishments. Servers were taught about the effects of alcohol and how to encourage responsible drinking. They used role playing to practice intervening with customers. Managers were taught to adopt policies to change the drinking environment.

Servers and managers from 26 establishments received the 1-day training, and 14 other establishments served as controls. Pairs of observers, who did not know whether the establishment had received the training, conducted on-site evaluations.

Questionnaires revealed that servers and managers learned a great deal about alcohol and increased their belief that customers would respond favorably to responsible drinking interventions. However, they were not able to recall many of the actual interventions that were suggested.

During the on-site evaluation, one observer drank three drinks and ordered another in a 1-hour period. Servers were instructed how to deal with such a situation, but they did not use the interventions more than servers in the control establishments. Educated servers did not slow the delivery of drinks, suggest a nonalcoholic drink, offer to find transportation, or refuse to serve another drink more than the control servers. Establishments with educated managers did not differ from controls in checking IDs of young-looking customers, offering pitchers, or offering happy hours. There was a trend for a difference in advertising non-alcoholic drinks.

In summary, this program was not effective in changing the behavior of servers or managers. Perhaps training the workers on site during the normal work times would have been more effective. Trainers could have demonstrated how to intervene effectively with actual customers so that servers could see how it worked. Education programs may have to address concerns about reduced revenue and tips. Some states are moving to require training for alcohol servers, but the content of the program must be improved so that the training is worth the effort (Howard-Pitney, Johnson, Altman, Hopkins, & Hammond, 1991).

---

ment can lead to decreased drug use and more productive lives, but long-term treatment is needed.

Summary

In addition to the serious social and economic problems that can be caused by excessive drinking, severe health problems such as cirrhosis of the liver, cardiovascular diseases, and car crashes are directly related to alcohol intake. Alcohol is defined as an addictive substance because it produces both tolerance (the need for higher and higher doses) and withdrawal (unpleasant effects when consumption is stopped). Some people are able to drink small amounts of alcohol, and there is some evidence that these people live longer than those who abstain; others quickly lose control over their drinking. There may be a genetic basis for some forms of alcohol dependence. The disease model states that alcoholism is a disease that can be controlled but never cured. Alcoholics Anonymous is based on this model, and it is the largest treatment program. The behavioral model states that problem drinking is a learned behavior, and people can learn either to stop drinking or to drink in a controlled fashion. Alcohol prevention programs that teach adolescents to refuse offers of alcohol can be moderately effective. Comprehensive alcohol treatment programs not only teach patients the skills needed to stop drinking but also assist with the family, employment, financial, and health problems experienced by problem drinkers. While contemporary treatment programs are moderately effective, they need to be both improved and made available to more people in need. Promising trends include the incorporation of family members in the treatment and an emphasis on therapy outside the hospital.

Alcohol and tobacco have more direct negative health consequences than illicit drugs, but illicit drugs have very important indirect effects on crime, health of drug-exposed fetuses, and economic costs to society. Drug abuse typically starts during the teen years. Adolescents who use drugs tend to have a pattern of deviant behavior that includes aggression and poor school performance. Polydrug abuse is common. Prevention programs have not been very effective for marijuana, which is the most commonly used illicit drug. However, drug treatment programs for heroin, cocaine, and psychoactive prescription drugs are relatively effective. In most cases, drug treatment requires a long-term commitment and multiple treatment episodes. There is controversy over the effectiveness of the law enforcement emphasis of the current war on drugs.

KEY TERMS

Unintentional injuries. These used to be referred to as *accidents*, but it is now known that they are not random events. Car crashes, burns, and drownings are included in this category, but not suicide and homicide, because they are intentional.

BAC (blood alcohol content). Driving is impaired in almost everyone with a BAC of 0.10 percent. The legal limit in many states is now 0.08 percent.

Injury prevention. Efforts to reduce the risk of injuries before they happen. Passive approaches include child-proof caps on bottles. Active behavioral approaches include promoting seat belt and bicycle helmet use.

Homicide. The intentional killing of another person. The United States has one of the highest homicide rates in the world, and most of these are murders, not self-defense killings.

Domestic violence. Violence between persons living in the same house. Women and children are the usual victims. This problem tends to continue over a period of time and does not often correct itself without external assistance.

Battered woman syndrome. Women who are beaten often develop a variety of physical and psychological disorders. Although they have frequent contacts with the health care system, this syndrome is often not detected unless the practitioner does a trauma history.

Child abuse. Physical, sexual, and psychological maltreatment of a child, including neglect. This is the fifth leading cause of death for children aged 1 to 18.

Child Protective Services. Social service agency responsible for responding to all reports of child abuse. Workers must decide whether abuse has occurred and whether the child should remain in the home or be removed for his or her protection.

Elder abuse. Includes physical and psychological abuse, misuse of property or finances, and neglect by an identified caretaker.

Mandatory abuse reporting laws. All professionals suspecting child or elder abuse are required to make a report to authorities in all 50 states.

Social drinker. One who is experiencing no social or health problems as a result of drinking. Social drinkers are at risk of injury if they drive after having a few drinks.

Alcohol abuser. One with a high-risk drinking pattern. This person may not drink every day, but gets drunk regularly. Drinking is not out of control, but this person is at risk of injury from drinking.

Alcohol dependent. One who cannot control drinking. Daily drinking quickly leads to im-

paired judgment, social problems, and severe damage to health.

Alcohol addict. This term is now preferred by scientists as opposed to *alcoholic*.

AA (Alcoholics Anonymous). A worldwide self-help organization devoted to helping people quit drinking. AA groups can be found in virtually every city and town in the United States and in many other countries.

Antabuse (disulfiram). A drug that makes one violently ill if one drinks even a small amount of alcohol.

Polydrug abuse. Abuse of more than one drug. It is common for drug abusers to use more than one illicit drug, as well as alcohol and tobacco.

Health Behavior and Health Promotion

CHAPTER 14

Dietary Risk Factors and Interventions

When Brian Triandis was a child, his mother made sure to serve him what she believed to be a healthful diet. Fresh vegetables and fruits, whole grain bread, and chicken dishes were plentiful in Brian's house. Red meat was eaten occasionally, but microwave dinners, potato chips, and sweets were in short supply. Brian took his mother's delicious home cooking for granted, but he preferred to munch pretzels while watching television and had fast-food lunches on the weekends. After his first year of college he moved into an apartment, and he was responsible for feeding himself for the first time in his life. At first, Brian indulged all his fast-food fantasies and kept the apartment stocked with essentials like chips, soda, beer, and ice cream. Although he enjoyed his diet, he soon found that eating all those convenience foods cost a bundle. He really had to start thinking about his diet when he had a checkup at Student Health Services and they told him his blood cholesterol was high. He was advised to cut down on high-fat foods. Brian did not know where to start. Would you?

BOX 14·1

HEALTH OBJECTIVES FOR THE YEAR 2000

By the year 2000:

1. Reduce dietary fat intake to an average of 30 percent of all calories or less and average saturated fat intake to less than 10 percent of all calories among people aged 2 and older (baseline: 36 percent of all calories from total fat and 13 percent of all calories from saturated fat).

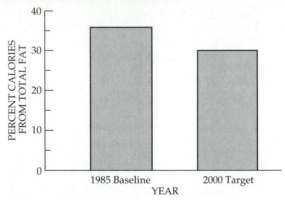

2. Reduce the mean serum cholesterol level among adults to no more than 200 mg/dl (baseline: 213 mg/dl).

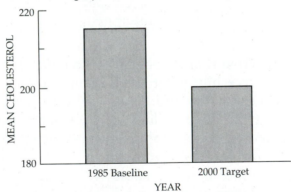

3. Reduce the prevalence of blood cholesterol levels of 240 mg/dl or greater to no more than 20 percent among adults (baseline: 27 percent for ages 20 to 74).

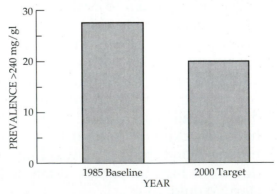

It's hard to eat properly as a college student. Time and money are in short supply, and there are many distractions. Most college campuses are surrounded by McDonald's, Jack-in-the-Box, and other fast-food outlets. Hamburgers taste good, you can get them quickly, and they don't cost much. When you are done with the burger, the challenges really start. Ice cream, for example, is always difficult to turn down. Your parents, your friends, and television programs seem to always have something to say about cholesterol, heart disease, and low-fat diets. What is that all about? In this chapter, we will explore the relationship between diet and disease, and we will look into the evidence that dietary habits can be changed.

THE INFLUENCE OF DIET ON HEALTH

In many developing countries, and until the 1940s in the United States, most diet-related diseases were due to a lack of specific nutrients. You probably do not know anyone who has had one of the following nutrient deficiency diseases:

Disease	Associated nutrient deficiency
rickets	vitamin D
pellagra	niacin (a B vitamin)
scurvy	vitamin C
beriberi	thiamine (a B vitamin)
goiter	iodine

These diseases that were once common are now virtually eliminated in the United States because of an abundant food supply, effective distribution system, and improvements in food products and nutritional science. Once it was found that goiter was caused by lack of iodine, the addition of iodine to salt solved the problem. Modern cases of nutritional deficiency diseases are usually due to severe illness or injury, child neglect, being either housebound

or homeless, or alcoholism (U.S. Department of Health and Human Services, 1988).

Dietary habits still contribute to ill health, but the problem now is an excess of nutrients. We are suffering the effects of dietary overabundance and imbalance. Of the top ten causes of death, dietary habits are related to five: coronary heart disease, some cancers, stroke, diabetes mellitus, and atherosclerosis. Excessive intake of the nutrient alcohol is related to cirrhosis of the liver, injuries, and suicides. Because the food we eat every day affects so many common diseases, we must conclude that eating is an important health-related behavior that should be taken seriously. As you read about the relation of diet to the diseases listed below, notice which nutrients are most important and how healthful or unhealthful your usual dietary practices are.

Coronary Heart Disease

There are more than 1.25 million heart attacks in the United States each year, and 500,000 people in the United States die from coronary heart disease (CHD). Saturated fat, total fat, and cholesterol are the nutrients most closely linked with CHD. Excessive alcohol can contribute as well. Diets high in complex carbohydrates (starches) are recommended to reduce the risk, partly to replace fats in the diet. There is some evidence that water-soluble fibers found in oat bran, guar gum, psyllium seeds, pectin, and certain beans have the effect of lowering blood lipids. Because of the importance of the relation between dietary fat and heart disease, this topic will be covered in depth in this chapter.

Stroke and High Blood Pressure

The 500,000 yearly strokes in the United States kill about 150,000 people and produce long-term disabilities for many more. About 2 million Americans currently suffer from stroke-related disabilities. High blood pressure is a major risk factor for both stroke and coronary heart disease. About 58 million people in the United States have hypertension, and 39 million of these are younger than 65. Three dietary factors are well known to produce increased blood pressure: obesity (through excess intake of calories), sodium, and alcohol. Potassium and calcium tend to decrease blood pressure, while caffeine causes short-term increases.

Cancer

Each year 900,000 new cases of cancer are detected in the United States, and there are about 475,000 cancer deaths. Most people are not aware that dietary habits may be responsible for about 35 percent of all cancer deaths. Diet may influence cancer by several mechanisms. Carcinogens can be naturally present in foods, or they can be contaminants. Foods may activate or deactivate other carcinogens. Nutrients may speed up (for example, fats) or slow down (for example, vitamin A) the growth of cancer cells. Nutrients may also impair the effectiveness of the immune system to fight cancer.

Table 14-1 summarizes studies of the relation between cancers at various sites and specific nutrients.

Diabetes Mellitus

Diabetes mellitus kills about 38,000 people every year, and it contributes to 95,000 other deaths from cardiovascular and kidney diseases. Although obesity is strongly linked with non-insulin-dependent diabetes, specific nutrients are important in the etiology and treatment of diabetes. Contrary to popular belief, excess sucrose (refined sugar) intake does not lead to diabetes, except through obesity. Diets high in complex carbohydrates improve the diabetic's ability to use sugars, which is very helpful. Reduced fat diets and increased fiber intake are a key part of the treatment.

Obesity

About 34 million American adults are obese, and obesity is a risk factor for several chronic diseases. Although it seems obviously true, it has been difficult to document that excess intake of energy (calories) is a major cause of

---

TABLE 14-1

DIETARY COMPONENTS IN RELATION TO CANCERS

Cancer site	Incidence per 100,000 people	Fat	Body weight & calories	Fiber	Fruits and vegetables	Alcohol	Smoked, salted, & pickled foods
Lung	55				−	+	
Breast	51	+	+			+	
Colon	36	+	+	−	−		
Prostate	34	+	+		−		
Rectum	15	+				+	
Endometrium	13	+	+				
Oral cavity	11				−	+	
Stomach	8				−		+
Cervix	5		+		−		
Esophagus	4					+	+

Source: U.S. Department of Health and Human Services, 1988.
Note: " − " means that the component protects against the cancer. " + " means that the component promotes the cancer.

obesity. However, decreased energy intake, with emphasis on reducing fat intake, is a primary treatment of obesity. Dietary fat appears more likely to be stored as body fat than carbohydrates or alcohol.

Osteoporosis

In osteoporosis, the bones lose calcium and become weak. About 15 to 20 million Americans are affected by osteoporosis, which leads to 1.3 million bone fractures per year. Hip fractures are particularly common in older women, and they lead to death in 12 to 20 percent of the cases. There is moderate to strong evidence that the risk factors listed in Table 14-2 influence bone health.

Dental Diseases

Dental diseases cause pain, restriction of activity, and loss of work time. Some forms of dental disease are declining, especially cavities in children. However, in 1985, the costs of dental care were estimated at $21.3 billion. Sugars of all kinds lead to tooth decay. Sugars interact with bacteria in the mouth to produce acids that dissolve the enamel on the tooth. Fluoride is an element that prevents tooth decay. When it is not added to the water supply, it can be taken as a supplement by children.

Did you notice that dietary fats increase risk of coronary heart disease, stroke, several cancers, diabetes, and obesity? Overconsumption of fat is certainly the most important dietary behavior that affects health.

The study of diet and health is most advanced in the area of cardiovascular disease (CVD). There is a long history of interest in the hypothesis that diet affects heart disease, and this area has seen the collaboration of physicians, nutritionists, psychologists, public health experts, and policymakers. The remainder of this chapter focuses on different aspects of the diet-heart question.

THE DIET-HEART HYPOTHESIS

The diet-heart theory states that diet is a major cause of CVD. Although thousands of studies related to the question have been performed over the last 60 years, it is still one of today's most controversial issues among medical researchers and the lay public. The news media regularly reports each new study, and it seems like each one contradicts many of the others. One study confirms that dietary cholesterol affects serum cholesterol, and the next one says that no link could be found. One study says that coffee increases blood cholesterol, and another finds that only decaffeinated coffee affects cholesterol. The many conflicting studies that are publicized so heavily have created more confusion than understanding in the general public, but there is a great desire for information on what people can eat to improve their health. Here are some of the questions about diet and health that are often asked:

Is pork high in fat or low in fat?
Is white cheese better for you than yellow cheese?
How much calcium does skim milk have?
Should I take fish oil supplements?
Should I cook with safflower oil or olive oil?

TABLE 14-2

RISK FACTORS FOR OSTEOPOROSIS

Factors that increase risk	Factors that decrease risk
Age	Obesity
Removal of ovaries before menopause	Black ethnicity
Extremely sedentary lifestyle	Heavy exercise
Low dietary calcium	

Source: U.S. Department of Health and Human Services, 1989.

BOX 14·2

DIETARY RECOMMENDATIONS FROM THE SURGEON GENERAL'S REPORT ON NUTRITION AND HEALTH

After collecting and evaluating the evidence linking diet with the current health problems, the Surgeon General's Report on Nutrition and Health (1988) made the following recommendations for the general public.

ISSUES FOR MOST PEOPLE

Fats and cholesterol: Reduce consumption of fat (especially saturated fat) and cholesterol. Choose foods relatively low in these substances, such as vegetables, fruits, whole grain foods, fish, poultry, lean meats, and low-fat dairy products. Use food preparation methods that add little or no fat.

Energy and weight control: Achieve and maintain a desirable body weight. To do so, choose a dietary pattern in which energy (caloric) intake is consistent with energy expenditure. To reduce energy intake, limit consumption of foods relatively high in calories, fats, and sugars and minimize alcohol consumption. Increase energy expenditure through regular and sustained physical activity.

Complex carbohydrates and fiber: Increase consumption of whole grain foods and cereal products, vegetables (including dried beans and peas), and fruit.

Sodium: Reduce intake of sodium by choosing foods relatively low in sodium and by limiting the amount of salt in food preparation and at the table.

Alcohol: To reduce risk for chronic disease, take alcohol only in moderation (no more than two drinks a day), if at all. Avoid drinking any alcohol before or while driving, operating machinery, taking medications, or engaging in any other activity requiring judgment. Avoid drinking alcohol while pregnant.

ISSUES FOR SOME PEOPLE

Fluoride: Community water systems should contain fluoride at optimal levels for prevention of tooth decay. If such water is not available, use other appropriate sources of fluoride.

Sugars: Those who are particularly vulnerable to dental caries (cavities), especially children, should limit the consumption and frequency of use of foods high in sugars.

Calcium: Adolescent girls and adult women should increase consumption of foods high in calcium, including low-fat dairy products.

Iron: Children, adolescents, and women of childbearing age should be sure to consume foods that are good sources of iron, such as lean meats, fish, certain beans, and iron-enriched cereals and whole grain products. This issue is of special concern for low-income families.

How can I choose the most healthful frozen dinners?·

How much sodium is in processed foods?

What kinds of fiber will lower my blood cholesterol?

The study of diet and nutrition is a specialized science, but since eating is a behavior, psychologists have a role to play. People must eat to stay alive, but in developed societies eating is an activity that serves many purposes. We eat for pleasure, we eat to enhance social interactions, we eat to change the way we feel, we eat to change the way we look, and sometimes we eat to influence our health.

Not only do we eat for different purposes, but we eat a wide variety of foods. An American supermarket may have 10,000 different food products, and most of us eat different foods every day. When you consider that many of these foods can be prepared several different ways, you begin to understand some of the difficulties in studying eating behavior and nutrition. The assessment of diet is a problem with which researchers have been struggling for decades, and the struggle continues. Except in studies conducted in hospitals, diet is virtually always assessed by self-report. Participants in studies are asked to either keep a record of their diet or recall what they ate during the previous day. Although these methods have been shown to have adequate validity, there are still important limitations. Some people will fail to remember everything they ate or they will report something they did not eat. Some people will be inaccurate in reporting amounts. Of course, some people will simply lie about what they ate because they are embarrassed about it or for other reasons. The limitations of dietary assessment make nutrition research difficult, yet knowledge in this area is advancing rapidly.

Foods are made up of hundreds of nutrients and compounds, but only a limited number have been found to be related to CVD. Those nutrients and foods will be the focus of this discussion.

1. Total caloric intake. Calories indicate the amount of energy in food. Calories are important in the etiology of obesity.

2. Cholesterol. Cholesterol is a waxy substance that is found only in foods of animal origin. The cell walls of animals are made of cholesterol. Because the cell walls of plants are made of "fiber," no cholesterol is in animal foods. The human body produces all the cholesterol that is needed for cells, hormones, and other uses, so it is not necessary to eat cholesterol in foods. Dietary cholesterol increases serum cholesterol, but only slightly.

3. Total fats. Fats are found in both animal and vegetable foods. Total fats are related to serum cholesterol, but there are three types of

fats that are important to distinguish. It is essential to have fats in the diet.

a. Saturated fats. *Saturated* means that all the bonds on the carbon atoms are filled, while *unsaturated* means that some of the bonds are not filled. Saturated fats are more difficult to break down. They are solid at room temperature, like butter, while unsaturated fats are liquid, like vegetable oils. Saturated fats have a strong effect on serum cholesterol. Most saturated fats are from animal products. However, coconut oil and palm oil are highly saturated fats and are used in many processed foods.

b. Monounsaturated fats. *Monounsaturated* means that all the carbon bonds are filled except one. Until recently it was believed that monounsaturated fats did not have much effect on serum cholesterol, but new studies indicate that monounsaturated fats like olive and peanut oils can produce significant decreases in serum cholesterol.

c. Polyunsaturated fats. These fats have several carbon bonds that are not filled. The cholesterol-lowering effects of polyunsaturated fats like safflower and corn oils have been known for many years. Fish oils are polyunsaturated, unlike fat from most meats, which is highly saturated.

4. Carbohydrates. Sugars of all kinds are simple carbohydrates, and starches are complex carbohydrates. Starches used to be avoided by people on weight reduction diets because they were felt to be high in calories. Now complex carbohydrates are recommended to the obese because they have many fewer calories per bite than fats. It is not the bread and potatoes that promote weight gain; it is the butter, jelly, and sour cream that add large amounts of calories.

5. Fiber. There are two major categories of fiber. Water-insoluble fibers, like wheat bran, may be helpful in preventing some types of cancer because they decrease the time that foods stay in the intestines. Water-soluble fibers—like oat bran, pectin, and psyllium—may reduce serum cholesterol. Fiber is often

taken out of food when it is processed, such as with white bread and white rice. Fiber intake can be increased by eating whole unprocessed foods or by supplementing the diet with fiber.

6. Sodium, potassium, and calcium. These minerals have been shown in several studies to affect blood pressure. Sodium increases, while potassium and calcium decrease, blood pressure.

7. Alcohol. Alcohol increases blood pressure. However, in small amounts alcohol increases HDL cholesterol, and this may be a beneficial effect.

EPIDEMIOLOGY: WHAT ARE PEOPLE EATING?

Although people eat *foods*, most dietary studies discuss *nutrients*. As seen in Figure 14-1 (Wadden & Brownell, 1984), the current American diet consists of about 42 percent fat, 12 percent protein, and 46 percent carbohydrates. (Since this figure was developed, fat intake has dropped to about 36 percent, and carbohydrate intake has increased to about 50 percent.) To help prevent heart disease, the American Heart Association and other agencies have developed dietary guidelines, and these are also shown in Figure 14-1. It is recommended that Americans reduce fat intake to 30 percent or less of all calories and increase carbohydrate intake to 58 percent of all calories. Heart disease patients are frequently prescribed diets with less than 20 percent of all calories from fat. Typical sodium intake is about 5000 to 6000 mg per day, and the recommendation is to consume less than 3000 mg per day. Average cholesterol intake is about 500 mg per day, and the recommendation is below 250 mg per day.

The diets of children are similar to those of adults. Dietary assessments were collected on 1251 white children aged 6 to 19 (Salz et al., 1983). These children ate 38 percent of their calories as fat, and 15 percent was saturated fat. Protein was 15 percent of the diet, and

carbohydrates were 48 percent of the diet. Sucrose, or ordinary table sugar, made up 11 percent of the total calories. For both boys and girls, fat intake increased with age, suggesting that diets become less healthful during adolescence.

Because fat is of particular relevance for CVD, it is important to know where the dietary fat comes from. On the basis of dietary assessments of almost 12,000 Americans (Block, Dresser, Hartman, & Carroll, 1985), these foods were found to contribute the most fat to the diet:

hamburgers, cheeseburgers, and meatloaf: 7.0 percent

hot dogs, ham, and lunch meats: 6.4 percent

whole milk: 6.0 percent

These foods—along with steaks, cheese, and pork—contributed about half of the saturated fat in the diet. Therefore, a small number of foods with high amounts of fat are eaten so frequently that they account for much of the dietary fat. Beef products by themselves contribute 18 to 20 percent of the total saturated fat and 16 to 18 percent of the total cholesterol in the American diet. In contrast, butter and ice cream contribute only about 2 percent each of total dietary fat. Thus, most adults could reduce their dietary fat and cholesterol substantially by substituting low-fat entrées for beef dishes.

The patterns are slightly different for children. Dietary intake of 185 ten-year-old black and white children in Louisiana was studied (Frank, Webber, & Berenson, 1982). The largest contributors of saturated fats for children were as follows:

milk: 26 percent
desserts: 13 percent
beef: 9 percent
pork: 9 percent

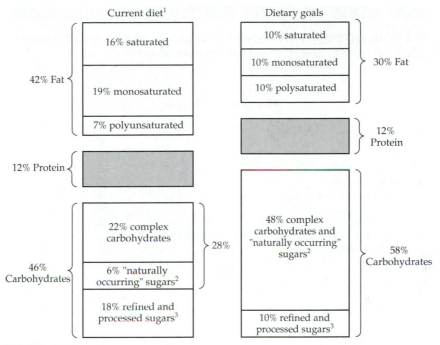

FIGURE 14-1

Dietary goals for the United States proposed by a Senate select committee compared with the current U.S. diet. (1) These percentages are based on calories from food and nonalcoholic beverages. Alcohol adds approximately another 210 calories per day to the average diet of drinking-age Americans. (2) "Naturally occurring": sugars which are indigenous to a food, as opposed to refined (cane and beets) and processed (corn sugar, syrups, molasses, and honey) sugars that may be added to a food product. (3) In many ways alcoholic beverages affect the diet in the same way as refined and other processed sugars. Both add calories (energy) to the total diet but contribute little or no vitamins or minerals. (From the U.S. Select Committee on Nutrition and Human Needs, 1977.)

Even fewer foods accounted for most of the saturated fats eaten by children. Changing from whole milk to skim milk could decrease fat intake significantly. There are other reasons to be concerned about children's diets. In a study conducted with children aged 10 to 15 in Norway, dietary habits were studied by questionnaire (Tell, 1982). About 18 percent said that they had not eaten any fruit the day before the survey, and over 40 percent had not eaten any vegetables. However, over 95 percent had drunk milk (mostly whole milk), 40 percent said that they drank soft drinks, and almost 30 percent said that they had eaten sweets. This is similar to the diets of American youth,

and it is not the kind of diet that is likely to lead to healthy hearts.

Two respected researchers (Connor & Connor, 1985) in the field of diet and CVD have developed a cholesterol–saturated fat index (CSI) so that foods can be rated on their potential to increase serum cholesterol:

$$\text{CSI} = (1.01 \times \text{g saturated fat}) + (0.05 \times \text{mg cholesterol})$$

Table 14-3 shows the CSI score and kilocalories for several common foods. Using this index you can determine which foods are more and less likely to increase serum cholesterol.

	CSI	Kilocalories

TABLE 14·3

THE CHOLESTEROL–SATURATED FAT INDEX (CSI) AND KILOCALORIE CONTENT OF SELECTED FOODS (1000 g OR $3\frac{1}{2}$ oz)

	CSI	Kilocalories
Fish, poultry, red meat		
Whitefish—snapper, perch, sole, and so forth.	4	91
Shellfish	6	104
Salmon	5	149
Poultry, no skin	6	171
Beef, pork, and lamb		
10% fat (ground sirloin, flank steak)	9	214
15% fat (ground round)	10	258
20% fat (ground chuck; pot roasts)	13	286
30% fat (ground beef, pork, and lamb; steaks; ribs; pork and lamb chops; roasts)	18	381
Eggs		
White	0	51
Egg substitute	1	91
Whole	29	163
Fats		
Most vegetable oils	13	884
Soft vegetable margarines	16	720
Soft shortenings	26	884
Bacon grease	39	902
Butter	54	716
Coconut oil, palm oil, cocoa butter (chocolate)	78	884

THE EPIDEMIOLOGY BEHIND THE DIET-HEART HYPOTHESIS

Nicolai Anitschkow is often credited with proposing the diet-heart hypothesis in 1933 (Gordon, 1988). He concluded from two decades of work with rabbits and from other human studies that cholesterol in the food we eat is transported in the blood and deposited on the walls of arteries. At about the same time it was observed that rich countries with high levels of fat and cholesterol in the diet had high rates of CVD, while poor countries with mostly vegetarian diets had low rates of CVD. This led to the famous Seven Countries Study, directed by Ancel Keys of the University of Minnesota (Keys, 1970). Almost 13,000 mid-

dle-aged men were studied between 1958 and 1964 in countries with varied rates of CVD. Diets were studied either by personal interviews or by chemical analysis. Across the 14 groups studied, the correlation between saturated fats and serum cholesterol was .89, indicating a very strong relationship. Figure 14-2 shows the scatterplot for this association.

Most international studies have confirmed the association between dietary saturated fats and serum cholesterol, but studies of single populations have produced conflicting results. For example, the Framingham Study has shown no association between dietary fats or cholesterol and serum cholesterol. This lack of association is felt to be due to the fact that

T A B L E 14·3 continued

	CSI	Kilocalories
Cheeses		
Count-down, dry-curd cottage cheese, tofu (bean curd), pot cheese, low-fat cottage cheese, St. Otho	1	98
Cottage cheese, Lite-Line, Lite 'n Lively, part-skim ricotta	6	139
Cheezola, Scandic or Min Chol, Hickory Farm Lyte, Pizza Pal, Saffola American*	6	317
Green River (lower-fat Cheddar), part-skin mozzarella, Neufchâtel (lower-fat cream cheese), Kell Kase, Skim American, Olympia Low Fat	12	256
Cheddar, roquefort, Swiss, brie, jack, American, cream cheese, Velveeta, cheese spreads (jars), and so forth	26	386
Frozen desserts		
Water ices or sorbets	0	105
Sherbet or frozen yogurt	1	119
Ice milk	4	152
Ice cream, 10% fat	9	193
Milk		
Skim milk (0.1% fat) or buttermilk	<1	36
1% milk	1	47
2% milk	2	59
Whole milk (3.5% fat)	4	65
Liquid nondairy creamers: store brands, Cereal Blend, Coffee Rich	9	141
Liquid nondairy creamers: Mocha Mix, Poly Rich	3	154

* Cheeses made with skim milk and vegetable oils.
From Connor and Connor, 1985.

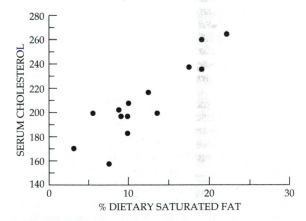

FIGURE 14-2
Saturated fat and serum cholesterol in seven countries. (From Keys, 1970.)

people in Framingham tend to eat the same types of foods (Blackburn & Jacobs, 1984). It is difficult to find correlations when there is a small range of differences in the population. Studies comparing largely vegetarian Seventh-Day Adventists with the general population typically do find that dietary fats and cholesterol are strongly related to serum cholesterol (Fraser, 1986).

If most of the data indicate that diet and serum cholesterol are correlated, what is the data to document a causal effect? In the study of Western Electric employees in Chicago (Shekelle et al., 1981) change in dietary fat and cholesterol predicted change in serum cholesterol. The dietary fat and cholesterol score also predicted CVD mortality over a 19-year period. This study suggests that diet changes serum cholesterol, but it does not prove the hypothesis. There are many small-scale experimental studies of animals and humans in hospital metabolic wards showing that dietary fats and cholesterol do cause changes in serum cholesterol. These tightly controlled studies indicate that dietary cholesterol and saturated fats increase serum cholesterol, while monounsaturated fats and polyunsaturated fats decrease serum cholesterol (Grundy et al., 1982).

Two large-scale intervention studies with controlled diets have been conducted in institutional settings. In Finland one mental hospital was assigned to serve a diet low in saturated fat and cholesterol for 6 years, while a second mental hospital continued its usual diet (Miettinen, Turpeinen, Karvonen, Elosuo, & Paavilainen, 1972). In Los Angeles, elderly residents of a Veterans Administration hospital were randomly assigned to receive either a low-fat or a regular diet (Dayton, Pearce, Hashimoto, Dixon, & Tomiyasu, 1969). In both studies serum cholesterol was reduced significantly, and cardiovascular mortality rates were lowered as well.

Thus, animal studies as well as small-scale and large-scale experimental studies in humans suggest that diet can lower cholesterol. While this conclusion is still somewhat controversial, most physicians and public health professionals agree that serum cholesterol and CVD mortality could be reduced by changing the diet. This has led to recommendations from the American Heart Association (Grundy et al., 1982). and the National Heart, Lung, and Blood Institute for the entire population to lower saturated fat and cholesterol intake.

SPECIFIC DIETARY RECOMMENDATIONS

Connor and Connor (1985) from the University of Oregon have used the American Heart Association recommendations to develop specific dietary guidelines that they call the *Alternative Diet*. There are three phases, and with each phase there is a greater restriction of saturated fats and cholesterol. The types of behaviors targeted in each phase are summarized in Table 14-4. In phase 1 the goal is to decrease consumption of high cholesterol and saturated fat foods such as egg yolks, butterfat, lard, and organ meats by making substitutions.

In phase 2 the main goal is to decrease the intake of meat and cheese. The typical American diet may contain up to a pound of meat per day, and the goal of phase 2 is to decrease meat consumption to 6 to 8 oz per day. In this phase it is necessary to find new recipes and to experiment with dishes from other cultures. Asian dishes use many fresh vegetables and rice. Mexican foods are high in complex carbohydrates and make use of tortillas and beans. Mediterranean diets from Greece and Italy emphasize pastas and vegetable sauces. Middle Eastern cuisines use wheat and different types of beans in their meals. Exploring international recipes helps avoid monotony when changing from a meat-centered to a low-fat diet.

To achieve phase 3 goals, meat must be used as a ''condiment'' rather than a main dish. Fish and skinless poultry are eaten in modest quantities, and red meats and shellfish are eaten infrequently and in very small quantities. Phase 3 is referred to as ''a new way of eating'' and requires many changes in menu planning, shopping, cooking, and eating out.

Examples of menus for the Alternative Diet are shown in Table 14-5. On the basis of the observed effects of changes in dietary fats and cholesterol on serum cholesterol in previous studies, the amount of change in serum cholesterol with each phase of the Alternative Diet can be estimated. In the first phase, when total fat is reduced to about 35 percent of all calories, total blood cholesterol will decrease by 18 percent. In phase 2, with 25 percent total fat, blood cholesterol is decreased by 39 per-

TABLE 14·4

SUMMARY OF THE THREE PHASES OF THE ALTERNATIVE DIET

Phase 1: substitutions

This is accomplished by:

Avoiding egg yolks, butterfat, lard, and organ meats (liver, heart, brains, kidney, gizzards)

Substituting soft margarine for butter

Substituting vegetable oils and shortening for lard

Substituting skim milk and skim milk products for whole milk and whole-milk products

Substituting egg whites for whole eggs

Trimming fat off meat and removing skin from chicken

Choosing commercial food products lower in cholesterol and fat (low-fat cheeses, egg substitutes, soy meat substitutes, frozen yogurt, and so forth)

Modifying favorite recipes by using less fat or sugar and vegetable oils instead of butter or lard.

Phase II: new recipes

This step involves:

Reducing amounts of meat and cheese eaten and replacing them with chicken and fish

Eating meat, chicken, or fish only once a day

Cutting down on fat as spreads and salad dressings and fat used in cooking and baking

Eating more grains, beans, fruits, and vegetables

When eating out, making low-fat, low-cholesterol choices

Finding new recipes to replace those that cannot be altered

Phase III: a new way of eating

The final phase means:

Eating meat, cheese, poultry, and fish as "condiments" to other foods, rather than as main courses

Eating more beans and grain products as protein sources

Using no more than 3–5 teaspoons of fat/day in spreads and salad dressings, and in cooking and baking

Drinking 4–6 glasses of water per day

Keeping extra meat, shellfish, regular cheese, chocolate candy, coconut, and richer home-baked or commercially prepared food for special occasions (once a month or less)

Enjoying a wide variety of new foods and a repertoire of totally new and savory recipes

From Connor and Connor, 1985.

TABLE 14·5

ALTERNATIVE DIET SAMPLE MENUS

Day 1	Day 2	Day 3	Day 4	Day 5	Day 6	Day 7
			Breakfast			
Cantaloupe Raisin bran cereal Skim milk English muffin with jam	Orange juice Whole-wheat pancakes topped with unsweetened applesauce	Plain low-fat yogurt with banana Cereal Bran muffins*	Berries Shredded wheat Skim milk Whole-grain toast	Grapefruit half Potatoes (hash-browned with small amount of oil in nonstick pan) Whole-grain toast with marmalade	Blueberries Hot whole-grain cereal Skim milk English muffin	Fresh melon German oven pancakes.*
			Lunch			
Tuna sandwich (water-packed tuna mixed with tangy dressing* or imitation mayonnaise) Carrot sticks Fresh fruit	Chili bean salad* in whole-wheat pocket bread Tomato soup (Campbell's low-sodium) Fresh fruit Graham crackers	Lentil soup* Low-fat crackers Laughing Cow reduced calorie cheese Fresh fruit	Bean burritos Lettuce and sliced tomato Fresh fruit	Salad bar (greens topped with kidney beans, tomato, radishes, garbanzo beans, and cucumbers) Low-calorie commercial or Western dressing* Bagel Fruit	Peanut butter and jelly sandwich Vegetable sticks (carrot, celery, and so forth) Fresh orange Whole-wheat fig bar	Minestrone soup Wheat berry rolls Low-fat cottage cheese Fresh fruit

Dinner

Bean lasagna*	Cashew chicken*	Easy tuna noodle casserole*	Pizza rice casserole*	Baked herbed fish*	Corn chip* with bean dip*	Spaghetti with marinara sauce*
Tossed salad with Western dressing*	Steamed rice	Steamed broccoli	Green peas	Baked potato with mock sour cream*	Creamy enchiladas*	Tossed salad with low-calorie dressing
French bread	Fresh pineapple slices	Confetti appleslaw*	Green salad with low-calorie dressing	Steamed zucchini	Meatless Spanish rice	Steamed green beans seasoned with lemon and pepper
Fresh berries	Wheat berry rolls	Wheat rolls	Sourdough rolls	Waldorf salad*	Shredded lettuce and tomato	French bread
	Hot fudge pudding cake*	Strawberry ice*	Gingersnaps	Caraway dinner rolls*	Fresh fruit	Fresh fruit

* Recipes from Connor W. E. Connor S. L., Becker N. et al. *The Best from the Family Heart Kitchens*, Portland, Oregon. Oregon Health Sciences University Press, 1981. From Connor and Connor, 1985.

cent. If a phase 3 diet of 20 percent total fat is eaten, total blood cholesterol will decrease by 53 percent from baseline. However, it must be kept in mind that relatively few people are successful in achieving phase 3 goals.

ETIOLOGY

Although it is obvious that people eat to survive, what determines the types of foods that are eaten? Throughout most of human history people ate what was grown locally, so availability was the primary determinant of eating patterns. With modern techniques of preservation and transportation, many types of foods are available to us most of the time. Therefore, other more complex influences on diet are now more important. The influences on eating habits are commonly classified into biological, cultural, and psychological factors.

Biological Factors

The most widely documented biological influence is the preference for sweet tastes. Infants strongly prefer sweets, and this preference continues throughout life (Rozin, 1984). There is a mild aversion to bitter and salty tastes among infants, but this pattern is altered as the child ages. There seems to be some adaptive value in these preferences, because sweet foods tend to be the source of nutrients and toxic substances often have bitter tastes (Rozin & Fallon, 1980). While this taste for sweets may have stimulated people to stock up on calories in preparation for famine in past times, the situation is different today. Processed sugar is now in many foods with very few nutrients, and the strong preference for sweets has probably been a factor in the development of obesity for many people.

Recall the studies of animals who were given the supermarket diet (Sclafani & Springer, 1976). The availability of a variety of foods that were high in sugar and fat led to almost all the animals becoming grossly obese. We all know some people who have a great deal of difficulty controlling their intake of sweets and baked goods, and they may be victims of the supermarket diet phenomenon. With our current unlimited access to many foods it seems that our biological preferences are leading us to overeat.

Food aversions are more powerful than food preferences. When animals are given a food with a toxin that makes them sick, they develop an aversion to the taste of that food which is often permanent (Garcia, Hankins, & Rusiniak, 1974). Similar long-term taste aversions have been observed in humans (Rozin & Kalat, 1971).

There are metabolic differences that affect eating patterns. A high percentage of adults from some ethnic groups have lactose intolerance. Lactose (or milk sugar) creates gas, bloating, and diarrhea in these people. Ethnic groups with a long tradition of cow herding, such as northern Europeans, do not have much lactose intolerance, but most of the world's people cannot drink milk. It appears that lactose intolerance is an inherited trait that determines a culture's use of milk in foods.

Cultural Factors

Each culture creates its own cuisine, and those foods and dishes in large part define that culture. Each cuisine is defined by its staple foods, cooking methods, and added flavorings (Rozin, 1982). Cultures differ by the social setting in which food is eaten, the sequence in which courses are presented, and the significance of eating.

The family is the primary agent for transmitting the culture from one generation to another, so it is reasonable to expect to find similarities in food preferences and eating habits among family members. Rozin (1984) summarizes the literature by suggesting that the diets of older children resemble their parents' habits because there have been 16 or 17 years of exposure. The diets of young children are less similar to their parents' diets. However, Klesges and colleagues (Klesges et al., 1983) found that parents actively influence young children's eating habits by encouraging, praising, and punishing.

Food is often used as a reward for children. ("If you are good, then you can have dessert.") Sweet foods are used more frequently because they are more preferred. However, using sweets as a reward may further increase the child's preference for them. Birch, Zimmerman, and Hind (1980) found that foods paired with praise became more preferred by youngsters. Children even began to like carrots more when they were given as a reward by an adult. This study suggests that we condition children to like sweets even more by pairing them with positive social events, such as birthdays, and giving them as rewards.

Another major agent for transmitting culture is television. Over the course of a year most children spend more time watching television than they spend in a classroom. Much of television advertising directed at children is specifically designed to alter their food preferences. Each year, the average American child watches 20,000 commercials, and 10,000 of them are for food. Commercials during the weekend daytime viewing hours were studied for 9 months on the three commercial networks. There were 7515 food commercials: 51 percent were for cereals, 22 percent were for candy and gum, and 11 percent were for cookies. Nonsugared products were featured in only 4.3 percent of the ads, and vegetables were not advertised at all. Cereals were the most frequently advertised food, but most cereals for children are 40 percent sugar (some are even as high as 70 percent). It is clear that after 10,000 exposures a year, children are learning from food commercials, and this learning is affecting behavior. Of 591 mothers who were interviewed, fully 75 percent who

purchased sugared products said that they were influenced by their child's request (Wadden & Brownell, 1984).

There have been very few attempts to use television to increase children's preferences for nutritious foods. In one study kindergarten children watched ten 20-minute videotapes on healthy nutrition over a 2-week period (Peterson, Jeffrey, Bridgwater, & Dawson, 1984). Compared with their exposure to commercial advertisements, this was a very limited amount of time. Although there was evidence of recall of the information and increased knowledge of nutrition concepts, there was no change in preference or actual food choices. Even so, the potential power of television for stimulating healthy eating habits was demonstrated. If children are going to learn to eat health-promoting diets, then attempts will have to be made to counter their massive exposure to the promotion of sugar-laden foods on television commercials.

Socioeconomic status is an influence on all cultures. Levels of income, education, and occupational status are related to dietary behaviors. A recent study suggested that socioeconomic status may be more important than race or ethnicity as an influence on data. Diets of black men and women were studied in North Carolina. The beneficial minerals potassium and calcium were eaten more frequently by high socioeconomic status blacks. Those with higher education also believed more strongly that diet affects health and were less likely to use salt at the table (Gerber et al., 1991).

Psychological Factors

There is mounting evidence that despite the common elements of biology and culture, each individual develops his or her own personal preferences that may differ from those of others in the same culture. Rozin (1984) has developed a classification system for describing food preferences. The classes are (a) sensory-affective factors, (b) anticipated consequences, and (c) ideational factors. Sensory-affective factors are based on the taste of food. Good tastes produce a positive emotional response. While some tastes are biologically influenced, there appears to be great individual variation for most foods. Anticipated consequences of food may refer to immediate effects such as nausea or a feeling of fullness. Ideas about the delayed consequences of eating often refer to health issues. That is, a food may be seen as high in vitamins, low in fat, or carcinogenic. There are also social consequences. For example, even if you do not like pizza, you will tend to eat it if it is highly valued in your social circle. In some groups you can improve your social status by eating jalapeño peppers. Foods are often rejected for ideational reasons. Some substances are seen as ''inappropriate'' as foods, and this varies greatly by culture. Most Americans will not eat insects or dogs, but in other cultures these are considered good foods. Wood shavings, on the other hand, are rarely seen as appropriate food.

The study of beliefs about foods may help us understand more about why people eat diets that increase risk of CVD. The Nutrition Attitude Survey was developed to measure attitudes about adopting a low-fat, low-cholesterol diet (Hollis, Carmody, Connor, Fey, & Matarazzo, 1986). The 40-item survey was administered to 415 healthy men and women. Four types of attitudes were identified in this survey. The Helpless and Unhealthy factor suggested that people felt helpless about their ability to change unhealthy eating habits. The Food Exploration factor measured flexibility in trying new foods, recipes, and restaurants. The Meat Preference factor reflected a belief that meat should be the central dish of most meals. The Health Consciousness factor indicated an awareness of the role of nutrition in disease and a willingness to alter the diet. Those who scored high on the Helpless and Unhealthy factor were high on all of the fol-

lowing measures: meat intake, weight, emotional distress, medical and psychological symptoms, total cholesterol, and LDL cholesterol. Those who scored high on the Food Exploration factor were relatively young, and the men participated more in food preparation. Meat Preference scores were correlated positively with meat consumption and negatively with consumption of meatless meals, fruit, and beans. Those who scored high on Health Consciousness ate less meat and more meatless meals. This is an interesting description of how adults think about food, and it suggests that attitudes about food are related to actual intake.

A variety of psychological theories and models can be applied to the study of eating behaviors. Self-efficacy is a strong predictor of change in eating habits (Shannon, Bagby, Wang, & Trenkner, 1990). The stages of change model also helps explain eating behavior, and not surprisingly, men were more likely to be in the precontemplation stage, suggesting they were not ready to reduce fat in their diets (Curry, Kristal, & Bowen, 1992).

Stress has long been suspected as being a powerful influence on eating, and some experimental data support this idea. Grunberg and Straub (1992) either exposed subjects to a stressful (industrial accidents) or a nonstressful film. Afterward, they observed what subjects ate in the laboratory. Men and women responded very differently. Men in the stress condition ate much less, but women in the stress condition ate more, than those in the nonstress condition. Stressed women doubled their intake of sweet foods. Does this study sound true to you?

Psychological factors also appear to help explain why some people respond well to dietary change programs, and others do not. In the Women's Health Trial, a study of dietary change to prevent breast cancer, maintenance of the low-fat diet was assessed one year after the program. Those women who felt deprived by the healthy diet and who found it costly in time or money were unlikely to continue the healthful diet (Urban, White, Anderson, Curry, & Kristal, 1992). Diet change programs need to address these barriers to success.

Other researchers have studied how adolescents think about food. Contento, Michela, and Goldberg (1988) identified motivational factors that affected food choices in 355 children and adolescents aged 11 to 18. The subjects rated various attributes of 20 foods. The foods included ones that adolescents liked and disliked and ones that they ate frequently and infrequently. Each food was rated on eight scales representing these attributes:

tasty

healthful

likely to cause heart disease

contained sugar

fattening

easy to get

eaten by friends

served by parents

The investigators found that adolescents could be categorized as to how they made food choices. There were five main groups. For all of the groups taste was an important factor, as would be expected based on Rozin's (1984) theory as described above. However, for the group labeled "hedonistic," taste was the most important attribute of food. Health was not an important consideration for this group, and they had the highest intake of fat, sugar, and sodium. The second group was named the "socially/environmentally controlled" cluster because their most important attributes of food were "easy to get" and "served by parents." They ate what was around them, and health was not a consideration.

The next three groups were motivated to obtain healthful foods and avoid harmful foods. In all of these groups food choice was positively correlated with health, but negatively correlated with "contains sugar, fattening, and likely to cause heart disease." The motivation of these three groups was similar, but the source of the motivation seemed to be different. In the third group, there were low correlations with friend and parent factors, so this group was named "personal health." In the fourth group food choices were highly correlated with "eaten by friends," so this group was named "peer-supported health." Here both the subject and his or her friends appeared to be motivated by health. The fifth group was named "parent-supported health" because their food choices were related to what their parents served as well as the strong effect of health attributes.

This study shows that adolescents are not alike in how they make food choices. Some are strongly motivated by taste and convenience, while others are concerned about how the foods they eat will affect their health. Understanding how both adults and adolescents make their food choices may help health promotion experts devise dietary change programs that are effective for each major segment of the population.

TREATMENT

There is nearly unanimous agreement among health professionals that people who have already developed a clinical manifestation of CVD or who have elevated risk factors should make dramatic changes in their diets. The usual recommendations are as follows:

Reduce saturated fat and cholesterol intake to lower serum cholesterol.

Reduce calories to control weight.

Reduce sugar intake to lower triglycerides and control weight.

Reduce sodium and increase potassium and calcium to control blood pressure.

Reduce alcohol to control blood pressure.

One of the largest and most successful dietary change programs that incorporated prin-

BOX 14-3

FOCUS ON WOMEN

Why Are Women More Likely to Have Eating Disorders?

There has been a great deal of concern about the apparent increases in the incidence of eating disorders in recent years. *Anorexia nervosa* is a serious disorder with a mortality rate between 5 and 20 percent. It is characterized by low body weight, cessation of menstruation, extreme fear of fatness, and distorted body image. Although an anorexic may be very thin, they may perceive themselves as fat and severely restrict their food intake to lose even more weight. About 1 percent of all adolescent girls are anorexic; the condition is rare among boys. *Bulimia nervosa* is a behavioral pattern of binge eating followed by efforts to get rid of the excess calories by vomiting, laxative use, diet pills, or fasting. Bulimics have a fear of fatness, but they are usually normal weight or even overweight. One to four percent of young women may have this disorder; very few men engage in the binge-purge pattern. Many adolescent women have some of the symptoms of bulimia, but not the full-blown syndrome. Although bulimia is typically not a life-threatening disorder, bulimics tend to be psychologically troubled, and frequent vomiting and other bulimic behaviors can lead to numerous health problems.

Although relatively few women have eating disorders, it is extremely common for girls and women to be dissatisfied with their body shapes. The vast majority of men are satisfied with their body weight, but most women want to be thinner. Nearly half of all adolescent girls want to lose weight, and this percentage is higher in girls from affluent families. It is believed that women's dissatisfaction with their bodies is largely due to societal definitions of attractiveness and increases their risks of eating disorders.

Women's status in the community is historically more dependent on their physical attractiveness than men's, so women are more affected by shifts in ideal body types. Greek statues portrayed women with moderate amounts of body fat, and artists in the sixteenth through nineteenth centuries tended to paint women who today would be considered obese. The ideal female body type changed in the 1920s. Very thin bodies came to be preferred, and both medical and popular literature commented on the rising prevalence of eating disorders in girls who were starving themselves to achieve the ideal thin shape. As the styles changed in the 1930s, the incidence of dieting decreased. In the 1960s thinness again became a hallmark of female attractiveness. Over the past several decades, *Playboy* centerfolds, fashion models, and Miss America contestants have become increasingly thin, while the general female population has increased considerably in body weight. It is not surprising that more women are dieting.

Even young girls are experiencing conflict about eating. Nearly half of all 7- to 13-year-old girls want to be thinner, and almost that many have already tried dieting. It is believed that a number of women who restrict their eating will develop a disordered eating style. Thus, the more dieting they engage in, the more likely they will develop eating disorders. What are some of the factors that influence this process?

Sociocultural factors are important. Affluent women between the ages of 12 and 25 are most likely to be bulimic or anorexic. Although weight dissatisfaction and dieting are normative for females, those who are extreme in these beliefs and who equate thinness with success are most likely to develop an eating disorder. Dancers, models, and athletes are at very high risk, because there is intense pressure to have thin, attractive bodies. Male wrestlers and jockeys are at risk of developing eating disorders because of the same pressures.

Psychological correlates of eating disorders have been identified. Anorexics tend to be perfectionistic and have limited spontaneity. Both anorexics and bulimics tend to be obsessive, particularly about food, and they usually have low self-esteem. Bulimics are likely to have various types of maladjustment throughout childhood, and a history of attempted suicide is fairly common.

Family characteristics may predispose some girls to eating disorders. Families of anorexics have been described as overprotective and achievement-oriented. Families of bulimics demonstrate overt conflict, rejection, and neglect. Family histories of eating disorders have been documented, and some studies suggest a genetic role.

There are several likely reasons for the increased risk of eating disorders among women, and many of these factors, such as societal ideals of female beauty, are not easy to change. The high incidence of dieting, even in young girls, indicates that many females have conflicts about food. These findings should be taken into account in dietary change programs so as not to stimulate any more guilt about eating (Rolls, Fedoroff, & Guthrie, 1991).

ciples of behavior change occurred in the Multiple Risk Factor Intervention Trial, also known as MRFIT. Over 12,000 men with established risk factors for CVD were studied for 6 years. Half the men were randomly assigned to the Usual Care condition, and they were only evaluated each year. The other half took part in a Special Intervention that focused on dietary change, smoking cessation, and hypertension treatment with medication. The overall results of the study are very controversial. Partly because the Usual Care group reduced their risk factors more than expected, there was no difference in CVD mortality at the end of the study. However, it is instructive to examine the effects of the diet change program in the Special Intervention group.

Dolecek and colleagues (Dolecek et al., 1986) reported the effects of the MRFIT dietary change program on both eating habits and serum cholesterol. The intervention program changed over the years, but it included both group and individual counseling (Gorder et al., 1986). In the first phase both patients and their spouses attended 10 group sessions and received instruction in behavior modification methods. The goals of the intervention were to alter food choices, cooking methods, and shopping habits rather than to provide a specific diet. After the initial sessions, nutrition counseling was accomplished in individual sessions. Weight reduction groups were conducted for overweight patients. Throughout the 6 years new materials and new methods were developed to promote further dietary change. During periodic visits with project nutritionists, adherence to the dietary recommendations was monitored with 3-day diet records that were scored for fat intake. Using these records the nutritionist would either highlight progress or identify areas for further work.

There were large and significant differences between Usual Care and Special Intervention groups in the amount of dietary changes across the 6 years of the study. Special Intervention subjects decreased calorie intake, all types of fats, and cholesterol; while the Usual Care subjects made few changes. Table 14-6 shows some of the differences.

Participants in the Special Intervention group were classified as high, medium, and low adherers to the diet (Dolecek, Milas, Van Horn, et al., 1986) based on their 3-day records. Sixty percent were low adherers, meaning that they may have made some changes but there was need for additional dietary alterations. Thirty-three percent of the men were classed as medium adherers, meaning that they met the goals of the basic MRFIT diet. Only seven percent of the men were adhering

---

TABLE 14·6

CHANGES IN SELECTED NUTRIENTS IN USUAL CARE (UC) AND SPECIAL INTERVENTION (SI) SUBJECTS ACROSS 6 YEARS IN THE MULTIPLE RISK FACTOR INTERVENTION TRIAL

Nutrient	Baseline	Change in SI	Change in UC
Calories	2433.1	−531.6	−176.5
Total fat (%)	38.2	−4.4	−0.2
Saturated fat	14.3	−3.9	−0.3
Monounsaturated fat	15.0	−2.5	−0.2
Polyunsaturated fat	6.3	2.1	0.2
Cholesterol (mg)	450.7	−186.2	−22.1

Note: All differences between groups are significant at $p < .001$. Adapted from Gorder, Dolecek, Coleman, et al., 1986.

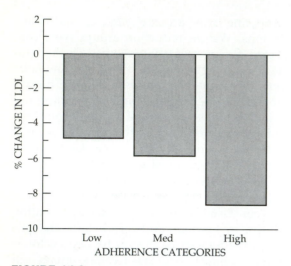

FIGURE 14-3

Adherence to MRFIT diet and LDL change over 6 years. (From Dolecek, Milas, Van Horn, et al., 1986.)

to the most advanced diet recommended in the intervention. As shown in Figure 14-3 the extent of adherence was strongly related to the amount of reductions in LDL-cholesterol. The same pattern was seen for total cholesterol.

The MRFIT study shows that with behavioral counseling, patients at high risk for CVD can achieve important reductions in dietary fat and cholesterol and sustain those changes over 6 years. Similar effective programs have also been carried out in clinics (Meyer & Henderson, 1974) and work sites (Bruno, Arnold, Jacobson, Winick, & Wynder, 1983) with high-risk patients.

PREVENTION

It is often argued that those with identified risk factors are motivated to change, but it is very difficult to engage the general population in dietary change programs because they do not see the need to change their diets. Public health professionals stress that it is important to promote dietary changes in the entire population because the typical American diet leads

to heart disease. One common approach is to teach children and adolescents healthful eating habits, because it is felt to be easier for children to change their diets than adults, who have eaten high-fat diets for several decades. Young children do not have much choice over what they eat, but adolescents are increasingly making their own decisions in this area. Several effective nutrition education programs for adolescents have been reported, but the study by King and colleagues (King et al., 1988) combined a good behavioral intervention with a comprehensive measurement plan.

Tenth grade classes in two California high schools were randomly assigned to intervention or control conditions. The five-session dietary change curriculum was implemented over a 3-week period and emphasized nutrition information and cognitive-behavioral strategies. Intervention methods included dietary self-assessment, problem solving, goal setting, food tasting, role playing, food preparation, and a nutrition quiz. Slides, in-class contests, and food demonstrations increased student interest. Homework promoted behavior change outside of class.

The observation of students' actual food choices was particularly innovative. After taking the paper-and-pencil measures, students were offered their choice of four snacks. Two snacks were heart healthy (bagels and unsalted nuts) and two were not (cookies and potato chips). Their choices were recorded. In addition, students were given a coupon redeemable for one snack at the school lunchroom. The snack choice was written on the coupon, and it was returned to the experimenters after it was redeemed.

At the end of the brief intervention there were significant improvements in dietary knowledge, and the improvement was maintained at the 1-year follow-up. The improvement in frequency of eating heart healthy foods seen at posttest did not maintain for 1 year, nor did the initial improvement in

BOX 14·4

FOCUS ON DIVERSITY
Promoting Healthful Diets in African American Families

As in other segments of U.S. society, the diets of African Americans typically contain too much sodium and fat. However, there have been few programs designed to improve diets in this population, despite the cultural differences in food selection and preparation. Baranowski and colleagues developed a program for African American families in Texas so that parents and children could help one another make the dietary changes.

The program was based at a convenient community center, where the intervention could be controlled and individual diet counseling could be offered. A community advisory council assisted in making the program relevant to the needs of the local African American community, and people from the local community were hired as staff members. Families were encouraged to attend as a group, and a family photo album was developed showing each family member engaged in healthful activities. The center was decorated with pictures of African American celebrities and articles from black magazines that were consistent with the messages in the intervention. Personal testimonials, which are a popular interaction format, were included in the educational sessions.

The goal of the dietary intervention was to decrease sodium, total fat, and saturated fat. Families were counseled regarding diet change and were assisted in setting goals, finding social support, and problem solving. Group education sessions helped participants identify, shop for, and prepare healthful foods. Each session ended with a healthful snack that was often provided by participating families. Educational sessions were held in the evenings for 14 weeks.

All African American families with fifth through seventh grade children in Galveston were invited to participate in the study. Of the 96 families who volunteered, half were randomly assigned to the intervention and the others were controls. Dietary behaviors were measured by a food frequency questionnaire and an intensive 24-hour diet recall interview.

There were significant differences across groups in high total fat, high saturated fat, and high sodium foods, indicating that the intervention had the desired effects on the food frequency measure. However, no differences were found on the 24-hour recall. Although only 17 percent of the adults attended more than half of the sessions, those who attended most of the sessions reported substantial dietary improvements. Those who attended a few sessions reported little dietary change. Therefore, it is important to identify methods of increasing attendance.

The investigators interviewed subjects in their home to determine reasons for nonattendance. Conflicts with work and school activities were the primary barriers. The authors suggested that it might be more effective to conduct the intervention in a more convenient setting in which families are already gathering, such as at churches (Baranowski et al., 1990).

availability of healthy foods at home. Self-efficacy for making dietary changes did not improve at all. While the intervention did not increase healthy snack choices, intervention students who used lunchroom coupons made more healthy choices than control students.

The King and colleagues (1988) study shows that a very brief diet change program can produce improvements in knowledge and behavior in a general population of high school students. Although the diet changes were not large, a five-session program may not be ex-

BOX 14·5

FOCUS ON RESEARCH

High-Tech Health Behavior Change at Your Local Supermarket

Programs to prevent diet-related health problems can also be directed toward adults. Richard A. Winett and colleagues (1991) reported an innovative use of computers to help people eat more healthy foods. The authors reasoned that an important part of eating healthful foods is to have them available at home. They developed a computerized program, called the Nutrition for a Lifetime System, to help supermarket shoppers select low-fat and high-fiber foods. The system consists of a kiosk (or display) in a supermarket full of the latest technology, including a computer, color monitor with touchscreen capability, videodisc player, printer, and optical scanner.

Each shopper identified him or herself with a social security number so that the computer could keep track of purchases over time and give individualized feedback. Shoppers indicated their intended purchases by filling out a 209-item checklist. The computer read the shopping list and printed out an aisle-by-aisle guide for finding the items.

During a 6-week intervention phase additional information and feedback were presented to shoppers in the treatment group. A brief video program (2 to 8 minutes) showed them how to make gradual changes in food selection and meal preparation. Reviews of the previous week's program were available. The program gave specific suggestions for trying new foods and asked the shopper to commit to changing behavior by using touchscreens. The computer then gave feedback, such as "You're off to a good start."

The computer-printed shopping guides contained prompts for low-fat and high-fiber foods. When a shopper put a new healthful food on the shopping list, the computer printed a note of congratulations.

The study included baseline, experimental, and follow-up phases for the 26 treatment and 23 control subjects who returned their actual store receipts. During the experimental phase the treatment group intended to purchase less (and actually did purchase less) meats and dairy products than the control groups. The differences in dairy products remained significant at follow-up. The difference for high-fiber grains was in the correct direction, but was not significant. Amount spent on food did not differ between groups.

Improvements planned for the system include more options for information (such as healthy snacks and reading food labels), graphing of shoppers' progress, a coupon incentive system, and a maintenance program. This use of computer technology in a behavior-change program was very popular and helped people improve their diets at no extra cost. Look for the Nutrition for a Lifetime System at your local supermarket (Winett et al., 1991).

pected to induce major modifications in eating behavior. A long-term nutrition education curriculum for elementary students that included parent involvement through homework produced changes in diet that persisted throughout the full year of the program (Perry et al., 1988). These and other studies indicate that children and adolescents who are not identified as having high CVD risk factors can learn to eat more healthful diets.

SUMMARY

Diet-related health problems in the developed world are primarily due to overconsumption. Dietary habits are related to five of the top ten causes of death in the United States: coronary heart disease, stroke, diabetes mellitus, cancers, and atherosclerosis. Dietary fat increases risk of developing all these diseases, so it should be considered the most important dietary component. A few other nutrients also influence important health problems. For example, diabetics are instructed to eat more fiber. Some dietary fibers decrease risk of CVD, while others decrease risk for some cancers. Sodium can increase blood pressure. Calcium can decrease blood pressure and help maintain bone health. Sugars promote tooth decay. The health effects of other nutrients and specific foods continue to be investigated.

Studies have demonstrated a systematic relationship between saturated fat in the diet and serum cholesterol. Other studies link serum cholesterol to death from heart disease. Several influential studies have been conducted throughout the world. These include a study in seven countries, an important study of workers in Chicago, and two intervention studies conducted in Finland and Los Angeles. Research with other groups that use a vegetarian diet (such as Seventh-Day Adventists) also suggests that nonmeat eaters have low levels of blood cholesterol and heart disease. The diet-heart hypothesis suggests that consumption of high levels of dietary fat and cholesterol leads to high levels of serum cholesterol. High serum cholesterol, in turn, is associated with development of CVD. High levels of saturated fat and cholesterol are found in common foods such as hamburgers, steaks, cheese, and whole milk. Fried foods are also high in saturated fats. Other dietary risk factors for heart disease include high levels of salt and low levels of calcium and potassium. These minerals are related to high blood pressure, another important risk factor for CVD.

Food choices may be affected by a variety of factors: biological, cultural, and psychological. The American Heart Association recommends a prudent diet to prevent cardiovascular disease. For someone with a high risk of developing CVD, treatment might include reduction of saturated fats, reduction in calories, and reduction in sugar and sodium intake. It might also include increases in potassium and calcium intake. Major programs such as the Multiple Risk Factor Intervention Study have demonstrated that these changes can be achieved. Other studies involving high school students and other community groups suggest that the high-fat, high-salt diet that leads to heart disease can be prevented or modified.

KEY TERMS

Total caloric intake. The amount of energy consumed, typically reported for one meal or one day.

Cholesterol. A waxy substance only found in foods of animal origin. Most cholesterol in the blood of humans is produced by the body, but cholesterol levels can also be influenced by dietary intake.

Fats. Substances found in animal and vegetable foods. Saturated fats raise blood cholesterol, whereas monosaturated and polysaturated fats lower blood cholesterol.

Carbohydrates. Sugars (simple carbohydrates) and starches (complex carbohydrates).

Fiber. An undigestible part of vegetable foods. Water-soluble fiber may reduce serum cholesterol, and water-insoluble fiber may prevent some cancers.

Sodium, potassium, calcium. Minerals that may affect blood pressure. Sodium increases blood pressure, while potassium and calcium decrease it.

Serum cholesterol. The level of cholesterol found in the serum of blood. The higher the level of serum cholesterol, the higher the risk of cardiovascular disease.

Cholesterol–saturated fats index (CSI). A formula that provides an estimate of the likelihood that foods will increase serum cholesterol. CSI = (1.01 × g saturated fat) + 0.05 × mg cholesterol.

Seven Countries Study. A large study demonstrating a strong relationship between saturated fats consumed in the diet and serum cholesterol levels found in blood.

Western-Electric Study. A study of Chicago workers that demonstrated a relationship between dietary fat and cholesterol and cardiovascular disease over a 19-year period.

Lactose intolerance. The inability to properly digest the sugars in milk. This characterizes most people in the world.

MRFIT (the Multiple Risk Factor Intervention Trial). This study of 12,000 men was unable to show that attempts to modify risk factors reduce heart disease. However, those participants who adhered to the treatment achieved significant reductions in blood cholesterol levels.

CHAPTER 15

Physical Activity

When Celine Baker was growing up, she was not a tomboy but she loved being outdoors playing games with other children. During adolescence she developed other interests, and most of those interests involved boys. Although she did not notice it, she spent much less time being active. During college she spent a lot of time reading, studying, and partying. Recreation included tennis and swimming only on rare occasions. Right after she graduated, she got married, got a job, and had two children. Now her daughter Tiffany is starting high school, and Celine is starting to see a change in her daughter's lifestyle. Tiffany quit the swim team a couple of years ago, and now she spends most of her free time watching videos at home or hanging out with other teens at the mall.

Celine is seeing the same pattern of decreasing physical activity in her daughter that she now realizes occurred in her own life. Celine is not too sure this is a good idea. When she graduated from high school, she weighed 120 lb. Now 20 years later, she has crept up to 145 lb. She also feels tired most of the time, and she finds it hard to walk from the supermarket to the car carrying even one bag of groceries. Not only is Celine now thinking about starting an exercise program for herself, but she also wants to get Tiffany involved so that she will not develop a sedentary lifestyle like her mother's. What is the best way for them to start exercising? What will exercise really do for them? What makes it hard for most people to stick with an exercise program?

Think about how easy life has become. Most people have cars, so walking is not necessary. Although there are stairs, there are also elevators. There are other mechanical devices to perform almost any task. In past centuries physical activity was not a major health concern, because it was a part of everyone's life. If you wanted to go somewhere, you usually walked. Most people's work involved manual labor, such as construction, farm tasks, and movement of commodities. In more primitive times, people had to track down animals or work the earth to get something to eat. Sedentary lifestyles are a recent innovation in human existence made possible by the mechanical devices that transport us and do heavy work for us. While a great deal of creativity has been expended in developing labor-saving machines, there appears to be a side effect to them that affects health in important ways. Before taking a look at the health effects of physical activity, it is necessary to define a few terms.

TERMS

Physical activity is a broad term that has been defined as "any bodily movement produced by skeletal muscles that results in energy expenditure" (Caspersen, Powell, & Christenson, 1985). Thus, physical activity covers everything from twiddling your thumbs and fidgeting in your seat during a test to Olympic weight lifting and participation in triathlons. Physical activity can be done as part of work or during leisure time, and it is often measured as caloric expenditure.

Exercise is a subset of physical activity since it involves bodily movement, but exercise should be used in a limited sense. Exercise has been defined as "planned, structured, and repetitive bodily movement done to improve or maintain one or more components of physical fitness" (Caspersen et al., 1985). Conditioning activities and sports are likely to be exercise, while household chores and work activities are unlikely to be exercise because they are not done to improve fitness. The concept of intention seems to be necessary in defining exercise. If I walk to the store because my car is broken, that is not exercise. If I walk to the store to burn some extra calories, that is exercise.

Physical fitness is "a set of attributes that people have or achieve that relates to the ability to perform physical activity" (Caspersen et al., 1985). Several types of health-related physical fitness have been identified: (a) cardiorespiratory endurance, (b) muscular endurance, (c) muscular strength, (d) body composition, and (e) flexibility. There are also performance-related physical variables that apply to sports performance rather than health. Physical fitness refers to physiological function and not to behavior. However, physical activity can improve physical fitness, and physical fitness improves one's ability to be physically active.

EPIDEMIOLOGY

While much is known about the epidemiology of smoking and health, the study of physical activity as it relates to health is in its infancy. Such basic questions as "What percentage of the population is sedentary, and what percent-

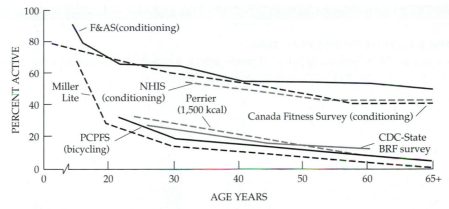

FIGURE 15-1

Leisure-time physical activity and age, United States and Canada, 1972–1983. (From Stephens, Jacobs, & White, 1985.)

age is active?'' are difficult to answer. There is no standard measure of physical activity because physical activity can vary by type, duration, intensity, frequency, and intermittency. Thus, it is difficult to specify what is "active." Every survey uses a different definition of physical activity and exercise, so comparisons across studies are difficult to make. However, several representative surveys of the U.S. and Canadian populations have been conducted. Some of these results are shown in Figure 15-1

(Stephens et al., 1985). Percentage of subjects classified as active in leisure time, for example at age 30, varied from more than 60 percent to less than 20 percent. The discrepancy is caused mainly by different definitions of *active*. However, all studies agree that activity decreases with age. As shown in Figure 15-2 (Stephens et al., 1985), physical activity increases with education, and the same result is seen with family income.

One of the conclusions that can be reached

FIGURE 15-2

Leisure-time physical activity and education, United States and Canada, 1972–1983. (From Stephens, Jacobs, & White, 1985.)

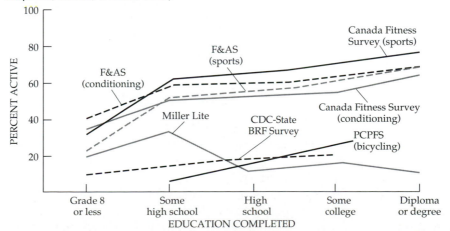

BOX 15·1

HEALTH OBJECTIVES FOR THE YEAR 2000

1. Increase to at least 30 percent the proportion of people aged 6 and older who engage regularly, preferably daily, in light to moderate physical activity (baseline: 22 percent).

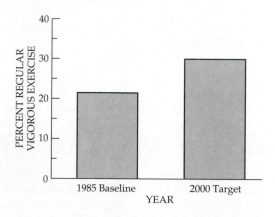

2. Increase to at least 20 percent the proportion of people aged 18 and older—and to at least 75 percent the proportion of children and adolescents aged 6 through 17—who engage in vigorous physical activity that promotes the development and maintenance of cardiorespiratory fitness 3 or more days per week for 20 or more minutes per occasion (baseline: 12 percent for people aged 18 and older in 1985, 66 percent for youth aged 10 through 17 in 1984).

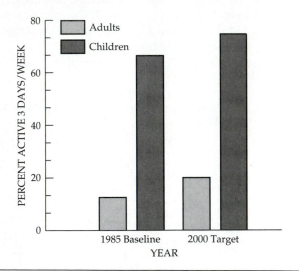

BOX 15·1 *continued*

3. Reduce to no more than 15 percent the proportion of people aged 6 and older who engage in no leisure-time physical activity (baseline: 24 percent for people aged 18 and older in 1985).

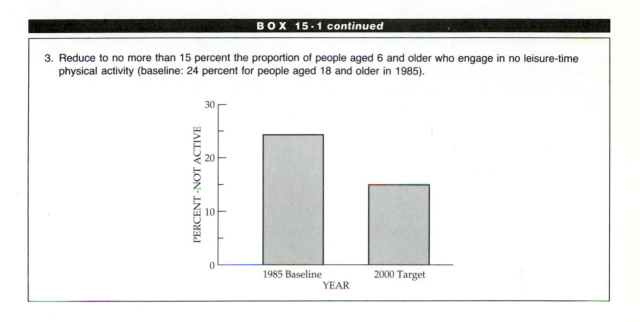

about patterns of activity is that younger, better educated, and more affluent persons are more likely to be active in their leisure time. Many people with low levels of education are likely to be active in their work, so they may not feel a need to be active after work. In most studies men are more active than women (King et al., 1992).

It is not clear to what extent physical activity differs by race and ethnic group. Most studies find blacks, especially black women, to be less active than whites. Latino women may also be less active than whites. When income and education are taken into account, there are still differences between race and ethnic groups, but those differences tend to be small (Shea et al., 1991; Washburn, Kline, Lackland, & Wheeler, 1992).

The most common standard for physical activity was developed by the American College of Sports Medicine (ACSM) (1991). A panel of scientists reviewed the literature on physical activity and physical fitness and defined a minimal amount of recommended physical activity based on the amount required to increase car-diorespiratory fitness. The recommendation is summarized in Box 15-2.

When the ACSM definition of exercise is used, the U.S. adult population seems very sedentary. On the basis of the 1985 National Health Interview Survey, only 8 percent of all men and 7 percent of all women regularly performed the type of vigorous activity recommended (Caspersen, Christenson, & Pollard, 1986). From these data, one can conclude that there is an epidemic of sedentary lifestyles among U.S. adults.

BOX 15·2

AMERICAN COLLEGE OF SPORTS MEDICINE RECOMMENDATIONS FOR EXERCISE

Type: large-muscle activity that is rhythmic and repetitive (for example, walking, running, swimming, and cycling)

Duration: at least 20 minutes continuously

Frequency: 3 to 4 times per week

Intensity: vigorous (defined as at least 60 to 80 percent of maximal capacity)

The latest revision of the American College of Sports Medicine (1991) guidelines makes a distinction between physical activity to promote fitness and physical activity to promote health. Less vigorous physical activity that is performed regularly is now viewed as adequate to provide protection from CVD. Both the ACSM and the year 2000 objectives for the nation place a major emphasis on recommending moderate-intensity activities as a necessary part of a healthy lifestyle. Walking, gardening, and easy cycling are moderate-intensity activities that improve health. Many people are intimidated by the thought of having to run or do aerobics, but going for a brisk walk is not threatening at all. Everyone can do it. Therefore, the recommendation to do moderate-intensity activity is good news for many people, and it encourages them to get out of their chair and do something to improve their health.

It is useful to think about vigorous exercise (running, cycling, aerobics, swimming laps, and singles tennis) for increasing fitness and optimal health and moderate-intensity activities (walking, gardening, hiking, slow cycling) for some health benefits. (Blair, Kohl, Gordon, & Paffenbarger, 1992). The current message from health authorities is that it is important to do some amount of physical activity on a regular basis, but it does not have to be strenuous. Being a total couch potato is hazardous to your health, but forget about "no pain, no gain."

What about the activity levels of children? Everyone knows that children are constantly running around and expending enormous amounts of energy. However, the physical activity of children has been studied less than that of adults. One study monitored the heart rates of 6- to 7-year-old children during an entire summer day when they could be as active as they wanted (Gilliam et al., 1981). Heart rates can be used to estimate physical activity, because activity causes the heart rate to increase. As can be seen in Figure 15-3 these young children spent only 3 percent of their

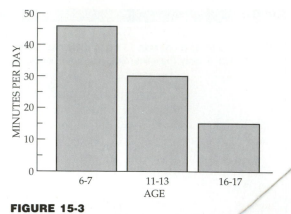

FIGURE 15-3

Minutes of vigorous activity per day in children, based on heart rate recordings.

day, or less than 1 hour, in vigorous activity (heart rate 140 or greater). Other studies show that children become even less active as they get older. Figure 15-3 indicates that the average 17-year-old does not spend even 20 minutes per day in vigorous physical activity.

It seems that neither adults nor children are getting much exercise, despite what we keep hearing about the fitness boom. But is it important to be physically active? What are the health effects of physical activity?

These types of questions have not been seriously asked until recently. It was not until the 1970s that large numbers of scientists began to strongly suspect that physical activity played a role in CVD. Several studies were reported in the 1950s and 1960s, but many of them had very poor measures of physical activity and had inconsistent results. Enough data have been reported now to indicate that sedentary lifestyle is a major risk factor for CVD. Over 120 articles reporting 54 studies of physical activity and CVD were reviewed by Powell, Thompson, Caspersen, and Kendrick (1987). Forty-three studies were good enough to carefully scrutinize, and the conclusion was that inactive adults are twice as likely to die from CVD as those who are very active. Thus, the risk of inactivity is about the same as having high blood cholesterol, having high blood pressure, or smoking. Not only does physical activity help to prevent CVD, but there is evidence that physical activity aids rehabilitation from heart attacks, prevents second attacks, and has beneficial effects on several physiological risk factors (Haskell et al., 1992).

One of the most influential studies was the Harvard Alumni Study reported by Paffenbarger and colleagues (Paffenbarger, Wing, & Hyde, 1978). They studied almost 20,000 male alumni of Harvard University, aged 35 to 74, over a 16-year period. They found that not only were physically active men less likely to die from CVD, but they lived longer on average than the inactive men (Paffenbarger, Hyde, Wing, & Hsieh, 1986). Some people have joked that they don't want to live longer if they use all their extra time exercising. However, Paffenbarger and coworkers (1986) found that for every minute of activity, their subjects lived about 2 minutes longer. So you don't spend all your additional life exercising.

Paffenbarger and associates (1978) calculated calories expended in different types of activity, and each type offered protection from CVD mortality. While subjects who played a lot of vigorous sports received the most protection, even subjects who walked a modest amount received about 80 percent of the maximal protection. This illustrates an important point about physical activity and exercise. You can get most of the protective effects of physical activity just by walking, but you can get some extra protection by doing vigorous exercises like running.

Does physical activity protect you if you smoke or if you have high blood cholesterol? Again Paffenbarger and his colleagues (1978) studied this question. Whether they had another risk factor or not, those men who were physically active had lower CVD rates. There are now numerous epidemiologic studies showing that physically active people lower

their risk of CVD mortality. Physical inactivity is as strong a risk factor as blood pressure, blood cholesterol, and smoking. Therefore, most health scientists have accepted that physical activity is important, even though no randomized intervention study has shown that physical activity reduces CVD deaths.

Physical activity has beneficial effects on many health problems. Risk factors for nine major chronic diseases were studied (Hahn, Teutsch, Rothenberg, & Marks, 1990). The diseases included CVD, lung disease, several cancers, and diabetes. The percent of deaths that could be attributed to several risk factors were calculated. These are the findings:

Risk factor	Percent of deaths from nine chronic diseases
Smoking	33
Obesity	24
Sedentary lifestyle	23
High blood cholesterol	23
Hypertension	21

It may surprise you that lack of physical activity is believed to cause as many deaths as obesity, high blood cholesterol, and hypertension. The growing evidence of the importance of physical activity is leading the health care community to study this behavior much more carefully.

Physical fitness is also related to health status. Because physical activity is hard to measure, levels of physical fitness may tell us more about the health effects of regular physical activity. Blair and colleagues (1989) studied over 10,000 men and 3000 women who had their cardiovascular fitness measured with a maximal treadmill exercise test. They were followed for an average of 8 years, and the findings were dramatic. Men and women who were at least moderately fit lived longer, had less heart disease, and had less cancer than those with low fitness levels. The results also showed that men and women would be better off if they were high-fit smokers than if they were low-fit nonsmokers. In this study, fitness was more strongly related to mortality than smoking. In addition, moderate to high levels of fitness were protective even if subjects were fat, had high blood cholesterol, had high blood pressure, or were smokers. This is strong evidence that fitness has a large influence on health, but it must be remembered that the only way to increase your fitness is to do regular physical activity.

OK, physical activity may have some benefits, but what about the risks? Most people have heard that Jim Fixx, author of *The Complete Book of Running*, died just after a workout. A study conducted by Siscovick and colleagues (Siscovick, Weiss, Fletcher, & Lasky, 1984) illustrates the risk-benefit ratio of exercise. By studying cases of sudden death in the Seattle area they found that during exercise, risk of sudden death was increased about 700 percent. However, men who exercised had half the death rate of those who did not exercise. How can exercise both increase and decrease risk? Exercise stresses the cardiovascular system, so during exercise you are at increased risk of mortality, especially if you have advanced atherosclerosis. However, exercise has many effects that protect against CVD. Since one exercises only a few minutes on any particular day, a small fraction of the day is spent at increased risk, and the great majority of the day is spent at decreased risk. The net result is that the CVD benefits of exercise greatly outweigh the risks.

The story of Jim Fixx is a sad one. He had a strong family history of early death from CVD; and for 30 years he smoked, ate a high-fat diet, and did little physical activity. He made many lifestyle changes later in life, but he unwisely refused to have medical examinations that were indicated based on his age and family history. He had severe narrowing of his coronary arteries that was found on autopsy. While some people draw the conclusion from this well-publicized case that running will kill you, it is actually possible that his running and healthy diet helped him live longer than he otherwise would have.

The Jim Fixx case also illustrates the need to use common sense while exercising. Anyone who has known risk factors for CVD, including a family history, should obtain medical clearance before making large increases in physical activity. Most of the risks of exercise are dose-related, meaning that the risks increase as you do more vigorous physical activity. This is another reason to recommend low-intensity exercise, like walking.

Two primary conclusions may be drawn from this overview of epidemiologic data on physical activity. First, physical activity probably reduces CVD risk and total mortality significantly. Second, not many people are physically active. Look back to Box 15-1. It is estimated that only about 12 percent of adults do regular vigorous activity, and about 22 percent of Americans do regular moderate activity. That leaves about 66 percent of the population that is very sedentary. When you put these two facts together, you discover that more CVD deaths can be attributed to physical inactivity than to hypertension, hypercholesterolemia, or smoking. This is illustrated in Figure 15-4.

This figure shows what percentage of U.S. adults are doubling their risk by having each of the CVD risk factors. A systolic BP of 150 mmHg represents about a 2.0 relative risk, as does a total cholesterol of 268 mg/dl and smoking a pack of cigarettes or more per day. Being active 3 times per week for 20 minutes each time decreases risk by about one-half. Blood pressure is a risk factor for about 10 percent of the population, cholesterol is a risk factor for about 10 percent, and about 18 percent of all adults smoke at least a pack a day. However, almost 50–70 percent of all adults are so inac-

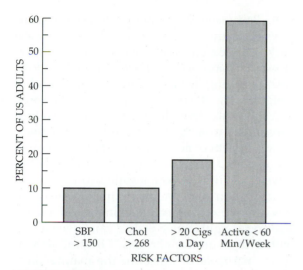

FIGURE 15-4

Percentage of U.S. adults doubling CVD risk, by risk factor.

tive that they are doubling their risk of CVD. Thus, these data suggest that more heart attacks could be prevented by increasing activity levels than by controlling any of the other risk factors. Because physical activity is certainly a behavior that is related to health, it is important to apply psychological methods to its measurement and promotion.

PATHOPHYSIOLOGY

Because the CVD benefits of physical activity have not been well documented until recently, our understanding of the mechanisms of this benefit is limited. There are several known mechanisms by which physical activity could reduce CVD, but we just do not know which are most important. These mechanisms are briefly discussed here.

1. Cardiovascular (CV) fitness. Cardiovascular fitness, also known as *aerobic power*, refers to the ability of the body to use oxygen. Oxygen is needed to fuel the muscles, so the more oxygen that can be taken into the body

and used, the greater the capacity for muscular exertion. CV fitness is measured by the rate of oxygen use at maximal exertion. This is referred to as the volume of oxygen at maximal exercise, and is abbreviated VO_2 max. CV fitness itself has been found to be associated with CVD mortality (Blair et al., 1989; Ekelund et al., 1988). While CV fitness is partially determined by genetics, regular physical activity can increase it by 25 percent or more.

Improving the body's ability to use oxygen is just one of physical activity's effects on the CV system. The heart is a muscle, so vigorous exercise strengthens the heart, increases its size, and improves several of its functions. Placing stress on the CV system through physical activity forces it to adjust by growing stronger.

2. HDL-cholesterol. Recall that HDL-cholesterol is the protective lipoprotein in the blood that may take cholesterol away from the arteries. Physical activity, especially if it is vigorous, produces large increases in HDL-cholesterol (Haskell, 1984). Figure 15-5 shows the relationship between average weekly running

FIGURE 15-5

Running mileage and change in HDL-cholesterol. (After Wood et al., 1983.)

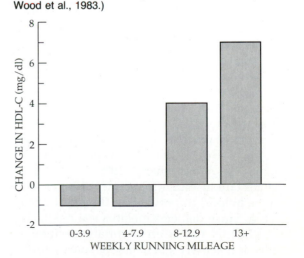

mileage and change in HDL-cholesterol over 1 year in initially sedentary middle-aged men (Wood et al., 1983).

This study showed that unless a person runs at least 8 mi per week, they are unlikely to obtain increases in HDL-cholesterol. While HDL-C may explain some of the benefits of physical activity in those who exercise vigorously, there must be another mechanism that accounts for the benefits of moderate-intensity physical activity.

3. Other lipids and lipoproteins. Physical activity does not have reliable effects on total cholesterol or LDL-cholesterol, since in most studies physical activity influences only HDL-cholesterol. However, triglycerides, which are fats in the blood, are reduced by physical activity.

4. Blood pressure. Many studies have reported that physically active people have lower blood pressures than those who are sedentary. Most of the epidemiologic studies indicate that physical activity may lower diastolic blood pressures by about 2 to 5 mmHg (Hicky, Mulcahy, Bourke, Graham, & Wilson-Davis, 1975; Siegel & Blumenthal, 1991). Men who are active throughout life are much less likely to develop hypertension than men who are sedentary (Paffenbarger, Wing, Hyde, & Jung, 1983). On the basis of these and other studies, it seems that reduced blood pressure is a potentially important mechanism of the CVD benefits of physical activity.

5. Glucose metabolism. Disturbed metabolism of glucose and insulin is involved in diabetes mellitus, and physical activity affects these metabolic factors. Physical activity reduces blood glucose, increases insulin receptors, and increases the effectiveness of insulin (Vranic & Wasserman, 1990). All these changes are useful in treating diabetes and may be helpful in preventing the onset of the disease. Since diabetes mellitus is a risk factor for CVD, this may be an important mechanism of physical activity's benefits for some people.

6. Body weight and body fat. The effects of physical activity on body weight and fat are very complex and are not completely understood. Physical activity burns calories and increases resting metabolic rate, so it is useful in weight loss. However, clinical studies show that physical activity by itself does not produce substantial weight loss, but physical activity is an effective addition to dietary change (Thompson, Jarvie, Lahey, & Cureton, 1982). Physical activity is better suited to producing fat reduction than weight reduction. Because physical activity can promote increased muscle size and weight, active people can have fat loss with little or no weight loss. Physical activity seems particularly critical in the maintenance of weight loss (Epstein & Wing, 1980).

Weight loss itself can have many of the same effects as physical activity. Weight loss produces increases in HDL-cholesterol, decreases in triglycerides, decreases in blood pressure, improved glucose metabolism, and even increases in CV fitness (Brownell & Stunkard, 1980). Because weight and fat loss and physical activity are so closely connected, it is difficult to distinguish the effects of fat loss from those of physical activity. It is possible that many of the physiological benefits of physical activity are a result of decreases in body weight and body fat.

7. Fibrinolysis. Fibrinolysis is the activity of fibrins in the blood. Fibrins are the blood components that stick together to form scabs and clots. For people with advanced atherosclerosis, clots can be dangerous because they precipitate heart attacks. Thus, reducing the activity of fibrins is generally beneficial. Physical activity reduces the stickiness of fibrins, so this may be a mechanism of its CVD benefits. (Haskell, Leon, Caspersen et al., 1992).

Although the most important health effects of physical activity may concern CVD, physical activity has been found to beneficially affect several diseases and body systems. A brief review of these diverse benefits follows.

1. **Cancer.** In the past few years more than 10 studies have been published showing that physical activity has a protective effect against certain cancers (Calabrese, 1990). There is strong evidence regarding colon cancer. Cancers of the breast and reproductive organs are less likely in women who are physically active. It is hypothesized that physical activity may protect against cancers by improving immune functioning, although most studies do not find fewer infections in active people.

2. **Bone health.** There is interest in physical activity as a means of preventing osteoporosis, or bone loss. This is a major concern, especially for elderly women. Weight-bearing exercise helps the bones take up more calcium in early life, before bone density peaks in the thirties. Physical activity helps in later life by slowing loss of calcium from the bones. It is interesting that, despite concerns that running creates diseases of the joints, studies of older runners have failed to find bone or joint problems (for example, arthritis) associated with moderate levels of running (Smith, Smith, & Gilligan, 1990).

3. **Mental health.** There is substantial evidence that physical activity can be an effective treatment for some emotional disorders. Clinical studies show that mild anxiety and depression are improved by physical activity, so exercise is gaining acceptance as a supplement to psychotherapy (Brown, 1990). The results of four large surveys consistently showed that physically active people are less anxious and depressed than sedentary people (Stephens, 1988). This finding indicates that physical activity may have a limited effect on reducing risk of developing emotional disorders. The top three reasons people give for being active suggest that the mental health benefits are highly motivating: to feel better mentally and physically (62 percent), to control weight or look better (42 percent), and to relax or reduce stress (36 percent) (Stephens, 1988).

The psychological effects of physical activity on the elderly are of particular interest because of declines in cognitive functioning. Though the findings are not completely consistent, it seems that the elderly with cognitive or emotional impairments can be helped to some degree by physical activity. Among the elderly with high levels of functioning, physical activity may not have a noticeable effect (Emery & Blumenthal, 1992).

4. **Quality of life.** The ability of physical activity to lengthen life has been demonstrated, but many people are interested in whether physical activity enhances quality of life. This issue was discussed by Stewart and King (1991), who were mainly concerned with the elderly. Quality of life can be thought of in many ways. They included these factors in their definition: physical functioning, cognitive functioning, daily activities, bodily well-being, emotional well-being, self-concept, and satisfaction with health and life. Few studies have addressed these questions, but there was some indication that physical activity has positive effects on physical functioning, emotional functioning and well-being, and self-esteem. It is important for future studies to determine whether regular physical activity truly improves quality of life.

HEALTH BENEFITS FOR CHILDREN

Most of the health effects of physical activity have been studied for adults. Though physical activity will not protect them from a heart attack in childhood, it could reduce their risk of future heart attacks. In general, physical activity has similar effects on CVD risk factors in childhood as it does in adulthood. Physical activity appears to increase HDL-cholesterol in children. High blood pressures are reduced by physical activity, but normal blood pressures are not affected. The association between physical activity and obesity is not clear because the studies are conflicting. However, it is logical that regular physical activity will burn calories and help prevent obesity. Physical activity is commonly used in the treatment of children with lung diseases, such as asthma and cystic fibrosis (Baranowski et al., 1992).

An additional benefit is expected for girls, but it has not been well-studied. It is believed that girls who deposit large amounts of calcium in their bones during youth will be protected from osteoporosis later in life when the calcium starts to dissolve from the bones. It appears that regular physical activity enhances the ability of the bone to deposit calcium. Because girls probably receive this extra benefit from physical activity, there is concern because girls are less active than boys.

ETIOLOGY

In more primitive societies people were physically active because they had to run from danger and hunt for food. They had to carry everything with their arms. Sedentary lifestyles were unheard of, but they were desired. The motivation to avoid activity must be strong, because a great deal of brainpower and money have been spent on labor-saving and step-saving devices. We have become so successful in avoiding physical activity that sedentary lifestyles are now a major threat to health in industrialized societies. Is there something inherently punishing or unpleasant about physical activity? A study by Epstein and colleagues (Epstein, Smith, Vara, & Rodefer, 1991) indicates that even children prefer being sedentary. This preference for inactivity means that people avoid activity, and special efforts must be made to increase physical activity levels. Lest we paint too bleak a picture, we should point out that many people enjoy their workouts very much. One of the major challenges for health psychology is to figure out how to make physical activity enjoyable for more people.

Given the health benefits of physical activity and the generally low level of activity in the population, it is important to find out why some people exercise and others do not. The problem is not so simple, because there are actually three questions that must be studied. Most people are not very physically active, so the first question is, "Why do people start exercising?" Most people who become physically active do not continue this habit throughout their life. In fact, of those who start an exercise program, at least half will drop out within 1 year. Interestingly, this dropout rate is similar for people who exercise in programs, for those who exercise on their own, and for heart attack patients (Sallis & Hovell, 1990). The second question is, "Why do people drop out from exercise?" Not everybody who drops out remains sedentary. An unknown percentage of dropouts take up regular exercise again. The third question is, "Why do dropouts resume exercise?" To understand the etiology of physical activity, all of these questions must be studied.

There is another complicating factor. Determinants may be different for various types of activity. More important, the determinants of vigorous activities like running may be different from the determinants of moderate-intensity activities like walking.

The first question about starting exercise has rarely been researched. One large study examined differences between those who did and those who did not begin vigorous or moderate physical activity over a 1-year period (Sallis et al., 1986). Exercise self-efficacy, attitudes toward exercise, and health knowledge predicted the adoption of both types of activity. Increases in moderate activity were most likely in those with high levels of knowledge about the benefits of exercise and those who were less obese. Thus, it appears that there are some differences in the determinants of moderate and vigorous activities.

The second question of who drops out of exercise has been studied many times. This area of research is often referred to as *exercise*

BOX 15·3

FOCUS ON DIVERSITY

Is Physical Activity Related to Hypertension in African Americans?

While it is known that physically active people are less likely than sedentary people to become hypertensive, most of the studies have been conducted with whites. Because blacks have very high rates of hypertension, it is important to know if physical activity is related to blood pressure in this population. The hypothesis that low levels of physical activity in black men and women are partly responsible for high blood pressure was tested in a large epidemiologic study.

About 1100 women and 650 men aged 25 to 50 were selected to form a representative sample of blacks in Pitt County, North Carolina. Eighty percent of those eligible for the study agreed to participate, which is an excellent response rate. While these subjects may not be representative of blacks across the nation, they are probably a good sample of blacks in rural North Carolina.

Resting blood pressure was measured 3 times during an interview, and other data were also collected. Hypertension was defined as an average diastolic blood pressure of 90 mmHg or greater, or current use of antihypertensive medication. Those who reported doing exercise or work hard enough to cause them to sweat for at least 20 minutes 3 times per week were classified as active. All others were classified as sedentary. While we can be confident that most of those in the "active" group were very active, many people in the "sedentary" group were probably also active enough to obtain many physiological benefits.

Forty-four percent of the men and 65 percent of the women were classified as sedentary. This is a very consistent finding. Virtually every study—regardless of the age, nationality, or race of subjects—finds males to be more active than females. Thus, it is not surprising to find that pattern again in this group of black adults.

The relation between physical activity and hypertension was unexpected. Thirty-one percent of the men were hypertensive, and there was no difference at all between sedentary and active men. However, a difference was found for women. Twenty-six percent of the sedentary women were hypertensive, compared with 20 percent of the active women. Although the difference may not seem big, it was highly statistically significant. Looking at it another way, sedentary women were 31 percent more likely to be hypertensive than active women. This difference was not explained by other factors known to influence blood pressure—such as age, obesity, or alcohol consumption.

This large study indicates that physical activity is related to hypertension in black adults, but only in women. The authors noted that several studies of whites had similarly found that physical activity and blood pressure were more strongly related in women than in men. The reason for this gender difference needs to be explored in future research. However, these results suggest that physical activity may be one important part of hypertension treatment and prevention programs for black women (Ainsworth, Keenan, Strogatz, Garrett, & James, 1991).

---

adherence, and most studies have examined the characteristics of people who drop out of organized programs that emphasize vigorous activity. The results of many studies were summarized in Table 15-1 by Dishman, Sallis, and Orenstein (1985). This table shows the factors that predict dropout of participants in supervised programs as well as those who exercise on their own (free-living activity). For supervised programs, blue-collar workers, smokers,

TABLE 15-1

SUMMARY OF VARIABLES THAT MAY DETERMINE THE PROBABILITY OF EXERCISE

Changes in Probability

Determinant	Supervised program	Spontaneous program
Personal characteristics		
Past program participation	+ +	
Past extra-program activity	+	
School athletics, 1 sport	+	0
School athletics, > 1 sport		+
Blue-collar occupation	− −	−
Smoking	− −	
Overweight	− −	
High risk for coronary heart disease	+ +	
Type A behavior	−	
Health, exercise knowledge	−	0
Attitudes	0	+
Enjoyment of activity	+	
Perceived health	+ +	
Mood disturbance	− −	− −
Education	+	+ +
Age	00	−
Expect personal health benefit	+	
Self-efficacy for exercise		+
Intention to adhere	0	0
Perceived physical competence	00	
Self-motivation	+ +	0
Evaluating costs and benefits	+	
Behavioral skills	+ +	
Environmental characteristics		
Spouse support	+ +	+
Perceived available time	+ +	+
Access to facilities	+ +	0
Disruptions in routine	− −	
Social reinforcement (staff, exercise partner)	+	
Family influences		+ +
Peer influences		+ +
Physical environment		+
Cost		0
Medical screening	−	
Climate	−	
Incentives	+	
Activity characteristics		
Activity intensity	00	−
Perceived discomfort	− −	−

Key + + = repeatedly documented *increased* probability; + = weak or mixed documentation of *increased* probability; 00 = repeatedly documented that there is *no change* in probability; 0 = weak or mixed documentation of *no change* in probability; − = weak or mixed documentation of *decreased* probability; − − = repeatedly documented *decreased* probability. Blank spaces indicate no data.

Source: Dishman, Sallis, & Orenstein, (1985).

those who perceive a lack of time, and those who perceive exercise as effort are most likely to drop out. Those with past participation, high self-motivation, spouse support, available time, access to facilities, and perception of good health are most likely to continue. A wide range of behavior-change approaches is also effective.

Free-living activity has been studied less often, so strong conclusions cannot be made. However, for both supervised and free-living activity, some cognitive, health, demographic, social, and activity characteristics have been found to be important influences. These findings suggest that not just one but many factors determine participation in physical activity. This means that behavior-change programs must take several factors into account.

One of the limitations of many of these studies is that the determinants for various populations have not been examined. Most of the studies were conducted with young and middle-aged white men (King et al., 1992). However, there is some evidence that similar determinants are important for Latino women and men (Hovell et al., 1991). Most of these studies only measured vigorous activities, like running or singles tennis. Because less-vigorous activities, like walking, also have health benefits, it is important to study them. It appears that the determinants of walking are quite different (Hovell et al., 1989). Thus, different approaches may be needed to encourage people to walk.

The third question deals with resumption of physical activity after dropout. The reasons for restarting may be different from the reasons for starting in the first place. However, no studies have investigated this question.

Several different theories have been used in the study of determinants of physical activity. Both the health belief model (Sonstroem, 1988) and the theory of reasoned action (Olson & Zanna, 1987) have been employed often, and several variables suggested by these theories have been found to be related to physical ac-

tivity. However, both of these theories focus almost exclusively on cognitive variables and assume that people make rational choices. Even the limited knowledge available indicates that environmental variables such as support from others and access to facilities play a role in determining physical activity habits (Dishman, 1990). Thus, theories that include only cognitive factors will provide an incomplete picture of determinants of physical activity. It appears that theories which are based on learning principles (Bandura, 1986) and which include both cognitive and environmental variables will be needed to produce the most complete possible understanding of determinants of physical activity.

Regular physical activity appears to reduce CVD risk factors in children the same as it does in adults (Sallis, Patterson, Buono, & Nader, 1988), so the determinants of physical activity in children are also of interest. Unfortunately, this topic has been studied less in children than in adults. Two factors have been investigated in several studies. First, it has been hypothesized that obese children are less active than thin children. Because some studies have found such a difference (Berkowitz, Agras, & Korner, 1985; Klesges et al., 1984) and other studies have not (Sallis, Patterson, McKenzie, & Nader, 1988; Waxman & Stunkard, 1980), this issue is undecided (Shah & Jeffery, 1991).

Families appear to influence children's physical activity in a number of ways. Parents' beliefs about exercise (Godin & Shephard, 1984) and direct encouragements to be active (Klesges et al., 1984) influence children's activity levels. The power of the parent as a role model is suggested by findings that parental physical activity is significantly correlated with the physical activity of preschool children (Sallis et al., 1988) and teenagers (Gottlieb & Chen, 1985; Sallis, Patterson, Buono, Atkins, & Nader, 1988). What parents say and do have a large impact on their children's physical activity.

Studies of psychological factors indicate that

BOX 15-4

FOCUS ON RESEARCH

Exercise and Self-Schemata Theory

One of the psychological theories being used to increase understanding of the determinants of physical activity is self-schemata theory. Deborah Kendzierski (1990) is studying the role of these self-perceptions in predicting exercise behavior. Self-schemata related to exercise are based on past experience with exercise as well as the perceived importance of exercise to the person's self-perceptions.

To assess exercise self-schemata, Kendzierski developed a rating scale with three primary items. First, subjects rate the extent to which these three phrases described them: someone who exercises regularly, someone who keeps in shape, and someone who is physically active. These ratings mainly describe their activity patterns, so the second rating is essential for defining self-schemata. Here each item is rated again based on how important it is to them. Subjects are then placed into three categories based on their ratings. Exerciser schematics rate two of the three items high on "describes me" and high on "importance." It is important for them to be exercisers. Nonexerciser schematics rate two of the three items low on "describes me" and high on "importance." For this group, it is important to be nonexercisers. Aschematics rate the items in the middle range on "describes me" and low to moderate on "importance." Exercise is just not an important topic for aschematics.

In the first study 22 college students in each self-schemata category took a number of additional tests. Kendzierski found that exerciser schematics rated a large number of exercise-related words and phrases as being descriptive compared with nonexerciser schematics. This showed that subjects were consistent in their self-images across different tests. Exerciser schematics gave more examples of behaviors from their own life to justify why they described themselves with exercise-related words, such as energetic. Finally, exerciser schematics were more likely than the other groups to predict that they would choose active or sedentary behaviors. For example, exerciser schematics generally said that they would take stairs rather than an escalator.

Because it is easy to say that you will choose active behaviors in the future, Kendzierski (1990) conducted a second study to determine whether exerciser schematics were more likely to start an exercise program. Few studies have attempted to predict adoption of exercise, so this is an important application of the theory. Ninety-five college students took the exercise self-schema test and reported on their exercise behavior 12 weeks later. About 20 percent of the nonexerciser schematics and aschematics said that they had started an exercise program during the 12 weeks. However, about 50 percent of the exerciser schematics who were not initially physically active reported that they had started to exercise during the 12 weeks.

These studies show that exercise self-schemata play a role in the development of exercise behavior. It is noteworthy that this simple questionnaire predicted whether subjects adopted an exercise program. However, these studies looked at only one psychological variable. While self-schemata may be useful, they are not the only factors leading to changes in exercise behavior.

BOX 15·5

FOCUS ON WOMEN

Do Men and Women Start Exercising for Different Reasons?

However you measure it, females appear to be less physically active, on average, than males. This is true for children as young as 6 years of age, and it remains true during adulthood. Women can receive the same health benefits from physical activity as men, but they are more likely to be sedentary; thus, it may be more important to understand why women become active. Unfortunately, most studies of influences on physical activity have not included women. Furthermore, most studies have tried to explain why people drop out of exercise, not why they start in the first place, even though the majority of American adults are largely sedentary. Only a few studies have tried to determine whether women and men start exercise, or physical activity, for different reasons.

In one study a survey was mailed to a random sample of households, and respondents were followed up 2 years later. There were over 700 women and 1000 men in the study, aged 18 to 90. Twenty-five variables believed to be influences on physical activity were measured at baseline. Environmental variables included how much exercise equipment was at home and how many exercise facilities were conveniently located. Social variables included role models and social support. Cognitive variables included exercise knowledge and perceptions about barriers to exercise. Physiological variables included an index of obesity. Health behavior variables included smoking, a diet index, and history of exercise during childhood. About 300 women and 400 men were sedentary at baseline, so analyses were conducted to find out which characteristics at baseline predicted whether participants took up exercise in the 2-year period.

The results were quite different for men and women. Self-efficacy was a strong predictor of adoption for both gender groups. All three environmental variables predicted adoption for men. The most interesting finding was that women whose friends and family supported exercise and who had many exercise role models were the most likely to be adopters.

While it is important for everyone to feel confident about their ability to be physically active, men and women appear to be responding to different cues in their environments. Men tended to respond to stimuli in the physical environment, so intervention programs may need to focus on creating new exercise facilities or more visual cues to be effective for men. Social influences were much more important for women, so a totally different approach may be called for; for example, programs that emphasize personal influence and social support. Current exercisers may be the most effective people to convince sedentary female friends and family members to take up a very healthful habit. This is an example of why it is important to study gender differences in health behaviors, so that interventions can be developed that will have a chance of being effective for both women and men (Sallis, Hovell, & Hofstetter, 1992).

---

personality variables do not help explain physical activity in youth. Knowledge, beliefs, and attitudes are weakly related to activity habits. Only specific beliefs about personal physical activity, such as self-efficacy, have been strongly associated with physical activity (Sallis et al., 1992).

Characteristics of the physical environment have strong influences on children's physical activity. Children are more active on the weekends, because they do not sit at school most of the day. They are also much more active when they are out-of-doors. There is a great deal of concern that television may be stealing time that children could use for activity (Sallis, Simons-Morton, Stone, et al., 1992).

TREATMENT

Exercise is a commonly prescribed treatment for many medical conditions. In the typical medical encounter a patient will be told to exercise regularly, and the conversation will end there. Patients with CVD often have exercise tests to determine what level of exercise they can safely tolerate. They are then given a detailed exercise prescription that specifies type of activity, frequency, and duration. Intensity of exercise is monitored by heart rate. In many cases the exercise is done in a medically supervised program or community fitness program run by certified exercise leaders. Although physicians who make exercise prescriptions are well versed in the physiological risks and benefits of exercise, the exercise treatment programs themselves are run by health professionals with limited knowledge of behavior-change principles and methods. Thus, not surprisingly, there are large dropout rates in these programs. There is a great need for training in behavior change techniques that could improve adherence to exercise prescriptions in supervised programs.

Many more people exercise on their own than in a supervised program. Various governmental and voluntary health agencies recommend regular physical activity as a means of promoting health and preventing disease, but these recommendations do not usually include suggestions on how to effectively modify this difficult behavior. Therefore, in both clinical treatment and prevention programs, behavior-change principles need to be applied.

Even though 50 to 70 percent of the adult population in the United States is very sedentary, there have been few efforts to promote adoption of regular activity. The notable exception is a study by King, Haskell, Taylor, and colleagues (1991), where the researchers dialed random telephone numbers to identify sedentary adults between the ages of 50 and 65. After excluding people for medical reasons, 357 were randomly assigned to one of four groups. In the first group, subjects were encouraged to attend 1-hour vigorous exercise sessions at a community center at least 3 times per week. In the second group, subjects were instructed to do similar vigorous exercise on their own, and periodic phone contacts were made to promote adherence. The third group was instructed to do lower-intensity exercise for 30 minutes 5 days per week on their own. Those in the fourth group (the controls) were only measured.

Adherence to exercise was much higher in the home-based programs than in the group-based program. This supports the use of the telephone contact method as a means of encouraging subjects to continue their activity. All three groups increased their cardiovascular fitness more than the controls. Not surprisingly, fitness increased most in those who were regular in their physical activity. Although blood lipids, weight, and blood pressure did not change significantly in these healthy adults, the modest 5 percent increase in fitness suggests that more exercise may be necessary for risk factor changes. However, there was no evidence of increased injuries in the exercising groups. Subjects preferred to do moderate-intensity activities at home. This study by King and associates indicates that sedentary adults can be motivated to adopt a pattern of regular physical activity with a minimum of assistance. This appears to be a low-cost method of stimulating inactive people to be active.

Several studies have demonstrated the effectiveness of behavior-change techniques for promoting maintenance in people who are already doing physical activity. Behavioral contracts with specific reinforcement contingencies were effective with both healthy adults (Wysocki, Hall, Iwata, & Riordan, 1979) and cardiac rehabilitation patients (Oldridge & Jones, 1983).

In the Oldridge and Jones (1983) study, 120 cardiac patients were randomly assigned to a control condition or to a behavioral contracting experimental treatment. In the control group, patients were supervised twice a week in a cardiac rehabilitation program. They were given individual prescriptions to exercise at a heart rate between 65 and 85 percent of their maximal capacity. These patients also had educational lectures and regular group discussions. The experimental subjects received the same treatment with the addition of a behavioral self-management program. The patient and program provider signed a contract stating agreement to participate for at least 6 months. Exercise heart rates were self-monitored each month, and physical activity was monitored 6 days each month. The primary outcome was attendance at the exercise sessions. After 6 months, 52 percent of the subjects dropped out. Although the 42 percent compliance or attendance rate in the control group was lower than the 54 percent rate in the experimental group, this difference was not significant ($p <. .20$). However, 15 of the 63 experimental subjects did not sign the contract. When the signers and nonsigners were analyzed separately, it was found that the signers attended significantly more sessions than the nonsigners ($p < .005$). The signers also attended significantly more sessions than the controls.

While this study indicates that behavioral techniques can increase adherence to exercise prescriptions, these self-management procedures work only with those who agree to use them in the first place. Signing an adherence contract could be used as a screening procedure so that program resources would not be wasted on patients who did not intend to complete the program. This study shows that self-management can work, but the benefits are limited to motivated subjects.

Martin and colleagues (Martin et al., 1984) conducted a series of six studies to systematically evaluate the effectiveness of several behavior-change techniques in promoting adherence to exercise. Subjects were healthy sedentary adults who signed up for a noncredit exercise course offered by a small college. Their use of healthy subjects instead of cardiac patients indicates that the investigators were interested in developing a program that could be used in preventing heart disease in the general adult population. Of the 143 subjects who participated in the studies, 38 percent said that they wanted to exercise for "improved physical health" and 27 percent wanted to lose weight.

In each of the six studies, participants were randomly assigned to one of two exercise programs, and one or more behavioral techniques were evaluated. All classes met twice per week for 10 to 12 weeks. One session per week included a brief lecture on an exercise-related topic such as proper jogging form, flexibility, and injury prevention; while the other session included training in the specific adherence strategies being tested. Every session included 30 to 45 minutes of brisk walking or jogging, and subjects planned to exercise outside of class as well.

The results of the Martin and coworkers (1984) studies showed that attendance at the sessions was significantly increased by instructor praise and feedback, flexible goal setting by the subject, and a strategy of distraction (that is, thinking about something other than exercise) during exercise. An attendance lottery and relapse prevention training did not influence exercise adherence. Overall, the treatment groups had attendance rates of 80 to 85 percent, while a true control group had attendance rates of only about 50 percent. Therefore, the package of cognitive-behavioral interventions improved adherence to a clinically significant degree, meaning that there was an important effect.

Although most of the interventions were designed to improve session attendance, adherence interventions must be judged on their long-term effects. In the superior intervention in each study, 3-month adherence ranged from about 50 to 90 percent, while in the less effective intervention, 3-month adherence ranged from about 20 to 40 percent. Thus, the cognitive-behavioral interventions in the Martin and colleagues (1984) studies improved long-term adherence. This set of studies is a good model of behavioral health research because a series of well-controlled experiments was used to develop an effective multicomponent package.

PREVENTION

Efforts to prevent the development of a sedentary lifestyle have primarily involved changes in school physical education programs. Although most people believe that children are very active, studies indicate that first-graders spend only about 3 percent of a usual summer day in vigorous activity (Gilliam, Freedson, Geenen, & Shahraray, 1981). Time spent watching television, playing video games, and staying indoors limits the amount of time available for active play. The current thinking is that children need to be active on a regular basis, and they should learn activities that can be carried over into adulthood. Most physical education programs teach sports and activities that most adults do not play, such as football, kickball, dodge ball, and capture the flag. Fitness activities such as running and aerobic dance are rarely taught to children. Physical education programs do not even provide students with large amounts of activity, since in many games children stand while they wait their turn. Thus, it is believed that physical education is not living up to its potential to improve the health of children by teaching them how to live an active lifestyle (Sallis & McKenzie, 1991).

Even in elementary schools physical education can be modified to emphasize fitness activities that should help improve health. Running and other aerobic activities have been introduced in a gradual and positive manner. These programs are feasible and lead to im-

provements in fitness. Figure 15-6 shows the results of one study (Dunan, Boyce, Itami, & Puffenbarger, 1983). The mile run time decreased during the school year when the program was in effect, showing an increase in cardiovascular fitness. However, fitness decreased in the summer, when children were not in the program. This finding suggests that children did not keep up their activity level during the summer months. Future studies should include cognitive-behavioral skills to teach children how to maintain their activity, much as the Martin and associates (1984) study promoted long-term exercise adherence in adults.

Though schools are the obvious site for physical activity promotion programs for children, there are other possibilities. Families can be involved in programs at any site, though this approach has not been effective with healthy children. Community organizations such as youth sports, YMCA/YWCA, church groups, and social service agencies could become engaged in efforts to promote children's physical activity. It is possible that developing

FIGURE 15-6

A fitness-oriented physical education program for fifth grade. Change in mile run time of fitness program and control children. (From Duncan, Boyce, Itami, & Puffenbarger, 1983.)

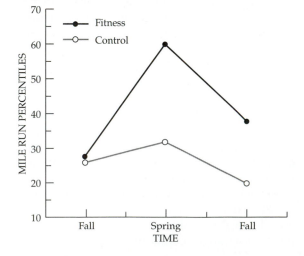

more and safer parks and playgrounds could be as effective as educational programs. As credible sources of health information, pediatricians could play a significant role as well. To help keep children active, all of the groups will probably have to work together (Sallis, Simons-Morton, Stone, et al., 1992).

SUMMARY

Physical activity, exercise, and fitness appear to prevent heart disease, some cancers, osteoporosis, diabetes, hypertension, and emotional disorders. Epidemiologic studies suggest that regular physical activity can reduce the risks of cardiovascular disease by decreasing blood pressure, obesity, and cholesterol. Exercise may also stabilize glucose metabolism and reduce dangerous blood clotting factors.

The U.S. population appears to be very sedentary, or inactive. It is difficult to predict who will exercise regularly. However, those who engage in moderate activity tend to be knowledgeable about the benefits of exercise and less obese. Those with high self-motivation, behavioral skills, supportive spouses, available time, and access to facilities are more likely to continue exercising. As in other intervention areas, social learning and other learning theories have contributed to the development of intervention programs. Participation in exercise programs is enhanced by social support, praise, feedback, flexible goal setting, and (perhaps) distraction during an exercise session. More studies are needed to determine what factors predict long-term participation in exercise programs. Newer programs are attempting to promote adoption of exercise by sedentary adults and are trying to change long-term exercise patterns in school-aged children. Unfortunately, we still know very little about methods for preventing the sedentary lifestyle that characterizes most Americans.

KEY TERMS

Physical activity. Any bodily movement produced by a skeletal muscle that results in energy expenditure.

Exercise. A subset of physical activity that involves bodily movement but is planned, structured, and done repetitively to improve and maintain one or more components of fitness.

Physical fitness. A set of attributes that people have or achieve that relates to the ability to perform physical activity.

ACSM (American College of Sports Medicine). A group of professionals who encourage scientific studies of physical activity and oversee the credentialing of exercise specialists.

Harvard Alumni Study. An important study of Harvard graduates which established that regular moderate activity predicts long-term survival. College athletes were not necessarily the ones who remained in the best shape as they aged.

Jim Fixx. The author of *The Complete Book of Running*, who died of a heart attack after exercising. It was later discovered that Fixx had a serious heart disease, and his exercise program may have prevented him from dying even earlier.

Glucose metabolism. The use of sugars as fuels by the body (see Chapter 9). Physical activity releases blood glucose and increases insulin sensitivity. Supervised exercise may be valuable for people with glucose metabolism problems, such as diabetes.

Fibrinolysis. Activities of fibrins in the blood. Fibrins are important in blood clotting. Physical activity may reduce the likelihood that a clot will be formed which could cause a heart attack.

Exercise adherence. The level of participation in exercise programs, once people have been advised to exercise. Typically, exercise adherence is poor.

CHAPTER 16

Smoking

If Maria Rubio could do one thing over again, she would not have started smoking. A couple of years ago, smoking was just something she did when she was bored; it was no big deal. Now, she is obsessed with the thought that she has to quit. Two weeks ago, Maria learned she was pregnant. Her physician immediately told her that she must give up smoking. Maria heard that her smoking could cause her baby to be abnormally small, and this could threaten the baby's life. Her physician told her many harmful effects of her smoking on the baby in her body. Maria walked out of the office confused about how she was going to be able to afford to take care of her baby and fearful that she would not be able to quit smoking. She really wants to quit, because she would never want to harm her baby. But smoking has become such a constant part of her life that she is not sure how she will react to quitting. Will the stress of quitting be worse for the baby than the smoking? Maria talked to her husband about it, and he said he would help her any way he could. For several days she has been trying to quit, but she keeps on buying and smoking cigarettes. Because of her failure to quit so far, Maria has decided she needs some help. Where can she get help? Her friends have used hypnosis.

Others have told her about nicotine gum. Which method is best for her? How can she find out? What are her chances of success?

These are real issues faced by people every day. In spite of growing social disapproval of smoking, millions of Americans still smoke. Hundreds of thousands die each year because of smoking. This is one of the most important health issues of our times.

INTRODUCTION

Tobacco has been used in many cultures for centuries, but the mass consumption of tobacco is unique to the twentieth century. The development of the modern cigarette is largely responsible for the widespread use of tobacco throughout the world. As opposed to cigars, pipes, and chewing tobacco, cigarettes are convenient to carry and easy to use. Many people find cigarettes less offensive than other types of tobacco, and cigarettes are the only tobacco product used by large numbers of women. The real breakthrough in cigarette technology was the addition of chemicals to ensure that the cigarette would not go out when left unattended. This combination of convenience and free distribution of cigarettes to soldiers in both world wars led to the mass addiction to tobacco in the latter part of the twentieth century. Figure 16-1 shows the increase in per capita consumption of cigarettes during this century.

Scientists first became concerned about the health consequences of smoking in the 1930s because of the increase in lung cancers. In 1930 fewer than 3000 deaths were attributed to lung cancer, but 50 years later lung cancer was blamed for over 100,000 deaths in the United States (U.S. DHHS, 1980a). Those early concerns led to thousands of studies that have linked cigarette smoking with a variety of cancers, several serious respiratory ailments, and cardiovascular diseases (CVD). We have

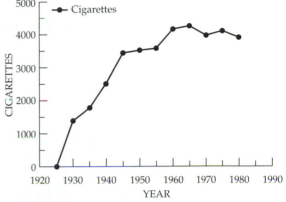

FIGURE 16-1

Annual per capita consumption of cigarettes by U.S. adults. (After *Smoking, Tobacco, and Health: A Fact Book*. U.S. DHHS, Public Health Service, DHHS Pub. No. 80-50150. Washington, D.C.: U.S. Government Printing Office, 1980.)

learned that cigarette smoking is the number one preventable cause of disease and death in the United States and that smoking is responsible for over 350,000 deaths per year. That is more than drugs, alcohol, traffic-related deaths, AIDS, suicides, and homicides combined. Warner (1986) put these numbers into perspective: "The death toll associated with smoking is the equivalent of three fully loaded jumbo jets crashing and leaving no survivors, every single day of the year" (p. 7).

Smoking is now a social issue as well as a health issue, because nonsmokers are concerned about the effects of secondhand smoke and are increasingly vocal about their unwillingness to inhale the smoke of other people's cigarettes. Smoking is also a political and economic issue. While the U.S. government funds antismoking research and programs with one hand, the other hand is providing subsidies to tobacco growers and permitting massive tobacco advertising and promotional

B O X 16·1

HEALTH OBJECTIVES FOR THE YEAR 2000: SMOKING

Reduce cigarette smoking to a prevalence of no more than 15 percent among people aged 20 and older (baseline: 29 percent in 1987; 32 percent for men and 27 percent for women).

YEAR 2000 GOAL FOR CIGARETTE SMOKING

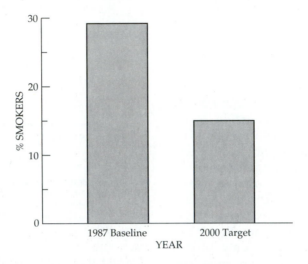

Increase smoking cessation during pregnancy so that at least 60 percent of the women who are cigarette smokers at the time they become pregnant quit smoking early in pregnancy and maintain abstinence for the remainder of their pregnancy (baseline: 39 percent of white women smokers aged 20 through 44 quit at some time during pregnancy in 1985).

YEAR 2000 GOAL FOR SMOKING CESSATION DURING PREGNANCY

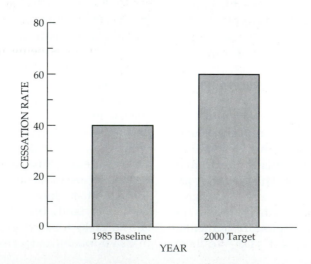

campaigns. The government has attempted to force several Asian nations to advertise and sell tobacco in their countries, and this has prompted an outcry around the world.

With an advertising budget of nearly $3 billion annually in the United States, the tobacco industry is a powerful economic force that uses its money to cast doubt on the negative health effects of smoking. The industry constantly fights tax increases and limits on advertising. As the biggest advertiser in the nation, the tobacco industry is able to limit the flow of negative information on smoking in major magazines. Despite these efforts, cigarette use is declining in the United States.

Cigarette smoking is one of the most controversial behaviors in this country. Health, political, and economic interests converge on smoking, and the result is a fascinating drama with life and death consequences. This chapter touches on many aspects of the smoking issue, because any informed citizen should be aware of this controversy.

EPIDEMIOLOGY

Patterns of Cigarette Use—Who Smokes?

There are approximately 50 million smokers in the United States, or a little less than 30 percent of the adult population (U.S. DHHS, 1987). Almost half of the smokers are women. This equality between the sexes is a recent occurrence, reflecting a decrease among men and an increase among women during the past 40 years. The sex distribution of smokers is continuing to change, because the smoking rate of teenage girls is increasing while the smoking rate of teenage boys is decreasing. Figure 16-2 shows these trends for the 1970s, but the same general trends were seen throughout most of the 1980s as well, with the increase in girls' smoking leveling out recently.

In earlier years when cigarette smoking was on the rise, the upper class was at the forefront of the trend. Cigarette advertisements at the

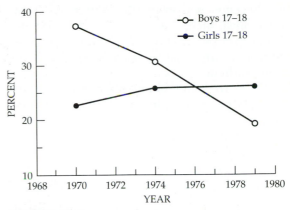

FIGURE 16-2

Percentage of teenage smokers. (From USDHEW, National Institute of Education. *Teenage smoking: Immediate and long-term patterns*. Washington, D.C.: U.S. Government Printing Office, 1979.)

time showed physicians promoting their favorite brand. Now the situation is reversed. The current trend in the United States is a decrease in the prevalence of smoking, and the affluent and well-educated are again leading the way. Less than 20 percent of all physicians smoke now, while nearly 50 percent of all blue-collar workers smoke (Beuchner, Perry, Scott, et al., 1986). In general, health professionals have low smoking rates, with the exception of nurses, whose smoking rate is still over 35 percent (U.S. DHEW, 1975). In countries where American-style cigarettes and promotion have just been introduced, the early pattern in the United States is being repeated. In many African and some Asian nations smoking is being advertised as a sophisticated habit to appeal to the more affluent people who can afford the expense.

There are racial and ethnic differences in cigarette use, but they probably reflect socioeconomic differences. Blacks are more likely to smoke than whites, but blacks smoke fewer cigarettes per day (Remington, Forman, Gentry, et al., 1985).

Latino men may also have higher smoking rates than whites, but Latino women have the lowest smoking rates (Haynes, Harvey, Mentes, Nickens, & Cohen, 1990; Marcus & Crane, 1985; Shea, Stein, Basch, et al., 1992). In some ethnic groups those with less than high school education are twice as likely to smoke as college graduates.

There are some ethnic differences in smoking habits of youth. In a California study, Latino middle-school students had the highest rate of tobacco use (14 percent), followed by whites (12 percent), African Americans (11 percent), and Asians (9 percent) (De Moor, Elder, Young, Wildey, & Molgaard, 1989).

In 1965 the percentage of smokers in the United States began to decline, and that decline continues to the present time. The event that triggered this major change in smoking habits was the first Surgeon General's Report on the health consequences of smoking. This compilation of the voluminous data linking smoking to cancer, heart disease, and other illnesses received wide publicity. Up until this time the public questioned the growing evidence of the effects of smoking on morbidity and mortality, largely because of the well-

---

BOX 16-2

FOCUS ON WOMEN

A Worldwide Perspective on Women and Smoking

When we think about gender differences in smoking, we usually consider whether women or men smoke more. In addition, Americans tend to think only about the situation in the United States. A recent review by Grunberg, Winders, and Wewers (1991) attempted to broaden our concept of differences between men and women in tobacco use. They point out that women's use of tobacco differs from country to country. In some countries like Japan, China, Greece, and Indonesia, women smoke much less than men. In India, 52 percent of the men smoke, but only 3 percent of the women. In Hong Kong, smoking rates are 23 percent for men and 4 percent for women. In other countries like the United States, Canada, England, New Guinea, and Uruguay, smoking rates are very similar for men and women. In some countries smoking is high for both genders. In New Guinea 85 percent of the men and 80 percent of the women smoke.

It is difficult to find patterns in these gender differences in smoking rates. Men and women do not consistently have similar rates in western countries, in rich countries, or in countries with high smoking rates. These differences suggest that cultural influences on women's tobacco use are important. Even in the United States, it is generally considered unacceptable for women to smoke pipes or cigars or to use chewing tobacco, so few women use these products. As pointed out in Virginia Slims ads, there used to be cultural sanctions against women who smoked, but the acceptance of women's smoking changed with women's increased civil rights. Before the twentieth century it was acceptable for both men and women to smoke pipes, but during this century pipe smoking changed to a predominantly male behavior. Improved understanding of the gender differences in

smoking in various nations may lead to culture- and gender-appropriate methods of smoking control.

Grunberg and colleagues (1991) suggest that consideration of different stages of tobacco use may help explain gender differences. The three main stages are initiation, maintenance, and cessation. Over the past decades there has been a clear trend in the United States for females to experiment more with smoking. In the 1960s 80 percent of the men and 34 percent of the women had tried smoking, but the figures for 1980 were 72 percent for men and 83 percent for women. Adolescent girls are now more likely to smoke (26 percent) than adolescent boys (19 percent).

Among regular smokers, there are also gender differences. Males smoke more cigarettes per day, inhale more deeply and more often, and take larger puffs. Thus, women who smoke appear to expose themselves to lower doses of nicotine. Gender differences in smoking pattern could be due to social factors, biological differences such as body size, or differences in the way men and women respond to the drug nicotine. Differences in cessation have not been well studied, but there is some evidence that men who attend smoking cessation programs are more likely to quit successfully than women.

Reasons for differences between men and women in smoking behavior have not been well researched. Grunberg and colleagues (1991) reviewed many hypotheses and studies and conclude that there are both psychosocial and biological reasons for the differences. The rising rate of smoking-related diseases in women throughout the world makes it important to understand the specific factors that affect smoking in women (Grunberg, Winders, & Wewers, 1991).

financed efforts of the tobacco industry. This landmark report was the first time the mountain of incriminating evidence against tobacco was gathered together. The report was convincing to physicians and to many smokers. Since that time 64 percent of all smoking physicians have quit, and over 30 million other Americans have quit smoking as well. What is the evidence that caused so many people to go to the trouble of stopping such a difficult behavior?

The Epidemiology—Smoking OR Health?

Since the 1964 Surgeon General's Report, our understanding of the health effects of smoking has improved, but the basic conclusions are still the same. Cigarette smoking is the single largest hazard to health in the industrialized world.

Mortality   A two-pack-a-day smoker between the ages of 30 and 35 has a life expectancy 8 to 9 years shorter than a nonsmoker of the same age (Schwartz, 1987). Chances of dying are related to the overall lifetime exposure to smoking. This is measured in pack-years, which is the number of packs per day usually smoked times the number of years smoking. Of the approximately 350,000 Americans who die each year from smoking, about 170,000 of those deaths are from heart disease, about 130,000 are from various cancers, and about 50,000 are from chronic obstructuve lung diseases (Warner, 1986).

Smokers who quit improve their chances of living. Risk of heart disease after 1 year of quitting is similar to that of never-smokers. However, it takes 10 to 15 years of quitting before the total mortality rates of former smokers resemble those of people who never smoked (U.S. DHEW, 1979).

Morbidity   It is estimated that there are 145 million days of disability and over 80 million days of work lost that are the result of smoking-related illnesses each year. While smoking is the leading cause of mortality, it is also the leading cause of avoidable illness and disability (Warner, 1986). Smokers have more emphysema and bronchitis, peptic ulcers, chronic sinusitis, and hospitalizations than nonsmokers (Schwartz, 1987).

CVD   There are hundreds of studies showing that myocardial infarction, sudden death, peripheral artery disease, and cerebrovascular disease are all strongly related to cigarette smoking (Dawber, 1980; U.S. DHHS, 1983). The Pooling Project combined three major U.S. epidemiologic studies of men, and the results are typical of many other studies conducted throughout the world. Over 7000 middle-aged men were followed for 8.6 years (Pooling Project, 1978). The main results are shown in Figure 16-3. Men who smoked over a pack a day tripled their risk of dying from CVD.

The risk of smoking has also been documented in various racial and ethnic groups and among women. While women have lower rates of heart disease than men, women who use oral contraceptives and who smoke greatly increase their risk of heart disease. Using oral contraceptives increases risk of myocardial infarction twofold, but the increased risk is ten-

FIGURE 16-3

Mortality and smoking in the Pooling Project. (From Pooling Project, 1978.)

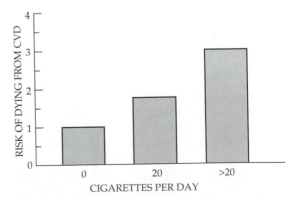

fold (that means 1000 percent) if the woman also smokes (Ory, 1977).

In most studies cigar and pipe smokers have lower risk of CVD than cigarette smokers. However, smokers who switch from cigarettes to cigars or pipes continue to have high risks because they inhale the smoke, while lifetime cigar and pipe smokers do not usually inhale (Aronow & Kaplan, 1983). Many people who continue smoking are concerned about reducing their health risks as much as possible, and some have switched to low-tar and low-nicotine cigarettes because they are believed to be "safer." (There is little evidence to support such beliefs since CVD rates are similar in smokers of both high-tar and low-tar cigarettes (Kuller, Meilahn, & Ockene, 1985). Several studies have shown that low-tar and low-nicotine cigarettes are smoked in such a way that they deliver similar amounts of nicotine as regular cigarettes. For example, smokers of low-nicotine cigarettes inhale them more deeply or cover up holes in the filter with their fingers. Thus, there probably is no "safe cigarette."

Cancer   About 130,000 Americans a year die from smoking-related cancers, and that is about one-third of all cancer deaths. Smokers are 10 times more likely to get lung cancer than those who never smoked, and that translates into a 1000 percent higher risk for smokers. Lung cancer was almost unknown at the beginning of the twentieth century, but now it makes up one-quarter of all cancer deaths. Lung cancer has long been the most frequent cancer for men, and in the late 1980s lung cancer bypassed breast cancer and became the most common form of cancer for women (Warner, 1986).

Smoking causes cancers at other sites as well. It is a major cause of (or a contributor to) cancers of the oral cavity, esophagus, bladder, kidney, and pancreas. In a study of Japanese-Americans, smoking accounted for 29 percent of all cancers and 85 percent of lung cancers (Chyou, Nomura, & Stemmermann, 1992).

Chronic Obstructive Pulmonary Disease   Almost all long-term smokers develop some degree of emphysema, and smoking is virtually the only cause of this disabling condition. Persons with chronic obstructive pulmonary disease have great difficulty breathing, so their lives become more and more restricted as the condition worsens.

Involuntary Smoking   Because of the profound and multiple health effects of tobacco smoke, it is not surprising that it also affects those who are exposed to the smoke of others. The passive smoker most affected is the unborn child. Mothers who smoke have more low-birthweight children, and low birthweight is itself a risk factor for spontaneous abortion, fetal death, and neonatal death (U.S. DHHS, 1980b). Thus, it is very important for women to stop smoking, especially during pregnancy.

After birth, children continue to be affected by their parents' smoking. Respiratory infections are more common among children who have smoking parents, from birth all the way through adolescence. Studies with children of a wide range of ages show that those with two smoking parents have more respiratory symptoms and illnesses than children with one smoking parent, who in turn have more symptoms than children with nonsmoking parents (Weiss, Tager, Schenker, & Speizer, 1983).

There is another threat to children from smoking that is rarely discussed. Cigarettes are the cause of between 30 and 40 percent of all home fires, and there are many children among the 2300 Americans who die each year as a result. An additional 5000 are burned but do not die from cigarette-caused fires (Warner, 1986).

A few studies have examined whether passive smoking is associated with CVD. This question has been studied in an elderly population in southern California (Garland, Barrett-Connor, Suarez, Criqui, & Wingard, 1985). It was found that nonsmoking spouses of smokers had twice as great a risk of having a myocardial infarction as nonsmoking spouses of nonsmokers. Thus, it appears that living in the same environment with a smoker for many years may significantly increse your own risk of heart diseae.

If you are a nonsmoker living with a smoker, you are most exposed to cigarette smoke at home. Otherwise, you receive most of your exposure at work. Among 186 nonsmokers who monitored their exposure to cigarette smoke, the average exposure was 60 minutes per day (Emmons et al., 1992).

The Smoking and Health "Controversy"

The number of studies indicating that cigarette smoking is the major cause of the deaths of millions of tobacco users around the world is literally in the thousands. The links between cigarette smoking, CVD, and various cancers are considered to be the most thoroughly researched epidemiologic questions in history. However, the smoking and health issue is often referred to as a ''controversy.'' The tobacco companies and their public relations organization, The Tobacco Institute, are among the small handful of individuals and organizations that question the major role tobacco plays in the epidemic of CVD and cancer in the industrialized world. The tobacco companies contend that the evidence against tobacco is circumstantial, so they say there is no scientific basis for all the concern over its health effects.

It is instructive to examine this argument. There is a kernel of truth in it. Recall that cause and effect can be proved only by randomized, controlled experiments. It is correct that no such study has been carried out which proves that smoking causes cancer and CVD, but what would such a study look like? First, you would have to enlist a large number of children before any of them start smoking. Second, you would randomly assign half of them to start smoking on a regular basis for many years and half of them to never smoke. Third,

you would have to make sure that all the children followed the instructions for about 40 years. Finally, you would compare the two groups on their medical history throughout life and on the age and cause of death.

It is safe to say that no such study will ever be conducted. Why not? Because it is unethical and unnecessary. This definitive study that the tobacco industry wants before it will accept that smoking is harmful is unethical because half of the subjects would be deliberately exposed to highly toxic substances (tobacco smoke). The study is unnecessary because it is already known that smoking is harmful. There are criteria that can be used to judge whether nonexperimental data support a cause-effect relationship:

1. the consistency of the association
2. the strength of the association
3. the specificity of the association
4. the temporal relationship of the association
5. the availability of a mechanism

Rarely have all these criteria been fulfilled as completely as in the smoking and health issue. Since the tobacco industry requires data that will never be gathered, it will maintain its position that the health hazards of cigarette smoking are unproven. This is how the smoking and health "controversy" is kept alive. To most health professionals, it is a question of smoking *or* health.

PATHOPHYSIOLOGY

Tobacco smoke can contain more than 4000 compounds since it results from the burning of hundreds of additives as well as the tobacco and paper. The purpose of additives is to improve the flavor and ensure that the cigarette burns evenly and does not self-extinguish. Additives can vary from chocolate to petroleum products. While they are included in small quantities, the smoker is exposed to large doses of additives over a lifetime of smoking. The three major components of tobacco smoke with implications for CVD and cancer are nicotine, tars, and carbon monoxide.

Nicotine

Nicotine, which is believed to be the primary addictive substance in tobacco, has several effects that increase CVD risk.

1. Nicotine produces the release of norepinephrine (noradrenaline), which increases resting heart rate, systolic blood pressure, and diastolic blood pressure.
2. Nicotine promotes disturbances in cardiac rhythms that may increase risk of fibrillation.
3. Nicotine causes a rise in free fatty acids in the blood.
4. Nicotine increases platelet stickiness, which promotes clotting (Aronow & Kaplan, 1983).

Tars

Cigarette smoke is composed of gases and solids. A great variety of harmful gases are produced by burning tobacco and the hundreds of additives. Several components are known to be carcinogenic, and many others are suspected of being cancer-causing. Some of the more commonly known toxic gases are ammonia, hydrogen cyanide, and formaldehyde. The solid parts of the smoke are known as *tars* because, when collected, they resemble a sticky black tar. Tars include such chemicals are benzene, hydrocarbons, acids, arsenic, nickel, cadmium, pesticides such as DDT, and radioactive elements (Warner, 1986). It is believed that radioactive polonium and potassium are delivered to the lungs, where they sit for many years, radiating the lung tissue and promoting cancer.

Carbon Monoxide

Carbon monoxide (CO) is believed to be the major component of tobacco smoke that causes CVD. CO is produced as a result of combustion, and it is inhaled along with the other gases and solids that constitute tobacco smoke. Because hemoglobin prefers to bind with CO rather than O_2, the availability of large amounts of CO in the blood means that less oxygen will be circulating. The increase in heart rate and blood pressure caused by nicotine means that the heart needs additional oxygen, and the reduced supply of oxygen caused by high levels of CO places the heart muscle under strain.

Exposure to CO from any source is harmful. Among men who worked in an iron foundry, the presence of angina pectoris was related to CO exposure whether it was from the industrial combustion, cigarette smoking, or a combination. Heavy smokers routinely subject themselves to 8 times the level of CO that is allowed in the workplace (Aronow & Kaplan, 1983).

ETIOLOGY

Different influences on cigarette smoking are important at different stages in the natural history of smoking. The four major stages are shown in Table 16-1, along with an indication of whether psychosocial factors, physiological factors, or both are important at each stage.

Initiation of Smoking

Almost everyone who starts smoking does so during the teen years, and most of these start during junior high school. Cigarette smoking (and tobacco use of any kind) is just one of the many issues faced by teens. Adolescents are in the transition to adulthood, and they have to make many decisions about their lives. Will I finish school? Will I go to college? Will I drink alcohol, use drugs, smoke cigarettes, have sex?

These decisions are not made in a vacuum. It seems that everyone wants to have some input, from churches and schools to parents and friends. For most teens it is clear that

TABLE 16·1	
STAGES IN THE NATURAL HISTORY OF CIGARETTE SMOKING	
Stage	**Influences**
Stage 1. Initiation	Psychosocial
Stage 2. Regular smoking	Physiological + psychosocial
Stage 3. Cessation	Physiological + psychosocial
Stage 4. Maintenance	Psychosocial

Source: Adapted from Lichtenstein & Brown, 1983.

the influence of peers is the greatest. This is shown by studies of teenagers' first experimentation with tobacco. Possibly 90 percent of us have tried smoking at least once (Flay, d'Avernas, Best, Kersell, & Ryan, 1983), and 50 percent of all adolescents try their first cigarette with a friend. While a substantial percentage experiment with an older sibling, only 16 percent of the boys and 9 percent of the girls report having their first cigarette alone (Friedman, Lichtenstein, & Biglan, 1985). Peer pressure to smoke is usually the most direct and effective, but there are other factors that influence the initiation of smoking. As shown in Table 16-2, all these influences are social or psychological (reviewed in Flay et al., 1983).

While knowledge, attitudes, and beliefs are associated with smoking, it is clear that direct pressure from peers is the most important influence on the initiation of smoking in adolescence. Until recently, most studies of influences on the adoption of smoking included mainly white children. More recent studies have confirmed that the same influences are important for Latino (Dusenbury et al., 1992) and African American youth (Botvin, Baker, Goldberg, Dusenbury, & Botvin, 1992).

Regular Smoking

Not everyone who experiments with cigarettes becomes a regular smoker, but 70 to 90 percent of all adolescents who smoke four or more cigarettes will become regular smokers (Salber,

Freeman, & Albalin, 1968). The transition to regular smoker is marked by developing a smoking routine (style of holding the cigarette, where cigarettes are carried, when and where to smoke) and by acquiring the necessary paraphernalia (ashtrays, lighters). Adoption of a personal brand tends to alter one's self-image from nonsmoker to smoker. There are also changes that take place in reasons for smoking. Social reasons for smoking grow in importance during adolescence and then decline throughout adult life. Smoking for social confidence decreases dramatically during the first 2 or 3 years of smoking. On the other hand, there is a rapid increase in smoking to relieve nervous irritation during the first 2 years. This suggests that it may take some time to become dependent on cigarettes.

Physiological-pharmacological factors become important after the initiation of smoking. Russell (1974) summarized the early work on the role of nicotine, which is the addictive component of tobacco. Smoking delivers nicotine to the brain about 7 seconds after each puff, so there is strong and immediate reinforcement. The importance of nicotine is captured in this quote: "There is little doubt that if it were not for the nicotine in tobacco smoke, people would be little more inclined to smoke than they are to blow bubbles or light sparklers" (Russell, 1974, p. 793).

Addiction is characterized by tolerance and withdrawal. *Tolerance* is the need to administer increasing amounts of the drug to achieve the

---

T A B L E 16 · 2

INFLUENCES ON SMOKING INITIATION AMONG ADOLESCENTS

Adolescents with parents or siblings who smoke are likely to become smokers.

Teenagers generally have a favorable image of smokers. Adolescents report that appearing more mature is one of the most important benefits of smoking. Other perceived benefits are appearing tougher, more sociable, and more like a leader.

There is no direct evidence that mass media and advertising influence the initiation of smoking. However, it is commonly believed that the media stimulate smoking by portraying the use of cigarettes as a sign of maturity and autonomy. These images are particularly attractive to adolescents.

Boys from low socioeconomic status families are more likely to smoke than high status boys, but this trend is not so clear for girls.

Teens who smoke are those who are likely to be doing poorly in school and who do not plan to go to college. Thus, smoking rates are usually low among college freshman and high among high school dropouts.

Hundreds of studies have failed to detect personality differences between smoking and nonsmoking teens. The one exception appears to be the finding that smoking is more common in extroverted boys and girls.

Cigarette smoking appears to be the primary "gateway" drug that predicts use of other substances. Teens who smoke are more likely to use alcohol, marijuana, and other drugs. Most users of smokeless tobacco also smoke cigarettes.

While most adolescents know that cigarettes cause health problems, smoking adolescents are less knowledgeable about the negative consequences of smoking and have fewer negative attitudes about smoking than nonsmoking teens.

Most nonsmoking teens are unaware of the addictiveness of smoking and believe that if they start, they will be able to stop any time they want.

Adolescents view smoking as the norm. An American Cancer Society (1976) study found that 83 percent of the teens believed that most other teens smoked, while only 15 to 30 percent of them actually do.

---

same response. Jarvik (1979) asserts that tolerance to tobacco has been demonstrated in both humans and animals. A tobacco *withdrawal syndrome* has also been identified (Shiffman, 1979), although it varies greatly from person to person. Common objective symptoms are changes in EEG (brain waves) and cardiovascular function as well as decreases in motor performance. The subjective symptoms are more troublesome and include irritability, anxiety, inability to concentrate, insomnia, and an intense craving for cigarettes. These symptoms usually subside after a few days or a couple of weeks, except that a less intense craving for cigarettes may persist.

Schachter (1978) proposes that smokers regulate the amount of nicotine in their blood by changing their smoking behavior. This hypothesis is consistent with the view that nicotine is addictive and is supported by several studies. For example, Schachter (1977) found that, when given low-nicotine cigarettes, heavy smokers increased their smoking rate by 25 percent and light smokers increased 18 percent. It was suggested that urinary pH was the physiological mechanism for regulating nicotine in the body. When the urine is acid, much more nicotine is excreted than when the urine is alkaline. Since urinary acidity is increased during times of stress (Schachter, Silverstein, Kozlowski, Herman, & Liebling, 1977), this may account for increased rates of smoking as a result of stress. The nicotine regulation hypothesis is still controversial, but it is a good example of the interaction of physiological and psychological influences on smoking behavior.

The powerful reinforcing and addictive qualities of nicotine may be enough to produce a tenacious habit, but there are also powerful behavioral, social, and psychological factors that help explain why it is more difficult to stop smoking than to stop using heroin. First, consider the opportunities for learning. A pack-a-day smoker smokes about 7300 cigarettes in a year. Since each puff delivers reinforcement to the brain via nicotine, and smokers take at least 10 puffs per cigarette, that is 73,000 learning trials per year. We do very few other activities in life this frequently, so it is easy to see how smoking becomes overlearned to the point where a smoker can on occasion take out a cigarette, light it, and start smoking, without even being aware of doing it.

Because smoking is legal, it can be performed in a wide variety of situations. These settings over time become cues for smoking. When driving, talking on the phone, having a cup of coffee, or finishing a good meal are paired with smoking day after day, smoking becomes reinforced by the feelings associated with these activities. Since smoking is paired with so many situations and feelings, the same smoker may reach for a cigarette when bored, excited, depressed, happy, relaxed, or tense.

Smoking appears to be stimulated by consumption of alcohol and coffee, because use of these three substances is clustered. In detoxified alcoholics, smoking rates were from 26 to 170 percent higher when alcohol was provided, in contrast to a placebo drink (Griffiths, Bigelow, & Liebson, 1976). College students were found to smoke more when given either caffeinated or noncaffeinated coffee in comparison with students who were given water (Marshall, Epstein, & Green, 1980).

Casual observation will reveal that smokers tend to light up when they see someone else do so. You can conduct a simple study by watching smokers in a small group. Measure the amount of time from when the first person in the group lights up until the other smokers light up. This modeling effect has been validated in numerous studies. For example, a heavy smoking model induced significantly more smoking than a light smoking model (Antonucio & Lichtenstein, 1980).

The reasons that cigarette smoking is acquired with some ease and given up with such difficulty were summarized very well by Lichtenstein and Brown (1983):

> In sum, cigarette smoking is a highly practiced, overlearned behavior reinforced by both physiological events and a wide variety of psychosocial events. It is cued by a large array of environment and internal stimuli, and is socially and legally acceptable in most settings. No other substance can provide so many kinds of reinforcement, is so readily and cheaply available, and can be used in so many settings and situations. While there are numerous immediate positive consequences, the negative consequences are delayed and probabilistic.

Smoking Cessation

About 90 percent of all current smokers would like to quit, and almost all of them have made at least one serious attempt. While the success of quitting on your own is only about 5 percent for any given attempt, most of the 30 million Americans who have quit smoking have done so without any formal program. Smokers quit or try to quit for many reasons. The most important reason to quit is for health problems. Smokers who experience a smoking-related health problem are more successful at quitting than those who are motivated to quit for some other reason. Some may be motivated by a persistent cough, while others do not try to quit until they have a heart attack or develop cancer. Social pressure to quit has increased

BOX 16·3

FOCUS ON DIVERSITY

Are White Teenagers More or Less Likely Than Other Ethnic Groups to Smoke Cigarettes?

A great deal is known about factors that lead to the initiation of smoking. However, one of the most basic questions is also one of the most difficult to answer. Which ethnic groups are most and least likely to take up smoking? A major study has been attempting to document smoking and other drug use among U.S. high school seniors since 1975. About 17,000 seniors from 130 high schools across the country are surveyed each year. This is a large enough sample to look at both ethnic differences and changes over time.

Below are the percentages of students in different ethnic groups who reported smoking in the past 30 days on the 1985–1989 surveys.

Group		% smoking in past 30 days
White	Male	30
	Female	34
African American	Male	16
	Female	13
Mexican American	Male	24
	Female	19
Puerto Rican/Latino	Male	22
	Female	25
Asian American	Male	17
	Female	14
Native American	Male	37
	Female	44

By far, those with the highest rate were the Native Americans, and whites had the second highest rates. The Latino groups smoked at intermediate rates. The African American and Asian samples had the lowest rates. It is interesting that in some groups females smoked more than males, while in other groups males smoked more. When trends across time were analyzed,

smoking rates declined for just about every group from the mid-1970s to the late 1980s.

The data on ethnic differences are clear-cut, but the interpretation of these findings is not. The biggest problem with this study is that it includes only high school seniors, and up to 40 percent of some groups drop out before this time. It is known that smoking rates (as well as drinking and drug use) are higher in dropouts. Therefore, it is unclear what the smoking rates are for the entire population of 17-year-olds. Because Latinos have high dropout rates, their true smoking rates are probably higher than reported. Asian Americans have low dropout rates, so their true smoking rates are probably close to the reported figures. Native Americans have very high dropout rates, so the reported data are underestimates. African American and white dropout rates are about the same, so the smoking rates of these groups are both underestimated. However, the black-white difference in smoking rates in this study is probably equivalent to differences in the total population.

One of the most surprising findings is the low smoking rate for African Americans, because it is known that black adults smoke more than white adults. The authors suggest that the low rates for Latinos and African Americans are not due to parental presence or education. However, differences in religious affiliations as well as family, peer, and community norms about smoking are probably operating. Other studies confirm low smoking rates among African American adolescents, but black-white differences are small in early adulthood. By middle adulthood African Americans are more likely to smoke than whites.

This study shows that smoking rates are lower among nonwhite high school seniors compared with their white classmates. The exception is that Native Americans in this group are the most likely to smoke. Smoking prevention programs should be a high priority for Native Americans, and prevention programs for African Americans and Latinos may need to be continued into early adulthood, because these groups may start smoking later in life than whites (Bachman et al., 1991).

dramatically as evidence has surfaced about the hazards of secondhand smoke. Many smokers now report that they want to quit to avoid the glares and comments of friends, co-workers, and even strangers. Other reasons cited by smokers include saving money, set-

ting a good example for their children, and getting lower insurance rates. Because there is so much interest in smoking cessation, many approaches and a sizable industry have developed (Schwartz, 1987).

Most smoking cessation methods are based

BOX 16·4

FOCUS ON RESEARCH

Do You Gain Weight When You Quit Smoking?

Unfortunately, many studies show that those who quit smoking are likely to gain a few pounds. The amount of weight gain is not as much as most people fear. A lot of people gain no weight at all, most gain less than 10 lb., and a few gain more than 10 lb. Most people seem to know someone who quit smoking and gained 20 lb., and that story discourages many from trying to quit. For your health, you are much better off quitting and gaining 10 to 15 lb. than continuing to smoke.

However, we live in a weight-conscious society, and the pressure is especially strong on women to be thin. Concern about weight gain may explain why fewer women try to quit smoking and why women's relapse rates are higher than men's. Because of the importance of this issue, researchers in Pittsburgh tried to find out what accounts for the women's weight gain following smoking cessation.

They reasoned that the weight gain must be the result of increased calorie intake, decreased calorie expenditure, or both. Seven young women smokers who were near ideal weight were subjects in this study. Calorie intake was measured by food diaries, and sweet taste preference was measured to see if quitting smoking increased the desire for sweet foods that might lead to overeating. Leisure-time physical activity was also assessed with a diary. Resting metabolic rate was carefully measured, because smoking is known to increase the rate of metabolism, which means that smokers burn calories faster than nonsmokers. Each woman participated in the study for 3 weeks. During week 1, she smoked as usual. During week 2, she had to quit smoking entirely. She resumed her normal rate of smoking in week 3.

The results are as follows:

Subjects gained about 1 lb. during week 2 and did not lose any weight during week 3.

Resting metabolic rate decreased slightly during week 2 but increased significantly during week 3.

Calorie intake increased during week 2 and then went down to baseline levels during week 3. Most of the extra calories came from alcohol.

Leisure-time physical activity did not change.

There were no changes in sweet taste preference.

These results may help explain the weight gain following smoking cessation. After they stopped smoking, these women experienced a disruption in their energy balance that would result in weight gain. That is, their resting metabolic rate declined slightly, and their calorie intake increased. They did not increase their physical activity to make up for these changes, and the subjects gained 1 pound in their week of not smoking. If these patterns persisted over time, more weight gain could be expected. The authors suggest that increased caloric intake is temporary. The women may have increased their alcohol intake to help them cope with the stress of quitting smoking (Perkins, Epstein, & Pastor, 1991).

on research concerning the influences on smoking. Smokers report using cigarettes to control their feelings, so approaches using relaxation have appeared. Increasing data on the pharmacologic factors in smoking have led to nicotine chewing gum and gradual fading of nicotine to prevent the withdrawal syndrome. Evidence of conditioning influences has led to stimulus control procedures, reinforcement for nonsmoking, and aversive conditioning for smoking. Therapies have been developed to modify smoking-related attitudes and beliefs. Specific programs and their effectiveness are reviewed later in this chapter.

Maintenance or Relapse

Mark Twain reportedly said, "Quitting smoking is the easiest thing I have ever done. I've done it thousands of times." Smokers quickly realize that quitting is not hard to do, but staying quit (or maintaining abstinence) is one of the most challenging tasks of their lives. Many studies report about the same success rates for quitting heroin, alcohol, and cigarettes.

Alan Marlatt and Judith Gordon (1985) proposed a model of the relapse process in all addictive behaviors that has become influential in stimulating research and treatments. This cognitive-behavioral model emphasizes the choice points that set the stage for maintenance or relapse. For example, whether to attend a party soon after quitting, whether to have a beer, and whether to talk with a group of smokers or a group of nonsmokers—these are all decisions that alter the probability of relapse. Therapies have been devised to teach ex-smokers to identify high-risk situations and develop effective coping responses.

If the ex-smoker does have a cigarette, Marlatt and Gordon found a common cognitive-emotional reaction that they termed the *abstinence violation effect*. This effect has two parts: (a) guilt from smoking, which is discrepant from the new self-image as a nonsmoker, and (b) an attribution that the smoking episode was due to personal weakness. The abstinence violation effect decreases self-efficacy and the will to keep trying. Marlatt and Gordon teach their clients to separate a slip from a relapse. A *slip* is temporary, but a *relapse* is long term, and slips do not need to turn into relapses. Interventions based on this model focus on identifying high-risk situations, developing coping strategies, and learning to counteract the abstinence violation effect with positive thoughts.

There is evidence that smokers can correctly identify their high-risk situations, and these situations are related to relapse. Condiotte and Lichtenstein (1981) had participants in a smoking cessation program complete a questionnaire in which they rated their self-efficacy that they could resist the urge to smoke in several potential smoking situations. The subjects were asked months later whether they relapsed and what circumstances led to their first cigarette. The results confirmed their ratings. If they felt that they would be unable to resist a smoking urge when drinking or when depressed, then they were more likely to actually relapse in that situation. The Marlatt and Gordon (1985) model was supported by findings of guilt reactions and decreases in self-efficacy following the first abstinence violation. The effectiveness of relapse prevention training based on this model is presented in the next section.

TREATMENT

Smokers who want to quit are faced with a difficult choice. Which of the dozens of types of smoking cessation programs should they choose? Which programs are the most effective at helping them quit permanently? Hundreds of studies have been conducted over the past 20 years to examine almost every conceivable approach to smoking cessation. Early studies of specific components have now given way to studies of multicomponent or "broad spectrum" programs. Approaches have been developed to decrease both psychological and physiological dependence on tobacco, and the most promising methods are described in this section.

Reducing Psychological Dependence

Aversion *Aversive approaches* attempt to alter the environment so that smoking behavior is punished instead of reinforced. The first method used was electrical aversion produced by mild shock after each puff from a cigarette. Since this method was not successful, it is rarely used. Imaginal aversion techniques, such as covert sensitization, have also been used. Covert sensitization involves having the smoker imagine an aversive event, such as throwing up, each time he or she takes a puff. This method adds little or nothing to other self-control treatments (Lichtenstein & Brown, 1983).

Current research is concerned with making cigarette smoke itself the aversive stimulus. Several of these methods are based on the principle of satiation. When one's desire for something is satiated, continued exposure to that stimulus becomes punishing. Just as the fourth hot fudge sundae is not nearly as good as the first, excessive tobacco smoke becomes aversive even to smokers. In the early 1970s rapid smoking seemed like a powerful aversive smoking cessation method. In *rapid smoking* treatment, smokers sit in a closed room and take a puff every 6 seconds until they can smoke no more. Although rapid smoking is relatively effective at producing long-term abstinence (Danaher, 1977) , it is rarely used in practice because of the side effects. Because more tobacco smoke than usual is consumed, rapid smoking causes large increases in carboxyhemoglobin (that is, carbon monoxide in the blood), blood nicotine, heart rate, and cardiac arrhythmias (Lichtenstein & Brown, 1983). These side effects require medical screening before rapid smoking can be used, and it is not recommended for heart patients. While it is recommended for use only in supervised medical settings, it is now rarely employed because safer aversive smoking procedures are available.

Several safe alternatives to rapid smoking have been developed and tested. These methods have been used as the primary smoking cessation treatments, but they are more commonly used to produce cessation in multicomponent programs. In *focused smoking*, subjects smoke at a normal rate while they are instructed by the therapist to concentrate on the negative sensations associated with smoking. This procedure is no more risky than regular smoking, and it was found to be effective in early studies (Hackett & Horan, 1978). However, this early success has not been replicated. The most promising aversive procedure at this time is *smoke holding*, which consists of holding smoke in the mouth and concentrating on the negative sensations. When smoke is held in the mouth, not only does the taste become aversive but the lining of the mouth becomes mildly irritated. This safe procedure's ability to produce abstinence was demonstrated in an early study (Kopel, Suckerman, & Baksht, 1979). As shown in Figure 16-4, smoke holding was a more effective aversive smoking method than focused smoking (Walker & Franzini, 1985).

Controlled Smoking There is substantial controversy in the field about *controlled smoking*. On one side, experts argue that millions of smokers are unwilling or unable to give up cigarettes entirely, and if they reduced their intake of tobacco, they would also reduce the associated health risks. Smokers can learn to

FIGURE 16-4

Comparison of focused smoking and smoke holding. (From Walker and Franzini, 1985.)

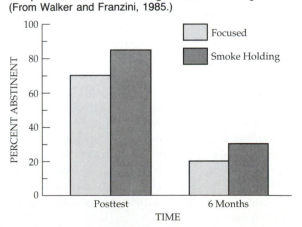

control the rate of smoking, the nicotine content of the cigarette, and the topography of smoking. Topography includes such things as the frequency of puffs, depth of inhalation, puff duration, and amount of cigarette smoked (Frederiksen, Miller, & Peterson, 1977). Smokers who are taught to control their smoking have not increased their rate of smoking or exposure to nicotine or carbon monoxide (Lichtenstein & Brown, 1983).

On the other side, scientists argue that since many individuals smoke so as to maintain nicotine intake at a constant level, there is a tendency to make adjustments for changes in rate or topography. They point to studies showing that smokers of low-nicotine cigarettes take deeper or more frequent puffs to maintain former nicotine intake. This results in higher carbon monoxide levels (Benowitz, 1983; Russell, 1978; Schachter, 1978). Although this debate continues, most smoking treatment programs recommend abstinence from cigarettes.

Hypnosis *Hypnotic approaches* to smoking cessation are more commonly advertised in newspapers than subjected to scientific scrutiny. Therefore, there is limited information on the effectiveness of hypnosis in smoking cessation. One-session hypnosis treatments have not been studied in controlled experiments, so reports of high long-term abstinence rates cannot be verified. Holroyd (1980) reviewed 18 studies of more individualized therapies in which hypnosis was one of several treatment components. These programs included multiple sessions, self-hypnosis training, and in-person or telephone follow-up. Six-month abstinence rates were typically greater than 50 percent in these uncontrolled studies. In later studies when patients were randomly assigned to hypnosis or control conditions, hypnosis produced only 20 percent abstinence (Frank, Umlauf, Wonderlich, & Ashkanazi, 1986). This discrepancy reemphasizes the need to conduct rigorous controlled studies of all therapies.

Restricted Environmental Stimulation Techniques (REST) *REST* is based on the hypothesis that removing external stimuli promotes increased receptivity to new ideas or suggestions. In the typical treatment, subjects spend from 1 to 24 hours in a dark silent chamber or a flotation tank. During this time taped messages about smoking cessation may be played. Investigations have shown that in controlled studies REST combined with self-management training has produced 12-month abstinence rates of 25 to 50 percent (Suedfeld & Kristeller, 1982). These studies have caught the interest of smoking cessation researchers, but this procedure is considered too poorly understood to be recommended for wide use.

Even the foregoing list is incomplete because these cessation methods require personal contact with a therapist. Other educational approaches are meant to be easily available to large numbers of people. For example, printed stop smoking kits or video programs could be used in one's home. Telephone counseling is an alternative to face-to-face sessions. When smokers in Australia were asked which cessation services they would like to try, 46 percent said "none." Of those who expressed a preference, almost 70 percent chose to have personal contact with a practitioner. About 12 percent chose a group, and 23 percent chose printed materials. Only 3 percent chose mail or telephone services. Heavy smokers, and those unsure of their ability to stop, tended to choose personal services (Owen & Davies, 1990). These findings are in some conflict with earlier studies suggesting most people did not want to use intensive methods. However, now that many smokers have already quit, the remaining recalcitrant smokers feel they need the most powerful methods.

Reducing Physiological Dependence

Nicotine Fading The *nicotine fading* procedure calls for smokers to switch to brands of cigarettes that have progressively lower levels of nicotine and to decrease the number of cigarettes smoked (tapering). Since smokers are dependent on nicotine, this procedure helps to slowly wean them from nicotine so that they can stop altogether. When nicotine intake is reduced to a low level, it is expected that those who quit will have milder withdrawal reactions. If the smoker is unable to stop, then he or she will be prepared to achieve controlled smoking. The results of studies on nicotine fading suggest that, by itself, it has minor effects on cessation, but that it can be effective when combined with other components such as self-management, relapse prevention, or smoke holding (Brown, Lichtenstein, McIntyre, & Harrington-Kostur, 1984; Lando & McGovern, 1985). However, given the small impact of this procedure, the time spent in explaining how to change brands does not seem well spent.

Nicotine Replacement Numerous pharmacologic treatments for tobacco dependence have been tried over the years. Each drug has been selected to mimic an effect of nicotine that is supposedly responsible for maintaining tobacco use (U.S. DHHS, 1987). Drugs that have been studied and found to be generally ineffective include sedatives, antianxiety agents, stimulants, propranolol (a drug used in the treatment of hypertension), and sodium bicarbonate.

The pharmacologic approach of greatest current interest is actual *nicotine replacement*. Nicotine chewing gum is designed to treat the physiological addiction to cigarettes and to prevent severe withdrawal reactions caused by abrupt smoking cessation. Although nicotine in any form is an addictive and toxic substance, it is reasoned that, unlike cigarettes, nicotine gum does not contain the noxious tars and gases that have severe health consequences. Nicotine gum is used only during the first 3 to 6 months after cessation, and then the gum is withdrawn. Because it takes 20 to 30 minutes for peak nicotine levels to occur in

the blood after chewing the gum, as opposed to 7 seconds for cigarettes, withdrawal from the gum is not usually difficult.

After several years of clinical trials, nicotine gum was approved in 1984 by the Food and Drug Administration as the first pharmacologic treatment for smoking cessation. In virtually all studies, nicotine gum is ineffective unless it is used in combination with behavioral treatments. When it was combined with behavioral treatments nicotine gum was superior to a placebo in producing cessation in eight of nine studies (U.S. DHHS, 1987). However, most studies show that nicotine gum does not improve long-term maintenance of abstinence (Hall & Killen, 1985).

Nicotine patches came onto the market in 1992, and nicotine nasal spray is currently being studied. These forms of nicotine administration may have some advantages, but we cannot count on the pharmacologists to solve the smoking cessation problem for us. Therefore, health psychologists must continue to improve methods of long-term behavior change that can be applied to smoking cessation.

Maintenance and Relapse Prevention

Many programs that use aversive smoking and other methods are able to produce immediate cessation in 90 percent or more of the smokers, but this success is illusory since relapse continues to be the major problem in smoking cessation. However, improvements in short-term cessation rates now allow more attention to be devoted to maintenance and relapse prevention. Because early experience with booster sessions indicated no benefit, the two primary approaches to maintenance are social support and cognitive-behavioral relapse prevention interventions.

Social support in the natural environment is consistently found to predict the success of smoking cessation (Mermelstein, Cohen, Lichtenstein, Baer, & Kamarck, 1986), since smokers with high levels of support are more likely to quit. Surprisingly, efforts to promote social support in intervention programs have typically had disappointing results (Lichtenstein, Glasgow, & Abrams, 1986). At least five studies have been conducted recently, and in none of them did the social support condition improve smoking cessation rates. The only notable success in this area was an early study of a buddy system that showed short-term effects. Very long term follow-up 10 years after treatment indicated that subjects in the buddy system condition continued to have better abstinence rates (Janis, 1983). This extraordinary finding encourages researchers to try to harness social support, but no one has yet reported such positive results.

Marlatt and Gordon's (1985) model of relapse prevention discussed above has stimulated a few studies. The program developed by Brown and Lichtenstein (1980) included five components: identifying high-risk situations, practicing coping strategies, cognitive change to avoid turning "slips" into relapses, incorporating pleasant activities into one's lifestyle, and self-rewards. When this package was tested, it was found to be no more effective than an unstructured discussion group. Hall and colleagues (Hall, Hall, Sachs, & Benowitz, 1984) developed a similar cognitive and behavioral intervention and tested it as part of a multicomponent program. At 1 year the abstinence rate in the relapse prevention condition was 46 percent and for the discussion condition it was 30 percent. Thus, relapse prevention programs show some promise, but work in this area is just starting.

In an effort to improve long-term maintenance of cessation, the process of relapse has been studied. Shiffman's (1982) early work showed that ex-smokers were most likely to relapse during periods of negative affect, such as anxiety, anger, and depression. One-third of relapses occurred during encounters with other smokers or while drinking alcohol. Use of either cognitive or behavioral coping responses were more effective in avoiding a relapse than no coping at all.

Condiotte and Lichtenstein (1981) first determined that ex-smokers could use self-efficacy ratings to predict the situations in which they would be most likely to relapse. Haaga and Stewart (1992) have extended this work by examining self-efficacy that the ex-smoker can recover abstinence after an initial lapse. This was termed self-efficacy for recovery. During simulated high-risk situations, subjects were asked to describe their thought processes about having a lapse and to rate their self-efficacy for recovery. The authors found that ex-smokers with moderate levels of self-efficacy maintained abstinence longer than those with either low or high self-efficacy. This pattern agreed with Bandura's (1986) hypothesis that self-efficacy should be high enough that ex-smokers would not be depressed if they had a lapse, but not so high that they are tempted to experiment with smoking.

Comprehensive Programs for Cessation and Relapse Prevention

Most smokers who seek treatment eventually find themselves in a multicomponent program, and such programs are also the focus of most of the current research in clinical smoking cessation. Thus, it is useful to review two rather typical and effective comprehensive programs.

Harry Lando (1977) developed one of the more effective programs that has served as a model for other clinic-based smoking cessation treatments. Up until this time most clinic-based programs scheduled 8 to 16 weekly sessions. The first component of Lando's program consisted of six sessions of aversive smoking over a 1-week period. During the sessions subjects smoked continuously for 25 minutes. They also doubled their usual daily smoking rate outside the sessions. Control subjects received only the aversive smoking component, but experimental subjects attended seven additional sessions over the next 2 months. At the follow-up sessions subjects identified problems they were having in maintaining abstinence and came up with ways to overcome those problems. Subjects also made self-reward and self-punishment contracts. These formal contracts stated that they would forfeit a small amount of money ($0.25 to $3.00) for each cigarette smoked and give themselves rewards (for example, a new sweater) for nonsmoking.

The results strongly indicated that the broad-spectrum behavioral approach was more successful than the aversion-only treatment, as shown in Figure 16-5.

The 76 percent abstinence rate at 6 months was very promising and indicated that Lando (1977) had come upon a very effective comprehensive program. In a later study (Lando & McGovern, 1982) the same program achieved a 46 percent abstinence rate at 12 months, and the same 46 percent success rate was maintained at the 36-month follow-up. Unfortunately, there was no objective verification of abstinence in these studies, so success rates are likely to be overestimated because smokers are known to misreport their smoking status.

FIGURE 16-5

Abstinence rates. Broad-spectrum smoking cessation program versus a control condition. (After Lando, 1977.)

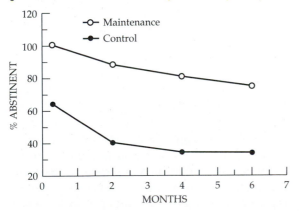

Nevertheless, the general pattern of results suggests that the broad-spectrum approach is more effective than almost any other published approach. One of the primary innovations of Lando's treatment was the high frequency of sessions devoted to aversive smoking in the first week of the program. Even the controls who got no further treatment achieved a 35 percent abstinence rate at 6 months (Lando, 1977), which is more effective than other complete programs. Thus, the initial grouping of daily aversive smoking sessions has been adopted by other investigators.

One study that used several elements of Lando's ground-breaking approach supplemented it with a pharmacological component designed to ease withdrawal from nicotine. Killen, Maccoby, and Taylor (1984) reasoned that because there are both psychological and physiological factors involved in tobacco addiction, treatments should be directed at both kinds of factors. Because the aim of the study was to evaluate the effects of interventions on relapse prevention, all subjects received a 1-week intensive cessation treatment. This consisted of three daily sessions of problem-solving and behavioral skills training plus aversive smoking. The aversive procedure was smoke holding, in which subjects held smoke in the mouth for 30 seconds and focused on the negative sensations produced by it. Subjects were instructed to quit smoking on day 3 and to attend a final cessation meeting on day 4.

Smokers were randomly assigned to one of three conditions. In the nicotine gum condition they started using the gum on day 1 of the cessation phase. Nicotine gum contains 2 to 4 mg of nicotine, and when it is chewed properly, it produces relatively stable blood levels of nicotine. The gum prevents many of the withdrawal symptoms that occur when people stop cold turkey. Subjects were instructed to chew gum each time they had a craving to smoke. Gum usage was reduced at week 3 and was no longer available after week 7. The second condition was skills training. These subjects met weekly with a therapist in weeks 2 and 3. They identified high-risk situations and designed appropriate treatment strategies, based on a relapse prevention framework. In weeks 4 through 7, self-administered maintenance programs were supervised in weekly drop-in clinic sessions. Thus, responsibility for maintenance was transferred to the subjects. In the third condition, subjects received both skills training and nicotine gum components. The results are shown in Figure 16-6.

Eighty-three percent of the subjects quit smoking for at least 24 hours during the cessation phase. This abstinence rate is similar to the findings from Lando (1977) and much higher than most programs that employ only weekly sessions. It can be seen that the combined treatment was superior to the other conditions at all measurements. Reports of abstinence were verified with two biochemical measures, so one can be certain that the quit rates are accurate. This study suggests that both psychological/behavioral and pharmacological treatments are needed to produce long-term abstinence. The nicotine gum seems to help smokers get past the early withdrawal

and cravings, while the behavioral skills training prepares them to deal effectively with relapse-inducing episodes. This study agrees with several others that the combination of behavioral skills and nicotine gum offers the most potent smoking cessation treatment at this time.

SMOKING PREVENTION

Will it be possible to make further dramatic reductions in smoking rates by continuing to improve smoking cessation programs? Many experts believe that the limited effectiveness of even the best smoking cessation programs means that other approaches must be explored. The primary alternative to smoking cessation has been smoking prevention. Smoking prevention programs are invariably aimed at teenagers, since almost all smokers take up the habit during adolescence.

Smoking prevention programs during the 1950s and 1960s were based on the notion that informing teens of the dangers of smoking would lead to decreased smoking rates. These programs presented the health hazards of smoking dramatically, using many visual aids such as specimens of healthy and diseased lungs. While these programs often produced the desired changes in knowledge and attitudes toward smoking, the expected changes in actual smoking did not occur (Thompson, 1978).

In the mid-1970s social psychologist Richard Evans was influential in changing the approach to smoking prevention. He noted that the major influences on the initiation of smoking were social in nature. Pressure from peers, smoking by parents and siblings, and probably modeling through the media had the most impact on adolescent smoking. Thus, intervention programs should counter those influences. Borrowing from McGuire's (1964) social inoculation theory, Evans developed a new type of smoking prevention program. Social

FIGURE 16-6

Abstinence rates. Behavioral treatment and nicotine gum in smoking cessation. (After Killen et al., 1984.)

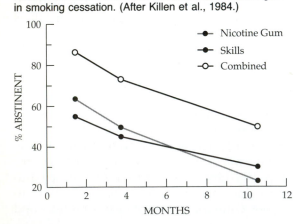

BOX 16·5

FOCUS ON RESEARCH

A New Approach: Smoking Policies at the Workplace

In the past few years nonsmokers have become vocal about their right to breathe air that is not polluted by cigarette smoke. They have asserted their rights by lobbying for restrictions on smoking. Work sites have been frequently targeted, because nonsmokers may be involuntarily exposed to tobacco smoke for 40 hours per week or more at work. As a result, many companies have adopted policies that range from restricting smoking to certain areas to banning smoking altogether at the workplace. A group of investigators in Boston studied the effects of a work site smoking policy on smoking cessation by employees.

The New England Telephone Company employs about 27,000 people at 600 different sites. A smoking policy was implemented that prohibited smoking in all work areas, including individual offices. There were designated smoking areas in cafeterias, lounges, hallways, and rest rooms. A full-time coordinator of the policy was hired, and free on-site smoking cessation classes were offered.

Twenty months after the policy went into effect, over 1000 employees from top management to secretaries were surveyed anonymously regarding the policy. The response rate was about 75 percent. About 21 percent of the employees who were smokers when the policy began said they had quit smoking. Cessation rates were about twice as high among managers than among nonmanagers. Nine percent of the original smokers said they quit because of the policy, and 32 percent said they reduced the number of cigarettes smoked as a result of the policy.

Almost 40 percent of the smokers said they received some kind of smoking cessation assistance, but they were no more likely to quit than those who received no assistance. Thus, smoking cessation programs at this company did not appear to help smokers quit. However, those who quit were more likely to work in areas where other employees complied with the policy.

This study indicates that restrictive work site smoking policies may encourage workers to quit. The 21 percent cessation rate is much higher than the 2 to 5 percent of the people who quit per year in the general U.S. population. This is a promising approach to reducing the amount of exposure to the harmful effects of tobacco smoke.

Smoking bans have been instituted in workplaces in other nations, such as Australia. Public service workers were surveyed following smoking bans in 44 government office buildings in 3 cities. Initially, there was a great deal of discontent, with many smokers feeling inconvenienced. Six months after the ban, attitudes of both smokers and nonsmokers improved dramatically. Many smokers were willing to put up with the inconvenience, because they recognized the benefits of the ban. However, one-third of the smokers still disapproved of the ban. Only about 2 percent of the smokers quit the first 6 months of the ban, but no smoking cessation assistance was provided (Sorenson, Rigotti, Rosen, et al., 1991; Borland, Owen, Hill, et al., 1990).

---

inoculation theory is analogous to physiological inoculation in that small doses of an infectious agent (pressure to smoke, in this case) can protect one from a full-blown infection later (habitual smoking). Smoking prevention programs, therefore, present teens with pressure to smoke in a classroom setting and train the students to resist those pressures. These skills can then be used when the teens are pressured to smoke in the "real world."

Students are taught to identify, analyze, and resist pressures from peers, adults, and the media. While resistance skills training is the core of the approach, students also learn about the short-term disadvantages of smoking, and they are encouraged to make public commitments to remain nonsmokers. Most smoking prevention programs are conducted with seventh-graders, because initiation rates start to climb rapidly in that grade. Usually between 6 and 10 classroom sessions are delivered, with a few booster sessions in the eighth grade. The programs are brief and can be integrated into the regular curriculum.

Flay (1985) reviewed 27 studies of the social inoculation approach to smoking prevention. In general the results have shown that this type of program is effective in reducing the number of teens who begin smoking. Some studies have shown dramatic results in which differences between intervention and control conditions lasted for several years. Figure 16-7 shows the results of a program (Telch, Killen, McAlister, Perry, & Maccoby, 1982) in which students were followed for almost 3 years. Some studies have less dramatic effects (Luepker, Johnson, Murray, & Pechacek, 1983).

FIGURE 16-7

Seventh grade smoking prevention: 3-year follow-up. (From Telch et al., *J. Behav. Med. 5*, 1–8, 1982).

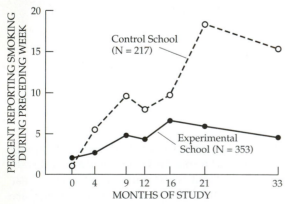

One interesting variation on the now-standard approach has been studied by Botvin and colleagues in New York (Botvin, Eng, & Williams, 1980). They have developed an intervention for junior high school students called Life Skills Training, with smoking prevention being only a portion of the entire program. Students are taught a variety of skills that are important to teens, such as basic communication skills, decision making, resisting pressure to use alcohol and drugs, and anxiety reduction. The researchers feel that smoking serves a function for adolescents since it is perceived as an "adult" behavior, and smoking prevention is just one skill that they need to help them successfully make it through the teen years. This program is as effective as other social inoculation approaches (Botvin et al., 1980).

Research in smoking prevention is becoming very complex, and current studies typically involve 20 to 50 schools (Flay, 1985). While the early results generally showed the effectiveness of smoking prevention programs in schools, more recent studies have questioned the long-term success. Two follow-up studies have shown that after 5 to 7 years the smoking rates of treatment and control subjects are identical (Flay et al., 1989; Murray, Pirie, Luepker, & Pallonen, 1989). Maybe 6 to 10 sessions in the seventh and eighth grades are not sufficient to produce permanent effects, and additional methods of discouraging smoking must be developed if smoking-related diseases are going to be reduced drastically in the next generation.

New Approaches to Tobacco Control

Traditional psychological approaches to reducing tobacco use consist of behavioral and pharmacological treatments for current smokers and behavioral and social skills training to prevent young people from starting to smoke. However, a wide variety of other approaches have been developed in recent years to limit access to cigarettes and to protect non-smokers. These innovative methods were summarized by Novotny, Romano, Davis, & Mills (1992). Some of them are listed here.

Clean-Indoor-Air Laws and Policies Workplace smoking bans fit into this category (see Box 16-5), but cities and states are passing laws to minimize nonsmokers' exposure to smoke. Before the mid-1970s almost no states had these laws. Now, 45 states and the District of Columbia have clean-indoor-air laws.

Restricting Access to Tobacco by Minors While many states have laws against the sale of tobacco to minors, these laws were not enforced. In the past few years there have been many efforts to strengthen enforcement of these laws. Cigarette vending machines are being banned in many areas. In many convenience stores, signs are posted, and clerks wear buttons stating that tobacco will not be sold to minors.

Restricting Advertising While cigarette ads have been banned on television and radio since 1971, new approaches include banning billboards (Utah) and signs in sports stadiums (cities in 7 states). At least 14 cities ban the free distribution of tobacco product samples. However, tobacco companies undermine these restrictions by sponsoring sports events that are shown on television. There are also at least a dozen companies in Hollywood that work to get products, such as cigarettes, shown prominently in movies.

Increasing Taxes Although increased taxation probably has a limited effect on current smokers, the price of cigarettes has a large impact on access to tobacco by young people. However, there are usually substantial decreases in cigarette sales when tobacco taxes are raised. In 1988, California voters passed Proposition 99, which put an extra 25-cent tax on a pack of cigarettes. There was an immediate 15 percent decline in cigarette sales, but this was due to the combined effects of the tax and a massive education program paid for by the tax. However, the effect of the tax decreased over time, suggesting that many smokers simply stocked up before the tax went into effect.

Increasing Research Large-scale research studies are now underway that serve to increase knowledge about smoking control and to have a large impact on tobacco use across the nation. The largest is the COMMIT trial, sponsored by the National Cancer Institute. More than 2 million smokers in 22 sites are involved. This study focuses on heavy smokers who have tended not to be successful in previous studies. In addition to COMMIT, at least 10 million people in 300 cities are involved in other smoking control research studies.

Intensifying Public Information Campaigns Major efforts are being made to involve health departments, health agencies of all types, and governments in coordinated public information campaigns. Some of these target special groups such as minorities and pregnant women, while others use mass media to reach the whole population. California, Michigan, and Minnesota are among a growing list of states using public funds to buy media time for nonsmoking messages. California spent almost $29 million of Proposition 99 money in 1989–1990 alone.

Networking Because of the growing knowledge and rapidly changing situation related to smoking control, new efforts are made to keep health professionals up to date. Computer networks focus specifically on smoking and health. Organizations such as Doctors Ought to Care (DOC) have extensive newsletters.

Coalitions of varied groups within states and nationwide share information. The Office on Smoking and Health has a Technical Information Center that is available to all.

Even with all of these activities, the $3.3 billion spent on cigarette advertising each year buys a lot of political influence and effectively gets the protobacco message out. A good measure of the effectiveness of the tobacco industry is that about 400,000 people will die this year because of their tobacco use.

SUMMARY

Cigarette smoking is the major preventable cause of death in the western world today. A report by Surgeon General Antonia C. Novello, released in 1990, stated that "smoking cessation represents the single most important step smokers can take to enhance the length and quality of their lives." Cigarette smoking increased rapidly in the twentieth century. Although there has been some downturn in recent years, smoking is still the major public health problem in the developed world today. There has been some decline in cigarette smoking by males, but females are more likely to take it up.

The evidence that smoking is damaging to health is overwhelming. Two-pack-a-day smokers can expect to live 8 to 9 years less than nonsmokers. More than 350,000 Americans die each year from cigarette smoking. In addition, smoking causes ill health prior to death. Not only are smokers damaging their own health, but increasing evidence suggests that a smoky environment can have ill effects on nonsmokers. Nicotine and carbon monoxide increase the risk of cardiovascular disease, and there are 15 known cancer-causing compounds in cigarette smoke.

The initiation of the smoking habit is most likely influenced by peer pressure. The majority of people start smoking cigarettes in their teen years. Once established, smoking may become addictive. There are important bene-fits to stopping. However, overcoming the smoking habit is very difficult. People become irritable, gain weight, and often try many times before they are successful. Relapse is common. Modern treatments deal with psychological factors through aversive smoking and relapse prevention, and physiological factors through nicotine gum or patches. Youth programs for smoking prevention can also be successful. Although smoking rates are declining, we expect cigarette smoking to remain one of the major health problems of the nineties.

KEY TERMS

Surgeon General's Report. This report, first published in 1964, put together the scientific evidence against cigarettes. The report has been updated several times, and the evidence against cigarette smoking has continued to grow.

Pooling Project. A project that combined data from several epidemiologic studies. The combined data show a strong relationship between cigarette smoking and mortality.

Involuntary smoking. Exposure to cigarette smoke among nonsmokers. This occurs when nonsmokers are in the presence of smokers. Growing evidence identifies health consequences of exposure to involuntary smoke.

Smoking and health "controversy." Tobacco companies continue to argue that the evidence suggesting that cigarettes harm health is inconclusive. Thus, they refer to a "controversy." Most scientists agree that the evidence against cigarette smoke is overwhelming.

Nicotine. The primary addictive substance in tobacco products.

Carbon monoxide (CO). A product of cigarette combustion. Carbon monoxide occupies red cells in the blood and reduces the amount of oxygen that can be delivered to tissues of the body.

Tars. The solid portions of tobacco smoke containing many toxic compounds like arsenic and radioactive polonium.

Smoking initiation. The process of beginning to smoke cigarettes.

Smoking addiction. Some evidence supports an addiction model of smoking. This suggests that smoking is physiologically addictive, and when tobacco is withdrawn, people experience symptoms including irritability, anxiety, inability to concentrate, insomnia, and cigarette craving.

Smoking cessation. The act of quitting the cigarette habit.

Maintenance. The process of maintaining nonsmoker status once a smoker has quit.

Relapse. The process by which a former smoker becomes a smoker once again.

Aversion. An approach to smoking treatment that requires smoking behavior to be punished.

Rapid smoking. A technique in which the smoker takes a puff every 6 seconds. The rapid exposure to nicotine causes the smoker to feel sick. This can be used to produce a conditioned aversive response to smoking cigarettes.

Smoking prevention. Efforts to help young people remain nonsmokers. Most programs teach teenagers how to resist peer pressure to smoke.

CHAPTER 17

Obesity

Susan Brown is a healthy and intelligent teenager, but she is unhappy. She is at school sitting in the waiting room of the principal's office. She is thinking about what a tough childhood she had. Every single day the other kids made fun of her, and at times she had no friends with whom she could talk about her frustrations. Now she is unhappy because boys do not ask her out on dates. She is in the principal's office because she was caught skipping class. Instead of going to physical education she went out to the parking lot to smoke a cigarette. She hates going to P.E. class because she is embarrassed to change clothes in front of the other girls, and she is embarrassed to play basketball because she is so slow and clumsy. She feels that all her problems are due to her obesity. She has tried to do something about it. Several times a year she tries to diet by fasting as long as she can. Usually she lasts only a day or two, and then she is starving so much she really loads up on sweets for days afterward. Reading novels is always more interesting than working out, so exercise has never appealed to her. Last year she started smoking, because she heard that would help her lose weight. She may have lost a few pounds, but she feels like giving up. Both her parents are overweight, and they are already starting to have health problems. Her mother is diabetic, and her father has high blood pressure. All she can see in the future is more unhappiness, no boyfriends, and health problems on top of all that. Life is difficult for the obese, but is it really this bad? What health problems is she risking if she stays overweight? Is there any way for her to lose weight, or is she going to be obese all her life?

The risk factor of most concern to the general public is obesity, if concern is measured by conversation, magazine articles, books, and commercial treatment programs. Obesity is as much a cosmetic issue as it is a health issue. The societal ideal—as seen in movies, television, and magazines—is to be very thin. While the average adult in the United States is overweight, the pressure to be lean has led an increasing number of people, especially women, to develop eating disorders such as anorexia and bulimia that are partly the result of an unhealthy desire for thinness. While there may be too much concern about obesity in the United States, the fact remains that obesity is a health hazard.

Obesity refers to an excessive amount of body fat. While obesity is the condition of most concern, overweight is usually measured in clinical settings. Overweight is simply weight that is above some standard, defined in relation to height. The definitions of overweight and obesity depend on the measurement method used.

Several indexes of overweight and obesity are based on weight and height. The well-known Metropolitan Life Insurance Company tables provide guidelines for ideal weight, which was determined by observing which weights were associated with the lowest death rates. A person's relative weight is determined by dividing their actual weight by their ideal weight. Thus, a person at their ideal weight would have a relative weight of 1.0. A person with a relative weight of 1.17 would be 17 per-

cent overweight. A person with a relative weight of 0.90 would be 10 percent below ideal weight for height. Body weight guidelines are shown in Table 17-1 (Bray, 1983). A person is considered obese if he or she is 20 percent or more above ideal weight; that is a relative weight of 1.20 or greater.

Various ratios of weight to height have also been studied. The most commonly used ratio is the body mass index (BMI), also known as the Quetelet index, for the man who first proposed it over 100 years ago. The body mass index is most highly correlated with percentage of body fat. Body mass index is weight divided by height squared. The nomogram for computing body mass index (Figure 17-1) can also be used. Find your weight and height, and connect them with a straightedge. Your body mass index is where the line crosses the center scale. You can see that *overweight* is defined as a BMI between 24 and 30 for women and between 25 and 30 for men. A BMI greater than 30 has arbitrarily been defined as *obesity*.

These methods do not truly measure obesity, since they do not determine the amount of body fat. Body fat is most often assessed by measuring the size of skinfolds with special calipers. A pinch of skin that contains a double layer of skin plus the fat underneath is pulled and measured. If several skinfolds are taken at defined parts of the body, the percentage of body fat can be well estimated. Newer methods of assessing body fat include electrical conductance that is used to estimate body density. Because the conductance and density of fat is

TABLE 17-1

FOGARTY TABLE OF DESIRABLE WEIGHTS

Height (cm)*	Men		Women	
	Average weight (kg)*	Acceptable weight range*	Average weight (kg)*	Acceptable weight range*
Metric				
145			46.0	42–53
148			46.5	42–54
150			47.0	43–55
152			48.5	44–57
154			49.5	44–58
156			50.4	45–58
158	55.8	51–64	51.3	46–59
160	57.6	52–65	52.6	48–61
162	58.6	53–66	54.0	49–62
164	59.6	54–67	55.4	50–64
166	60.6	55–69	56.8	51–65
168	61.7	56–71	58.1	52–66
170	63.5	58–73	60.0	53–67
172	65.0	59–74	61.3	55–69
174	66.5	60–75	62.6	56–70
176	68.0	62–77	64.0	58–72
178	69.4	64–79	65.3	59–74
180	71.0	65–80		
182	72.6	66–82		
184	74.2	67–84		
186	75.8	69–86		
188	77.6	71–88		
190	79.3	73–90		
192	81.0	75–93		
Nonmetric				
4′10″			102	92–119
4′11″			104	94–122
5′0″			107	96–125
5′1″			110	99–128
5′2″	123	112–141	113	102–131
5′3″	127	115–144	116	105–134
5′4″	130	118–148	120	108–138
5′5″	133	121–152	123	111–142
5′6″	136	124–156	128	114–146
5′7″	140	128–161	132	118–150
5′8″	145	132–166	136	122–154
5′9″	149	136–170	140	126–158
5′10″	153	140–174	144	130–163
5′11″	158	144–179	148	134–168
6′0″	166	152–189		
6′1″	166	152–189		
6′2″	171	156–194		
6′3″	176	160–199		
6′4″	181	164–204		

Source: G. A. Bray, ed., *Obesity in Perspective,* vol. 2, part 1. DHEW Publication no. (NIH) 75-708. Washington, D.C.: U.S. Government Printing Office, p. 72.
* Height without shoes, weight without clothes.

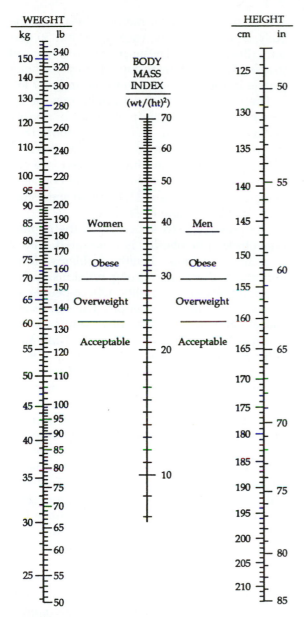

FIGURE 17-1

Nomogram for body mass index (BMI). To determine BMI, place a ruler or other straightedge between the body weight column on the left and the height column on the right and read the BMI from the point where it crosses the center. (From G. A. Bray, 1978. Definitions, measurements, and classification of the syndromes of obesity, *International Journal of Obesity* 2:99–112. Reprinted by permission of the publisher.)

different from that of muscle and bone, the electrical conductivity of obese persons is different from that of lean persons. This method is still undergoing study, but it is a quick and easy way of estimating body fat.

The most accurate method of assessing body fat is called *hydrostatic weighing*, or underwater weighing. This method is also based on the principle that fat has a different density from other body tissues. Thus, fat tends to float. By measuring weight out of the water, and then underwater, the amount and percentage of body fat can be accurately measured. This is a time-consuming and expensive test that is not often used in clinical practice.

Recent research has indicated that the distribution of body fat may be more important than the amount of body fat, so there is renewed interest in studying where the fat is located. Excessive upper-body or abdominal

BOX 17·1

HEALTH OBJECTIVES FOR THE YEAR 2000: OBESITY

By the year 2000, we should reduce overweight to a prevalence of no more than 20 percent among people aged 20 and older and no more than 15 percent among adolescents aged 12 through 19 (baseline: 26 percent for people aged 20 through 74 in 1976–1980, 24 percent for men and 27 percent for women; 15 percent of adolescents aged 12 through 19 in 1976–1980).

YEAR 2000 GOALS FOR % OVERWEIGHT

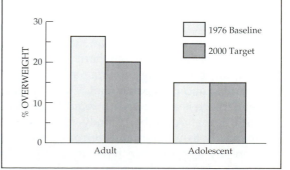

fat has higher health risks than lower-body fat that is concentrated on the hips and thighs. Note that upper-body fat is characteristic of men and lower-body fat is characteristic of women. This distribution can be assessed simply by measuring circumferences. The ratio of waist to hip circumference is a good indicator of fat distribution. The higher the ratio is, the higher the risk of CVD will be.

To assess your waist to hip ratio, measure your waist with a tape measure just above your navel. Stand relaxed, and do not suck in your stomach. Make sure the measuring tape is level. Measure around your hips at the largest part of your buttocks.

Divide your waist measurement by your hip measurement. Your waist to hip ratio is too high if it is above 0.95 for men or 0.80 for women.

EPIDEMIOLOGY

Obesity is a very common condition. Using the definition of 20 percent overweight, the prevalence of obesity increases from about 7 percent of 20- to 24-year-old men to 17 percent of 35-to 44-year-old men. The prevalence is higher in women, increasing from about 10 percent in 20- to 24-year-olds to about 35 percent in 55- to 64-year-olds. Therefore, obesity is more common in women and in the middle-aged. There is a strong tendency for lower socioeconomic status individuals, especially women, to develop obesity. In addition, obesity is more prevalent in black and Latino women than in white women (Bray, 1983).

The amount of body fat shows characteristic changes with age. The newborn is about 12 percent fat, but during the first 6 months, this increases to about 30 percent fat. Over the next 10 years there is a decrease to about 18 percent in both sexes. At puberty body fat increases dramatically in women and decreases slightly in men. By age 18, men have about 15 to 18 percent body fat, and women have about 20 to 25 percent body fat. Between the ages of 20 and 50 the body fat of men doubles, and the body fat of women increases by about 50 percent (Bray, 1983). These are all averages, of course. There is tremendous diversity among people in their changes over time in body fat.

The percentage of obese adults may be increasing slowly, but the prevalence of obesity in children may have increased by more than 50 percent in the past 15 years (Gortmaker & Dietz, 1987). If this finding is correct, we can expect to see ever-increasing numbers of obese persons in the years ahead, because obese children tend to become obese adults.

Not only are 15 to 30 percent of the population obese, but obesity is associated with a long list of serious health problems. Most important, there is a strong relationship between obesity and mortality. Obese people die much sooner than lean people. The results of a study conducted by insurance companies on obesity (defined by body mass index) and mortality are shown in Figure 17-2 (Bray, 1986). About 3.5 million people were included in this study. The figure shows that highly obese individuals were 3 times as likely to die during the study as individuals at ideal weight. Though this figure was based mainly on whites, the general findings apply to other groups, such as Mexican-Americans (Stern, Patterson, Mitchell, Hafner, & Hazuda, 1990). Individuals in the "overweight" category (BMI between 25 and 30) were found to have low risk. Most studies show, as this one did, that underweight individuals have a slightly higher death rate than those at ideal weight. It is believed that some of the underweight people may already be suffering from a disease. Unless you have an eating disorder, you should not be concerned about being somewhat thin.

The major cause of excess mortality of the obese is CVD. However, there is a controversy over whether obesity is an independent risk factor or whether it increases CVD risk by affecting other risk factors. In any case, the Framingham Study (Dawber, 1980) showed that obese persons were at least twice as likely as

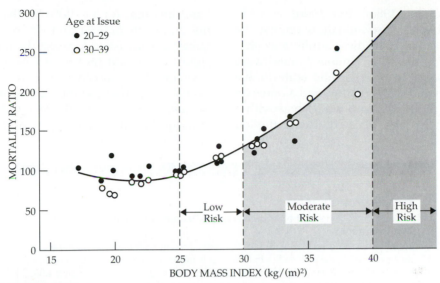

FIGURE 17-2

Relation of body mass index (BMI) to excess mortality. The U- or J-shaped relationship between the mortality ratio and the BMI is apparent. The dashed lines indicate
the various levels of risk associated with ranges from the BMI (From Bray, 1986.)

lean persons to have myocardial infarction, sudden death, and stroke. Obesity also increases risk of hypertension, hypercholesterolemia, low HDL-cholesterol, and diabetes. There are many mechanisms by which obesity increases the risk of CVD, so maintenance of ideal weight is an important goal for its prevention and treatment.

OTHER HEALTH RISKS OF OBESITY

In addition to increasing probability of CVD, there are numerous health risks of obesity (Bray, 1986).

1. Impaired pulmonary function. Impairments range from mild restrictions in work capacity to the severe shortness of breath that is seen in the morbidly obese. These individuals also have disturbed sleep.

2. Digestive diseases. Gallbladder disease is much more common in the obese. Since gallstones are composed largely of cholesterol, the hypercholesterolemia in the obese is thought to be a factor in gallbladder disease.

3. Orthopedic problems. Most studies show that the obese are at increased risk of osteoarthritis, especially of the weight-bearing joints such as the ankle.

4. Obstetric problems. Obese women are more likely to become hypertensive during pregnancy. Labor is longer and caesarean section is more common in obese women.

5. Cancer. Obesity is a risk factor for several types of cancer. Obese men are at increased risk of developing prostate and colon-rectal cancer. Obese women are at increased risk of gallbladder, breast, cervical, endometrial, uterine, and ovarian cancer.

6. Endocrine and metabolic disorders. Some endocrine abnormalities—such as increased production of insulin, impaired growth hormone response, and decreased testosterone—are reversed by weight loss. Alterations in adrenal or thyroid function may not change after weight loss.

7. Emotional and social problems. Most studies do not show that the obese are more likely to be anxious or depressed (Streigel-

Moore & Rodin, 1986), but there is well-documented social discrimination against the obese. In a series of studies, adults and children from across the United States were shown photographs of (a) a child with no disability, (b) a child with crutches and a brace on the left leg, (c) a child in a wheelchair with a blanket over the legs, (d) a child with the left hand missing, (e) a child with the left side of the mouth disfigured and (f) an obese child. Subjects were asked to select the picture of the child they would find most easy to like. That photograph was taken away and the next most likable child was selected until only one remained. The obese child was rated less likable than all the others regardless of age, sex, so-

---

BOX 17·2

FOCUS ON DIVERSITY

Is Body Fat Found at the Same Places on People of Different Racial and Ethnic Groups?

There has been a great deal of recent interest among both scientists and the lay public concerning where on the body the fat is found. People with more fat on the trunk are at particularly high risk of developing CVD and diabetes compared with those whose fat is concentrated on the extremities. Different ethnic groups vary in their risk for these diseases, and it is possible that ethnic differences in fat patterning may partly explain variations in disease risk. However, little is known about fat distribution patterns in different ethnic groups.

This study by Greaves and colleagues examined fat distribution in black, white (referred to as "Anglo"), and Mexican American adults in Texas, as well as their preschool children. Not only could they answer the question about ethnic differences, but they could determine whether any differences started early in life. They measured skinfold thickness at seven different sites on 222 three- and four-year-old children, 245 mothers, and 101 fathers. There were approximately equal numbers of subjects from each ethnic group.

Mothers did not differ in weight, but Mexican American mothers had more total fat than Anglo or black mothers. Mexican American mothers also had significantly more trunk fat. Fathers did not differ in weight. However, black fathers had less total body fat than the other groups. The waist-hip ratio was highest for Mexican American fathers, but it was also high for black fathers. Children did not differ in weight. Black children had less total body fat than Anglo or Mexican American children. Ethnic differences in fat distribution were not as consistent for children as they were for adults.

Adults in the three ethnic groups had different patterns of fat distribution. Those differences are generally consistent with known levels of disease risk. Mexican American women and men are at the highest risk for diabetes, so their high levels of trunk fat are consistent with this risk. Black men are at the highest risk for CVD, and their high levels of trunk fat are consistent with their disease risk, even though they have low levels of total fat. Few ethnic differences were seen in children, except that black children had less fat than Mexican American or Anglo children.

Further research is needed to determine which specific patterns of fat distribution are most related to specific diseases. It is also not known whether fat distribution is affected by health behaviors, such as diet, physical activity, and smoking. We need to find out whether it may be possible to change not only the amount of fat but the distribution of fat through alterations in lifestyle (Greaves, Puhl, Baranowski, et al., 1989).

cioeconomic status, and race of the rater (Goodman, Richardson, Dornbusch, & Hastorf, 1963; Richardson, Hastorf, Goodman, & Dornbusch, 1961). Obesity is a powerful social stigma. Studies have found evidence that obese individuals are less likely to be accepted for college and hired for jobs at any level (Bray, 1986; Streigel-Moore & Rodin, 1986). There is also some evidence that obese persons earn less after employment than thin persons.

ETIOLOGY

Obesity is a very complex condition. There are several types of obesity, and there are multiple causes. Genetic, physiological, psychological, and social factors all contribute to obesity. Thousands of human and animal studies have been conducted to increase our understanding of the etiology of obesity, and only a few types of research can be summarized here.

Genetic Factors

Genes are important contributors to obesity, and obesity runs in families. Only 20 percent of the children with no obese parents are overweight, while 40 percent of the children with one obese parent are overweight. However, if both parents are obese, almost 80 percent of the children will become overweight (Garn, Bailey, Solomon, & Hopkins, 1981). Family studies do not indicate whether the similarities in obesity are due to genetic or environmental influences. However, studies of twins in adopted and biological families allow one to make inferences about nature versus nurture. The most impressive research of this type is a recent study by Stunkard, Foch, and Hrubec (1986). They studied a large number of twins and found similarities only between children and biologic parents. This study and others indicate that genetic influences are very important in the etiology of obesity.

Some people draw the wrong conclusions about the genetic causes of obesity. They incorrectly believe that genetics dooms some people to a lifetime of obesity, but that is not true. In a classic study, Mayer kept genetically obese mice thin by reducing their food consumption and increasing their physical activity (Mayer, 1953). Caloric intake and expenditure are still important influences on body composition, and many people achieve and maintain near-ideal body weight through diet and exercise.

It is easy to overemphasize the genetic contributions, but some important trends in obesity cannot be explained by genes. For example, nationwide surveys indicate that the prevalence of obesity in childhood may have increased by about 50 percent between 1970 and 1985 (Gortmaker, Dietz, Sobol, & Wehler, 1987). Although this is a major increase, it was found only with a measure of skinfold. Body mass index did not show this trend. However, the causes of any increase in this short time are certainly environmental and not genetic. The authors of the report hypothesized that a large increase in time spent viewing television was correlated with the increase in childhood obesity.

Physiological Factors

There are numerous metabolic, endocrine, cardiovascular, and other changes that are associated with obesity, and there is evidence that many of these changes may make it more difficult to achieve and maintain weight loss. Two theories of the physiology of obesity are currently supported by research and are receiving the most attention in the literature (Brownell, 1982).

Fat Cell Theory The fat cell theory states that there are at least two types of obesity. *Hyperplastic* obesity is an excess number of fat cells, and *hypertrophic* obesity refers to fat cells of excess size. Obesity that begins in childhood is usually due to hyperplastic cells; obese children may have 5 times the number of fat cells of normal-weight children. Obesity with adult onset tends to be due to hypertrophic cells. Weight loss is typically accomplished by reducing the size of fat cells, but it is extremely difficult to reduce the number of fat cells. There are limits to reducing the size of fat cells, and Bjorntorp and colleagues (1975) showed that when fat cell size reached normal levels, women stopped losing weight and tended to drop out of the weight loss program. Thus, both fat cell number and fat cell size may be biologic limits to weight loss.

It appears that the health risks of obesity may be more related to fat cell size than fat cell number (Sjostrom, 1980). If this is confirmed, then a hyperplastic obese individual could reduce risk of disease by decreasing fat cell size, although they would remain obese due to excess fat cell number. Such an outcome would satisfy health professionals, but it may not satisfy the obese individual because they would still be obese. In order to make the best use of our growing knowledge of fat cells, it is necessary to measure fat cell size and number. However, this is rarely done in practice because it requires a painful biopsy of fat tissue (Brownell, 1984) in which a large needle is inserted through the skin so that a sample of fat can be removed and studied in the laboratory.

In addition to the type of fat cell, the distribution of fat is a very important determinant of the health risks of obesity. It has been obvious for some time that men and women have different characteristic patterns of fat distribution, but it has only been recently learned that different levels of risk were associated with each pattern. Women tend to accumulate fat on the hips and thighs (pear shape), and this pattern does not increase CVD risk very much whether it is found on men or women. Men characteristically accumulate fat in the abdomen (apple shape), and this pattern of fat increases CVD risk substantially as well as risk of diabetes in both men and women (Krotkiewski, Bjorntorp, Sjostrom, et al., 1983). Gillum (1987) studied fat distribution in the 1960 National Health Examination Survey of 2669 adults. Excessive abdominal fat was associated with blood pressure, total serum cholesterol, and diagnosed coronary artery disease. The best index of CVD risk from obesity now appears to be the ratio of waist to hip circumference, and this measure is being used increasingly in obesity and CVD research.

Set Point Theory A second physiological theory of obesity is called the *set point theory*. The set point is thought of as the body's ideal weight, and the body will work to stay as close to that ideal weight as possible. The set point acts like a thermostat that attempts to keep temperature in an ideal range. While a set point may be "ideal" to an individual's body, it may be well above the cultural ideal and it may be at a level that increases health risks. Two classic studies suggest that the set point theory may be valid. Ancel Keys and colleagues (Keys, Brozek, Henschel, Mickelson, & Taylor, 1950) studied 36 men who were maintained for an extended period on a starvation diet of half their usual calories. The men became preoccupied with food and had numerous psychological problems. However, they also conserved calories so as to lose as little weight as possible. They became listless and ceased most activities. Their resting metabolic rates also decreased dramatically so that they were burning very few calories. The same phenomenon has been documented with dieters. The more that food is restricted, the more the body resists losing weight by reducing caloric expenditure. Sims and Horton (1968) studied prison inmates who volunteered to gain 20 to 25 percent of their body weight. Many of the men had difficulty gaining weight even though they ate large amounts of food. They lost interest in food and required more calories than expected to maintain their weight gains. After the experiment the men returned to their starting weights quickly. It seems that the body has a preferred weight, and it is difficult to change that weight very much because metabolism changes to preserve that weight.

A landmark animal study by Brownell and colleagues (Brownell, Greenwood, Stellar, & Shrager, 1986) indicates that repeated dieting may create physiological changes but does not change the set point. The Control rats were fed regular chow. The Obese Controls were fed high-fat chow consistently. The Obese Cycling rats were put on a cyclic diet (they did not pedal a cycle!). They were fed high-fat chow until they became obese. Then they were subjected to two cycles of food restriction and refeeding. Weight loss was rapid during the first restriction period, but it was twice as slow during the second restriction. Weight gain was 3 times faster during the second refeeding than during the first one. The dieting pattern was designed to be like the "yo-yo" dieting of many obese humans, who diet and regain weight repeatedly. This study shows that frequent dieting may make it more difficult to lose weight later. The yo-yo effect implies that it is important to maintain weight that is lost, because repeated cycles of loss and regain can lead to increases in fat stores.

All these studies indicate that the body makes adjustments to maintain a body weight. The resting metabolic rate increases or decreases, and there are changes in the desire for food. While these studies and others support the set point theory, it is far from proven. There is no way to know what an individual's set point is. If it is true, set point theory suggests that losing weight is not as simple as decreasing food intake. Dieters may be fighting a formidable physiological foe.

Psychological Factors, Diet, and Physical Activity

Views of psychological causes of obesity have undergone tremendous change over the years. There has been a move away from simplistic views, such as the search for the "obese personality," to a consideration of multiple and changing psychological factors. The psychodynamic explanation of obesity centered on two hypotheses. First, there were unconscious conflicts arising from childhood that led to overeating. Obese individuals were said to be passive, frustrated, and looking for love. Second, overeating was seen as a means of coping with emotional distress such as depression and anxiety. Increases in emotional distress during dieting were presented as evidence for the psychodynamic point of view (Streigel-Moore & Rodin, 1986). These explanations have lost favor as more scientific theories have been developed and as little evidence has supported the psychodynamic theories. The unconscious conflicts hypothesis is not testable. The increases in distress that accompany dieting are now thought to be due to dieting itself. The emotionality is transient and is also observed in normal-weight people who are on restricted diets.

There are numerous studies showing that levels of depression and anxiety are similar in obese and normal-weight individuals. For example, on a variety of measures of adjustment, the only difference was that normal-weight children had a more positive self-concept than obese children (Sallade, 1973). Of course, this might be expected in a culture that teaches children early that being fat is very undesirable.

An influential psychological theory of obesity is Schachter's (1971) internality-externality hypothesis. It is proposed that the eating of normal-weight people is controlled by internal cues such as gastric motility (stomach movements) and central cues for hunger and satiety. The eating of obese persons is thought to be controlled more by external cues such as the presence of palatable foods, location, and time of day. Although everyone may occasionally overeat when confronted with a tempting array of foods, it is reasonable to suppose that obese persons are much more responsive to these stimuli, and their restraint will be overcome with regularity. After 15 years of research, some aspects of the theory have been supported and some have not. Obese persons are more responsive to some food cues than normal-weight people. For example, when cashews were under dim light, obese and nonobese subjects ate about the same number. When the cashews were under bright lights, the obese doubled their consumption (Ross, 1974). The obese seem to be particularly responsive to food cues only when they are very salient.

Palatability is an important determinant of eating for everyone, but it is an especially powerful factor for the obese. In a supposed cracker-tasting study, obese and nonobese subjects ate the same number of disliked crackers. However, the obese ate significantly more well-liked crackers than the nonobese (Price & Grinker, 1973). The obese only eat more good-tasting foods, not more foods in general.

Responsiveness to external cues is not a product of obesity since this responsiveness does not decrease when the obese person loses weight. However, it is not known whether external responsivity is itself genetically or environmentally determined (Rodin, 1980).

Herman and Polivy (1980) hypothesized that the external responsivity of the obese was produced by the nearly constant dieting and conscious dietary restraint. Most laboratory studies disrupted the dietary regulation of the restrained eaters. When their restraint was broken, they responded by overcompensating and overeating. Disruptions included a high-calorie preload, alcohol, emotional arousal, and cognitive manipulations. Most studies showed that restrained eaters who had their restraint disrupted responded by overeating in the presence of external cues. In one study by Polivy (1976) restrained subjects who were told they had just eaten a high-calorie rich pudding ate 61 percent more food in a subsequent tasting experiment than subjects who were told they had just eaten a low-calorie diet pudding. Later studies with a refined measure of restraint have indicated that restraint may be more important for normal-weight than for obese individuals (Streigel-Moore & Rodin, 1986).

One of the ironic findings from the studies of dietary restraint is that trying to restrain eating leads to overeating. If this holds true, then the more people who are trying to lose weight through restraint, the more who are expected to overeat. There are reasons to believe that women in the United States are under increasing pressure to become thin by dieting. Two ideals of feminine shape are transmitted through *Playboy* magazine centerfolds and Miss America contestants. There has been a steady decline in the weights of these women throughout the 1960s, 1970s, and 1980s. These supposedly "ideal" women weighed 13 to 19 percent less than the average woman during this time. If women's satisfaction with their own weights were decreased by these unrealistic "ideal" images, they may have been motivated to lose weight. During these same decades the number of articles in women's magazines on diet and exercise for weight loss more than doubled (Wiseman, Gray, Mosimann, & Ahrens, 1992). These articles may have further motivated women to reduce their eating and attempt weight loss. It is interesting that there are many more diet articles and advertisements in magazines targeting young women than in those targeting young men. In a study of 20 magazines in 1987, those for women had 5.6 articles or ads for diets versus an average of 0.5 in magazines for men (Anderson & DiDomenico, 1992). Thus, the culture is putting strong and increasing pressure on young women to lose weight through restrained eating.

The Role of Diet Since obesity literally means "to overeat," it is generally believed that obese people overeat. However, such evidence is very difficult to find. Although some studies show that obese people eat more than the nonobese, more studies show that there is no difference (Spitzer & Rodin, 1981). Several epidemiological studies show that the obese eat fewer calories per day than the nonobese (Garrow, 1974). In an interesting study Stunkard and colleagues (Coll, Meyers, & Stunkard, 1979) observed patrons in nine fastfood and other restaurants. Over 5000 food choices for lunch and snacks were observed. While eating habits differed greatly by setting, there were no significant differences in food choices or calories consumed by obese and nonobese subjects. The results of this large study are typical of research in this area (Streigel-Moore & Rodin, 1986), indicating that there are very few differences in the amount or style of eating between the obese and the nonobese whether they are children or adults. These findings are, of course, puzzling. It may be that improvements in research methods will lead to different findings, but if there were major differences in eating behavior, they would probably have been detected. Changing the amount and style of consumption can be effective in promoting weight loss, so there is a discrepancy between the etiologic and the treatment research.

One aspect of the diet that appears to be very important is the composition, particularly the percentage of fat. High-fat diets stimulate the appetite and increase the efficiency with which food is converted into energy, at least in animals (Rozin, 1984). That is, fat in the diet is more easily stored as body fat than other nu-

trients. High-fat diets also tend to reduce the metabolic rate, which can have a large impact on energy expenditure over a day (Shah & Jeffery, 1991).

A series of animal studies have demonstrated one major reason that the prevalence of obesity may be so high in modern societies. Rats first maintained their normal weight on regular chow. Then they were given a diet that was high in fat, sugar, and variety. At least seven foods were provided each day, and the types of foods were varied frequently. The menu looks like what a typical American teenager eats: chocolate chip cookies, condensed milk, milk chocolate, salami, marshmallows, cheese, peanut butter, and bananas. This "supermarket diet" was given along with the regular chow, but the rats rarely ate the regular chow. Virtually all the animals on the supermarket diet became obese, and the supermarket diet group gained 269 percent more weight than the regular chow group (Sclafani, 1980). In affluent societies we have constant access to an amazing variety of foods, and it seems that mostly high-fat and high-sugar foods are advertised on television, radio, newspapers, and magazines. Ingesting calories is such a pleasant experience for most of us that the average American adult is now 13 percent above ideal weight.

The Role of Physical Activity The determinant of obesity that is most often overlooked is physical activity. Some scientists have concluded that obesity is simply a disease of physical inactivity, because the prevalence of obesity has doubled since 1900 but calorie consumption has decreased 10 percent (Pi-Sunyer, 1988). However, the relationship between obesity and physical activity is probably a bit more complex. Some studies show that the obese are less active, and some show that they are about as active as the nonobese (Shah & Jeffery, 1991).

However, it may be important to look at

different types of activity. When a representative sample of adults in northern California was studied, there were no differences between obese and nonobese subjects in the amount of vigorous exercise they reported, such as jogging, swimming laps, and long-distance cycling (Sallis, Haskell, Wood, Fortmann, & Vranizan, 1986). There were large differences in all age groups between the obese and nonobese in the amount of moderate activities they reported (Sallis, Haskell, Fortmann, & Vranizan, 1986), with the obese consistently reporting less activity. Moderate activities included walking instead of driving, taking daily walks, and taking stairs instead of elevators. Thus, all weight groups may do about the same amount of vigorous exercise, which is usually not much, but it appears that the obese may do less of the more common physical activities such as walking. This suggests that moderate intensity activities could be helpful for weight loss.

There are at least two effects of physical activity that aid in the maintenance of ideal weight (Pi-Sunyer, 1988):

1. In animal studies, exercise inhibits food consumption. For example, in the study by Oscai and Holloszy (1969), experimental rats ate less than control rats on exercise days, but they ate the same as control rats on nonexercise days. It is very difficult to conduct adult studies on this effect, but the available studies generally support the animal finding that exercise decreases appetite.

2. Resting metabolic rate decreases when food is restricted, but exercise while dieting largely offsets much of the decrease in metabolic rate. Since resting metabolic rate accounts for most of the energy expenditure during the day, this long-term effect of exercise may be a major factor in weight control (Thompson, Jarvie, Lahey, & Cureton, 1982).

TREATMENT

There is tremendous public interest in the treatment of obesity. On any given day at least 20 percent of all Americans say that they are dieting to lose weight (U.S. DHEW, 1979). Women are particularly interested in weight loss, with 56 percent of all women between 25 and 34 years of age dieting at any one time (Stunkard, 1984). The intense interest in weight loss has led to a weight loss industry that consists of million-selling diet books, clinics, surgeries, special food products, self-help organizations, and weight loss resorts. Obese people seeking treatment are confronted with a dizzying variety of choices, with each diet book or program claiming spectacular results or "guaranteed" success. However, the long-term success of almost every weight loss method is notoriously poor. The chances of maintaining significant weight loss for 5 years are less than the 5-year survival rate for most cancers (Stunkard & Penick, 1979).

Although many weight loss programs are simply ineffective, some are dangerous. Early liquid-protein diets had unbalanced nutrition and caused several deaths. Some surgical procedures such as intestinal bypass had severe side effects. Ads for parasitic worms are obviously promoting a questionable approach to weight loss. Fortunately, responsible medical and psychological researchers have developed relatively safe and effective weight loss treatments for obese individuals.

Behavior modification is the most effective and most widely used professional approach to treating mild obesity. Initial behavior modification approaches were based on Ferster and coworkers' assertion that obesity was due to an obese eating style that consisted of taking large bites at frequent intervals. As discussed earlier, this assumption is not true (Stunkard & Kaplan, 1977), but the treatments that were

BOX 17-3

FOCUS ON WOMEN

Weight Gain and Weight Loss in Black and White Women

Studies consistently show that black women are more likely to be overweight than white women, even when differences in income and education are taken into consideration. However, most studies have looked at differences only at one point in time. That does not tell how women came to their present weights. The study described here identified a group of women who had their weights and other variables measured in the early 1970s and were then remeasured 10 years later. The authors were interested in whether black and white women differed in their weight loss and weight gain over the 10-year period.

This study used data from the National Health and Nutrition Examination Survey (NHANES), which collects data on a wide variety of health issues. Follow-up data were available on 89 percent of the original sample of women. Weight change was examined for 514 black and 2770 white women who were 25 to 44 years of age at the first survey. Major weight gain was defined as an increase of 13 kg or more (about 29 lb; 1 kg = 2.2 lb), and a major weight loss was a decrease of 7 kg or more (about 15 lb). Black women gained an average of 3.8 kg, and white women gained an average of 2.8 kg; this was a significant difference. In their analyses, the authors have tried to adjust for the effects of variables that may influence weight changes, such as baseline weight, smoking, physical activity, number of children, and rural/urban background. These adjustments are made to determine whether the observed differences are truly due to race and socioeconomic status.

Even though black women were more likely to have a major weight gain (13 percent) than white women (7 percent) during the 10 years, when all other variables were considered, there were no racial differences. Regardless of race, women who had a major weight gain tended to be poor, have a high school education or less, and be heavier at baseline. Women who became married during the follow-up interval tended to have a major weight gain.

Major weight loss was more common in white than black women. Women with very low incomes were more likely to lose weight, but education was not related. Those who became married were less likely to have a major weight loss than other groups.

Even though this study did not describe all weight changes during the 10 years, it sheds light on the black-white differences in weight among women. Black women appeared to have a greater mean increase in weight because they are less likely than white women to lose weight. Other studies have shown that black women are less concerned with their weight, so this study is consistent with less motivation for weight loss.

These findings suggest that obesity prevention programs need to be targeted to poor women with relatively low educational achievement. Women in these groups were most likely to gain weight, regardless of race, although blacks in the United States are more disadvantaged in income and education than whites. Another target for prevention may be women who get married. More studies need to be done to find out whether women tend to change their diet, physical activity, or both, when they get married (Kahn, Williamson, & Stevens, 1991).

based on this faulty premise have been quite effective.

Stuart (1967) published a series of case studies that stimulated great enthusiasm for behavioral treatments of obesity. Stuart's program and subsequent typical treatments are based on four components. First, careful self-monitoring of food intake increases awareness of what foods are eaten and under what circumstances. Second, numerous self-control strategies are included, such as limiting access to high-calorie foods by not buying them or placing them on high shelves. Because eating tends to become associated with other pleasant activities, patients are told to eat only at the table and to do nothing but eat. For example, they should not watch television. The same table setting is used at all meals, and the use of small plates is encouraged. Third, the act of eating is slowed by putting down silverware between bites, chewing each bite a specified number of times, and purposefully adding delays between bites. Fourth, therapist-delivered or self-controlled reinforcement is made contingent on weight loss. In Stuart's (1967) initial study, 8 of 10 patients who stayed in treatment for 12 months lost an average of about 35 lb, which was a real breakthrough at the time.

On the basis of these promising results, hundreds of studies have been conducted over the past 20 years attempting to improve behavior modification programs for obesity. For example, a study by Mahoney (1974) showed that self-reinforcement for weight loss was more effective than self-punishment. Behavioral programs focus on changing dietary habits to produce gradual weight losses of 1 to 2 lb per week. The stimulus control and self-control skills are designed to be used after the formal program ends to enable maintenance of losses.

Behavior modification programs are typically superior to no treatment or psychotherapy. Penick, Filion, Fox, and Stunkard (1971) treated 34 severely overweight subjects with either behavior therapy or a supportive psychotherapy group that included nutrition counseling. To make this a difficult test of behavior modification, an experimental psychologist with no clinical experience and a technician led the behavioral group, while an experienced internist/psychiatrist and research nurse led the psychotherapy group. The results after 3 months showed the superiority of the behavioral treatment. In the psychotherapy group, 24 percent lost more than 20 lb, while in the behavioral group, 53 percent lost more than 20 lb.

In more recent years, the focus in behavioral treatment of obesity has shifted to a concern with what types of foods are eaten, the need for increasing physical activity, the use of social support, improving weight loss during treatment, improving maintenance, and treatment of obesity in childhood.

1. Types of food. Classic behavior modification programs dealt only with how much was eaten, not with the types of food. Increasing evidence indicates that not only do high-fat diets tend to increase serum cholesterol, but fat in the diet is turned into body fat more easily than carbohydrates. Thus, obese patients need assistance in choosing foods that are low in fat as well as low in calories. After 1 year in a low-fat diet change program, obese men and women lost about 10 lb of body fat, while control subjects gained a slight amount of body fat (Wood, Stefanick, Williams, & Haskell, 1991).

2. Physical activity. At one time the goal of obesity treatment was weight loss, but that goal is being modified to one of fat loss. Caloric restriction tends to produce more loss in lean body mass than fat mass. Physical activity, when combined with dieting, builds lean body mass while promoting fat loss. While programs including both diet and physical activity lead to slower weight loss, combined programs produce superior fat loss. The most important effect of physical activity may be that it is the best way to prevent the regain of weight after treatment (Bray, 1990).

3. Social support. Most weight loss programs include only the obese patient in the treatment. However, the family is affected by and affects dietary changes of all its members. This recognition has led to programs that include family members, usually spouses, in the treatment programs. In the first such study (Brownell, Heckerman, Westlake, et al., 1978) patients whose spouses participated in the program lost significantly more weight (30 lb) than patients whose spouses refused to participate (19 lb) or those in a control group (15 lb). However, other studies have not replicated this finding that spouse participation is important (Brownell & Stunkard, 1981), so the area is controversial. When the results of all 12 studies on this subject were combined in one analysis, it was found that couples training was more successful than individual programs in producing weight loss at both posttreatment and 2- to 3-month follow-up (Black, Gleser, & Kooyers, 1990). Thus, this is a promising strategy.

Support from peers, such as those in self-help weight loss programs like TOPS (Take Off Pounds Sensibly), may also be important. Perri and colleagues (1984) studied peer support by assigning patients either to a control group with a typical behavioral program or to a group in which treatment was supplemented with a buddy system. At the end of treatment, patients in the "buddy group" continued to meet, monitor one another's progress, and help one another overcome problems with maintenance. At the 2-year follow-up the buddy group maintained 10 lb of their original 13.5-lb loss, but the group without buddies only maintained 0.8 lb of their original 12.4-lb

loss. Most people who have tried to lose weight will tell you that it is much easier if your family and friends are working with you rather than against you.

4. Improving weight loss. Many patients are dissatisfied with weight losses that average 1 to 2 lb per week, and severely obese patients feel that they will never achieve significant weight losses at these rates. Medically supervised very low calorie diets of 1000 to 1200 calories per day have become popular as a method of producing rapid weight loss. Modern approaches not only are safe but typically produce weight losses of 45 lb in 12 weeks. Obese patients are impressed and encouraged with these results, but the major problem is that maintenance of losses is poor. Health psychologists have developed programs combining very low calorie diets with behavior modification that appear to be among the most effective weight loss programs ever devised. Wadden and Stunkard (1986) randomly assigned obese patients to behavior therapy alone, very low calorie diet alone, or a combined program. At the end of the 4- to 6-month treatment, weight losses were 31.0, 31.5, and 42.5 lb, respectively. While all three treatments led to meaningful weight losses, the combined treatment was superior. However, the real test is maintenance of the losses. At the 12- month follow-up, losses from pretreatment were 20.9 lb for the behavior therapy group, 10.1 lb for the very low calorie diet group, and 28.4 lb for the combined group. Thus, it appears that behavioral treatment is needed to maintain the rapid losses produced by very low calorie diets.

5. Improving maintenance. While the Wadden and Stunkard (1986) study indicates that maintenance of weight loss with state-of-the-art behavior modification is good, there is still need for improvement. Probably the most effective method of improving weight loss maintenance is exercise. Studies consistently show that while exercise has a small impact on weight loss, it is necessary for successful weight maintenance (Dahlkoetter, Callahan, & Linton, 1979; Epstein, Wing, Koeske, & Valoski, 1984; Harris & Hallbauer, 1973; Stalonas, Johnson, & Christ, 1978). Even moderate-intensity exercise such as walking is effective, although the mechanism of the effect is not known. It may be that exercise burns calories, increases metabolic rate, decreases appetite, adjusts the set point, improves self-esteem and mood, or all of the above.

The social support studies discussed here indicate that support may be particularly important in maintaining weight loss. Even though they seem like a good idea, booster sessions by themselves have not been found to be effective in promoting maintenance, but training in relapse prevention skills can be useful (Foreyt, 1987).

6. Treatment of childhood obesity. With the increasing prevalence of childhood obesity, it is becoming more and more important to develop effective treatments for children. Epstein and colleagues at the University of Pittsburgh have been testing behavioral programs for obese children for more than 15 years (Epstein, 1986). They have focused their study on obese children with two obese parents, because these children are at the highest risk for sustained and severe obesity. There are four stages in the program, based upon the child's age. Between the ages of 1 and 5 the focus is exclusively on parental management, because the children are not able to be engaged in the treatment process, nor are they interested in controlling their weight. Between 5 and 8 years the children are exposed to more influences on diet and physical activity as they go to school. While parental management is still the focus, the children are trained to handle social situations in which food is offered. In the third stage, ages 8 to 12, children become involved in self-monitoring and goal setting, and they are usually motivated to lose weight. Behavioral contracting between children and parents

is still an important part of the program. Adolescents are taught self-management skills, much like in adult programs, because the adolescents have the necessary capability and motivation. Contracts must be handled carefully to avoid conflict between parents and teens who are developing their independence.

It is obvious that childhood obesity treatment programs must be family-based, although parents and children are usually seen separately. The focus is on changes in diet and physical activity, along with developing supportive behaviors within the family. Epstein's studies have shown that behavioral treatment is effective in producing meaningful and safe weight losses at all ages, that even untreated family members tend to lose weight either during or after treatment, and that low-intensity exercise is more effective over the long term than aerobic exercise. The most important finding is that the approach has long-term benefits, as shown in Box 17-4. Weight loss programs for children may be more effective than treatment of adults, so this argues for starting early in life.

Current practice in the area of weight loss has been affected by the research performed by health psychologists. Many good examples of behavioral medicine can be found in the weight loss field because health psychologists are collaborating closely with physicians, dietitians, exercise physiologists, and others to develop, evaluate, and apply effective weight loss programs.

One of the ironies of the weight loss field is that many of the treatments are apparently unrelated to the documented causes. This is particularly true with respect to eating habits. Eating habits of the obese are usually found to be no different from those of the nonobese, either in eating style or number of calories. Nevertheless, changes in eating style and reduction of calories are powerful methods of weight loss. Obesity appears to be strongly influenced by genetics, but environmental manipulations can produce significant weight

---

BOX 17·4

FOCUS ON RESEARCH

Can People Keep the Weight Off?

Someone who wants to lose weight usually spends a great deal of time and effort trying to reach some goal, and many of them never get there. For the persistent ones who do lose weight, their troubles are just starting. Whether it is set points, the lure of supermarket diets, or a low resting metabolic rate, there seems to be a conspiracy to make it hard to keep the weight off. A couple of recent studies show the continuing problems in weight loss maintenance, but they also point to promising directions.

Hovell and colleagues (Hovell et al., 1988) studied 485 adults who had signed up for an intensive weight loss program. A medically supervised very low calorie diet was used until participants reached their goal weight. Behavior modification group sessions were used for support during the modified fast and afterward to teach new, healthier eating patterns. Most of the participants were women (81 percent), and they were followed for 30 months after treatment. Over half of the participants never reached their weight goal or dropped out of the program, but half of them lost substantial amounts of weight. Patients who completed treatment lost about 85 percent of their excess weight, or about 55 lb. At the follow-up measurement, only about 15 percent were still close to their weight goal. This small percentage who kept their weight off for a long period of time is disappointing to both the participants and to weight loss therapists. However, this study demonstrates again the challenge faced by adults who want to lose weight.

The continuing poor long-term results in treating obesity in adults have led a few investigators to examine whether treatment in childhood is more effective. The program developed by Epstein and colleagues is described in this chapter, and several studies have found this to be a promising approach. The real proof of the effectiveness of the program was published in 1990 in the *Journal of the American Medical Association*, where the 10-year results of their family-based treatment were

reported (Epstein, Valoski, Wing, & McCurley, 1990). This in itself is a rare event, because virtually no one tracks people for 10 years to see if the treatment has truly long term effects.

The families of 76 obese children aged 6 to 12 were randomly assigned to groups where (a) parents and children were reinforced for behavior change and weight loss, (b) only children were reinforced for behavior change and weight loss, and (c) families were reinforced for attendance only (control group). At the end of the 8-month treatment, weight loss was greatest in the parent and child group and least in the control group. This same pattern of results continued to be evident at the 5- and 10-year follow-ups. After 10 years the child and parent group decreased percentage overweight by 7.5 percent, while the control group increased percentage overweight by 14.3 percent. That difference was very statistically significant. The child reinforcement group was in the middle and showed an increase in percentage overweight of 4.5 percent. On average the parents increased their percentage overweight, and there were no differences between groups. The weight changes in the children did not affect their heights, so it appeared to be a safe treatment.

Is treating obesity in childhood more effective than treating it in adulthood? The Epstein and coworkers study suggests that this is a possibility. These long-term results for children are certainly better than the results for any behavioral treatment of adult obesity. It is interesting that the parents increased their percentage overweight during the follow-up, regardless of the group they were in. Even in this study, the children had better results than their parents. Maybe there is something to the idea that it is easier for children to change their health behavior because they have not spent so many years practicing the habits that created their health problems (Epstein, Valoski, & Wing, et al., 1990; Hovell et al., 1988).

---

loss. Obesity is such a complex problem that these apparent contradictions merely point out the limits of our understanding.

PREVENTION OF OBESITY

Despite the national obsession with obesity, hundreds of studies of weight loss methods,

and a vast menu of weight loss treatments, the prevalence of obesity continues to rise in the United States. Because weight loss treatments are only modestly effective at best, there is a need to prevent the initial development of obesity. A program called "A Pound of Prevention" was developed to test interest among normal-weight adults in preventing obesity

(Forster, Jeffery, Schmid, & Kramer, 1988). This innovative program was based on the rationale that a simple, low-cost program to raise awareness of the risk of adult weight gain and to educate about methods of normal-weight maintenance might be effective for adults who had so far avoided becoming obese.

Subjects were selected from people who had been screened for cardiovascular risk factors in a community program and had been found to be less than 115 percent of ideal weight, based on standard tables. Three thousand potential subjects were sent a letter describing the program. Of those who received the letter, 25 percent returned a postcard expressing interest. Eventually 366 were enrolled in the study, and they were randomly assigned to treatment or control conditions.

The treatment subjects received 12 monthly newsletters that included information on diet, physical activity, psychological topics related to weight management, and the health risks of obesity. The newsletter was intended to provide weight-related information rather than direct behavior-change guidance. Each newsletter contained a postcard on which subjects were asked to record their current weight and what they were doing to control their weight. There was a monthly financial incentive for those who maintained their weight. The final component was an optional four-session educational program that offered assistance to those who had gained weight during the year or who were over their ideal weight.

Participation in the program was high. An average of 75 percent returned the monthly postcards, and 29 percent attended at least one of the four sessions. The mean weight change in the treatment group was −2.1 lb, and the mean change in the control group was −0.3 lb. This was a significant difference. Over the 12-month period, 82 percent of the treatment group and only 56 percent of the control group maintained their baseline weight or lost weight.

This simple intervention was surprisingly effective. About 13 percent of the eligible subjects enrolled in the program, and instead of gaining the usual 1 to 2 lb per year, the treatment subjects lost 2 lb. The authors estimated that the total cost per treatment subject for recruitment and the year of intervention was only $35, certainly a modest amount. Although this 1-year study must be considered a pilot program, it is a very promising approach to reducing the health burden caused by obesity. Future research needs to address the long-term maintenance of normal weight. In addition, early prevention programs involving children should be conducted.

SUMMARY

Obesity is defined as having excess amounts of body fat. Obesity leads to a number of severe medical conditions such as CVD, some cancers, digestive problems, bone and joint problems, complications of pregnancy, and metabolic disorders. The obese have social problems because they are the object of discrimination. About 15 to 30 percent of all American adults are obese, and the number of obese children may have increased 50 percent in the past 15 years.

The most common measures of obesity, weight in relation to height, are actually measures of overweight. Body fat can be estimated by skinfold assessment, circumferences, electrical resistance of the body, and underwater weighing. Distribution of fat is also important, with central (abdominal) fat being more dangerous to health than lower-body fat. Obesity is genetically transmitted to a large extent, but there are many other factors. Physiological theories of obesity stress the importance of the number of fat cells and the set point, or the body's ideal weight. The obese are believed to be more responsive to external cues to eat. Short-term fluctuations in body weight and body fat are usually due to energy balance, or the relationship between calorie intake and expenditure. Thus, diet and physical activity are the targets in behavioral weight loss treatments.

At least 20 percent of all U.S. adults are dieting at any one time, and there are many ineffective and dangerous weight loss methods available. Behavior modification is a safe and moderately effective approach. It includes self-monitoring, stimulus control, and reinforcement. Current studies are incorporating low-fat diets, physical activity, social support, very low calorie diets, and maintenance strategies. Methods of preventing adult obesity include treatment of overweight children and programs to prevent the usual 1- to 2-lb per year weight gain in adults.

KEY TERMS

Obesity. A condition of having excessive amounts of body fat.

Overweight. A condition of having too much weight for a specified height, based on standard tables of ideal weight.

Skinfold thickness. Measuring a pinch of skin indicates the thickness of the layer of fat beneath the skin.

Hydrostatic weighing. Weights taken while a person is totally submerged in a tank of water. Because of the different densities of fat and lean tissue, body fat can be accurately measured by a formula using dry weight and underwater weight.

Fat distribution. It is important to know not only how much fat one has but also where the fat is on the body.

Waist-hip ratio. The ratio of these circumferences is a common index of fat distribution. A high number reflects central obesity, which has higher health risks.

Fat cell theory. Obesity can be due to increased fat cell number or fat cell size. It is possible to reduce cell size, but it may not be possible to reduce cell number.

Set point theory. Each person may have a set point weight that the body attempts to maintain, despite efforts to change. Personal set points may differ from societal ideal weights.

Weight cycling. The yo-yo diet syndrome of repeated weight losses and regains. Weight cycling may make it more and more difficult to lose body fat.

Internality-externality hypothesis. Obese people are more responsive to external cues, such as the presence of food. Nonobese people use internal cues such as hunger.

Metropolitan Life Insurance Weight Tables. Using the relationship between weight and longevity, this insurance company developed tables for ideal weights for men and women at a variety of heights. These tables are commonly used in weight loss studies.

Resting metabolic rate (RMR). The rate at which calories are burned when a person is sitting quietly at rest. A low RMR makes it difficult to lose weight. RMR decreases when one diets and increases during and after physical activity.

Very low calorie diet. These 1000- to 1200-calorie-per-day diets are used to create rapid weight losses. However, weight is quickly regained unless behavior modification and physical activity are incorporated.

Self-help groups. Organizations such as Take Off Pounds Sensibly (TOPS) and Overeaters Anonymous (OA) have been formed to give social support to obese people who want to lose weight.

CHAPTER 18

Person Factors: Personality and Demographic Influences on Health

John was a hard-driving business executive. He smoked two packs of cigarettes per day and was always at his desk by 7:30 A.M. On weekends he could not relax. Whatever he did he took it to the extreme. On the ski slope, for example, he always chose the steepest run (even though his ability level did not suggest that this was a wise choice). If he attended a football game, he had to sit on the 50-yd line, and he was always extremely disappointed when his team lost. With his employees and his family, John lost his temper if things were not done perfectly. At age 54, John had a severe heart attack. This was the first time in his life he had to confront slowing down.

Are easygoing people less likely to get ill than those who are always nervous? Does anger lead to heart attacks? Are extroverts more healthy than introverts? If you know someone's personality, is it possible to predict what illnesses they may get in the future? Should you be concerned about your health if people say that you are a hard-driving, ambitious Type A person?

The role of personality in health and illness has been of interest for centuries. Before the era of modern medicine, philosophers thought that most disease was associated with certain personality types. Hippocrates, Galen, and other ancient Greek physicians thought that imbalances in bodily "humors" (fluids) were associated with most physical and mental illnesses. Humors were thought to be vital fluids of the body. Ancient Greeks believed that there were four humors that were associated with these problems: phlegm, black bile, blood, and yellow bile. Sluggishness was thought to be the result of excess phlegm. Ancient Greeks described a person who was sluggish or lethargic as phlegmatic. People who were depressed were thought to have an overabundance of black bile. They were described as melancholic. An excess of blood was believed to be associated with a sanguine personlity. People in this category were cheerful, confident, or optimistic. If the person had too much yellow bile, they might be described as bilious or choleric. People in this category are quick-tempered. For centuries, physicians used these theories about humors in medical treatment. Blood letting, for example, was used in an attempt to find the appropriate balance for sanguine personalities.

The field of psychosomatic medicine was developed by those who were concerned about how personality affected health (Alexander, 1939). Psychosomatic medicine explored connections between mind and body, and there was particular interest in the effects of personality and psychological factors on different diseases. Some diseases were believed to be mainly caused by personality, so they were called *psychosomatic diseases*. These included hypertension, heart disease, cancer, asthma, ulcerative colitis, and ulcers. Not until recently have there been scientific studies devoted to these questions. As you will see, these studies have generally added to the controversy more than they have settled it.

The psychosomatic viewpoint has changed over the years. With the modern age of biological science, traditional thinking about personality correlates of illness was pushed aside. However, there has been a rebirth of interest in the relationship between personality and illness. This has been stimulated by repeated observations that there is a relationship between stress and illness (see Chapter 6). Today, there is considerable debate about the relationship between personality and disease. Perhaps the most extreme position was represented in a 1985 editorial in the *New England Journal of Medicine* which argued that there is no scientific evidence for an association between mental state and illness (Angell, 1985). This position was countered by a significant number of critical letters to the editor in the same journal. Furthermore, Friedman (1991) has systematically reviewed the evidence that there is a significant association between personality factors and several disease states. This is the lesson of Engel's biopsychosocial model, which teaches that all illnesses are subject to many influences. We will not be able to review the entire literature in this chapter. Instead, we will provide several examples of studies linking personality to illness. The first focus is on Type A behavior and heart disease.

TYPE A BEHAVIOR AND ITS COMPONENTS

The most well-known psychological risk factor for cardiovascular disease (CVD) was "discovered" by two physicians. In the early 1950s cardiologists Meyer Friedman and Ray Rosenman were treating heart patients in San Francisco. Being careful observers of human behavior, they began to notice that their patients shared many common characteristics. Friedman and Rosenman continued their observations and identified a constellation of behaviors that characterized their cardiac patients. In addition to conducting scientific studies, they published a book titled *Type A Behavior and Your Heart* (Friedman & Rosenman, 1974). That best-selling book provoked a great deal of interest in this new behavioral risk for heart disease and started a public controversy that continues to this day.

The Type A behavior pattern has been defined as "an action-emotion complex that can be observed in any person who is aggressively involved in a chronic, incessant struggle to achieve more and more in less and less time, and if required to do so, against the opposing efforts of other things and other persons" (Friedman & Rosenman, 1974, p. 67). There are several major components of the Type A behavior pattern that are frequently discussed. If a person has several of the following characteristics, they are referred to as "Type A." If few of these characteristics are present, the person is referred to as "Type B."

Competitiveness and Achievement Striving

Type A's have a strong need to win in all situations. They are motivated to achieve more and more at work and are never satisfied with their positions or earnings. They are compelled to compete even when winning is trivial, such as when playing games with children. This competitiveness can be so extreme that it causes conflicts and alienates family, friends, and coworkers.

Time Urgency and Impatience

Type A's feel that there is not enough time to do what they feel needs to get done. They are in a hurry at work, so they may be very productive. However, Type A's are usually not more productive than Type B's, because Type A's try to do so many things that they are often disorganized or fatigued. They are in a hurry at home, so they may spend little time with their family. They talk fast, drive fast, and interrupt others frequently. They become upset when standing in line and do several things at once, like reading while talking on the phone.

BOX 18·1

HEALTH OBJECTIVES FOR THE YEAR 2000

There are no health objectives for the year 2000 that directly target changes in personality variables. Research on personality and health has a long history, but it has been controversial. The experts who assembled the year 2000 objectives were not convinced that the evidence supported the inclusion of targets for changes in personality variables. After reading this chapter, see whether you agree or disagree with their conclusion.

Hostility and Aggressiveness

Type A's become angered easily. While they are not necessarily physically aggressive, they show hostility in interactions by acting bored, condescending, or challenging. They create conflict at work and in other situations.

An additional characteristic has been suggested by David Glass (1977). He sees Type A behavior as a coping style that is used to deal with stressful events. Type A's may be more threatened by loss of control over situations, so they try harder to maintain control or at least a sense of control. The need to maintain control may lead to frequent experiences of helplessness, frustration, and depression in response to life's many uncontrollable situations. This psychological characteristic of Type A is very consistent with the classic description of Type A. If one is highly motivated to maintain control, that might lead to competitiveness, aggression against those who are interfering with control, and frequent impatience about things that cannot be controlled.

ASSESSING TYPE A BEHAVIOR

Because these characteristics are somewhat vague and can be manifested by many different behaviors, the assessment of Type A is difficult. The signs of Type A include rate and volume of speech, and nonverbal mannerisms such as gesturing and tense smiling; so paper-and-pencil self-report scales are usually felt to be inadequate. The best available method of assessment is the Structured Interview. This is a standardized interview that takes 10 to 15 minutes to administer. The trained interviewer reads a script, and the interview is audiotaped or videotaped to be scored by another rater. The purpose of the interview is to present standardized challenges to which the subject must react. Type A behavior is more pronounced in stressful situations, so the interview is designed to produce mild stress.

The Structured Interview includes questions about ambition, aggressiveness, and time urgency, but the interviewer's behavior is designed to provoke the subject. First, the interviewer is "coldly professional." Second, the interviewer directly challenges the subject's response. If the subject says that the spouse has never asked him or her to slow down or speed up while working, the interviewer challenges by asking *"Never?"* Third, the interviewer interrupts frequently because this is felt to anger the subject. Before the subject is finished answering whether he or she is satisfied with the present job level, the interviewer will interrupt with "Why?" or "Why not?" Fourth, the interview script calls for the interviewer to stutter during some questions to provoke the Type A behavior of completing someone else'e sentence. Here is one such question: "Most people who work have to get up fairly early in the morning, in your particular case, uh-what-time-uh-do-you-uh, ordinarily uh-uh-uh-get-up?" Fifth, some questions ask the subject to recall challenging situations, and the subject's behavior during their answer is noted. An example would be: "What *irritates* you most about your work, or the people with whom you work?"

On the basis of the subject's behavior and answers during the Structured Interview, a rater scores the subject as one of the following types (Chesney, Eagleston, & Rosenman, 1981):

A-1: Fully developed pattern of Type A

A-2: Many Type A characteristics, but not the complete pattern

  X: Equal mix of Type A and B characteristics

  B: Few or no Type A characteristics

In recent years scoring systems have been developed to provide separate scores for hostility, achievement striving, time urgency, and other characteristics. The definition and assessment of Type A have been problematic. Price (1982) counted 31 different proposed characteristics of Type A appearing in the literature, so not everyone is defining Type A behavior in the same way. Other measures of Type A behavior have been used. The most common is the Jenkins Activity Survey (Jenkins & Friedman, 1967). This self-report scale was based on questions in the Structured Interview.

Type A is even assessed in children, with the most commonly used measure being the Matthews Youth Test for Health (MYTH) (Matthews & Angulo, 1980). Child behaviors that would seem to be early indicators of Type A behavior are rated by parents or teachers. However, not everyone agrees that the MYTH is actually measuring Type A behavior, since ratings of aggression, achievement striving, and time urgency in children may reflect conduct disorders rather than Type A behavior.

TYPE A BEHAVIOR AS A CVD RISK FACTOR

The Type A classification was developed because this constellation of behaviors was felt to be a risk factor for CVD. Friedman and Rosenman immediately set out to confirm this hypothesis. They organized the Western Collaborative Group Study (WCGS), which involved over 3400 healthy middle-class men working in the San Francisco Bay Area. In 1960 these men were assessed for cholesterol, blood pressure, diet, medical history, and smoking. Their Type A behavior was assessed with an early version of the Structured Interview. After 8.5 years of follow-up, the rates of CVD were compared in Type A and Type B men. After statistical adjustment for other risk factors, Type A men were twice as likely as Type B men to develop symptoms of coronary heart disease, to have a first MI, to have a second MI, and to die from CVD (Rosenman et al., 1975). This large study is a landmark and provided convincing evidence that Type A behavior is indeed a strong risk factor for CVD that is independent of other risk factors.

Although the WCGS was a carefully conducted study, some scientists were skeptical because it was directed by the same investigators who discovered the Type A pattern. Therefore, it was important to have the link between Type A and CVD confirmed by other teams. The Framingham Heart Study included questionnaire items that assessed behaviors that were similar to Type A, and Suzanne Haynes led a study to determine whether Type A predicted CVD over an 8-year period in the Framingham population (Haynes, Feinleib, & Kannel, 1980). This study substantiated most of the results of the WCGS. Type A predicted coronary heart disease and myocardial infarction in white-collar men but not in blue-collar men. Because all the men in the WCGS were white-collar workers, this study was taken as general confirmation of the WCGS results. The Haynes and coworkers (1980) study also showed for the first time that Type A women were twice as likely to suffer from coronary heart disease and angina as Type B women.

Largely because of the WCGS and the Framingham Study, along with other findings that Type A men tended to have more atherosclerotic obstructions in their coronary arteries than Type B men (Frank, Heller, Kornfeld, Sporn, & Weiss, 1978), a panel organized by the National Heart, Lung, and Blood Institute (NHLBI) concluded that Type A behavior was a risk factor for coronary heart disease (Review Panel on Coronary-Prone Behavior and Coronary Heart Disease, 1981). The panel's report was published in 1981, and this document accepted that Type A behavior was a risk factor equal in magnitude with blood pressure, blood cholesterol, and smoking. This report represented a major victory for those seeking recognition of the importance of psychological factors in the etiology of CVD.

At least two European epidemiologic studies published after the Review Panel report supported the conclusion that Type A behavior is a risk factor for coronary heart disease (DeBacker, Kornitzer, Kittel, & Dramaix, 1983; French-Belgian Collaborative Group, 1982). However, several other large, well-conducted studies have found no association between Type A behavior and coronary heart disease. These contradictory findings have produced a tremendous controversy in both the scientific and lay press, because just about the time that Type A was accepted as a risk factor, new data caused the validity of that conclusion to be seriously questioned.

In the Honolulu Heart Study, Japanese American Type A's were no more likely to develop coronary heart disease than Type B's (Cohen & Reed, 1985). However, since fewer Japanese Americans were rated Type A and they have lower rates of heart disease, it is possible that this study is not comparable to the WCGS.

Although the WCGS showed that Type A men were more likely to have a second heart attack that Type B's, at least three other long-term studies found that Type A scores on the same test did *not* predict new coronary events in high-risk men (Matthews & Haynes, 1986). More important, in the Multiple Risk Factor Intervention Trial, which included mainly high-risk white-collar men similar to those in the WCGS, Type A behavior did not predict coronary heart disease (Shekelle et al., 1985). The lack of relationship was found whether the Structured Interview or the Jenkins Activity Survey was used as the measure of Type A.

Perhaps the most damaging blow to the status of Type A behavior as a coronary heart disease (CHD) risk factor came with the report of the 22-year follow-up of the original subjects from the WCGS (Ragland & Brand, 1988). Almost 99 percent of the men were accounted for, and 214 of the subjects had died from CHD. The predictors of CHD death were systolic blood pressure, serum cholesterol, cigarette smoking, and age. Type A men were no more likely to die of CHD than Type B men. The 8.5-year findings of the WCGS had been the primary evidence for the risk associated with Type A behavior, but the 22-year results from that same landmark study have essentially laid to rest the idea that Type A is a cardiovascular disease risk factor.

The changing fortunes of the Type A behavior concept have been one of the most baffling chapters in the history of health psychology. In the 1960s and 1970s most studies found that Type A was strongly associated with coronary heart disease morbidity and mortality, but since that time almost no one has found such a relationship. Moreover, there is no widely accepted explanation for this turn of events. Very few health scientists currently accept that Type A behavior, as it was originally understood, is a major risk factor for coronary heart disease, but many laypeople, after years of reports that Type A behavior can kill you, have not digested the new, more confusing message that it looks like Type A behavior is OK now.

There is a need to understand why Type A was first accepted and then rejected as a risk factor. Dimsdale (1985) has suggested several possible explanations.

1. One possibility is that Type A behavior is simply not a risk factor for coronary heart disease. This would mean that the early results of the WCGS were a fluke and cannot be generalized. Since the Framingham Study showed that Type A behavior was a risk factor only for certain subsets of the population, it is possible that Type A is not a risk factor for everyone.

2. The assessment and classification of Type A behavior may have changed over the years. The Structured Interview is very difficult to standardize, and it is possible that either the interview procedures, the rating of the taped interviews, or both have changed. One piece of evidence for this explanation is that in the WCGS about 50 percent of the subjects were classified as Type A (Ragland & Brand, 1988), but in the Multiple Risk Factor Intervention Trial 15 years later, about 75 percent of the men were classified as Type A (Shekelle et al., 1985). Has society become more Type A, or did the assessment technique change?

3. Because Type A is a combination of several components, maybe some components increase risk and others do not. This hypothesis has been supported by research that will be described later in this chapter. These studies, including rescoring of Structured Interviews in the WCGS, indicate that anger and hostility is the component of Type A that is most likely to be a risk factor. Because classification as Type A does not require the person to have all the characteristics, some Type A's were high in the hostility component and some were not. These differences in the Type A groups may have accounted for some of the conflicting results.

4. A final possibility is that coronary heart disease may have changed between the time of WCGS in the 1960s and the studies with nega-

tive findings that appeared mostly in the 1980s. The CVD mortality rate decreased 26 percent from 1968 to 1980 (National Heart, Lung, and Blood Institute, 1985). Changes in diet, physical activity, and smoking have been more pronounced in high-income groups, and all these changes could have altered the impact of Type A behavior in ways that we do not understand.

The concept of the Type A behavior pattern has always been controversial, but it has also generated a great deal of research that has benefited both medical and behavioral science. Stress-related behavior is now widely considered to be relevant to the field of cardiology, even if the original Type A behavior pattern is not now believed to be a risk factor. Dozens of studies have shown that Type A's and Type B's differ on many psychological, physiological, and behavioral factors. Some of these studies suggest that Type A's may be at risk of developing headaches and other health problems, so Type A may still be a relevant topic of study for health psychologists. All these studies now need to be reinterpreted in light of the more recent evidence that Type A is not a risk factor for coronary heart disease.

Type A behavior may be indirectly related to CHD risk because it appears to be correlated with other risk factors. For example, Type A's tend to smoke more than Type B's (Shekelle, Schoenberger, & Stamler, 1976), but most studies find no differences in serum cholesterol or resting blood pressure. Type A men have been found to drink about 30 percent more alcohol than Type B's (Folsom et al., 1985).

Type A does appear to be a relatively long-lasting behavior pattern. Men in the original WCGS were reinterviewed 27 years later to examine changes in Type A. Sixty-one percent were classified the same. However, self-rated changes in Type A had no relation to changes

observed in the Structured Interview. This suggests that self-perceptions are very different from the way others see Type A behavior. This study suggested Type A has some beneficial effects. Type B subjects who were later scored Type A were younger, retired earlier, and reported better health than those who changed from A to B (Carmelli, Dame, Swan, & Rosenman, 1991). This study only adds to the confusion surrounding Type A.

There are many studies showing that Type A's generally have greater and longer-lasting elevations in blood pressure, heart rate, and catecholamines than Type B's in response to stressful tasks in the laboratory. Those tasks that produce the largest physiological reactions in Type A's tend to be frustrating, difficult, and competitive (Matthews, 1982). Originally it was felt that exaggerated physiological reactivity was a mechanism by which Type A behavior increased the risk for CHD. Now Type A behavior pattern is seen as only one of several influences on physiological reactivity. It has even been suggested that Type A behavior may be a result of excessive responsivity to challenging situations. Because blood pressure responses to stress have been found to be higher in Type A's even when they are under general anesthesia (Krantz, Arabian, Davia, & Parker, 1982), as well as in the usual laboratory situations, it appears that psychological factors do not account for some of the physiological reactivity differences between Type A's and Type B's.

Components of Type A Behavior

Booth-Kewley and Friedman (1987) reviewed studies of Type A components and other psychological variables. Through a technique known as *meta-analysis* they were able to compare the effects of all psychological/behavior variables on coronary heart disease. They combined both prospective epidemiological studies and cross-sectional studies of patients with angiography, which is a technique for measuring the obstruction in the coronary arteries. The size of the effect is summarized as a correlation coefficient (r). Some of their findings are presented in Table 18-1.

The table shows that the Structured Interview was associated with CHD both before and after 1977. However, the apparent strength of the Structured Interview decreased over time. The effect of time urgency and job involvement also decreased, while competition/aggression maintained a high effect size. The effect of anger/hostility, which is related to competition/aggression, decreased over the years, but the effect size remained relatively high. The effect size for depression increased substantially, but the effect size for anxiety decreased.

The constellation of behaviors associated with competition, aggression, anger, and hostility appears to be confirmed as related to CHD in most studies. This evidence comes both from component scorings of the Structured Interview and from studies with specialized measures, particularly the Cook-Medley Hostility Scale. When the Structured Interviews collected in the Multiple Risk Factor Intervention Trial were scored for components of Type A, only the two hostility-related scores were significant predictors of future CHD (Dembroski, MacDougall, Costa, & Grandits, 1989). This study provides particularly strong support for the importance of hostility, because global Type A did not predict CHD at all in the MRFIT study.

The Cook-Medley is a subscale of the Minnesota Multiphasic Personality Inventory that appears to measure hostility and cynical mistrust of people (Smith & Frohm, 1985). Those who score high on the Cook-Medley tend to expect the worst of others and dwell on people's negative characteristics. Several studies have found that Cook-Medley scores predict CHD mortality. For example, Barefoot, Dahlstrom, and Williams (1983) administered the Cook-Medley scale to medical students. Twenty-five years later they found that physicians with high scores were 6 to 7 times more likely to die than those with low hostility scores while in medical school. Williams (1987) proposes that the hostility complex is truly a coronary-prone behavior and offers several possible biological mechanisms including exaggerated catecholamine and corticosteroid release in response to provocations. The rela-

---

TABLE 18-1

THE ASSOCIATION OF TYPE A COMPONENTS AND OTHER PSYCHOLOGICAL VARIABLES WITH CORONARY HEART DISEASE

Variable	Association with CHD Pre-1977®	Association with CHD Post-1977®
Type A Structured Interview	.27	.17
Type A Jenkins Survey	.10	.07
Time urgency	.15	.08
Job involvement	.10	.00
Competition/aggression	.18	.20
Anger/hostility	.19	.11
Depression	.19	.28
Anxiety	.18	.05

Source: Adapted from Booth-Kewley and Friedman (1987).

tionship between hostility/anger and CHD is currently stimulating a great deal of research.

This research on hostility and health was reviewed by Timothy Smith (1992). At least 10 studies have examined whether hostility predicts CVD, and most of them found a significant effect of hostility, even though they used very different measures. There is limited support for the idea that hostile people may be more physiologically reactive. However, hostile people may respond more dramatically to social stressors, and high levels of reactivity may be more dangerous for people with advanced atherosclerosis. Hostile people appear to experience more interpersonal conflict, and some of this could be due to their own actions. By anticipating mistreatment from others, and by interpreting many actions of others as hostile, they may create conflict in their daily lives. This conflict would then strengthen their own hostility. Another mechanism of hostility's influence on health could be an association with health habits. In fact, there is evidence that hostile people have less healthful lifestyles than others, including less physical activity, more alcohol use, more frequent drinking and driving, and more smoking. Though not much is known about the etiology of hostility, there is a small genetic contribution.

Table 18-1 indicates that depression may be the psychological variable that is most strongly related to coronary heart disease. The mechanisms of such an effect have rarely been discussed, and surprisingly this is not an active area of research. However, we need to understand more clearly why depressed people seem to be experiencing more heart disease. Are depressed people less likely to exercise and eat a good diet? Does depression promote the release of hormones that damage the heart? Does depression affect cholesterol level? Do drugs used as depression treatments have side effects that promote CVD? These questions need to be answered. In addition, car-diologists need some direction from mental health clinicians in the evaluation and treatment of depression in their heart disease patients.

Treatment of Type A Behavior

Over the years several treatments for Type A behavior have been tested. Levenkron, Cohen, Mueller, and Fisher (1983) found that both cognitive-behavior therapy and group support significantly reduced some Type A components as measured by the Jenkins Activity Survey. Roskies and colleagues (Roskies et al., 1986) found that Type A behavior measured by the Structured Interview was reduced by cognitive-behavioral stress management but not by aerobic exercise or weight lifting. These studies show that Type A behavior can be altered, but they do not show whether changing Type A behavior reduces coronary heart disease.

The Recurrent Coronary Prevention Project (Powell, Friedman, Thoresen, Gill, & Ulmer, 1984) has been designed to assess the effect on CHD of changing Type A behavior. Over 1000 nonsmokers who had experienced an MI were randomly assigned to receive a Type A behavior-change program or to receive an educational program about heart disease and risk factors. A comprehensive cognitive-behavioral program was developed for the Type A subjects that was implemented in group sessions that continued over several years. Patients identified their Type A behaviors and changed them through cognitive techniques, behavioral drills and assignments between sessions, and practice of relaxation exercises. Postinfarction patients were recruited as subjects because they were felt to be motivated to change their behavior, and because their high rates of disease would allow the study to detect differences between groups.

FOCUS ON RESEARCH

What Kinds of People Are Cynically Hostile?

The ability of the Cook-Medley Hostility Scale to predict mortality in several studies has increased interest in this questionnaire. B. Kent Houston and Christine R. Vavak (1991) conducted a study to identify factors that might influence the early development of cynical hostility and describe the health habits of cynically hostile people.

They hypothesized that cynical hostility may develop in childhood. Cynical hostility is likely to develop in children whose parents have low levels of genuine acceptance. Parents who interfere with their children's desires by being strict and discouraging independence may tend to raise cynically hostile children. A final developmental factor may be inconsistent discipline.

Sixty-five undergraduates who scored high on cynical hostility and 69 students who scored low were selected from an initial group of 930. Students later reported on their parents' child-rearing practices and their own health behaviors.

Eight of the nine parent behaviors were significantly different between high and low hostility groups. These results strongly supported hypotheses that mothers and fathers of cynically hostile students were less accepting of their children, more strictly controlled them, gave them less independence, and used more punitive controls and inconsistent discipline. These results were similar for male and female students. In addition, those in the high-cynical hostility group had lower self-esteem and were much more likely to suppress their angry feelings. This pattern of suppressing anger has itself been associated with negative health effects.

Associations with health behavior provided clues about why cynical hostility may lead to health problems. Cynically hostile students tended to drink more alcohol, to drive a car after drinking more often, and to be more obese. There were no significant differences in cigarette smoking, exercise, or preferences for healthy foods.

The authors indicate that, although the apparent effects of parent behavior on child cynical hostility may reflect learning, there may be genetic influences on these variables. That is, the child could both inherit a tendency to be cynical hostility and learn such a behavior pattern from the parents. The study suggests that cynical hostility is a tendency developed in childhood to be oppositional and mistrustful of other people. Cynically hostile people appear to be psychologically vulnerable, as reflected by low self-esteem and suppressed anger. In addition to the potential health-damaging effects of being cynically hostile, these people are further increasing their risk by their drinking and driving habits.

After 2 years of intervention, significant reductions in the Type A intervention group were observed in global Type A as assessed by a videotaped Structured Interview. Moreover, the greatest reductions in Type A components were seen for time urgency and hostility. Of those with clear reductions in Type A behavior 2.2 percent had another MI, compared with 4.9 percent of those with no reduction in Type A behavior. This difference was not statistically significant.

The Type A intervention studies are difficult

B O X 18-3

FOCUS ON DIVERSITY

Who Was John Henry, and What Does He Have to Do with Hypertension in Blacks?

Many investigators are trying to understand why blacks have unusually high rates of hypertension, and personality may provide a partial explanation. Sherman A. James developed a theory, a measure, and a line of research that attempts to explain some earlier findings. James was intrigued by a study of Detroit residents that was published in the 1960s. Blacks living in high-stress environments had higher blood pressures than blacks living in low-stress environments. A high-stress environment was characterized by low income, high unemployment, high crime, and a high rate of marital breakups. The association between stressful environment and blood pressure was highest in black males under age 40, but there was no association at all among whites.

James and others hypothesized that the young black men were coping actively with their stressful environment by trying to change it. This style of active coping may lead to more sympathetic nervous system activity (fight or flight response pattern) and put the active copers at higher risk of developing hypertension than others who are more accepting of their situation.

This pattern of active coping reminded James of the legend and song about John Henry, the "steel-driving man." John Henry was a black manual laborer with extraordinary strength and determination. He competed against a mechanical steel drill and won the contest against great odds. However, after he won, he dropped dead from mental and physical exhaustion. Therefore, James created the John Henryism Scale for Actively Coping to measure the personality disposition to cope actively with stressors in the environment. Subjects report whether 12 statements are true or false regarding them on a five-point scale. Sample items include "I've always felt that I could make of my own life pretty much what I wanted to make of it" and "When things don't go the way I want them to, that just makes me work even harder."

The John Henryism hypothesis is that people living in stressful environments with high levels of John Henryism are more likely to become hypertensive than people in similar environments with low levels of John Henryism. Among other studies, James tested this hypothesis in a survey of 1548 randomly selected black and white adults living in a poor section of North Carolina with high rates of stroke.

As in the earlier Detroit study, socioeconomic status (environmental stress) was related to blood pressure in blacks but not in whites. The main hypothesis was also supported. In high socioeconomic status blacks, hypertension rates were only slightly higher in high John Henryism subjects than in low John Henryism subjects. However, in blacks with high environmental stress, those high in John Henryism were almost 3 times as likely to be hypertensive as those low in John Henryism (31 percent versus 11 percent).

This is a classic interaction between personality and environment. Only for blacks living in a stressful environment did personality make a difference. In this case, the personality characteristic of John Henryism made a large difference in the risk of hypertension. The lack of relation between John Henryism and blood pressure for whites could not be explained. However, for both whites and blacks, those high in John Henryism tended to be satisfied with their lives and to perceive their health as very good. Having a sense of mastery over your environment may be psychologically very healthy. However, when you have little power to change a stressful environment, heroic attempts to change your situation may have detrimental effects on your health.

These results help explain why the poor have an excessive number of health problems. They also suggest that the social and economic hardships of poverty may have to be improved before we see large improvements in the health status of poor people of all racial and ethnic backgrounds (James, Strogatz, Wing, et al., 1987).

---

to interpret. Given the decreasing evidence that Type A behavior is a risk factor, there seems to be little justification to conduct intervention studies. However, if these programs improve hostility, depression, or psychological and behavioral factors that seem to be related to CVD, then some impact on CVD could be

expected. To the extent that people are unsatisfied with their competitiveness, obsession with achievement, time urgency, hostility, and need for control, then interventions to alter these dysfunctional characteristics would be a contribution to mental health. However, for the field of heart disease, it seems most important to study the effects of changing hostility and depression on coronary heart disease morbidity and mortality.

HEALTH LOCUS OF CONTROL

Have you ever felt that you have no control over your life? Many researchers have demonstrated that a sense of control is very important. The term *internal control* describes the expectation that rewards and punishments in life are under direct personal control. For example, a person who believes in internal control thinks that getting a promotion, achieving in school, or avoiding the flu result from something they have done. A belief in external control suggests that positive or negative things that happen in one's life are the result of luck or chance. In 1978 Wallston, Wallston, and DeVellis developed the Multidimensional Health Locus of Control Scales (MHLC). These measures evaluate whether information about health is perceived to be determined by internal or external factors. In addition, the scale evaluates a third dimension known as "powerful others." This aspect of control is relevant to beliefs about health outcomes being determined by powerful people in their environment, such as health care providers.

Beliefs about control may be particularly important for people with chronic illnesses. It has been suggested that people who believe in internal control may be more able to make positive adjustment when they become chronically ill. Many chronic illnesses—such as arthritis, heart disease, and diabetes—are associated with unexpected exacerbations, or flare-ups. There has been some debate about whether beliefs in personal control are good or bad for people with these chronic illnesses. For example, one study of people with arthritis evaluated beliefs in control over the course of the illness. For patients who had severe rheumatoid arthritis, beliefs in internal control were associated with greater mood distur-

bance. It might be argued that it is bothersome to have exacerbations of a serious illness while one thinks that these events are under their control (Affleck et al., 1987). However, other studies have suggested that those who believe that they have control over the environment are more likely to have positive outcomes (Devins et al., 1982).

An example of the research on the control concept is provided by a study of end-stage renal disease. There are nearly 125,000 Americans who suffer chronic kidney diseases. These people must undergo lifetime medical therapy in order to compensate for their poor kidney function. The therapies might involve renal dialysis, a treatment in which waste material is filtered periodically using an artificial kidney machine. When dialysis is not effective, other options such as kidney transplantation are considered. However, a significant number of patients develop complications in the transplanted kidneys and need to return to renal dialysis in order to survive. Because of these problems, depression is common among patients with end-stage kidney diseases.

Ninety-six hemodialysis patients completed the Health Locus of Control Scale along with measures of depression. Among these patients, sixty-six were on dialysis but had not received a kidney transplant. The remaining thirty patients had returned to dialysis after an unsuccessful attempt at transplantation. The Health Locus of Control Scale is shown in Table 18-2. One of the most interesting results of the study is shown in the Figure 18-1. Depression was related to internal locus of control. However, the relationship between locus of control and depression differed for the two patient groups. For those who had experienced failure in a transplanted kidney, high internal control was related to higher depression. In other words, those who had experienced a major setback were more depressed if they felt they had control over their health status. For the patients who had not received a

TABLE 18·2

MULTIDIMENSIONAL HEALTH LOCUS OF CONTROL (MHLC) SCALES (Form A).

(For each item, respondent indicates: Strongly Disagree, Moderately Disagree, Slightly Disagree, Slightly Agree, Moderately Agree, or Strongly Agree)

Internal health locus of control (IHLC)

If I get sick, it is my own behavior which determines how soon I get well again.

I am in control of my health.

When I get sick I am to blame.

The main thing which affects my health is what I myself do.

If I take care of myself, I can avoid illness.

If I take the right actions, I can stay healthy.

Powerful others health locus of control (PHLC)

Having regular contact with my physician is the best way for me to avoid illness.

Whenever I don't feel well, I should consult a medically trained professional.

My family has a lot to do with my becoming sick or staying healthy.

Health professionals control my health.

When I recover from an illness, it's usually because other people (for example, doctors, nurses, family, friends) have been taking good care of me.

Regarding my health, I can only do what my doctor tells me to do.

Chance health locus of control (CHLC)

No matter what I do, if I am going to get sick, I will get sick.

Most things that affect my health happen to me by accident.

Luck plays a big part in determining how soon I will recover from an illness.

My good health is largely a matter of good fortune.

No matter what I do, I'm likely to get sick.

If it's meant to be, I will stay healthy.

Source: Wallston, Wallston, and DeVellis, (1978).

transplanted kidney, the relationship was the reverse. Those who felt they had control over their health were less depressed that those who were low on the internal locus of control scale. A similar result was obtained for the "powerful other" locus of control measure. These results occurred for patients who had more serious kidney disease. For those with less serious kidney disease, there appeared to be no relationship between locus of control and depression for either transplanted or untransplanted patients.

These findings suggest that the personality variable of perceived control may be very important. However, the results also help us recognize how complicated these relationships can be. The sense of personal control over outcomes combined with the misfortune of having a kidney rejected may be difficult to cope with. Some people may feel that they caused their own misfortune. When faced with rejection of a kidney, other interventions may be worthwhile. For example, someone with a high sense of personal control may benefit

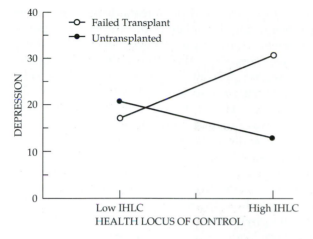

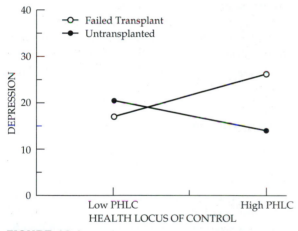

FIGURE 18-1

Relationship between internal locus of control and depression for those experiencing rejection or nonrejection of a kidney transplant. (From Christensen et al., 1991.)

from switching attention. Instead of focusing on their sense of control over the outcomes, they might be encouraged to direct their attention toward controlling their use of appropriate medications (Christensen, Turner, Smith, Holman, & Gregory, 1991). The concept of health locus of control has become extremely popular. Yet investigations linking locus of control to health outcomes have produced in-

consistent results. As this study suggests, the relationship between control and health may be very complicated.

Not everyone likes the concept of health locus of control. Aaron Antonovsky, a sociologist from Israel, believes that the locus of control concept is too heavily influenced by the American culture. The issue is not whether a person can control outcomes but rather whether there is control. Antonovsky describes this belief as a sense of coherence. People may believe that the resources required to manage stress are at their disposal, even though they personally may not control them. For example, for many people religious beliefs give a sense of security. According to Antonovsky (1990), those who have a sense of coherence are more likely to resist disease and to engage in healthful behaviors. Indeed, he has presented some evidence that those with a high sense of coherence are more resistant to illness.

OPTIMISM

Have you ever heard that maintaining a positive attitude is important for staying healthy? It is widely believed that having a positive outlook, or an adaptive attitude, toward illness is associated with longer life (Friedman, 1991). But what is the evidence? Overall, scientific evidence does not clearly answer the question. However, there are some studies demonstrating that those with a more optimistic outlook are better able to adapt to surgery and serious illness. In these studies the optimistic attitude is typically measured using a scale called the Life Orientation Test (LOT) (Scheier & Carver, 1985). The LOT is a brief scale that attempts to determine whether people have a positive or negative orientation toward life. Those with a positive orientation are called *optimists*, while those with a negative orientation are called *pessimists*. In one study, patients undergoing coronary artery bypass surgery were interviewed the day before the surgery and then 6 days, 8 days, and 6 months following the surgery. At each follow-up the patients were given a series of measures evaluating their mood and rate of recovery from this major surgical procedure.

BOX 18·4

FOCUS ON WOMEN

Breast cancer is a major source of distress. However, as a result of early detection, many women undergo surgery for breast cancer during early stages. Those with stage 1 or stage 2 breast cancer have tumors that are well localized. This means that their chances of survival following the surgery are very good. Nevertheless, stage 1 or stage 2 breast cancer still requires disfiguring surgery and usually chemotherapy that produces unpleasant side effects. One of the intriguing questions is why some women adapt relatively well to this threatening situation while others do more poorly. One potential explanation is that optimism may be related to better adaptation.

In one study, women diagnosed with breast cancer were given the Life Orientation Test (LOT) that measures optimism and pessimism. They were interviewed the day before their surgery and then again 7 and 10 days following surgery. Furthermore, they were reinterviewed 3 months later. Around the time of the surgery, women who scored higher on the optimism scale were more likely to view the situation in a positive light and to accept its reality. Women who scored higher on pessimism were more likely to deny the reality of the situation and to report giving up or feeling that the surgery was hopeless. However, it is important to point out that relatively few women reported that the situation was completely hopeless. Among women undergoing this stressful experience, optimism was associated with a positive mood and the ability to maintain a sense of humor. Pessimism was associated with more reports of emotional distress, denial, and disengagement. These studies also demonstrated that acceptance of the reality of the situation is important. Those who demonstrated acceptance prior to the surgery were less likely to show serious distress after the surgery had been completed (Carver, Scheier, & Pozo, 1991).

Optimists and pessimists differed from the beginning. Even before the surgery, the pessimists were reporting higher levels of hostility and depression than the optimists. After the surgery, pessimists reported themselves to be less happy and less relieved than the optimists. The optimists seemed to be less focused on the negative experiences associated with surgery. For example, they reported less distressed emotions and fewer symptoms than the pessimists. After the surgery the optimists were more likely to seek information that would help them in the recovery process. On the physical recovery side, the optimists were more likely to be up and walking around their rooms after surgery than the pessimists. Six months after surgery optimists were more likely to have returned to vigorous exercise. Overall, the optimists seemed to be making a better adaptation to the surgery and appeared to return to their normal lives at a more rapid pace (Carver, Scheier, & Pozo, 1991).

PERSONALITY AND CANCER OUTCOME

For many years oncologists have reported that some patients are much hardier and likely to survive cancer than others. There are many different explanations for this. For example, it has been suggested that natural killer cells (NK) play an important role in resistance to cancers (Lotzova & Herberman, 1986). Yet the exact reasons why some people survive and some do not have not been well understood. Some studies have demonstrated that social isolation may be an important factor in survival. For example, Reynolds and Kaplan (1990) found that male cancer patients who were socially isolated from other people had significantly poorer survival than those who were better socially integrated. In another study that followed women with breast cancer for 20 years, Funch and Marshall determined that those in the youngest and the oldest age groups with good social support survived longer than those with poorer support networks. However, this effect did not occur for those in the middle ranges of social support.

Other studies have suggested that a sense of helplessness or hopelessness might be associated with poorer cancer outcomes. Learned helplessness is a phenomenon that has been well demonstrated in psychological laboratories. *Helplessness* is defined as a state that results from perceived uncontrollability of events in one's environment (Seligman, 1975). Originally, learned helplessness was demonstrated in laboratory animals who were exposed to random painful shock. Once exposed to shock on a random schedule, the animals were unable to learn a simple task that would help them avoid the punishment. This phenomenon became known as *learned helplessness* because the animals had learned not to respond.

A variety of animal studies have shown that the learned helplessness paradigm is associated with increased growth of tumors (Greenberg, Dyck, & Sandler, 1984). In one intriguing study, tumors were implanted in three groups of rats. One group was put in an environment where they could learn to escape electrical shocks. A second group received inescapable shock, while a third group served as a control. When tumors were implanted in these laboratory animals, the control group and the group receiving escapable shock had the same rates of tumor rejection, while those receiving the inescapable shock were significantly less likely to reject the tumors (Visintainer, Volpicelli, & Seligman, 1982). These studies may help explain why a perceived sense of helplessness is related to poor outcomes in cancer.

Patients who show a fighting spirit seem to do better than those who do not. In one study, it was demonstrated that patients' rating of hopelessness and negative beliefs about the future had poorer outcomes (Goodkin, Antoni, & Blaney, 1986). Greer, Pettingale, Monis, and Haybittle (1985) have also reported that patients with a "fighting spirit" are more likely to survive breast cancer. A series of studies by Levy and her colleagues at the University of Pittsburgh have also demonstrated that patients who exhibit repression, hopelessness, and helplessness seem to have poorer outcomes than patients with a more positive view. These studies are prospective. In other words, they rule out the explanation that the women have poor attitudes because they are sick. Levy and her colleagues have also shown that natural killer (NK) cell activity is reduced by depression and helplessness and compromised immunal function results. The functioning immune system, in turn, is related to tumor rejection (Levy & Heiden, 1990; Levy, Herberman, Lippman, & D'Angelo, 1987). More details on the relationship between immune functioning and personality are provided in Chapters 6 and 12.

In this chapter we have covered only a few of the many personality variables that may be related to health. A subtantial number of studies now address these problems (Friedman, 1991). Several years ago the belief that personality could affect illness was seriously challenged (Angell, 1985). Now, there is substantial evidence that personality and personal resources probably play a very important role in the development of illness and in the process of coping with serious health problems.

In addition to personality factors, other social resources probably play a key role in adaptation to health. For example, poverty almost certainly is associated with many measures of health status. Furthermore, there are significant problems associated with being of advanced age. In the next sections we will explore the role of social disadvantage and advanced age as they affect health outcomes. These are not truly personality variables. However, they do describe the importance of personal resources.

DEMOGRAPHIC FACTORS

Social Class, Race, and Poverty

Nearly 1 in 8 Americans lives in a family that is below the poverty level, and 1 child in every 6 comes from a low-income family (Special Center for Children in Poverty, 1990). For virtually all the major causes of death, there are significant differences between high- and low-income people. For example, children with low income experience more cancer with lower survival rates. With the exception of breast and colon-rectal cancer, most other cancers are more common in low-income than higher-income individuals (Amler & Doll, 1987). Low-income people also experience more infectious diseases, including HIV infection and tuberculosis. They are more likely to become addicted to drugs and are more likely to die in an accident or to be murdered. Figure 18-2 summarizes the relationship between activity limitations and income. As the figure suggests, there is a systematic relationship between low

income level and likelihood of being limited in the activities essential to daily life.

One of the reasons for the relationship between low income and poor outcomes may be related to health behavior. Low-income individuals are more likely to be overweight and to have high blood pressure and other risk factors for heart disease (Public Health Service, 1988). Although the use of cigarettes has declined in the population in general, rates of tobacco use among low-income adults have remained essentially unchanged in the last 20 years (Kaplan, Pierce, & Gilpen, Johnson & Bal, 1992).

There are special problems for particular groups. African Americans make up about 12 percent of the U.S. population. About one-third of all American blacks live below the property line, a rate that is 3 times higher than for white citizens. Although the life expectancy is about 75 years for Americans in general, it is only about 69 years for black citizens. Furthermore, the life expectancy for white citizens is increasing, while it has shown a small decrease for black groups. Figure 18-3 summarizes the leading causes of death for blacks and whites in the United States. As the figure clearly shows, there are significantly higher death rates for blacks in several categories including heart disease, cancer, stroke, and homicide. Thus, there are important concerns relevant to decreasing the gap between white and nonwhite groups. One of the major overall goals for the year 2000 is to reduce the health discrepancy among ethnic groups in the United States.

In order to make progress toward narrowing the gap, we will need to consider the environments in which people live in addition to their personal characteristics. A poverty environment may be one important factor that influences health outcomes. Considerable evidence suggests that there are associations between poverty and health that may not be explained by known risk factors or lack of access to medical care. The relationship between

FIGURE 18-2

Percentage of people who experience limitation of major activity by income level. (From *Healthy People 2000*, p. 30).

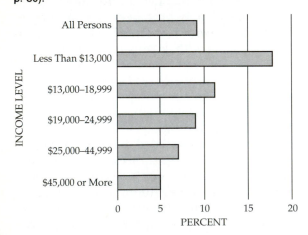

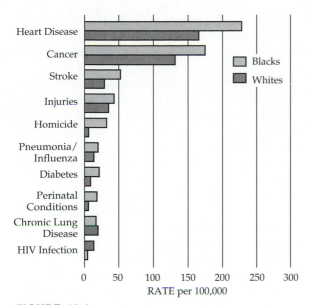

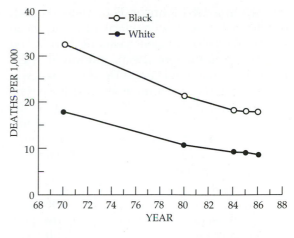

FIGURE 18-3

Leading causes of death for white and Afro-Americans. (*Healthy People 2000*, p. 32.)

social disadvantage and health status is well known and well documented. Although black and white families inhabit all income levels, we still face a situation in which the average income and environment for black Americans is significantly more disadvantaged than that for the white majority. Many studies make inferences about effects of social disadvantage on the basis of minority-white differentials. Such analyses confound (or confuse) ethnic effects with the effects of poverty and education per se. Nevertheless, we can learn something from the study of minority-white differentials, since black families remain disproportionately represented below the poverty line.

According to 1988 data from the National Center for Health Statistics, the black-white differences in infant mortality are striking. Figure 18-4 summarizes white-nonwhite differences in infant mortality, which is defined as the number of children born alive who do not survive until their first birthday. In addition to

infant mortality, the probability of early death is higher for nonwhites in a variety of different categories. By adulthood, the differences become even stronger. In 1988 the life expectancy for a white male was 72 years, while for a black male it was 65.2 years, a difference of nearly 7 years. A white female has a life expectancy of 78.8 years, while a black female can expect to live 73.5 years. In comparison with whites, black Americans have nearly twice the rate of death due to stroke, and there are about 1.5 deaths from cancer in black men for each death due to cancer in a white man. Blacks are more than twice as likely as whites to die from diabetes and have a significantly higher rate of death from diseases of the liver. In some categories, the differences are more extreme. For example, 6.65 black men die of homicide for each white man who is murdered. Black women are more than 4 times as likely as white women to die from homicide.

Many explanations have been proposed to account for these differences, but some are proving to be either oversimplified or incorrect. For example, differential access to medical care has been proposed as the reason for the well-known differences. Yet, as documented in a 1983 Johnson Foundation report, differential access to medical care has been greatly reduced in recent years (Robert Wood Johnson Foundation, 1983). Although there has been some reduction in the discrepancy in health status between the poor and those who are better off (Feldman, 1982), the differential remains large. It is possible that poor people do get access to the health care system but that the quality of service they receive is substandard. Some of these problems were reviewed in Chapter 4.

One of the most common explanations for the health status differential is that the poor engage in riskier health behaviors. Yet the evidence does not always support this view. One of the most interesting studies on this point involved 17,530 civil servants in England. These employees were graded by social class. As expected, there was a steep inverse relationship between social class and mortality from all causes. The data also revealed that those in lower social grades had more mortality, with risk factors removed as covariates in a statistical model. In other words, there appeared to be differences in mortality independent of the major risk factors. As all participants had access to the U.K. National Health System, it is difficult to attribute the differences to unequal access to care (Marmot et al., 1984).

Another intriguing explanation for the differential in health status concerns the effects of living in a poverty area. A report using data from the Alameda County Study raises some interesting questions about the effects of a poverty environment. Haan and colleagues (1984) analyzed the mortality experiences of a random sample of residents in Oakland, California. Citizens who dwell in a poverty area were compared with matched inhabitants of nearby areas outside the poverty district. The poverty area was designated by the federal government on the basis of unemployment and income reported in the 1960 census. Most of the impoverished census tracts would remain in the poverty area based on the 1990 census.

Although the concentration of poverty is greater in the poverty areas, there are still a substantial number of residents in nonpoverty areas who have equally low levels of income and education. Thus, Haan and colleagues were able to statistically control for education and income in order to evaluate the effects of living in the poverty environment. An analysis adjusting for age, sex, health status, and ethnicity demonstrated that there were 1.47 deaths in the poverty area for each death in the comparison area. Over a series of analyses, adjustments were made for income, lack of medical care, unemployment, ethnicity, health practices, social connections, and psychological factors. None of these adjustments had a substantial impact upon the differential mortality in the two areas. Haan and colleagues include as possible explanations for the effects of poverty upon health the effects of the physical environment, higher levels of social stressors, and higher risks associated with low-status occupations. Whatever the explanation, there appears to be an effect of living in a poverty area that is independent of access to medical care and to traditional behavioral risk factors.

The relationship between social disadvantage and health status presents some interesting challenges for future research. Although the gap in access to care has declined in recent years, it is possible that the quality of care received by low-income people is less comprehensive than that given to people with higher socioeconomic status (Howard, Ound, & Bell, 1980). In addition, low educational attainment may be associated with a lower probability of following complex directions and complying with medical regimens (Jenkins, 1982). Furthermore, it has been suggested that disadvantaged persons wait longer to have cancers diagnosed at later stages in the disease process (Howard, 1982).

Despite these suggestions, it is interesting to consider the effects of providing easier access to care for the general public. The RAND health insurance experiment demonstrated that those randomly assigned to have 100 percent of their health care paid for use services significantly more often than those required to share in their medical care costs. With the exception of those with poor vision plus low income and persons with high blood pressure, free medical care and greater utilization were unrelated to improved health status (Brook, Ware, Rogers, et al., 1983).

Older Adults

Older Americans are another group that will deserve even more attention in the future. The numbers of people in this category have increased sharply over the course of this century. In 1900, people over the age of 65 represented only about 4 percent of the U.S. population. Today, older people are 12.4 percent of the population, and this number will increase to 22 percent by the year 2030. More older people are living into their eighties. Many older Americans suffer from a variety of illnesses including chronic lung disease, cancer, heart disease, and arthritis. These problems were described in the preceding chapters. However, we also need to take into consideration that many old people suffer from more than one of these problems at the same time. New approaches are necessary to prevent ill older citizens from becoming more disabled, and other interventions are needed to rehabilitate those with chronic conditions (Institute of Medicine, 1991).

Several lines of evidence suggest that we can prevent many of the disabilities associated with aging. This might be done by preventing

the use of cigarettes or getting people to stop smoking early. In addition, dietary interventions may be helpful in reducing risk factors for chronic diseases such as cancer and heart disease.

There is also growing evidence that physical activity is important for older adults. Over 40 percent of all people over 65 report that they have no leisure-time physical activity, and less than a third of all older adults report moderate physical activity such as walking or gardening. Less than 10 percent exercise vigorously on a regular basis. As we have shown in preceding chapters, regular exercise may be helpful in reducing the burden of several problems, including coronary heart disease, high blood pressure, non-insulin-dependent diabetes, and depression (Caspersen, 1989). The numerous health and daily function problems associated with sedentary lifestyle in older adults are being documented (Wagner, LaCroix, Buchner, & Larson, 1992). There may also be significant benefits for the elderly associated with more prudent use of health services, obtaining regular vaccinations, and appropriate compliance with medical regimens.

SUMMARY

Many theories of the effect of personality on health and disease have been proposed, and the most well known theory is that Type A behavior causes heart disease. The Type A concept was developed by cardiologists Friedman and Rosenman. Type A people are described as hard-driven, time-urgent, competitive, and aggressive. Several early studies found that Type A was indeed a risk factor for CVD and was related to the amount of atherosclerosis in coronary arteries. These findings led to the acceptance of Type A as a CVD risk factor. More recent studies have consistently found that Type A is not related to CVD. When the 22-year follow-up of Friedman and

Rosenman's original study found that Type A was unrelated to CVD, most people were forced to conclude that Type A was probably not a risk factor.

Current research on personality and CVD focuses on the Type A component of hostility and aggression. It appears that hostile people are more likely to have heart attacks than those who are more easygoing. The theory that hostility leads to hypertension and heart disease was one of the primary theories in psychosomatic medicine early in the twentieth century, so it is interesting that this theory is finally receiving scientific support.

Several other personality variables may be related to health outcomes. For example, the perception of control over an environment may be associated with lower levels of stress and depression. However, the results of studies on control and illness are often very complex. Optimism is a personality variable that seems to be related to several positive health outcomes. For example, people with optimistic outlooks show faster recoveries from surgery than those who are pessimistic.

Although not personality variables, poverty, low socioeconomic status, and advanced age are individual difference factors that are associated with poor health outcomes. These need our attention for planning health care interventions.

KEY TERMS

Psychosomatic medicine. A subfield of psychiatry interested in the effects of psychological and personality factors on disease.

Type A behavior. A pattern of behavior and emotion characterized by competitiveness, aggression, hostility, and time urgency that has been suspected of being a risk factor for CVD.

Hostility. A component of Type A behavior. Psychosomatic theorists believed that hostility was related to CVD, and modern studies are supporting the theory.

Structured Interview. The preferred method of assessing Type A behavior. The style of responding is more important than the actual answers to questions.

Western Collaborative Group Study (WCGS). An epidemiological study of Type A behavior and CVD conducted by Friedman and Rosenman. In the 8.5-year follow-up Type A was a risk factor, but it did not predict CVD death at the 22-year follow-up.

Cook-Medley Hostility Scale. A measure of cynical mistrust of other people that has been found to predict CVD and all-cause mortality.

Recurrent Coronary Prevention Project. A study conducted by Meyer Friedman and colleagues to treat Type A behavior in men who have already had a heart attack.

Locus of control. The perception of control over the environment. Those with an internal locus of control believe that positive or negative events are under their control, while those with external control beliefs think that important outcomes are the result of luck or chance.

Optimism. A positive outlook on life.

Pessimism. A negative outlook on life.

CHAPTER 19

Community Interventions

Ingrid Knutsen lives in rural North Dakota. She is a mother of three who likes to enjoy her good health by cross-country skiing in the winter and roller skating in the town park in the summer. She has been active for many years, but recently she has been working hard on changing her diet. She has been hearing a lot of information lately on the harmful effects of fatty foods, and she wants her children to grow up eating foods that will keep them healthy. After dinner tonight she served the family nonfat frozen yogurt that she got free with a coupon. Her 10-year-old son just asked her to help with his homework. His assignment was to take an inventory of all the supplies and equipment at their home that could be used for physical activity and sports. Ingrid's husband was talking with her last week about signing up for a stress management class that was being offered by his company at lunchtime. The week before that a woman from her church called and asked her to volunteer to help organize a cholesterol screening program that is planned one Sunday next month. After seeing an ad on television for a smoking cessation program offered at the local hospital, she starts to wonder if all this health information was always around or if something new is happening.

THE COMMUNITY APPROACH TO DISEASE PREVENTION

Something new is happening, and Ingrid's family is among the first to experience it. Her town was part of a large study to find out whether health can be improved through programs for the whole community. The goal is to motivate people to adopt more healthful lifestyles and to change the environments in which people live to make it easier to continue those lifestyles. Notice that Ingrid's family was being encouraged to make healthful behavior changes through work sites, churches, schools, hospitals, local businesses, and even television.

Communitywide intervention may be part of the evolution of health care. Health care of the future will take place not only in clinics and hospitals. Health professionals, legislators, business leaders, the media, educators, and others are starting to work together to encourage people to behave in ways that will keep them healthy and avoid many of the chronic diseases we already know how to prevent. Often, the environment can have a major impact on what we do. The World Health Organization supports a variety of programs designed to create healthy environments. For example, there is now a major campaign for a smoke-free Europe. There is also a major European campaign for healthy schools and healthy communities. In this chapter we will explore the concepts behind community intervention approaches. The major theme is that we can modify risky behavior by modifying the whole environment in which people live.

CONTRASTING INDIVIDUAL AND COMMUNITY APPROACHES TO HEALTH BEHAVIOR CHANGE

Community interventions usually represent a hybrid of different approaches to health behavior change that have arisen from different disciplines. Roberts (1987) contrasts the approaches of public health and health psychology. The traditional approach to solving public health problems emphasizes passive protection of the population. Putting fluoride in the water supply, requiring safety caps on medicine bottles, and ensuring the safety of food supplies are all examples of the public health approach. Virtually everyone in the population is protected, but behavior change is not required from each citizen.

The usual psychological approach emphasizes individual responsibility for one's own health-related behaviors. This is an outgrowth of a clinical psychology perspective that puts the highest priority on the most extreme cases. The application of the psychological approach has led to educational and motivational programs to promote the use of seat belts, to help people eat low-fat diets, and to help smokers quit.

The public health advocates point out that strategies which work automatically are often more effective than strategies which require behavior change. They point to the examples of sanitation regulations and air bags in automobiles. Health psychology advocates argue that legislative approaches often restrict personal choice and are politically impossible in many cases. Laws requiring motorcyclists to wear helmets definitely save lives. However, these laws are often repealed because the cyclists do not want to wear helmets and put heavy pressure on lawmakers. It is not feasible to outlaw fatty foods, so the only practical alternative at this time is to attempt to change people's dietary practices.

Both of these approaches are typically used in community interventions. A cancer prevention program may work with food companies to reduce the fat and increase the fiber in their products. At the same time educational programs will inform people about healthful eating, prompt them to make specific behavioral changes, and motivate them to use low-fat food items by providing discount coupons.

BOX 19·1

HEALTH OBJECTIVES FOR THE YEAR 2000: COMMUNITY-BASED PROGRAMS

Increase to at least 50 percent the proportion of postsecondary institutions with institutionwide health promotion programs for students, faculty, and staff. (Baseline: at least 20 percent of higher education institutions offered health promotion activities for students in 1989–1990).

YEAR 2000 GOAL FOR HEALTH PROMOTION IN HIGHER EDUCATION

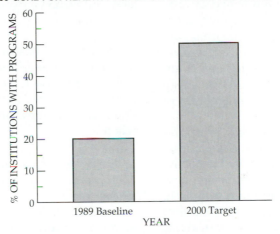

Increase to at least 75 percent the proportion of local television network affiliates in the top 20 television markets that have become partners with one or more community organizations in addressing one of the health problems discussed in the Healthy People 2000 objectives (baseline data not available).

Increase to at least 5000 brand items the availability of processed food products that are reduced in fat and saturated fat (baseline: 2500 items reduced in fat in 1986).

YEAR 2000 GOAL FOR LOW-FAT FOOD ITEMS

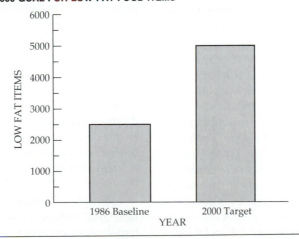

Jeffery (1989) demonstrates that public health and psychology advocates have different models for understanding behavior. A psychologist will ask, "Why do people differ?" He or she will then study individual differences in attitudes, biology, social upbringing, and social status. The public health professional will ask, "Why do populations differ?" He or she will tend to focus on environmental factors. Maybe there is more violence in the United States because there are more firearms, not because Americans are more aggressive. Maybe there is more smoking in some countries because there are many ads for cheap cigarettes, not because people are ignorant of the hazards of smoking.

Psychologists have developed principles and methods of behavior modification that were based on the desire to change the behavior of individuals. These methods are now being applied in community interventions to change the behavior of populations. This shift in focus from changing behavior in individuals to changing behavior in populations has led psychologists to learn about public health approaches. Three types of public health approaches are being applied in community programs.

1. Economic incentives. Increasing taxes reduces consumption of alcohol or tobacco. Discounts on insurance for nonsmokers encourage smokers to quit. These policies affect everyone in the community, but they are generally accepted because people still have the right to choose to do or not to do the behavior.

2. Passive protection from hazards. If unhealthful products are restricted, people have fewer chances to be exposed to them. Prohibiting alcohol sales to minors, improving highway design, and water sanitation are common examples of this approach. These measures will be supported when the population perceives that the health improvements outweigh the loss of choice. Although gun control would

save many lives, many voters feel strongly about restrictions being placed on gun ownership. Therefore, there is very limited gun control in the United States.

3. Controlling the promotion of health behaviors. In this approach, the product is not restricted, but the promotion of the product is controlled. The ban on cigarette ads on television and radio is a good example of restricted promotion.

For effective health behavior change, both individual and public health strategies are usually required. Each strategy works well under certain conditions. Jeffery (1989) states that individual behavior-change strategies work best when:

1. the benefits to the individual are substantial and almost guaranteed
2. the benefits are received quickly (within days or weeks)
3. there are few costs involved

These conditions apply with such behaviors as birth control and fluoridated toothpaste, so behavior change is relatively successful. The conditions do not apply well to such behaviors as diet change, because the costs are high in terms of inconvenience and the benefits are long-term. Predictably, dietary change programs have modest success.

Community or public health strategies work best when:

1. changing a well-defined environment will strongly affect the population
2. the environments are controlled by governments, not businesses
3. the intervention is economically and politically feasible

Examples of successes include water sanitation and building codes. On the other hand, legislative approaches to regulating private behaviors such as drug use and violence have not been successful. The behaviors occur in a variety of environments, they are difficult to detect, and it is not feasible to intervene effectively without a massive loss of personal freedom.

Although psychologists may not appreciate population-based approaches, and public health professionals may not consider individual approaches effective, the designer of community interventions must understand and combine each of these strategies. There are now many examples of psychologists and public health professionals working together to create new models and intervention approaches.

An example of an integrative model is Ewart's (1991) social action theory. This theory is concerned with personal control of behavior, but the influence of social interaction and environmental structures are emphasized. The social, physical, and policy environments can influence cognitive action schemas, self-goals, and problem-solving activities that are necessary for long-term behavior change. This theory has the potential to lead to improved methods of health behavior change in populations.

One of the primary reasons for pursuing the community approach as opposed to reliance on the clinical strategy of treating only high-risk individuals is that the community approach should be more effective in reducing the total level of disease risk in the population. The community approach attempts to reduce, for example, serum cholesterol and blood pressure by a small amount in everyone. In contrast, the clinical strategy attempts to reduce risk factors by a large amount in a small group of high-risk patients. Kottke and colleagues (Kottke, Puska, Salonen, Tuomilehto, & Nissinen, 1985) have discussed the extent of CVD reduction in the population that can be expected with each approach. Using risk factor data from Finland, they calculated that the clinical approach would treat 12 percent of the population for hypercholesterolemia and 10 percent of the population for hypertension. If treatment goals of 20 percent reduction in serum cholesterol and 10 percent reduction in diastolic blood pressure to 90 mmHg were met in all patients, a 28 percent reduction in the CVD death rate would be expected.

This is a substantial effect, but it must be compared with what could be achieved in the community approach. First, assume that the community program was only half as effective as the clinical approach so that serum cholesterol decreased by 10 percent and diastolic blood pressure decreased by 5 percent in the entire population. In this case CVD death rates should be reduced by 31 percent, and this is more than could be achieved by the clinical approach. If the community program reduced serum cholesterol by 20 percent and diastolic blood pressure by 10 percent in the population, a 51 percent decrease in CVD deaths could be expected. The main reason the community approach is more effective is that it affects risk factors in the entire population, not just in a few high-risk patients. Because most of the CVD deaths occur in people with "average" risk factor levels, it is not sufficient to devote all the resources to only the most high-risk people.

Changing health behaviors and risk factors in an entire community is a challenging undertaking. A team of experts from a variety of disciplines is required to mount the complex programs that are needed. In addition to physicians and psychologists, many community programs receive input from dietitians, exercise physiologists, health educators, statisticians, and survey researchers. Larger projects often require publishing and marketing teams consisting of writers, media experts, and graphic designers. Although community-based prevention projects are expensive, their costs are very small compared with clinical treatments of CVD.

THEORETICAL BASIS FOR COMMUNITY-BASED PROGRAMS

There is no one theory that guides all of the community approaches to health promotion, but most existing programs have used the following theories and models in designing their interventions.

Social Cognitive Theory

Bandura's ideas about social, cognitive, and environmental influences on behavior have heavily influenced all the community studies. All programs focus on behavior change and incorporate self-management principles and methods into both media and face-to-face educational programs. See Chapter 3 for a review of Bandura's theories.

The Communication-Behavior Change Framework

This model was described in Chapter 3. A hierarchy of steps in the learning process is proposed, and this herarchy is useful in designing messages and programs. For example, most smokers know that smoking is bad for them and want to quit, but they do not know how to quit. Thus, interventions to increase knowledge or motivation are deemphasized, while skills training is emphasized. In the area of dietary change, confusion about which foods are high in fat would suggest that the program should begin with the goal of increasing knowledge and then progress up the hierarchy. This type of analysis allows health messages and programs to be targeted to the proper audience.

The Social Marketing Framework

Social marketing was developed by Kotler (1982) to apply marketing principles and techniques when the goal is not to sell a product but to create a social change. The basic dictum of marketing is summarized by the four P's: the right *product* backed by the right *promotion* and put in the right *place* at the right *price*. Another essential element of social marketing is that consumer surveys must be done to determine where on the communication-behavior change hierarchy the target population is. The four P's can then be readily applied to community-based health promotion.

The community program must determine what *products* and services that will further health promotion goals are also acceptable to the community. Products such as low-fat cookbooks and services such as work site exercise groups can then be developed.

Promotion of products and services can be accomplished through the mass media, word of mouth, or special events at community festivals, malls, or work sites.

It is sometimes challenging to find the right *place* to distribute products and services. Health educational materials have been made available through public libraries, supermarkets, work sites, churches, and direct mailings to residences.

The *price* element includes not only monetary costs but time costs and convenience costs as well. A free smoking cessation course may take too much time, a low-fat cooking course may be too far from home, or a televised program on exercise may be opposite a favorite sitcom. Because health promotion programs are competing for time and attention with many other factors in people's lives, careful planning is needed to successfully market the programs.

The Community Organization Framework

The purpose of community organization is to stimulate towns and cities to use their own social structures and resources to accomplish health goals that are consistent with local values (Bracht & Kingsbury, 1990). Some group must take responsibility for initiating the community organization effort, and frequently this group has come from outside the target community. The sponsor is interdependent with the community and its organizations, so community organizations must be involved in the development and implementation of the program. This involvement promotes community ownership of the program so that there is a commitment to maintain the prevention efforts into the indefinite future.

It is important to clearly define the community of interest. The community can be a place, like a town or work place. Other communities are not bound to a particular place. Communities can be made up of a specific ethnic group, of members of a type of church, or of members of a political group. You could have a community of people in the same profession or of users of a computer network. When a meaningful community is defined, the work begins.

The community becomes stimulated to work toward the health objective one step at a time. If the community was already working hard to solve the problem, there would be little need for community organization. The first step is to make the community aware of the health issue, whether it is CVD, cancer, AIDS, drunk driving, or physical activity. The next step is for the community or its representatives to agree that change in this health issue is a priority. The third step is to make plans for relevant changes. Finally, the community must establish structures to implement and maintain the relevant programs. The process of stimulating community action can be very complicated, but the benefits of success are that important resources of time and money can be identified or created, and the health promotion programs can be carried on indefinitely (Bracht & Kingsbury, 1990).

Because community organization is just one piece of the total community approach, it is important to understand what it can and cannot do. There are several roles of community organization in health promotion that were suggested by Farquhar, Maccoby, and Solomon (1984).

1. Community organization can augment the effects of mass media.
2. Community organization can multiply the effects of other programs by increasing interpersonal communication about the health issue.
3. Organizations can expand the distribution of educational products and programs.
4. Organizations can sponsor programs on a long-term basis.
5. Formation of new organizations can increase the number of organizations committed to health promotion.

There is no limit to the type of organization that can be involved in the community program. Health organizations such as hospitals, medical societies, nursing societies, the local Heart Association or Cancer Society, and Weight Watchers are obvious. Educational institutions like colleges and continuing education centers can add courses related to health promotion. Programs for children and adolescents can be started in public schools. Local government can be involved through the parks and recreation departments and others. Social and professional groups of all types can sponsor activities. Businesses and chambers of commerce can be involved in many ways. Work sites have become a popular location for health promotion programs because so many people spend so much time there.

The Social Ecology Framework

You might be familiar with the term *ecology*, which is often used in biology; it means the study of relationships between an organism and its environment. The field of social ecology is concerned with how people interact with their social, institutional, and cultural environments, as well as with their physical environments. Stokols (1992) has described how a social ecology perspective can contribute to health promotion in the community. Social ecology can give clues about what changes in the environment would facilitate healthful behaviors.

First, the characteristics of the physical and social environments that affect health must be identified. Stress may be influenced by uncontrollable noise or a change of residence in the physical area. Social environment factors may be chronic conflict or social isolation. Health behavior may be influenced by geographic accessibility to health care facilities or by having a workout room at the work site. Social environment influences may include others who model seat belt wearing or religious teachings for abstinence from alcohol. Careful analyses of factors in the physical and social environments that affect a specific health behavior, access to health care, or safety can lead to health promotion programs that focus on changing those aspects of the environment.

The social ecology perspective stresses the need for intervention at multiple levels. Policies and interventions can be implemented at the municipal, regional, national, and international levels. Although behavioral medicine and community intervention approaches already stress the need for a variety of disciplines to work together, social ecologists suggest new disciplines to add to the mix. Geographers can contribute to land use policies that may reduce stress and provide better access to health care facilities. Architects can make sure safety is a priority in building design. Engineers and technologists can design safer and more healthful products and reduce use of, and exposure to, toxic substances. Social scientists can improve methods of conflict resolution in organizations, promote corporate health programs, and develop methods of influencing the behavior of legislators regarding

health. Diplomats must be involved in efforts to protect enviromental quality on an international scale.

Interventions at multiple levels are expected to complement one another so that media messages to change behavior are facilitated by governmental policies and business practices. For example, media campaigns to promote physical activity may be enhanced by educational programs at the work site, by locating exercise facilities close to work, and by insurance discounts for regular exercisers. Researchers are just beginning to consider how important environmental changes may be for health promotion. As you go through your day, try to think of changes in the social or physical environment that would make the environment healthier or would make it easier for you to have healthier habits.

COMMUNITY-BASED HEALTH PROMOTION PROGRAMS

The major community intervention studies are summarized here. These studies have helped define the field and have inspired many similar programs around the world. Community interventions are not developed in the CVD prevention area.

The North Karelia Project

The state of North Karelia in Finland had been found to have the world's highest death rate from CVD in the Seven Countries Study. Of course, this made big headlines in the local papers. The population was alarmed and circulated a petition to call on the government to do something to improve the health of the people in their state. It was decided that a test program would be conducted in North Karelia, and if successful, the program would be expanded nationwide. This is how the North Karelia Project was born (Puska, 1984). The program was started in 1972 and involved all sectors of the community. For example, low-fat cooking classes were set up, food makers were asked to develop lower-fat products, schoolchildren were taught how to live a "heart healthy lifestyle," and programs like smoking cessation classes were started at work sites. The results in North Karelia were compared with a neighboring state that did not have the intensive program. After 5 years the risk of CVD in North Karelia decreased by 17 percent in men and 11 percent in women. These improvements maintained over 10 years of follow-up, but it was impossible to compare the results with a control community because a nationwide program had been started.

The Stanford Three-Community Study

At the same time that plans were being made for the Finnish project, John W. Farquhar, a physician and researcher at Stanford University, put together a multidisciplinary team to conduct an ambitious community-based trial to lower risk of CVD. The emphasis of the study was to determine whether mass media programs could be effective in reducing CVD risk. Three small towns in northern California with a population of about 15,000 each were enrolled in the study.

Gilroy, one of the towns, received 3 years of mass media intervention that included television spots, radio ads and programs, mass mailings of printed information, newspaper columns and stories, and billboards. Watsonville, another town, received the same mass media intervention because it shared radio and television stations with Gilroy, but high-risk persons identified by the risk factor assessments were also targeted for a face-to-face behavior modification program. This intervention targeted smoking cessation, weight loss, low-fat diet, and increases in physical activity. Tracy, the third town, was the control community and received only the risk factor assessments.

The results of this study indicated that CVD risk factors could indeed be changed in an entire community. Levels of risk decreased significantly in both Watsonville and Gilroy, but because of the face-to-face program in Watsonville, changes occurred more quickly there. Interestingly, risk in Tracy increased over the 3 years of the project. The intervention communities reduced CVD risk 25 to 30 percent, indicating that community-based interventions can have important effects (Meyer, Nash, McAlister, Maccoby, & Farquhar, 1980). These results stimulated several other larger projects in the United States, Europe, and Australia.

The Stanford Five-City Project

The Five-City Project (FCP) was designed to answer several questions that were not addressed by the Three-Community Study. The intervention began in 1980. The major differences between the two studies are as follows:

1. The FCP communities were larger and more complex. They ranged in population from 44,000 to 130,000.
2. The intervention in the FCP lasted 9 years and involved a more comprehensive mass media plus community organization strategy.
3. The FCP included a major youth education component.
4. There was an emphasis on establishing permanent programs that would be continued by community agencies.
5. Not only would risk factors be monitored, but the long-term intervention allowed evaluation of changes in CVD morbidity and mortality.

Monterey and Salinas were chosen as the intervention cities because they share television and radio stations. Educational products

BOX 19·2

FOCUS ON RESEARCH

Results of a 5-Year Community Intervention: The Stanford Five-City Project

A 1990 report in the *Journal of the American Medical Association* described the Five-City Project intervention methods and results on knowledge and CVD risk factors (Farquhar, Fortmann, Flora, et al., 1990). The study was designed to see if the comprehensive educational program reduced heart attacks and death from CVD, but that will be reported later.

The program promoted diet change, increased physical activity, decreases in cigarette use, and control of weight, blood pressure, and blood cholesterol through personal change and medical care. In addition to ongoing educational programs, there were four or five campaigns each year consisting of special events, like contests, new classes, and media programs.

The investigators estimated how much each person in the community heard, saw, or participated in some aspect of the educational program. Each adult in the community was exposed to an average of about 100 educational episodes per year, accounting for about 26 hours per person over the 9 years. Only about 7 percent of the exposure was in classes or lectures. Mass media reached people the most, with 34 percent of the exposure coming from television and radio, 41 percent from booklets, and 18 percent from newspapers and newsletters.

Even though people in the control cities made changes in their risk factors over the course of the study, the intervention cities improved significantly more on knowledge, blood pressure, and smoking. There were no significant differences concerning cholesterol or obesity. When all these risk factors were combined into an overall risk score, the intervention cities were found to have decreased their CVD risk by 16 percent more than the control cities. A reduction of CVD death rates by 16 percent would be dramatic, so these findings support the effectiveness of community interventions.

The authors indicate some of the reasons why the 5-year program did not have even larger effects. The average adult in an intervention city spent about 1 hour each year watching or listening to 70 television or radio ads from the Five-City Project. During that same year, they spent about 292 hours watching 35,000 other ads on television. Many of these ads encouraged people to eat *more* of the foods the Five-City Project was trying to get people to eat *less* of. The intervention provided just a drop in the big ocean of information that surrounds people each day. Because of the relatively low quantity of educational exposure, the Five-City Project was constantly challenged to produce materials and messages of high quality so that they would attract attention.

Conducting a health behavioral change program for entire cities is expensive when you look at the total dollar cost, but the Five-City Project intervention was estimated to cost about $4 per resident per year. This is 4 percent of what the same population spends on cigarettes each year. How much health behavior change could be accomplished and how many lives could be saved if health promoters had the same budgets as "un-health" promoters?

and services were developed at Stanford, based on consultation with community agencies and feedback from community surveys. The products were then distributed through community organizations. A small community organization staff was hired in each city, and it was responsible for working with community agencies and media outlets to involve them in the health promotion effort (Farquhar et al., 1985). The intervention has been completed, and most program components have been transferred to community control with limited input from Stanford University staff. See Box 19-2 for a summary of the effects of the program on risk factors.

The Minnesota Heart Health Program

The Minnesota Heart Health Program (MHHP) involves three intervention communities and three control communities. The MHHP operates in a staged approach, such that intervention began in a small town of 30,000. Two years later, the intervention was started in a city of 110,000; and finally, a suburban area of 80,000 entered the program.

Media programs were similar to the Stanford Five-City Project, and they were organized by annual campaigns focusing on the four targeted risk factors of smoking, normal blood pressure, physical activity, and diet. A "direct education" program was organized around a Health Education Center located in each intervention community. Sixty percent of the adult population was targeted for risk factor screening. Each person screened was given a Health Passport, high-risk individuals were referred for medical care, and there were health education classes in smoking cessation, diet change, and physical activity. Direct heart health education was also conducted in the schools. Physician education about CVD prevention was a major program component.

A comprehensive community organization plan guided efforts to involve every segment of the intervention communities in the program. The intervention began in 1981, and the evaluation will include changes in CVD risk factors, morbidity, and mortality (Carlaw, Mittelmark, Bracht, & Luepker, 1984). The MHHP is directed by Henry Blackburn, an epidemiologist who believes that our detailed knowledge of what causes heart disease gives us the basic knowledge needed to mount programs to reduce CVD in an entire population.

The Pawtucket Heart Health Program

The Pawtucket Heart Health Program (PHHP) targets a largely blue-collar Rhode Island city of 72,000. This program was initiated by Richard Carleton, chief of cardiology at the local community hospital, who felt that prevention would be more effective in improving the health of the city than reliance on treatment of only those with clinical CVD. The PHHP developed a model for intervening on four levels of social structure: individual, small group, organization, and community. Because electronic media use was not practical in this community, the emphasis of the intervention that began in 1982 was community organization. One unique feature of the PHHP was the extensive use of volunteers. Communitywide intervention events included volunteer-run risk factor screenings, quit-smoking contests, monthly weigh-ins, and an exercise program developed jointly with the city's parks and recreation department. The effective use of volunteers kept down the costs of this community-based program (Elder et al., 1986).

Each of the current generation of community-based CVD prevention programs uses similar methods. They all use media programs, face-to-face interventions, and community organization, but the emphases vary from project to project. Each project has already published promising results from some intervention components, but the major results on CVD morbidity and mortality are still being

BOX 19·3

FOCUS ON WOMEN

A Community Approach to Promoting Breast Self-Examination

Although many of the large community-based health behavior-change programs focused on reducing risk of CVD, other programs have targeted alcohol use and HIV disease prevention. Cancer researchers are interested in changing smoking and dietary habits, along with cancer screening practices. An important cancer screening practice for women is breast self-examination, and an effort to reduce cancer risk in women was conducted in New England.

It is recommended that women systematically examine their breasts monthly for early detection of breast lumps. Women who do some form of breast self-exam have been found to detect cancers at an earlier stage and survive longer than women who do not do regular self-exams. Although the behavior takes only a few minutes a month, most women do not conduct self-exams, and the most common barriers are lack of confidence that they are doing exams correctly, forgetting, and anxiety about detecting breast cancer. A community intervention was designed to overcome these barriers and improve the quality of the technique and the frequency of breast self-examinations (BSE).

In the first year the intervention was delivered to groups of women in various community groups, such as clubs, work sites, clinics, churches, and groups of friends in homes. The 30- to 60-minute program included a discussion of breast cancer, a videotape demonstrating proper BSE technique, BSE practice with silicone breast models, and a calendar booklet to remind women to practice. Mass media was used to change community norms about BSE and provide some training to women who did not attend groups. Television was used to recruit women for the groups, and a 30-minute program showed a complete training session. Women presented testimonials about the benefits of BSE on the radio and in newspaper articles. One of the most effective recruiting methods was inviting women who had participated in the groups to host training sessions in their homes.

The intervention in year 2 was designed to reduce barriers to long-term adherence. To combat forgetting, a variety of reminders were developed. Menstruating women were told to practice the day after their period ends, and they were given a tampon container and message pad with the project logo. Nonmenstruating women selected a consistent day each month (for example, payday), and they were given reminder message pads. All women were given self-reward cards that suggested various ways women could reward themselves after performing BSE (for example, call a friend, listen to favorite music). To help women maintain high BSE confidence, newsletters and television spots reminded them of correct BSE technique, and physicians urged regular practice on radio spots. To reduce anxiety associated with BSE, newspaper and radio spots stressed that 80 percent of all breast lumps are not cancerous and that early detection leads to less extensive treatment and higher cure rates. A hot line was advertised throughout the year.

Four communities in Vermont, with populations ranging from 3000 to 8000, participated in the study. Two were intervention, and two were control. At least 320 from each community were surveyed by phone to determine BSE practice. A sample of these women were interviewed in their homes to assess their BSE skills with silicone breast models.

At the end of the first year, about 40 percent of the women in the experimental communities reported attending a training session, compared with none of the controls. About 45 percent of the intervention community women remembered reading something about BSE in the newspaper, and more than 20 percent saw something on television. Almost no control women reported media exposure to program materials. The second year evaluation also indicated that large percentages of women in the intervention communities were affected by the media campaign.

Over the 2 years, the intervention communities improved regular BSE practice by about 12 to 15 percentage points, while the controls improved by only 5 percentage points. Thus, the campaign had a significant influence on BSE practice. Observations of BSE technique during home interviews showed that women in the intervention communities were significantly better than women in control communities. The intervention increased women's confidence in their BSE skills as well as social support from friends and family.

This study showed that an important health behavior for women can be changed over a substantial period of time. The group training was effective for both frequency of practice and BSE skills. The mass media maintenance program was also effective. The first year costs were about $46,000 per community, including staff, educational materials, and mass media production and airtime. The project received important assistance from women in the community who recruited others to the group sessions. To combat a disease that will strike 1 of 10 women, this type of program may be a good investment (Worden et al., 1990).

awaited. Similar programs that are less comprehensive and are not being so carefully evaluated are being implemented by health departments and other agencies throughout the world, so these pacesetting community health promotion programs have already begun to impact the practice of health care.

Now that the basic concepts and approaches to community intervention are well-known, they are being applied to communities with specific needs. The current trend is to bring these interventions to ethnic communities that typically have limited access to other health programs. The Washington Heights-Inwood Healthy Heart Program targets a population of 200,000 residents in northern Manhattan, New York City. The population is primarily immigrants from the Dominican Republic, and the average income and educational level is low. The program is working closely with community organizations and makes extensive use of volunteers (Shea, Basch, Lantigua, & Wechsler, 1992). A more limited program focused on the single risk factor of weight loss. This program targeted overweight African American women and was conducted in churches in Baltimore. Participating women not only lost weight, but their blood pressures decreased as well (Kumanyika & Charleston, 1992).

STRATEGIES OF COMMUNITY-BASED HEALTH PROMOTION

People receive information and other influences on their behavior from a wide variety of sources, so many types of health behavior-change programs can be appropriate. Examples of some of the major strategies of community intervention are described in this section.

Mass Media

Mass media is a part of our lives, and more often than not it promotes unhealthful lifestyles. However, there are at least four ways that mass media can contribute to community health promotion (Flora & Cassady, 1990). First, the media can be used as the primary change agent. A television show or printed booklet may be used to teach people how to change behavior. Second, the media can complement other interventions. For example, similar information could be provided via radio, mailings, and special classes during a given month to provide a focus on drunk driving. Third, media can be used to promote other programs. Because the mass media reach so many people, this is an effective means of letting people know about health promotion materials or programs. Fourth, media messages can support lifestyle change by encouraging maintenance of behavior, providing role models for healthful behavior, and generally keeping health on the public's agenda. Community interventions often use the media for all of these purposes.

On any given day about 80 percent of the U.S. population watches television (Comstock & Paik, 1991), so it is a source of information that cannot be ignored. Television is not the only medium that can be used for health promotion. Newspapers can carry articles and columns on health promotion, and they can advertise products or services. Radio can be used effectively to promote programs, and they allow access to targeted populations. For example, in the Stanford Community Studies, the local Spanish-language station aired a soap opera–like series that dealt with smoking and diet change. This was very successful.

Printed materials can also be used effectively. Behavioral tip sheets, low-fat cookbooks, and instructions for changing diet and exercise have been developed by many community programs to fit the needs of their own populations. Print and electronic media can be combined. For example, a smoker's Quit Kit was promoted by a week-long series on group smoking cessation methods that was aired on the local television evening news. The news show demonstrated ways of quitting in groups or on your own, and this information was reinforced in the Quit Kit that was available for free. Smokers who requested the kit were surveyed by phone. Of these smokers, 52 percent reported watching at least one of the television news segments, and 69 percent said that they used at least one behavioral recommendation from the program. At a 1-year follow-up, 18 percent of the smokers had quit. It was estimated that about 3900 smokers, or 12.5 percent of the smokers in the country, watched at least one of the shows, so this appeared to be a cost-effective way of promoting cessation in the community (Sallis, Flora, Fortmann, Taylor, & Maccoby, 1985).

Risk Factor Screening

Several community programs emphasize screening of the population to detect elevations in serum cholesterol and blood pressure, and to motivate high-risk individuals to make behavioral changes or seek appropriate medical care. A study was conducted as part of the Minnesota Heart Health Program to assess the effectiveness of risk factor screening as part of a comprehensive community-based prevention program (Murray et al., 1986).

One group was randomly assigned to attend a screening at a central Heart Health Center, while the control group was not invited until 1 year later. Of those invited to be screened, about 50 percent were actually screened. During the screening session, results were returned and educational messages were delivered by videotape, printed materials, or both. Each screenee spent 20 minutes with a health counselor who provided them with personalized interpretations of results and instructions on changing health behaviors and risk factors. Both groups were assessed for risk factors 1 year later to determine what effect the screening had on behavior and risk factors.

It appeared that the screening group decreased serum cholesterol and systolic blood pressure and increased physical activity significantly in the year after the screening. These variables were also different from those of the control group. Thus, screening, when it is combined with immediate and personalized counseling that includes specific recommendations for behavior change, can produce substantial risk factor changes. The counseling received during the screening may have also made the participants more aware of the many messages and programs that were available to them in the community as part of the overall Minnesota Heart Health Program intervention.

A somewhat different approach toward screening was adopted by the Pawtucket Heart Health Program (Lefebvre et al., 1986). Rather than conduct screenings at a central site, screenings were organized at numerous community events. They also focused exclusively on cholesterol screening and diet assessment for an intensive 2-month campaign called "Know Your Cholesterol." Physicians in the community were contacted to prepare them for an expected increase in desire for treatment of hypercholesterolemia. Local restaurants were enrolled in a supporting campaign to mark their low-fat, low-cholesterol menu items with "Four-Heart" stickers. The program was kicked off when the "Heart Check" van with a "Know Your Cholesterol" banner participated in the St. Patrick's Day parade. Coupons for $1 off the $5 price of two screenings were given out along the parade route. A Cook-Off contest and newspaper articles on cholesterol and diet change reinforced the 39 screening events that were held at work sites, churches, and community sites.

Over 1400 people were screened, and more than 60 percent of them had serum cholesterol levels over the goal of 200 mg/dl. Besides receiving an interpretation of their cholesterol level, each participant received a self-help Nutrition Kit that was designed to help them make healthful dietary changes. More than 70 percent of those screened returned for a follow-up cholesterol measurement, and the average reduction was 29 mg/dl. This is a good example of a well-planned community program that included the right product, promotion, place, and price to make it a success in improving an important risk factor. This program also required a great deal of planning and cooperation from many different community organizations.

Programs at Work Sites and Other Community Settings

Although churches and other community settings are sometimes used for CVD prevention programs (Lasater, Wells, Carleton, & Elder, 1986), work sites have most commonly been incorporated into community intervention programs. Work sites are desirable settings for

---

BOX 19·4

FOCUS ON DIVERSITY

Screening for Elevated Cholesterol in the African American Community

Although religious organizations have been used for health promotion in many locations, churches have emerged as a particularly important site for reaching African Americans. There is a tradition in the black church of supplying social, emotional, and material support, in addition to religious services. Community norms are set there, and churches are a focal point for social networks and a catalyst for change in the black community. This pattern of ministering to multiple needs of the congregation and the greater community is compatible with health promotion efforts. Because of the high incidence of CVD in the black population, there have been a variety of risk reduction programs in black churches. One such program was conducted in Oklahoma City.

After consultation with the local association of black ministers, six churches ranging in size from 200 to 1200 members were selected, along with one public library in the area. Risk factor screening was conducted before and after Sunday services, and it was promoted through ministers' announcements, church bulletin boards, radio spots, and community newspaper stories. Health professionals and students volunteered to conduct the screenings.

Six hundred sixty-one adults aged 21 to 89 were screened for blood pressure, pulse rate, height, weight, and serum cholesterol. Total cholesterol was measured using the finger-stick method, and a portable analyzer provided prompt feedback. All participants received their results and a brief interpretation.

Two different interventions were conducted with the 348 persons found to have total cholesterol over 200 mg/dl, which is higher than optimal according to the National Cholesterol Education Program guidelines. The education group was invited to attend six weekly diet modification classes at the church, offered at a variety of times. The program covered substituting low-fat and low-sodium foods, shopping, food preparation, label reading,

and eating in restaurants. Self-monitoring, role playing, and food sampling were among the behavior-change methods used. An important part of the program was that it was implemented by trained members of the church. This use of "natural helpers" in the community means that the program can continue once the researchers are gone. This is a way of "empowering" the community to meet its own needs. Instructional materials were mailed to those in the education condition who did not attend the program. Almost 50 percent attended half the sessions. The 174 participants in the referral condition had their results mailed to their primary physician.

Six months after the initial screening, the 348 with elevated cholesterol were invited for a second assessment. Although 75 percent of the education group was remeasured, only 36 percent of the referral group returned, so it is difficult to make conclusions about that group. Total cholesterol levels decreased 10 percent in the education group, which is similar to other diet-change programs. Among the referral subjects who returned, a 16 percent decrease in serum cholesterol was found. Although this might suggest that screening and feedback to the individual and the physician is a more effective intervention, the small number of referral subjects who were rescreened makes it impossible to come to a conclusion.

Despite the fact that this is not a carefully controlled study, it is a good example of how the church can be used as an effective site for organizing health promotion activities in the African American community. A large number of people were screened, nutrition education was delivered by people from the community, and important changes in blood cholesterol were detected. Programs like this need to be expanded on a long-term basis if they are to make a contribution to improving the health of African Americans. Because not all blacks attend church regularly, church-based programs cannot be considered the only appropriate approach for this segment of society (Wiist & Flack, 1990).

health promotion because most adults are employed, people spend a great deal of time at work, there are existing communication channels that can be used for health education, and companies are motivated to keep employees healthy and productive. A wide variety of programs have been conducted at work sites to address every CVD risk factor (Sallis, Hill, Fortmann, & Flora, 1986). Although small-group behavior- change programs are most common, at work sites it is possible to influence the environment and policies that will affect the entire work force.

A comprehensive work site program designed to promote physical activity and other health-promoting behaviors employed screening, behavior-change groups, environmental changes, and policy changes (Blair, Piserchia, Wilbur, & Crowder, 1986). Four Johnson and Johnson companies (N = 2600) were offered a comprehensive health promotion program, and three other Johnson and Johnson companies (N = 1700) received only yearly health screenings. In both conditions 75 percent of the employees participated in the health screenings. In the health promotion companies, the screening was followed by a 3-hour seminar on the variety of programs available to the employees and how the work site would support a healthy lifestyle. Classes were available on the employee's own time either at the work site or at nearby facilities. Frequent educational and promotional information was distributed through newsletters, health fairs, contests, and displays throughout the work sites. All of these companies make exercise space available and convenient. Employees were strongly encouraged to take advantage of these opportunities. Thus, the environment supported the educational messages.

After 2 years the employees in the health promotion companies increased their vigorous physical activity by 104 percent, while the control employees increased by only 33 percent. Not only was this large difference seen after 2 years, but improvement was seen in women as well as men and in blue-collar as well as white-collar employees. Figure 19-1 shows the percentage of women and men who began vigorous activity during the program.

Health Promotion Competitions

A relatively new technique in health promotion is the competition or contest, and there are several reasons to believe that they should be more effective than other types of programs (Brownell & Felix, 1987). A contest that is promoted well is a highly visible event that should be effective in stimulating more participation than a class or other standard type of program. Prizes are an important aspect of competitions, and these are felt to be effective reinforcers for behavior change. Finally, since groups will compete against each other to lose the most weight or to have the highest smoking cessation rate, this may stimulate increased cooperation and social support within groups.

FIGURE 19-1
Percentage of participants who started vigorous exercise by year 2. These individuals did not participate in vigorous exercise at baseline. Light bars indicate health promotion program employees; dark bars, health screen only employees. (From Blair S. N., et al.) A Public Health Intervention Model for work-site Health Promotion, *Journal of American Medical Association* 1986, *255*(7), 921–926, Copyright © 1986 American Medical Association.

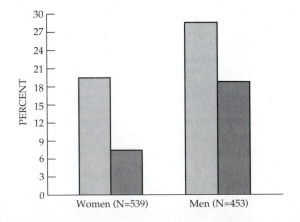

One of the first competitions involved three banks that challenged one another to a weight loss contest (Brownell, Cohen, Stunkard, Felix, & Cooley, 1984). Each participant was given a 12-week goal, and results were publicly posted in the lobby of each bank. Participants paid $5 to join, and this pool of money was awarded to the winner. There were no group meetings, but each participant was given a behavioral weight loss manual. Across the three banks, 31 percent of the work force participated. The mean weight loss was 13 pounds, which is similar to results of intensive clinic programs. At the 6-month follow-up, 80 percent of the initial weight loss was maintained. Not only was the program popular and effective, but it was cost-effective as well. As shown in Figure 19-2 the cost per pound lost was much less for work site competition than for traditional weight loss programs.

Smoking cessation contests have been conducted in communities as part of the Stanford Five-City Project (King, Flora, Fortmann, & Taylor, 1987) and the Pawtucket Heart Health Program (Elder et al., 1987). Both programs had follow-up quit rates of a respectable 15 percent.

In most studies competitions have had high participation rates, reasonable success rates, and low cost. They are also exciting for participants and make health promotion fun. Although competitions are not appropriate for all health promotion programs, this is a promising method that will surely continue to be used in many community programs.

ENVIRONMENTAL AND POLICY CHANGES

Some health behaviors are so deeply ingrained in the society that they are very difficult to change through educational programs (Winett, King, & Altman, 1989). In these cases alterations in the environment or in public policies may be more effective in changing behavior of the population. Some health-promoting policies can be implemented only on a state or federal level, such as improved food labeling or tobacco taxation. However, other policies can be changed by communities, such as im-

FIGURE 19-2

Weight loss costs for different programs (the cost per 1 percent reduction in percentage overweight for different weight loss programs). Estimates were obtained from a university clinic (Stanford Eating Disorders Program), from a popular commercial group, and from two work site programs using either lay or professional leaders. (From Brownell et al., 1984.)

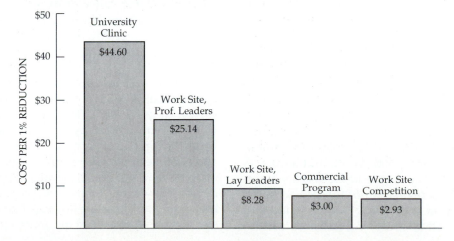

provement of local parks to encourage exercise, information on healthy choices in restaurants or food stores, and regulation of smoking in public places. Achieving these policy changes often requires working through the political process. Since most health professionals are unaccustomed to this type of work, progress in this area has been slow. However, there are great opportunities there for community-based prevention programs. Some examples of environmental and policy changes can be found in the nutrition and smoking areas.

Mayer, Dubbert, and Elder (1989) reviewed several interventions that promoted healthy nutrition at the point of choice, that is, at restaurants and food markets. At restaurants and cafeterias, most of the interventions consisted of posters and labels to encourage the selection of low-fat or low-calorie foods. These simple informational strategies were successful in fast-food restaurants and public, work site, and dormitory cafeterias. Thus, it appears that merely providing consumers with information highlighting healthy food choices can influence their behavior.

Interventions conducted in food markets have generally been less successful. All such attempts have consisted of posters in aisles, signs on shelves, or brochures promoting healthful choices. Some interventions targeted broad categories of low-fat foods, while others focused specifically on dairy products, oils, or breakfast cereals. Of six studies conducted, only two changed sales in targeted categories. Since there is so much competing printed information in supermarkets, perhaps announcements over loudspeakers or video presentations would draw more attention to the health message.

Winett, King, and Altman (1989) presented several policy changes that could affect smoking behavior among both youth and adults. A great deal of policy debate in the last few years has focused on regulation of tobacco advertising. In 1 year alone the tobacco industry spends over $3 billion on advertising, including 40,000 billboards in the United States, about six full-page ads in most magazines, and sponsorship of many entertainment and sporting events.

The effect of tobacco advertising on magazines is particularly apparent. The content of stories in 12 women's magazines was studied from 1967 to 1979 (Whelan, Sheridan, Meister, & Mosher, 1981). The mean number of anti-smoking or smoking cessation articles was two; however, *Good Housekeeping*, the only magazine that did not accept cigarette ads, ran 11 antismoking articles in that time period. The magazines that did accept cigarette ads featured many health stories on other topics: an average of 4.5 articles on stress, 8.6 on nutrition, 9.3 on contraceptives, and 21.5 on mental health.

Many health professionals are convinced that cigarette advertising has the effect of censoring coverage of the health consequences of smoking. A ban on cigarette advertising would clearly make it more difficult for tobacco companies to replace the 1 million smokers lost each year through death or quitting. The tobacco industry must recruit 5000 new smokers in the United States per day to replace these losses. There are currently proposals in Congress to severely restrict or entirely ban promotion of tobacco products. The arguments for the ban cite the fact that tobacco is the number one preventable cause of death in the United States. The arguments against the ban emphasize First Amendment guarantees of free speech and insist that applies to the tobacco companies.

Taxation can be used as an intervention to modify health behavior, and tobacco tax rates vary widely by state. The price of cigarettes, which is influenced by the tax rate, affects young people much more than committed adult smokers. Regular smokers will smoke no matter what the price, because they are addicted. However, young people have much less money to spare for luxuries like cigarettes, so the price of cigarettes influences their smoking habits substantially. It has been estimated that an 8- to 16-cent increase per pack in the cigarette tax would influence 1 to 2 million young people to quit smoking or not to start (Warner, 1986). Income from state taxes on tobacco can be directly applied to health-related research or to school health education. Only seven states use tobacco tax money for health programs: Alaska, California, Idaho, Kentucky, Louisiana, Nebraska, and New Jersey.

Tobacco is readily available to virtually everyone. This includes teenagers, even though it is illegal to sell cigarettes to minors in most states. In California, the law states that tobacco products can be sold only to those 18 or older. However, in one test, teens aged 14 to 16 were able to buy cigarettes at 74 percent of the stores and 100 percent of the vending machines they visited (Altman, Foster, Rasenick-Douss, & Tye, 1989). A community program was then begun to reduce the sale of cigarettes to minors. The program had three parts:

1. Community education. Public service announcements were produced and distributed to 13 television stations and 23 radio stations. The program was covered on local news shows. The media campaign was supported by talks given to community groups.

2. Direct merchant education. Merchants were randomly assigned to receive no contact, mailed information, or a personal visit from project staff. Stores with mailed information or personal contact received a kit that included facts about tobacco use by teens, information on how to train employees to not sell tobacco to minors, a copy of the state law, and warning signs stating that they would not sell tobacco to minors.

3. Education of chief executive officers. Since many of the stores that sell tobacco are chains, it was felt that company policies needed to be changed to make refusal to sell tobacco to minors a high priority. Chief executive officers received a letter urging them to

make it a policy not to make illegal tobacco sales to minors, all stores would post warning signs stating this policy, employees would be trained to implement the policy, and compliance with the law and policy would be monitored. Twenty-three of twenty-four executives promised to take action on this matter.

After 6 months of the community program, the same teens tried to buy cigarettes from the same stores. They were only able to buy cigarettes at 39 percent of the stores, and this was almost a 50 percent decrease from the pretest. The community program appeared to be very effective. All categories of stores were less likely to sell cigarettes to the teens.

The study of direct merchant education indicated that the type of information used did not make a difference, because stores in all three experimental conditions decreased sales to minors. However, there was a significant difference in posting of warning signs. Very few stores with no education posted signs, but sizable percentages of stores with either mail information or personal visits posted the signs, as shown in Figure 19-3. This study shows that the availability of cigarettes to teenagers can be reduced by community education, making it more difficult for young people to take up the smoking habit.

FIGURE 19-3

Effect of education on posting signs about sales of cigarettes to minors. (From Altman et al., 1989.)

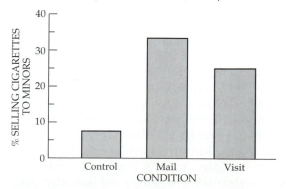

HEALTH PROMOTION ACTIVITIES IN COMMUNITIES

The research on community interventions is well known to health professionals, and there is great public interest in health promotion. However, the health care system has not responded by offering programs. It is assumed that people are seeking health promotion services in other settings. A few studies have explored the extent to which these services are available in communities. In a survey of four midwestern cities, the most programs were available for exercise, followed by smoking cessation, nutrition, heart disease education and screening, weight loss, stress management, and cancer education. Forty-one percent of the programs were sponsored by work sites, and other nontraditional health organizations such as schools, churches, and commercial businesses accounted for another 33 percent. Only 28 percent of health promotion programs were sponsored by traditional providers such as government, medical institutions, and nonprofit agencies (Weisbrod, Bracht, Pirie, & Veblen-Mortenson, 1991).

Another study also examined nontraditional sources of health promotion interventions. Nearly two-thirds of churches and labor unions had some sort of program for their members. The most frequent programs were single-session presentations and distribution of materials. About one-third of supermarkets reported distributing brochures on healthful nutrition. About one-third of restaurants reported they promoted the health of customers by enforcing no-smoking policies. Though large numbers of community organizations report participation in health-promotion programs, most of the programs were minimal. However, about 10 to 15 percent of churches and labor unions sponsored multiple-session educational programs, and a similar percentage of supermarkets and restaurants had signs to encourage healthful food choices (Elder, Sallis, Mayer, Hammond, & Peplinski, 1989). The question remains whether the quantity and quality of health-promotion programs in community settings will increase over time. Hopefully, the improved programs that are developed in research studies will be used in community settings. These studies clearly show that health promotion programs and information are available in many places in many communities. Community interventions are becoming part of the health care delivery system.

SUMMARY

Community interventions attempt to use resources in the local environment to motivate health behavior change. A variety of major health promotion studies have been conducted in North Karelia, Finland; northern California; the state of Minnesota; Pawtucket, Rhode Island; Cardiff, Wales; Germany; Sydney, Australia; and other locations. Most of these studies demonstrate that community-based approaches using mass media and social marketing can reduce the community risk for cardiovascular disease.

These approaches are based on a variety of different theories and models including social cognitive theory, communication-behavior change theory, social marketing, and social ecology. In other words, the community-based campaigns use modern behavioral science theory to promote healthful behaviors in entire cities. In addition, some of the projects use community organization to improve the chances that the project will succeed and continue on its own, once the original promoters of the program have to leave the area. This is a crucial element, because if programs do not continue, it is unlikely that the healthful behaviors will persist.

Community interventions can be applied to many health behaviors and disease conditions. CVD prevention programs are the most common, but programs to change cancer-related diet and smoking behaviors, cancer screening behaviors, drug and alcohol use, seat belt and child restraint use, dental hygiene, and other behaviors are already under way. It is clear that community-based programs will be seen more often in future years, although the scope of such programs will depend on the enthusiasm of the public and government funding agencies. Whatever the form future prevention efforts take, behavior change will play a central role. Therefore, behavioral scientists need to continue to develop more effective methods of changing health behaviors that can be applied to improve the cardiovascular health of individuals, communities, and nations.

KEY TERMS

Community strategy. An approach to the modification of health habits through campaigns at the community level. Community interventions typically combine the psychological approach of individual behavior change, and the public health approach of environmental and policy changes that do not require individual actions.

Community organization. Activation of a community to use its own social structures and resources to accomplish health goals decided mainly by community residents and consistent with local values.

North Karelia Project. An experimental project in Finland in which risk factors were modified in one area (North Karelia) and compared with surrounding states.

Stanford Three-Community Study. A study that compared coronary heart disease risk factors in three small northern California towns. The communities receiving special interventions reduced the risks of cardiovascular disease 25 to 30 percent.

Stanford Five-City Project. A project sponsored by Stanford University in medium-sized California cities. This project was designed to affect risk factors through mass media and permanent changes in community organizations.

Minnesota Heart Health Program. A large-scale program to produce changes in cardiovascular disease risk factors in three cities of varying size in the state of Minnesota.

Pawtucket Heart Health Program. A communitywide intervention in Pawtucket, Rhode Island. The program attempted to intervene at four levels: individual, small group, community organization, and community at large.

Media programs. Mass media are often used to facilitate behavior change, complement other interventions, promote other programs, and maintain behavior. Mass media include television, radio, newspaper, and magazines. Other media include printed materials and videos.

Environmental approach. Attempts to change individual behavior or health risks through changes in the physical and social environments.

Communication-behavior change framework. An approach developed by McGuire that is used to design messages for health promotion campaigns that are appropriate for specific audiences.

Social marketing framework. The use of marketing techniques to promote change in health behavior. This approach is based on the four P's: product, promotion, place, and price.

Social ecology framework. The study of social, institutional, and cultural contexts in the interaction between people and their environments.

Risk factor screening. Screening for risk factors such as serum cholesterol or blood pressure is a method for motivating individuals to make a behavior change.

Work site health promotion. The use of programs in the work setting to encourage health behavior change. These can be either educational, such as smoking cessation classes, or environmental, such as smoking restrictions. Often, companies can boost their own productivity along with the health of their employees through organized programs.

Competition. Competitions between companies or organizations can be used to motivate health behavior change.

Summary

CHAPTER 20

For Those Interested in More Information about Health and Human Behavior

We have covered a lot of ground in this book. However, a textbook can contain only a limited amount of information. We hope that this will be only the beginning and that you will want to learn more about our field. In this final chapter, we offer just a few comments on the field of health psychology. We describe the organizations that health psychologists belong to and how to get more information.

ORGANIZED HEALTH PSYCHOLOGY

The development of health psychology has been fostered by formal organized groups. The American Psychological Association (APA) is one of the largest academically based societies in the world. In 1978, the APA formally recognized a Division of Health Psychology as their Division 38. Although the APA has 47 divisions, the Division of Health Psychology has become one of the larger and more influential groups. In the early years of the division, the membership expanded very rapidly and drew from most of the established areas of psychology. The division now has more than 3500 members. In order to help shape the field, the division also held two major conferences.

The first set priorities for training in health psychology (Arden House Publications, 1987), while the second set priorities for research in the field (Harpers Ferry Conference, 1989).

The second major organization relevant to health psychology is the Society for Behavioral Medicine. This organization, which includes approximately 3000 members, is more multidisciplinary than APA Division 38. While the APA division includes mostly psychologists, the Society for Behavioral Medicine includes physicians from a variety of different specialties, dietitians, nurses, public health professionals, anthropologists, sociologists, and other groups. The goals of the organization include the encouragement of multidisciplinary research and practice. Other organizations that promote health psychology include the American Public Health Association (APHA), the Society of Public Health Educators (SOPHE), the American Psychosomatic Society (APS), the American Psychological Society (also APS), the Society for Medical Decision Making, and a variety of others.

Although health psychology is a relatively new field, it is well represented in several organizations. Research in health psychology is

461

reported in a wide variety of journals and discussed in many different professional organizations and societies. Some journals with a primary focus on health psychology include *Health Psychology, Psychology and Health, Journal of Behavioral Medicine,* and *Annals of Behavioral Medicine.*

WHAT DO HEALTH PSYCHOLOGISTS DO?

Since health psychology is such a new field, the roles that specialists in this area will play are still becoming defined. Some of the major areas include patient care, community work, teaching, and research.

Patient Care

The majority of the members in both Division 38 of the American Psychological Association and the Society for Behavioral Medicine are involved in patient care. These individuals are typically trained as clinical psychologists or in a related clinical discipline. Most provide care directly to patients. This might involve stress management training, smoking counseling, weight management, or pain management. Many of these individuals are also involved in psychological testing and treatment planning. Some work in private practice, while others are employed by hospitals, medical schools, or Heath Maintenance Organization (HMO's).

Community Work

A smaller but important group of health psychologists are employed in community work. This might involve the development of campaigns to change health behavior or programs designed to improve delivery of health services.

Teaching

A substantial number of health psychologists describe their primary role as university teaching. Your professor for this course might serve as a good example. An increasing number of health psychologists teach in medical schools. They teach medical students, residents, and even faculty about the issues you read about in this book. Nearly all health psychologists are trained to do research, and most are actively engaged in some research project.

RELATIONSHIPS WITH OTHER PROFESSIONALS

Health psychologists work with people from many disciplines in their patient care, community teaching, and research work. These relationships have generally been very productive and have led to breakthroughs in many areas. However, Harris (1991), Altmaier (1991), and Alcorn (1991) suggest that there will be boundary disputes between psychologists and other health care providers in the future. Those currently offering psychological services in health settings include nurses, health educators, psychologists, social workers, dietitians, exercise physiologists, chiropractors, and a variety of consultants in fields for which there is no recognized specialty or license. Each of these specialties claims to have some specific expertise in patient counseling, and there are arguments in the literature of each field for why they should be the unique provider of some services. Most psychology providers claim to offer the application of behavioral sciences. Yet nurses have long offered programs in stress management, adherence, and patient support. Although physicians have been slow to become involved in psychological services, there are growing numbers of physicians now offering behavioral services, and many residency programs in preventive medicine and family medicine offer some training in counseling.

There are opportunities to offer counseling services in health care. The challenge for psychologists and other behavioral scientists is to demonstrate their unique training and their unique effectiveness.

Other serious turf wars are just beginning to develop. One of them concerns the revision of the *Diagnostic and Statistical Manual (DSM)* of the American Psychiatric Association. Although this document is much maligned, it does provide the basis upon which many providers obtain reimbursement for their services. One of the classifications in the *DSM-III* is the category "psychological and behavioral factors affecting medical conditions." The psychiatric establishment has challenged this classification, suggesting that there is not enough evidence that psychological and behavioral factors influence the expression of physical symptoms or the onset, exacerbation, or clinical course of medical illness. Each feature of this category is being seriously debated for future editions of the *DSM*, and the wording of the revision may impact upon the way health psychology providers are reimbursed. Thus another challenge for psychologists is to continue providing evidence that psychological factors do, indeed, affect the expression and course of medical illness (Stoudemire & Hales, 1991).

The interface between psychologists and psychiatrists will be severely tested by some new proposals arising from the American Psychological Association. Currently, the APA is studying proposals to allow psychologists to prescribe medications. The Department of Defense has funded a demonstration program at Walter Reed Medical Center, and this evaluation has produced some favorable results. One survey of clinical psychologists suggested that the majority (65 percent) support the idea of psychologists prescribing medication (Barkley et al., 1990). Such proposals are certain to stimulate a major fight with psychiatry, and lively debates are expected for the next few years.

However, very little attention has been devoted to the impact of prescription privileges on health care costs and upon the ultimate outcomes for patients. Psychologists and other behavioral scientists should be prepared to participate in this debate.

TRAINING ISSUES

If you have been interested in the topics described in this book, you might want to learn more about how to get further training. Two organizations have published booklets describing available training programs. The Society of Behavioral Medicine and the Health Psychology Division of the American Psychological Association each describe training opportunities. There is considerable overlap in these two booklets. The APA booklet is reproduced as Appendixes A and B. This will describe some of the training opportunities for those who wish careers in psychology. We must warn you, however, that this list may be incomplete. New programs are beginning all the time, and not all programs are listed in the booklet.

If you are considering further training, there are several options. These include medical school, public health school, and graduate training in psychology or other behavioral sciences.

Medical School

One pathway to further training in health and behavior is to attend medical school. Typically, medical school requires a premedical curriculum during the undergraduate years. Most medical schools focus on 2 years of basic science with emphasis on classroom learning. During this time classes are typically taught in large groups. At the end of the second year, students take national board examinations to assess their competencies in basic science. The second 2 years in medical school focus on clinical experiences. Typically, students participate in the practice of surgery, internal medicine, and a variety of other specialty areas. Following medical school most physicians complete a 1-year internship and continue on in specialty training. Those interested in health and behavior might elect a residency in preventive medicine, psychiatry, family medicine, pediatrics, or internal medicine. The psychiatry specialty focuses on mental illness and may be less relevant to issues such as smoking, exercise, and weight control. However, the psychiatry residency may place greater emphasis on substance abuse and related problems. Pediatrics training programs

are devoting greater attention to issues of health and behavior, as are training programs in preventive medicine, family medicine, and internal medicine.

Public Health School

Another option is to attend public health school. There are currently 20 schools of public health in the United States (see Table 20-1). Public health schools typically offer a variety of degrees. The main degree is the Masters of Public Health (M.P.H.). These degrees are offered in several areas. Those most rele-

---

TABLE 20·1

HOW TO CONTACT ACCREDITED SCHOOLS OF PUBLIC HEALTH

For more information simply call or write the schools listed below:

Ms. Linda H. Potts
School of Public Health
University of Alabama at Birmingham
TH 308
University Station
Birmingham, Alabama 35294
(205) 934–4993

Ms. Barbara St. Onge
School of Public Health
Boston University
80 E. Concord St., A-403
Boston, Massachusetts 02118
(617) 638–5052

Mr. G. Nicholas Parlette
School of Public Health
University of California-Berkeley
19 Earl Warren Hall
Berkeley, California 94720
(415) 642–2773

Ms. Peggy K. Convey
UCLA School of Public Health
16–035 CHS
Los Angeles, California 90024–1772
(213) 825–5140

Dr. E. H. Krick
School of Public Health
Loma Linda University
Loma Linda, California 92350
(800) 422–4558

Mr. Jesse Ortiz
Division of Public Health
University of Massachusetts
Amherst, Massachusetts 01003–0037
(413) 545–1303

Ms. Lila Breitner
School of Public Health
University of Michigan
109 South Observatory Street
Ann Arbor, Michigan 48109–2029
(313) 764–5425

Dr. James Boen
School of Public Health
University of Minnesota
420 Delaware Street, SE
Minneapolis, Minnesota 54555–0318
(612) 624–6669

Dr. William T. Small
School of Public Health
University of North Carolina
Rosenau Hall 201-H
Chapel Hill, North Carolina 27514
(919) 966–2177

Dr. Donna Richter
School of Public Health
University of South Carolina
Columbia, South Carolina 29208
(803) 777–4845

Dr. Rita G. Bruce
College of Public Health
University of South Florida
13301 Bruce B.Downs Blvd.
MHH 104
Tampa, Florida 33612–3899
(813) 974–3623

Ms. Peggy Amante
School of Public Health
University of Texas
Health Sciences Center at Houston
P.O. Box 20186
Houston, Texas 77225
(713) 792–4425

Ms. Elaine Boston
School of Public Health and Tropical Medicine
Tulane University
1430 Tulane Avenue
New Orleans, Louisiana 70112
(504) 588–5387

vant to health and behavior are degrees in epidemiology, health promotion, and health education. The curriculum typically involves classroom learning along with practical and research experience. Most students complete the M.P.H. degree within 2 years. Those interested in further training within schools of public health can obtain Ph.D., Dr.P.H., or Sc.D. degrees. Among these degrees the Ph.D. is the most research-oriented, with the Dr.P.H. and the Sc.D. being more practically oriented. Most doctoral programs are designed to be completed within 4 to 5 years, although the actual amount of time taken to complete the program varies from student to student.

Psychology Training in Programs

There are a wide variety of psychology training programs relevant to health psychology and health and human behavior. Some of these are clinical psychology programs which prepare the student for a career in the clinical application of behavior principles. Other doctoral programs are oriented toward research or other applications. Some emphasize social psycho-

T A B L E 20 · 1 *continued*

Dr. William A. Van Wie
School of Public Health
Columbia University
600 West 168th Street
New York, New York 10032
(212) 305–3852

Ms. Bernita L. Anderson
School of Public Health
Harvard University
677 Huntington Avenue
Boston, Massachusetts 02115
(617) 732–1036

Ms. Nancy R. Kilonsky
School of Public Health
University of Hawaii
1960 East-West Road
Honolulu, Hawaii 96822
(808) 948–8267

Dr. Louis Rowitz
School of Public Health
University of Illinois at Chicago
P.O. Box 6998
Chicago, Illinois 60680
(312) 996–6620

Dr. Roger A. Lanier
School of Hygiene and
Public Health
Johns Hopkins University
615 North Wolfe St.
Baltimore, Maryland
21205–2179
(301) 955–3610

Dean Charles M. Cameron
College of Public Health
University of Oklahoma
Health Sciences Center
P.O. Box 26901
Oklahoma City, Oklahoma 73190
(405) 271–2232

Ms. Karen S. Peterson
Graduate School of Public Health
University of Pittsburgh
115 Parran Hall
Pittsburgh, Pennsylvania 15261
(412) 624–3002

Ms. Miriam Marquez
School of Public Health
University of Puerto Rico
Medical Sciences Campus
G.P.O. Box 5067
San Juan, Puerto Rico 00936
(809) 758–2525

Ms. Carol Anderson
School of Public Health
San Diego State University
San Diego, California 92182–0405
(619) 265–6317

Dr. Patrician Wahl
School of Public Health and
Community Medicine
University of Washington
SC-30
Seattle, Washington 98195
(206) 543–1144

Ms. Joan Stenner
Department od Epidemiology and
Public San Health
Yale University
School of Medicine
P.O. Box 3333—60   College
Street
New Haven, Connecticut
06510

Dr. Judith Magee
Director of Research
Association of Schools of
Public Health
1015 - 15th Street, NW
Suite 404
Washington, DC 20005
(202) 842–4668

logical issues, while others concentrate on applications of behavioral principles. Appendix A provides a good overview.

If you are considering a career in health and human behavior, we encourage you to discuss the options with your instructor.

SUMMARY

Health will always be one of our most important assets. In this book we have elaborated on the connections between health and behavior. Substantial evidence suggests that behavior and health are intimately intertwined. Many serious chronic illnesses may be caused by poor health habits. Conversely, illness clearly disrupts behavior.

We have only scratched the surface of the many theoretical and practical issues relevant to health and human behavior. We hope that this book has stimulated your interest in the field and that you will pursue further study. Health and behavior is a relatively new field of study, and there will be significant opportunities for research and practical applications in the future. Because we prize health so dearly, there will always be a market for knowledge on how to achieve better health status.

KEY TERMS

APHA. American Public Health Association.

SOPHE. Society of Public Health Educators.

APS. American Psychosomatic Society.

APS. (in addition to the above) American Psychological Society.

APA. American Psychological Association. Division 38 focuses on the field of health psychology.

Health Psychology Doctoral Programs*

QUEBEC

Graduate Secretary
Department of Psychology
Concordia University
1455 Maisonneuve Boulevard
West Montreal, Quebec H3G 1M8

Specialty areas: stress/anxiety/coping: sexual dysfunction

ALABAMA

Thomas J. Boll, Ph.D.
Director, Department of Psychology
Campbell Hall
University of Alabama at Birmingham
Birmingham, AL 35294

Specialty areas: numerous

CALIFORNIA

Charlie Bresler, Ph.D.
Director, Behavioral Medicine
California School of Professional Psychology
1350 M Street
Fresno, CA 93720

Specialty areas: community health: cardiovascular disease

Dr. Michael Jospe
Director, Health Psychology
Professor of Clinical Program
California School of Professional Psychology
2234 Beverly Blvd.
Los Angeles, CA 90057

Specialty areas: pediatrics; cognitive-behavioral oriented

* Compiled by Committee on Education and Training, APA Divisiion 38. Reproduced by permission, Division of Health Psychology, American Psychological Association.

Richard Gervirtz, Ph.D.
Associate Professor
California School of Professional Psychology
6212 Ferris Square
San Diego, CA 92121-1664

Specialty areas: psychosocial factors in health and illness: treatment of psychophysiological disorders; stress, chronic pain

Shelley Taylor, Ph.D.
Professor, Department of Psychology
University of California
1283 Franz Hall
Los Angeles, CA 90024

Specialty areas: social support; chronic disease; primary prevention

Sue O'Donnell
Administrative Assistant II
Graduate Program in Health Psychology
1350 Seventh Avenue, C.S.B.S.
201 University of California
San Francisco, CA 94143-0844

Specialty areas: health psychology; psychophysiology; biopsychology; stress/coping

Dennis P. Saccuzzo, Ph.D.
Director, Joint Doctoral Program
in Clinical Psychology
University of California, San Diego
San Diego State University Psychology Research
and Training Facility (PART)
6363 Alyarado Road
San Diego, CA 92120

Specialty areas: behavioral medicine, clinical neuro-psychology

COLORADO

Thomas F. Dietvorst, Ph.D.
Assistant Professor
School of Professional Psychology
University of Denver
2300 South Gaylord Street
Denver, CO 80208-0208

Specialty areas: illness behavior; biofeedback; neuropsychology

CONNECTICUT

Jane Olejarczyk
Registrar of Psychology
Department of Psychology
Yale University
2 Hillhouse Avenue
New Haven, CT 06520-7447

Specialty areas: biofeedback; chronic illness; alcoholism attitudes/personality/cognition/eating disorders

DISTRICT OF COLUMBIA

Rolf Peterson, Ph.D.
Director of Clinical Training
Department of Psychology
George Washington University
2125 G. Street, N.W.
Washington, DC 20052

Specialty areas: pain; stress; coping with illness; psychophysiological disorders

FLORIDA

Hugh Davis, Ph.D.
Director of Clinical Training
Department of Clinical & Health Psychology
University of Florida
Box J-165 JHMHC
Gainesville, FL 32610

Specialty areas: chronic pain; behavioral cardiology; behavioral pediatrics

Neil Schneiderman, Ph.D.
Director, Behavioral Medicine
Department of Psychology
University of Miami
Box 248185
Coral Gables, FL 33124

Specialty areas: cardiovascular disorders; diabetes; psychoimmunology

GEORGIA

Kenneth B. Matheny, Ph.D.
Director of Counseling Psychology
Department Counseling & Psychiatric Services
Georgia State University
Atlanta, GA 30303

Specialty areas: stress management; wellness; lifestyle redesign; compliance/adherence

HAWAII

John G. Carlson, Ph.D.
Professor, Department of Psychology
University of Hawaii at Manoa
2430 Campus Road
Honolulu, HI 96822

Specialty areas: stress management; cardiovascular disease compliance

ILLINOIS

Patrick Tolan, Ph.D.
Coordinator, Graduate Clinical Admissions
Department of Psychology
DePaul University
2219 North Kenmore
Chicago, IL 60614

Specialty areas: behavioral assessment; behavior modification; behavioral medicine seminar in community psychology

Frank Gruba-McCallister, Ph.D.
Chairman, Health Psychology Committee
Illinois School of Professional Psychology
220 South State Street
Chicago, IL 60604

Specialty areas: health psychology; holistic orientation

Robert Moretti, Ph.D.
Chairman, Health Psychology
Division of Psychology
Northwestern University
Medical School
303 E. Chicago, Ward 12-138
Chicago, IL 60611

Specialty areas: neuropsychology; diabetes; psychosocial factors in illness; health risk behavior change;
psychodynamic orientation

Joe Hatcher, Ph.D.
Director of Clinical Training
Department of Psychology
University of Health Sciences/Chicago
Medical School
3333 Green Bay Road, Building 51
North Chicago, IL 60064

Specialty areas: anxiety; behavioral pediatrics; behavioral medicine; neuropsychology

IOWA

Barbara L. Andersen, Ph.D.
Associate Professor
Department of Psychology
University of Iowa
Spence Laboratories
Iowa City, IA 52242

Specialty areas: pain; hypertension; social psychophysiology; diabetes; cancer and chronic illnesses

MARYLAND

Andrew Baum, Ph.D.
Director of Graduate Studies
Uniformed Services University of the Health
Sciences
F. Edward Hebert School of Medicine
4301 Jones Bridge Road
Bethesda, Maryland 20889-4799

Specialty areas: stress and coping; psychophar-
macology; behavioral cardiology; eating behavior,
psychoneuroimmunology; gender and health

Theodore M. Dembroski, Ph.D.
Director, Behavioral Medicine Program
University of Maryland at Baltimore County
Catonsville, MD 21228

Specialty areas: Reactivity, smoking, personality,
coronary-prone behavior, stress

MINNESOTA

Gloria R. Leon, Ph.D.
Director of Clinical Psychology
Department of Psychology
University of Minnesota
75 East River Road
Minneapolis, MN 55343

Specialty areas: stress and coping; eating disorders;
biological/psychological interactions

Robert Filbeck, Ph.D.
Training Director
Counseling Psychology
University of Nebraska-Lincoln
30 Bancroft Hall
Lincoln, NE 68588-0345

Specialty areas: disability substance abuse; biofeedback and stress management

NEW MEXICO

Graduate Admissions
Department of Psychology
University of New Mexico
Albuquerque, NM 87131

Specialty areas: pain; addictive behaviors; cognitive-behavioral orientation

NEW YORK

Camille Wortman, Ph.D.
Department of Psychology
State University of New York
Stony Brook, NY 11794

Specialty areas: stress/coping and immune function; coronary heart disease risk; chronic disease

Rafael Klorman, Ph.D.
Director, Clinical Psychology Program
Department of Psychology
University of Rochester
Meliora Hal—River Station
Rochester, NY 14627

Specialty areas: smoking; cardiovascular disease; motivation

Gilbert Levin, Ph.D.
Director of Health Psychology Program
Ferkauf Graduate School of Psychology/
Albert Einstein School of Medicine
Belfer Building, Room 1303
1300 Morris Park Avenue
Bronx, NY 10461

Specialty areas: numerous

Robert Thompson, Ph.D.
Department of Psychology
Duke University
Durham, NC 27706

Specialty areas: health and behavioral medicine

OHIO

Danny R. Moates, Ph.D.
Assistant Chairman for Graduate Affairs
Department of Psychology
Ohio University
Athens, OH 45701-2979

Specialty areas: respiratory and cardiovascular disease; stress/coping; health promotion; biofeedback; psychophysiology

OREGON

Christopher Cunningham, Ph.D.
Chair, Doctoral Studies Committee
Department of Medical Psychology
Oregon Health Sciences University
3171 S.W. Sam Jackson Park Road
Portland, OR 97201

Specialty areas: behavioral cardiology; substance abuse

PENNSYLVANIA

Sheldon Cohen, Ph.D.
Department of Psychology
Carnegie Mellon University
Pittsburgh, PA 15213

Specialty areas: stress, coping, social support, self-regulation, personality and health, gender differences; coronary heart disease; infectious disease; psychoneuroimmunology

Karen A. Matthews, Ph.D.
Program Director
Western Psychiatric Institute and Clinic
3811 O'Hara Street
Pittsburgh, PA 15213

Specialty areas: cardiovascular diseases; diabetes; obesity; smoking

TENNESSEE

Robert C. Klesges, Ph.D.
Associate Professor
Department of Psychology
Center for Applied Psychology Research
Memphis State University
Memphis, TN 38152

Specialty areas: health promotion; cardiovascular risk

David G. Schlundt, Ph.D.
Department of Psychology
323 A & S Psychology Bldg.
Vanderbilt University
Nashville, TN 37240

Specialty areas: chronic illness; health and health risk behaviors; pain

TEXAS

G. Frank Lawlis, Ph.D.
Director, Health Psychology/Behavioral Medicine
Doctoral Program—Psychology Department
North Texas State University
Denton, TX 76201

Specialty areas: pain; cancer; environmental disease

Richard I. Evans, Ph.D.
Distinguished University Professor
Director, Social Psychology/Behavioral Medicine
Research and Graduate Training Group
Department of Psychology
University of Houston
3801 Cullen Boulevard
Houston, TX 77204-5341

Special areas: application of social psychological theory to prevention of adolescent health risk behaviors (e.g. tobacco use, chemical substance abuse, exposure to HIV/AIDS), disease prevention evaluation

UTAH

Timothy W. Smith, Ph.D.
Associate Professor of Psychology
Department of Psychology
University of Utah
Social & Behavioral Science Building
Salt Lake City, UT 84112

Specialty areas: cardiovascular disease; chronic pain; pediatrics

VERMONT

James C. Rosen, Ph.D.
Director of Clinical Psychology Program
Department of Psychology
University of Vermont
Burlington, VT 05405

Specialty areas: stress, eating disorders; sexual dysfunction; pain; cardiovascular risk

VIRGINIA

Richard McCarty, Ph.D.
Associate Chairman
Department of Psychology
University of Virginia
102 Gilmer Hall
Charlottesville, VA 22903

Specialty areas: diabetes; stress and coping; aging; hypertension

Joseph P. Bush, Ph.D.
Behavioral Medicine Track Coordinator
Psychology Department,
Box 2018 Virginia
Commonwealth University
806 West Franklin Street
Richmond, VA 23284-2018

Specialty areas: rehabilitation; pain stress management; crisis intervention; psychophysiology; pediatrics

Health Psychology Postdoctoral Fellowships

CALIFORNIA

Dr. Doris Penman
Department of Psychiatry
Kaiser Permanente Medical Center
4747 Sunset Boulevard
Los Angeles, CA 90027

Specialty areas: cardiac rehabilitation headache/pain management; coping with illness

Shelly Taylor, Ph.D.
Professor
Department of Psychology
University of California
1283 Franz Hall
Los Angeles, CA 90024

Specialty areas: social support: chronic disease; primary prevention

Charles McCreary, Ph.D.
UCLA Neuropsychiatric Institute
760 Westwood Plaza
Los Angeles, CA 90024-1759

Specialty areas: chronic pain; assessment and management

Thomas J. Coates, Ph.D.
University of California
School of Medicine, Room A 405
San Francisco, CA 94143-0320

Specialty areas: AIDS - PNI

COLORADO

Robin Dee Post, Ph.D.
Container Box C258
University of Colorado Health Sciences Center
4200 East Ninth Avenue
Denver, CO 80262

Specialty areas: clinical neuropsychology; pediatric psychology

CONNECTICUT

Jane Olejarczyk
Registrar of Psychology
Department of Psychology
Yale University
2 Hillhouse Avenue
New Haven, CT 06520-7447

Specialty areas: biofeedback; chronic illness; attitudes/personality/cognition; eating disorders; alcoholism

FLORIDA

Cynthia Belar, Ph.D.
Director of Clinical Training
Department of Clinical & Health Psychology
University of Florida—Box J165 JHMHC
Gainesville, FL 32610

Specialty areas: chronic pain; diabetes; cancer; behavioral cardiology; behavioral pediatrics; clinical health psychology; neuropsychology

Neil Schneiderman, Ph.D.
Director, Division of Health Psychology
Department of Psychology
University of Miami
Box 248185
Coral Cables, FL 33124

Specialty areas: training grant programs in cardiovascular disorders and psychoimmunology and AIDS

Wendy Stone, Ph.D.
Director, Clinical Psychology
Mailman Center for Child Development
University of Miami Medical School
P. O. Box 016820
Miami, FL 33101

Specialty areas: prevention and/or management of developmental handicapping conditions

GEORGIA

Steve H. Sanders, Ph.D.
Executive Director
Pain Control & Rehabilitation Institute
350 Winn Way
Decatur, GA 30030

Specialty areas: chronic pain; stress management; biofeedback

ILLINOIS

Robert Moretti, Ph.D.
Chairman, Health Psychology
Division of Psychology
Northwestern University Medical School
303 E. Chicago, Ward 12-138
Chicago, IL 60611

Specialty areas: AIDS education/research

Yvonne Shade-Zeldow, Ph.D.
Director, Department of Psychology
Rehabilitation Institute of Chicago
345 E. Superior
Chicago, IL 60611

Specialty areas: hypnosis/biofeedback; disability rehabilitation; neuropsychology

IOWA

Barbara L. Andersen, Ph.D.
Associate Professor
Department of Psychology
University of Iowa
Spence Laboratories
Iowa City, IA 52242

Specialty areas: pain; hypertension; social psychophysiology; cancer and chronic diseases

KENTUCKY

Kathleen DeWalt, Ph.D.
Director of Graduate Studies
Department of Behavioral Science
University of Kentucky Medical Center
Lexington, KY 40536-0086

Specialty areas: stress; substance abuse; adherence/psychosocial factors in cancer

MARYLAND

Richard Waranch, Ph.D.
Co-Director, Behavioral Medicine
& Biofeedback Clinic
Johns Hopkins Medical Institutions
Department of Psychiatry—Moyer 144
Baltimore, MD 21205

Specialty areas: biofeedback and relaxation; stress management; smoking; obesity; medical hypnosis

MASSACHUSETTS

Daniel Brown, Ph.D.
Director of Behavioral Medicine
Cambridge Hospital
Harvard Medical School
493 Cambridge Street
Cambridge, MA 02139

Specialty areas: psychophysiological disorders; health risk behaviors

Dennis C. Russo, Ph.D.
Director, Behavioral Medicine
Department of Psychiatry
Children's Hospital
Harvard Medical School
300 Longwood Avenue
Boston, MA 02115

Specialty areas: chronic illness; headache/pain; children

Perry L. Belfer, Ph.D.
Clinical Coordinator
Eating Disorders Program
Newton-Wellesley Hospital
Newton, MA 02162

Specialty areas: eating disorders

MINNESOTA

Robert Ivnik, Ph.D.
Director, Section of Psychology (W9B)
Mayo Clinic
Rochester, MN 55905

Specialty areas: general psychological

MISSOURI

Joseph E. Brown, Ph.D.
Director of Postdoctoral Training
Division of Behavioral Medicine
St. Louis University School of Medicine
1221 South Grand Boulevard
St. Louis, MO 63104

Specialty areas: biobehavioral treatment; neuro-psychology; women's issues; pain, anxiety, agora-phobia

NEW HAMPSHIRE

Tim Ahles, Ph.D.
Behavioral Medicine Section
Dartmouth Medical School
Hanover, NH 03756

Specialty areas: stress & pain management; cog-nitive therapy; relaxation; hypnosis

NEW MEXICO

Graduate Admissions
Department of Psychology
University of New Mexico
Albuquerque, NM 87131

Specialty areas: pain; addictive behaviors

NEW YORK

James J. Blascovich, Ph.D.
Director, Behavioral and Social Aspects of Health
State University of NY at Buffalo Park Hall
Amherst, NY 14260

Specialty areas: cardiovascular health; cancer; neu-ropsychology; oral health; alcohol

Rafael Klorman, Ph.D.
Director, Clinical Psychology Program
Department of Psychology
University of Rochester
Meliora Hall—River Station
Rochester, NY 14627

Specialty areas: cigaratte smoking/relapse; car-diovascular disease; motivation

NORTH CAROLINA

Redford B. Williams, Jr., Ph.D.
Duke University Medical Center
Box 3926
Durham, NC 27710

Specialty areas: several health psychology areas

OHIO

Tom Creer/Kenneth Holroyd
Professors
Institute of Health & Behavioral Sciences
and Psychology Department
Ohio University
Athens, OH 45701-2979

Specialty areas: respiratory disorders, pain disorders

Janice Kiecolt-Glaser, Ph.D.
Associate Professor
College of Medicine Ohio State University
473 West 12th Avenue
Columbus, OH 43210

Specialty areas: behavioral immunology; psychoimmunology

OKLAHOMA

C. Eugene Walker, Ph.D.
Director, Pediatric Psychology Program
Department of Psychiatry
University of Oklahoma Health Sciences Center
P. O. Box 26901, 5SP 138
Oklahoma City, OK 73190

Specialty areas: stress management; biofeedback; effects of chronic illness

OREGON

Christopher Cunningham, Ph.D.
Chair, Doctoral Studies Committee
School of Medicine
Oregon Health Sciences University
3171 S.W. Sam Jackson Park Road
Portland, OR 97201

Specialty areas: behavioral cardiology; substance abuse

PENNSYLVANIA

Kelly D. Brownell, Ph.D.
Professor, Department of Psychiatry
University of Pennsylvania
133 South 36th Street
Philadelphia, PA 19104

Specialty areas: obesity; eating disorders

Karen A. Matthews, Ph.D.
Program Director
Western Psychiatric Institute and Clinic
3811 O'Hara Street
Pittsburgh, PA 15213

Specialty areas: cardiovascular diseases; diabetes obesity; smoking

RHODE ISLAND

David B. Abrams, Ph.D.
Associate Director, Postdoctoral Program
Division of Behavioral Medicine
The Miriam Hospital
164 Summit Avenue
Providence, RI 02906

Specialty areas: risk factor modification; pain

TENNESSEE

Thomas G. Burish, Ph.D.
Department of Psychology
Vanderbilt University
A&S Psychology Bldg.
Nashville, TN 38105

Specialty area: psychosocial oncology

William D. Murphy, Ph.D.
Department of Psychiatry
University of Tennessee, Memphis
66N Pauline, Suite 633
Memphis, TN 38105

Specialty areas: pain and stress management; physical rehabilitation; cardiac neuropsychology

Kenneth A. Wallston, Ph.D.
School of Nursing
Godchaux Hall
Vanderbilt University
Nashville, TN 37240

Specialty areas: rheumatoid arthritis; smoking cessation; health beliefs

TEXAS

Richard I. Evans, Ph.D.
Distinguished University Professor
Director, Social Psychology/Behavioral Medicine
Research and Graduate Training Group
Department of Psychology
University of Houston
3801 Cullen Boulevard
Houston, TX 77204-5341

Pre- and post-doctoral fellowships, National Heart, Lung and Blood Institute-funded (National Research Awards)

Specialty areas: application of social psychological theory to prevention of adolescent health risk behaviors (e.g., tobacco use, chemical substance abuse, exosure to HIV/AIDS), disease prevention evaluation

William J. Kelleher, Ph.D.
Director of Behavioral Health Division of
Mental Health
Wilford Hall Medical Center
ATC Lackland Air Force Base
San Antonio, TX 78236-5300

Specialty areas: smoking cessation; weight control; cardiac risk; behavioral dentistry

UTAH

Scot W. Russell, Ph.D.
Clinical Director, Division of Behavioral Medicine
University of Utah Medical Center
50 North Medical Drive
Salt Lake City, UT 84132

Specialty areas: chronic pain; somatization disorders

VIRGINIA

Richard McCarty, Ph.D.
Associate Chair, Department of Psychology
University of Virginia
102 Gilmer Hall
Charlottesville, VA 22903

Specialty areas: diabetes; hypertension; stress and coping; aging

Anne Newman, Ph.D.
Assistant Professor
Box 203
University of Virginia Medical Center
Charlottesville, VA 22901

Specialty areas: neuropsychology; chronic disease rehabilitation; headache; pain

Bibliography

Abraham S., & Johnson, C. L. (1979). Overweight adults in the United States. *Vital and Health Statistics of the National Center for Health Statistics*, No. 51, 11.

Achtenberg-Lawlis, J. (1982). The psychological dimensions of arthritis. *Journal of Consulting and Clinical Psychology, 50*, 984–992.

Ackerman, S. J. (1992). Exercise in NIDDM may be a prescription for protection. *Diabetes Care, 15*(1), 136–137.

Ader, R. (Ed.). (1981). *Psychoneuroimmunology.* New York: Academic Press.

Ader, R., & Cohen, N. (1982). Behaviorally conditioned immunosuppression and murine systemic lupus erythematosus. *Science, 215*, 1534–1536.

Affleck, G., Tennen, H., Pfeiffer, C., & Fifield, J. (1987). Appraisals or control and predictability in adapting to a chronic disease. *Journal of Personality and Social Psychology, 53*, 273–279.

Agras, W. S. (Ed.) (1978). *Behavior modification: Principles and clinical applications* (2nd ed.). Boston: Little, Brown.

Ainsworth, B. E., Keenan, N. L., Strogatz, D. S., Garrett, J. M., & James, S. A. (1991). Physical activity and hypertension in black adults: The Pitt County Study. *American Journal of Public Health, 81*, 1477–1479.

Ajzen, I. (1985). From intention to actions: A theory of planned behavior. In J. Kuhl & J. Beckman (Eds.), *Action-control: From cognition to behavior.* Heidelberg: Springer, pp. 11–39.

Akeson W. H., & Murphy, R. W. (1977). Low back pain. *Clinical Orthopedics, 2*, 129.

Akiskal, H. S., & McKinney, W. T. (1973). Depressive disorders: Toward a unified hypothesis. *Science, 182*, 20–28.

Alcorn, J. D. (1991). Counseling psychology and health applications. *The Counseling Psychologists.*

Alexander, B. H., Rivara, F. P., & Wolf, M. E. (1992). The cost and frequency of hospitalization for fall-related injuries in older adults. *American Journal of Public Health, 82*, 1020–1023.

Alexander, F. (1939). Emotional factors in essential hypertension. *Psychosomatic Medicine, 1*, 153–216.

Altmaier, E. N. (1991). Research and practice roles for counseling psychologists in health care studies. *The Counseling Psychologist.*

Altman, D., Foster, V., Rasenick-Douss, L., & Tye, J. (1989). Reducing the illegal sale of cigarettes to minors. *Journal of the American Medical Association, 261*, 80–83.

American Cancer Society. (1990). *Cancer facts and figures.* New York: American Cancer Society.

American Cancer Society. (1985). *(1992) Cancer facts and figures.* New York: American Cancer Society.

American College of Sports Medicine. (1986). *Guidelines for exercise testing and prescription* (3rd ed.). Philadelphia: Lea & Febiger.

American College of Sports Medicine. (1991). *Guidelines for exercise testing and prescription* (4th ed.). Philadelphia: Lea & Febiger.

American Diabetes Association (ADA). (1979). Policy statement. *Diabetes Care, 2,* 1–3.

American Diabetes Association (ADA). (1984). *Physicians guide to type II diabetes (NIDDM) diagnosis and treatment.* New York: American Diabetes Association.

American Diabetes Association. (1986). *Diabetes facts and figures.* Alexandria, Va.: American Diabetes Association.

American Heart Association (AHA). (1986). *Heart facts.* Dallas, Tex.: American Heart Association.

American Heart Association. (1988). *Heart facts.* Dallas, Tex.: American Heart Association.

Amler, R. W., & Doll, H. B. (1987). *Closing the gap: The burden of unnecessary illness.* New York: Oxford University Press.

Andersen, R., & Newman, J. F. (1973). Societal and individual determinants of medical care utilization in the United States. *Millbank Memorial Fund Quarterly/Health in Society, 51,* 95–124.

Anderson, A. E., & DiDomenico, L. (1992). Diet vs. shape content of popular male and female magazines: A dose-response relationship to the incidence of eating disorders? *International Journal of Eating Disorders, 11,* 283–387.

Anderson, G., Svensson, H., & Anders, O. (1983). The intensity of work recovery in low back pain. *Spine, 8*(8), 880–885.

Anderson, J. W., Zeigler, J. A., Deakins, D. A., Floore, T. L., Dillon, D. W., Wood, C. L., Oeltgen, P. R., & Whitley, R. J. (1991). Metabolic effects of high-carbohydrate, high-fiber diets for insulin-dependent diabetic individuals. *American Journal of Clinical Nutrition, 54*(5), 936–943.

Anderson, K. M., Castelli, W. P., & Levy, D. (1987). Cholesterol and mortality: 30 years of follow-up from the Framingham Study. *Journal of the American Medical Association, 257,* 2176–2184.

Anderson, R. M., Giachello, A. L., & Aday, L. A. (1986). Access of Hispanics to health care and cuts in services: A state-of-the-art overview. *Public Health Reports, 101*(3), 238–252.

Andrews, G., & Tennant, C. (1978). Being upset and becoming ill: An appraisal of the relationship between life events and physical illness. *Med. J. Aust., I,* 324–327.

Andrykowski, M. A., & Gregg, M. E. (1992). The role of psychological variables in postchemotherapy nausea: Anxiety and expectation. *Psychosomatic Medicine, 54*(1), 48–58.

Angell, M. (1985). Disease as a reflection of the psyche. *New England Journal of Medicine, 312,* 1570–1572.

Annis, H. M., & Davis, C. S. (1988). Self-efficacy and the prevention of alcoholic relapse: Initial findings from a treatment trial. In T. B. Baker & D. Cannon (Eds.), *Assessment and treatment of addictive disorders.* New York: Praeger, pp. 88–112.

Antonovsky, A. (1974). Conceptual and methodological problems in the study of resistance resources and stressful life events. In B. S. Dohrenwend & B. P. Dohrenwend (Eds.), *Stressful life events: Their nature and effects.* New York: Wiley.

Antonovsky, A. (1990). Personality and health: Testing the sense of coherence model. In H. Friedman (Ed.), *Personality and disease.* New York: Wiley, pp. 155–177.

Antonovsky, A., Leibowitz, U., Medalie, J. M., Smith, H. A., Halpern, L., & Alter, M. (1968). Reappraisal of possible etiologic factors in multiple sclerosis. *American Journal of Public Health, 58,* 836–848.

Antonuccio, D. O., & Lichtenstein, E. (1980). Peer modeling influences on smoking behavior of heavy and light smokers. *Addictive Behaviors, 5,* 299–307.

Appelbaum, S. A. (1977). The refusal to take one's medicine. *Bulletin of the Menninger Clinic, 41,* 511–521.

Aronow, W. S., & Kaplan, N. M. (1983). Smoking. In N. M. Kaplan & J. Stamler (Eds.), *Prevention of coronary heart disease.* Philadelphia: Saunders, pp. 51–60.

Ardon House Conference (1983). National working conference on education and training in health psychology. *Health Psychology, 2*(5), 1–153.

Arky, R. A. (1978). Current principles of dietary therapy of diabetes mellitus. *Medical Clinics of North America, 62,* 655–662.

Arnetz, B. B., Wasserman, J., Petrini, B., Brenner, S. O., Levi, L., Eneroth, D., Salovana, H., Hielm, R., Solovaara, L., Theorell, T., & Petterson, I. L. (1987). Immune function in unemployed women. *Psychosom. Med., 19,* 3–12.

Aronow, W. S., & Kaplan, N. M., (1983). Smoking. In N. M. Kaplan & J. Stamler (Eds.), *Prevention of coronary heart disease.* Philadelphia: Saunders, pp. 51–60.

Arria, A. M., Tarter, R. E., & Van Thiel, D. H. (1991). The effects of alcohol abuse on the health of adolescents. *Alcohol Health and Research World, 15,* 52–57.

Arthritis Foundation. (1983). *Basic facts: Answers to questions,* Atlanta: Arthritis Foundation.

Ary, D. D., Toobert, D., Wilson, W., & Glasgow, R. E. (1986). Patient perspectives on factors contributing to non-adherence to diabetes regimen. *Diabetes Care, 9,* 168–172.

Asher, W. L., & Harper, H. W. (1973). Effect of human chorionic gonadotropin on weight loss, hunger, and feeling of well-being. *American Journal of Clinical Nutrition, 26,* 211–218.

Atkins, C. J., Kaplan, R. M., & Toshima, M. T. (1991). Close relationships in the epidemiology of cardiovascular disease. In W. H. Jones & D. Perlman (Eds.), *Advances in personal relationships.* Vol. 3 London: Jessica Kingsley, pp. 207–231.

Atkinson, J. H., Grant, I., Kennedy, C. J., Richman, D. D., Spector, S. A., & McCutchan, J. A. (1988). Prevalence of psychiatric disorders among men infected with human immunodeficiency virus. *Arch. Gen. Psychiatr., 45,* 859–864.

Atkinson, R. L., Atkinson, R. C., Smith, E. E., & Bem, D. J. (1990). *Introduction to psychology* (10th ed.). San Diego: Harcourt, Brace, and Jovanovich.

Azjen, I. (1985). From intentions to actions: A theory of planned behavior. In J. Kuhl & J. Beckman (Eds.), *Action control: From cognition to behavior.* New York: Springer-Verlag, pp. 11–39.

Bachman, J. G., Wallace, J. M., O'Malley, P. M., Johnston, L. D., Kurth, C. L., & Neighbors, H. W. (1991). Racial/ethnic differences in smoking, drinking, and illicit drug use among American high school seniors, 1976–89. *American Journal of Public Health, 81,* 372–377.

Bagdade, J. D., Dierman, E. L., & Porte, D. (1967). Diabetic limpemia—A fat of acquired fat-induced lipemia. *New England Journal of Medicine, 276,* 427–433.

Baker, G. H. B. (1981). Psychological management. *Clinics in Rheumatological Disease, 7,* 455–466.

Baker, S. P., O'Neill, B., & Karpf, R. (1984). *The injury fact book.* Lexington, Mass.: Lexington.

Bandura, A. (1977a). Self-efficacy: Toward a unifying theory of behavioral change. *Psychological Review, 84,* 191–215.

Bandura, A. (1977b). *Social learning theory.* Englewood Cliffs, N.J.: Prentice-Hall.

Bandura, A. (1982). Self-efficacy mechanism in human agency. *American Psychologist, 37,* 122–147.

Bandura, A. (1986). *Social foundations of thought and action.* Englewood Cliffs, N.J.: Prentice-Hall.

Bandura, A., & Simon, K. M. (1977). The role of proximal intentions in self-regulation of refractory behavior. *Cognitive Therapy and Research, 1,* 177–184.

Baranowski, T., Bouchard, C., Bar-Or, O., Bricker, T., Heath, Kimm, S. Y. S., Malina, R., Oburzanek, E., Pate, R., Strong, W. B., Truman, B., & Washington, R. (1992). Assessment, prevalence, and cardiovascular benefits of physical activity and fitness in youth, *Medicine and Science in Sports and Exercise, 24,* 5237–5247.

Baranowski, T., Henske, J., Simons-Morton, B., Palmer, J., Tiernan, K., Hooks, P. C., & Dunn, J. K. (1990). Dietary change for cardiovascular disease prevention among black-American families. *Health Education Research, 5,* 433–443.

Barbarin, O. A., & Chesler, M. (1986). The medical context of parental coping with childhood cancer. *American Journal of Community Psychology, 14,* 221–235.

Barefoot, J. C., Dahlstrom, W. G., & Williams, R. B. (1983). Hostility, CHD incidence, and total mortality: A 25-year follow-up study of 255 physicians. *Psychosomatic Medicine, 45,* 59–63.

Barkley, R. A., et al. (1990). Task force report: The appropriate role of clinical child psychologists in the prescribing of psycho-active medication for children. *Journal of Clinical Child Psychology, 19,* Supplement, 1–38.

Barrera, M. (1981). Preliminary development of a scale of social support. *American Journal of Community Psychology, 9,* 435–447.

Barry, P. Z. (1975). Individual versus community orientation in the prevention of injuries. *Preventive Medicine, 4,* 47–56.

Bartlett, E. E. (1983). Educational self-help approaches in childhood asthma. *Journal of Allergy and Clinical Immunology, 72,* 545–554.

Bartrop, R. W., Lockhurst, E., Lazarus, L., et al. (1977). Depressed lymphocyte function after bereavement. *Lancet, 1,* 834–836.

Baum, A., Singer, J. E., & Baum, C. S. (1981). Stress

and the environment. *Journal of Social Issues, 37,* 4–35.

Beck, A. T. (1976). *Cognitive therapy and the emotional disorders.* New York: International Universities Press.

Becker, M. H. (Ed.). (1974). The health belief model and personal health behavior. *Health Education Monographs, 2,* 324–473.

Becker, M. H. (1974). The health belief model and sick role behavior. *Health Education Monographs, 2,* 409–419.

Becker, M. H. (1985). Patient adherence to prescribed therapies. *Medical Care, 23,* 539–555.

Becker, M. H., & Joseph, J. C. (1988). AIDS and behavioral change to reduce risk: A review. *American Journal of Public Health, 78,* 394–410.

Becker, M. H., & Maiman, L. A. (1980). Strategies for enhancing patient compliance. *Journal of Community Health, 6,* 113–135.

Becker, M. H., & Maiman, L. A. (1981). Patient compliance. In K. K. Melmon (Ed.), *Drug therapeutics: Concepts for physicians.* New York: Elsevier, pp. 65–79.

Belisle, M., Roskies, E., & Levesque, M. M. (1987). Improving adherence to physical activity. *Health Psychology, 7,* 159–172.

Bellack, A. S. (1976). A comparison of self-reinforcement and self-monitoring in a weight reduction program. *Behavior Therapy, 7,* 68–75.

Belloc, N. B., & Breslow, L. (1972). Relationship of physical health status and health practices. *Preventive Medicine, 1,* 409–421.

Belloc, N. B., & Breslow, L. (1972). Relationship of physical health status and health practices. *Preventive Medicine, 1,* 409–421.

Benden, S. N., & Brain, P. F. (1982). Studies on the effect of social stress on measures of disease resistance in laboratory mice. *Aggr. Behav., 8,* 126–129.

Benowitz, N. L. (1983). The use of biologic fluid samples in assessing tobacco smoke consumption. In J. Grabowski & C. S. Bell (Eds.), *Measurement in the analysis and treatment of smoking behavior.* NIDA Research Monograph No. 48, U.S. Department of Health and Human Services, Public Health Service, Alcohol, Drug Abuse and Mental Health Administration, DHHS Pub. No. (ADM), 83–1285.

Benson, H. (1975). *The relaxation response.* New York: Morrow.

Berenson, G. S. (1980). *Cardiovascular risk factors in children.* New York: Oxford University Press.

Bergman, A. B., Rivara, F. P., Richards, D. D., & Rogers, L. W. (1990). The Seattle children's bicycle helmet campaign. *American Journal of Diseases of Children, 144,* 727–731.

Bergner, M., Bobbitt, R. A., Carter, W. B., et al. (1981). The sickness impact profile: Development and final revision of a health status measure. *Medical Care, 19,* 787–805.

Berkman, L., & Syme, S. L. (1979). Social networks, host resistance, and mortality: A nine-year follow-up study of Alameda County residents. *American Journal of Epidemiology, 109,* 188–204.

Berkman, L. F., & Breslow, L. (1983). *Health and ways of living: Findings from the Alameda County Study.* New York: Oxford University Press.

Berkman, L. F. (1986). Social networks, support, and health: Taking the next step forward. *American Journal of Epidemiology, 123,* 559–562.

Berkowitz, R. I., Agras, W. S., & Korner, A. F. (1985). Physical activity and adiposity: A longitudinal study from birth to childhood. *Journal of Pediatrics, 106,* 434–438.

Bettelheim, B. (1943). Individual and mass behavior in extreme situations. *Journal of Abnormal Social Psychology, 38,* 417–452.

Bevan, A., Honour, A., & Stott, F. (1969). Direct arterial pressure recording in unrestricted man. *Clinical Science, 37,* 329–344.

Bibring, G. et al. (1961a). A study of the psychological processes in pregnancy and of the earliest mother-child relationship I: Some prepositions and comments. *Psychoanal. Stud. Child, 16,* 9–24.

Bibring, G., et al. (1961b). A study of the psychological processes in pregnancy and of the earliest mother-child relationship II. Methodological considerations. *Psychoanal. Stud. Child, 16,* 25–72.

Bijur, P. E., Kurzon, M., Overpeck, M. D., & Scheidt, P. C. (1992). Parental alcohol use, problem drinking, and children's injuries. *Journal of the American Medical Association, 267,* 3166–3171.

Billings, A. F., & Moos, R. H. (1982). Social support and functioning among community and clinical groups. A panel model. *Journal of Behavioral Medicine, 5,* 295–311.

Birch, L. L., Zimmerman, S. I., & Hind, H. (1980). The influence of social-affective context on the formation of children's food preferences. *Child Development, 51,* 856–861.

Bistrian, B. R., Blackburn, G. L., & Serimshaw, N. S. (1975). Cellular immunity in semistarved states in hospitalized adults. *Am. J. Clin. Nutr., 28,* 1148–1155.

Bjorntorp, P., Carlgren, G., Isaksson, B., Krotkiewski, M., Larsson, B., & Sjostrom, L. (1975). Effect of an energy-reduced dietary regimen in relation to adipose tissue cellularity in obese women. *American Journal of Clinical Nutrition, 28,* 445–452.

Black, D. R., Gleser, L. J., & Kooyers, K. J. (1990). A meta-analytic evaluation of couples weight-loss programs. *Health Psychology, 9,* 330–347.

Blackburn, H., & Jacobs, D. (1984). Sources of the diet-heart controversy: Confusion over population versus individual correlations. *Circulation, 70,* 775–780.

Blackwell, B. (1973). Patient compliance. *New England Journal of Medicine, 289,* 249–253.

Blair, S. N., Kohl, H. W., Gordon, N. F., & Paffenbarger, R. S. (1992). How much physical activity is good for health? *Annual Review of Public Health, 13,* 99–126.

Blair, S. N., Kohl, H. W., Paffenbarger, R. S., Clark, D. G., Cooper, K. H., & Gibbons, L. W. (1989). Physical fitness and all-cause mortality: A prospective study of healthy men and women. *Journal of the American Medical Association, 262,* 2395–2401.

Blair, S. N., Piserchia, P. V., Wilbur, C. S., & Crowder, J. H. (1986). A public health intervention model for work-site health promotion: Impact on exercise and physical fitness in a health promotion plan after 24 months. *Journal of the American Medical Association, 255,* 921–926.

Blanchard, E. B., Khramelashvili, V. V., McCoy, G. C., Aivazyan, T. A., McCaffrey, R. J., Salenko, B. B., Musso, A., Wittrock, D. A., Berger, M., Gerardi, M. A., & Pangburn, L. (1988). The USA-USSR collaborative cross-cultural comparison of autogenic training and thermal biofeedback in the treatment of mild hypertension. *Health Psychology, 7* (suppl.), 175–192.

Blanchard, E. B., Martin, J. E., & Dubbert, P. M. (1988). *Non-drug treatments for essential hypertension.* New York: Pergamon.

Blazer, D. (1982). Social support and mortality in an elderly community population. *American Journal of Epidemiology, 115,* 684–694.

Block, G., Dresser, C. M., Hartman, A. M., & Carroll, M. D. C. (1985). Nutrient sources in the American diet: Quantitative data from the NHANES II survey. *American Journal of Epidemiology, 122,* 27–40.

Blumenthal, J. A., Williams, R. G. J., Kong, Y., Shanberg, S. J., & Thompson, L. W. (1978). Type A behavior pattern in coronary atherosclerosis. *Circulation, 58,* 634–639.

Bond, G. G., Aiken, L. S., & Somerville, S. C. (1992). The health belief model and adolescents with insulin-dependent diabetes mellitus. *Health Psychology, 11,* 190–198.

Bonica, J. J. (1980). Pain research therapy: Past and current status and future needs. In L. K. Ng & J. J. Bonica (Eds.), *Pain discomfort and humanitarian care.* New York: Elsevier, pp. 1–46.

Bonica, J. J. (1991). History of pain concepts and pain therapy. *Mount Sinai Journal of Medicine, 58*(3), 191–202.

Booth-Kewley, S. & Friedman, H. S. (1987). Psychological predictors of heart disease: A quantitative review. *Psychological Bulletin, 101,* 343–362.

Boranic, M., Poljack-Blazi, M., Sverko, V., & Pericic, D. (1983). Suppression of the immune response of rats by prolonged overcrowding stress. *Iugoslav. Hysiol. Pharmacol. Acta, 19,* 347–351.

Borland, R., Owen, N., Hill, D., & Chapman, S. (1990). Changes in acceptance of workplace smoking bans following their implementation: A prospective study. *Preventive Medicine, 19,* 314–322.

Borysenko, M., & Borysenko, J. (1982). Stress, behavior, and immunity: Animal models and mediating mechanisms. *General Hospital Psychiatry, 4,* 56–67.

Botvin, G., Eng, A., & Williams, C. (1980). Preventing the onset of cigarette smoking through life skills training. *Preventive Medicine, 9,* 135–143.

Botvin, G. J., Baker, E., Goldberg, C. J., Dusenbury, L., & Botvin, E. M. (1992). Correlates and predictors of smoking among black adolescents. *Addictive Behaviors, 17,* 97–103.

Bovbjerg, D. H. (1991). Psychoneuroimmunology. Implications for oncology? *Cancer, 67*(3 Suppl); 828–832.

Bovbjerg, D. H., Redd, W. H., Maier, L. A., Holland, J. C., Lesko, L. M., Niedzwiecki, D., Rubin, S. C., & Hakes, T. B. (1990). Anticipatory immune suppression and nausea in women receiving cyclic chemotherapy for ovarian cancer.

Journal of Consulting and Clinical Psychology, 58(2), 153–157.

Bracht, N., & Kingsbury, L. (1990). Community organization principles in health promotion: A five-stage model. In N. Bracht (Ed.), *Health promotion at the community level.* Newbury Park, Calif.: Sage, pp. 66–88.

Bradley, L. A., Young, L. D., Anderson, K. O., Turner, R. A., Agedelo, C. A., et al. (1987). Effects of psychological therapy on pain behavior of rheumatoid arthritis patients: Treatment outcome and 6-month follow-up. *Arthritis and Rheumatism, 30,* 1105–1114.

Brandt, P. A., & Weinert, C. (1981). The PRQ—A social support measure. *Nursing Research, 30,* 277–280.

Brashear, R. E. (1980). Chronic obstructive pulmonary disease. In D. H. Simmons (Ed.), *Current Pulmonology, Vol. 2.* Boston: Houghton Mifflin, pp. 1–39.

Bray, G. A. (1983). Obesity. In N. M. Kaplan & J. Stamler (Eds.), *Prevention of coronary heart disease.* Philadelphia: Saunders, pp. 73–85.

Bray, G. A. (1986). Effects of obesity on health and happiness. In K. D. Brownell and J. P. Foreyt (Eds.), *Handbook of eating disorders.* New York: Basic Books, pp. 3–44.

Bray, G. A. (1990). Exercise and obesity. In C. Bouchard, R. J. Shephard, T. Stephens, J. R. Sutton, & B. D. McPherson (Eds.), *Exercise, fitness, and health: A consensus of current knowledge.* Champaign, Ill.: Human Kinetics, pp. 497–510.

Breed, W., & De Foe, J. R. (1981). The portrayal of the drinking process on primetime television. *Journal of Communication, 31,* 58–67.

Brehm, J. W. (1966). *A theory of psychological reactants.* New York: Academic Press.

Brenner, G. F., Williamson, D. J., & Melamed, B. G. (1989). *Transactions of social support in rheumatoid arthritis patients and their support providers.* Presented at the annual meeting of the Society of Behavioral Medicine, San Francisco, 1989.

Breslow, L., & Enstrom, J. E. (1980). Persistence of health habits and their relationship to mortality. *Preventive Medicine, 9,* 469–483.

Bright-See, E., & Levy, S. M. (1985). Dietary intervention in cancer prevention trials and clinical practice: Some methodological issues. In T. G.

Burish, S. M. Levy, & B. E. Meyerowitz (Eds.), Cancer, nutrition, and eating behavior. Hillsdale, N.J.: Lawrence Erlbaum, pp. 149–163.

Brim, O. G., & Ryff, C. D. (1980). On the properties of life events. In P. B. Baltes & O. G. Brim (Eds.), *Life-span development and behavior, Vol. 3.* New York: Academic Press.

Broad, M. I., & Hall, S. M. (1984). Joiners and nonjoiners in smoking treatment: A comparison of psychosocial variables. *Addictive Behavior, 9,* 217–221.

Brook, R. H., Ware, J. E., Rogers, W. H., et al. (1983). Does free care improve adults' health? Results from a randomized controlled trial. *New England Journal of Medicine, 309,* 1426.

Brown, D. R. (1990). Exercise, fitness, and mental health. In C. Bouchard, R. J. Shephard, T. Stephens, J. R. Sutton, & G. D. McPherson (Eds.), *Exercise, fitness, and health: A consensus of current knowledge.* Champaign, Ill.: Human Kinetics, pp. 607–626.

Brown, G. W., (1989). Life events and measurement. In G. W. Brown & T. Harris (Eds.), *Life events and illness.* New York: Guilford.

Brown, G. W., & Harris, T. O. (Eds.). (1989). *Life events and illness.* New York: Guilford.

Brown, G. K., Nicassio, P. M., & Wallston, K. A. (1989). Pain coping strategies and depression in rheumatoid arthritis. *Journal of Consulting and Clinical Psychology, 57,* 652–657.

Brown, G. W., & Harris, T. (1978). *The social origins of depression: A study of psychiatric disorder in women.* Tavistock Publications, London. New York: Free Press.

Brown, G. W., & Harris, T. O. (1978). *Social origins of depression.* New York: Free Press.

Brown, J. H., Spitz, P. W., & Fries, J. F. (1980). Unorthodox treatments in rheumatoid arthritis. *Arthritis and Rheumatism, 23,* 657–658.

Brown, J. M. (1984). Imagery coping strategies in the treatment of migraine. *Pain, 18,* 157–167.

Brown, R. A., & Lichtenstein, E. (1980). *Effects of a cognitive-behavioral relapse prevention program for smokers.* Paper presented at the 88th Annual Convention of the American Psychological Association, Montreal, Canada.

Brown, R. A., Lichtenstein, E., McIntrye, K., & Harrington-Kostur, J. (1984). Effects of nicotine fading and relapse prevention on smoking cessation. *Journal of Consulting and Clinical Psychology, 52,* 307–308.

Brownell, K. D. (1982). Obesity: Understanding and treating a serious, prevalent, and refractory disorder. *Journal of Consulting and Clinical Psychology, 50,* 820–840.

Brownell, K. D. (1984). The psychology and physiology of obesity: Implications for screening and treatment. *Journal of the American Dietetic Association, 84,* 406–413.

Brownell, K. D., & Felix, M. R. J. (1987). Competitions to facilitate health promotion: Review and conceptual analysis. *American Journal of Health Promotion, 7,* 28–36.

Brownell, K. D., Greenwood, M. R. C., Stellar, E., & Shrager, E. E. (1986). The effects of repeated cycles of weight loss and regain in rats. *Physiology & Behavior, 38,* 359–464.

Brownell, K. D., Heckerman, C. L., Westlake, R. J., Hayes, S. C., & Monit, P. M. (1978). The effects of couples training and partner cooperativeness in the behavioral treatment of obesity. *Behavioral Research and Therapy, 16,* 323–333.

Brownell, K. D., Marlatt, G. A., Lichtenstein, E., & Wilson, G. T. (1986). Understanding and preventing relapse. *American Psychologist, 41,* 765–782.

Brownell, K. D., & Stunkard, A. J. (1980). Physical activity in the development and control of obesity. In A. J. Stunkard (Ed.), *Obesity.* Philadelphia: Saunders, pp. 300–324.

Bruno, R., Arnold, D., Jacobson, L., Winick, E., & Wynder, E. (1983). Randomized controlled trial of a nonpharmacologic cholesterol reduction program at the worksite. *Preventive Medicine, 12,* 523–532.

Buchanan, W. W. (1982). Assessment of joint tenderness, grip strength, digital joint circumference, and morning stiffness in rheumatoid arthritis. *Journal of Rheumatology, 9,* 763–766.

Buchner, D. M., Beresford, S. A. A., Larson, E. B., LaCroix, A. Z., & Wagner, E. H. (1992). Effects of physical activity on health status in older adults I: Observational studies. *Annual Review of Public Health, 13,* 469–488.

Buechner, J. S., Perry, D. K., Scott, H. D., Freedman, B. E., Tierney, J. T., & Waters, W. J. (1986).

Cigarette smoking behavior among Rhode Island physicians, 1963–83. *American Journal of Public Health, 76,* 285–286.

Budzynski, T. H., & Stoyva, J. (1984). Biofeedback methods in the treatment of anxiety and stress. In R. Woolfolk & P. M. Lehner (Eds.), *Principles and practice of stress management.* New York: Guilford.

Bureau of the Census (1984). *Conditions of Hispanics in America today.* Washington, D.C.: Government Printing Ofice, Department of Commerce.

Bureau of the Census. (1985). Persons of Spanish origin in the United States: March 1985 (advanced report). *Current Population Reports.* Series P-20 (403). Washington, D.C.: U.S. Department of Commerce.

Burish, T. G., & Jenkins, R. A. (1992). Effectiveness of biofeedback and relaxation training in reducing the side effects of cancer chemotherapy. *Health Psychology, 11*(1), 17–23.

Byrne, D. (1964). Repression-sensitization as a dimension of personality. In B. A. Maher (Ed.), *Progress in experimental personality research* (vol. 1). New York: Academic Press, pp. 170–220.

Cahill, G. F. (1971). The physiology of insulin in man. *Diabetes, 20,* 785–799.

Cahill, K. M. (Ed.) (1984). *The AIDS epidemic, 1983.* New York: St. Martin's.

Calabrese, J. R., Kling, M. A., & Gold, P. W. (1987). Alterations in immunocompetence during stress, bereavement, and depression: Focus on neuroendocrine regulation. *The American Journal of Psychiatry, 144,* 9.

Calabrese, L. H. (1990). Exercise, immunity, cancer, and infection. In C. Bouchard, R. J. Shephard, T. Stephens, J. R. Sutton, & B. D. McPherson (Eds.), *Exercise, fitness, and health: A consensus of current knowledge.* Champaign, Ill.: Human Kinetics, pp. 567–579.

Calfas, C. J., Kaplan, R. M., & Ingram, R. E. (1992). One year evaluation of cognitive-behavioral intervention in osteoarthritis. *Arthritis Care and Research,* in press.

Cannon, W. B. (1932). *The wisdom of the body.* New York: Norton.

Capilouto, G. I., Weinstein, M. C., Hemenway, D., & Cotton, D. (1992). What is a dentist's occupational risk of being infected with the hepatitis B or human immuno deficiency virus? *American Journal of Public Health, 82,* 587–589.

Caplan, G. (1981). Mastery of stress: Psychosocial aspects. *The American Journal of Psychiatry, 138,* 413–420.

Caplan, R., Robinson, E. A. R., French, J. R., Caldwell, J. R., & Shinn, M. (1976). *Adhering to medical regiment.* Presented at the Institute for Social Research, Ann Arbor, Michigan.

Carlaw, R. W., Mittlemark, M. B., Bracht, N., & Luepker, R. (1984). Organization for a community cardiovascular health program: Experiences from the Minnesota heart health program. *Health Education Quarterly, 11,* 243–252.

Carmelli, D., Dame, A., Swan, G., & Rosenman, R. (1991). Long-term changes in Type A behavior. A 27-year follow-up of the Western Collaborative Group Study. *Journal of Behavioral Medicine, 14,* 593–606.

Carmody, T., Senner, J., Mailinow, M., & Matarazzo, J. (1980). Physical exercise rehabilitation: Long-term drop out rate in cardiac patients. *Journal of Behavioral Medicine, 3,* 163–168.

Caron, H. S., & Roth, H.P. (1971). Objective assessment of cooperation with an ulcer diet: Relation to antacid intake and to assigned physician. *American Journal of the Medical Sciences, 261,* 61–66.

Carter, W. B. (1990). Health behavior as a rational process: Theory of reasoned action and multiattribute utility theory. In K. Glanz, F. M. Lewis, & B. K. Rimer (Eds.), *Health behavior and health education: Theory, research, and practice.* San Francisco: Jossey-Bass, pp. 63–91.

Carvalho, J. J. M., Baruzzi, R. G., Howard, P. F., Poulter, N., Alpers, M. P., Franco, L. J., Marcopito, L. F., Spooner, V. J., Dyer, A. R., Elliott, P., Stamler, J., & Stamler, R. (1989). Blood pressure in four remote populations in the INTERSALT study. *Hypertension, 14,* 238–246.

Carver, C. S., Scheier, M. F., & Pozo, C. (1991). Conceptualizing the process of coping with health problems. In H. Friedman (Ed.), *Hostility, coping and health.* Washington, D.C.: American Psychological Association, pp. 167–187.

Carey, M. P., & Burish, T. G. (1988). Etiology and treatment of the psychological side effects associated with cancer chemotherapy: A review and discussion. *Psychological Bulletin, 104,* 307–325.

Case, R. B., Moss, A. J., Case, N., McDermott, M., & Eberly, S. (January 22–29, 1992). Living alone after myocardial infarction. Impact on prognosis. *Journal of the American Medical Association, 267*(4), 515–519.

Caspersen, C. J. (1989). Physical activity epidemiology: Concepts, methods, and applications to exercise science. *Exercise and Sport Science Reviews, 17,* 423–473.

Caspersen, C. J., Christenson, G. M., & Pollard, R. A. (1986). Status of the 1990 physical fitness and exercise objectives—Evidence from NHIS 1985. *Public Health Reports, 101,* 587–592.

Caspersen, C. J., Powell, K. E., & Christenson, G. M. (1985). Physical activity, exercise, and physical fitness. Definitions and distinctions for health-related research. *Public Health Reports, 100,* 126–131.

Centers for Disease Control. (1987). Revision of the CDC surveillance case definition for acquired immunodeficiency syndrome. Morbid monitor. *Weekly Reports, 35* (supp. 1).

Centers for Disease Control. (1988). Trends in diabetes mortality. *Morbidity and Mortality Weekly Report, 37,* 769–773.

Centers for Disease Control. (August 1990). Prevalence of HIV. *Weekly Report.*

Centers for Disease Control. (1991). AIDS in women—United States. *Morbidity and Mortality Weekly Report, 23.*

Chalmers, T. C., Celano, P., Sacks, H., & Smith, H. (1983). Bias in treatment assignment in controlled clinical trials. *New England Journal of Medicine, 309,* 1358–1361.

Chaney, E., O'Leary, M., & Marlatt, G. (1978). Skill training with alcoholics. *Journal of Consulting and Clinical Psychology, 46,* 1092–1104.

Chapman, C. R., & Bonica, J. J. (1985). *Chronic pain.* Kalamazoo, Mich.: Upjohn.

Charney, E., et al. (1976). Childhood antecedents of adult obesity: Do chubby infants become obese adults? *New England Journal of Medicine, 295,* 6–10.

Chen, M. M., & Bush, J. W. (1976). Maximizing health system output with political and administrative constraints using mathematical programming. *Inquiry, 13,* 215–227.

Chesney, M. A., Eagleston, J. R., & Rosenman, R. H. (1981). Type A behavior: Assessment and intervention. In C. K. Prokop & L. A. Bradley

(Eds.), *Medical psychology: Contributions to behavioral medicine.* New York: Academic Press, pp. 19–36.

Chodoff, P., Friedman, S., & Hamburg, D. (1964). Stress, defenses, and coping behavior: Observations in parents of children with malignant diseases. *American Journal of Psychiatry, 120,* 743–749.

Christensen, A., Phillips, S., Glasgow, R. E., & Johnson, S. M. (1983). Parental characteristics and interactional dysfunctions in families with child behavior problems: A preliminary investigation. *Journal of Abnormal Child Psychology, 11,* 153–166.

Christensen, A. J., Turner, C. W., Smith, T. W., Holman, J. N., & Gregory, M. C. (1991). Health locus of control and depression in end-stage renal disease. *Journal of Consulting and Clinical Psychology, 59,* 419–424.

Christoffel, K. K. (1990). Violent death and injury in U.S. children and adolescents. *American Journal of Diseases of Children, 144,* 697–706.

Chu, S. Y., Buehler, J. W., & Berkelman, R. L. (1990). Impact of the human immunodeficiency virus epidemic on mortality in women of reproductive age, United States. *JAMA, 264,* 225–229.

Chyou, P. H., Nomura, A. M. Y., Stemmermann, G. N. (1992). A prospective study of the attributable risk of cancer due to cigarette smoking. *American Journal of Public Health, 82,* 37–40.

Cinciripini, P. M., & Floreen, A. (1982). An evaluation of a behavioral program for chronic pain. *Journal of Behavioral Medicine, 5,* 375–390.

Cloninger, C. R., Bohman, M., & Sigvardsson, S. (1981). Inheritance of alcohol abuse. *Archives of General Psychiatry, 38,* 861–868.

Clot, J., Charmasson, E., & Brochier, J. (1972). Age-dependent changes of human blood lymphocyte subpopulations. *Clin. Exp. Immunol., 32,* 346–351.

Coates, T. J., McKusick, L., Morin, S. F., Charles, K. A., Wiley, J. A., Stall, R. D., & Conant, M. D. (August 1985). *Differences among gay men in desire for HTLV-III/LAV antibody testing and beliefs about exposure to the probable AIDS virus: The behavior AIDS project.* Presented at the Annual Meeting of the American Psychological Association, Los Angeles.

Coates, T. J., Stall, R. D., & Hoff, C. C. (1990).

Changes in sexual behavior among gay and bisexual men since the beginning of the AIDS epidemic. In *Psychosocial perspectives on AIDS.* Hillsdale, N.J.: Lawrence Erlbaum, pp. 103–137.

Coats, J. J., Stall, R. D., Ekstrand, M., & Solomon, G. F. (1989). *Psychosocial predictors as co-factors for disease progression in men infected with HIV: The San Francisco men's health study.* VIth Conference on AIDS, Montreal.

Cobb, S. (1976). Social support as a moderator of life stress. *Psychosomatic Medicine, 38,* 300–313.

Cobb, S., & Lindemann, E. (1943). Coconut Grove burns: Neuropsychiatric observations. *Ann. Surg., 117,* 814–824.

Cohen, F., & Lazarus, R. S. (1973). Active coping processes, coping dispositions, and recovery from surgery. *Psychosomatic Medicine, 35,* 375–389.

Cohen, F., & Lazarus, R. S. (1979). Coping with the stresses of illness. In G. C. Stone, F. Cohen, N. E. Adler (Eds.), *Health psychology.* San Francisco: Jossey-Bass.

Cohen, J. B., & Reed, D. (1984). The Type A behavior pattern and coronary heart disease risk among Japanese men in Hawaii. *Journal of Behavioral Medicine, 8,* 343–352.

Cohen, S., & Hoberman, H. (1983). Positive events and social supports as buffers of life change stress: Maximizing the prediction of health outcome. *Journal of Applied Social Psychology, 13,* 99–125.

Cohen, S., Mermelstein, R., Kamarck, T., & Hoberman, N. H. (1985). Measuring the functional components of social support. In I. Sarason & B. Sarason (Eds.), *Social support: Theory, research, and applications.* Dordrecht, Netherlands: Martinus Nijhoff, pp. 73–94.

Cohen, S., & Syme, S. L. (1985). *Social support and health.* San Francisco: Academic Press.

Cohen, S., Tyrell, A. J., & Smith, A. P. (1991). Psychological stress and susceptibility to the common cold. *New England Journal of Medicine, 325,* 606–612.

Cohen, S., & Williamson, G. M. (1991). Stress and infectious disease in humans. *Psychological Bulletin, 109,* 5–24.

Cohen, S., & Willis, T. H. (1985). Stress, social support, and the buffering hypothesis. *Psychological Bulletin, 98,* 310–357.

Cohen-Cole, S., Gogen, R., Stevens, A., Kirk, K.,

Gaitan, E., Hain, J., & Freeman, A. (1981). Psychosocial, endocrine, and immune factors in acute necrotizing ulcerative gingivitis. *Psychosomatic Medicine, 43,* 91.

Coll, M., Meyers, A., & Stunkard, A. J. (1979). Obesity and food choices in public places. *Archives of General Psychiatry, 36,* 795–797.

Colvey, A., & Blauchett, M. (1981). Disability trends in the United States population, 1966–76: Analysis of reported causes. *American Journal of Public Health, 71,* 464–471.

Committee on Diet, Nutrition, and Cancer of the National Research Council. (1983). *Diet, nutrition and cancer.* Washington, D.C.: National Academy of Sciences Press.

Committee on Trauma Research. (1985). *Injury in America: A continuing public health problem.* Washington, D.C.: National Academy Press.

Compton, W. M., Cottler, L. D., Decker, S. H., Meager, D., & Stringfellow, R. (1992). Legal needle buying in St. Louis. *American Journal of Public Health, 82,* 595–596.

Comstock, G., & Paik, H. (1991). *Television and the American child.* New York: Academic Press.

Condiotte, M. M., & Lichtenstein, E. (1981). Self-efficacy and relapse in smoking cessation programs. *Journal of Consulting and Clinical Psychology, 49,* 648–658.

Connolly, J. (1976). Life events before myocardial infarction. *Journal of Human Stress, 3,* 3–17.

Connor, W. E., & Connor, S. L.(1985). The dietary prevention and treatment of coronary heart disease. In W. E. Connor & J. D. Bristow (Eds.), *Coronary heart disease: Prevention, complications, and treatment.* Philadelphia: Lippincott, pp. 43–64.

Contento, I. R., Michela, J. L., & Goldberg, C. J. (1988). Food choice among adolescents: Population segmentation by motivations. *Journal of Nutrition Education, 20,* 289–298.

Cook, P. (1981). Effect of liquor taxes on drinking, cirrhosis, and auto accidents. In M. H. Moor & D. R. Gerstein (Eds.), *Alcohol and public policy.* Washington, D.C.: National Academy Press.

Cook, T. D., & Campbell, D. G. (1979). *Quasi-experimentation: Design and analysis issues for field studies.* Chicago: Rand-McNally.

Cooperating Clinics of the American Rheumatism Association. (1965). A seven day variability study of 499 patients with peripheral rheumatoid arthritis. *Arthritis and Rheumatism, 8,* 302–334.

Corish, C. D., Richard, B., & Brown, S. (1989). Missed medication doses in rheumatoid arthritis patients: Intentional and unintentional reasons. *Arthritis Care and Research, 2,* 3–9.

Coronary Drug Project Research Group. (1980). Influence of adherence to treatment and response of cholesterol on mortality in the Coronary Drug Project. *New England Journal of Medicine, 303,* 1038–1041.

Cotton P. (1992). Women's health initiative leads way as research begins to fill gender gaps. *Journal of the American Medical Association. 267*(4) Jan. 22–29, 469–470, 473.

Council on Scientific Affairs, American Medical Association. (1992). Violence against women: Relevance for medical practitioners. *Journal of the American Medical Association, 267,* 3184–3189.

Cousins, N. (1976). Anatomy of an illness (as perceived by the patient). *New England Journal of Medicine, 195,* 1458–1463.

Cox, D. J., Gonder-Frederick, L., Julian, D., Cryer, P., Lee, J. H., Richards, F. E., & Clarke, W. (1991). Intensive versus standard blood glucose awareness training (BGAT) with insulin-dependent diabetes: Mechanisms and ancillary effects. *Psychosomatic Medicine, 53*(4), 453–462.

Craig, T. K. J., & Brown, G. W. (1984). Life events, meaning and physical illness—A review. In A. Steptoe and A. Mathews (Eds.) *Health care and human behavior.* London Academic Press, pp. 7–34.

Crary, B., Borysenko, M., Sutherland, D., Kutz, I., Borysenke, J., & Benson, H. (1983). Decrease in mitogen responsiveness of mononuclear cells from peripheral blood after epinephrine administration in humans. *Journal of Immunology, 130,* 694–697.

Creer, T., & Leung, P. (1982). The development and evaluation of a self-management program for children with asthma. In *Self-management education programs for childhood asthma,* vol. 2. Bethesda, Md.: National Institute for Allergic and Infectious Disease.

Creer, T. L. (1982). Asthma. *Journal of Consulting and Clinical Psychology, 50,* 912–921.

Creer, T. L., Ipacs, J., & Creer, P. P.(1983). Changing behavioral and social variables at resident treatment facilities for childhood asthma. *Journal of Asthma, 20,* 11–5.

Criqui, M. H. (1985). Alochol and cardiovascular mortality. In R. M. Kaplan & M. H. Criqui (Eds.), *Behavioral epidemiology and disease prevention.* New York: Plenum, pp. 67–90.

Criqui, M. H. (1987). Alcohol and hypertension: New insights from population studies. *European Heart Journal, 8*(suppl.), 19–26.

Criqui, M. H., Wallace, R. B., Heiss, G., et al. (1980). Cigarette smoking and plasma high-density lipoprotein cholesterol. *Circulation, 62* (suppl.), 70–75.

Cromwell, C. J., & Schmidtt, M. H., (1990). Perceived health status, self-esteem and body image in women with rheumatoid arthritis or systemic lupus erythematosus. *Research in Nursing and Health, 13,* 99–107.

Cronan, T. A., Kaplan, R. M., Posner, L., Blumberg, E., & Kozin, F. (1990). Prevalence of the use of unconventional remedies for arthritis in a metropolitan community. *Arthritis and Rheumatisim, 32*(12), 1604–1607.

Cropp, G. J. A. (1985). Special features of asthma in children. *Chest, 87,* 55S–62S.

Cummings, K., Jette, A., Brock, B., & Haefner, D. (1979). Psychosocial determinants of immunization behavior in a swine influenza campaign. *Medical Care, 17,* 639–649.

Cunningham, L. S., & Kelsey, J. L. (1984). Epidemiology of musculoskeletal impairment and associated disability. *American Journal of Public Health, 74,* 574–579.

Cupps, T., & Fauci, A. (1982). Corticosteroid-mediated immunoregulation in man. *Immunology Review, 65,* 133–135.

Curbow, B., Somerfield, M., Legro, M., & Sonnega, J. (1990). Self-concept and cancer in adults: Theoretical and methodological issues. *Social Science and Medicine, 31*(2), 115–128.

Curry, S. J., Kristal, A. R., & Bowen, D. J. (1992). An application of the stage model of behavior change to dietary fat reduction. *Health Education Research: Theory and Practice, 7,* 97–105.

Dahlkoetter, J., Callahan, E. J., & Linton, J. (1979). Obesity and the unbalanced energy equation: Exercise versus eating habit change. *Journal of Consulting and Clinical Psychology, 47*(5), 898–905.

Danaher, B. G. (1977). Rapid smoking and self-control in the modification of smoking behavior. *Journal of Consulting and Clinical Psychology, 45,* 1068–1075.

Darko, D. F., Gillin, J. C., Rock, S. C., Bulloch, K., Golshan, S., Tasevska, Z., & Hamburger, R. N. (1988). Immune cells and the hypothalamic-pituitary axis in major depression. *Psychiatry Res., 215,* 173–179.

Davidson, D. M., & Shumaker, S. A. (1987). Social support and cardiovascular disease. *Atherosclerosis, 7,* 101–104.

Davidson, M. D. (1986). *Diabetes mellitus: Diagnosis and treatment* (2nd ed.). New York: Wiley.

Davidson, T. N., Bowden, L., & Tholen, D. (1979). Social support as a moderator of burn rehabilitation. *Archives of Physical Medicine and Rehabilitation, 60,* 556.

Davis, M. S. (1968). Physiologic, psychological and demographic factors in patient's compliance of doctors' orders. *Medical Care, 6,* 115–122.

Dawber, T. R. (1980). *The Framingham Study: The epidemiology of atherosclerotic disease.* Cambridge: Harvard University Press.

Dawes, R. M. Faust, P., & Meehl, P. E. (1989). Clinical versus actuarial judgment. *Science, 243,* 1668–1674.

Dayton, S., Pearce, J. L., Hashimoto, S., Dixon, W. J., & Tomiyasu, U. (1969). A controlled clinical trial of a diet high in unsaturated fat in preventing complications of atherosclerosis. *Circulation, 40* (suppl. 2), 1–63.

DeBacker, G., Kornitzer, M., Kittel, F., & Dramaix, M. (1983). Behavior, stress, and psychosocial traits as risk factors. *Preventive Medicine, 12,* 32–36.

Dembroski, T. M., MacDougall, J. M., Costa, P. T., Jr., & Grandits, G. A. (1989). Components of hostility as predictors of sudden death and myocardial infarction in the Multiple Risk Factor Intervention Trial. *Psychosomatic Medicine, 51*(5), 514–522.

DeMoor, C., Elder, J. P., Young, R. L., Wildey, M. B., & Molgaard, C. A. (1989). Generic tobacco use among four ethnic groups in a school age population. *Journal of Drug Education, 19,* 257–270.

Depue, R. A., & Monroe, S. M. (1984). *Life stress and human disorder: Conceptualization and measurement of the disordered group*. Univ. of Pittsburgh. Unpublished paper.

Derogatis, L. R., Abeloff, M. D., & Melisaratos, N. (1979). Psychological coping mechanisms and survival time in metastatic breast cancer. *Journal of the American Medical Association, 242,* 1504–1508.

Derogatis, L. R., & Spencer, P. M. (1982). *The Brief Symptom Inventory (BSI), administration, scoring, and procedures manual I.* Baltimore: Clinical Psychometrics Research.

Descartes, R. (1662). Depression and immunity: Lymphocyte function in ambulatory depressed patients, hospitalized schizophrenic patients, and patients hospitalized for herniorrhaphy. *Archives of General Psychiatry, 42,* 129–133; reprinted in R. Eaton (Ed.) (1955). *Selections.* New York: Scribner's.

Des Jarlais, D. C., & Friedman, S. (1987) HIV infection among intravenous drug users: Epidemiology and risk reduction (editorial review). *AIDS, 1,* 67–76.

Des Jarlais, D. C., & Friedman, S. R. (1990). Target groups for preventing AIDS among intravenous drug users. In *Psychosocial perspectives on AIDS.* Hillsdale, N.J.: Lawrence Erlbaum, pp. 35–50.

Devesa, S. S., & Schneiderman, M. A. (1977). Increase in the number of cancer deaths in the United States. *American Journal of Epidemiology, 106,* 1–5.

DeVita, V. T., & Kershner, L. M. (1980). Cancer, the curable disease. *American Pharmacy,* April.

Deyo, R. A. (1988). Measuring "quality of life" in patients with rheumatoid arthritis. In S. Walker & R. Rosser (Eds.), *Quality of life: Assessment and application.* London: MTP Press, pp. 205–222.

Deyo, R. A., Inui, T. S., Leininger, J. D., et al. (1983). Measuring functional outcomes in chronic disease: A comparison of traditional scales and a self-administered health status questionnaire in patients with rheumatoid arthritis. *Medical Care, 21,* 180–192.

DHEW. (1979). *Health people: The surgeon general's report on health promotion and disease prevention.* Publication no. 79-55071. Washington, D.C.

Diamond, E. L. (1982). The role of anger and hostility in essential hypertension and coronary heart disease. *Psychological Bulletin, 92,* 410–433.

DiClemente, C. C., & Hughes, S. O. (1990). Stages of change profiles in outpatient alcoholism treatment. *Journal of Substance Abuse, 2,* 217–235.

DiClemente, C. C., Prochaska, J. O., Fairhurst, S. K., Velicer, W. F., Velasquez, M. M., & Rossi, J. S. (1991). The process of smoking cessation: An analysis of precontemplation, contemplation, and preparation stages of change. *Journal of Consulting and Clinical Psychology, 59,* 295–304.

DiClemente, R. J. (1990). Adolescents and AIDS: Current research, prevention strategies, and policy implications. In *Psychosocial perspectives on AIDS.* Hillsdale, N.J.: Lawrence Erlbaum, pp. 51–64.

DiClemente, R. J., Boyer, C. B., & Morales, E. S. (1988). Minorities and AIDS: Knowledge, attitudes, and misconceptions among black and adolescents. *American Journal of Public Health, 78,* 55–57.

DiMatteo, M. R., & DiNicola, D. D. (1982). *Achieving patient compliance.* New York: Pergamon.

Dimond, M. (1979). Social support and adaptation to chronic illness: The case of maintenance hemodialysis. *Research in Nurisng and Health, 2,* 101–108.

Dimsdale, J. E. (1974). The coping behavior of Nazi concentration camp survivors. *American Journal of Psychiatry, 131,* 792–797.

Dimsdale, J. E. (1985). Controversies regarding Type A and coronary heart disease. *Cardiology Clinics, 3,* 259–267.

Dimsdale, J. E. (1988). A perspective on Type A behavior and coronary disease. *New England Journal of Medicine, 318,* 110–112.

Dishman, R. K. (1990). Determinants of participation in physical activity. In C. Bouchard, R. J. Shephard, T. Stephens, J. R. Sutton, & G. D. McPherson (Eds.), *Exercise, fitness, and health: A consensus of current knowledge.* Champaign, Ill.: Human Kinetics, pp. 75–101.

Dishman, R. K., Sallis, J. F., & Orenstein, D. M. (1985). The determinants of physical activity and exercise. *Public Health Reports, 100,* 158–172.

Division of Injury Control. (1990). Childhood injuries in the United States. *American Journal of Diseases of Children, 144,* 627–646.

Dohrenwend, B. P., & Shrout, P. E. (1985). Hassles in the conceptualization and measurement of life stresses variables. *American Psychologist, 40,* 780–785.

Dohrenwend, B. S., & Dohrenwend, B. P. (1984). Life stress and illness: Formulation of the issues. In *Stressful life events and their contexts.* pp. 1–23.

Dolecek, T. A., Milas, N. C., Van Horn, L. V., Farrand, M. E., Gorder, D. D., Duchene, A. G., Dyer, J. R., Stone, P. A., & Randall, B. L. (1986). A long-term nutrition intervention experience: Lipid responses and dietary adherence patterns in the Multiple Risk Factor Intervention Trial. *Journal of the American Dietetic Association, 86,* 752–758.

Doll, R., & Peto, R. (1981). *The causes of cancer.* New York: Oxford University Press.

Dorian, B. J., Keystone, E., Garfinkel, P. E., & Brown, G. M. (1982). Aberrations in lymphocyte subpopulations and functions during psychological stress. *Clinical and Experimental Immunology, 50,* 132–138.

Dubbert, P. M., Martin, J. E., Zimering, R. T., Burkett, P. A., Lake, M., & Cushman, W. C. (1984). Behavioral control of mild hypertension with aerobic exercise: Two case studies. *Behavior Therapy, 15,* 373–380.

Dubbert, P. M., & Wilson, G. T. (1984). Goal-setting and spouse involvement in the treatment of obesity. *Behaviour Research and Therapy, 13,* 227–242.

Duffy, J. (1987). Quackery in arthritis. *Minnesota Medicine, 70, 700.*

Dunbar, J. (1990). Predictors of patient adherence: Patient characteristics. In S. A. Shumaker, E. B. Schron, & J. D. Ockene (Eds.), *The handbook of health behavior change.* New York: Springer, pp. 348–360.

Dunbar, J., & Stunkard, A. J. (1979). Adherence to diet and drug regimen. In R. Levi, B. Rifkind, B. Dennis, & N. Ernst (Eds.), *Nutrition, lipids, and coronary heart disease.* New York: Raven.

Dunbar-Jacob, J., Dwyer, K., & Dunning, E. J. (1991). Compliance with antihypertensive regimen: A review of the research in the 1980s. *Annals of Behavioral Medicine, 13,* 31–39.

Duncan, B., Boyce, W. T., Itami, R., & Puffenbarger, N. (1983). A controlled trial of a physical fitness program for fifth grade students. *Journal of School Health,* 153–160.

Duncan, J. J., Farr, J. E., Upton, J., Hagan, R. D., Oglesby, M. E., & Blair, S. N. (1985). The effects of aerobic exercise on plasma catecholamines and blood pressure in patients with essential hypertension. *Journal of the American Medical Association, 254,* 2609–2613.

Dunkel-Schetter, C., Feinstein, L. G., Taylor, S. E., & Falke, R. L. (1992). Patterns of coping with cancer. *Health Psychology, 11*(2), 79–87.

Dusenbury, L., Kerner, J. F., Baker, E., Botvin, G., James-Ortiz, S., & Zauber, A. (1992). Predictors of smoking prevalence among New York Latino youth. *American Journal of Public Health, 82,* 55–58.

Eaton, R. P. (1979). Lipids and diabetes: The case for macrovascular disease. *Diabetes Care, 2,* 46–50.

Ekelund, L. G., Haskell, W. L., Johnson, J. L., Whaley, F. S., Criqui, M. H., & Sheps, D. S. (1988). Physical fitness as a predictor of cardiovascular mortality in asymptomatic North American men. *New England Journal of Medicine, 319,* 1379–1384.

Ekerdt, D. J. (1987). Why the notion persists that retirement harms health. *The Forum, 27,* 454–457.

Ekerdt, D. J., Baden, L., Bosse, R., & Dibbs, E. (1983). The effect of retirement on physical health. *American Journal of Public Health, 73,* 779–783.

Elder, J., McGraw, S., Abrams, D., Ferreira, A., Lasater, T., Longpre, H., Peterson, G., Schwertfeger, R., & Carleton, R. (1986). Organizational and community approaches to community-wide prevention of heart disease: The first 2 years of the Pawtucket heart health program. *Preventive Medicine, 15,* 107–117.

Elder, J. P., McGraw, S. A., Rodrigues, A., Lasater, T. M., Ferreira, A., Kendall, L., Peterson, G., & Carleton, R. A. (1987). Evaluation of two community-wide smoking cessation contests. *Preventive Medicine, 16,* 221–234.

Elder, J. P., Sallis, J. F., Mayer, J. A., Hammond, N., & Peplinski, S. (1989). Community-based health promotion: A survey of churches, labor unions, supermarkets, and restaurants. *Journal of Community Health, 14,* 159–168.

Ellis, A., & Greiger, R. (1977). *Handbook of rational-emotive therapy.* New York: Springer.

Emery, C. F., & Blumenthal, J. A. (1991). Effects of physical exercise on psychological and cognitive functioning of older adults. *Annals of Behavioral Medicine, 13,* 99–107.

Emmons, C. A., Joseph, J. G., Kessler, R. C., et al. (1986). Psychosocial predictors of reported behavior change in homosexual men at risk for AIDS. *Health Education Quarterly, 13,* 331–345.

Emmons, K. M., Abrams, D. B., Marshall, R. J., Etzel, R. A., Novotny, T. E., Marcus, B. H., & Kane, M. E. (1992). Exposure to environmental tobacco smoke in naturalistic settings. *American Journal of Public Health, 82,* 24–28.

Engel, B. T., Glasgow, M. S., & Gaarder, K. R. (1983). Behavioral treatment of high blood pressure: III. Follow-up results and treatment recommendations. *Psychosomatic Medicine, 45,* 23–30.

Engel, G. L. (1977). The need for a new medical model: A challenge for biomedicine. *Science, 196,* 129–136.

Enthoven, A., & Kronick, R. (1989). A consumer-choice health plan for the 1990's: Universal health insurance in a system designed to promote quality and economy. *New England Journal of Medicine, 320,* 29–37.

Epstein, L. H. (1984). The direct effects of compliance upon outcome. *Health Psychology, 3,* 385–393.

Epstein, L. H. (1986). Treatment of childhood obesity. In K. D. Brownell & J. P. Foreyt (Eds.), *Handbook of eating disorders.* New York: Basic Books, pp. 159–179.

Epstein, L. H., & Clauss, P. A. (1982). A behavioral medicine perspective on adherence to long-term medical regimens. *Journal of Consulting and Clinical Psychology, 50,* 950–971.

Epstein, L. H., Smith, J. A., Vara, L. S., & Rodefer, J. S. (1991). Behavioral economic analysis of activity choice in obese children. *Health Psychology, 10,* 311–316.

Epstein, L. H., Valoski, A., Wing, R. R., & McCurley, J. (1990). Ten-year follow-up of behavioral, family-based treatment for obese children. *Journal of the American Medical Association, 264,* 2519–2523.

Epstein, L. H., Wing, R. R., Koeske, R., & Valoski, A. (1984). Effects of diet plus exercise on weight change in parents and children. *Journal of Consulting and Clinical Psychology, 52,* 429–437.

Epstein, L. H., Wing, R. R., Koeske, R., & Valoski, A. (1985). A comparison of lifestyle exercise, aerobic exercise, and calisthenics on weight loss in obese children. *Behavior Therapy, 16,* 345–356.

Epstein, L. H., Wing, R. R., Thompson, J. K., & Griffin, W. (1980). Attendance and fitness in aerobic exercise: The effects of contract and lottery procedures. *Behavior Modification, 4,* 465–479.

Etinger, L. (1964). *Concentration camp survivors in Norway and Israel.* London: Allen & Unwin.

Evans, D., Clark, N. M., Feldman, C. H., Wasilewski, Y., Levison, M. J., Zimmerman, B. J., Levin, B., & Mellins, R. B. (1990). School-based health education for children with asthma: Some issues for adherence research. In S. A. Shumaker, L. B. Schron, & J. K. Ockene (Eds.), *The handbook of health behavior change.* New York: Springer, pp. 144–152.

Evans, M. G. (January 1991). The problem of analyzing multiplicative composites. In *American Psychologist,* pp. 6–15.

Evans, R. I., Rozelle, R. M., Mittelmark, M. B., Hansen, W., Bane, A. L., & Havis, J. (1978). Deterring the onset of smoking in children: Knowledge of immediate physiological effects and coping with peer pressure, media pressure, and parent modeling. *Journal of Applied Social Psychology, 8,* 126–136.

Ewart, C. K. (1991). Social action theory for a public health psychology. *American Psychologist, 46,* 931–946.

Ewart, C. K., Taylor, C. B., Reese, C. B., & DeBusk, R. F. (1983). Effects of early postmyocardial infarction exercise testing on self-perception and subsequent physical activity. *American Journal of Cardiology, 51,* 1076–1080.

Farley, T. A., & Flannery, J. T. (1989). Late-stage diagnosis of breast cancer in women of lower socioeconomic status: Public health implications. *American Journal of Public Health, 79,* 1508–1512.

Farquhar, J. W., Fortmann, S. P., Flora, J. A., Taylor, C. B., Haskell, W. L., Williams, P. T., Maccoby, N., & Wood, P. D. (1990). Effects of communitywide education on cardiovascular disease risk factors: The Stanford Five-City Project. *Journal of the American Medical Association, 264,* 359–365.

Farquhar, J. W., Fortmann, S. P., Maccoby, N., Haskell, W. L., Williams, P. T., Flora, J. A., Taylor, C. B., Brown, B. W., Solomon, D. S., & Hulley, S. B. (1985). The Stanford five-city project: Design and methods. *American Journal of Epidemiology, 122,* 323–334.

Farquhar, J. W., Maccoby, N., & Solomon, D. S. (1984). Community applications of behavioral medicine. In W. D. Gentry (Ed.), *Handbook of behavioral medicine.* New York: Guilford, pp. 437–478.

Federal Register. (November 25, 1987). *52,* 227.

Feinleib, M. (1983). Genetics. In N. M. Kaplan & J. Stamler (Eds.), *Prevention of coronary heart disease: Practical management of the risk factors.* Philadelphia: Saunders, pp. 120–129.

Feinstein, A. R. (1971). Clinical biostatistics, VIII: An analytical appraisal of the university group diabetes program (UDGP). *Clinical Pharmacology, 12,* 167–191.

Feinstein, A. R., Wood, H. F., & Epstein, J. A. (1959). A controlled study of three methods of prophylaxis against streptococcal infection in a population of rheumatic children. ii. Results of the first three years of the study including methods for evaluating the maintenance of oral prophylaxis. *New England Journal of Medicine, 260,* 697–702.

Feldman, J. J. (1982). Health of the disadvantaged: An epidemiological overview. In D. C. Parron, F. Solomon, & C. D. Jenkins (Eds.), *Behavior, health risks, and social disadvantage.* Washington, D.C.: National Academy Press, pp. 13–18.

Felten, D., Felten, S., Carlson, S. Olschawka, J., & Livnat, S. (1985). Noradrenergic and peptidergic innervation of lymphoid tissue. *Journal of Immunology, 135* (2 Supple.), 755s–765s.

Felten, S. Y., Felten, S. Y., Bellinger, D. L., et al. (1987). Noradrenergic sympathetic neural interactions with the immune system: Structure and function. *Immunol. Rev., 100,* 225–260.

Felton, B. J., & Revenson, T. A. (1987). Age differences in coping with chronic illness. *Psychology and Aging, 2,* 164–170.

Ferguson, J. M., & Birchler, G. (1978). Therapeutic packges: Tools for change. In W. S. Agras (Ed.), *Behavior modification: Principles and clinical applications* (2nd ed.). Boston: Little Brown.

Ferster, C. B., Nurnberger, J. I., & Levitt, E. D. (1962). The control of eating. *Journal of Methetics, 1,* 87–109.

Finlayson, A. (1976). Social support networks as coping resources: Lay help and consultation patterns used by women in husband's post-infarction careers. *Social Science and Medicine, 10,* 97–103.

Finnegan, D. L., & Suler, J. R. (1984). Psychological factors associated with maintenance of improved health behaviors in postcoronary patients. *Journal of Psychology, 119,* 87–94.

Fischl, M. A., Richman, D. D., Grielo, M. H., et al. (1987). The efficacy of azidothymidine (AZT) in the treatment of patients with AIDS and the AIDS-related complex. *New England J. of Medicine, 317,* 185–191.

Fishman, B., & Loscalo, M. (1987). Cognitive-behavioral interventions in management of cancer pain: Principles and applications. *Medicine and Clinical Practice in North America, 71,* 271–287.

Flay, B. R. (1985). Psychosocial approaches to smoking prevention: A review of findings. *Health Psychology, 4,* 449–488.

Flay, B. R., d'Avernas, J. R., Best, J. A., Kersell, M. W., & Ryan, K. B. (1983). Cigarette smoking: Why young people do it and ways of preventing it. In P. J. McGrath & P. Firestone (Eds.), *Pediatric and adolescent behavioral medicine.* New York: Springer, 132–183.

Flay, B. R., Koepke, D., Thomson, S. J., Santi, S., Best, J. A., & Brown, K. S. (1989). Six-year follow-up of the first Waterloo school smoking prevention trial. *American Journal of Public Health, 79,* 1371–1376.

Flay, B. R., Ryan, K. B., Best, J. A., Brown, K. S., Kersell, M. W., d'Avernas, J. R., & Zanna, M. P.

(1985). Are social-psychological smoking prevention programs effective? The Waterloo Study. *Journal of Behavioral Medicine, 8,* 37–59.

Flora, J. A., & Cassady, L. (1990). Roles of media in community-based health promotion. In N. Bracht (Ed.), *Health promotion at the community level.* Newbury Park, Calif.: Sage, pp. 143–157.

Folkman, S., & Lazarus, R. S. (1980). An analysis of coping in a middle-aged community sample. *Journal of Health and Social Behavior, 21,* 219–239.

Folkman, S., & Lazarus, R. S. (1988). *Manual for the Ways of Coping Questionnaire* (Research edition). Palo Alto: Consulting Psychologists Press.

Folsom, A. R., Hughes, J. R., Buehler, J. F., Mittelmark, M. B., Jacobs, D. R., & Grimm, R. H. (1985). Do Type A men drink more frequently than Type B men? Findings in the Multiple Risk Factor Intervention Trial (MRFIT). *Journal of Behavioral Medicine, 8,* 227–236.

Fordyce, W. E. (1976). *Behavioral methods in chronic pain and illness.* St. Louis: Mosby.

Fordyce, W. E. (1988). Pain and suffering. A reappraisal. *American Psychologist, 43,* 276–283.

Foreyt, J. P. (1987). Issues in the assessment and treatment of obesity. *Journal of Consulting and Clinical Psychology, 55,* 677–684.

Foreyt, J. P. Goodrick, G. K., & Gotto, A. M. (1981). Limitations of behavioral treatment of obesity: Review and analysis. *Journal of Behavioral Medicine, 4,* 159–174.

Forster, J. L., Jeffery, R. W., Schmid, T. L., & Kramer, M. (1988). Preventing weight gain in adults: A pound of prevention. *Health Psychology, 7,* 515–525.

Fox, B. H. (1989). Depressive symptoms and risk of cancer. *Journal of the American Medical Association, 262*(9), 1231.

Frank, G. C., Webber, L. S., & Berenson, G. S. (1982). Dietary studies of infants and children: The Bogalusa Heart Study. In T. J. Coates, A. C. Petersen, & C. Perry (Eds.)., *Promoting adolescent health: A dialog on research and practice.* New York: Academic Press, 329–354.

Frank, K. A., Heller, S. S., Kornfeld, D. S., Sporn, A. A., & Weiss, M. B. (1978). Type A behavior pattern in coronary angiographic findings. *Journal of the American Medical Association, 240,* 761–763.

Frank, R. G., Umlauf, R. L., Wonderlich, S. A., & Ashkanazi, G. S. (1986). Hypnosis and behavioral treatment in a worksite smoking cessation program. *Addictive Behaviors, 11,* 59–62.

Frankl, V. (1963). *Man's search for meaning.* New York: Washington Square Press.

Franz, I. D. (1913). On psychology and medical education. *Science, 38,* 555–566.

Fraser, G. E. (1986). Blood lipids and ischemic heart disease in vegetarians. In G. E. Fraser (Ed.), *Preventive cardiology.* New York: Oxford, 75–88.

Frederiksen, L. W., Miller, P. M., & Peterson, G. L. (1977). Topographical components of smoking behavior. *Addictive Behaviors, 2,* 55–61.

Fredikson, M., Robson, A., & Ljungdell, T. (1991). Ambulatory and laboratory blood pressure in individuals with negative and positive family history of hypertension. *Health Psychology, 10,* 371–377.

Freedman, D. S., Lee, S. L., Byers, T., Kuester, S., & Sell, R. D. (1992). Serum cholesterol levels in a multiracial sample of 7,439 preschool children from Arizona. *Preventive Medicine, 21,* 162–176.

Freeman, G. L. (1940). *Introduction to physiological psychology.* New York: Ronald.

French, T. M., & Alexander, F. (1941). Psychogenic factors in bronchioasthma. *Psychosomatic Medicine Monographs* (Number 4). Menasha, Wis.: George Banta.

French-Belgian Collaborative Group. (1982). Ischemic heart disease and psychological patterns: Prevalence and incidence studies in Belgium and France. *Advances in Cardiology, 29,* 25–31.

Frerichs, R. R., Chapman, J. M., & Maes, E. F. (1984). Mortality due to all causes and to cardiovascular diseases among seven race-ethnic populations in Los Angeles County, 1980. *International Journal of Epidemiology, 13,* 291–298.

Friedman, H. S. (1991). The self-dash healing personality. New York: Henry Holt.

Friedman, H. S., & DiMatteo, M. R. (1989). *Health psychology.* Englewood Cliffs, N.J.: Prentice-Hall.

Friedman, L. S., Lichtenstein, E., & Biglan, A. (1985). Smoking onset among teens: An empirical analysis of initial situations. *Addictive Behaviors, 10,* 1–13.

Friedman, M., & Rossenman, R. H. (1974). *Type A behavior and your heart.* New York: Knopf.

Friedman, S., et al. (1963). Behavioral observations on parents anticipating the death of a child. *Pediatrics, 32,* 610–625.

Fries, J. F. (1983). Toward an understanding of patient outcome measurement. *Arthritis and Rheumatism, 26,* 697–704.

Fries, J. F., Spitz, P. W., Kraines, R., et al. (1980). Measurement of outcome in arthritis. *Arthritis and Rheumatism, 23,* 137.

Fries, J. F., & Vickery, D. M. (1990). *Take care of yourself* (4 ed.). Reading, Mass., Addison-Wesley.

Ganda, O. P. (1980). Pathogenesis of macrovascular disease in the human diabetic. *Diabetes, 29,* 931–942.

Ganz, P. A. (1990). Current issues in cancer rehabilitation. *Cancer, 65*(3 Suppl), 742–751.

Ganz, P. A. (1992). Treatment options for breast cancer—beyond survival. *New England Journal of Medicine, 326*(17), 1147–1149.

Garcia, J., Hankins, W. G., & Rusiniak, K. W. (1974). Behavioral regulation of the milieu interne in man and rat. *Science, 185,* 824–831.

Garland, C., Barrett-Connor, E., Suarez, L., Criqui, M. H., & Wingard, D. L. (1985). Effects of passive smoking on ischemic heart disease mortality of nonsmokers: A prospective study. *American Journal of Epidemiology, 121,* 645–650.

Garland, C. F., Garland, F. C., Gorham, E. D. (1991). Can colon cancer incidence and death rates be reduced with calcium and vitamin D? *American Journal of Clinical Nutrition, 54* (1 Suppl.), 193S–201S.

Garn, S. M., Bailey, S. M., Solomon, M. A., & Hopkins, P. J. (1981). Effects of remaining family members on fatness prediction. *American Journal of Clinical Nutrition, 34,* 148–153.

Garrity, T. F. (1973). Vocational adjustment after first myocardial infarction: Comparative assessment of several variables suggested in the literature. *Social Science and Medicine, 7,* 705–717.

Garrow, J. (1974). *Energy balance and obesity in man.* New York: Elsevier.

Gaston-Johnasson, F., Albert, M., Fagon, E., & Zimmerman, L. (1990). Similarities in pain descriptions of four different ethnic-cultural groups. *Journal of Pain and Symptom Management, 5,* 94–100.

Gauthier, Y., Fortin, C., Drapeau, P., Breton, J. J., Gosselion, J., Quintal, L., Weifnagel, J., & Lamarre, A. (1978). Follow-up study of 35 asthmatic preschool children. *Journal of the American Academy of Child Psychology, 17,* 679–694.

Gerber, A. M., James, S. A., Ammerman, A. S., Keenan, N. L., Garrett, J. M., Strogatz, D. S., & Haines, P. S. (1991). Socioeconomic status and electrolyte intake in black adults: The Pitt County study. *American Journal of Public Health, 81,* 1608–1612.

German, P. S., & Klein, L. E. (1986). Adverse drug experience among the elderly. In Pharmaceutical Manufacturers Association (Ed.), *New research and new concerns: Pharmaceuticals for the elderly.* Washington: Hill and Knowlton, pp. 40–48.

Gilliam, T. B., Freedson, P. S., Geenen, D. L., & Shahraray, B. (1981). *Medicine and Science in Sports and Exercise, 13,* 65–67.

Gillum, R. F. (1987). The association of body fat distribution with hypertension, hypertension heart disease, coronary heart disease, diabetes, and cardiovascular risk factors in men and women aged 18–79 years. *Journal of Chronic Diseases, 40,* 421–428.

Gisler, R. H. (1974). Stress and hormonal regulation of the immune system in mice. *Psychotherapy and Psychosomatics, 23,* 197–208.

Glasgow, N. S., Gaarder, K. R., & Engel, B. T. (1982). Behavioral treatment of high blood pressure: II. Acute and sustained effects of relaxation in systolic blood pressure biofeedback. *Psychosomatic Medicine, 44,* 155–170.

Glasgow, R. E., McCaul, K. D., & Schafer, L. C. (1987). Self-care behaviors and glycemic control in Type I diabetes. *Journal of Chronic Diseases, 40,* 399–412.

Glasgow, R. E., Toobert, D. J., Riddle, M., Donnelly, J., Mitchell, D. L., & Calder, D. (1989).

Diabetes-specific social learning variables and self-care behaviors among persons with Type II diabetes. *Health Psychology, 8,* 265–303.

Glass, D. C. (1977). *Behavior patterns, stress, and coronary disease.* Hillsdale, N.J.: Erlbaum.

Gleser, G. C., & Ihilevich, D. (1969). An objective instrument for measuring defense mechanisms. *Journal of Consulting and Clinical Psychology, 33,* 51–60.

Godin, G., & Shephard, R. J. (1984). Normative beliefs of school children concerning regular exercise. *Journal of School Health, 54,* 443–445.

Goldberg, E. L., & Comstock, G. W. (1980). Epidemiology of life events: Frequency in general populations. *American Journal of Epidemiology, 111*(6), 736–752.

Goldert, J. J., Biggar, R. J., Weiss, S. H., et al. (1986). Three-year incidence of AIDS in five cohorts of HTLV-III-infected risk group members. *Science, 231,* 992–995.

Goldstein, I. B., Jamner, L. D., & Shapiro, D. (1992). Ambulatory blood pressure and heart rate in healthy male paramedics during a workday and a nonworkday. *Health Psychology, 11,* 48–54.

Goldstein, M. J. (1973). Individual differences in response to stress. *American Journal of Community Psychology, 1,* 113–137.

Gonder-Frederick, L. A., Cox, D. J., Bobbitt, S. A., & Pennebaker, J. W. (1989). Mood changes associated with blood glucose fluctuations in insulin-dependent diabetes mellitus. *Health Psychology, 8,* 45–59.

Goodall, T. A., & Halford, W. K. (1991). Self-management of diabetes mellitus: A critical review. *Health Psychology, 10,* 1–8.

Goodenow, C., Reisine, S. T., & Grady, K. E. (1990). Quality of social support and associated social and psychological functioning in women with rheumatoid arthritis. *Health Psychology, 9,* 266–284.

Goodkin, K., Antoni, M., & Blaney, P. H. (1986). Stress and hopelessness in the promotion of cervical intapithelial neoplasia to invasive squamous cell carcenoma of the cervix. *Journal of Psychosomatic Research, 30,* 67–76.

Goodman, J. I., Richardson, S. A., Dornbusch, S. M., & Hastorf, A. H. (1963). Variant reactions to physical disabilities. *American Sociological Review, 28,* 429–435.

Goodrich, D. W., & Boomer, D. S. (1963). Experimental assessment of modes of conflict resolution. *Family Process, 2,* 15–24.

Goodwin, P. J. (March 1992). Economic factors in trials of palliation. In F. Porzsolt, *Goals of palliative cancer therapy. International workshop.* Reisenburg Castle, Germany.

Gorder, D. D., Dolecek, T. A., Coleman, G. G., Tillotson, J. L., Brown, H. B., Lenz-Litzow, K., Bartsch, G. E., & Grandits, G. (1986). Dietary intake in the Multiple Risk Factor Intervention Trial (MRFIT): Nutrient and food changes over 6 years. *Journal of the American Dietetic Association, 86,* 744–751.

Gordis, L. (1979). Conceptual and methodological problems in measuring patient compliance. In R. B. Haynes, D. W. Taylor, & D. L. Sackett (Eds.), *Compliance in health care.* Baltimore: Johns Hopkins University Press.

Gordon, T. (1988). The diet-heart idea. *American Journal of Epidemiology, 127,* 220–225.

Gordon, T., Castelli, W. P., Hjortland, M. C., et al. (1977). High density lipoprotein as a protective factor against coronary heart disease. The Framingham Study. *American Journal of Medicine, 62,* 707–712.

Gorham, E. D., Garland, C. F., & Garland, F. C. (1989). Acid haze air pollution and breast and colon cancer mortality in 20 Canadian cities. *Canadian Journal of Public Health. Revue Canadienne de Sante Publique, 80*(2), 96–100.

Gortmaker, S. L., Dietz, W. H., Sobol, A. M., & Wehler, C. A. (1987). Increasing pediatric obesity in the United States. *American Journal of Diseases of Children, 141,* 535–540.

Gottlieb, N. H., & Chen, M. S. (1985). Sociocultural correlates of childhood sporting activities: Their implications for heart health. *Social Science and Medicine, 21,* 533–539.

Graham, J. W., Johnson, C. A., Hansen, W. B., Flay, B. R., & Gee, M. (1990). Drug use prevention programs, gender, and ethnicity: Evaluation of three seventh-grade Project SMART cohorts. *Preventive Medicine, 19,* 305–313.

Grant, I., Atkinson, H., Hesselink, J. R., Kennedy, C. J., Richman, D. D., & Spector, S. A. (1987). Evidence for early central nervous system involvement in the acquired immunodeficiency syndrome (AIDS) and other human immunodeficiency virus (HIV) infections. *Annals of Internal Medicine, 107,* 828–836.

Grant, I., & Atkinson, J. H. (1990). The evolution of neurobehavior complications of HIV infection. *Psychological Medicine, 20,* 747–754.

Grant, I., Brown, G. W., Harris, T., McDonald, W. I., Patterson, T. L., & Trimble, M. R. (1989). Severely threatening events and marked life difficulties preceding onset or exacerbation of multiple sclerosis. *Journal of Neurology, Neurosurgery and Psychiatry, 51,* 143–148.

Grant, I., Gerst, M., & Yager, J. (1976). Scaling of life events by psychiatric patients and normals. *Journal of Psychosomatic Research, 20,* 141–149.

Grant, I., & Heaton, R. K. (1990). Human immunodeficiency virus-type I (HIV-1) and the brain. *Journal of Consulting and Clinical Psychology, 58*(1), 22–30.

Grant, I., Patterson, T. L., Yager, J., et al. (1987). Life events do not predict symptoms: Symptoms predict symptoms. *Journal of Behavioral Medicine, 10,* 231–240.

Grant, I., Yager, J., Sweetwood, H. L., & Olshen, R. (May 1982). Life events and symptoms. *Arch. Gen. Psychiatry, 39,* 598–605.

Greaves, K. A., Puhl, J., Baranowski, T., Gruben, D., & Seale, D. (1989). Ethnic differences in anthropometric characteristics of young children and their parents. *Human Biology, 61,* 459–477.

Green, D. E. (1979). *Teenage smoking: Immediate and long-term patterns.* Department of Health, Education, and Welfare, National Institute of Education. Washington, D.C.: U.S. Government Printing Office.

Green, L. W., & Kreuter, M. W. (1991). *Health promotion planning: An educational and environmental approach.* Mountain View, Calif.: Mayfield.

Green, L. W., Kreuter, M. W., Deeds, S. G., & Partridge, K. B. (1980). *Health education planning: A diagnostic approach.* Palo Alto, Calif.: Mayfield.

Green, L. W., Mullen, P. D., & Stainbrook, G. L. (1984). Programs to reduce drug errors in the elderly: Direct and indirect evidence from patient education. In *Improving medication compliance.* Reston, Va.: National Pharmaceutical Council, pp. 59–70.

Green, L. W., Wilson, A.L., & Lovato, C. Y. (1986). What changes can health promotion achieve and how long do these changes last? The trade-offs between expendiency and durability. *Preventive Medicine, 15,* 508–521.

Greenberg, A., Dyck, D., & Sandler, L. (1984). Opponent processes, neurohormones, and natural resistance. In B. Fox & B. Newbury (Eds.), *Psychoneuroendocrine systems in cancer and immunity.* Toronto: C. J. Hogrefe.

Greenfield, S., Kaplan, S. H., Ware, J. E., et al. (1988). Patients' participation in medical care: Effects on blood sugar and quality of life in diabetes. *Journal of General Internal Medicine, 3,* 448–457.

Greenwald, P., & Sondik, E. (1986). Diet and chemoprevention in NCI's research strategy to achieve national cancer control objectives. In L. Breslow, J. E., Fielding, & L. B. Lave (Eds.), *Annual Review of Public Health, 7,* 267–292. Palo Alto: Annual Reviews, Inc.

Greer, S., Petdingile, K., Morris, T., & Haybittle, J. (1985). Mental attitudes to cancer: An additional prognostic factor. *Lancet, 3,* 750.

Griffiths, R. R., Bigelow, G. E., & Liebson, I. (1976). Facilitation of human tobacco self-administration by ethanol: A behavior analysis. *Journal of the Experimental Analysis of Behavior, 25,* 279–292.

Gruber, B. L., Hall, N. R., Hersh, S. P., & Dubios, P. (1988). Immune system and psychological changes in metastatic cancer patients using relaxation and guided imagery: A pilot study. *Scandinavian Journal of Behavior Therapy, 17,* 25–44.

Grunberg, N. E., & Straub, R. O. (1992). The role of gender and taste class in the effects of stress on eating. *Health Psychology, 11,* 97–100.

Grunberg, N. E., Winders, S. E., & Wewers, M. E. (1991). Gender differences in tobacco use. *Health Psychology, 10,* 143–153.

Grundy, S. M., Bilheimer, D., Blackburn, H., Brown, W. V., Kwiterovich, P. O., Mattson, F., Schonfeld, G., & Weidman, W. H. (1982). Rationale of the diet-heart statement of the American Heart Association: Report of the Nutrition Committee. *Circulation, 65,* 839A–854A.

Gustafsson, P. A., Kjellman, N. I. M., & Cederblad, M. (1986). Family therapy in the treatment of severe childhood asthma. *Journal of Psychosomatic Research, 30,* 369–374.

Guyer, B., Gallagher, S. S., Chang, B. H., Azzara, C. V., Cupples, L. A., & Colton, T. (1989). Prevention of childhood injuries: Evaluation of the statewide childhood injury prevention program (SCIPP). *American Journal of Public Health, 79,* 1521–1527.

Gwinn, T. S., Bailey, G. J., & Mecklenburg, R. S. (1988). Factors related to discontinuation of continuous subcutaneous insulin-infusion therapy. *Diabetes Care, 11,* 46–51.

Haaga, D. A. F., & Stewart, B. L. (1992). Self-efficacy for recovery from a lapse after smoking cessation. *Journal of Consulting and Clinical Psychology, 60,* 24–28.

Haan, M. N., Kaplan, G. A., & Camacho-Dicky, T. (June 1984). *Poverty and health: A prospective study of Alameda County residents.* Presented at the Annual Meeting of the Society for Epidemiologic Research. Houston, Tex.

Haan, N. (1977). *Coping and defending: Processes of self-environment organization.* New York: Academic Press, pp. 162–165.

Hackett, G., & Horan, J. J. (1978). Focused smoking: An unequivocably safe alternative to rapid smoking. *Journal of Drug Education, 8,* 261–265.

Hahn, R. A., Teutsch, S. M., Rothenberg, R. B., & Marks, J. S. (1990). Excess deaths from nine chronic diseases in the United States, 1986. *Journal of the American Medical Association, 264,* 2654–2659.

Hall, R. G., Hall, S. M., Sachs, D. P. L., & Benowitz, N. L. (1984). Two-year efficacy and safety of rapid smoking therapy in patients with cardiac and pulmonary disease. *Journal of Consulting and Clinical Psychology, 52,* 574–581.

Hall, S. M., & Killen, J. D. (1985). Psychological and pharmacological approaches to smoking relapse prevention. In J. Grabowski & S. M. Hall (Eds.), *Pharmacological adjuncts in smoking cessation.* NIDA Research Monograph No. 53, U.S. Department of Health and Human Services, Public Health Service, Alcohol, Drug Abuse and Mental Health Administration, DHHS, Pub. No. (ADM), 85–133.

Hamberg, D. A., Elliott, G. R., & Parron, D. L. (1982). *Health and behavior: Frontiers of research in the behavioral sciences.* Washington, D.C.: National Academy Press.

Hamburg, D., & Adams, J. E. (1967). A perspective on coping behavior: Seeking and utilizing information in major transitions. *Archives of General Psychiatry, 17,* 277–284.

Hamburg, D., Hamburg, B., & DeGoza, S. (1953). Adaptive problems and mechanisms in severely burned patients. *Psychiatry, 16,* 1–20.

Hansen, W. B., Johnson, C. A., Flay, B. R., Graham, J. W., & Sobel, J. L. (1988). Affective and social influences approaches to the prevention of multiple substance abuse among seventh grade students: Results from Project SMART. *Preventive Medicine, 17,* 135–154.

Hanson, C. L., Henggeler, S. W., Harris, M. A., Burghen, G. A., & Moore, M. (1989). Family system variables and the health status of adolescents with insulin-dependent diabetes mellitus. *Health Psychology, 8,* 239–283.

Harpers Ferry Conference. (1989). Proceedings of the National Working Conference on Research in Health and Behavior. *Health Psychology, 8*(6), 629–779.

Harris, J. K. (1991). Evolution of a health focus: Old values—new practices in counseling psychology, education and training. *The Counseling Psychologist.*

Harris, M. (1985). The prevalence of non-insulin-dependent diabetes mellitus in National Diabetes Data Group. *Diabetes in America: Diabetes data compiled, 1984.* Bethesda, Md.: National Institutes of Health. NIH Publication 85-1468, Chapter 6.

Harris, M. B., & Hallbauer, E. S. (1973). Self-directed weight control through eating and exercise. *Behaviour Research and Therapy, 11,* 523–529.

Harris, M. I. (1985). *Diabetes in America: National Diabetes Data Group,* NIH Publication 85-1468. Bethesda, Md.: National Institutes of Health.

Harris, M. I. (1990). Epidemiology of diabetes mellitus among the elderly in the United States. *Clinics in Geriatric Medicine, 6*(4), 703–719.

Harris, M. I. (1991). Epidemiological correlates of NIDDM in Hispanics, whites, and blacks in the U.S. population. *Diabetes Care, 14*(7), 639–648.

Harris, M. I., Haiden, W. C., Knowler, W. C., & Bennett, P. H. (1987). Prevalence of diabetes and impaired glucose tolerance and plasma glucose levels in U.S. population age 20–74 years. *Diabetes, 36,* 523–534.

Harris, R. P., O'Malley, M. S., Fletcher, S. W., & Knight, B. P. (1990). Prompting physicians for preventive procedures: A five-year study of manual and computer reminders. *American Journal of Preventive Medicine, 6*(3), 145–152.

Harris, R. P., Fletcher, S. W., Gonzalez, J. J., Lannin, D. R., Degnan, D., Earp, J. A., & Clark, R. (1991). Mammography and age: Are we targeting the wrong women? A community survey of women and physicians. *Cancer, 67*(7), 2010–2014.

Haskell, W. L. (1984). Exercise-induced changes in plasma lipids and lipoproteins. *Preventive Medicine, 13*, 23–36.

Haskell, W. L., Camargo, C., Williams, P. T., et al. (1984). The effect of cessation and resumption of moderate alcohol intake on serum high-density lipoprotein subfractions. A controlled study. *New England Journal of Medicine, 310*, 805–810.

Haskell, W. L., Leon, A. S., Caspersen, C. J., Froelicher, V. F., Hagberg, J. M., Harlan, W., Holloszy, J. O., Regensteiner, J. G., Thompson, P. D., Washburn, R. A., & Wilson, P. W. F. (1992). Cardiovascular benefits and assessment of physical activity and fitness in adults. *Medicine and Science in Sports and Exercise, 24*, S201–220.

Haynes, R. B. (1979). Determinants of compliance: The disease and the mechanics of treatment. In R. B. Haynes, D. W. Taylor, & D. L. Sackett (Eds.), *Compliance in health care*. Baltimore: Johns Hopkins University Press.

Haynes, R. B., Taylor, D. W., & Sackett, D. L. (1979). *Compliance in health care*. Baltimore: Johns Hopkins University Press.

Haynes, R. B., Taylor, D. W., Snow, J. C., & Sackett, D. L. (1979). Annotated and indexed bibliography on compliance with therapeutic and preventive regimens. In R. B. Haynes, D. W. Taylor, & D. L. Sackett (Eds.), *Compliance in health care*. Baltimore: Johns Hopkins University Press.

Haynes, S., Feinleib, M., & Kannel, W. (1980). The relationship of psychosocial factors to coronary heart disease in the Framingham Study. III, Eight-year incidence of CHD. *American Journal of Epidemiology, 107*, 37–58.

Haynes, S. G., & Feinleib, M. (1980). Women, work and coronary heart disease: Prospective findings from the Framingham Heart Study. *American Journal of Public Health, 70*, 133–141.

Haynes, S. G., Harvey, C., Montes, H., Nickens, H., & Cohen, B. H. (1990). Patterns of cigarette smoking among Hispanics in the United States: Results from HHANES 1982–84. *American Journal of Public Health, 80*(Suppl.), 47–53.

Haynes, S. G., & Matthews, K. A. (1988). Coronary-prone behavior. Continuing evolution of the concept. *Annals of Behavioral Medicine, 10*, 47–59.

Hayward, R. A., Shapiro, M. F., Freeman, H. E., & Corey, C. R. (1988). Inequities in health services among insured Americans. Do working-age adults have less access to medical care than the elderly? *New England Journal of Medicine, 318*(23), 1507–1512.

Heitzmann, C. A., & Kaplan, R. M. (1988). Assessment of methods for measuring social support. *Health Psychology, 7*, 75–109.

Hench, P. K., & Mitler, M. M. (1986). Fibromyalgia: Review of a common rheumatologic syndrome. *Post Graduate Medicine, 80*, 47–56.

Henderson, S., Duncan-Jones, P., Byrne, D. G., & Scott, R. (1980). Measuring social relationships. The Interview Schedule for Social Interaction. *Psychological Medicine, 10*, 723–734.

Henry, J. P., & Stephens, P. M. (977). *Stress, health, and the social environment: A sociobiologial approach to medicine*. New York: Springer-Verlag.

Henry R. R., Crapo, P. A., & Thorburn, A. W. (1991). Current issues in fructose metabolism. *Annual Review of Nutrition, 11*, 21–39.

Henry, R. R., & Edelman, S. V. (1992). Advances in treatment of Type II diabetes mellitus in the elderly. *Geriatrics, 47*(4), 24–30.

Herman, C. P., & Polivy, J. (1980). Restrained eating. In A. J. Stunkard (Ed.), *Obesity*. Philadelphia: Saunders, pp. 208–225.

Herman, W. H., Toetsch, S. M., & Gies, L. S. (1988). Diabetes mellitus. In R. Amler & H. B. Dull (Eds.), *Closing the gap: The burden of unnecessary illness*. New York: Oxford, pp. 72–82.

Hersch, M. S. (1992). The treatment of cytomegalovirus in AIDS—more that meets the eye. *New England Journal of Medicine, 326*, 264–266.

Heyward, W. L., & Curran, J. W. (1988). The epidemiology of AIDS in the U.S. In *The science of AIDS*, New York: W. H. Freeman, pp. 39–49.

Hicky, N., et al. (1975). Study of coronary risk factors related to physical activity in 15,171 men. *British Medical Journal, 5982*, 507–509.

Higham, C., & Jayson, M. I. V. (1982). Non-prescribed treatments in rheumatic patients. *Annals of Rheumatic Diseases, 41*, 203.

Hill, S. (1982). Biological consequences of alcoholism and alcohol-related problems among women. In *Alcohol and health monograph no. 4: Special population issues*. Rockville, Md.: NIAAA, pp. 43–73.

Hines, E. A., & Brown, G. E. (1936). The cold pressor test for measuring the reactivity of blood pressure: Data concerning 571 normal and hypertensive subjects. *American Heart Journal, 31*, 1–9.

Hinkle, L. E. (1974). The concept of "stress" in the biological and social sciences. *International Journal of Psychiatry in Medicine, 5*(4), 335–357.

Hippocrates. (approximately 400 B.C.). *On air, water, and places.*

Hirschfeld, R. M., & Cross, C. K. (1982). Epidemiology of affective disorders: Psychosocial risk factors. *Archives of General Psychiatry, 39*, 35–46.

Hochhauser, M. (August 1987). *Readability of AIDS educational materials.* Presented at the Annual Meeting of the American Psychological Association, New York.

Hoffman, J. W., Benson, H., Arns, P. A., Stainbrook, G. L., Landsberg, L., Young, J. B., & Gill, A. (1982). Reduced sympathetic nervous system responsivity associated with the relaxation response. *Science, 215*, 190–192.

Holland, J. C., Morrow, G. R., Schmale, A., Derogatis, L., Stefanek, M., Berenson, S., Carpenter, P. J., Breitbart, W., & Feldstein, M. (1991). A randomized clinical trial of alprazolam verses progressive muscle relaxation in patients with cancer. *Journal of Clinical Oncology, 9*, 1004–1011.

Hollis, J. F., Carmody, T. P., Connor, S. L., Fey, S. G., & Matarazzo, J. D. (1986). The nutrition attitude survey: Associations with dietary habits, psychological and physical well-being, and coronary risk factors. *Health Psychology, 5*, 359–374.

Holman, H., & Lorig, K. (1992). Perceived self-efficacy in self-management of chronic disease. In R. Schwarzer (Ed.), *Self-efficacy: Through control of action*. Washington: Hemisphere, pp. 305–323.

Holmes, T. H., & Masuda, M. (1974). Life change and illness susceptibility. In B. S. Dohrenwend & B. P. Dohrenwend (Eds.), *Stressful life events: Their nature and effects*. New York: Wiley, pp. 45–72.

Holmes, T. H., & Rahe, R. H. (1967). The social readjustment rating scale. *Journal of Psychosomatic Research, 11*, 213–218.

Holroyd, I. (1980). Hypnosis treatment for smoking: An evaluation review. *International Journal of Clinical and Experimental Hypnosis, 23*, 341–357.

Horton, E. S. (1991). Exercise in the treatment of NIDDM. Applications for GDM? *Diabetes, 40*(Suppl. 2), 175–178.

Horwitz, R. I., Viscoli, C. M., Berkman, L., Donaldson, R. M., Horwitz, S. M., Murray, C. J., Ransohoff, D. F., & Sindelar, J. (1990). Treatment adherence and risk of death after a myocardial infarction. *Lancet, 336*(8714), 542–545.

House, J. S., Landis, K. R., & Unberson, D. (1988). Social relationships and health. *Science, 241*, 540–545.

House, J. S., Robbins, C., & Metzner, H. L. (1982). The association of social relationships and activities with mortality. Prospective evidence from the Tecumseh community health study. *American Journal of Epidemiology, 116*, 123–140.

Houston, B. K., & Vavak, C. R. (1991). Cynical hostility: Developmental factors, psychosocial correlates, and health behaviors. *Health Psychology, 10*, 9–17.

Hovell, M., Sallis, J., Hofstetter, R., Barrington, E., Hackley, M., Elder, J., Castro, F., & Kilbourne, K. (1991). Identification of correlates of physical activity among Latino adults. *Journal of Community Health, 16*, 23–36.

Hovell, M. F. (1982). The experimental evidence for weight-loss treatment of essential hypertension: A critical review. *American Journal of Public Health, 72*, 359–367.

Hovell, M. F., Kaplan, R. M., & Hovell, F. (1991). Analysis of preventive medical services in the United States. In P. A. Lamal (Ed.), *Behavior analysis of societies and cultural practices*. New York: Hemisphere, pp. 181–200.

Hovell, M. F., Koch, A., Hofstetter, C. R., Sipan, C., Faucher, P., Dellinger, A., Borok, G., Forsythe, A., & Felitti, V. J. (1988). Long-term weight loss maintenance: Assessment of a behavioral and supplemented fasting regimen. *American Journal of Public Health, 78,* 663–666.

Hovell, M. F., Sallis, J. F., Hofstetter, C. R., Spry, V. M., Faucher, P., & Caspersen, C. J. (1989). Identifying correlates of walking for exercise: An epidemiologic prerequisite for physical activity promotion. *Preventive Medicine, 18,* 856–866.

Howard, J. (1982). An approach to the secondary prevention of cancer. In D. L. Parron, F. Solomon, & C. D. Jenkins (Eds.), *Behavior, health risks, and social disadvantage.* Washington, D.C.: National Academy Press, 51–61.

Howard, J., Ound, P., & Bell, G. (1980). Hospital variations in metastatic breast cancer. *Medical Care, 18,* 442.

Howard-Pitney, B., Johnson, M. D., Altman, D. G., Hopkins, R., & Hammond, N. (1991). Responsible alcohol service: A study of server, manager, and environmental impact. *American Journal of Public Health, 81,* 197–199.

Hsiao, W., Braun, P., Becker, E. R., & Dunn, D. (1992). RBRVS: Objections to Maloney, I. *JAMA, 267*(13), 1822–1823.

Hsiao, W. C., Braun, P., Dunn, D., & Becker, E. R. (1988) Resource-based relative values. An overview. *JAMA, 260*(16), 2347–2353.

Hubert, H. B. (1986). The importance of obesity in the development of coronary risk factors and disease: The epidemiologic evidence. *Annual Review of Public Health, 7,* 493–502.

Hudgens, A. (1979). Family-oriented treatment of chronic pain. *Journal of Marital and Family Therapy, 58–67.

Hughes, P. M., & Lieberman, S. (1990). Troubled parents: Vulnerability and stress in childhood cancer. *British Journal of Medical Psychology, 63*(Pt 1), 53–64.

Hunt, W. A., Barnett, L. W., & Branch, L. G. (1971). Relapse rates in addiction programs. *Journal of Clinical Psychology, 27,* figure on p. 456.

Hurwitz, N. (1969). Predisposing factors in adverse reactions to drugs. *British Medical Journal, 1,* 536; In R. Ader (Ed.), *Psychoneuroimmunology.* New York: Academic Press.

Institute of Medicine. (1991). *Disability in America: A national agenda for prevention.* M. A. Pope & A. Tarloff (Eds.). Washington, D.C.: National Academy Press.

Institute of Medicine, National Academy of Sciences. (1982). *Frontiers of research in biobehavioral sciences.* Washington, D.C.: National Academy Press.

Inui, T. S., & Carter, W. B. (1985). Problems and prospects for health services research on provider-patient communication. *Medical Care, 23,* 521–538.

Ireland, J. T., Thomson, W. S. T., & Williamson, J. (1980). *Diabetes today: A handbook for the clinical team.* New York: Springer.

Irion, J. C., & Blanchard-Fields, F. (1987). A cross-sectional comparison of adaptive coping in adulthood. *Journal of Gerontology, 42,* 502–504.

Irwin, M., Brown, M., Patterson, T., Hauger, R., Mascovich, A., & Grant, I. (1991). Neuropeptide Y and natural killer cell activity: Findings in depression and Alzheimer caregiver stress. *FASEB, 5,* 3100–3107.

Irwin, M., Daniels, M., Bloom, E., Smith, T., & Weiner, H. (1987). Life events, depressive symptoms, and immune function. *American Journal of Psychiatry, 144,* 437–441.

Irwin, M., Daniels, M., Bloom, E., & Weiner, H. (1986). Life events, depression and natural killer cell function. *Psychopharmacol. Bull., 22,* 1093–1096.

Irwin, M. R., Patterson, T. L., Smith, T. L., Caldwell, C., Brown, S. A., Gillin, J. C., & Grant, I. (1990). Reduction of immune function in life stress and depression. *Biological Psychiatry, 27,* 22–30.

Irwin, M. R., Segal, D. S., Hauger, R. L., & Smith, T. L. (1989). Individual behavior and neuroendocrine differences in responsiveness to repeated audiogenic stress. *Pharmacol. Biochem. Behav., 32,* 913–917.

Istvan, J., & Matarazzo, J. D. (1984). Tobacco, alcohol, and caffeine use: A review of their interrelationships. *Psychological Bulletin, 95,* 301–326.

Jacob, R. G., Chesney, M. A., Williams, D. M., Ding, Y., & Shapiro, A. P. (1991). Relaxation therapy for hypertension: Design effects and treatment effects. *Annals of Behavioral Medicine, 13,* 5–17.

Jacobs, D. R., Mebane, I. L., Bangdiwala, S. I., Criqui, M. H., & Tyroler, H. A. (1990). High density lipoprotein cholesterol as a predictor of cardiovascular disease mortality in men and women: The follow-up study of the lipid research clinics prevalence study. *American Journal of Epidemiology, 131,* 32–47.

Jacobs, S. C., Prusoff, B. A., & Paykel, E. S. (1974). Recent life events in schizophrenia and depression. *Psychological Medicine, 4,* 44–453.

James, S. A., Strogatz, D. S., Wing, S. B., & Ramsey, D. L. (1987). Socioeconomic status, John Henryism, and hypertension in blacks and whites. *American Journal of Epidemiology, 126,* 664–673.

James, W. (1890). *The principles of psychology.* New York: Holt, Rinehart & Winston.

Janis, I. (1958). *Psychological stress.* New York: Wiley.

Janis, I. L. (1983). The role of social support in adherence to stressful decisions. *American Psychologist, 38,* 143.

Janssen, R. S., Saykin, A. K., Kaplan, J. E., Spira, T. J., Pinsky, P. F., Sprehn, G. S., Hoffman, J. C., Mayer, W. B., & Schonberger, L. B. (1988). Neurological symptoms and neurological abnormalities in lymphadenopathy syndrome. *Ann. Neurol., 23*(Suppl.), 517.

Jeffery, R. W. (1989). Risk behaviors and health: Contrasting individual and population perspectives. *American Psychologist, 44,* 1194–1202.

Jemmott, J. B., & Locke, S. E. (1984). Psychosocial factors, immunologic mediation, and human susceptibility to infectious diseases: How much do we know? *Psychological Bulletin, 95*(1), 78–108.

Jenkins, C. D. (1967). Appraisal and implications for theoretical development. *Milbank Memorial Fund Quarterly, 65,* 141–152.

Jenkins, C. D. (1982). Overview: Behavioral perspectives on health risks among the disadvantaged. In D. L. Parron, F. Solomon, & C. D. Jenkins (Eds.), *Behavior, health risks, and social disadvantage.* Washington, D.C.: National Academy Press, pp. 3–12.

Jenkins, C. D., Rosenman, R. H., & Friedman, M. (1967). Development of an objective psychological test for the determination of the coronary-prone behavior pattern in employed men. *Journal of Chronic Diseases, 20,* 371–379.

Jessor, R., & Jessor, L. J. (1977). *Problem behavior in psychosocial development.* New York: Academic Press.

Jones, D. R., Goldblatt, P. O., & Leon, D. A. (1984). Bereavement and cancer: Some data on deaths of spouses from the longitudinal study of Office of Population Census and Surveys. *British Medical Journal, 239,* 461–464.

Joossens, J. V. (1973). Salt and hypertension, water hardness and cardiovascular death rate. *Triangle, 12,* 9–12.

Joseph, J. G., Kessler, R. C., Ostrow, D. G., et al. (June 12–16, 1988). *Psychosocial predictors of symptom development in HIV-infected gay men.* IV Intl. Conf. on AIDS, Stockholm, Sweden.

Joseph, J. G., Montgomery, S. B., Emmons, C. A., Kessler, R. C., Ostrow, D. B., Wortman, C. B., O'Brien, K., Eller, M., & Eshleman, S. (1987). Magnitude and determinants of behavior risk reduction: Longitudinal analysis of a cohort at risk for AIDS. *Psychological Health, 1,* 73–96.

Kahn, H. S., Williamson, D. F., & Stevens, J. A. (1991). Race and weight change in women: The roles of socioeconomic and marital status. *American Journal of Public Health, 81,* 319–323.

Kaloupek, D. G., White, H., & Wong, M. (1984). Multiple assessment of coping strategies used by volunteer blood donors: Implications for preparatory training. *Journal of Behavioral Medicine, 7,* 35–60.

Kandel, D. B. (1978). *Longitudinal research on drug use: Empirical findings and methodological issues.* New York: Wiley.

Kannel, W. B. (1987). New perspectives on cardiovascular risk factors. *American Heart Journal, 114,* 213–219.

Kannel, W. B., Thom, T. J., & Hurst, J. W. (1986). Incidence, prevalence, and mortality of cardiovascular diseases. In *The heart* (6th ed.). New York: McGraw-Hill.

Kanner, A. D., Coyne, J. C., Schaefer, C., & Lazarus, R. S. (1981). Comparison of two modes of stress measurement: Daily hassles and uplifts versus major life events. *Journal of Behavioral Medicine, 4,* 1–39.

Kaplan, G. A. (1985). Psychosocial aspects of chronic illness: Direct and indirect associations with ischemic heart disease mortality. In R. M. Kaplan & M. H. Criqui (Eds.), *Behavioral epi-*

demiology and disease prevention. New York: Plenum, pp. 237–269.

Kaplan, G. A., Lazarus, N. B., Cohen, R. D., & Lew, D. J. (1991). Psychosocial factors in the natural history of physical activity. *American Journal of Preventive Medicine, 7,* 12–17.

Kaplan, N. M., & Stamler, J. (1983). *Prevention of coronary heart disease: Practical management of the risk factors.* Philadelphia: Saunders.

Kaplan, R. M. (1985). Behavioral epidemiology, health promotion, and health services. *Medical Care, 23,* 564–583.

Kaplan, R. M. (1985). Social support and social health: Is it time to rethink the WHO definition of health? In I. R. Sarason & B. R. Sarason (Eds.). *Social support Theory, Research and Applications,* The Hague: Nijhoff pp. 95–113.

Kaplan, R. M. (1988). Health-related quality of life in cardiovascular disease. *Journal of Consulting and Clinical Psychology, 56*(3), 382–392.

Kaplan, R. M. (1989). Models of health outcome for policy analysis. *Health Psychology, 8*(6), 723–735.

Kaplan, R. M. (1992). A quality-of-life approach to health resource allocation. In M. A. Strosberg, J. M. Wiener, R. Baker, & I. A. Fein (Eds.), *Rationing America's medical care: The Oregon plan and beyond.* Washington, D.C.: The Brookings Institution, pp. 60–77.

Kaplan, R. M., & Anderson, J. P. (1988). The general health policy model: Update and applications. *Health Services Research, 23,* 203–235.

Kaplan, R. M., & Atkins, C. J. (1987). Selective attrition causes overestimates of treatment effects in studies of weight loss. *Addictive Behaviors, 12,* 297–302.

Kaplan, R. M., & Atkins, C. J. (1989). The well-year of life as a basis for patient decision making. *Patient and Education Counseling, 13,* 281–295.

Kaplan, R. M., Atkins, C. J., & Lenhard, L. (1982). Coping with a stressful sigmoidoscopy: Evaluation of cognitive and relaxation preparations. *Journal of Behavioral Medicine, 5*(1), 67–82.

Kaplan, R. M., Atkins, C. J., & Reinsch, S. (1984). Specific efficacy expectations mediate compliance in patients with COPD. *Health Psycholoy, 3,* 223–242.

Kaplan, R. M., & Bush, J. W. (1982). Health-related quality of life measurement for evaluation research and policy analysis. *Health Psychology, 1*(1), 61–80.

Kaplan, R. M., Bush, J. W., & Berry, C. C. (1976). Health status: Types of validity and the index of well-being. *Health Services Research, 11*(4), 478–507.

Kaplan, R. M., Bush, J. W., & Berry, C. C. (1978). The reliability, stability, and generalizability of a health status index. *American Statistical Association, Proceedings of the Social Status Section,* 704–709.

Kaplan, R. M., Chadwick, M. W., & Shimmel, L. E. (1985). Social learning intervention to promote metabolic control and Type I diabetes mellitus. Pilot experiment results. *Diabetes Care, 8,* 152–155.

Kaplan, R. M., Metzger, G., & Jablecki, C. (1983). Brief cognitive and relaxation training increases tolerance for a painful clinical electromyographic examination. *Psychosomatic Medicine, 45,* 155–162.

Kaplan, R. M., Pierce, J. P., & Gilpen, E., Johnson, M. & Bal, D. (1992) Stages of self-initiated smoking in the California Baseline Tobacco Survey. Submitted for publication.

Kaplan, R. M., Pierce, J. P., Gilpen, E., & Burns, D. (1991). *Failure to quit among black smokers: The California Baseline Tobacco Survey.* Unpublished manuscript, University of California, San Diego.

Kaplan, R. M., & Ries, A. L. (1992). Adherence in the patient with pulmonary disease. In J. Hodgkin & J. Bell (Eds.), *Pulmonary rehabilitation: Guidelines to success* (2nd ed.). Philadelphia: Lippincott.

Kaplan, R. M., Reis, A., & Atkins, C. J. (1985). Behavioral management of chronic obstructive pulmonary disease. *Annals of Behavioral Medicine, 7,* 5–10.

Kaplan, R. M., & Simon, H. J. (1990). Compliance in medical care: Reconsideration of self-predictions. *Annals of Behavioral Medicine, 12*(2), 66–71.

Kaplan, R. M., & Toshima, M. T. (1990). Social relationships in chronic illness and disability. In I. G. Sarason, B. R. Sarason, & G. R. Pierce (Eds.), *Social support: An interactional perspective.* New York: Wiley.

Karasek, R. A., Baker, D., Marxer, R., Ahlbom, A., & Theorell, T. (1981). Job decision latitude, job demands, and cardiovascular disease: A prospective study of Swedish men. *American Journal of Public Health, 71,* 694–705.

Karasek, R. A., Jr., Russell, R. S., & Theorell, T. (1982). Physiology of stress and regeneration in job related cardiovascular illness. *Journal of Human Stress, 8,* 29–42.

Kathey, M., Wolfe, F., Kleinheksel, S., et al. (1986). Socioeconomic impact of fibrositis. A study of 81 patients with primary fibrositis. *American Journal of Medicine, 81,* 78–84.

Katz, S. T., Downs, H., Cash, H., & Grotz, R. (1970). Progress and Development of an index of ADL. *Gerontologist, 10,* 20–30.

Katz, R. C., & Zlutnick, S. (Eds.). (1975). *Behavior therapy and health care: Principles and applications.* New York: Pergamon.

Kazis, L. E., Meenan, R. F., & Anderson, J. J.(1983). Pain in the rheumatic diseases. *Arthritis and Rheumatism, 26,* 1017–1022.

Keefe F. G., & Gill, K. M. (1986). Behavioral concepts in the analysis of chronic pain syndromes. *Journal of Consulting and Clinical Psychology, 54,* 776–783.

Keefe, F. J., Caldwell, D. S., Wueen, K., Gill, M. K., Martinez, S., Crisson, J. E., Ogden, W., & Nunley, J. (1987). Osteoarthritic knee pain: A behavioral analysis. *Pain, 28,* 309–321.

Keefe, F. J., Wilkins, R. H., Cook, W. A., Crisson, J. E., & Muhlbaier, L. H. (1986). Depression, pain, and pain behavior. *Journal of Consulting and Clinical Psychology, 54,* 665–669.

Keller, S. W., Weiss, J. M., Schleifer, S. J., Miller, N. E., & Stein, M. (1981). Suppression of immunity by stress: Effect of a graded series of stressors on lymphocyte proliferation. *Science, 213,* 1397–1400.

Kelly, J. A., & St. Lawrence, J. S. (1988). *The AIDS health crisis: Psychological and social interventions.* New York, Plenum.

Kelly, J. A., St. Lawrence, J. S., Brasfield, T. L., & Hood, H. V. (June 1–5, 1987). *Relationship between knowledge about AIDS and actual risk behavior in a sample of homosexual men: Some implications for prevention.* Presented at the Third International AIDS Conference, Washington, D.C.

Kelsey, J. L., White, A. A., Pastides, H., & Bisbee, G. E. (1979). The impact of musculoskeletal disorders on the population of the United States. *Journal of Bone and Joint Surgery, 61A,* 959–964.

Kendzierski, D. (1990). Exercise self-schemata: Cognitive and behavioral correlates. *Health Psychology, 9,* 69–82.

Kennedy, D. L., Piper, J. M., & Baum, C. (1988). Trends in the use of oral hypoglycemic agents, 1964–1986. *Diabetes Care, 11,* 558–562.

Kessler, R. C., Joseph, J., G., et al. (June 1988). *Psychosocial predictors of symptom development in HIV-infected gay men.* IV International Conference on AIDS, Stockholm, Sweden.

Kessler, R. C., Price, R. H., & Wortman, C. B. (1985). Social factors in psychopathology: Stress, social support, and coping processes. *Annual Review of Psychology, 36,* 531–572.

Keys, A. (1970). Coronary heart disease in seven countries. *Circulation, 41* (suppl. 1), entire issue.

Keys, A., Brozek, J., Henschel, A., Mickelson, O., & Taylor, H. L. (1950). *The biology of human starvation* (Vols. 1 & 2). Minneapolis: University of Minnesota Press.

Keys, A. Taylor, H. L., Blackburn, H., Brozek, J., Anderson, J. T., & Simonson, E. (1971). Mortality and coronary heart disease among men studied for 23 years. *Archives of Internal Medicine, 128,* 201–214.

Kiecolt-Glaser, J. K., Fisher, L., Ogrochi, P., Stout, J., Speicher, C., & Glaser, R. (1987). Marital quality, marital disruption, and immune function. *Psychosomatic Medicine, 49,* 13–34.

Kiecolt-Glaser, J. K., & Glaser, R. (1988). Psychological influences on immunity. Implications for AIDS. *American Psychologist, 43*(11), 892–898.

Kiecolt-Glaser, J. K., Glaser, R., Strain, E. C., Stout, J. C., Tar, K. L., Holliday, J. E., & Speicher, C. E. (1986). Modulation of cellular immunity in medical students. *J. Behav. Med., 9,* 5–21.

Kiecolt-Glaser, J. K., Glaser, R., Williger, D., Stout, Messick, G., Sheppard, S., Ricker, D., Romisher, S. C., Briner, W., Bonnerill, G., & Donnerberg, R. (1985). Psychosocial enhancement of immunocompetence in a geriatric population. *Health Psychology, 4,* 25–41.

Kiecolt-Glaser, J. K., Kennedy, S., Malkoff, S., Fisher, L., Speicher, C. E., & Glaser, R. (1988). Marital discord and immunity in males. *Psychosom. Med., 50,* 213–219.

Kiecolt-Glaser, J. K., Ricker, D., George, J., Messick, G., Speicher, C., Garner, W., & Glaser, R. (1984). Urinary cortisol levels, cellular immunocompetency, and loneliness in psychiatric inpatients. *Psychosomatic Medicine, 46*(1), 523–535.

Kielcot-Glaser, J. K., Garner, W., Speicher, C., Penn, G., Holliday, E. S., & Glaser, R. (1984). Psychosocial modifiers of immunocompetence in medical students. *Psychosomatic Medicine, 46*(1), 7–14.

Kikuchi, D. A., Srinivasan, S. R., Harsha, D. W., Webber, L. S., Sellers, T. A., & Berenson, G. S. (1992). Relation of serum lipoprotein lipids and apolipoproteins to obesity in children: The Bogalusa Heart Study. *Preventive Medicine, 21,* 177–190.

Killen, J. D. (1985). Prevention of adolescent tobacco smoking: The social pressure resistance training approach. *Journal of Child Psychology and Psychiatry, 26,* 7–15.

Killen, J. D., Maccoby, N., & Taylor, C. B. (1984). Nicotine gum and self-regulation training in smoking relapse prevention. *Behavior Therapy, 15,* 234–248.

Kilo, C., Miller, J., & Williamson, J. R. (1980). The crux of the UGDP: Spurious results and biologically inappropriate data analysis. *Diabetologia, 18,* 179–185.

King, A. C., Blair, S. N., Bild, D. E., Dishman, R. K., Dubbert, P. M., Marcus, B. H., Oldridge, N. B., Paffenbarger, R. S., Powell, K. E., & Yeager, K. K. (1992). Determinants of physical activity and interventions in adults. *Medicine and Science in Sports and Exercise, 24,* S221–S237.

King, A. C., Flora, J. A., Fortmann, S. P., & Taylor, C. B. (1987). Smokers' challenge: Immediate and long-term findings of a community smoking cessation contest. *American Journal of Public Health, 77,* 1340–1341.

King, A. C., & Frederiksen, L. W. (1984). Low-cost strategies for increasing exercise behavior: Relapse preparation training and social support. *Behavior Modification, 8,* 3–21.

King, A. C., Haskell, W. L., Taylor, C. B., Kraemer, H. C., & DeBusk, R. F. (1991). Group- vs. home-based exercise training in healthy older men and women: A community-based clinical trial. *Journal of the American Medical Association, 266,* 1535–1542.

King, A. C., Saylor, K. E., Foster, S. Killen, J. D., Telch, M. J., Farquhar, J. W., & Flora, J. A. (1988). Promoting dietary change in adolescents: A school-based approach for modifying and maintaining healthful behavior. *American Journal of Preventive Medicine, 4,* 68–74.

Kirmayer, L., Robbins, J., & Kapusta, M. (1988). Somatization and depression in fibromyalgia syndrome. *American Journal of Psychiatry, 145,* 950–954.

Kirsch, J. P. (1988). The health belief model and predictions of health actions. In D. S. Gochman (Ed.), *Health behavior: Emerging research perspectives.* New York: Plenum, pp. 27–42.

Kishimoto, S., Tomino, S., Inomata, K., et al. (1978). Age-related changes in the subsets and functions of human T lymphocytes. *J. Immunol., 121,* 1773–1780.

Klatsky, A. L., & Armstrong, M. A. (1991). Cardiovascular risk factors among Asian Americans living in Northern California. *American Journal of Public Health, 81,* 1423–1428.

Klatzman, D., & Gluckman, J. C. (1986). HIV infection: Facts and hypotheses. *Immunology Today, 7*(10), 291–295.

Klesges, R. C., Coates, T. J., Brown, G., Sturgeon-Tillisch, J., Moldenhauer-Klesges, L. M., Holzer, B., Woolfrey, J., & Vollmer, J. (1983). Parental influences on children's eating behavior and relative weight. *Journal of Applied Behavior Analysis, 16,* 371–378.

Klesges, R. C., Coates, T. J., Moldenhauer-Klesges, L. M., Holzer, B., Gustavson, J., & Barnes, J. (1984). The FATS: An observational system for assessing physical activity in children and associated parent behavior. *Behavioral Assessment, 6,* 333–345.

Kobasa, S. C., Hilker, R. R. J., & Maddi, S. R. (1979). Who stays healthy under stress? *Journal of Occupational Medicine, 21*(9), 595–598.

Kolterman, O. G., Rivers, R. R., & Fink, R. I. (1985). Assessment of receptor and post-receptor defects in target tissue insulin action. In R. DePirro & R. Lauro (Eds.), *Handbook of receptor research fields.* Rome: Educational Italia acta medica.

Kopel, S. A., Suckerman, K. R., & Baksht, A. (December 1979). *Smoke holding: An evaluation of physiological effects and treatment efficacy of a new nonhazardous aversive smoking procedure.* Paper presented at the 13th Annual Meeting of the Association for the Advancement of Behavior Therapy, San Francisco.

Koss, M. P., Gidycz, C. A., & Wisniewski, N. (1987). The scope of rape: Incidence and prevalence of sexual aggression and victimization in a national sample of higher education students. *Journal of Consulting and Clinical Psychology, 55,* 162–170.

Koss, M. P., Koss, P. G., & Woodruff, W. J. (1991). Deleterious effects of criminal victimization on women's health and medical utilization. *Archives of Internal Medicine, 151,* 342–347.

Koster, F. T., Darwin, L. P., Chakraborty, J., Jackson, T., & Curlin, G. C. (1987). Cellular immune competence and diarrheal morbidity in malnourished Bangladeshi children: A prospective field study. *American Journal of Clinical Nutrition, 46,* 115–120.

Kotler, P. (1982). *Marketing for nonprofit organizations.* Englewood Cliffs, N.J.: Prentice-Hall.

Kottke, T. E., Puska, P., Salonen, J. T., Tuomilehto, J., & Nissinen, A. (1985). Projected effects of high-risk versus population-based prevention strategies in coronary heart disease. *American Journal of Epidemiology, 121,* 697–704.

Krall, L. P., Entmacher, P. S., & Drury, T. F. (1985). Life cycle in diabetes: Socioeconomic aspects. In Marble, A. (Ed.) *Joslin's diabetes mellitus* (12th ed.). Philadelphia: Lea & Febiger.

Krantz, D. S., Arabian, J. M., Davia, J. E., & Parker, J. S. (1982). Type A behavior and coronary artery bypass surgery: Intraoperative blood pressure and perioperative complications. *Psychosomatic Medicine, 44,* 273–284.

Krantz, D. S., & Manuck, S. B. (1984). Acute psychophysiologic reactivity and risk of cardiovascular disease: A review and methodologic critique. *Psychological Bulletin, 96,* 435–464.

Krotkiewski, M., Bjorntorp, P., Sjostrom, L., et al. (1983). Impact of obesity on metabolism in men and women: Importance of regional adipose tissue distribution. *Journal of Clinical Investigation, 72,* 1150–1162.

Kulik, J. A., & Mahler, H. I. M. (1987). Effects of pre-operative roommate assignment on pre-operative anxiety and recovery from coronary-by-pass surgery. *Health Psycholoy, 6,* 525–543.

Kulik, J. A., & Mahler, H. I. (1989). Social support and recovery from surgery. *Health Psychology, 8*(2), 221–238.

Kuller, L., Meilahn, E., & Ockene, J. (1985). Smoking and coronary heart disease. In W. E. Connor & J. D. Bristow (Eds.), *Coronary heart disease: Prevention, complications, and treatment.* Philadelphia: Lippincott, pp. 65–84.

Kumanyika, S. K., & Charleston, J. B. (1992). Lose weight and win: A church-based weight loss program for blood pressure control among black women. *Patient Education and Counseling, 19,* 19–32.

Kuttner, M. J., Delamater, A. M., & Santiago, J. V. (1990). Learned helplessness in diabetic youths. *Journal of Pediatric Psychology, 15,* 518–594.

LaGreca, A. M., Auslander, W., Spetter, D., Greco, P., Skyler, J. S., Fisher, E. B., & Santiago, J. V. (March 1991). *Adolescents with IDDM: Family and peer support of diabets care.* Proceedings of the Society of Behavioral Medicine 12th Annual Scientific Session. Washington, D.C.: p. 110.

Lando, H. A. (1977). Successful treatment of smokers with a broad-spectrum behavioral approach. *Journal of Consulting and Clinical Psychology, 45,* 361–366.

Lando, H. A., & McGovern, P. G. (1982). Three-year data on a behavioral treatment for smoking: A follow-up note. *Addictive Behaviors, 7,* 177–181.

Lando, H. A., & McGovern, P. G. (1985). Nicotine fading as a nonaversive alternative in a broad-spectrum treatment for eliminating smoking. *Addictive Behaviors, 10,* 153–161.

Lang, A. R., & Marlatt, G. A. (1982). Problem drinking: A social learning perspective. In R. J. Gatchel, A. Baum, & J. E. Singer (Eds.), *Handbook of psychology and health. Vol. 1. Clinical psychology and behavioral medicine: Overlapping disciplines.* Hillsdale, N.J.: Erlbaum, pp. 121—169.

Laporte, R. E., Fishbein, H. A., Drash, A. L. et al. (1981). The Pittsburgh insulin dependent diabetes mellitus registry. The incidence of NIDDM in Allegheny County, Pennsylvania (1965–1976). *Diabetes, 30,* 279–284.

Lasater, T. M., Wells, B. L., Carleton, R. A., & Elder, J. P. (1986). The role of churches in disease prevention research studies. *Public Health Reports, 101,* 125–131.

Lask, B., & Matthew, D. (1979). Childhood asthma.

A controlled trial of family psychotherapy. *Archives of Diseases of Childhood, 55,* 116–119.

Laudenslager, M., Capitano, J. P., & Reite, M. (1985). Possible effects of early separation experiences on subsequent immune function in adult macaque monkeys. *American Journal of Psychiatry, 142,* 862–864.

Laudenslager, M. L., Ryan, S. M., Drugan, R. C., Hyson, R. L., & Maier, S. F. (1983). Coping and immunosuppression: Inescapable but not escapable shock suppresses lymphocyte proliferation. *Science, 221,* 568–570.

Lawson, D. M., (1986). Alcoholism. In M. Hersen (Ed.), *Outpatient behavior therapy: A clinical guide.* New York: Grune & Stratton, pp. 143–172.

Lazarus, R. S. (January 6–10, 1973). *The psychology of stress and coping: With particular reference to Israel.* Address at international conference on psychological stress and adjustment in time of war and peace. Tel Aviv, Israel.

Lazarus, R. S. (1981). The stress and coping paradigm. In C. Eisdorfer, D. Cohen, A. Kleinman, & P. Maxim (Eds.), *Models for clinical psychopathology.* New York; Spectrum.

Lazarus, R. S., DeLongis, A., Folkman, S., & Gruen, R. (1985). Stress and adaptational outcomes: The problem of confounded measures. *American Psychologist, 40,* 770–779.

Lazarus, R. S., & Folkman, S. (1984). *Stress, appraisal, and coping.* New York; Springer, p. 205.

Lazzarin, A., Mella, L., & Trombini, M. (1984). Immunologic status in heroin addicts: Effects of methadone maintenance treatment. *Drug and Alcohol Dependency, 13,* 117–123.

Lefebvre, R. C., Peterson, G. S., McGraw, S. A., Lassater, T. M., Sennett, L., Kendall, L., & Carleton, R. A. (1986). Community intervention to lower blood cholesterol: The "know your cholesterol" campaign in Pawtucket, Rhode Island. *Health Education Quarterly, 13,* 117–129.

Lenaway, D. D., Ambler, A. G., & Beaudoin, D. E. (1992). The epidemiology of school-related injuries: New perspectives. *American Journal of Preventive Medicine, 8,* 193–198.

Levenkron, J. C., Cohen, J. D., Mueller, H. S., & Fisher, E. B. (1983). Modifying the Type A coronary-prone behavior pattern. *Journal of Consulting and Clinical Psychology, 51,* 192–204.

Leventhal, H., Zimmerman, R., & Gutmann, M. (1984). Compliance: A self-regulation perspective. In W. D. Gentry (Ed.), *Handbook of behavioral medicine.* New York: Guilford, pp. 369–436.

Levi, L. (1972). Introduction: Psychosocial stimuli, psychophysiological reactions, and disease. In L. Levi (Ed.), *Stress and distress to psychosocial stimuli.* Oxford: Pergamon.

Levy, S., Herberman, R., Lippman, M., & D'Angelo, T. (1987). Correlation of stress factors and sustained depression of natural killer cell activity and predicted prognosis in patients with breast cancer. *Journal of Clinical Oncology, 5,* 348–353.

Levy, S. M., & Heiden, L. A. (1990). Personality and social factors in cancer outcome. In H. S. Friedman (Ed.), *Personality and disease.* New York: Wiley, pp. 254–279.

Lewicki, R., Tchorzewski, H., Denys, A., Kowalska, M., & Golinska, A. (1987). Effect of physical exercise on some parameters of immunity in conditioned sportsmen. *International Journal of Sports Medicine, 8,* 309–314.

Lewis, C. E. (1966). Factors influencing the return to work of men with congestive heart failure. *Journal of Chronic Diseases, 19,* 1193–2013.

Lex, B. W. (1991). Some gender differences in alcohol and polysubstance users. *Health Psychology, 10,* 121–132.

Liang, M. H., Larson, M. G., Cullen, K. E., & Schwartz, J. A. (1988). Comparative measurement efficiency and sensitivity of five health status instruments in arthritis research. *Arthritis and Rheumatism, 28,* 542–547.

Libow, M., & Schlant, R. C. (1982). Smoking and heart disease. In P. N. Yu & J. F. Goodwin (Eds.), *Progress in cardiology. Vol. 11.* Philadelphia: Lea & Febiger, pp. 131–161.

Lichstein, K. L. (1988). *Clinical relaxation strategies.* New York: Wiley.

Lichtenstein, E., & Brown, R. A. (1983). Current trends in the modification of cigarette dependence. In A. S. Bellack, M. Hersen, & A. E. Kazdin (Eds.), *International handbook of behavior modification and therapy.* New York: Plenum.

Lichtenstein, E., Glasgow, R. E., & Abrams, D. B. (1986). Social support in smoking cessation: In search of effective interventions. *Behavior Therapy, 17,* 607–619.

Liebman, R., Minuchin, S., & Baker, L. (1974). The use of structural family therapy in the treatment of intractable asthma. *American Journal of Psychiatry, 121,* 535–540.

Liebman, R., Minuchin, S., & Rosman, B. (1976). The role of the family in the treatment of childhood asthma. In T. J. Guerin (Ed.), *Family therapy theory and practice.* New York: Gardner.

Lifson, A., Hessol, N., Rutherford, G. W., et al. (1989). *The natural history of HIV infection in a cohort of homosexual and bisexual men: Clinical manifestations, 1978–1989.* Vth Int. Conf. AIDS, Montreal.

Lifton, R. (1967). *Death in life.* New York: Random House.

Light, K. C. (1981). Cardiovascular responses to effortful active coping: Implications for the role of stress in hypertention development. *Psychophysiology, 18,* 216–225.

Lin, N., Simeone, R., Ensel, W., & Kuo, W. (1979). Social support, stressful life events and illness: A model and an empirical test. *Journal of Health and Social Behavior, 20,* 108–119.

Lindemann, E. (1944). Symptomatology and management of acute grief. *American Journal of Psychiatry, 101,* 141.

Link, B. (1978). On the etiological role of stressful life-change events (comment on Gersten et al., September 1977). *J. Hlth. Soc. Behav., 19,* 343–345.

Linn, S., Fulwood, R., Carroll, M., Brook, J. G., Johnson, C., Kalsbeek, W. D., & Rifkind, B. M. (1991). Serum total cholesterol: HDL cholesterol ratios in U.S. white and black adults by selected demographic and socioeconomic variables (HANES II). *American Journal of Public Health, 81,* 1038–1043.

Linton, S. J., & Gotestam, K. G. (1985). Controlling pain reports through operant condition. *Perceptual and Motor Skills, 60,* 427–437.

Lipid Research Clinics Program. (1984). The Lipid Research Clinics coronary primary prevention trial results. I. Reduction in incidence of coronary heart disease. *Journal of the American Medical Association, 251,* 351–364.

Lippman, M., & Barr, R. (1977). Glucocorticoid receptors in purified subpopulations of human peripheral blood lymphocytes. *Journal of Immunology, 118,* 1977–1981.

Litt, I. F. (1985). Know thyself—Adolescents' "self-assessment" of compliance behavior. *Pediatrics, 75,* 693–696.

Little, R. E., Streissguth, A. P., & Guzinski, G. M. (1980). Prevention of fetal alcohol syndrome: A model program. *Alcoholism: Clinical and Experimental Research, 4,* 185–189.

Livnat, S., Felton, S. J., Carlton, S. L., Bellinger, D. L., & Felton, D. L. (1985). Involvement of peripheral and central catecholamine systems in neural-immune interactions. *Neuroimmunology, 10,* 5–30.

Livnat, S., Madden, K. S., Felton, D. L., & Felton, S. Y. (1987). Regulation of the immune system by sympathetic neuronal activity. *Progress in Neuropsychoimmunology and Biological Psychiatry, 11,* 145–152.

Lloyd, C. (1980). Life events and depressive disorder reviewed. *Archives of General Psychiatry, 37,* 529–548.

Lochman, J. E. (1992). Cognitive-behavioral intervention with aggressive boys: Three-year follow-up and preventive effects. *Journal of Consulting and Clinical Psychology, 60,* 426–432.

Locke, S. E., Kraus, L., Leserman, J., Hurst, M. W., Heisel, J. S., & Williams, R. M. (1984). Life change stress, psychiatric symptoms, and natural killer cell activity. *Psychosomatic Medicine, 46*(5), 441–451.

Loehrer, P. J., Sr., Greger, H. A., Weinberger, M., Musick, B., Miller, M., Nichols, C., Bryan, J., Higgs, D., & Brock, D. (October 1, 1991). Knowledge and beliefs about cancer in a socioeconomically disadvantaged population. *Cancer, 68*(7), 1665–1671.

Loeser, J. E. (1980). Perspectives on pain. In *Proceedings of the First World Conference on Clinical Pharmacology and Therapeutics.* London: MacMillan, pp. 313–316.

Lorig, K., Holman, H. R. (1989). Long-term outcomes of an arthritis self-management study: Effects of reinforcement efforts. *Social Science and Medicine, 29*(2), 221–224.

Lowman, C. (August 30, 1982). *FAS researchers studying increased public knowledge.* NIAAA Information and Feature Service, p. 5.

Luepker, R. V., Johnson, C. A., Murray, D. M., & Pechacek, T. F. (1983). Prevention of cigarette smoking: Three-year follow-up of an education program for youth. *Journal of Behavioral Medicine, 6,* 53–62.

Lui, K., Darrow, W. W., & Rutherford, G. W.

(1988). A model-based estimate of the mean incubation period for AIDS in homosexual men. *Science, 240,* 1333–1335.

Maccoby, N., Farquhar, J. W., & Fortmann, S. P. (1985). The community studies of the Stanford heart disease prevention program. In R. M. Kaplan & M. H. Criqi (Eds.). *Behavioral epidemiology and disease prevention.* New York: Plenum, pp. 385–400.

MacGregor, G. A. (1983). Dietary sodium and potassium intake and blood pressure. *Lancet,* 750–753.

Maciewicz, R., & Martin, J. B. (1987). Pain. In E. Braunwald et al. (Eds.). *Harrison's principles of internal medicine* (11th ed.). New York: McGraw-Hill, pp. 13–17.

Maddi, S. R., & Kobasa, S. C. (1984). *The hardy executive: Health under stress.* Homewood, Ill.: Dow Jones-Irwin.

Mahaffey, K. R., Annest, J. L., Roberts, J., & Murphy, R. S. (1982). National estimates of blood lead levels: United States, 1976–1980: Association with selected demographic and socioeconomic factors. *New England Journal of Medicine, 307,* 573–579.

Mahler, H. I., & Kulik, J. A. (1991). Health care involvement preferences and social-emotional recovery of male coronary-artery-bypass patients. *Health Psychology, 10*(6), 399–408.

Mahoney, M., & Arnkoff, D. B. (1979). Self-management. In O. F. Pomerleau & J. P. Brady (Eds.), *Behavior medicine: Theory and practice* New York: Williams & Wilkins, pp. 75–96.

Mahoney, M., & Mahoney, K. (1976). *Permanent weight control.* New York: W. W. Norton.

Mahoney, M. J. (1974). Self-reward and self-monitoring techniques for weight control. *Behavior Therapy, 5,* 48–57.

Mahoney, M. J., Moura, N. G. M., & Wade, T. C. (1973). The relative efficacy of self-reward, self-punishment, and self-monitoring techniques for weight loss. *Journal of Consulting and Clinical Psychology, 40,* 404–407.

Maiman, L. A., & Becker, M. H. (1974). The health belief model: Origins and correlates in psychological theory. *Health Education Monographs, 2,* 336–353.

Malott, J. M., Glasgow, R. E., O'Neill, H. K., & Klesges, R. C. (1984). Co-workers social support in a worksite smoking control program. *Journal of Applied Behavioral Analysis, 17,* 485–495.

Mann, J. M., Chin, J., Piot, P., & Quinn, T. (1988). The international epidemiology of AIDS. In *The science of AIDS,* New York: W. H. Freeman, pp. 51–61.

Manuck, S. B., Kaplan, J. R., Adams, M. R., & Clarkson, T. B. (1988). Studies of psychosocial influences on coronary artery atherogenesis in cynomolgus monkeys. *Health Psychology, 7,* 113–124.

Marangoni, C., & Ickes, W. (1989). Loneliness: A theoretical review with implications for measurement. *J. Personality Assess., 51*(1), 61–81.

Marcus, A. C., & Crane, L. A. (1985). Smoking behavior among U.S. Latinos: An emerging challenge for public health. *American Journal of Public Health, 75,* 169–172.

Marcus, B. H., Selby, V. C., Niaura, R. S., & Rossi, J. S. (1992). Self-efficacy and the stages of exercise behavior change. *Research Quarterly for Exercise and Sport, 63,* 60–66.

Marks, G., Garcia, M., & Solis, J.M. (1990). Health risk behaviors of Hispanics in the United States: Findings from HHANES, 1982–84. *American Journal of Public Health, 80* (Suppl.), 20–26.

Marlatt, G. A. (1982). Relapse prevention: A self-control program for the treatment of addictive behaviors. In R. B. Stuart (Ed.), *Adherence, compliance and generalization in behavioral medicine.* New York: Brunner/Mazal.

Marlatt, G. A., Demming, B., & Reid, J. B. (1973). Loss of control drinking in alcoholics: An experimental analogue. *Journal of Abnormal Psychology, 81,* 233–241.

Marlatt, G. A., & Gordon, J. R. (Eds.) (1985). *Relapse prevention: Maintenance strategies in addictive behavior change.* New York: Guilford.

Marmot, M. G., Shipley, N. J., & Rose, G. (1984). Inequalities in death-specific explanations of a general pattern. *Lancet, 5,* 103.

Marquis, K., & Ware, J. E. (1979). *New measures of diabetic patient knowledge, behavior, and attitudes.* Santa Monica, Calif.: Rand.

Marshall, W. R., Epstein, L. H., & Green, S. B. (1980). Coffee drinking and cigarette smoking: I. Coffee, caffeine and cigarette smoking behavior. *Addictive Behaviors, 5,* 389–394.

Martin, J. E., & Dubbert, P. M. (1982). Exercise applications and promotion in behavioral medicine: Current status and future directions. *Journal of Consulting and Clinical Psychology, 30,* 1004–1017.

Martin, J. E., Dubbert, P. M., & Cushman, W. C. (1990). Controlled trial of aerobic exercise in hypertension. *Circulation, 81,* 1560–1567.

Martin, J. E., Dubbert, P. M., Kattell, A. D., Thompson, J. K., Raczynski, J. R., Lake, M., Smith, P. O., Webster, J. S., Sikora, T., & Cohen, R. E. (1984). Behavioral control of exercise in sedentary adults. Studies 1 through 6. *Journal of Consulting and Clinical Psychology, 52,* 795–811.

Martin, J. L. (1988). Psychological consequences of AIDS-related bereavement among gay men. *Journal of Consulting and Clinical Psychology, 56(6),* 856–862.

Masi, A. T., & Medsger, T. A., Jr. (1979). Epidemiology of rheumatic diseases. In D. J. McCarty (Ed.), *Arthritis and allied conditions.* Philadelphia: Lea and Febiger, pp. 131–147.

Massie, M. J., & Holland, J. C. (1991). Psychological reactions to breast cancer in the pre- and postsurgical treatment period. *Seminars in Surgical Oncology, 7(5),* 320–325.

Massie, M. J., & Holland, J. C. (1992). The cancer patient with pain: Psychiatric complications and their management. *Journal of Pain and Symptom Management, 7(2),* 99–109.

Mason, J. (1975). A historical view of the stress field. *Journal of Human Stress, 1,* 6–12.

Matarazzo, J. D. (1980). Behavioral health and behavioral medicine: Frontiers for a new health psychology. *American Psychologists, 35,* 807–817.

Matthews, K. A. (1982). Psychological perspectives on the Type A behavior pattern. *Psychological Bulletin, 91,* 293–323.

Matthews, K. A., & Angulo, J. (1980). Measurement of the Type A behavior pattern in children: Assessment of children's competitiveness, impatience-anger, and aggression. *Child Development, 51,* 466–475.

Matthews, K. A., & Haynes, S. G. (1986). Type A behavior pattern and coronary disease risk: Update and critical evaluation. *American Journal of Epidemiology, 123,* 923–960.

Matthews, K. A., Manuck, S. B., & Saab, P. G. (1986). Cardiovascular responses of adolescents during a naturally occurring stressor and their behavioral and psychophysiological predictors. *Psychophysiology, 23,* 198–209.

Matthews, K. A., & Stoney, C. M. (1988). Influences of sex and age on cardiovascular responses during stress. *Psychosomatic Medicine, 50,* 46–56.

Matthews, T. J., & Bolognesi, D. P. (1988). AIDS vaccines. In *The science of AIDS.* New York: W. H. Freeman, pp. 101–110.

Maugh, T. H., II. (1982). Cancer is not inevitable. *Science, 217,* 36–37.

Maurer, K. (1979). *Basic data of arthritis—Knee, hip, and sacroiliac joints in adults ages 25–74 years: United States. 1971–1975.* Hyattsville, Md.: NCHS, Publication No. PHS 79-1661.

Mayer, J. (1953). Decreased activity and energy balance in the hereditary obesity-diabetes syndrome of mice. *Science, 117,* 504–505.

Mayer, J. A., Dubbert, P. M., & Elder, J. P. (1989). Promoting nutrition at the point of choice: A review. *Health Education Quarterly, 16,* 31–43.

Mayers, D., Wilson, D. B., Wagner, K. F. (1989). *Progression of HIV1 disease in population of seropositive Navy and Marine Corps personnel.* V Int. Conf. AIDS, Montreal.

Mazze, R., Shamoon, H., & Pasmantier, R. (1984). Reliability of blood glucose monitoring by patients with diabetes mellitus. *American Journal of Medicine, 198(77),* 211–217.

Mazzuca, S. A. (1982). Does patient education in chronic disease have therapeutic value? *Journal of Chronic Diseases, 35,* 521–529.

McAlister, A., Perry, C., Killen, J., Slinkard, L. A., & Maccoby, N. (1980). Pilot study of smoking, alcohol, and drug abuse prevention. *American Journal of Public Health, 70,* 719–721.

McArthur, J. C., Cohen, B. A., Selnes, O. A., Kumar, A. J., Cooper, K., McArthur, J. H., Souci, G., Cornblath, D. R., Chmiel, J. S., Wang, M. C., Starkey, D. L., Ginzburg, H., Ostrow, D. G., Johnson, R. T., Phair, J. P., & Polk, B. S. (1989). Low prevalence of neurological and neuropsychological abnormalities in otherwise healthy HIV-1-infected individuals: Results from the Multicenter AIDS Cohort Study. *Ann. Neurol., 26(5),* 601–611.

McCarron, D. A., Morris, C. D., Henry, H. J., & Stanton, J. L. (1984). Blood pressure and nutrient intake in the United States. *Science, 224,* 1392–1398.

McCarty, D. J. (1979). Clinical assessment of arthritis. In D. J. McCarty (Ed.), *Arthritis and allied conditions* (9th ed.). Philadelphia: Lea & Febiger.

McClelland, D. C., Patel, V., Brown, D., & Kelner, S. P., Jr. (1991). The role of affiliative loss in the recruitment of helper cells among insulin-dependent diabetics. *Behavioral Medicine, 17*(1), 5–14.

McCrady, B. S., Noel, N. E., Abrams, D. B., Stout, R. L., Nelson, H. F., & Hay, W. M. (1986). Comparative effectiveness of three types of spouse involvement in outpatient behavioral alcoholism treatment. *Journal of Studies on Alcohol, 47*, 459–467.

McCrae, R. R., & Costa, P. T., Jr. (1986). Personality, coping, and coping effectiveness in an adult sample. *Journal of Personality, 54*, 385–405.

McDuffie, F. C., Felts, W. R., & Hochberg, M. C. (1987). Arthritis and musculoskeletal diseases. In R. W. Amler & H. B. Dull (Eds.), *Closing the gap.* New York: Oxford Press, pp. 19–29.

McFarlane, A. H., Neale, K. A., Norman, G. R., Roy, R. G., & Streiner, D. L. (1981). Methodological issues in developing a scale to measure social support. *Schizophrenia Bulletin, 7*, 90–100.

McGuire, W. J. (1964). Inducing resistance to persuasion. In L. Berkowitz (Ed.), *Advances in experimental social psychology* (1st ed.). New York: Academic Press.

McGuire, W. J. (1981). Theoretical foundations of campaigns. In R. E. Rice & W. J. Paisley (Eds.), *Public communication campaigns.* Beverly Hills, Calif.: Sage, 41–70.

McKinlaey, J. B., & McKinlay, S. M. (1977). The questionable contribution of medical measures to the decline of mortality in the United States in the twentieth century. *Millbank Memorial Fund Quarterly—Health and Society, 55*(3), 405–428.

McKinlay, J. B., McKinlay, S. M., & Beaglehole, R. (1989). A review of the evidence concerning the impact of medical measures on recent mortality and morbidity in the United States. *International Journal of Health Services, 19*(2), 181–208.

McNamara, J. J., Molot, M. A., Stremple, J. F., et al. (1971). Coronary artery disease in combat casualties in Vietnam. *Journal of the American Medical Association, 216*, 1185–1187.

McNaughton, M. E., Smith, L. W., Patterson, T. L., & Grant, I. (1990). Stress, social support, coping resources, and immune status in the elderly. *Journal of Nervous and Mental Disease, 178*(7), 460–461.

Mechanic, D. (1962). *Students under stress: A study in the social psychology of adaptation.* Glencoe, Ill.: Free Press of Glencoe.

Mechanic, D. (1977). Illness behavior, social adaptation, and the management of illness. A comparison of educational and medical models. *Journal of Nervous and Mental Disorders, 165*, 79–87.

Meehan, P. J., & O'Carroll, P. W. (1992). Gangs, drugs, and homicide in Los Angeles. *American Journal of Diseases of Children, 146*, 683–687.

Meenan, R. F. (1982). AIMS approach to health status measurement: Conceptual background and measurement properties. *Journal of Rheumatology, 9*, 785–788.

Meenan, R. F., & Pincus, T. (1987). The status of patient status measures. *Journal of Rheumatology, 14*, 411–414.

Meenan, R. F., Yelin, E. H., Nevitt, M., & Epstein, W. (1981). The impact of chronic disease— A sociomedical profile of rheumatoid arthritis. *Arthritis and Rheumatism, 24*, 544–549.

Meerson, F. Z., Sukhikh, G. T., Fuks, B. B., Sbiryaev, V. I., & Ivanov, V. T. (1984). Prevention of stress depression of the activity of natural killers by sodium hydroxybutyrate and the delta-sleep peptide. *Dokl. Biol. Sci., 279*, 122–124.

Meichenbaum, D. (1975). *Cognitive behavior modification.* Lexington, Mass.: Heath.

Meichenbaum, D. (1977). *Cognitive behavior modification.* New York: Plenum.

Melzack, R., & Wall, P. D. (1982). *The challenge of pain.* New York: Basic Books.

Mermelstein, R., Cohen, S., Lichtenstein, E., Baer, J., & Kamarck, T. (1986). Social support and smoking cessation and maintenance. *Journal of Consulting and Clinical Psychology, 54*, 447–453.

Meyer, A. J., & Henderson, J. B. (1974). Multiple risk factor reduction in the prevention of cardiovascular disease. *Preventive Medicine, 3*, 225–236.

Meyer, A. J., Nash, J. D., McAlister, A. L., Maccoby, N., & Farquhar, J. W. (1980). Skills training in a cardiovascular health education campaign. *Journal of Consulting and Clinical Psychology, 48*, 129–142.

Meyerowitz, B. E., Heinrich, R. L., Schag, C. A. (1989). Helping patients cope with cancer. *Oncology, 3*(11), 120–129; discussion 129–131.

Miettinen, M., Turpeinen, O., Karvonen, M. J., Elosuo, R., & Paavilainen, E. (1972). Effect of cholesterol-lowering diet on mortality from coronary heart-disease and other causes. A twelve-year clinical trial in men and women. *Lancet, 2,* 835–837.

Miller, A. B. (1991). Is routine mammography screening appropriate for women 40–49 years of age? *American Journal of Preventive Medicine, 7*(1), 55–62.

Miller, L., Goldstein, G., & Murphy, M. (1982). Reversible alterations in immunoregulatory T cells in smoking. *Chest, 82,* 526–529.

Miller, P. (1975). A behavioral intervention program for chronic public drunkenness offenders. *Archives of General Psychiatry, 32,* 915–918.

Miller, P., Wikoff, R. L., McMahon, M., Garrett, M. J., & Ringel, K. (1985). Indicators of medical regimen adherence for myocardial infarction patients. *Nursing Research, 34,* 268–272.

Millon, C., Morgan, R., Blaney, N., & Szapoczynik, J. (June 12–16, 1988). *Personality style, psychosocial variables and immune status in an HIV positive population.* IV Intl. Conf. on AIDS, Stockholm, Sweden.

Mills, K., Sobell, M., & Schaefer, H. (1971). Training social drinking as an alternative to abstinence for alcoholics. *Behavior Therapy, 2,* 18–27.

Mischel. W. (1979). On the interface of cognition and personality: Beyond the person-situation debate. *American Psycholoogist, 34,* 740–754.

Monjan, A. A. (1981). Stress and immunologic competence: Studies in animals. In R. Ader (Ed.), *Psychoneuroimmunology.* New York: Academic Press.

Monroe, S. M., Thase, M. E., Hersen, M. (1985). Life events and the endogenous-nonendogenous distinction in the treatment and post-treatment course of depression. *Comprehensive Psychiatry, 26,* 175–186.

Moore, T. J. (1989). *Heart failure.* New York: Random House.

Moos, R. E. (1973). *Illness, immunity and social interaction.* New York: Wiley-Interscience.

Mor, V. (1992). QOL measurement scales for cancer patients: Differentiating effects of age from effects of illness. *Oncology, 6*(2 Suppl), 146–152.

Most, R. S., & Sinnock, P. (1983). The epidemiology of lower extremity amputations in diabetic individuals. *Diabetes Care, 6,* 87–91.

Motzova, E., & Herberman, R. (Eds.). (1982). *Immunobiology of natural killer cells.* Boca Raton, Fla.: CRC Press.

Muldoon, M. F., & Manuck, S. B. (1992). Health through cholesterol reduction: Are there unforeseen risks? *Annals of Behavioral Medicine, 14,* 101–108.

Murphy, E., et al. (1963). Development of autonomy and parent-child interaction in late adolescence. *American Journal of Orthopsychiatry, 33,* 643–652.

Murphy, L. B. (1962). *The widening world of childhood: Paths toward mastery.* New York: Basic Books.

Murray, D. M., Luepker, R. V., Pirie, P. L., Grimm, R. H., Bloom, E., Davis, M. A., & Blackburn, H. (1986). Systematic risk factor screening and education: A community-wide approach to prevention of coronary heart disease. *Preventive Medicine, 15,* 661–672.

Murray, D. M., Pirie, P., Luepker, R. V., & Pallonen, U. (1989). Five- and six-year follow-up results from four seventh-grade smoking prevention strategies. *Journal of Behavioral Medicine, 12,* 207–218.

Murray, M. D., Darnell, J., Weinberger, N., & Martz, B. L. (1986). Factors contributing to medication noncompliance in elderly public housing tenants. *Drug Intelligence and Clinical Pharmacy, 20,* 146–151.

Mustacchi, P. (1990). Stress and hypertension. *Western Journal of Medicine, 153,* 180–185.

Nachenson, A. L. (1976). The lumbar spine: An orthopedic challenge. *Spine, 1,* 59–71.

Nathan, P. E. (1985). Prevention of alcoholism: A history of failure. In J. C. Rosen & L. J. Solomon (Eds.), *Prevention in health psychology.* Hanover, N. H.: University Press of New England, pp. 34–71.

Nathan, P. E., & Skinstad, A. H. (1987). Outcomes of treatment for alcohol problems: Current methods, problems, and results. *Journal of Consulting and Clinical Psychology, 55,* 332–340.

National Academy of Science. (1980). *Toward healthful diets.* Food and Nutrition Board, Division of Biological Sciences, Assembly of Life Sciences, National Research Council of the National Academy of Sciences. Washington, D.C.

National Breast Screening Consortium. (1990). Screening mammography: A missed clinical opportunity? Results of the NCI Breast Cancer Screening Consortium and National Health Interview Survey Studies. *Journal of the American Medical Association, 264,* 54–58.

National Center for Health Statistics. (1977). *Limitation of activity due to chronic conditions.* Department of Health and Services, Series 10, No. 111.

National Center for Health Statistics. (1982). *Current estimates from the National Health Interview Survey, United States.* Series 10, No. 141, 1981. DHHS Publication No. (PHS) 82-1569. Hyattsville, Md.: U.S. Department of Health and Human Services.

National Center for Health Statistics. (1983a). *Physicians' visits, volume, and interval since last visit, United States, 1980.* Data from the National Health Interview Survey. Series 10, No. 144, 1983. DHHS Publication No. (PHS) 83-1572. Hyattsville, Md.: U.S. Department of Health and Human Services.

National Center for Health Statistics. (1983b). *Health and prevention profile, United States, 1983.* The HHS Publication (PHS)84-1232, Washington, D.C.: National Center for Health Statistics.

National Center for Health Statistics. (1985). *Health, United States.* Public Health Service. Washington, D.C.: U.S. Government Printing Office, DHHS Pub. No. PHS86-1232.

National Center for Health Statistics. (1986). *Current estimates from the National Health Interview Survey.* Washington, D.C.: U.S. Department of Health and Human Services.

National Diabetes Data Group. (1979). Classification and diagnosis of diabetes mellitus and other categories of glucose intolerance. *Diabetes, 28,* 1039–1057.

National Heart, Lung, & Blood Institute. (1985). *Fact book, fiscal year 1985.* Bethesda, Md.: National Institutes of Health.

National Institutes of Health. (1979). *Epidemiology of respiratory diseases: Task force report on state of knowledge, problems, needs.* NIH Publication No. 81-2019. Washington, D.C.: National Institutes of Health.

NCEP Expert Panel on Blood Cholesterol Levels in Children and Adolescents. (1992). National Cholesterol Education Program (NCEP): Highlights of the report of the expert panel on blood cholesterol levels in children and adolescents. *Pediatrics, 89,* 495–501.

Ndetei, D. M., & Vadher, A. (1981). The relation between contextual and reported threat due to life events: A controlled study. *British Journal of Psychiatry, 139,* 540–544.

Neel, J. B. (1986). Diabetes mellitus: A geneticists nightmare. In W. Creutzfeldt, J. Kobberling, & J. D. Neel (Eds.), *Genetics of diabetes mellitus.* Berlin: Springer-Verlag, pp. 1–11.

Neilson, E., Brown, G., & Marmot, M. (1989). Myocardial infarction. In G. W. Brown & T. Harris (Eds.), *Life events and illness,* New York: Guilford.

Nelson, R. O. (1977). Self-monitoring: Procedures and methodological issues. In J. D. Cone & R. P. Hawkins (Eds.). *Behavioral assessment: New directions in clinical psychology.* New York: Brunner/Mazel.

Newacheck, P. W., Halfon, N., & Budetti, P. (1986). Prevalence of activity limiting chronic conditions among children based on household interviews. *Journal of Chronic Diseases, 39,* 63–71.

Newberger, E. H. (1992). Child abuse. In J. M. Last & R. B. Wallace (Eds.), *Public health and preventive medicine* (13th ed.). Norwalk, Conn.: Appleton & Lange, pp. 1046–1048.

Newberger, E. H., Hagenbuch, J. J., Ebeling, N. B., et al. (1973). Reducing the literal and human cost of child abuse: Impact of a new hospital management system. *Pediatrics, 51,* 840–844.

Newman, W. P., Freedman, D. S., Voors, A. W., Gard, P. D., Srinivasan, S. R., Cresanta, J. L., Williamson, G. D., Webber, L. S., & Berenson, G. S. (1986). Relation of serum lipoprotein levels and systolic blood pressure in early atherosclerosis: The Bogalusa Heart Study. *New England Journal of Medicine, 314,* 138–144.

Niaura, R. S., Herbert, P. H., Saritelli, A., Follick, M. J., Gorkin, L., & Ahern, D. K. (1988). Relation of lipoprotein profiles to occupational stress and response style. Brown University, unpublished.

Noll, R. B., Bukowski, W. M., Rogosch, F. A., LeRoy, S., & Kulkarni, R. (1990). Social interactions between children with cancer and their peers: Teacher ratings. *Journal of Pediatric Psychology, 15*(1), 43–56.

Norbeck, J. S., Lindsey, A. M., & Carrieri, V. L. (1981). The development of an instrument to measure social support. *Nursing Research, 30,* 264–269.

Norell, S. E. (1981). Accuracy of patient interviews

and estimates by clinical staff determining medication compliance. *Social Science and Medicine, 15,* 57–61.

Novotny, T. E., Romano, R. A., Davis, R. M., & Mills, S. L. (1992). The public health practice of tobacco control: Lessons learned and directions for the states in the 1990s. *Annual Review of Public Health, 13,* 298–318.

Noyes, R., Jr., Kathol, R. G., Debelius-Enemark, P., Williams, J., Mutgi, A., Suelzer, M. T., & Clamon, G. H. (1990). Distress associated with cancer as measured by the illness distress scale. *Psychosomatics, 31*(3), 321–330.

Nutrition Sub-Committee of the British Diabetic Association. (1982). Dietary recommendations for diabetics for the 1980's: A policy statement by the British Diabetic Association. *Human Nutrition, Applied Nutrition, 15,* 36A.

O'Connell, D. O., & Velicer, W. F. (1988). A decisional balance measure and the stages of change model for weight loss. *International Journal of the Addictions, 23,* 729–750.

O'Connor, G. T., Buring, J. E., Yusuf, S., Goldhaber, S. Z., Olmstead, E. M., Paffenbarger, R. S., & Hennekens, C. H. (1989). An overview of randomized trials of rehabilitation with exercise after myocardial infarction. *Circulation, 80,* 234–244.

Office of the Actuary, Division of National Cost Estimates. (1987). Health care financing administration. National health expenditures, 1986–2000. *Health Care Financing Review, 8*(4), 1–36.

Office of Smoking and Health, U.S. Department of Agriculture. (1985). Nutrition and your health: Dietary guidelines for Americans. *Home and Garden Bulletin,* No. 232.

Oldridge, N. B., & Jones, N. L. (1983). Improving patient compliance in cardiac exercise rehabilitation: Effects of written agreement and self-monitoring. *Journal of Cardiac Rehabilitation, 3,* 257–262.

Olds, D. L., Henderson, C. R., Chamberlin, R., & Tatelbaum, R. (1986). Preventing child abuse and neglect: A randomized trial of nurse home visitation. *Pediatrics, 78,* 65–78.

Olson, J. M., & Zanna, M. P.(1987). Understanding and promoting exercise: A social psychological perspective. *Canadian Journal of Public Health, 78,* S1–S8.

Onions, T. (1933). *Shorter Oxford English dictionary.* Oxford: Clarendon Press.

Orne, C. M., & Binik, Y. M. (1989). Consistency in adherence across regimen demands. *Health Psychology, 8,* 27–43.

Ornish, D., Brown, S. E., Scherwitz, L. W., Billings, J. H., Armstrong, W. T., Ports, T. A., McLanahan, S. M., Kirkeeide, R. L., Brand, R. J., & Gould, K. L. (1990). Can lifestyle changes reverse coronary heart disease? *Lancet, 336,* 129–133.

Orth-Gomer, K., & Unden, A. L. (1990). Type A behavior, social support and coronary risk: Interaction and significance for mortality in cardiac patients. *Psychosomatic Medicine, 52,* 59–72.

Ory, H. W. (1977). Association between oral contraceptives and myocardial infarction. A review. *Journal of the American Medical Association, 237,* 2619–2622.

Oscai, L. B., & Holloszy, J. O. (1969). Effects of weight changes produced by exercise, food restriction, or overeating on body composition. *Journal of Clinical Investigation, 48,* 2124–2128.

Osler, W. (1910). The Lumleian lectures on angina pectoris. *Lancet, 1,* 696–700, 838–844, 974–977.

Ostrow, D. G. (1990). Psychiatric aspects of human immunodeficiency virus infection. In *Current concepts,* Kalamazoo, Mi.: The Upjohn Company.

Owen, N., & Davies, M. J. (1990). Smokers' preferences for assistance with cessation. *Preventive Medicine, 19,* 424–431.

Paffenbarger, R. S., Hyde, R. T., Wing, A. L., & Hsieh, C. C. (1986). Physical activity, all-cause mortality, and longevity of college alumni. *New England Journal of Medicine, 314,* 605–613.

Paffenbarger, R. S., Wing, A. L., & Hyde, R. T. (1978). Physical activity as an index of heart attack risk in college alumni. *American Journal of Epidemiology, 108,* 161–175.

Paffenbarger, R. S., Wing, A. L., Hyde, R. T., & Jung, D. L. (1983). Physical activity and incidence of hypertension in college alumni. *American Journal of Epidemiology, 117,* 245–256.

Page, L. B. (1980). Dietary sodium and blood pressure: Evidence from human studies. In R. M. Lauer & R. B., Shekelle (Eds.), *Childhood prevention of atherosclerosis and hypertension.* New York: Raven, pp. 291–303.

Pelletier, K. R. (1989). University of California, San

Francisco, unpublished. UCSF corporate health promotion research program: Overview.

Palmblad, J. (1981). Stress and immunocompetence: Studies in man. In R. Ader (Ed.), *Psychoneuroimmunology*. New York: Academic Press.

Palmblad, J., Petrini, B., Wasserman, J., et al. (1979). Lymphocyte and granulocyte reactions during sleep deprivation. *Psychosoma. Med., 41*(4), 273–278.

Panush, R. S., (1991). Does food cause or cure arthritis? *Rheumatic Diseases Clinics of North America, 17*(2), 259–272.

Parker, J. C., Smarr, K. L., Buescher, K. L., Phillips, L. R., Frank, R. G., Beck, N. C., Anderson, S. K., & Walker, S. E. (1989). Pain control and rational thinking. Implications for rheumatoid arthritis. *Arthritis and Rheumatism, 32*, 984–990.

Parkes, C. M., Benjamin, B., & Fitzgerald, R. G. (1969). Broken heart: A statistical study of increased mortality among widowers. *British Medical Journal, 1*, 740–743.

Patterson, T. L., Kaplan, R. M., Sallis, J. F., & Nader, P. R. (1987). Aggregation of blood pressure in Anglo-American and Mexican-American families. *Preventive Medicine, 16*, 616–625.

Pattison, E. M., Sobell, M. B., & Sobell, L. C. (1977). *Emerging concepts of alcohol dependence*. New York: Springer.

Pavlov, I. (1927). *Conditioned reflexes*. London: Oxford University Press.

Paykel, E. S. (1978). Contribution of life events to causation of psychiatric illness. *Psychol. Med., 8*, 245–253.

Paykel, E. S. (1983). Methodological aspects of life events research. *Journal of Psychosomatic Research, 27*, 341–352.

Paykel, E. S. (1987). Methodology of life events research. *Advances in Psychosomatic Medicine, 17*, 13–29.

Pearlin, L. I. & Aneshensel, C. S. (1986). Coping and social supports: Their functions and applications. In L. Aiken & B. Mechanic (Eds.), *Applications of social science to clinical medicine and health policy*. New Brunswick: Rutgers University Press.

Pearlin, L. I., & Schooler, (1978). The structure of coping. *Journal of Health and Social Behavior, 19*(1), 2–21.

Penick, S. B., Filion, R., Fox, S., & Stunkard, A. J. (1971). Behavior modification in the treatment of obesity. *Psychosomatic Medicine, 33*, 49–55.

Perkins, K. A., Epstein, L. H., & Pastor, S. (1991). Changes in energy balance following smoking cessation and resumption of smoking in women. *Journal of Consulting and Clinical Psychology, 58*, 121–125.

Perri, M. G., McAdoo, W. G., Spevak, P. A., & Newlin, D. B. (1984). Effects of a multicomponent maintenance program on long-term weight loss. *Journal of Consulting and Clinical Psychology, 52*, 480–481.

Perry, C. L., Luepker, R. V., Murray, D. M., Durth, C., Mullis, R., Crockett, S., & Jacobs, D. R. (1988). Parent involvement with children's health promotion: The Minnesota home team. *American Journal of Public Health, 78*, 1156–1160.

Perry, S., Belsky-Barr, D., Barr, W. B., & Jacobsberg, L. (1989). Neuropsychological function in physically asymptomatic, HIV-seropositive men. *J. Neuropsychiat. 1*(3), 296–302.

Perry, S., & Jacobsen, P. (1986). Neuropsychiatric manifestations of AIDS-spectrum disorders. *Hosp. Community Psychiatry, 37*, 135–142.

Peshkin, M. M. (1930). Asthma in chldren: Role of environment in the treatment of a selected group of cases: A plea for a "home" as a restorative measure. *American Journal of Diseases of Children, 39*, 774–781.

Peterson, L., Farmer, J., & Kashani, J. H. (1990). Parental injury prevention endeavors: A function of health beliefs? *Health Psychology, 9*, 177–191.

Peterson, P. E., Jeffrey, D. B., Bridgwater, C. A., & Dawson, B. (1984). How pronutrition programming affects children's dietary habits. *Developmental Psychology, 20*, 55–63.

Peto, R. (August 1990). *Future world-wide health effects of present smoking patterns*. Presented at the 15th International Cancer Congress. Hamburg, Germany.

Peto, R., Lopez, A. D., Boreham, J., Thun, M., & Heath, C. Jr. (1992). Mortality from tobacco in developed countries: Indirect estimation from national vital statistics. *Lancet, 339*, 1268–1278.

Phibbs, C. S., Bateman, D. A., & Schwartz, R. M. (1991). The neonatal costs of maternal cocaine use. *Journal of the American Medical Association, 266*, 1521–1526.

Pickering, T. G., & Gerin, W. (1990). Cardiovascular reactivity in the laboratory and the role of behavioral factors in hypertension: A critical review. *Annals of Behavioral Medicine, 12*, 3–16.

Pillemer, K., & Frankel, S. (1992). Elder abuse. In J. M. Last & R. B. Wallace (Eds.), *Public health and preventive medicine* (13th ed.). Norwalk, Conn.: Appleton & Lange, pp. 1051–1054.

Pincus, T., Sunney, J., Soraci, S., Wallston, K., & Hummon, N. (1983). Assessment of patient satisfaction in activities of daily living using a modified Stanford Health Assessment questionnaire. *Arthritis and Rheumatism, 26*, 1346–1353.

Pi-Sunyer, F. X. (1988). Exercise in the treatment of obesity. In R. T. Frankle and M-U. Yang (Eds.), *Obesity and weight control.* Rockville, Md.: Aspen, pp. 241–255.

Plaut, S. M., & Friedman, S. B. (1981). *Psychosocial factors in infectious disease.* In R. Ader (Ed.), *Psychoneuroimmunology* New York: Academic Press, (pp. 3–30).

Polivy, J. (1976). The perception of calories and regulation of intake in restrained and unrestrained subjects. *Addictive Behaviors, 1*, 237–244.

Pooling Project Research Group. (1978). Relationship of blood pressure, serum cholesterol, smoking habit, relative weight and ECG abnormalities to incidence of major coronary events: Final report of the Pooling Project. *Journal of Chronic Disease, 31*, 201–306.

Porritt, D. (1979). Social support in crisis: Quantity or quality? *Social Science and Medicine, 13A*, 715–721.

Powell, K. E., Thompson, P. D., Caspersen, C. J., & Kendrick, J. S. (1987). Physical activity and the incidence of coronary heart disease. *Annual Review of Public Health, 8*, 253–287.

Powell, L. H., Friedman, M., Thoresen, C. E., Gill, J. J., & Ulmer, D. K. (1984). Can the Type A behavior pattern be altered after myocardial infarction? A second year report from the Recurrent Coronary Prevention Project. *Psychosomatic Medicine, 46*, 293–313.

Pratt, R. T. C. (1951). An investigation of the psychiatric aspects of disseminated sclerosis. *Journal of Neurology, Neurosurgery, and Psychiatry, 14*, 326–336.

Prentice-Dunn, S., & Rogers, R. W. (1986). Protection motivation theory and preventive health: Beyond the health belief model: *Health Education Research, 1*, 153–161.

Price, J. M., & Grinker, J. (1973). Effects of degree of obesity, food deprivation and palatability on eating behavior of humans. *Journal of Comparative and Physiological Psychology, 85*, 265–271.

Price, R. W., Brew, B., Sidtis, J., Rosenblum, M., Scheck, A. C., Clearloy, P. (1988). The brain in AIDS: Central nervous system HIV-1 infection and AIDS dementia complex. *Science, 239*, 586–592.

Price, V. A. (1982). *Type A behavior pattern.* New York: Academic Press.

Prochaska, J. O., & DiClemente, C. C. (1984). *The transtheoretical approach: Crossing traditional boundaries of therapy.* Homewood, Ill.: Dow Jones Irwin.

Procidano, M. E., & Heller, K. (1983). Measures of perceived social support from friends and from family: Three validation studies. *American Journal of Community Psychology, 11*(1), 1–24.

Protective effect of physical activity on coronary heart disease. (1987). *Mortality and Morbidity Weekly Report, 36* (No. 26), 426–430.

Public Health Services. (1988). *The surgeon general's report on nutrition and health.* Washington, D.C.: U.S. Department of Health and Human Services.

Purcell, K., Brady, K., Chi, H., Muser, J., Mulk, L., Gordon, N., & Means, J. (1969). The effect on asthma in children of experimental separation from the family. *Psychosomatic Medicine, 31*, 144–164.

Puska, P. (1984). Community-based prevention of cardiovascular disease: The North Karelia project. In J. D. Matarazzo, S. M. Weiss, J. A. Herd, N. E. Miller, & S. M. Weiss (Eds.), *Behavioral health: A handbook of health enhancement and disease prevention.* New York: Wiley, pp. 1140–1147.

Raab, A., Dantzer, R., Michaud, B., Mormede, P., Taghzouti, K., Simon, H., & Le Moal, M. (1986). Behavioral, physiological, and immunological consequences of social status and aggression in chronically coexisting resident-intruder dyads of male rats. *Physiol. Behav., 36*, 223–228.

Rabkin, J. G., & Streuning, E. L. (1976). Life events, stress, and illness. *Science, 194*, 1013–1020.

Rabkin, S. W., Boyko, E., Wilson, A., & Streja, D. A. (1983). A randomized clinical trial comparing behavior modification and individual counseling in nutritional therapy of non-insulin-dependent diabetes mellitus: Comparison of the effect on blood sugar, body weight, and serum lipids. *Diabetes Care, 6,* 50–56.

Ragland, D. R., & Brand, R. J. (1988). Type A behavior and mortality from coronary heart disease. *New England Journal of Medicine, 318,* 65–69.

Rainwater, N., Aylllon, T., Frederiksen, L. W., Moore, E. J., & Bonar, J. R. (1983). Teaching self-management skills to increase diet compliance in diabetics. In R. B. Stuart (Ed.), *Adherence compliance and generalization in behavioral medicine.* New York: Brunner/Mazel.

Rakowski, W., Dube, C. E., Marcus, B. H., Prochaska, J. O., Velicer, W. F., & Abrams, D. B. (1992). Assessing elements of women's decisions about mammography. *Health Psychology, 11,* 111–118.

Rand, C. S. (1990). Issues in the measurement of adherence. In S. A. Shumaker, E. B. Schron, & J. K. Ockene (Eds.), *The handbook of health behavior change.* New York: Springer, 102–110.

Rapoport, R., & Rapoport, R. N. (1964). New light on the honeymoon. *Human Relations, 17,* 3–56.

Raskin, S. W., Boyko, E., Wilson, A., & Streja, D. A. (1983). A randomized clinical trial comparing behavior modification and individual counseling in nutritional therapy of non-insulin-dependent diabetes mellitus: Comparison of the effect on blood sugar, body weight, and serum lipids. *Diabetes Care, 6,* 50–56.

Rauramaa, R. (1984). Relationship of physical activity, glucose tolerance, and weight management. *Preventive Medicine, 13,* 37–46.

Ravelli, G. P., Stein, Z. A., & Susser, M. W. (1976). Obesity in young men after famine exposure in utero and early infancy. *New England Journal of Medicine, 295*(7), 349–353.

Ravenholt, R. T. (1985). Tobacco's impact on 20th century U.S. mortality patterns. *American Journal of Preventive Medicine, 1,* 4–17.

Redd, W. H., Andersen, G. V., & Minagawa, R. (1982). Hypnotic control of anticipatory nausea in patients undergoing cancer chemotherapy. *Journal of Consulting and Clinical Psychology, 50,* 12–19.

Redd, W. H., & Andrykrwski, M. A. (1982). Behavioral interventions in cancer treatment: Controlling adverse reactions to chemotherapy. *Journal of Consulting and Clinical Psychology, 50,* 1018–1029.

Redd, W. H., Silberfarb, P. M., Andersen, B. L., Andrykowski, M. A., Bovbjerg, D. H., Burish, T. G., Carpenter, P. J., Cleeland, C., Dolgin, M., & Levy, S. M. (1991). Physiologic and psychobehavioral research in oncology. *Cancer, 67*(3 Suppl), 813–822.

Reed, D., McGee, D., Yano, K., & Feinleib, M. (1983). Social networks and CHD among Japanese men in Hawaii. *American Journal of Epidemiology, 117,* 384–396.

Rees, D. W. (1985). Health beliefs and compliance with alcohol treatment. *Journal of Studies of Alcohol, 46,* 517–524.

Remington, P. L., Forman, M. R., Gentry, E. M., et al. (1985). Current smoking trends in the United States: The 1981–1983 behavioral risk factor surveys. *Journal of the American Medical Association, 253,* 2975–2978.

Renne, C. M., & Creer, T. L. (1985). Asthmatic children and their families. *Developmental and Behavioral Pediatrics, 6,* 41–81.

Report of the presidential commission on the human immunodeficiency virus epidemic. (1988). Washington, D.C.: U.S. Government Printing Office.

Reuben, N., Hein, K., Drucker, E., Bauman, L., & Lanby, J. (March 24–27, 1988). *Relationship of high-risk behaviors to AIDS knowledge in adolescent high school students.* Presented at the Annual Research Meeting, Society for Adolescent Medicine, New York City.

Review Panel on Coronary-Prone Behavior and Coronary Heart Disease. (1981). Coronary-prone behavior and coronary heart disease: A critical review. *Circulation, 63,* 1199–1215.

Reynolds, P., & Kaplan, G. A., (1990). Social connections and risk for cancer: prospective evidence from the Alameda County Study. *Behavioral Medicine, 16*(3), 101–110.

Richardson, S. A., Hastorf, A. H., Goodman, N., & Dornbusch, S. M. (1961). Cultural uniformity in reaction to physical disabilities. *American Sociological Review, 90,* 44–51.

Riley, V. (1981). Psychoneuroendocrine influences on immunocompetence and neoplasia. *Science, 212,* 110–119.

Rimm, A. A. (1985). Trends in cardiac surgery in the United States. *New England Journal of Medicine, 312,* 119–120.

Roark, G. (1971). Psychosomatic factors in the epidemiology of infectious mononucleosis. *Psychosomatics, 12,* 402–411.

Robert Wood Johnson Foundation. (1983). *Special report: Updated report on access to health care for the American people.* Princeton, N.J.: Robert Wood Johnson Foundation.

Roberts, A., & Reinhardt, L. (1980). The behavioral management of chronic pain: Long-term follow-up with comparison groups. *Pain, 8,* 151–162.

Roberts, M. C. (1987). Public health and health psychology: Two cats of Kilkenny? *Professional Psychology: Research and Practice, 18,* 145–149.

Rodin, J. (1978). Somatopsychics and attribution. *Personality and Social Psychology Bulletin, 4,* 531–540.

Rodin, J. (1980). The externality theory today. In A. J. Stunkard (Ed.), *Obesity.* Philadelphia: Saunders, pp. 226–239.

Rodwin, V. G. (1984). *The health planning predicament.* Berkeley: University of California Press.

Rokeach, M. (1973). *The nature of human values.* New York: Free Press.

Rolls, B. J., Fedoroff, I. C., & Guthrie, J. F. (1991). Gender differences in eating behavior and body weight regulation. *Health Psychology, 10,* 133–142.

Romano, P. S., Bloom, J., & Syme, L. (1991). Smoking, social support, and hassles in an urban African-American community. *American Journal of Public Health, 81,* 1415–1422.

Roos, N. P. (1984). Hysterectomy: Variations in rates across small areas and across physicians practices. *American Journal of Public Health, 74,* 327–355.

Rosenbaum, M., & Ben-Ari, S. K. (1986). Cognitive and personality factors in the delay of gratification of hemodialysis patients. *Journal of Personality and Social Psychology, 51,* 357–364.

Rosenberg, M. L., & Mercy, J. A. (1992). Assaultive violence. In J. M. Last & R. B. Wallace (Eds.), *Public health and preventive medicine* (13th ed.). Norwalk, Conn.: Appleton & Lange, pp. 1035–1039.

Rosenberg, M. L., Stark, E., & Zahn, M. A. (1986). Interpersonal violence: Homicide and spouse abuse. In J. M. Last (Ed.), *Public health and preventive medicine* (12th ed.). Norwalk, Conn.: Appleton-Century-Crofts, pp. 1399–1426.

Rosenman, R. H., Brand, R. J., Jenkins, C. D., Friedman, M., Straus, R., & Wurm, M. (1975). Coronary heart disease in the western collaborative heart study: Final follow-up experience of $8\frac{1}{2}$ years. *Journal of the American Medical Association, 233,* 872–877.

Rosenstock, I. M. (1966). Why people use health services. *Milband Memorial Fund Quarterly, 44,* 94–127.

Rosenstock, I. M. (1990). The health belief model: Explaining health behavior through expectancies. In K. Glanz, F. M. Lewis, & B. K. Rimer (Eds.), *Health behavior and health education: Theory, research, and practice.* San Francisco: Jossey-Bass, pp. 39–62.

Roskies, E., Seraganian, P., Oseasohn, R., Hanley, J. A., Collu, R., Martin, N., & Smilga, C. (1986). The Montreal Type A intervention project: Major findings. *Health Psychology, 5,* 45–69.

Ross, H., Bernstein, G., & Rifkin, H. (1983). Relationship of diabetes mellitus to long-term complications. In M. Ellenberg & H. Rifkin (Eds.), *Diabetes mellitus theory and practice* (3rd ed.). New Hyde Park, N.Y.: Medical Examination Publishing, pp. 907–926.

Ross, L. (1974). Effects of manipulating the salience of food upon consumption by obese and normal eaters. In S. Schachter & J. Rodin (Eds.), *Obese humans and rats.* Washington, D.C.: Erlbaum/Halsted.

Ross, L. (1977). The intuitive psychologist and his shortcomings. Distortions in the attribution process. In L. Berkowitz (Ed.), *Advances in experimental social psychology* (Voltan). New York: Academic Press.

Rossini, A. A., Mordeis, J. P., & Handlar, E. S. (1989). The "tumbler" hypothesis: The autoimmunity of insulin-dependent diabetes mellitus. *Diabetes Spectrum, 2*(3), 195–201.

Roth, H. P. (1990). Problems with adherence in the elderly. In S. A. Shumaker, E. B. Schron, & J. K. Ockene (Eds.), *The handbook of health behavior change.* New York: Springer, pp. 315–326.

Rozin, P. (1984). The acquisition of food habits and preferences. In J. D. Matarazzo, S. M. Weiss, J. A. Herd, N. E. Miller, & S. M. Weiss (Eds.), *Behavioral health: A handbook of health enhancement and disease prevention.* New York: Wiley, pp. 590–607.

Rozin, P., & Kalat, J. W. (1971). Specific hungers and poison avoidance as adaptive specializations of learning. *Psychological Review, 78,* 459–486.

Ruberman, W. (1992). Psychosocial influences on

mortality of patients with coronary heart disease, *Journal of the American Medical Association, 267*(4), 559–560.

Ruberman, W., Weinblatt, E., Goldberg, J. D., & Chaudhary, B. S. (1984). Psychosocial influences on mortality after myocardial infarction. *New England Journal of Medicine, 311,* 552–559.

Rudy, T. E., & Turk, D. C. (1991). Psychological aspects of pain. *International Anesthesiology Clinics, 29*(1), 9–21.

Rukeyser, L., & Cooney, J. (1988). *Louis Rukeyser's business almanac.* New York: Simon & Schuster.

Runyan, C. W., & Gerken, E. A. (1989). Epidemiology and prevention of adolescent injury: A review and research agenda. *Journal of the American Medical Association, 262,* 2273–2279.

Russell, L. (1986). *Is prevention better than cure?* Washington: The Brookings Institution.

Russell, M. A. H. (1974). The smoking habit and its classification. *The Practitioner, 212,* 791–800.

Russell, M. A. H. (1978). Smoking addiction: Some implications for cessation. In J. L. Schwartz (Ed.), *Progress in smoking cessation: Proceedings of the International Conference on Smoking Cessation.* New York: American Cancer Society.

Sackett, D. L. (1979). A compliance practicum for the busy practitioner. In R. B. Haynes, D. W. Taylor, & D. L. Sackett (Eds.), *Compliance in health care.* Baltimore, Md.: Johns Hopkins University Press, pp. 286–294.

Sackett, D. L., & Snow, J. C. (1979). The magnitude and measurement of compliance. In R. B. Haynes, D. W. Taylor, & D. L. Sackett (Eds.), *Compliance in health care.* Baltimore: Johns Hopkins University Press.

Sacks, H., Chalmers, D. C., & Smith, H. (1982). Randomized versus historical controls for clinical trials. *American Journal of Medicine, 72,* 233–240.

St. Leger, A., cochrane, A., & Moore, F. (1978). The anomaly that won't go away. *:Lancet, II,* 1153.

Salber, E. J., Freeman, H. E., & Abelin, T. (1968). Needed research on smoking: Lessons from the Newton study. In E. F. Borgatta & R. R. Evans (Eds.), *Smoking, health and behavior.* Chicago: Aldine.

Sallade, J. (1973). A comparison of the psychological adjustment of obese vs. nonobese children. *Journal of Psychosomatic Research, 7,* 89–93.

Sallis, J. F., Dimsdale, J. E., & Caine, C. (1988). Blood pressure reactivity in children. *Journal of Psychosomatic Research, 32,* 1–12.

Sallis, J. F., Flora, J. A., Fortmann, S. P., Taylor, C. B., & Maccoby, N. (1985). Mediated smoking cessation programs in the Stanford five-city project. *Addictive Behaviors, 10,* 441–443.

Sallis, J. F., Grossman, R. M., Pinsky, R. B., Patterson, P. L., & Nader, P. R. (1987). The development of scales to measure social support for diet and exercise behaviors. *Preventive Medicine, 16,* 825–836.

Sallis, J. F., Haskell, W. L., Fortmann, S. P., Vranizan, K. M., Taylor, C. B., & Solomon, D. S. (1986). Predictors of adoption and maintenance of physical activity in a community sample. *Preventive Medicine, 15,* 331–341.

Sallis, J. F., Haskell, W. L., Fortmann, S. P., Wood, P. D., & Vranizan, K. M. (1986). Moderate-intensity physical activity and cardiovascular risk factors. *Preventive Medicine, 15,* 561–568.

Sallis, J. F., Haskell, W. L., Wood, P. D., Fortmann, S. P., & Vranizan, K. M. (1986). Vigorous physical activity and cardiovascular risk factors in young adults. *Journal of Chronic Diseases, 39,* 115–120.

Sallis, J. F., Hill, R. D., Fortmann, S. P., & Flora, J. A. (1986). Health behavior change at the worksite: Cardiovascular risk reduction. *Progress in Behavior Modification, 20,* 161–197.

Sallis, J. F., & Hovell, M. F. (1990). Determinants of exercise behavior. *Exercise and Sport Sciences Reviews, 18.* Champaign, Ill.: Human Kinetics.

Sallis, J. F., Hovell, M. F., & Hofstetter, C. R. (1992). Predictors of adoption and maintenance of vigorous physical activity in men and women. *Preventive Medicine, 21,* 237–251.

Sallis, J. F., & McKenzie, T. L. (1991). Physical education's role in public health. *Research Quarterly for Exercise and Sport, 62,* 124–137.

Sallis, J. F., Patterson, T. L., Buono, M. J., Atkins, C. J., & Nader, P. R. (1988). Aggregation of physical activity habits in Mexican-American and Anglo families. *Journal of Behavioral Medicine, 11,* 31–41.

Sallis, J. F., Patterson, T. L., Buono, M. J., & Nader, P. R. (1988). Relation of cardiovascular fitness and physical activity to cardiovascular disease risk factors in children and adults. *American Journal of Epidemiology, 127,* 933–941.

Sallis, J. F., Patterson, T. L., McKenzie, T. L., & Nader, P. R. (1988). Family variables and physical activity in preschool children. *Journal of Developmental and Behavioral Pediatrics, 9,* 57–61.

Sallis, J. F., Simons-Morton, B. G., Stone, E. J., Corbin, C. B., Epstein, L. H., Faucette, N., Iannotti, R. J., Killen, J. D., Klesges, R. C., Petray, C. K., Rowland, T. W., & Taylor, W. C. (1992). Determinants of physical activity and interventions in youth. *Medicine and Science in Sports and Exercise, 24,* S248–S257.

Salz, K. M., Tamir, I., Ernst, N., Kwiterovich, P., Glueck, C., Christensen, B., Larsen, R., Pirhonen, D., Prewitt, T. E., & Scott, L. W. (1983). Selected nutrient intakes of free-living white children ages 6–19 years. The Lipid Research Clinics program prevalence study. *Pediatric Research, 17,* 124–130.

Sandler, L. (1965). Child-rearing practices of mothers of asthmatic children. *Journal of Asthma Research, 2,* 215–256.

Sarason, B. R., Sarason, I. G., & Pierce, G. R. (Eds.) (1990). *Social support: An interactional view.* New York: Wiley.

Sarason, I. G., Johnson, J. H., & Siegel, J. M. (1978). Assessing the impact of life changes: Development of the life experiences survey. *Journal of Consulting and Clinical Psychology, 46,* 932–946.

Sarason, I. G., Levine, H. M., Basham, R. B., & Sarason, B. R. (1983). Assessing social support: The Social Support Questionnaire. *Journal of Personality and Social Psychology, 44*(I), 127–139.

Sausen, K. P., Lovallo, W. R., Pincomb, G. A., & Wilson, M. F. (1992). Cardiovascular responses to occupational stress in male medical students: A paradigm for ambulatory monitoring studies. *Health Psychology, 11,* 55–60.

Schachter, S. (1971). *Emotion, obesity, and crime.* New York: Academic Press.

Schachter, S. (1978). Pharmacological and psychological determinants of smoking. *Annals of Internal Medicine, 88,* 104–114.

Schachter, S., Silverstein, B., Kozlowski, L. T., Herman, C. P., & Liebling, B. (1977). Effects of stress on cigarette smoking and urinary pH. *Journal of Experimental Psychology: General, 106,* 24–130.

Schafer, L. C., McCaul, K. D., & Glasgow, R. E. (1984). *Supportive and nonsupportive family behaviors: Relationships to adherence and metabolic control in persons with Type I diabetes.* Unpublished manuscript. Fargo: North Dakota State University.

Schafer, L. C., McCaul, K. D., & Glasgow, R. E. (1986). Supportive and non-supportive family behaviors: Relationships to adherence and metabolic control in persons with Type I diabetes. *Diabetes Care, 9,* 179–185.

Schag, C. A., Heinrich, R. L., Aadland, R. L., & Ganz, P. A. (1990). Assessing problems of cancer patients: Psychometric properties of the cancer inventory of problem situations. *Health Psychology, 9*(1), 83–102.

Schilling, R. F., El-Bassel, N., Schinke, S. P., Nichols, S., Botvin, G. J., & Orlandi, M. A. (1991). Sexual behavior, attitudes toward safer sex, and gender among a cohort of 244 recovering IV drug users. *The International Journal of the Addictions, 26,* 859–877.

Schinke, S., Orlandi, M., Vaccaro, D., Espinoza, R., McAlister, A., & Botvin, G. (1992). Substance use among Hispanic and non-Hispanic adolescents. *Addictive Behaviors, 17,* 117–124.

Schleifer, S. J., Keller, S. E., Camerino, M., Thornton, J. C., & Stein, M. (1983). Suppression of lymphocyte stimulation following bereavement. *Journal of the American Medical Association, 250,* 374–377.

Schleifer, S. J., Keller, S. E., Siris, S. G., Davis, K. L. & Stein, M. (1985). Depression and immunity: Lymphocyte function in ambulatory depressed patients, hospitalized schophrenic patients, and patients hospitalized for hermiorrhaphy. *Archives of General Psychiatry, 42,* 129–133.

Schless, A. P. (1979). Life events and affective illness. In J. E. Barrett, R. M. Rose, & G. L. Kierman (Eds.), *Stress and mental disorder.* New York: Raven Press.

Schneiderman, L. J., & Arras, J. D. (1985). Counseling patients to counsel physicians on future care in the event of patient incompetence. *Annals of Internal Medicine, 102,* 693–698.

Schniederman, L. J., & Kaplan, R. M. (1992). Fear of dying of HIV infection versus hepatitis B infection. *American Journal of Public Health, 82,* 584–586.

Schoenbach, V. J., Kaplan, B. H., Fredman, L., & Kleinbaum, D. G. (1986). Social ties and mortality in Evans County, Georgia. *American Journal of Epidemiology, 123*(4), 577–591.

Schor, S. (1971). The University Group Diabetes Program. A statistician looks at the mortality rate. *Journal of the American Medical Association, 217,* 1671–1675.

Schroeder, S. A. (1987). Strategies for reducing medical costs by changing physician's behavior. *International Journal of Technology in Health Care, 3,* 39–50.

Schuster, C. R., & Kilbey, M. M. (1992). Prevention of drug abuse. In J. M. Last & R. B. Wallace (Eds.), *Public health and preventive medicine* (13th ed.). Norwalk, Conn.: Appleton & Lange, pp. 769–786.

Schwartz, G. E., & Weiss, S. M. (1977). *Yale conference on behavioral medicine.* Washington, D.C.: Department of Health, Education, and Welfare; National Heart, Lung, and Blood Institute.

Schwartz, J. L. (1987). *Review and evaluation of smoking cessation methods: The United States and Canada, 1978–1985.* Washington, D.C.: National Cancer Institute (NIH Pub. No. 87-2940).

Sclafani, A. (1980). Dietary obesity. In A. J. Stunkard (Ed.), *Obesity.* Philadelphia: Saunders, pp. 208–225.

Sclafani, A., & Springer, D. (1976). Dietary obesity in adult rats: Similarities to hypothalamic and human obesity syndromes. *Physiology and Behavior, 17,* 461–471.

Seligman, M. P. (1975). *Helplessness: On depression, development and death.* San Francisco: Freeman.

Sella, D. F., Pratt, A., & Holland, J. C. (1986). Persistent anticipatory nausea, vomiting, and anxiety in cured Hodgkin's disease patients after completion of chemotherapy. *American Journal of Psychiatry, 143,* 641–643.

Selye, H. (1956). *The stress of life.* New York: McGraw-Hill.

Selye, H. (1980). The stress concept today. In I. L. Kutash, L. B. Schlesinger, et al. (Eds.), *Handbook on stress and anxiety.* San Francisco: Jossey-Bass, pp. 127–129.

Shah, M., & Jeffery, R. W. (1991). Is obesity due to overeating and inactivity, or to a defective metabolic rate? A review. *Annals of Behavioral Medicine, 13,* 73–81.

Shannon, B., Bagby, R., Wang, M. Q., & Trenkner, L. (1990). Self-efficacy: A contributor to the explanation of eating behavior. *Health Education Research: Theory and Practice, 5,* 395–407.

Shavit, Y., Lewis, J. W., Terman, G. W., Gale, R. P., & Liebeskind, J. C. (1984). Opioid peptides mediate the suppressive effects of stress on natural killer cell cytotoxicity. *Science, 223,* 188–190.

Shea, S., Basch, C. E., Lantigua, R., & Wechsler, H. (1992). The Washington Heights–Inwood Healthy Heart Program: A third generation community-based cardiovascular disease prevention program in a disadvantaged urban setting. *Preventive Medicine, 21,* 201–217.

Shekelle, R. B., Hulley, S. B., Neaton, J. D., Billings, J. H., Borhani, N. O., Gerace, T. A., Jacobs, D. R., Lasser, N. L., Mittlemark, M. B., & Stamler, J. (1985). The MRFIT behavior pattern study II: Type A behavior and incidence of coronary heart disease. *American Journal of Epidemiology, 122,* 559–570.

Shekelle, R. B., Schoenberger, J. A., & Stamler, J. (1976). Correlates of the JAS Type A behavior pattern score. *Journal of Chronic Diseases, 29,* 381–394.

Shekelle, R. B., Shryock, A. M., Paul, O., Leppar, M., Stamler, J., Liu, S., & Raynor, W. J. (1981). Diet, serum cholesterol, and death from coronary heart disease. The Western Electric Study. *New England Journal of Medicine, 304,* 65–69.

Sheley, J. F., McGee, Z. T., & Wright, J.D. (1992). Gun-related violence in and around inner-city schools. *American Journal of Diseases of Children, 146,* 677–682.

Shiffman, S. (1982). Relapse following smoking cessation: A situational analysis. *Journal of Consulting and Clinical Psychology, 50,* 71–86.

Shiffman, S. M. (1979). The tobacco withdrawal syndrome. In N. M. Krasnegor (Ed.), *Cigarette smoking as a dependence process (Monograph 23).* Rockville, Md.: National Institute on Drug Abuse, U.S. Department of Health Education and Welfare.

Siber, E., et al. (1961). Adaptive behavior in competent adolescents. *Archives of General Psychiatry, 5,* 354–365.

Sick Health Services. (July 16, 1988). *The Economist,* 19–22.

Sidle, A., Moos, R., Adams, J., & Cady, P. (1969). Development of a coping scale. *Archives of General Psychiatry, 20,* 226–232.

Siegel, J. M., & Kuykendall, D. H. (1990). Loss, widowhood, and psychological distress among the elderly. *Journal of Consulting and Clinical Psychology, 58,* 519–524.

Siegel, W. C., & Blumenthal, J. A. (1991). The role of exercise in the prevention and treatment of hypertension. *Annals of Behavioral Medicine, 13,* 23–30.

Siegrist, J., Dittman, K. H., Rittner, K., & Weber, I. (1982). The social context of active distress in patients with early myocardial infarction. *Social Science and Medicine, 16,* 443–454.

Sievers, M. L., & Fischer, J. R. (1985). Diabetes in North American Indians. In *National diabetes data group, diabetes in America.* NIH publication 85-1468, Chapter 11.

Silberstein, C. (1985). Major depressive illness in AIDS patients. *Einstein Quarterly Journal of Biology and Medicine, 3,* 135–143.

Silverman, M. M., Eichler, A., & Williams, G. D. (1987). Self-reported stress: Findings from the 1985 National Health Interview Survey. *Public Health Reports, 102,* 47–53.

Sims, E. A. H., & Horton, E. S. (1968). Endocrine and metabolic adaptation to obesity and starvation. *American Journal of Clinical Nutrition, 21,* 1455–1470.

Siscovick, D. S., Weiss, N. S., Fletcher, R. H., & Lasky, T. (1984). The incidence of primary cardiac arrest during vigorous exercise. *New England Journal of Medicine, 311,* 874–877.

Sjostrom, L. (1980). Fat cells and body weight. In A. J. Stunkard (Ed.), *Obesity.* Philadelphia: Saunders, pp. 72–100.

Skinner, B. F. (1938). *The behavior of organisms.* New York: Appleton-Century-Crofts.

Skinner, B. F. (1953). *Science and human behavior.* New York: Macmillan.

Sklar, L. S., & Anisman, H. (1981). Stress and cancer. *Psychology Bulletin, 89*(3), 369–406.

Skyler, J. S. (1979). Diabetes and exercise: Clinical implications. *Diabetes Care, 2,* 307–311.

Sleet, D. A. (1987). Motor vehicle trauma and safety belt use in the context of public health priorities. *Journal of Trauma, 27,* 695–702.

Sloan, J. H., Kellerman, A. L., Reay, D. T., et al. (1988). Handgun regulations, crime, assaults and homicide: A tale of two cities. *New England Journal of Medicine, 319,* 1256–1262.

Smith, E. L., Smith, K. A., & Gilligan, C. (1990). Exercise, fitness, osteoarthritis, and osteoporosis. In C. Bouchard, R. J. Shephard, T. Stephens, J. R. Sutton, & G. D. McPherson (Eds.), *Exercise, fitness, and health: A consensus of current knowledge.* Champaign, Ill.: Human Kinetics, pp. 517–528.

Smith, L. W., Patterson, T. L., & Grant, I. (1992). Work, retirement, and activity: Coping challenges for the elderly. In M. Hersen (Ed.), *Handbook of social development: A life-span perspective.* New York: Plenum, pp. 475–502.

Smith, M. B., & Glass, G. D. (1987). *Research and evaluation in education and the social sciences.* Englewood Cliffs, N.J.: Prentice-Hall, 1987.

Smith, T. W. (1992). Hostility and health: Current status of a psychosomatic hypothesis. *Health Psychology, 11,* 139–150.

Smith, T. W., & Frohm, K. D. (1985). What's so unhealthy about hostility? Construct validity and psychosocial correlates of the Cook and Medley Ho scale. *Health Psychology, 4,* 503–520.

Smith, T. W., Peck, J. R., & Ward, J. R. (1990). Helplessness and depression in rheumatoid arthritis. *Health Psychology, 9,* 377–389.

Snow, J. (1855). *On the mode of communication of cholera.* London: Churchill Press (reprinted by Hafner Press, 1965).

Sobolski, J., Kornitzer, M., De Backer, G., Dramaix, M., Abramowicz, M., Degre, S., & Denolion, H. (1987). Protection against ischemic heart disease in the Belgian physical fitness study: Physical fitness rather than physical activity? *American Journal of Epidemiology, 125,* 601–610.

Solomon, G. F., Kemeny, M. E., & Temoshok, L. (in press). Psychoneuroimmunological aspects of human immunodeficiency virus infection. In R. Ader, D. L. Felton, & N. Cohen (Eds.), *Psychoneuroimmunology II.* Orlando, Fla.: Academic Press.

Solomon, G. F., & Moos, R. H. (1964). The relationship of personality to the presence of rheumatoid factor in asymptomatic relatives of patients with rheumatoid arthritis. *Psychosomatic Medicine, 27,* 350–360.

Solomon, G. F., Temoshok, L., O'Leary, A., et al. (1987). An intensive psychoimmunologic study of long-surviving persons with AIDS: Pilot work background studies, hypotheses, and methods. *Ann. New York Academy of Sciences, 46,* 647–655.

Sonstroem, R. (1988). Psychological models. In

R. K. Dishman (Ed.), *Exercise adherence: Its impact on public health.* Champaign, Ill.: Human Kinetics.

Sorenson, G., Rigotti, N., Rosen, A., Pinney, J., & Prible, R. (1991). Effects of a worksite nonsmoking policy: Evidence for increased cessation. *American Journal of Public Health, 81,* 202–205.

Special Center for Children in Poverty. (1990). *A statistical profile of our poorest young citizens.* New York: The Center.

Spector, S. L., Kingsman, R., Mawhinney, H., Siegel, S. C., Rachelefsky, G. S., Katz, R. M., & Rohr, A. S. (1986). Compliance of patients with asthma with an experimental aerosolized medication: Implications for controlled clinical trials. *Journal of Allergy and Clinical Immunology, 77,* 65–70.

Spiegel, D., Bloom, J. R., Kraemer, H. C., & Gottheil, E. (1989). Effect of psychosocial treatment on survival of patients with metastatic breast cancer. *Lancet, 2*(8668), 888–891.

Spirito, A., Stark, L. J., Cobiella, C., Drigan, R., Androkites, A., & Hewett, K. (1990). Social adjustment of children successfully treated for cancer. *Journal of Pediatric Psychology, 15*(3), 359–371.

Spitzer, L., & Rodin, J. (1981). Human eating behavior: A critical review of studies in normal weight and overweight individuals. *Appetite, 2,* 293–329.

Stall, R., Wiley, J., McKusick, L., et al. (1986). Alcohol and drug use during sexual activity and compliance with safe sex guidelines for AIDS: The AIDS behavioral research project. *Health Education Quarterly, 13,* 359–371.

Stallones, R. A. (1983). Ischemic heart disease and lipids in blood and diet. *Annual Review of Nutrition, 3,* 155.

Stalonas, P. M., Johnson, W. G., & Christ, M. (1978). Behavior modification for obesity: The evaluation of exercise, contingency management, and program adherence. *Journal of Consulting and Clinical Psychology, 46,* 463–469.

Stamler, R., & Stamler, J. (1979). Asymptomatic hyperglycemia and coronary heart disease. *Journal of Chronic Disease, 32,* 683–691.

Stark, E., & Flitcraft, A. H. (1992). Spouse abuse. In J. M. Last & R. B. Wallace (Eds.), *Public health and preventive medicine* (13th ed.). Norwalk, Conn.: Appleton & Lange, pp. 1040–1043.

Staulcup, H., Kenward, K., & Frigo, D. (1979). A review of federal primary alcoholism prevention projects. *Journal of Studies on Alcohol, 40,* 943–968.

Stephens, T. (1988). Physical activity and mental health in the United States and Canada: Evidence from four population surveys. *Preventive Medicine, 17,* 35–47.

Stephens, T., Jacobs, D. R., & White, C. C. (1985). A descriptive epidemiology of leisure-time physical activity. *Public Health Reports, 100,* 147–158.

Stern, M. P., Patterson, J. K., Mitchell, B. D., Haffner, S. M., & Hazuda, H. P. (1990). Overweight and mortality in Mexican Americans. *International Journal of Obesity, 14,* 623–629.

Stetson, B. A., Virts, K., Gregory, B., Schlundt, D., Boswell, E., & Snyder, G. (March 1991). *Nutrition education vs. problem solving skills training in promoting adherence to the IDDM dietary regimen.* Proceedings of the Society of Behavioral Medicine 12th Annual Scientific Session. Washington, D.C.: p. 102.

Stewart, A. L., & King, A. C. (1991). Evaluating the efficacy of physical activity for influencing quality-of-life outcomes in older adults. *Annals of Behavioral Medicine, 13,* 108–116.

Stiler, C. R., Dupre, J., Gent, M., et al. (1984). Effects of cyclosporine immunosuppression in insulin dependent diabetes of recent onset. *Science, 223,* 1362–1366.

Stimson, G. V. (1974). Obeying doctors' orders: A view from the other side. *Social Science and Medicine, 8,* 97–104.

Stokols, D. (1992). Establishing and maintaining healthy environments: Toward a social ecology of health promotion. *American Psychologists, 47,* 6–22.

Stone, G. C. (1979). Patient compliance and the role of the expert. *Journal of Social Issues, 35*(1), 34–59.

Stoudemire, A., & Hales, R. E. (1991). Psychological and behavioral factors affecting medical conditions and DSM-IV. *Psychosomatics, 32,* 5–13.

Streigel-Moore, R., & Rodin, J. (1986). The influence of psychological variables in obesity. In K. D. Brownell & J. P. Foreyt (Eds.), *Handbook of eating disorders.* New York: Basic Books, pp. 99–121.

Strong, W. B. (1983). Atherosclerosis: Its pediatric roots. In N. M. Kaplan & J. Stamler (Eds.), *Prevention of coronary heart diease: Practical management of the risk factors.* Philadelphia: Saunders, pp. 20–32.

Stuart, R. B. (1967). Behavioral control of overeating. *Behaviour Research and Therapy, 5,* 357–365.

Stunkard, A. J. (1979). Behavioral medicine and beyond: The example of obesity. In O. G. Pomerleau & J. P. Brady (Eds.), *Behavioral medicine: Theory and practice.* Baltimore: Williams and Wilkins.

Stunkard, A. J. (1984). Current status of treatment of obesity in adults. In A. J. Stunkard & E. Stellar (Eds.), *Eating and its disorders.* New York: Raven, pp. 157–173.

Stunkard, A. J., Foch, T. T., & Hrubec, Z. (1986). A twin study of human obesity. *Journal of the American Medical Association, 256,* 51–54.

Stunkard, A. J., Harris, J. R., Pedersen, N. L., & McClearn, G. E. (1990). The body-mass index of twins who have been reared apart. *New England Journal of Medicine, 24,* 322(21), 1483–1487.

Stunkard, A. J., & Kaplan, D. (1977). Eating in public places: A review of reports of the direct observation of eating behavior. *International Journal of Obesity, 1,* 89–101.

Stunkard, A. J., & Penick, S. B. (1979). Behavior modification in the treatment of obesity. *Archives of General Psychiatry, 36,* 801–806.

Suedfeld, P., & Kristeller, J. (1982). Stimulus reduction as a technique in health psychology. *Health Psychology, 1,* 337–357.

Suleveda, M., & Swartz, K. (1986). *The uninsured and uncompensated care: A chart book.* Washington, D. C., National Health Policy Forum, George Washington University.

Surwit, R. S., Feinglos, M., & Scover, A. W. (1983). Diabetes and behavior: A paradigm for health psychology. *American Psychologist, 38,* 255–262.

Targan, S., Britvan, L., & Dorey, F. (1981). Activaton of human NKCC by moderate exercise: Increase frequency of NK cells with enhanced capability of effector-target lytic interactions. *Clinical Experimental Immunology, 45,* 352–360.

Taylor, C. B., Farquhar, J. W., Nelson, E., & Agras, S. (1977). Relaxation therapy and high blood pressure. *Archives of General Psychiatry, 34,* 339–342.

Taylor, S. E. (1990). Health psychology. The science and the field. *American Psychologist, 45(1),* 40–50.

Telch, M. J., Killen, J. D., McAlister, A. L., Perry, C. L., & Maccoby, N. (1982). Long-term follow-up of a pilot project on smoking prevention with adolescents. *Journal of Behavioral Medicine, 5,* 1–8.

Tell, G. S. (1982). Factors influencing dietary habits: Experiences of the Oslo Youth Study. In T. J. Coates, A. C. Petersen, & C. Perry (Eds.), *Promoting adolescent health: A dialog on research and practice.* New York: Academic Press, pp. 381–396.

Temoshok, L. (1988). Psychoimmunology and AIDS. In T. P. Bridge, A. F. Mirsky, & F. K. Goodwin (Eds.), *Psychological, neuropsychiatric, and substance abuse aspects of AIDS.* New York: Raven Press, pp. 47–64.

Temoshok, L. (1991). Malignant melanoma, AIDS, and the complex search for psychosocial mechanisms. *Advances: The Journal of Mind-Body Health, 7,* 20–28.

Temoshok, L., & Fox, B. H. (Eds.) (1986). *International Issue Advances, 4,* 1–179.

Temoshok, L., Sweet, D. M., Jenkins, S., Straits, K., Pivar, I., Moulton, J. M., & Sites, D. P. (1988). *Psychoimmunologic studies of men with AIDS and ARC.* Presented at the Fourth International Conference on the Acquired Immune Deficiency Syndrome (AIDS). Stockholm, Sweden.

Tevino, F. M., & Moss, A. J. (1984). Health indicators for Hispanic, black and white Americans. *Vital and Health Statistics,* Series 10 (148), DHHS Publication #(PHS) 84-1576. Washington, D.C.: U.S. Government Printing Office.

The Expert Panel. (1988). Report of the national cholesterol education program expert panel on detection, evaluation, and treatment of high blood cholesterol in adults. *Archives of Internal Medicine, 148,* 36–69.

Theorell, T., Lind, E., & Folderus, B. (1975). The relationship of disturbing life changes and emotions to the early development of myocardial infarction and some other serious illnesses. *International Journal of Epidemiology, 4,* 281–293.

Thoits, P. A. (1985). Social support and psychological well-being: Theoretical possibilities. In I. G. Sarason & B. R. Sarason (Eds.), *Social support: Theory, research, and application.* The Hague, Netherlands: Martinus Nijhoff.

Thoits, P. A. (1986). Social support as coping assistance. *Journal of Consulting and Clinical Psychology, 54,* 416–423.

Thomas, P. D., Goodwin, J. M., & Goodwin, J. S. (1985). Effect of social support on stress-related changes in cholesterol level, uric acid, and immune function in an elderly sample. *American Journal of Psychiatry, 142*(6), 735–737.

Thompson, E. L. (1978). Smoking education programs, 1960–1976. *American Journal of Public Health, 68*, 250–257.

Thompson, J. K., Jarvie, G. J., Lahey, B. B., & Cureton, K. J. (1982). Exercise and obesity: Etiology, physiology, and intervention. *Psychological Bulletin, 91*, 55–79.

Thorn, G. W. (1970). Alterations in body weight. In E. Wintrobe (Ed.), *Harrison's principles of internal medicine*. New York: McGraw-Hill.

Thum, D., Wechsler, H., & Demone, H. W. (1973). Alcohol levels of emergency service patients injured in fights and assaults. *Criminology, 10*, 487–497.

Tipton, C. M. (1991). Exercise, training, and hypertension: An update. *Exercise and Sports Sciences Reviews, 19*, 447–505.

Trevisan, M., Krogh, V., Freudenheim, J., Blake, A., Muti, P., Panico, S., Farinaro, E., Mancini, M., Menotti, A., & Ricci, G. (1990). Consumption of olive oil, butter, and vegetable oils and coronary heart disease risk factors. *Journal of the American Medical Association, 263*, 688–692.

Tugwell, P., & Bombardier, C. (1982). A methodologic framework for developing and selecting endpoints in clinical trials. *Journal of Rheumatology, 9*, 758–762.

Turk, D. (1986). Chronic pain. In K. A. Holroyd & T. L. Creer (Eds.), *Self-management of chronic disease: Handbook of clinical interventions and research*. Orlando, Fl.: Academic Press, pp. 441–472.

Turk, D. C. (1990). Customizing treatment for chronic pain patients: who, what, and why. *Clinical Journal of Pain, 6*(4), 255–270.

Turk, D. C., Michenbaum, D., & Genest, M. (1983). *Pain and behavioral medicine: A cognitive perspective*. New York: Gilford Crest.

Turk, D. C., & Rudy, T. E. (1986). Assessment of cognitive factors in pain: A worthwhile enterprise? *Journal of Consulting and Clinical Psychology, 54*, 760–768.

Turner, C. F., Miller, H. G., & Moses, L. E. (1989). *AIDS sexual behavior and intravenous drug use*. Washington, D.C.: National Academy Press.

Tversky, A., & Kahneman, D. (1982). Judgement under uncertainty: Heuristics and biases. In D. Kahneman, P. Slovic, & A. Tversky (Eds.), *Judgement under uncertainty: Heuristics and biases*. Cambridge: Cambridge University Press.

U.S. Department of Health and Human Services (U.S. DHHS). (1980a). *Smoking, tobacco & health*. PHS Pub. no. 80-50150. Washington, D.C.: U.S. Government Printing Office.

U.S. Department of Health and Human Services. (1980b). *Smoking, tobacco & health. The health consequences of smoking for women. A report of the surgeon general*. Washington, D.C.: U.S. Government Printing Office.

U.S. Department of Health and Human Services. (1983). *The health consequences of smoking: Cardiovascular disease. A report of the surgeon general*. Department of Health and Human Services, Public Health Service, Office on Smoking and Health, DHEW Pub. No. (PHS) 84-50204. Washington, D.C.: U.S. Government Printing Office.

U.S. Department of Health and Human Services. (1985) *Report of the secretary's task force on black and minority health. Volume I, executive summary*, Publication #491-313/44706. Washington, D.C.: U.S. Department of Health and Human Services.

U.S. Department of Health and Human Services. (1987). *Smoking and health: A national status report*. Pub. no. 87-8396. Washington, D.C.: U.S. Government Printing Office.

U.S. Department of Health and Human Services. (1988). *The surgeon general's report on nutrition and health*. DHHS (PHS) Publication No. 88-50210. Washington, D.C.: U.S. Government Printing Office.

U.S. Department of Health and Human Services. (1990). *Alcohol and health*. DHHS Pub. No. (ADM) 90-1656. Washington, D.C.: Government Printing Office.

U.S.Department of Health, Education and Welfare (U.S. DHEW). (1964). *Smoking and health: A report of the surgeon general*. Washington, D.C.: U.S. Government Printing Office.

U.S. Department of Health, Education, and Welfare. (1979a). *Health, United States*. Washington,

D.C.: U.S. Government Printing Office, Pub. No. (PHS) 80-1232.

U.S. Department of Health, Education, and Welfare. (1979b). *Smoking and health: A report of the surgeon general.* Department of Health, Education, and Welfare, Public Health Service, Office on Smoking and Health, DHEW Pub. No. (PHS) 79-50066. Washington, D.C.: U.S. Government Printing Office.

U.S. Office on Smoking and Health. (1990). *Smoking and health, a national status report: A report to Congress* (2nd ed.). Department of Health and Human Services. Rockville, Md.: U.S. Dept. of Health and Human Services, Public Health Service, Centers for Disease Control, Center for Chronic Disease Prevention and Health Promotion, Office on Smoking and Health.

U. S. Select Committee on Nutrition and Human Needs. (1977). U.S. Senate: *Dietary Goals for the United States*, pp. 4–5.

Uhlmann, R. F., Inui, T. S., Percoraro, R. E., & Carter, W. B. (1988). Relationship of patient request fulfillment to compliance, glycemic control, and other health care outcomes in insulin-dependent diabetes. *Journal of General Internal Medicine, 3,* 458–463.

Urban, N., White, E., Anderson, G. L., Curry, S., & Kristal, A. R. (1992). Correlates of maintenance of a low-fat diet among women in the women's health trial. *Preventive Medicine, 21,* 279–291.

Visintainer, M. A., Volpicelli J. R., & Seligman, M. E. P. (1982). Tumor rejection in rats after inescapable versus escapable shock. *Science, 216,* 437–439.

Vitaliano, P. P., Maiuro, R. D., Russo, J., & Becker, J. (1987). Raw versus relative scores in the assessment of coping strategies. *Journal of Behavioral Medicine, 10*(1), 1–19.

Voulgaropolous, D., Schneiderman, L. J., & Kaplan, R. M. (1989). *Recommendations against the use of medical procedures: Evidence, judgment and ethical implications.* Submitted for publication.

Vranic, M., Horvath, S., & Wahren, J. (1979). Proceedings on a conference on diabetes and exercise. M. Vranic, S. Horvath, & J. Wahren (Eds.), *Diabetes* (supplement 1), pp. 1–113.

Vranic, M., & Wasserman, D. (1990). Exercise, fitness, and diabetes. In C. Bouchard, R. J. Shep-hard, T. Stephens, J. R. Sutton, & G. D. McPherson (Eds.), *Exercise, fitness, and health: A consensus of current knowledge.* Champaign, Ill.: Human Kinetics, pp. 467–490.

Wachter, R. M. (1992). AIDS, activism, and the politics of health. *New England Journal of Medicine, 326,* 128–132.

Wadden, T. A., & Brownell, K. D. (1984). The development and modification of dietary practices in individuals, groups, and large populations. In J. D. Matarazzo, S. M. Weiss, J. A. Herd, N. E. Miller, & S. M. Weiss (Eds.). *Behavioral health: A handbook of health enhancement and disease prevention.* New York: Wiley, pp. 608–631.

Wadden, T. A., & Stunkard, A. J. (1986). A controlled trial of very-low-calorie diet, behavior therapy, and their combination in the treatment of obesity. *Journal of Consulting and Clinical Psychology, 54,* 482–488.

Wagner, E. H., LaCroix, A. Z., Buchner, D. M., & Larson, E. B. (1992). Effects of physical activity on health status in older adults I: Observational studies. *Annual Review of Public Health, 13,* 451–468.

Waldron, I. (1983). Sex differences in human mortality: The role of genetic factors. *Social Science and Medicine, 17,* 321–333.

Walker, W. B., & Franzini, L. R. (1985). Low-risk aversive group treatments, physiological feedback, and booster sessions for smoking cessation. *Behavior Therapy, 16,* 263–274.

Waller, J. A. (1985). *Injury control: A guide to the causes and prevention of trauma.* Lexington, Mass.: Lexington Books.

Waller, J. A. (1986). Prevention of premature death and disability due to injury. In J. M. Last (Ed.), *Public health and preventive medicine* (12th ed.). Norwalk, Conn.: Appleton-Century-Crofts, pp. 1543–1576.

Wallston, B. S., Whitcher-Alagna, S., DeVellis, B. M., & DeVellis, R. F. (1983). Social support and physical health. *Health Psychology, 2,* 367–391.

Wallston, K. A., Wallston, B. S., & DeVellis, R. (1978). Development of the multidimensional health locus of control (MHLC) scales. *Health Education Monographs, 6,* 160–170.

Wankel, L. M. (1984). Decision-making and social

support strategies for increasing exercise adherence. *Journal of Cardiac Rehabilitation, 4,* 124–135.

Warheit, G. (1979). Life events, coping, stress, and depressive symptomatology. *American Journal of Psychiatry, 136,* 502–507.

Warner, K. E. (1986). *Seeing smoke: Cigarette advertising and public health.* Washington, D.C.: American Public Health Association.

Warner, K. E., Wickizer, T. M., Wolfe, R. A., Schildroth, J. E., & Samuelson, M. H. (1988). Economic implications of workplace health promotion programs: Review of the literature. *Journal of Occupational Medicine, 30,* 102–112.

Warren, S. A., Greenhill, S., & Warren, K. G. (1982). Emotional stress and the development of multiple sclerosis: Case-control evidence of a relationship. *Journal of Chronic Diseases, 35,* 821–831.

Watson, J. B. (1950). *Behaviorism.* New York: Norton.

Watson, R., Eskelson, C., & Hartman, B. (1984). Severe alcohol abuse and cellular immune functions. *Arizona Medicine, 41,* 665–668.

Waxler-Morrison, N., Hislop, T. G., Mears, B., & Can, L. (1991). The facts on social relationships on survival with women with breast cancer: A prospective study. *Social Science and Medicine, 33,* 177–183.

Waxman, M., & Stunkard, A. J. (1980). Caloric intake and expenditure of obese boys. *Journal of Pediatrics, 96,* 187–193.

Weisbrod, R. R., Bracht, N. F., Pirie, P. L., & Veblen-Mortenson, S. (1991). Current status of health promotion activities in four midwest cities. *Public Health Reports, 106,* 310–317.

Weiss, J., Stone, E., & Harrell, N. (1980). Coping behavior and brain norepinephrine level in rats. *Journal of Comparative Physiology and Psychology, 72,* 153–160.

Weiss, S. T., Tager, I. B., Schenker, M., & Speizer, F. E. (1983). The health effects of involuntary smoking. *American Review of Respiratory Diseases, 128,* 933–942.

Welin, L., Svardsudd, K., Ander-Peciva, S., Tibblin, G., Tibblin, B., & Larsson, G. (1985). Prospective study of social influences on morality. *Lancet, II,* 915–918.

Wennberg, J. E. (April 1987). *Small area analysis.*

National Center for Health Services Research. Conference on strengthening causal interpretation of non-experimental data. Tucson, Arizona.

Wennberg, J. E. (1990). Small area analysis in the medical care outcome problem. In L. Sechrest, E. Perrin, & J. Bunker (Eds.), *Strengthening causal interpretations of non-experimental data.* Beverly Hills, Calif.: Sage.

Wennberg, J. E., Freeman, J. L., & Culp, W. S. (1987). Are health services rationed in New Haven or overutilized in Boston? *Lancet, 23,* 1185–1189.

Wertheimer, M. D., et al. (1986). Increasing the effort toward breast cancer detection. *Journal of the American Medical Association, 255,* 1311–1315.

Wertkin, R. A. (December 1985). Stress-inoculation training: Principles and applications. *Social Casework: The Journal of Contemporary Social Work,* 611–616.

West, K. M. (1978). *Epidemiology of diabetes and its vascular lesions.* New York: Elsevier.

Whelan, E. M., Sheridan, M. J., Meister, K. A., & Mosher, K. A. (1981). Analysis of coverage of tobacco hazards in women's magazines. *Journal of Public Health Policy, 2,* 28–35.

White, C. C., Tolsma, D. D., Haynes, S. G., & McGee, D. (1987). Cardiovascular disease. In R. W. Amler & H. B. Dull (Eds.), *Closing the gap: The burden of unnecessary illness.* New York: Oxford University Press, pp. 43–54.

Whitehead, W. E., Blackwell, B., DeSilva, H., & Robinson, J. (1977). Anxiety and anger in hypertension. *Journal of Psychosomatic Research, 21,* 383–389.

Wiist, W. H., & Flack, J. M. (1990). A church-based cholesterol education program. *Public Health Reports, 105,* 381–388.

Willett, W. C., & MacMahon, B. (1984). Diet and cancer: An overview. *New England Journal of Medicine, 310,* 697.

Williams, C. A., Beresford, S. A. A., James, S. A., La Croix, A. Z., Strogatz, D. S., Wagner, E. H., Kleinbaum, D. G., Cutchin, L. M., & Ibrahim, M. A. (1985). The Edgecome County high blood pressure control program: III. Social support, social stressors, and treatment dropout. *American Journal of Public Health, 75,* 483–486.

Williams, R. B., Barefoot, J. C., Califf, R. M., Haney, T. L., Saunders, W. B., Pryor, D. B.,

Hlatky, M. A., Siegler, I. C., & Mark, D. B. (1992). Prognostic importance of social and economic resources among medically treated patients with angiographically documented coronary artery disease. *Journal of the American Medical Association, 267*(4), 520–524.

Williamson, J., & Chapin, J. M. (1980). Adverse reactions to prescribed drugs in the elderly: A multicare investigation. *Age and Aging, 9,* 73–80.

Wilson, G. T. (1978). Alcoholism and aversion therapy: Issues, ethics, and evidence. In G. Marlatt & P. Nathan (Eds.), *Behavioral approaches to alcoholism.* New Brunswick, N.J.: Journal of Studies on Alcohol.

Wilson, G. T. (1987). Cognitive studies in alcoholism. *Journal of Consulting and Clinical Psychology, 55,* 325–331.

Wilson, W., Ary, D. D., Biglan, A., Glasgow, R. E., Toobert, D. J., & Campbell, D. R. (1985). Psychosocial predictors of self-care behaviors (compliance) and glycemic control in non-insulin dependent diabetes mellitus. *Diabetes Care, 9,* 614–622.

Wing, R. R. (1989). Behavioral strategies for weight reduction in obese Type II diabetes patients. *Diabetes Care, 12,* 139–144.

Wing, S., Barnett, E., Casper, M., & Tyroler, H. A. (1992). Geographic and socioeconomic variation in the onset of decline of coronary heart disease mortality in white women. *American Journal of Public Health, 82,* 204–209.

Wing, R. R., Caggiula, A. W., Nowalk, M. P., Koeske, R., Lee, S., & Langford, H. (1984). Dietary approaches to the reduction of blood pressure: The independence of weight and sodium/potassium interventions. *Preventive Medicine, 13,* 233–244.

Wing, R. R., Epstein, L. H., Paternostro-Bayles, M., et al. (1988). Exercise in a behavioral weight control program for obese patients with Type II (non-insulin dependent) diabetes. *Diabetologia, 31,* 902–909.

Wing, R. R., Epstein, L. H., Norwalk, M. P., et al. (1986). Does self-monitoring of blood glucose levels improve dietary compliance for obese patients with Type II diabetes. *American Journal of Medicine, 81,* 830–836.

Wing, R. R., Koeske, R., Epstein, L. H. et al. (1987). Long-term effects of modest weight loss in Type II diabetic patients. *Archives of Internal Medicine, 147,* 1749–1753.

Wing, R. R., Marcos, M. D., Epstein, L. H., & Jawad, A. (1991). A "family based" approach to the treatment of obese Type II diabetic patients. *Journal of Consulting and Clinical Psychology, 59,* 156–162.

Wingard, D. L. (1984). The sex differential in morbidity, mortality, and lifestyle. *Annual Review of Public Health, 5,* 433–458.

Wingard, D. L., Berkman, L. F., & Brand, R. J. (1982). A multivariate analysis of health-related practices: A 9-year mortality follow-up of the Alameda County Study. *American Journal of Epidemiology, 116,* 767–775.

Wingard, D. L., & Cohn, B. A. (1990). Variations in disease-specific sex-morbidity and mortality ratios: United States vital statistics data and prospective data from the Alameda County Study. In M. G. Ory & H. R. Warner (Eds.), *Gender, health and longevity: Multidisciplinary perspectives.* New York: Springer.

Winnett, R. A., King, A. C., & Altman, D. G. (1989). *Health psychology and public health: An integrative approach.* New York: Pergamon.

Winnett, R. A., Wagner, J. L., Moore, J. F., Walker, W. B., Hite, L. A., Leahy, M., Neubauer, T., Arbour, D., Walberg, J., Geller, E. S., Mundy, L. L., & Lombard, D. (1991). An experimental evaluation of a prototype public access nutrition information system for supermarkets. *Health Psychology, 10,* 75–78.

Wiseman, C. V., Gray, J. J., Mosimann, J. E., & Ahrens, A. H. (1992). Cultural expectations of thinness in women: An update. *International Journal of Eating Disorders, 11,* 85–89.

Wishner, A. R., Schwarz, D. F., Grisso, J. A., Holmes, J. H., & Sutton, R. L. (1991). Interpersonal violence-related injuries in an African-American community in Philadelphia. *American Journal of Public Health, 81,* 1474–1476.

Wittenberg, S. H., Blanchard, E. D., McCoy, G., et al. (1983). Evaluation of compliance in home and center hemodialysis patients. *Health Psychology, 2,* 227–237.

Wolf, T. M., & Kissling, G. E. (1984). Changes in life-style characteristics, health, and mood of freshman medical students. *Journal of Medical Education, 59,* 806–814.

Wolpe, J. (1981). Behavior therapy versus psycho-analaysis. *American Psychologist, 36,* 159–164.

Wood, P. D., Haskell, W. L., Blair, S. N., Williams, P. T., Krauss, R. M., Lindgren, F. T., Albers, J. J., Ho, P. H., & Farquhar, J. W. (1983). Increased exercise level and plasma lipoprotein concentrations: A one-year randomized, controlled study in sedentary, middle-aged men. *Metabolism, 32,* 31–39.

Wood, P. D., Stefanick, M. L., Williams, P. T., & Haskell, W. L. (1991). The effects on plasma lipoproteins of a prudent weight-reducing diet, with or without exercise, in overweight men and women. *New England Journal of Medicine, 325,* 461–466.

Worden, J. K., Solomon, L. J., Flynn, B. S., Costanza, M. C., Foster, R. S., Dorwaldt, A. L., & Weaver, S. O. (1990). A community-wide program in breast self-examination training and maintenance. *Preventive Medicine, 19,* 254–269.

World Health Organization. (1948). *Constitution of the World Health Organization.* Geneva: WHO Basic Documents.

Worsely, A., & Crawford, D. (1984). Australian dietary supplement or supplementation practices. *Medical Journal of Australia, 140,* 579–583.

Worth, R. M., Kato, H., Rhoads, G. G., et al. (1975). Epidemiologic studies of CHD and stroke in Japanese men living in Japan, Hawaii, and California: mortality. *American Journal of Epidemiology, 102,* 481–488.

Wortman, C. B., & Donkel-Schetter, C. (1979). Interpersonal relationships and cancer: A theoretical analysis. *Journal of Social Issues, 35,* 120–155.

Wurtele, S. K. (1990). Teaching personal safety skills to four-year-old children: A behavioral approach. *Behavior Therapy, 21,* 25–32.

Wybran, J., Schandene, L., Van Vooren, J., Vandermoten, G., Latinne, D., Sonnet, T., deBruyere, M., Toelman, H., & Plotnikoff, N. (1987). Immunologic properties of methionine-enkephalin, and therapeutic implications in AIDS, ARC, and cancer. *Annuals of the New York Academy of Science, 496,* 108–113.

Wynder, E. L., & Gori, G. B. (1977). Contribution of the environment to cancer incidence: An epidemiologic exercise. *Journal of the National Cancer Institute, 58,* 825–832.

Wysocki, T., Green, L., & Huxtable, K. (1989). Blood glucose monitoring by diabetic adolescents: Compliance and metabolic control. *Health Psychology, 8,* 267–284.

Wysocki, T., Hall, G., Iwata, B., & Riordan, M. (1979). Behavioral management of exercise: Contracting for aerobic points. *Journal of Applied Behavior Analysis, 12,* 55–64.

Yarchoan, R., Mitsuya, H., & Broder, S. (1988). AIDS therapies. In *The science of AIDS,* pp. 85–99. New York: W. H. Freeman and Co.

Yelin, E., Meenan, R., Nevitt, M., & Epstein, W. (1980). Work disability in rheumatoid arthritis: Effects of disease, social, and work factors. *Annuals of Internal Medicine, 93,* 551–556.

Zapka, J. G., Stoddard, A. M., Costanza, M. E., & Greene, H. L. (1989). Breast cancer screening by mammography: Utilization and associated factors. *American Journal of Public Health, 79,* 1499–1502.

Zimmerman, A. L. (1991). Peritoneal solute clearance in "diabetics." *Peritoneal Dialysis International, 11*(1), 89–90.

Zimmerman, B. R. (1989). Influence of the degree of control of diabetes on the prevention, postponement and amelioration of late complications. *Drugs, 38*(6), 941–956.

NAME INDEX

SUBJECT INDEX